FAITH IN PAPER

FAITH IN PAPER

The Ethnohistory and Litigation of Upper Great Lakes Indian Treaties

Charles E. Cleland

WITH

Bruce R. Greene, Marc Slonim, Nancy N. Cleland, Kathryn L. Tierney, Skip Durocher, and Brian Pierson

THE UNIVERSITY OF MICHIGAN PRESS

Ann Arbor

To the leaders of the
native people of the
Great Lakes region,
both ancient and modern,
who fought to preserve
the rights and culture
of their people

First paperback edition 2014

Published in the United States of America by
The University of Michigan Press
First Published October 2011

Library of Congress Cataloging-in-Publication Data

Cleland, Charles E., 1936–
Faith in paper : the ethnohistory and litigation of upper Great Lakes Indian treaties / Charles E. Cleland ; with Bruce R. Greene ... [et al.].
p. cm.
Includes bibliographical references and index.
ISBN 978-0-472-11729-1 (cloth : alk. paper)
1. Indians of North America—Great Lakes Region (North America)—Treaties—History. 2. Indians of North America—Legal status, laws, etc.—Great Lakes Region (North America)—History. 3. Indians of North America—Land tenure—Great Lakes Region (North America)—History. I. Greene, Bruce R. II. Title.
KF8205.C54 2011
346.7704'3208997—dc22 2011007376

ISBN 13: 978-0-472-03594-9 (pbk. alk. : paper)
ISBN 13: 978-0-472-90551-5 (OA e-book)

Preface

Faith in Paper is about the reinstitution of Indian treaty rights in the upper Great Lakes region during the last quarter of the twentieth century. This book focuses on the few treaties and legal cases that together have awakened a new day in Native American sovereignty and established the place of Indian tribes on the modern political landscape. Providing an account of these has been a daunting task. The reader should note that scores of other treaties also pertain to the same tribes under discussion here, but these treaties have not been litigated, at least by modern courts. The many treaties not described here, while perhaps of less importance in modern law, are nonetheless significant in cultural and historical perspective.

Since its inception, this book has been buffeted by difficult organizational eddies and crosscurrents. First, it has been difficult to find a satisfactory means to discuss a topic that originates in the esoterica of three separate academic and professional disciplines—namely, anthropology, history, and the law. Fortunately, the two broad categories of treaty litigation and treaty history offer a means of organization that, to some degree, bridges geographical, cultural, historical, and judicial boundaries. For example, treaty rights claims have been brought under the same treaties by different modern tribes that are the political successors in interest to those Indian bands that historically negotiated the treaties. Often these cases have been heard in the federal courts of different states and separate judicial districts. To simplify the organization of this discussion, I have grouped the cases into two large categories: those dealing with hunting, fishing, and gathering rights and those arising from reservation issues, such as boundary claims, tribal jurisdiction, and claims related to the benefits to Indian people who live and work within Indian reservations.

This organization, though providing a means to factor out problems related to geography and the inherent differences between modern tribes and judicial districts, involves problems as well. For example, knowledge of the basic historical background and the political objectives of federal Indian policy in creating Indian reservations is important for understanding the circumstances under which the different reservation treaties were negotiated. Since this is so, where historical particulars and legal theory related to specific treaty cases are being explained, the fundamentals of contemporary reservation policy become crucial to understanding each case. Since the various cases of the reservation section all evolve from the same policy, a certain amount of repetition is necessary so that each treaty and legal case can stand alone as a coherent statement. Since *Faith in Paper* will presumably be used by some as a reference text, I found it necessary to include somewhat more repetition than is usually found in a straightforward narrative. I hope the reader will be understanding in this regard.

Another organizational challenge involves the anticipated readership for this book and its parts. I am hopeful that its contents will be of interest to tribal members and to scholars and students of history, anthropology, and the law. I also hope this book will be of interest to members of the lay public, a crucial audience in bringing a new understanding to the role of modern Indian tribes in the affairs of the larger Great Lakes community. These separate audiences do not share the same vocabulary, means of conducting research, or theoretical perspectives. I have not tried to bridge these separate chasms but, instead, have made an effort to create a discussion that will be intelligible, useful, and accessible to the separate readerships by providing the legal, historical, and cultural perspectives necessary to understand and interpret Indian treaties.

Several different strategies have been adopted to make *Faith in Paper* available to readers and researchers. First, it will be available as a printed edition. Second, the material will be accessible electronically in a number of formats.

This book is about the struggle of Indian people to resurrect and to give meaning to these agreements, to explain their contexts, and to give them reality in the modern world. To native people, treaties are not ancient history but a living part of their cultural heritage. To succeed, the tribes had to confront many treasured historical myths in the mainstream as well as to convince the courts of the justice of their cause.

Part 1 of this book presents information on the development of the Indian treaties in historic time and their social and legal context. Treaty making, which involved direct face-to-face negotiation of people of totally distinct cultures, also required the negotiation of mutually satisfactory mechanisms for treaty making itself. Also considered in this part is the process that provided treaties cultural legitimacy in the context of both cultures.

Part 2 deals with the specific treaties that have been litigated for the right of Indian people to hunt, fish, and gather in the upper Great Lakes region. In each case, I provide an ethnohistorical account of the historical circumstances of the negotiation of the treaty or treaties in contention. Each historical narrative is followed by a commentary by one of the lawyers who organized and argued the case for the tribe or tribes. Here they explain the circumstances that led to litigation, the legal contentions of the tribe as well as the opposing parties, the legal cases relied on by the tribe, the track of the case through the court system, and, finally, the decision of the court. While the historical reports or legal views of the opposing parties are not provided, this account is oriented toward the Indian perspective and does not pretend to be totally balanced. The reader might keep in mind, however, that while the Indians' side did not win all the cases described here, it did prevail in most. In those latter cases, the court accepted the accounts presented as factual and relied on them.

Part 3, which is in the same format as part 2, deals with reservation issues. Finally, part 4 deals with the impact of treaty litigation on the modern Indian and non-Indian communities of the Great Lakes region.

I hope that each reader will find the story of the reinstitution of treaty rights to the upper Great Lakes region interesting and will come to understand the significance of the ancient treaty promises and what they have brought to the region and to its native people.

Charles E. Cleland
Norwood, Michigan

Acknowledgments

The separate reports that constitute much of my writing in this book originally evolved in response to specific cultural and historical questions posed by attorneys. These questions were not motivated by curiosity as much as by the need for hard evidence to support complex legal arguments. As such, my initial studies were read and reread by teams of lawyers who questioned every fact, nuance of meaning, and conclusion. Though at times painful, this legal scrutiny made the modified reports that appear here all the better. For their help in organization and presentation, I gratefully acknowledge the labors of the following legal colleagues: John Arnum, Jim Bransky, Howard Bickler, Bill Brooks, Henry Buffalo, Chris Duggan, Skip Durocher, Doug Endreson, Dan Green, Bruce R. Greene, Garfield Hood, Jim Jannetta, Frank Jozwiak, Anne Noto, Joseph O'Leary, Brian Pierson, Bill Rastetter, Milt Rosenberg, David Siegler, Marc Slonim, Paul Stenzel, Mary Streitz, Kathryn L. Tierney, and Alice Walker. In addition, I would especially like to mention my friend Larry Burgess, Michigan attorney-magistrate of the Ninetieth District Court, who helped me through the mysteries of legal citation and in finding obscure cases. Finally, for his reading of earlier drafts and general encouragement, I thank my brother, John M. Cleland, judge of the Superior Court of Pennsylvania.

I also owe a great debt to my historical and ethnological colleagues. First and foremost, I acknowledge James M. McClurken and Richard A. Carlson for their help in finding and collecting many of the documents used in preparing this volume. Many of the maps were drawn by Ellen White of the MSU Cartographic Center, and her work is greatly appreciated. For the enormous job of managing the many thousands of documents used in this writing, including those appearing in the endnotes and bibliography, my sincere thanks go to my wife, Nancy N. Cleland. These documents are now reposited at the Clarke Library at Central Michigan University, where they are in the safekeeping of director Frank Boles and archivist Marian Matyn.

The professional staff members of many archives were helpful and patient in helping with documentary research. Foremost of these are the Archives of the United States in Washington, D.C., Suitland, Maryland, and the Chicago Regional Archives of the National Archives. I also thank the staffs at the Library of Congress, the Sault Ste. Marie Agency and the Minneapolis Area Regional Office of the Bureau of Indian Affairs, the Michigan Historical Center Archives, the Historical Society of Wisconsin, and the Minnesota Historical Society. Many university, regional, and local archives contributed useful information to this book. Among these, thanks are due to the Michigan State University Library, the Bentley Library and Historical Collections at the University of Michigan, the Clarke Library and Archives at Central Michigan University, the Chicago Historical Society, and the Bishop Baraga Archive in Marquette, Michigan. Assistance from the tribal archives of the Bay Mills Indian Community and the Stockbridge-Munsee Band of Mohican Indian Community is gratefully acknowledged.

Apart from these institutions, I most gratefully thank the following professors for their intellectual influence and for sharing their tremendous knowledge of the ethnohistory and history of the Great Lakes region and its native people: Harry Brown, James Clifton, Harold Hickerson, Volney Jones, George Quimby, and Marshall Sahlins. I note also the stimulating influences among my contemporary colleagues especially: Bob Birmingham, Doug Burke, Rich Carlson, Jim McClurken, Paul Dribben, Helen H. Tanner, Jim Morrison, Larry Nesper, Jim Schlender, Ann Soltis, Don Wedll, Bruce White, and Jim Zorn.

Many native people contributed to my understanding of the historical and contemporary nuances of tribal life. Among those to whom I owe a special debt of gratitude are Armilla Parker, Jeff Parker, Paula Carrick, Wanda Perron, and Bucko Teeple of the Bay Mills Indian Community; Bernard Bouschor and Joe Lumsden of the Sault Ste. Marie Tribe of Chippewa Indians; Joe Chosa and Tom Molson of the Lac du Flambeau

Band of Lake Superior Chippewa Indians; George Aubin and Melanie Benjamin of the Mille Lacs Band of the Chippewa Indians; Ted Halopa of the Keweenaw Bay Indian Community; and Jim Schlender of the Lac Courte Oreilles Band of Lake Superior Chippewa. Thanks are also due to tribal governments that, through their officers, staff, elders, and legal counsels, helped in many ways in supporting historical research. In addition to those native communities already mentioned, I acknowledge the help of the Keweenaw Bay Indian Community, the Bad River Band of Lake Superior Chippewa, the Sokaogon, the Mole Lake Band of Lake Superior Chippewa, the Lac Vieux Desert Band of Lake Superior Chippewa, the Fond du Lac Band of Lake Superior Chippewa, the St. Croix Band of Lake Superior Chippewa, the Grand Portage Band of Lake Superior Chippewa, the Red Cliff Band of Lake Superior Chippewa, the Mille Lacs Chippewa Indians, the Little Traverse Bay Band of Odawa Indians, the Grand Traverse Bay Band of Odawa and Chippewa Indians, the Little River Band of Odawa Indians, the Saginaw Chippewa Tribe, the Menominee Tribe of Wisconsin, the Forest County Potawatomi Tribe, and the Stockbridge and Munsee Band of Mohican Indians.

For their good advice and generous gifts of time and talents, I offer my heartfelt thanks to the coauthors of this volume: Bruce R. Greene, Marc Slonim, Nancy N. Cleland, Kathryn L. Tierney, Skip Durocher, and Brian Pierson.

Finally, my sincere thanks go to Ellen McCarthy, Christina Milton, and Scott Hamm of the University of Michigan Press for their editorial skill and innovative thinking regarding the production of this volume.

Contents

PART 1. Exploring the Origins of Indian Treaties 1

CHAPTER 1. Introductory Notes 3

CHAPTER 2. The Treaty 12

CHAPTER 3. The Foundations of Treaty Making 19

CHAPTER 4. The Invention of Euro-American and Indian Treaty Making 30

CHAPTER 5. Treaties and American Law 40

PART 2. Usufructuary Litigation 45

CHAPTER 6. The Treaties of 1836 and 1855 49

CHAPTER 7. *United States v. Michigan,* by Bruce R. Greene 88

CHAPTER 8. *United States v. Michigan,* by Marc Slonim 93

CHAPTER 9. The Treaties of St. Peters (1837) and La Pointe (1842) 100

CHAPTER 10. *Lac Courte Oreilles Band v. Wisconsin,* by Kathryn L. Tierney 124

CHAPTER 11. *Milles Lacs Band of Chippewa Indians et al. v. State of Minnesota et al.,* by Marc Slonim 132

CHAPTER 12. The Menominee and the Coming of Europeans 140

CHAPTER 13. *Menominee Indian Tribe of Wisconsin v. Thompson,* by Bruce R. Greene 192

PART 3. Reservation Issues 199

CHAPTER 14. The Boundary of the Keweenaw Bay Reservation 203

CHAPTER 15. *Keweenaw Bay Indian Community v. Michigan,* by Bruce R. Greene 226

CHAPTER 16. Factionalism and Removal: The Stockbridge and Munsee, 1830–56 230

CHAPTER 17. *State of Wisconsin v. Stockbridge-Munsee Community and Robert Chicks,* by Brian Pierson 258

CHAPTER 18. The Ethnohistory of the Mille Lacs Reservation Boundary 265

CHAPTER 19. *County of Mille Lacs v. Melanie Benjamin et al.,* by Marc Slonim 279

CHAPTER 20. The Treaties of Detroit (August 2, 1855) and Saginaw (October 18, 1864) 286

CHAPTER 21. Allotment and Land Loss on the Keweenaw Bay Reservation 308

CHAPTER 22. *Keweenaw Bay Indian Community v. Naftaly,* by Skip Durocher 329

PART 4. Conclusions 335

CHAPTER 23. The Benefits of Reestablished Treaties 337

Notes 345

Acronyms and Bibliography, compiled by Nancy N. Cleland 379

Index 385

PART I

Exploring the Origins of Indian Treaties

CHAPTER 1

Introductory Notes

I hope the reader will forgive me for beginning this task by writing about myself. There are two reasons for this imposition. First, the reader deserves to know about my orientation toward the law, anthropology, and history. Second, I believe that in some small way, my experience in the application of these disciplines to treaty casework represents a significant aspect of the reemergence of treaty obligations in modern social and political contexts. The latter has resulted in the recognition by our society at large that our collective historical past has real consequences for the modern political life that, in this case, is represented by viable Native American tribal governments.

My learning experience in treaty rights work began in 1975. At that time, I was in my late thirties and an associate professor of anthropology at Michigan State University. I had been trained as an anthropologist and archaeologist at the University of Michigan, where I wrote my doctoral dissertation on a very esoteric subject. I had studied the remains of animals, mostly bones recovered from dozens of archaeological sites around the upper Great Lakes region, in order to better understand both the changing environments occupied by ancient Indian people and their food ways. This study was published in 1966 under the title *The Prehistoric Animal Ecology and Ethnozoology of the Upper Great Lakes Region* and soon was widely cited by scholars, though I suspect seldom read.

I was surprised and puzzled when, in the fall of 1975, I received a call from a lawyer in Sault Ste. Marie, Kathryn L. Tierney, who claimed not only to have read my book but to have been enthralled by it. She asked if she might make the six-hour trip to East Lansing to talk to me about ethnozoology. I was, of course, delighted. When we met, I learned that Ms. Tierney, along with a number of her colleagues, represented three Michigan Indian tribes that, with the aid of the U.S. Department of Justice, were suing the state of Michigan for the right of their members to fish in the open waters of the Great Lakes under a treaty concluded between the tribes and the United States in 1836. If their suit was successful, the State of Michigan, which had not been a party to the original treaty, would have no say in regulating a tribal fishery, and the state vigorously resisted the treaty claim. Among other reasons, the state argued that a nineteenth-century Indian agreement had no relevance or legal reality in modern times.

The state also claimed that gill nets, the main device used by the Indian fishermen to catch Great Lakes fish, were not native technology but were instead introduced by the French after their arrival to the New World in the early seventeenth century. As such, they could not, the state argued, be used by modern Indian fishermen, even if they had a fishing right under the treaty. In my work with fish bones from Indian sites and other evidence, I was able to show that Great Lakes Indians not only independently invented gill nets but had been effectively using them for nearly a thousand years by the time the French arrived. Thus, by a strange twist of fate, my research suddenly became "relevant." I became excited about its application to a "real-life" problem and agreed to become an expert witness for the tribes.

As I began to prepare a report in the Indian fishing case, I eventually met Kathryn Tierney's colleagues Bruce Greene, Jim Jannetta, Dan Green, Bill James, and Bill Ratstetter, all very bright young attorneys who, I discovered, had very similar social and political views to my own. I began for the first time to see how a proper alignment of law, anthropology, and history could be a powerful force for social change. Frankly, I was somewhat worried about what the attorneys would want me to say and whether I could remain true to the scientific evidence and still support their arguments. I was encouraged and reassured when Bruce Greene, the lead attorney in the case, officially called *United States v. Michigan,* gave me his instructions for preparing my report: "All we ask of you is your full and honest opinion, the complete truth as you understand the facts." I was to explain to the court the subsistence strategies of ancient Native American culture in the Great Lakes region, emphasizing subsistence and settlement practices at the time of European exploration and the development of these practices from archaeological evidence. Of course, the emphasis was to be on fishing.[1] The attorneys were building their arguments around what I had to say, instead of, as I had feared, expecting my statements to conform to their arguments.

At some point, I discovered that my part in the case was very small. The main question was about the very existence of the right to fish under authority of the Treaty of Washington negotiated in 1836. The expert witness in this central question was the eminent Indian historian Dr. Helen Hornbeck Tanner. Helen was very experienced in the legal realm from her work in the 1950s before the Indian Claims Commission as well as in other legal cases. Recognizing me as a complete neophyte, she took me under her wing, and we spent many hours talking about Indian history, federal Indian policy, the nineteenth-century Michigan frontier, and Ottawa and Ojibwe culture. This was a profitable exchange for both of us, but I am sure I came out well ahead.

I also learned that my friend Helen had a very jaundiced view of lawyers as well as the rules the court had evolved for the presentation of evidence.[2] She never tired of telling me how much easier and the better justice would be served if the judge would only let the opposing expert witnesses talk directly to each other in order to determine the points on which they disagreed. Helen believed it was silly to let lawyers, who did not know the facts of history, direct the content and flow of testimony by asking questions that were, in her view, mostly inane. Helen certainly had a style of her own, which in part, I tried to emulate. She was self-assured, scrappy, and especially good at establishing a rapport with the judge.

Although I much admired Helen and her vast knowledge of Indian history, I do not share her aversion to the legal process itself. Eventually, as I learned more about the law, I began to appreciate its sometimes arcane procedures. The rules of evidence, courtroom protocol, and the importance of precedent is a world unto itself, albeit a world born of a strange mixture of logic and tradition. It seemed to me that the trick to being an effective historical expert witness was to make the past relevant to the legal questions at hand.

There is another thing I realized when discussing Indian history with Helen as well as other historians. The way historians tend to view the past is much different from the way I viewed the past as an anthropologist. Helen's view of the past was filled with people, dates, and specific events; mine was filled with generalizations about the culture of the people who produced events and things (including history itself). To me, artifacts and documents were a means for understanding the intangible cultural values and beliefs that motivated people to behave in certain fairly predictable ways. For me, historical descriptions incorporated in ancient documents provide a view into an extinct culture and an aid to understanding that culture and the way it changed to accommodate the ever-fluctuating social and natural environment. I suppose it could be said that I was concerned not so much with historical specifics per se but, rather, with what these facts could contribute to developing an understanding of human behavior and cultural process.

I do not, by the way, mean that historians are not interested in general propositions or cultural problems, only that anthropologists have a different focus to their study. If anthropologists are obsessed with theory, historians often seem atheoretical and event centered. If historians treasure perspective in time and space, anthropologists often seem myopic, peeking into a tiny window for a glimpse of the here and now. Or is it the there and then?

It would seem obvious that a partnership between history and anthropology would have advantages for both disciplines. Indeed, something of a rapprochement occurred between the two fields during the 1980s and 1990s.[3] Anthropologists, particularly cultural anthropologists, began to see the advantages of using written sources in the study of culture change and learning their way around archives. Likewise, perhaps under the example of French historians, such as F. Baudel, Emmanuel Le Roy Ladurie, and Maurice Bloch of the Annales School, anthropologists started to appreciate the *longue durée,* that is, the benefit of time in understanding long-term cultural transformations as well as the effect of history on relatively short-term social oscillations.[4]

Why is culture an important variable in understanding the past, and why is the past equally important to understanding culture? In simple terms, our behavior is built on the foundation of our particular culture as well as historical experience. Our behavior embodies all the beliefs, values, morals, and knowledge that we accumulate as members of a society. We, in turn, pass what we learned on to our children, in some modified version, from one generation to the next. Historical conditions, resulting from environmental impacts or the impingement of intercultural competition, certainly influence cultural experience and thus modify culture through time. Culture determines what language we speak, what deities we worship, what foods we find palatable, and all the other factors central to our lives. Historical events may introduce new words into our language or religious practices, while food shortages may expand our definition of acceptable foods. History and culture are clearly interrelated in a major way.

Any serious analysis or understanding of the events surrounding the negotiation of nineteenth-century Indian treaties must include an understanding of the culture or cultures that critically affected the motivations of historical actors. Historic actors who were Potawatomi had a much different view of reality than those who were raised as Wyandots, who, in turn, saw the world differently from Ojibwe people. Thus, the same events were interpreted in different ways depending on the cultural perspective of the participants and observers.

It is problematic that the written documents that describe events related to the Native American history of the nineteenth century and before are almost exclusively written by non-Indians. Worse, most of the authors, though providing valuable contemporary accounts, were largely ignorant of Indian culture and language. Some reporters assumed that Indians perceived events in the same way they did and acted with the same motivations. At the time, this approach constituted a liberal construction, since more often than not, non-Indian reporters assumed that Indian actions and the rationale behind them (if any) derived from innate instincts of the basest kind. Indians, they assumed, were by nature cruel, ignorant, lazy, dirty, warlike, and otherwise depraved.

It should also be observed that although modern non-Indian Americans share a cultural tradition with their nineteenth-century ancestors, their culturally derived understandings of the world have changed radically from that day to this. Nineteenth-century Americans had much different beliefs about religion, politics, self-reliance, food, disease, and especially American Indians. Given their distinct cultural orientation, we might ask if the documents they left behind are in any way useful for understanding the Ojibwe, Ottawa, Menominee, Potawatomi, or other Indian people of the American frontier. It seems evident that even though such documents cannot be trusted on their face, they are indeed useful for analyzing the beliefs and motivations of both their authors as well as the Indian people who are the subjects of their descriptions.

To get the most from any archival source, it is necessary to understand the bias of the author. Historians are trained to do precisely this, but, unfortunately, few are knowledgeable about the cultural variables that are crucial to understanding the Indians the contemporary observer is describing. While the motivation of the author of the ancient document may be revealed, the motivation of the Indian actors remains opaque, ever mysterious. There are many well-documented histories of Indian tribes, Indian wars, Indian folklore, and the like that are written from primary documents but, at best, tell us little about Indians. It is possible to learn quite a lot about these very Indians by using the same documents but employing a different methodological approach, namely, ethnohistory.

Bias Explained

Before describing ethnohistory, I want to discuss bias. In my career as an expert witness, opposing attorneys have often accused me of being biased. Whether there is bias is also not only a fair question to ask oneself but a topic on which any reader should be informed by any author. In my own case, the short answer is yes; I am biased.

In the run-up to trials in the U.S. legal system, each side is obliged to disclose to the other the witnesses who will be called at trial as well as the general topic on which they will testify. This is part of the process known as discovery, by which opposing attorneys are afforded the opportunity to question the witnesses for the other side under oath and take their depositions—in short, to depose the witnesses. The object of the depositions is to give each side the opportunity to find out what witnesses will say at trial and what evidence they relied on in forming their opinions. In treaty trials, it is at this point that each side exchanges copies of the historical documents, which are the source material for many of the conclusions of the witnesses. Unlike witnesses to crimes or accidents who appear in court to testify about what they observed from their own experience, expert witnesses have wide latitude to express opinions. Treaty cases are almost always bench trials, meaning that no jury is impaneled, and the judge decides the case. As part of the judge's deliberation, she or he must decide how much weight to give the opinions of each expert witness. The expert witnesses' credibility is thus based on the soundness of their opinions given the evidence presented.

As an academic, I have always found the discovery process difficult. Often, opposing attorneys try to discredit the witness either by questioning their credentials or experience or probing for weaknesses and inconsistencies in their opinions. This process always reminded me of the PhD dissertation defense, with malice. In preparation for my first deposition, I was instructed to answer the questions asked but to volunteer no additional information. I found this to be a surprisingly tough assignment. Mostly, the opposing attorneys were smart, but sometimes they were woefully uninformed about the topics at hand, and my every instinct as a professor was to teach them. I was constantly tempted to point out that they were asking the wrong questions or to correct their assumptions, and, quite frankly, I was also strongly inclined to be argumentative. All of these are bad instincts for a good expert witness. As attorney Bruce Greene once pointed out to me, "Attorneys argue; witnesses opine."

The main idea behind the division of labor between attorneys and experts is that the expert is an unbiased and objective provider of facts and opinions, while the attorney uses facts and opinions to build an argument toward various points of law. On some levels, this division is a difficult proposition to sustain, since both sides in the lawsuit hire experts to provide objective and unbiased testimony using basically the same set of documents. The problem is that the experts for each side almost always come to opposite conclusions. There is, of course, nothing at all unusual about experts coming to different conclusions, after all; we remind ourselves of the common adage, honest people may differ. But beyond this, I remain uneasy about the bias issue.

While it is true enough that every argument has two sides, I had to ask myself why I always work on behalf of the tribes in case after case. Does this suggest a bias on my part? My answer is yes, but I hasten to add that this bias never interfered with my ability to evaluate the facts as I understand them. As a matter of fact, honest experts came to different conclusions because of their biases. After all, my interest and expertise are in the realm of Indian culture and history, and my particular take on these subjects has long ago been established in my academic writings. Indian tribes hire me because they agree with my views of the past, not because they know for sure that I will agree with theirs. It could also be said that my views are not the ones that the opponents of tribes are likely to want to hear in court. It is not surprising that nontribal interests have never approached me to testify in their behalf. I have, however, declined to testify for tribes in cases where I was not convinced that the historical evidence supported the legal positions they hoped to advance. In my view, there is no such thing as a purely objective or unbiased view of the world. In historical context, the "reality" incorporated into historical documents and, therefore, the "facts" on which cases are tried are, in the end, the product of an individual whose perception is influenced by their own gender, age, social position, education, religion, and life experience, as well as many other variables.

The question of author's bias should be of concern to the readers of this book, who should want to know if it contains a fair and honest account of the treaty litigation in the Great Lakes and its historical context. To be sure, in each of the cases that will be described, experts, both historians and anthropologists, have argued positions contrary to those presented here. Debates on these points will rage on in the academic arena. In the judicial context, the contrasting views are laid before a judge who must make a decision. In most, but not all, of the cases presented in this book, court decisions have supported the view of the past developed by the experts for the tribes. Nonetheless, it is my objective to lay out the arguments and some of the facts in each case so that the reader may reach his or her own judgment.

Treaty litigation touches such a raw nerve for many Americans. In effect, it drags modern native tribes out of a comfortable historical context, where Indians are either unfairly romanticized or vilified, and it forces the general public not only to confront the unpleasant realities of history but also to reconsider the popular mythology about the place of native people in modern society. Beyond this, if Indians actually succeed in reestablishing the legal provisions embodied in the treaty documents, such decisions by the courts have the effect of empowering the institution of the tribe itself. A favorable outcome not only provides the tribe with power but confirms the modern political reality of the tribal institution itself.

Different Kinds of History

I have mentioned that Great Lakes Indians, like other North American native people, had a nonliterate tradition. Theirs were not written languages. This does not mean, however, that Indian people were ahistorical; in fact, one of the lessons I learned from Ojibwe elders at Mille Lacs was how much rich detail was contained in oral history. This and other experiences in working with the Indian elders of the northern tribes convinced me that the formal telling and retelling of the past, which once was but is no longer a major part of America's mainstream historical tradition, is worthy of attention.

The U.S. legal system does not often accept oral history, because it is considered to be hearsay. Obviously it is hearsay, but in our discourse, there is no way to know what the nature of hearsay is. In the English language, there is no formal way to distinguish between what is known from secondhand information sources and what has been experienced firsthand—that is, whether what is being related is history, mythology, or merely gossip. This is not so in the Ojibwe language, where a distinction is made between *daebaudjimowin,* a chronicle known from personal experience, and *auwaetchigum,* truth that transcends personal experience. In fact, these two types of history can be rolled into one, because, for the Ojibwe, the concept of hearsay has no meaning. Thus, Mille Lacs elder George Aubin once related to me the facts of his tribe's historical past as *daebaudjimowin,* history as if he had personally experienced it. At the same time, given the context of the telling, it was a recitation of tribal truth, *auwaetchigum,* that is history. These are kinds of history our institutions can neither recognize nor accept as verifiable ways to understand the past. In our courts, we must weigh the credibility of the testimony of actual witnesses or the written accounts of actual observers. We do not recognize the institutional truths of *auwaetchigum,* which we would classify as "mythology," yet who would claim that a fact is true simply because it is committed to paper? Just as sure as we know that oral history is hearsay, we must recognize that written records are full of perceived truth, and, in fact, we do.

Since Indian oral history is given little credence in our courts, Indian history is effectively taken out of the hands of tribal elders, who are traditionally held responsible for this duty, and with very few exceptions is placed into the arena of non-Indian scholars who are empowered by the courts to speak as experts on behalf of the tribes. I have already mentioned the inevitable personal bias of the people who create the written records from which we must construct Indian history. In almost all cases, these people had no or only a little understanding or even curiosity about Indian culture, but they commonly slanted their descriptions to suit their own purposes. For example, Indian agents often stressed the "civilized" behavior of their Indian charges—wearing Western dress, living in log houses, or farming—in order to tout the success of government civilization programs as well as the fine job they were doing personally.[5] The fact that historic documents contained biases does not mean that such documents are useless for understanding the past; it does mean that they must be used with caution. It also means that these records can be used most effectively by those who understand the cultures of the people being described.

Another pitfall in working with ancient documents is a methodological one. Unfortunately, there is a temptation to read all the documents on one subject and then to select and cite only those that support a particular theory. Lawyers quite naturally tend to classify documents as "good" or "bad" depending on whether or not they support a particular argument. Some even make the pronouncement that they are under no legal obligation to reveal documents that do not support their views. This is, at best, a self-defeating proposition, because opposing experts will certainly bring these "bad" documents to light, since they are "good" documents for them. In fact, all documents pertaining to a topic should be acknowledged. If a document does not support a position, it needs to be explained, or the position needs to be modified. Properly, documents should be used as data to either support or refute a conclusion using the standard of civil procedures established by our courts, that is, "a preponderance of the evidence."

A good effect of the adversarial nature of the court proceedings is achieved in treaty rights cases because, in the end, opposing experts and lawyers are working from the same set of documents. Of the thousands of relevant documents discovered and exchanged during the discovery process, the argument crucial to the outcome of the case usually resolves itself around arguments over the meaning of a mere handful of documents. The disputed facts are those related to points of law and, I might add, are not often even remotely related to the factual quibbles that consume the experts. In my experience with the courts as an expert witness, I have concluded that the reemergence of treaty rights and much of the progress that has come to Indian people in recent decades have come as a benefit of our judicial system. Our courts seem to be the one institution in our society where a small and politically powerless minority, like Indian tribes, can get a fair hearing based on the merits of their case.

Ethnohistory Explained

My own interest in working with archival resources ultimately led me to the intellectual intersection of the fields of anthropology and history. By the late 1980s, I began to teach university courses in the relationship between these two disciplines as well as in the ethnohistory of the native peoples of the Great Lakes region. Ethnohistory is a field of inquiry that combines skills and subject matter that are generally more closely associated with the disciplines of either history or anthropology. Specifically, it is a field that deals with cultural bias that is either implicit or explicit in historical accounts.

As we have seen, such biases are common, if not universal, in written documents that contain descriptions of the actions of people belonging to cultures that differ from that of the writer. It should be noted that such bias is usually the result not of willful distortion but of ignorance of cultural details. Ethnohistory starts with the premise that people of different cultures have different ways of understanding and therefore different ways of trying to manipulate the world around them.

Let us say, for example, that we have a document in which an American military officer provides a description of a battle between Ojibwe and Dakota warriors that took place in 1825. The officer's account would likely be useful for such details as the number of warriors involved, the battle tactics used by each side, and an evaluation of the outcome of the combat. If an Ojibwe or Dakota Indian had been available and able to leave a description of the same events, such an Indian writer might have included information on the feuding that led to the battle, the names of the families involved, the role of magic and spells in determining the outcome, and the war honors earned by the leaders. Obviously, each account would have different information, but the problem is that we do not have accounts from Indian observers. What we do have is plenty of ethnographic information from many other sources about the way Indian warfare was conducted not only by the Ojibwe and Dakota but by similar tribal people. An ethnohistorian with this information in mind could likely get much more from the American officer's description even if the American officer did not understand the fine points of the Indian warfare he was observing. This is true because good descriptions often provide details that might not make much sense to the author.

For example, in 1802 the French Canadian fur trader Michael Curot was trading among the Ojibwe along the St. Croix River, which separates the modern states of Wisconsin and Minnesota.[6] At one point in his journal, he complained about the trouble being caused by one particular Ojibwe band because the men were getting into fights with each other and, when drunk on the rum provided by Curot, were stabbing each other or otherwise causing violence and misery. Curot said that he found this behavior difficult to explain, particularly because all of the men were brothers-in-law to each other, that is, relatives. An ethnohistorian would, hopefully, understand the problem immediately.

Among the Ojibwe, kinship, so important in regulating social interaction, is based on a patrilineal ethic. Unlike in the case of our own bilateral kinship system, where children are members of the families of both the parents, Ojibwe children of that era were members of the father's family only. Further, the father's family formed the nucleus of residence groups, so that a family was based on a male and his sons and grandsons. As these sons and grandsons married, they chose wives from other bands, that is, from unrelated families. These women would come to reside with their husband's families and their children would be members of the father's family. Since all the males of the families which composed the patrilineal band were closely related to each other, they would cooperate to reduce social tensions and to resolve conflicts within the extended family.

In the case of Curot's "problem band," it was composed of related women and their unrelated husbands, the opposite of the customary arrangement. Occasionally, in the course of the Ojibwa year, such social configurations temporarily formed when husbands were requisitioned to help women faced with tasks that required heavy labor. Such gatherings were troublesome, since they were composed of unrelated men who had little incentive to try to quell violent episodes. Further, when women quarreled in the context of this kind of group, the men would be expected to take the part of their wives. As a result, they would end up fighting with each other. Consequently, from an ethnohistorical point of view, there was every reason to expect that an Ojibwe group made up of brothers-in-law and their wives would be very unstable, and the addition of alcohol provided a formula for disaster. Ethnohistory is not simply the conventional history of people who have a different culture; it is the use of knowledge about that culture to fully understand the historical record and to include that information in the production of historiography and culture histories.

Indian Treaties and American Power

Indian treaties, with a few exceptions, were always initiated by the United States in order to advance some economic or political agenda, such as making peace, acquiring natural resources, or, most important, acquiring land. This is not to say that Indian tribes did not have their own objectives in treaty negotiations. In a few cases, they even advocated treaties in order to advance these causes. It would, however, be accurate to say that in all cases of treaties between the United States and Indian tribes, the Indians negotiated from a position of relative weakness. Even in some cases where Indians actually had superior military strength on the ground, they were subject to intimidation and threats.[7] From the Indian point of view, treaties were convened at times and places decided by the United States and were negotiated in a foreign language and translated by interpreters chosen and paid for by the government. When finally negotiated, treaties were set forth in a legal terminology that was difficult to understand and, at any rate, needed to be explained through third parties, using as many as three or four different languages. From the Indian point of view, much had to be accepted on faith. Few modern Americans would buy or sell even an inexpensive item under such a contract, yet in the nineteenth century, Indians were pressured to sell millions of acres of land under such conditions.

Why would Indians accede to such consequential arrangements under such unfavorable terms? Among other reasons, they agreed to treaties because they were forced to do so by the simple exercise of power, both covert and overt. As the frontiers of the United States expanded by settlement in the late eighteenth and early nineteenth centuries, native peoples had the choice of either staying in place as landless refugees while undergoing immense cultural change or maintaining their traditional cultures by moving ahead of the wave of American immigration. By one choice, they would lose their language, their mode of living, their political independence, and their social system and religion. The other choice would cost them their homeland. Among Americans living in the early nineteenth century, it was firmly believed that Indians and whites could not exist side by side in harmony. Despite the fact that frontier communities often found a practical means to accommodate both populations in a mutually beneficial division of labor, the government insisted on casting the relationship as a confrontation between "savagery" and "civilization." This characterization left no middle ground; Indians were either to be civilized or to be banished. The treaty was a device that could accommodate either choice.

In the 1830s Lewis Cass, who, as secretary of war, was in charge of Indian affairs by virtue of the fact that the Indian Office resided within the War Department, wrote an article in which he expounded on the immutable condition of the two races, which highlights the nineteenth-century distinction between savagery and civilization. Ironically, the Indians' failure to surrender to wholesale cultural change was, to many nineteenth-century Americans, a proof of their savage nature.

> The relative condition of the two races of men, who yet divide this portion of the continent between them, is a moral problem involved in much obscurity. The physical causes we have described, exasperated by the moral evils introduced by them, are sufficient to account for the diminution and deterioration of the Indians. But why were not these causes counteracted by the operation of other circumstances? As civilization shed her light upon them, why were they blind to its beams? Hungry or naked, why did they disregard, or regarding, why did they neglect, those arts by which food and clothing could be procured? Existing for two centuries in contact with a civilized people, they have resisted, and successfully too, every effort to meliorate their situation, or to introduce among them the most common arts of life. Their moral and their intellectual condition have been equally stationary. And in the whole circle of their existence, it would be difficult to point to a single advantage which they have derived from their acquaintance with the Europeans. All this is without a parallel in the history of the world. That it is not to be attributed to the indifference or neglect of the whites, we have already shown. There must then be an inherent difficulty, arising from the institutions, character, and condition of the Indians themselves.[8]

In this context, the treaty was the perfect instrument to accomplish the government's objectives. Land could be acquired by purchase, Indian savages could be removed from the path of settlement, and the government could provide educational and religious instruction as part of the land payment. Treaties thus became an important device for avoiding open warfare as well as for reducing racial and cultural strife. The method that treaties afforded for advancing civilization and pushing back savagery was not only relatively rapid and inexpensive but also provided a veil of legality. In these contexts, the treaty compared favorably to the exercise of raw military power and was thus used extensively as Americans expanded the boundaries of the nation westward.

Given this rationale, it seems puzzling that our modern historical mythology subscribes to the notion that the United States broke every treaty it ever concluded with Native Americans. While is true that most were broken by one side or the other, many—perhaps most—were kept, at least as far as their broad objectives were concerned. Perhaps, in concluding that all treaties were broken, Americans are indirectly confronting the realization that our ancestors forced and swindled Indians to sign agreements that were not to the Indians' advantage. It is perhaps also true that by saying that all treaties were broken, we are endorsing the supposition that this fact does not make much of a difference anyway.

For the general public today, the Indian treaties are just ancient agreements. Treaties therefore become simply old documents, which may be safely relegated to the long ago and far away. Certainly, such documents could have no relevance to the present or, just as surely, to the future. After acknowledging historical errors that reduce their credibility, we consign the treaties to the historic past, where they can do no damage to our sense of honor and fairness, which is so much at the forefront of the image Americans have of the United States as a country. It would seem a perfect way for Americans to exonerate ourselves from great historical injustices.

CHAPTER 2

The Treaty

The discovery and exploration of the non-Western world by Europeans during the fifteenth through the eighteenth centuries brought them into contact with native peoples whose very existence posed a host of perplexing philosophical topics. Many of these—such as the nature of civil government, the origin of kinship, the evolution of culture, the morality of slavery, and the justification for wars—were central to debates by scholars of the European Enlightenment. However, beyond the academic ruminations of John Locke, Adam Smith, David Hume, Herbert Spencer, John Stuart Mills, Jean Rousseau, and others lie a host of practical problems in the newly discovered lands of Asia, Africa, and the Americas. In this context, academic discourse was directed toward justification for the usurpation of land and resources from native people, their enslavement, and the waging of war against them.

None of these questions was ultimately more central than the justification for the expropriation of foreign land by European monarchs. This is the case because the taking of land from natives involved a myriad of assumptions related to the basic relationship between Europeans and non-European people and how this relationship reflected the perceived nature of both the natural and the cultural order. During the period of colonization, the rights that Europeans defined for themselves rested on the dual foundations of the importance of race and the idea of cultural evolution.

From at least the early seventeenth century through the nineteenth century, five widely held precepts in the Western world defined the relationship between Europeans and the alien occupants of foreign lands. The former were a priori regarded to be civilized; the latter, savage.

1. Civilized societies were, by definition, superior to savage societies in all important respects.
2. This superiority was, in large part, true because the races of civilized men were endowed by creation with superior characteristics, for example, great intelligence, ingenuity, refinement, and morality.
3. On the contrary, the races of savage men were endowed with characteristics of a less favorable nature, such as cunningness, cruelty, laziness, skill at hunting and warfare, and a pagan nature.
4. Since these characteristics were the result of divine creation, they were regarded to be immutable.
5. Members of civilized society had the right and duty to destroy savage society by education, Christian proselytism, and, if necessary, war.

From the European perspective, dependency on agricultural production (a civilized pursuit) was seen as both a more efficient use of the land than hunting and gathering (a habit of savage life) and also a better use of the land as sanctioned by biblical teachings. Transforming wilderness to productive farms, which required gaining control of native landholdings, was thus not only morally justified but, indeed, seen as a duty of civilized Christian people. This logic extended much further, however. Since savages were, by definition, warlike and hunters, they were also assumed to be wandering migratory people with no fixed abode. Thus, they did not own land but merely occupied it. These beliefs and assumptions justified the expropriation of land but did not square with the facts. Ironically, most of the Americas were occupied not by hunters but by native farmers, whose crops—such as corn, beans, squash, sunflowers, tobacco, potatoes, and peppers—were rapidly appropriated by European colonists, who quickly came to depend on them for sustenance and trade.

Notwithstanding this and other troubling inconsistencies in the civilized/savage dichotomy, European nations of the "age of discovery" adopted means to justify conquest and to divide the spoils. First, among themselves, they recognized the concept of the "right of discovery," by which explorers could lay claim to newly "discovered" land for the monarch who sponsored their expedition of discovery. Second, land could also be claimed as a result of the "right of conquest," which was obtained through "just wars." Presumably, these were wars waged on behalf of the civilized nations and Christianity. Since discovery was less costly than conquest, acquisition by the right of discovery was the preferred method of land theft. It is also why Europeans like to regard the lands that were unknown to them as undeveloped wilderness, which, by definition, would only be occupied by savages. In fact, however, every square foot of the "unexplored wilderness" was claimed by native families, clans, or political polities that were usually prepared to defend their claims against aggressors.

By the late eighteenth and early nineteenth centuries, when the process of colonization put real pressure on native land, several new ideas arose to help legitimize the taking of land acquired by the right of discovery. European nations and, later, the American state acknowledged that American natives had a vested residential right to the soil. This right, which remains a pillar of American Indian law even today, is referred to as "Indian title" or "aboriginal title." In law, Indian or aboriginal title is said to flow from the "undisturbed possession of the soil since time immemorial." Aboriginal title is unlike Western title in several major respects.

First, aboriginal title is a collective right of occupation, rather than ownership in fee. Writing in 1830, Lewis Cass, then secretary of war, explained this concept as a means of creating compatibility between Indian habit and pursuits and Americans' immediate jurisdiction and ultimate domain.[1] Cass also, however, acknowledged the logical conundrum of the United States acquiring title to land from Indians who did not recognize title as a concept.[2] As justification, he cited the observations of John Adams that "Indian tenure is not like our tenure." Explaining that Indians "have no idea of title to the soil itself," Adams said that "it is overrun by them rather than inhabited."[3] Cass was almost certainly influenced by a legal opinion written in 1823 by Chief Justice John Marshall in the case *Johnson v. MacIntosh*, in which Marshall laid out the rationale of right of discovery as the underlying authority of aboriginal title as well as the principle that aboriginal title was good only against the sovereign.[4]

The second departure from the concept of title in fee simple (i.e., freely negotiable) is that aboriginal title could only be acquired by the sovereign. During the seventeenth and eighteenth centuries, the sovereigns in North America were European kings. In the late eighteenth and nineteenth centuries, the government of the United States became the sovereign. As hegemony passed from one sovereign to another, the new sovereign, in turn, inherited the right to acquire aboriginal title. As we shall see, this is an important reason why Indian treaties required a sovereign-to-sovereign relationship.

The desire to acquire the land and, in effect, convert it to a private and salable commodity was not the only impetus for treaty making between the American government and the Indian tribes, but it was certainly the most important one. The process itself, however, also required that some attention be paid to the other rights that Indians associated with their occupation of the land.

The Era of American Treaty Making

The era of Indian treaty making began before the birth of the republic and ended when Congress unilaterally declared an end to treaty making as an instrument of Indian policy in 1871.[5] During that period of a little less than a hundred years, 364 Indian treaties that were negotiated between the United States and various tribes were ratified. Some tribes are parties to dozens of treaty agreements with the United States. Table 1 shows the number of ratified treaties negotiated with the tribes for each decade during the treaty-making era. This count does not include the treaties made between the tribes and the original colonies in the years prior to the American Revolution or the many treaties made between Indians and individual colonists.

The kinds of treaties as well as their frequency

TABLE 1. Number of Treaties Concluded with the U.S. Indian Tribes in the Nineteenth Century

Decade	Number of Treaties	Major Policies
Before 1800	19	Peace and friendship
1800–1809	29	Peace and friendship
1810–19	50	Land cession
1820–29	49	Land cession
1830–39	82	Removal
1840–49	17	Removal
1850–59	58	Reservation and civilization
1860–69	60	Reservation and civilization
Total	364	

Source: Data from Charles J. Kappler, ed., *Indian Treaties 1778–1883* (Mattituck, N.Y.: Amereon House, 1972).

depended on many factors, such as the intensity of the frontier dynamics in colonial expansion, the density of Indians on the active frontier, and the objectives of the U.S. Indian policy. Although treaties were often designed to meet special conditions or multiple objectives, there were four general treaty types. Arranged in chronological manner, reflecting the popularity of the treaty types as is manifest in the process of American settlement and the objectives of government policy, these types are treaties of peace and friendship, land cession treaties, removal treaties, and reservation and civilization treaties.

As American population expanded into the trans-Allegheny west in the years just before and after the War of Independence, it was expanding onto unceded Indian land. The result was many decades of vicious warfare in which both sides committed unspeakable atrocities. This violence in the Ohio Valley and the Southeast added to a long history of colonial Indian wars in New England, New York, and Pennsylvania, all of which bred intense hatred and fear on the part of both Indian and non-Indian populations. Although peace was temporarily restored to the Ohio country by the Treaty of Greenville in 1795, an alliance between a confederacy of tribes of the Old Northwest and the British during the War of 1812 rekindled the flames of mutual hatred on the frontier.

Following the War of 1812, the Great Lakes country produced a profusion of treaties whose main object was to establish peaceful relationships between the tribes and the United States and to promote an Indian-American alliance in case of a future war with Great Britain. Although promoting peace and friendship, such treaties had other objectives as well. Secondary objectives included regulating trade with the tribes, preventing trespass by Americans on Indian land, ascertaining the extent of land claims of each tribe, and discouraging intertribal warfare. For their part, the tribes were anxious to establish peace and to acquire long-term security to their lands, but they also hoped to extract presents from the government in exchange for future fidelity to the United States and to assure access to American traders.

With these peace and friendship objectives largely met by the early 1820s, the United States began to treat with the Great Lakes tribes for land cessions. In the upper Midwest, land cession treaties were negotiated one after another through the second and third decades of the nineteenth century and into the fourth. Typically, land cession treaties designated the land to be ceded to the United States, and since the land to be acquired was usually poorly known, the description of the area to be ceded was given in metes and bounds. Treaties of cession also specified the amount of payment and how the payment was to be made. Typically, payments were in the form of annuities paid over a period of several decades. Payment was usually made in a combination of coinage and benefits, such as schools, blacksmith shops, and the services of carpenters, physicians, teachers, and farmers. Other payments were rendered in goods, including, in part, guns, ammunition, fishnets, traps, clothing, and metal tools and implements. Reservations often were withheld from the land cession as permanent residences for the Indians selling the land; these lands were held in common by the tribe or by specifically named individuals for benefit of the tribe or band. The tribes were occasionally granted the privilege of hunting, fishing, and gathering on the land just ceded to the government.

It was a general hope of the United States that Indians would move to the reservations and confine themselves there while they obtained the skills and habits of civilized life under the guidance of teachers and missionaries. It was also hoped that at some point in the future, the newly civilized Indians would merge with the general population and be assimilated. But Indians usually ceded land as a necessity in order to pay their fur trade debts and to acquire the Western material goods on which they were now dependent. They hoped, also, that the reservations would be secure places of refuge against the advancing tide of American settlement. Most, but not all, Indians hoped to live as they had in the past, to preserve their language and culture and to maintain their political viability as independent people. They also believed they could use traditional skills to support themselves and to forge useful relationships with their new non-Indian neighbors.

During the late 1820s, it became apparent to many Americans and to the Indian Office that reservations could not shelter Indian people from the ill effects of intoxicating beverages and other bad outcomes resulting from contact with unscrupulous frontiersmen.[6] Eventually, a powerful coalition consisting of eastern intellectuals, clergy, and politicians joined with frontier Indian haters in the idea that the best means to deal with Indians was to remove them from the eastern settled states and territories and to form them into colonies west of the Mississippi River. The more benevolently inclined argued that once removed from close contact with frontiersmen and settlers, Indians could be colonized in peace and could be civilized under the supervision of missionaries and teachers. Other elements in the American body politic simply wanted to be rid of Indians in order to obtain their tribal domains.

The removal idea was supported by President Andrew Jackson, and on May 28, 1830, Congress approved the Indian Removal Act.[7] The act permitted Indian tribes in the states and territories east of the Mississippi to voluntarily exchange their land for new land in the West. In fact, the removal act was optional in name only; treaties with many tribes in the Southeast and the Midwest virtually forced removal.[8] In some cases, such as the Potawatomi, Indian people escaped to Canada or to the deep north woods rather than comply with the removal treaties.

Indians of virtually every tribe opposed removal from their ancestral homelands. Although treaties required Indians to remove, Indians delayed this outcome by all possible means. In the end, many were removed by force and transported west under conditions of severe hardship. The Cherokee removal, the Trail of Tears, is well known. The equally tragic removal episodes of other tribes remain obscure except in their own oral histories.

Almost before it began, it became apparent that removal policy would fail. By the mid-1830s, the American settlement frontier had already hopped the Mississippi River, so it became increasingly difficult to find isolated places to settle removed tribes. It was also problematic that land on which the government hoped to settle removed Indians was already occupied by local tribes who did not welcome competitors for the meager resources of their lands. In addition, the Indian colonies that had been established failed to produce "civilized" Indians who were eager for assimilation. In that day, it was popular to blame the Indians themselves for the failure of the Indian civilization effort, citing the supposed limitations inherent in the psychological makeup of the Indians themselves—that is, to conclude that they were incapable of learning civilized habits and pursuits.

In 1849 the Indian Office was reorganized and transferred from the War Department to the newly created Department of the Interior. The appointment of George Manypenny as commissioner of Indian affairs (1853–57) brought a new Indian policy and the many treaties that gave it effect.[9] Manypenny and his supporters believed that the fault for the failure of the removal effort as a means of civilizing and acculturating Indians lay not with the Indians but with government policy.[10] Commissioner Manypenny did, however, strongly believe that education was a key to assimilating Indians into the American mainstream. He also believed that this work could only succeed if Indians were isolated from the interference of frontier ruffians. To accomplish his mission, Manypenny proposed the creation of a new kind of reservation. It would be within the homelands of the particular tribe and would have well-defined and protected boundaries. The only non-Indians allowed to enter the reserve would be teachers, agents, and missionaries who were dedicated to Indian welfare.[11]

A key concept of the new reservation and civilization movement was the allotment of land in severalty. Each reservation would be surveyed into parcels, usually forty and eighty acres in size, sufficient to provide each family with its own farm. In time the farm would eventually be deeded to the head of the household in fee simple. Manypenny's hope was that the farm would promote free enterprise through market production and thus teach Indians the value of participation in the American economy as well as hard physical labor. After a few years, Manypenny believed, allotted Indians would be educated and self-sustaining, and the government would, in effect, be out of the Indian business.

Commissioner Manypenny negotiated fifty-three reservation and civilization treaties during his tenure. These treaties took different forms but contained similar terminology. Succinctly stated, Manypenny's objectives were as follows:

1. Concentrate Indians by reducing their land base and settling them on permanent reservations where they could be protected and where services could be provided effectively.
2. Consolidate money payments due under former treaties and sort out conflicting land claims in order to simplify the government's relations with each tribe.
3. Provide instruction in the arts of civilization to include instruction in the English language, Christianity, and Western agriculture; to foster these pursuits, the government would provide the services of blacksmiths, mechanics, millers, teachers, doctors, and missionaries who would work under the supervision of resident agents.
4. Demonstrate the benefits of private property ownership and labor by the allotment of family farms that would become the secure holdings of individuals.
5. Encourage Indians to eventually take an active role as citizens of their states and territories.

Manypenny often negotiated treaties personally, and if not, he illustrated a great deal of familiarity with the situation of the bands and tribes with whom the negotiations were taking place. He also often negotiated treaties in rapid order and used standard language, especially when dealing with less sophisticated tribes.

Allotment treaties recognized the problems of protecting Indian tenure to the allotments and included a variety of schemes to protect Indian interest in the land until the Indians were able to protect it for themselves. Unfortunately, none of these devices succeeded in keeping reservation lands in Indian hands. In the upper Great Lakes country, where numerous Manypenny treaties were negotiated in the 1850s, farming opportunities were limited by poor soils and a short growing season. Farming, likewise, had little appeal for the indigenous tribes who were, by tradition, fishermen and hunters. To the people of these tribes, allotted lands were virtually worthless. They were not worthless, however, to the lumber companies who coveted the pine and hardwood timber that covered the new allotments. During the post–Civil War lumber boom, non-Indian interest succeeded not only in doing business on the reservations but in swindling Indians out of their landholdings. By the early twentieth century, large corporations and non-Indian individuals owned practically all the land within the boundaries of the reservations that were created by the Manypenny treaties.

During the early decades of the twentieth century, most Great Lakes Indians were living as landless squatters: some crowded into the few remaining allotments of relatives, others formed communities on the margins of American towns, and still others followed traditional hunting rounds and lived on public land. Each year, Indians came increasingly under the authority of state and local laws, many of which were contrary to both traditional culture and the treaties they had signed with the United States. The Bureau of Indian Affairs supported, by and large, the efforts of the states to incorporate Indians. Both the state and the federal government seemed to regard treaties as historical anachronisms. Thus, between the late nineteenth century and the third quarter of the twentieth century, treaties were virtually ignored except by the Indian parties who believed them to remain in force.

In 1871 Congress decided to abolish treaty making with Indian tribes.[12] Apparently, this move was a result of the fact that the House of Representatives, which appropriated funds for the purpose of making treaties, had very little to say about their content and thus about the direction of Indian policy per se. The early 1890s brought yet another Indian policy shift when

Congress enacted the General Allotment Act, also called the Dawes Act.[13] This act allotted the large western reservations that were made by earlier treaties that provided that these reservations were to be held in common. After allotting parcels to individuals of small populations, the enormous tracts of unallotted land were declared to be "surplus" and were sold to non-Indian ranchers and farmers. It is estimated that at least 130 million acres of land were alienated from Indian control as a result of the General Allotment Act.[14] Even though the act had questionable application in the eastern part of the country, bureaucrats in the Indian Office used its provisions to try to define the status of individual Indian allottees with respect to landownership as well as access to government services.

By the early decades of the twentieth century, Indians all across the United States were largely landless and living in abject poverty. Fortunately, Congress took notice of these conditions and, in 1934, passed a sweeping reform of Indian policy known as the Indian Reorganization Act, or the Wheeler-Howard Act.[15] This legislation permitted disenfranchised tribes to reorganize under federal charter. The act also provided funds for reorganized tribes to reacquire reservation land and to fund economic development projects.[16] Clearly, the Indian Reorganization Act provided the legal and political basis for the resurgence of Indian tribes that has taken place in the last half of the twentieth century.

Western Assumptions of Treaty Making

From the Western perspective, treaties were political agreements. Although they may concern themselves with issues of war or peace, economic exchange, and a variety of other subjects, they are political in nature. The work of negotiating, agreeing, ratifying, and enforcing the terms of the treaty was undertaken and guaranteed by a sovereign state. Each state party was liable for the terms of the treaty irrespective of who acted as king, president, or emperor.

In Western context, a treaty implied certain assumptions about each sovereign party. The first and perhaps most important theoretical premise of state-sponsored treaty making is that the sovereigns are equal partners in the agreement. In ideological conception, a treaty could not be negotiated under duress and at the same time accepted as legitimate. The notion of equality of sovereigns was not a precondition of treaty making but a rationale of legitimacy. Thus, while treaty making sovereigns are seldom equal in power, the stronger partner cannot legitimatize a treaty that was forced on a weaker sovereign.

Another assumption is that both of the treaty partners have the political power to uphold their obligations under the treaty agreement. Thus, it might be rightly pointed out that treaties were instruments of both internal and external exercises of power. Western governments also assumed that over the term of the treaty, participating states would fulfill the treaty stipulation to which they agreed. For good reasons, states were suspicious of the motivations of each other, but the concept of honor (even among thieves) was a necessary component of treaty making.

Agreements among treaty parties had to be recorded as written documents, since, in literate society, such documents are recognized as the only reliable means to record the details of agreements. This process was complicated when two or more languages were involved in treaty conferences, since translators had to be employed in both negotiation and recording of the content of treaty agreements. Negotiated treaty agreements also had to be legitimized by a formal procedure set forth by both state parties, in order to approve the arrangements made on behalf of the state and to provide the sanction of state power in all aspects of the treaty's function.

In the case of the United States, the rules of treaty making are described in the U.S. Constitution, Article II, Section 2, which proscribes the duties of the president. Among these is the responsibility of treaty making: "He shall have power, by and with the advice and consent of the Senate, to make treaties provided that two thirds of the senators concur."[17] Thus, in the American system, the president has the power to negotiate treaties with foreign states but must lay them before the senators for approval.

In the normal course of affairs in the nineteenth century, American treaty making with Indian tribes was initiated by the Indian Office, headed by the commissioner of Indian affairs. The commissioner was appointed by the president, and the Indian Office was, of course, located within the executive branch of government. When a treaty seemed appropriate, the secretary of war or, after 1849, the secretary of the interior appointed one or, frequently, several treaty commissioners to actually negotiate the treaty. Congress would then be asked to appropriate funds to pay the commissioners and to provide for expenses to cover the cost of the negotiations. The treaty commissioners were then given a written charge by the appropriate cabinet secretary, by the commissioner of Indian affairs, or even, occasionally, by Congress. The treaty charge laid out the desired objectives of the proposed treaty in detail: when and where the negotiations would take place, which Indians were to be included, and even such details as what lands were to be purchased and the maximum price to be paid per acre. Recognizing, however, that negotiations required bargaining, the treaty commissioners were given the latitude necessary to conclude an agreement.

After the treaty was negotiated, the draft treaty was transmitted by the treaty commissioners to the commissioner of Indian affairs, along with a description of the content of the proposed treaty and an explanation of why its provisions were negotiated as they were. On some occasions, a journal of the proceedings of the actual negotiations was prepared by a treaty secretary. This journal was also forwarded to the commissioner. Once the draft treaty had been approved by the appropriate cabinet secretary, it was, with the recommendation of the commissioner of Indian affairs, forwarded by the president to the U.S. Senate for consideration. Here, it was assigned to the Senate Committee on Indian Affairs for discussion and, if approved, passed to the full Senate for floor debate. On some occasions, the Senate refused to ratify Indian treaties; on others, it gave approval either as the treaty was negotiated or with amendments. In the latter case, the treaty had to be returned to the Indian parties for discussion and for acceptance or rejection of the proposed amendments. Once having two-thirds approval of the senators, the treaty was returned to the president for his signature of final approval. The process of approving treaties sometimes required only a few weeks but could require several years.

Ratified treaties are dated in three separate ways: by the date of negotiation, the date the treaty was ratified by the Senate, and the date it was signed and proclaimed by the president. When approved, the treaties had the full force of federal law. Yet none of these elaborate and time-honored treaty protocols made much sense to Native Americans, who had their own means of understanding agreements with foreigners.

CHAPTER 3

The Foundations of Treaty Making

It is fashionable in social and historical debate to draw an invidious parallel between the slow rates at which Native Americans assimilated into American society and the rapid assimilation of nineteenth-century European immigrants. The immigrants arrived with little money, no English, and strange customs, yet they and their children rapidly assimilated, whereas the assimilation of the Indians, who also had different cultures, spoke no English, and had few economic means, has been very slow. Yet the comparison of these two episodes of assimilation is seriously flawed in a number of important respects.

First, Native Americans, unlike European immigrants who composed the greatest percentage of nineteenth-century immigrants, were not part of the Western tradition. They were not Christians, capitalists, or holders of democratic traditions. Nor did they subscribe to Western ideals concerning kinship, land tenure, inheritance, or political leadership. In short, Native Americans were people who constructed the world in a fundamentally different way than Westernized populations.

Beyond this, it is worth remembering that native people of the colonial era were overrun by force and that their cultures were under heavy assault from the outside. Quite naturally, they tended to respond to these pressures by reinforcing their own cultural beliefs, rather than willingly abandoning them. Unlike European immigrants who embraced change, Indian people resisted acculturation and assimilation as a mechanism of cultural and personal survival.

The fact that the native people who negotiated treaties with the United States did have a radically different view of their natural, social, and historical environments is a central starting point in both understanding the treaties they agreed to and adjudicating them in the modern courts of law. Understanding treaties is a cross-cultural exercise, and this fact explains the role of anthropologists and ethnohistorians in the judicial process.

The Great Lakes Indians

The native peoples of the New World developed a huge variety of languages and an equally impressive diversity of cultural traditions. These were the results of at least fourteen thousand years of cultural development over a period of time prior to discovery by Europeans. Today, we know only the bare remnants of this garden of cultural diversity, and even so, it is quite impressive. This book deals with only a small corner of the North American continent, the upper Great Lakes region of the United States—that is, the drainages of Lakes Superior, Michigan, and Huron. This region was occupied by speakers of the Algonquian languages, which are both ancient and grammatically complex. Tribal and ethnic labels present a difficult problem for the ethnohistorian, since there has been substantial change in preferred renderings in historic times as well as in the usage of contemporary native groups.

Most people are aware that the term *Indian,* long used to describe aboriginal or native people of the New World, has now fallen into disfavor because it is based on the mistaken belief of Spanish explorers that they had reached the Indian subcontinent. Nonetheless, the term is still widely used today, including by native peoples themselves, such as, for example, the "Sault Ste. Marie Tribe of Chippewa Indians." Great Lakes area native people today prefer the Algonquian term *Anishnabe* or its plural, *Anishnabeg,* which, in their languages, has reference to the original or true people. This term, however, is generic in the sense that it applies equally to ethnic categories, such as Ojibwe, Odawa, Potawatomi, or Menominee, among others.

Tribal designations have even more difficult problems. For example, the modern term *Ojibwe* refers to many named bands of native people scattered from Quebec to the Great Plains and from the Hudson Bay lowlands of Ontario to the upper Great Lakes states. Over this huge area, native Ojibwe people share a common dialect of the Algonquian language. At the time of the earliest European exploration of the region in the seventeenth century, these groups identified themselves with local names, such as *Amikwa, Temagami,* and *Marameg.* By the eighteenth century, these groups were known collectively as Ojibwa and in Canada as Ojibway. By the nineteenth century, the name for these groups had been corrupted into the English *Chippewa,* a term used in treaty documents. By the late twentieth century, a new spelling of *Ojibwa* emerged, and *Ojibwe* became the preferred spelling by American Ojibwe, as a more phonetically accurate version of the original.

For the purpose of this book, an attempt has been made to use terms in their historic context or, when referring to modern tribes, their preferred usage. Although admittedly confusing at times, consistency of usage—say, for example, changing the nineteenth-century *Chippewa* to follow the twentieth-century preference for *Ojibwe* or *Anishnabeg*—would not improve clarity. Consequently, the reader is asked to remember that *Chippewa* = *Chippeway* = *Ojibwa* = *Ojibwe* and that *Ottawa* = *Odawa.*

Great Lakes Algonquian speakers thus included the Ojibwe, who historically occupied the vast boreal forest from Quebec to Manitoba and south through the Ontario Peninsula, central Michigan, and Wisconsin, as well as northern and eastern Minnesota.[1] The Odawa originally occupied the northern and eastern rim of Lake Huron but today inhabit the eastern shore of Lake Michigan from the Straits of Mackinac south to Michigan's Grand River valley. South of the Odawa were the Potawatomi, who originally established their villages in southern Michigan and northern Indiana. In later times, they expanded around the south end of Lake Michigan, northward into northeastern Illinois, and along the western shore of Lake Michigan to the tip of the Door Peninsula of Wisconsin. The Ojibwe, Odawa, and Potawatomi spoke mutually intelligible dialects of an Algonquian language and consider themselves to be historically related. By the late eighteenth century, if not before, they referred to themselves collectively as the Confederacy of the Three Fires.

The Menominee, another Algonquian-speaking people, have traditionally occupied the area around Green Bay and Lake Winnebago in eastern Wisconsin and also established villages in the valleys of the Wolf and Menominee rivers. In the nineteenth century, their territorial claims extended south to the Milwaukee River and west into Wisconsin as far as the Mississippi River drainage. The Fox River valley of eastern Wisconsin was home to two Algonquian-speaking tribes that have close historical affiliation to the Sauk and Mesquakie, or Fox.[2]

East of the Algonquians lived speakers of the Iroquoian languages. These languages were as different from the Algonquian languages as English is from Chinese. The Five Nations Iroquois—that is, the Seneca, Cayuga, Oneida, Onondaga, and Mohawk—occupied what is now upstate New York. Iroquoian speakers also occupied both shores of eastern Lake Erie. These included the Erie and Wenro groups to the south of the lake and the Neutral, Tobacco, and Huron groups on the north.

West of the Algonquians were the Siouan-speaking Dakota, who inhabited the north plains and the prairie fringes of the eastern woodlands. The Dakota peoples occupied all of the country that now composes central and southern Minnesota. A related Siouan-speaking group, the Ho Chunk, or Winnebago, occupied south-central Wisconsin west of Lake Winnebago and south of the Wisconsin River.

From the mid-seventeenth century through the eighteenth, intertribal warfare, mostly resulting from competition between competing European powers, resulted in a great deal of geographic displacement of aboriginal tribes from their historic homelands. Nonetheless, the upper Great Lakes region remained solidly Algonquian in its linguistic affiliation and cultural affinities. Examples of such movement include the Petun, or Wyandot, an Iroquoian-speaking group who, during the late seventeenth century, moved from Ontario to the Straits of Mackinac area. In the early eighteenth century, the same group decided to relocate to the Detroit River valley and, still later, to the Sandusky area of northwestern Ohio. Other eastern Indians, including a group of Oneida, moved west to Green Bay, Wisconsin, in the early nineteenth century, as did some refugee Stockbridge and Munsee. These latter were actually coastal Algonquian speakers originally from New England who settled in central Wisconsin. All of these invading groups remained small and isolated minorities among resident Algonquian tribes. One exception is the Mississauga Ojibwe of the Ontario Peninsula who entered southeastern Michigan in large numbers during the late eighteenth century. These people became and remained the dominant group in the Saginaw Valley and along the eastern coast of Lake Huron.

Unfortunately, there are no comprehensive descriptions of any non-Western cultures before the mid-nineteenth century, when Lewis Henry Morgan published his description of the New York Iroquois.[3] Accordingly, Great Lakes Indian cultures of earlier times are known only from the casual references to Indian customs and behaviors that were recorded by explorers, traders, military officers, and adventurers who traveled the Great Lakes country in the seventeenth and eighteenth centuries. These accounts, though scattered, incomplete, and occasionally inaccurate, are nonetheless of great value. They have been widely cited by modern ethnographers and historians struggling to arrive at an understanding of Indian life and culture during the earliest centuries of European contact. What we know today of these topics is the result of traveler accounts, the work of twentieth-century ethnographers and historians, and information drawn from comparative ethnology, as well as the oral histories of the Indians themselves.

Some Cultural Principles

Given the scope and subject of this work, it is impractical to provide details regarding the customs and practices that are unique to specific Great Lakes tribal groups. It is, however, necessary to the understanding of treaty relations that the reader have a basic knowledge of the underlying cultural principles that organize the specific cultures of the tribes that were parties to the treaties that will be under discussion. It is necessary to keep in mind that the generalized description that follows is a reconstruction of the social and political organizations that would likely have been found as part of the basic organizing principles of all of the Algonquian tribes prior to extensive contact with Euro-Americans. These principles form the baseline from which historic cultural change may be monitored.

Economy and Technology

Upon the initial contact with Europeans, the Great Lakes tribes had what has been described as a Stone Age technology; that is, all their tools and implements were made from natural materials, those at hand in nature, such as stone, clay, wood, and hides. They did not possess smelted metal tools, glass, hard-fired ceramics, or woven fabrics. They did possess a vast store of knowledge concerning the resources of their environments as well as some indigenous devices that enhanced their survival in the natural world. The latter included such items as ceramic vessels, snowshoes, bows and arrows, canoes, netting, and medicines. It should be said that they also had access to domesticated food crops, particularly corn, beans, and squashes. In these precontact societies, everyone had access to essentially all of the same tools and implements; there was little difference between individuals as to the quality or quantity of their material possessions. Production was not aimed at personal acquisition of goods beyond immediate need; in fact, the accumulation of goods was seen as selfish and strongly discouraged.[4]

At the time of contact, the natives of the Great Lakes region had developed an economy that was the product of thousands of years of environmental and social adaptation. Sustaining life required hard work, but their economy was relatively stable and afforded relative security for their small populations. Those Algonquian groups living in the north were mainly hunters and fishermen who also availed themselves of plant foods that were naturally available in the mixed deciduous and conifer forests in which they lived. In historic times, these people became known as the Ojibwe. Farther to the south of the deciduous forest areas and where the eastern woodlands met the prairies, the climate was milder and the growing season longer. Although hunting and fishing was still an important element of the food quest, the native people of this region also produced food by horticulture. Here, such people as the Odawa and Potawatomi grew corn, beans, and squash, which provided both abundant and storable food.

Even with the addition of cultivated foods, the way of life dependent on hunting and gathering was tenuous. Noncultivated foods are, by nature, scattered over the landscape in patches and, in addition, only become available in quantity at certain times of the year. Thus, for example, blueberries, spawning fish, or migratory waterfowl are only available at certain times and in the specific habitats they favor. This fact necessitates that hunters and gatherers be highly mobile and know what foods are likely to be available in time and space. One strategy that evolved from these circumstances is the "seasonal round." In the Great Lakes region, the seasonal round is manifest in a settlement system in which native people lived in centralized villages of about 150 to 200 people during the warm season, when natural food was abundant.[5] In the winter, the time of scarcity, the villages fragmented as individual families spread out to visit remote hunting grounds. Thus, when food was scarce and dispersed, people distributed themselves in the same manner. In the spring and summer, villages were reoccupied in traditional locations that gave access to garden spots, sugaring groves, burial grounds, and fishing sites.

The Algonquian tribes also developed numerous social strategies to cope with the inevitable economic shortfalls resulting from natural cycles. Staking exclusive territorial claims is one such mechanism. As is typical among hunters and gatherers, each residential group claims exclusive use of the resources within a defined territory. These claims prevent use by other groups and enhance the local group's ability to reliably predict food availability within the territory. Although territories are not owned in the Western sense, families depend on the resources of their territory and are willing to defend them vigorously against surreptitious users.

It may seem strange, therefore, that when members of neighboring bands request the use of the resources of their neighbor's territory, they are seldom denied. This is true because economies dependent on hunting and gathering are reciprocal in nature. Denying a neighbor use of the resources exclusively claimed by a band would also necessarily foreclose future use by that band of the neighbor's territory. This result would be disastrous in the long run, since, over time, shortage inevitably comes to all areas. Thus, for example, a forest fire in the home territory of one band would be disastrous if the affected band was not able to make a reciprocal claim to the unburned territory of its neighbors.

Another important social coping mechanism is reciprocal sharing, which is accomplished by gift giving. As in modern circumstances, gift giving implies an obligation of return. The kin relationship between gift exchangers figures strongly into the nature of the gift exchange among Algonquians.[6] The closer the kin exchanging gifts are, the less immediate the return is, because the giving is expected to balance in the long run. If, however, the exchangers are more distant kin or even total strangers, such as occurred during the fur trade, then exchanges are expected to be equal in value, so that each party is immediately satisfied. Consider the advantage of reciprocal gift giving. Suppose a man who kills a deer gives the whole deer to others piece by piece. The benefit of giving is evident: since any man might only occasionally kill a deer, it would be a long, hungry time between kills; with a reciprocal exchange system, the hunter and his family will share in the venison brought in by all other hunters. The gift-giving ethic, which also extends to nonfood commodities, manufactured items, and even labor, puts emphasis on the survival of the group rather than the individual. In the preceding illustration, reciprocal giving benefits everyone equally, not just the best hunter. Gift giving works for everyone's benefit because it tends to even out the deficit created by constant demand in the presence of intermittent supply.

Kinship

The importance of kinship among hunters and gatherers cannot be overemphasized. As we saw in the case of economic exchange, the degree of kinship between individuals in Algonquian society determines how individuals interact. Among the Algonquians, unlike the Iroquoians, kin and residential groups are formed around males. Thus, the father, his sons and daughters, and his grandchildren form the patrilineal family. This family, along with attached wives and mothers, who are members of other kin groups, forms the minimal residential group. Put another way, women of unrelated families who marry into the group of related males become part of the husband's nuclear family but are never members of the patrilineal group to which their husbands and children belong. Marriage thus functions to create in-law bonds between the patrilineal families that form the basis of residential groups, and in this way, marriage creates bonds of mutual help and exchange. It is for this reason that an in-law obligation would likely be involved in a request to use resources in the territory of another residential group.

Large residential groups, such as summer villages, would be composed of several dozen nuclear families headed by related males—perhaps brothers, paternal uncles, and certain cousins. Together, these extended families constitute a band. The families of the band live together during the warm seasons, cooperate in the food quest, hold a territory in common, cooperate in offensive and defensive warfare, and form the largest political group of Algonquian society.

In the case of the Ojibwe, Menominee, and especially the Potawatomi, super groupings of families also exist. These are referred to as clans. Clans are nonresidential groups that are based on mythological concepts of descent from a common ancestor. In the case of Algonquian clans, the progenitors are animals, and the clans are, thereby, called totemic clans. Membership in a clan is a matter of birth, and as such, clan affiliation does not change during life. Certain patrilineal families say that they trace their ancestry to the wolf, others to the bear, martin, eagle, crane, sturgeon, or another of the dozens of clan progenitors. In all cases, individuals of the particular clan feel themselves more closely related to fellow clan members than to people of other clans. For this reason, men choose wives from unrelated clans; thus, clans are exogamous.

Since clans are not residential groups, members of any particular clan might live in any village of the tribe. Since clan members regard other members of their clan as close family, a member of the wolf clan visiting a distant village would likely find clan fathers, mothers, sisters, and brothers among the village residents. Even though they may be unknown to each other, they owe each other the status of close kin, and in this way, the web of clanship works to unite a dispersed society through familial obligations.

In some cases, such as the Menominee and Potawatomi, the clans are themselves grouped into larger divisions. These groups of clans make up groupings of kin who believe themselves to be more closely related to the clans of their group than to the clans of the other groups of clans. These large groupings of clans are called phratries, and these, too, are exogamous, meaning that each person must marry someone from a clan of another phratry. Phratries are often assigned special ceremonial duties, which helps to unify the social whole.

Among the Potawatomi, clans were, by tradition, assigned special ceremonial roles, such as supplying leaders for war and peace, hosting entertainment on special occasions, or providing skilled orators. Clans typically owned certain personal names, songs, and ritual prerogatives.[7] Although the Ojibwe had many clans, which seemed to mainly function in regulating marriage, they also played a role in providing political leadership in specific areas of the tribal domain. Apparently, the Odawa clan system was poorly developed compared to the other Great Lakes Algonquians, but the early historic Odawa grouped themselves into four regional tribes.

Polity

Just as there was no social stratification in Algonquian society, neither was there a political hierarchy. In fact, the Algonquians were truly egalitarian people who believed that no individual had the right or power to make a decision for anyone else. Every individual, regardless of sex or age, made their own decisions, and all group action was a result of consensus among the group's participants.

Those individuals who exhibited skill, wisdom, experience, and generosity became leaders because others followed their advice. Lack of political ambition was a characteristic to be admired in a leader. There was some tendency for the son of a successful chief to become chief in place of his father, but this only occurred when the son was competent in his own right. Men who became leaders of various endeavors were referred to as *ogamaw,* or *okamaw,* a term translated into English as "chief." In external affairs, an *ogamaw* represented a local band, which, as has been stated, was the largest decision-making group in Algonquian society. The "tribe" as we know it today—that is, as a political institution—did not exist at the time of European contact or for many years afterward. Of course, the Algonquian people did recognize that there were others living at some distance around them who spoke their language and had similar customs and to whom they felt related, but there was no collective political action with these people or common leadership. During the nineteenth century, some *ogamaw* achieved a degree of renown that extended beyond the local group. These were usually famous war leaders or civil chiefs who were skilled in diplomacy. Although perhaps respected beyond the band, these prominent leaders had no more authority than any other individual.

During the eighteenth century, warfare with powerful Euro-American enemies resulted in temporary military alliances between tribal groups. For example, a relatively short-lived confederacy of midwestern tribes included the Shawnee, Miami, Illini, Odawa, Wyandot, Ojibwe, and Kickapoo, among others. These tribes formed a loose alliance in hope of repelling American encroachment into the Ohio country.[8] Rather than a true political amalgamation, such confederacies were better thought of as temporary truces between tribes or tribal factions that were otherwise more or less hostile to each other—that is, a temporary alliance to fight a common enemy. In the north, the Ojibwe, Odawa, and Potawatomi referred to themselves collectively as the Confederacy of the Three Fires, but in actual practice, this relationship seems to have had to do more with origin mythology than with political action. It seems evident that outside of their utility for purposes of waging war, midwestern Indian confederacies had little real political import.

A Very Brief History of the Great Lakes Algonquians

Like all cultural groups, the culture of the Algonquian people of the upper Great Lakes was continuously evolving. Unfortunately, the absence of written records sometimes leads observers to conclude that the cultures of nonliterate societies were static or changeless. This is not true, and in the case of the Great Lakes natives, the prehistoric archaeological record is replete with evidence of thousands of years of cultural change brought about through adaptation to the changing environment and neighboring cultures. The pace of cultural adaptation, however, accelerated rapidly with European contact. In the early seventeenth century, Great Lakes natives were exposed to iron tools, firearms, woven clothing, and many other European technological items that they rapidly adopted and modified for their own purposes. Likewise, changes were taking place in social, political, and ideological realms of their culture.

It should be remembered that by the time of the nineteenth-century treaty-making era under discussion here, the native people who were partners in these treaties had been in contact with Europeans for nearly two hundred years. Yet we should also remember that culture change is usually a slow process; people of any society, particularly non-Western ones under pressure from alien cultures who have the power to overwhelm them, are often reluctant to modify their beliefs and values. It is also worth noting that culture change is not a one-way street. As Indians were changing to accommodate Western technology and cultural practices, Europeans were likewise adopting elements of Indian technology and culture. For the sake of convenience and brevity, the acculturative history of the Great Lakes Algonquians might be illustrated by a number of arbitrary periods, discussion of which follows.[9]

The Early Fur Trade: 1600–1650

This was the period of initial contact between the Indians and French explorers, traders, and missionaries. At this time, actual face-to-face contact between Indians and the French was a rare occurrence in the western Great Lakes country, as most of the French population was confined to the region east of Lake Huron. Likewise, the number of European trade goods in circulation was relatively small, and in many cases, these goods were acquired by trade with other tribes rather than through direct contact with the Europeans. In fact, the Algonquians were in intense competition with each other for access to trade goods, which was an important contributing cause to intertribal hostility. Trade and diplomacy between the French and Indians during the early period of the fur trade was largely dictated by Indian traditions.

The Middle Fur Trade: 1650–63

The establishment of French forts, mission stations, and trading houses in Indian country increased the availability of European goods and the quantity in actual circulation and, consequently, the degree of reliance the Indians placed on these goods. French-Indian mixed bloods, or métis, became influential in the trade as well as a strong political and social force in Indian communities. In addition to furs, Indian people produced a wide range of food and manufactured products for commerce with Europeans.

Algonquian warriors from the upper Great Lakes tribes became involved as fighters for the French interests in the eastern and southern campaigns against the British and their Indian allies. At the same time, European diseases, alcohol addiction, population loss, and population displacement became part of Indian life. Religious factionalism as a result of Christian influences as well as indigenous revivalism and revitalization movements began to affect the social and political solidarity of native communities. Many of the formal conventions of later Indian-European political negotiation had their origin in this period.

The British Period: 1763–1815

This period was marked by a great deal of warfare and violence that had its origin in British-American conflict as well as the encroachment of the American settlement frontier into the Ohio Valley. Intertribal alliances were formed to resist British trade policies and, later, to combat American settlement and to support British interests in the region. Although the War of 1812 and its aftermath resolved the international border between the two nations through the Great Lakes region, both the British and American governments provided huge quantities of presents to Great Lakes tribes in an attempt to curry their favor in case of future warfare between the two nations.

The fur trade was better organized and regulated during this time, and traders and trading establishments became more abundant in Indian country. Trade goods were becoming indispensable to Indian consumers. The dispersed clan system, which had evolved during the eighteenth century, helped to strengthen Indian societies that were being damaged by religious and political factionalism.[10]

The Treaty Era: 1815–71

The early part of this period marked the high point of the fur trade that collapsed in the Great Lakes region in the early 1840s. Mixed-blood individuals and communities were common on the Great Lakes frontier and grew increasingly influential in Indian affairs. The transition to American control south of the upper Great Lakes resulted in the initial surge of American settlement in the Old Northwest. The Indian land base began to decline as a result of land cession treaties associated with the removal policy.[11] The appearance of missions and schools established pursuant to treaty agreements began to erode the integrity of Indian culture but produced young people who were better able to cope with their new non-Indian neighbors. With the decline of the fur trade, Indians came to rely on traditional skills, such as fishing, hunting, and woodcraft, to participate in the American economy. The establishment of the Indian Office by the U.S. government, its appointment of Indian agents to reside in Indian country, and the passage of laws regulating Indian trade created a very forceful presence for the United States in the everyday affairs of the Algonquian tribes.

Treaty making with the United States matured in form and procedure during this period and had a variety of effects on Indian tribes. Certainly, the material benefits and services they provided made life more comfortable, and at least in the short run, the promise of land reservations and rights for land use decreased anxiety for the future. In those cases where treaties required long-distance removals and starting a new life in a radically different western environment, the treaties brought despair and anger.

The Post-treaty Era: 1871–1910

By the late nineteenth century, most of the extensive land allotments made to Indians by treaties were lost to land fraud and tax sales.[12] While economic times were relatively prosperous for Indians who engaged in opportunities for wage labor offered by lumber, mining, and fishing industries, the widespread use of alcohol and disease sapped the health and vitality of many Indian people. Indian boarding schools established by the federal government, which often required the attendance of school-age children, were very effective in disrupting the cultural and linguistic link between older and younger generations of Indian people.[13] Despite centuries of culture contact between Great Lakes Indians and Euro-Americans, most aspects of traditional culture and language were very much alive in Indian communities until the beginning of the twentieth century. By the third decade of the twentieth century, only the elders remembered the traditional ways.

The Period of Poverty and Neglect: 1910–40

The cycle of poverty, alcohol abuse, and land loss devastated several generations of Algonquian people. Lacking any viable alternative, Indians were forced to live in poor housing, suffered frequent sickness, lacked jobs, and had fewer educational opportunities. Throughout the Great Lakes region, Indians were romanticized for the burgeoning tourist industry, on the one hand, and yet, on the other, forced to endure intense racial prejudice on the part of their non-Indian neighbors.

After the loss of their landholdings, most Indian people formed small communities on the margins of American towns; others crowded onto the few remaining reservation lands or remaining allotments. At the same time, the federal government drastically reduced its stewardship over and presence among the Algonquian tribes. As the federal presence faded from the Great Lakes region, the states became more vigorous in exerting their authority over Indian people. Indians who had always been subject to federal authority were forced to endure abuse at the hands of local law enforcement, game wardens, and social welfare workers who refused to recognize either treaty rights or traditional social practices.

The Cultural Resurgence: 1940 to the Present

The Indian Reorganization Act passed by Congress in 1934 formed the political basis for the reestablishment of Indian self-government as well as vast improvements in the economic health of the tribes reorganized under this act.[14] Tribes reestablished under the Indian Reorganization Act are sometimes referred to as "recognized" or "acknowledged" tribes, a concept many Native Americans find a bit demeaning. The development of viable tribal economies and, particularly, congressional authorization of the National Indian Gaming Act of 1988, which permitted the establishment of Indian gaming, brought ready cash to many Indian families for the first time in their history. With the new economy have come enormous improvements in Indian housing, education, elderly care, health care, and the degree of tribal governmental sovereignty, as well as an expansion of tribal landholdings. Affluence has also made possible the legal fight to preserve treaty rights and to address the environmental issues so important to Indian people.

Pre-European Treaty Making among Indians

From the earliest record of European travelers among the Great Lakes tribes, there is every reason to believe that treaty making was a developed art long before the arrival of Europeans. It is from this baseline that we can begin to investigate the assumptions and practices that formed the understanding that the Algonquians brought to treaty making with Europeans and ultimately with the American negotiators. Since whatever agreements they made among themselves prior to the advent of written records are unknown to us, our understanding must be drawn from the few references to Indian treaty making in the earliest years of contact as well as an inference we can draw from our understanding of the principles under which their cultures were organized.

Our own membership in a very complex society with pansocietal institutions, overarching rules of social and political conduct, and easily segmented forms of engagement does not prepare us to understand the behavior of Great Lakes Algonquians.[15] Here, the expectations of proper behavior are highly contextualized rather than universal. Tribal behavior is tied to the closeness of kin relationship between actors rather than to abstract principles. Thus, for example, among tribesmen, stealing from family is strongly condemned, but stealing from strangers or enemies is considered meritorious.[16] Degrees of social and, therefore, spatial propinquity thus figure importantly into the rules of conduct that govern economic, social, political, or ideological behavior. In fact, unlike modern American society, these realms of human enterprise are not separable as distinct institutions. Within tribes, what is economic is also social, what is social is also political, and so forth. In fact, these constructs that we create to describe the various realms of human endeavor do not exist in any meaningful way within Algonquian society. In tribal context, all activities are to some degree also social, economic, political, and religious.

The degree of internal cohesion within tribal society can be correlated with social distance. The family, a group of related people living together and cooperating in subsistence, is the nucleus of all social, political, and economic interaction in Algonquian society. The band, a group of closely related families that reside in and claim a common territory, is the next most cohesive group. This is followed by the community, a group of intermarrying bands residing in adjoining territories. Beyond the community is the tribe, an amorphous group of communities who recognize themselves to be distantly related by virtue of language and custom. Finally, there are other people, strangers, who are at the very least potential enemies and thought to be people of a separate creation and therefore slightly less than human. As one moves outward from the nuclear family to the extended family and to the larger and more inclusive groups of people, the rules of social engagement change with distance. Economic exchange, diplomatic conventions, and etiquette are dependent on the degree of kinship that unites the interacting parties.

In regard to indigenous treaties, it is clear that the need to make treaties would occur with people on the outer reaches or beyond the kinship net of tribal groups. It is from these people that the most problems can be expected and the least consideration is due. It should, perhaps, be of no surprise, therefore, that aboriginal treaties are usually ineffective and of a short duration, normally lasting only as long as hostile factions were in actual contact with each other.[17] In the sense that tribal people would have understood treaties among themselves, there was really only need for one type—treaties of peace. In a world where each group was either partially or actively at war with all strangers, agreements of peace meant much more than a temporary cession of hostility. In the absence of war, tribes traded, could travel safely cross each other's territories, and could form political alliances and even intermarry, among other activities. These were all advantages that might otherwise accrue to in-laws. Thus, political alliance, like marriage, made strangers into a kind of distant and temporary kinsmen.

Such was the medium of all peaceful tribal interaction that the first requirement of any treaty agreement was that some kind of kinship link be found that would create a basis for intergroup discourse. The nineteenth-century Ojibwe historian William Warren cites an instance in which common clan members, as a result of earlier intertribal marriage, were used by the Dakota and Ojibwe as a basis to negotiate a peace agreement. In this case, intertribal marriage introduced the Dakota wolf clan into Ojibwe society, while another intertribal marriage introduced the Ojibwe water spirit clan among the Dakota.[18] Individuals belonging to these common clans on both sides of the tribal divide considered themselves close relatives and, in this way, were a perfect conduit for intertribal dialogue.

Since there were no political institutions per se among the natives of the upper Great Lakes, intertribal agreements seem to have been agreements between individuals rather than between political entities. Leaders who made such agreements on behalf of their bands or communities guaranteed the agreement with their own reputations; that is, both sides ascribed to the wisdom, experience, and truthfulness of these particular men to uphold the agreement by guaranteeing its provisions by their power of persuasion. Since leaders had no coercive powers, it was understood that any intertribal agreement would be temporary.[19] Here again is the parallel with tribal marriage.

One of the most important mechanisms for treaty making among tribal peoples was the giving of gifts, which, of course, produced good feelings. Among strangers, the value of the gifts to be exchanged was to be of equal value. There were many occasions for gift giving in treaty negotiations and in tribal contexts, including gifts to welcome guests, to seal agreements, and to emphasize important points during negotiation, to name only a few. As French explorer Nicholas Perot remarked, "Since Indians can't be commanded, gifts were an important form of *entreate*."[20] Wilbur Jacobs, who wrote of the importance of Indian gift giving, considered it a central feature in intertribal relations: "Relations between tribes and confederacies were often governed by presents. These were used for peace, for reward, for requests, for declaring war, as a tribute, as a mark of distinction, as a bribe, and for thanks and as a token of friendship."[21]

Aside from the goodwill that gift exchange created, there was an underlying expectation that if the agreement a gift symbolized was broken, there was an obligation to return the gift, which, of course, no one likes to do. Presumably, this obligation acted to strengthen the agreement on both sides. Here again, we can see a parallel with marriage, both ancient and modern, where gifts given to the bride and groom are not just "social" but "economic" and "political" at the same time. Perhaps in the case of traditional treaty making, it is not too far-fetched to again compare a tribal treaty to a marriage between groups.

Gifts were useful not only in making and maintaining intertribal agreements but also in repairing the breaches that inevitably occurred. This was an important mechanism, because there was no other effective way to stop disputes. Killing was perhaps the major source of intergroup conflict and was dangerous because it would set off waves of revenge killings. Gifts paid to aggrieved relatives, it was said, could "dry their tears," "cover the dead," or "raise up the dead" thus satisfying the need for revenge. The Ojibwe war chief Mihnehwehna explained this custom to the British at Fort Michilimackinac in 1763.[22] Presumably, the same procedure could heal the breach of an intertribal treaty agreement. The same speech by Mihnehwehna also illustrates a special form of oratory used in negotiations. Each principal point was made in a brief statement followed by the gift of a string of wampum.[23] Presumably, the wampum is symbolic of the point just rendered and serves as a mnemonic device so that the point would be recalled specifically in future years.

Treaty negotiations among tribes were also marked by a great deal of the ceremonialism. The greater the import of the negotiation was, the more elaborate were the ceremonies associated with it. People dressed and adorned themselves for these important occasions, and special arbors were prepared to shelter the negotiations. Both welcoming and arriving delegations made spectacular entrances featuring choreographed marching, dancing, and singing, as La Potherie reported on a meeting of Odawa and Potawatomi.[24] Speeches of welcome, prayers, blessings, and gift exchanges were part of both preliminary and closing ceremonies. Chiefs made introductory speeches that provided details of their own band affiliation and territory of origin and of the heroic deeds that were the basis for their renown. Among chiefs, there was a loose seniority with attendant protocols of respect, based partly on seniority and partly on deeds. Some chiefs mainly concerned themselves with external affairs and were usually referred to as war chiefs, while others concerned with domestic issues were known as peace chiefs. Particularly skillful orators were also involved in negotiations, though these gave voice to the consensus positions of the chiefs, who, in turn, represented the consensus positions of particular bands.

It would be badly amiss not to mention the importance of the spiritual dimensions of intertribal negotiations. Religious specialists were present, and it was their role to evoke the blessings of the spirits, to purify participants and grounds, and, if necessary, to ward off witchcraft by means of counterspells. Prayers were offered, and these were sent to the spirit world by the smoke from pipes. In some tribes, such as the Illini, a special type of redstone pipe, with a long wooden stem called the calumet, came to symbolize peace among many of the Algonquian, Dakota, and Iroquois tribes.[25] The calumet pipe ceremony and its attendant dances, songs, and feasting gave supernatural sanction to peace agreements. The counterpart of the calumet pipe was the war ax, or tomahawk, which symbolized a call to war.

The meeting and the negotiation between two foreign indigenous groups were fraught with danger, both physical and spiritual. Perhaps for this reason, it was also laden with psychic energy that manifested itself through parading, flags, music, singing, feasting, prayers, blessings, gift exchanges, and speeches. All of these elaborate activities were part of the dangerous process of reaching outside the boundaries of the kindred to build consensus with an alien people.

CHAPTER 4

The Invention of Euro-American and Indian Treaty Making

As we have seen, Western and native traditions developed two distinct means to conclude agreements with their foreign neighbors. When the need arose to seek peace, to collaborate in war, to conduct trade, or to join in other actions, neither convention of treaty making was acceptable to the other. This situation led to a series of experimental attempts to conduct negotiation and consummate agreements that were satisfactory not only in content but also in form. Historian Richard White, who perceptively wrote of Euro-American colonization of the Great Lakes region, referred to this process as a search for the "middle ground."[1]

The necessity to develop a mutually satisfactory solution was a long and difficult struggle that was never entirely perfected. Take, for example, the fact that Western societies could not accept treaty agreements in an oral form. Native people, who only chronicled events in oral tradition, placed little historical value on printed copy, which, in any case, they could not comprehend. Even by the mid-nineteenth century, when the treaty process reached its highest state of development, this particular clash of basic cultural values was never satisfactorily solved, a fact that remains one of the causes of treaty litigation to this day. Still, though the limitations of language and culture never permitted the type of treaty that would otherwise have been possible between two nations who spoke the same language and shared the same basic cultural principles, the United States and Indian tribes did indeed develop a mutually satisfactory process of treaty making.

The Issue of Power

In the consideration of Indian treaties, it is always necessary to keep in mind that treaties with Indian tribes were instruments in the exercise of political power. As the United States grew and forced its way west across the North American continent, land possessed by and used by native people came to be the property of the United States through the power of treaty making. Indians were either removed out of the path of settlement or swamped by it, so that they became concentrated on reservation enclaves, isolated and poverty-stricken. This process, too, was made possible by treaty agreements, which, by and large, were not seen by native people as being completely beneficial to their interests. The fact that they did agree to them, despite very fundamental objections, is an expression of the political power that the United States was then able to wield over them. The exercise of power in treaty making is usually well hidden in contemporary historical accounts, particularly official ones. After all, coercive force is not admissible in the context of Western treaty making, which assumes free and equal bargaining between peaceful sovereigns. To admit persuasion by force is to call the legitimacy of the entire process into question. Although we may suspect otherwise, in the context of popular history, we have the need to believe that treaties with the Indians were fair. As we shall see in the next chapter, our system of justice is not always so forgiving.

When we think of the coercive power of the state, we first think of military might. Surprisingly, this was seldom a direct factor in treaty making in the Great Lakes area. It is true that there were numerous military garrisons scattered around the Great Lakes region and that even the distant presence of American soldiers represented an implied threat. Sometimes, as in the case of the Treaty of Saginaw in 1819, the treaty commissioners—in this case, Lewis Cass—were accompanied to the treaty grounds by a company of the Third Infantry Division as well as a gunboat.[2] However, the overt display of military force was relatively rare in the context of Great Lakes treaty making. In the usual case, treaty negotiations relied on verbal descriptions of the terrible power at the disposal of an unhappy American president. In his negotiation of the

Treaty of Fond du Lac in 1826 on Lake Superior, the head of the Indian Office, Thomas McKenney, enlightened the Ojibwe in this respect.[3]

> Chippeways—we have spoken about your father's arm. You know nothing about it—because you have not seen it. Pe-zee-kee and Nodin have seen it—let them tell you. They know that if all your country was full of warriors, like leaves upon your trees, they could not lift it or turn it aside. Let them tell you if it is not so. I will tell you what it is like.
>
> You have all seen the sky grow black. You have heard the wind out of the clouds and seen it tear the leaves off the trees, and scatter them in the air, and blow them along the ground. You have seen the tree that was yesterday full of leaves, today all bare. And you have seen fire struck by the Great Spirit out of the sky, that splintered the big pine on the mountain. Then you have seen something that is like your great father's arm, when he is stirred, and when he paints himself and goes forth to war.
>
> But he is mild in peace:—and while you are good men and mind his counsels, he will never harm you, but use his arm to protect you and your wives and children.
>
> Yes, he is mild in peace. He is then like summer, when the streams open and the fishes swim;—when the hillside is warm and the birds do sing;—when your winter hunts have been good, and you have brought home plenty;—when you sit at your lodge with your pouch full of tobacco, and when your wives fill their kettles for you and for your children. This is like the arm and friendship of your great father, when that friendship is exercised.[4]

As in this case, American negotiators, like French and British diplomats before them, adopted a carrot-and-stick approach. They promised, on the one hand, the protection and support of the American president, the "Great Father," and, on the other, his terrible wrath. At least in the early years of treaty making, Indians realized that Euro-American forces were not sufficient to either protect or punish them. Likewise, these governments realized that treaties were far cheaper and easier than military conflict.

Euro-Americans had many other effective means to exert pressure on native peoples. One of these was the invidious comparison they frequently made between the status of themselves as "civilized and enlightened" people and the Indians as "savages" or "barbarians." American officials constantly contended to Indian people that they were a dependent people who were hungry, naked, and uneducated, while Americans were wealthy, numerous, powerful, and prosperous. As part of this informal conspiracy, American officials and missionaries warned that the game on which the Indians were dependent was becoming scarce and would finally disappear entirely and that, with its demise, the Indian way of life would necessarily end. Becoming civilized, the Americans said, required, as a necessary first step, agreeing to treaties in order to obtain the benefits of civilization for the survival of the Indian race. Superficially at least, Indians often seemed to buy into this idea. First, they often agreed that they wanted to be civilized, but as James M. McClurken has pointed out, this was a clever political ploy on their part.[5] By telling their agents and other American officials what they wanted to hear, Indians were often able to obtain not only goods and services from the government and missionary societies but also the freedom to work toward maintaining their own political autonomy and culture. Second, the frequent admission Indians made to the shrinking supply of game as well as their hunger, starvation, and nakedness was part of a deeply ingrained Algonquian form of supplication.

In a brilliant article, Mary Black-Rodgers investigated alternate uses of "starvation" terminology among the Ojibwe bands of the Canadian Shield during the era of the fur trade.[6] She found that claims of starvation and game shortages were not always literally true. Instead, the Ojibwa were using claims of starvation to solicit a gift of power. She warns that overlooking the message in this usage leads to a selective and inaccurate view of Indian culture, which suggests Indians to be dependent, childlike, begging, destitute, starving, and oriented toward welfare. Black-Rodgers explains the cultural background of manipulative usage as follows:

> In Ojibwa belief systems, events and conditions beyond one's control had special rules

> for handling, manifested by behavior referred to as "respect." The Indian perception did not separate natural and social environment; all of nature's things were living, and humans interacted with them. There was no accidental or non-purposive event; all were caused by "persons" whether human or other-than-human (to use the language of Hallowell). The natural elements and the animal, botanical, and mineral species had their own modes of "power." Power resided in all living things, but not with equal strength; the measure of every interaction was an assessment of *relative power,* which could change from day to day although a general continuum existed from the most powerful spirits to the lowest of insects, with humans scattered through the middle. Human beings, however, were dependent upon gifts of power in the form of "blessings" from their individual spirit helpers, with whom a private "respect/bless" relationship obtained. It was not good policy to speak of one's own powers (boasting and competitive motivations were frowned upon), and it was bad policy to try to control others against their will (coercive powers were recognized, but considered "bad medicine"). Individual autonomy and self-sufficiency were revered, but the facts of dependence and interdependence were not neglected. One had the most "respect" for those upon whom one was most dependent.[7]

According to Black-Rodgers, reports of game shortages could be metaphorical, deliberately ambiguous, or untrue statements. In Algonquian terminology and understanding, the solicitation of a gift of power, a promise of help in getting through life, refers to actions and not simply to a state. To give a blessing and to pity is one act. Chippewa preoccupation with relative power mixes human persons with all the others, and Europeans were placed rather high on the scale of power holders. White traders, with their goods and technology, were ranked with the bestowers of blessings and thus were the subject of solicitations. For the Algonquians, these took the form of complaints to elicit "pity" and, therefore, a "gift of power."[8] Thus, when visiting a trader or government agent, Indians often complained that the woods were bare of game, they had no food, their women and children were starving, and they were naked. Of course, on some occasions these claims may have been literally true, but on others they relate to the concept of "pity" and its role in establishing enduring relationships. As Black-Rogers described it, "For Ojibway [Chippewa] Indians, presenting oneself as powerless was not only accepted but recommended: the ignoble (and imprudent) thing would be to boast of a powerful position. They took measures to avoid being (or appearing) coercive."[9] The important point to be derived from this example is that when cultural variables are not given due consideration, complex cross-cultural interactions are fraught with opportunities for misrepresentation and misunderstanding.

The United States had at its disposal a large array of methods to exercise its power. In proposed treaty contacts, American negotiators often held out material inducements in the form of tools and implements, such as nets, guns, powder, axes, knives, and traps; woven cloth and blankets; decorative ornaments, such as glass beads, silver armbands, bracelets, and rings; and, of course, cash money. These items would be given over as annual benefits if the treaty was signed. Since, by the nineteenth century, Indians were dependent to a large degree on these goods, such offers were a huge inducement to sign the treaty.

The greatest inducement to agree to the treaties in the Great Lakes region was the trader debts system, a version of the "company store" gambit of later years. As the fur trade began to wind down because of the overharvest of high-quality fur species, such as beaver, otter, martin, and fisher, the American Fur Company and many independent traders began to advance credit to individual Indian trappers. This was done prior to the winter trapping season. In the spring the value of the fur produced would be balanced against the credits advanced. Given the falling price of fur on the international market, the net cash value for a winter's work was often a negative number. Knowing that the government would allow Indians to ask for funds earmarked for debt relief as part of treaty negotiations, fur interests purposely ran their businesses at a loss, sometimes for decades, knowing that a well-crafted treaty would produce a huge windfall profit. At the same time, they applied intense pressure on Indians to seek treaties that sold the Indians' one remaining asset of value, namely, their land. Such treaties provided traders a double benefit; the trader debt provision gave money directly to the trader and their companies, while cash annuity payments for the land usually were funneled directly into the pockets of the traders, who sold Indians the goods they could no longer get by trapping. Clearly, treaties were good business on the frontier. Perhaps ironically, as the fur trade declined, the "treaty business" became more important to Indians and the frontier economy in general, since treaties were one of the few sources of ready cash. Apart from the positive appeal of material items provided by treaties, American negotiators also frequently threatened to withdraw services that the Indians were already receiving. The threat to close blacksmith shops or other agency facilities was a potent inducement to bend to the government's will.

One other aspect of power relations needs to be explored, namely, the U.S. control over the treaty-making process from beginning to end. The American government initiated virtually every treaty, chose the location and time for the negotiations, indicated which Indian groups were to participate, determined the subjects to be discussed, hired the interpreters, wrote the treaty, and controlled the negotiations. These factors, of course, gave the government distinct advantages. Among the options open to the United States was to insist that the treaty negotiations be held in Washington, D.C. This ploy was expensive for the government, because Indian delegations had to be clothed, transported, housed, and fed. The advantages were, however, that the chiefs could be wined and dined, taken to meet the president and other officials, and impressed by the majesty of the capital city and the fecundity of the American population.

The disadvantages to the Indians were that they were in unfamiliar territory, far from their homeland and the advice and counsel of their kindred and fellow band members. Their isolation was further exacerbated by the presence of fur traders and other treaty claimants, who had the opportunity to apply pressure to achieve benefits of their own. Protesting against having to go to Washington to negotiate the Treaty of 1836,[10] the Grand River chief Noahquageshik and his fellow chiefs wrote to president Andrew Jackson through an intermediary, "Now we take a pen to communicate our thoughts. Not only what is in our mouths but that which comes from our whole hearts we shall speak. We are afraid and the reason is, because you already would take our land. We think not to shoulder this our land and carry it to where you are, it is too heavy. We hear that you would make a treaty for our land. We refuse to go, it is too hard for us."[11]

The Written Word and the Spoken Word

Cross-cultural negotiations are always difficult, but they are especially so when such negotiations must be accomplished across a language barrier. In the case of the Algonquian of the Great Lakes region, the dialects that were spoken by the Ojibwe, Odawa, Potawatomi, and Menominee were all mutually intelligible but considerably different in construction than Indo-European languages, such as English or French. Perhaps for this reason, no pidgin language developed in the region as a common trade language. Instead intergroup communication was conducted through bilingual individuals. In Indian and mixed-blood, or métis, communities, both French and one or more Algonquian dialects were commonly spoken. To this day it is not uncommon for native people in the Great Lakes region to greet each other with the salutation *boojoo,* clearly a local variant of the French *bonjour.* More individuals who had learned to speak both an Algonquian dialect as well as English were available in the last half of the eighteenth century and in the nineteenth century. Many of these bilingual individuals were Euro-American or Euro-Canadian males who were married to native women and had learned to speak a native dialect with various degrees of proficiency. Some of these individuals were employed by the government as agency interpreters, although most were métis fur traders.

For the purpose of treaty negotiations, English had to be rendered into an Algonquian dialect, such as Ojibwe or Odawa, and then from these languages back into English. Sometimes this task took the services of several individuals, one to translate English into an Indian dialect and another to go from that dialect back to English. On occasion three languages were required, to go, for example, from Ojibwe to French to English and then back again. Needless to say, the process left room for misunderstanding even given complete fluency, which was seldom the case.

Indians often complained about the quality of translation. One of the most common complaints was that the translator spoke the wrong Indian dialect—for example, Odawa rather than Potawatomi. During the negotiations of the Treaty of St. Peter's in 1837, the treaty secretary, Verplanck Von Antwerp, complained of the quality of translation, noting on the margins of his journal that the translation rendered into English for a particular sentence was "nonsense." He noted elsewhere that the interpreters were "unfit to act in that capacity."[12] An observer of the Treaty of La Pointe in 1842, missionary Alfred Brunson, remarked that the government interpreter Patrick Quinn was "a stammering Irishman not being able to speak intelligibly in either language [English or Ojibwe]."[13]

One wonders what understanding the Indian parties may have taken away from such treaties, given the vagueness of language. In the case of the Treaty of St. Peter's, we actually do know what at least some of the chiefs understood. This is a result of a written record made in the Ojibwe language twenty-seven years after the St. Peter's Treaty.[14] As far as the written treaty was concerned, the Ojibwe ceded several millions of acres of land, which today make up central Wisconsin and part of eastern Minnesota. The Ojibwe chiefs had a different view of the content of the treaty.

> So then Father, Our Great Father requests me to sell him my Pine Timber, our Great Father is mighty, therefore whatever he says would not be in vain, and whatever he promises to do he will fulfill.
>
> Very well, I will sell him the Pine Timber as he requests me to, From [the] usual height of cutting a tree down and upwards to [the] top is what I sell you, I reserve the root of the tree. Again this I hold in my hand the Maple Timber, also the Oak Timber, also this Straw which I hold my hand. Wild rice is what we call this. These I do not sell.[15]

The same misunderstanding also occurred after the Treaty of La Pointe in 1842, where the United States claims to have purchased all the land that now composes the western part of Michigan's Upper Peninsula and the northernmost part of Wisconsin. In that case, the Ojibwe believed they were accommodating the Great Father's wish that they sell him the minerals that his white children might find on the land.[16] In neither case did the Ojibwe understand that they had sold the land. When one considers that Ojibwe of that era did not think of land as a thing that could be owned, let alone sold, these understandings are completely logical from their perspective.

On another occasion, in 1855, George Manypenny, commissioner of Indian affairs, had opportunity to ask the great Lake Superior chief Nanawonggaybe what he understood of the 1854 treaty that he helped to negotiate and had signed the previous year. Nanawonggaybe replied, "My father I was here last year, when the treaty was made and I swallowed the words down my throat, and they have not yet had time to blister on my breast."[17] It is doubtful that the commissioner was expecting such an enigmatic reply. This is not to say that Indian chiefs could not understand what went on in treaty negotiations. They were, in fact, often skillful negotiators, even though working through a foreign language is difficult. Anyone who has tried to put together a complicated device using the instructions poorly translated into English from Japanese knows this frustration.

Another significant problem in negotiating treaties had to do with the unfamiliarity Americans had with the oral tradition of the Indian people. To Indians, what was said was more important than what was actually written down. They frequently took as fact statements that American diplomats regarded to be "negotiating positions." Veteran Indian agent Henry Gilbert made this point in a letter to the commissioner of Indian affairs in 1853: "The memory of an Indian is very tenacious. He treasures up everything that is said by a government officer and regards his statements and verbal assurances as equally binding upon the government as formal stipulations of the treaty."[18] Statements that are regarded as hearsay and not as factually reliable in American courts are what, in fact, constitute history in Algonquian traditional culture. These different views of what constitutes historical reality came into sharp focus in a conversation between the Mill Lacs Ojibwe chief Shobaushkung (Shobaushkum) and E. P. Smith, commissioner of Indian affairs, in 1875.

> SHOBAUSHKUNG: We signed the paper [the Treaty of 1863] because we were asked to sign with other Indians who were signing the paper for their land, and we did sign the paper giving our land away because the others wanted us to sign with them.
>
> COMMISSIONER SMITH: That is not here [in the treaty]. That was something that was spoken and it went away when they swept the room out in the morning.[19]

The Great Fathers

Given the centrality of kinship in tribal societies and the import of the role of the father in patrilineal kinship systems, it is not surprising that this term served the Algonquians well in dealing with Euro-Americans in an official capacity. The term *Great Father* and the behavior associated with it became important to the way Indians constructed their relationship with the omnipresent, powerful, yet invisible alien persona that eventually became so influential in their lives. The Great Father terminology was first used for the French king and later transferred, in turn, to the English king and finally to the American president. This type of fictive kin terminology was common in Algonquian social discourse and, in fact, necessary for any type of friendly interaction with strangers.

The role assigned to a father was one the Algonquians associated with a generous provider, a protector, and an experienced and wise counselor. By the use of the father term, these qualities, which described the ideal behavior expected of any father, were transferred and magnified when applied to the Great Father. In Algonquian concept, the Great Father would behave the same way toward his red children as he did toward his white children.

The father-child relationship embraced by the Algonquians also fit well with the pity-power gift relationship discussed earlier; both ideas were important themes in Algonquian culture. Thus, for example, a treaty's outpouring of wealth, guarantees of peace, and prospects of future trade, all to take place under the protection and supervision of the Great Father, were power gifts provided by the Great Father himself. In this sense a treaty agreement was a very personal arrangement between the people of Algonquian bands and the American president.

The Algonquians realized that the Great Father had helpers who spoke for him. American treaty negotiators almost always began negotiations by saying that they had been sent by the Great Father, who wished the best for his red children and implored them to agree to certain specific provisions of a proposed treaty because these would be for their own benefit. Intermediaries were also given appropriate father names; thus, an important official, such as an Indian superintendent, the negotiator for a proposed treaty, or a commissioner of Indian affairs, would simply be called "father." A local subagent might be referred to by a diminutive form, perhaps "little father."

Algonquian Indians did not hesitate to find fault with their Great Father. For example, they realized that their French Great Father was not capable of protecting them from attacks by the Iroquois, and they perceived that the English Great Father's trade policies were stingy. In regard to the latter, it must have mystified the English commandant at Detroit, Major De Peyster, when a chief complaining to him that the English Great Father did not provide sufficient rum, which they called "English milk," said, "Father you have only given milk at one breast."[20]

Since the Algonquians envisioned their relationship with the Great Father in purely personal terms, they were always anxious to go to Washington so that they could address their grievances directly and in person. In fact, many of the prominent chiefs of the nineteenth century had met an American president, and some had met several. To the great frustration of the Great Lakes Algonquians, American Indian agents strongly discouraged unofficial trips to Washington by tribal delegations. Apparently this policy was for financial reasons, since such delegations often tried to claim expenses for trips after the fact.

The concept of the Great Father was a concession made by Euro-Americans to the need of Indians to relate to each other through kin relationships and the appropriate behavior associated with them. Ultimately this convention served its purpose equally well from both the Indian and non-Indian perspective. From the perspective of the Americans, as well as the French and British before them, the Great Father symbolism implied a less stable and more ambivalent behavior. If Indians conformed to his wishes, the Great Father was supportive and generous; if not, he would be transformed into an authoritarian figure who could be punitive, a venue of terrible power. Lacking concepts of overarching authority or the use of punitive force against children, the Algonquians did not understand their Great Father in this light.

Presents

In dealing with native people, Euro-Americans soon learned that the exchange of presents was an important aspect of Indian social relations and good etiquette. When it came to exchanging with near relatives, such as the Great Father, the strictures in favor of exchanges of equal value were lifted. Given the enormous wealth and generosity of the Great Father in such things as treaty payments or gift giving that accompanied alliance making, there was no possibility that Indians could ever reciprocate with a gift of equal value. There was, however, the assumption in exchange with near relatives that value would balance in the long run. This was realistic because it allowed such factors as military service, trade concessions, and other favors that the Indians could provide to eventually balance the scales of giving. Thus, in treaty relationships gifts symbolized the mutual interdependence of the Great Father and his red children and had implications that went far beyond the treaty itself.

In the period of the initial French fur traders, the exchange of gifts was very complex. For example, some goods, like guns, seem to have mainly flowed through diplomatic channels, other kinds of goods through missionaries, and still others through the activities of traders. Likewise, the French tried to impose a status system on Algonquian society by providing different kinds of gifts for chiefs, as opposed to warriors, women, and even children.[21] This idea carried over, to some extent, to the British and also, to a lesser degree, to the Americans. Special gifts for chiefs during the nineteenth century included high-quality guns, American flags, silver peace metals engraved with the president's likeness, and fancy dress clothing. Occasionally treaties provided for money payments to chiefs of various classes, distinguishing between first- and second-class chiefs or between chiefs and headmen.[22] The distribution of goods in this manner had the effect of enhancing the personal status of the chiefs, because, as expected of good Algonquian leaders, they gave their goods away as presents to their kin and followers.

The Algonquians also had special diplomatic items, which they gave to foreigners with whom they wished to establish good relations. These included wampum belts and other jewelry, fur robes, native clothing and fancy handicraft items, and most important, carved catlinite stone pipes or calumets, which were symbolic of peace. Although American diplomats tended to think of presents that they gave to Indians as bribes, they were much more. To the Algonquians, gifting was a part of everyday life: the flow of presents assured survival, cemented social relationships, and symbolized open and peaceful foreign relations. In this way, gifts were essential to creating and maintaining treaty contracts.

Ceremonialism

Both Indians and Euro-Americans attached importance to the ceremonialism that surrounded the negotiation of a treaty. Both recognized the treaty as an agreement of importance, and proper ceremony helped to underscore the solemnity attached to this effort. From the Indian point of view, the more important the occasion was, the greater the ceremony was and the longer it lasted.

One of the most remarkable accounts of the actual ceremonials associated with treaty making is from an unofficial journal made during the negotiation of the Treaty of La Pointe in 1842.[23] This account was provided by Henry Blatchford, a métis who acted as interpreter for the Indian mission at Bad River, Wisconsin.[24]

> The making of a treaty with Indians is one of the most important occasions for which they ever assemble together. It is an occasion which calls out a greater number of people than ordinarily meet for the transaction of other business. It is a time when the wise men of the nation are called for, and when the talents and oratory of the people are brought into requisition. It is a time for paint and ornaments and all that display, which exhibits national character.[25]

The arrival of each delegation [bands from different parts of the country] seems to have been one of the ceremonial highlights. Blatchford was especially impressed with the entrance of the band led by the Minnesota Ojibwe chief Hole in the Day (the elder).

> They all came in canoes of course, but in large companies which we might call fleets or squadrons. The lake was perfectly calm, and the arrival in each of these companies was hailed by a salute from two vessels lying in the harbor and was returned by the Indians by the firing of muskets. There was one arrival which deserved a more particular description, as it attracted more attention than any other company which came. It consisted of a number of canoes headed by large batteau containing the braves of the greatest chief of the nation. His name was "Hole in the Sky [Hole in the Day]." Upon the top of this batteau a sort of deck or scaffold was raised, upon which the warriors were dancing to a war song, sung by a company of Indian musicians. When this party had landed they proce[e]ded to the council, ground in truly martial order. The leader at their head bearing the american [*sic*] colors, succeeded by the warriors and these followed by the musicians consisting of drummers and singers and rattlers, that is, men with rattles. These all proceeded in a slow military dance, peculiar to the Indians but difficult to describe.[26]

The solemn importance of the treaty for the Indians was signaled by their very movements, as Blatchford observed.

> You must not suppose however that the Indians are a people of dispatch in business. On such an occasion as this especially, they seem to associate dignity of character with the slowness of their movements, and to attach importance to what they are about to say, in proportion to the time they spend in smoking over the subject upon which they are to speak. After much deliberation the council assembled, seating themselves upon benches prepared for the purpose, in the open air. When a large keg of tobacco was brought forward placed before them.[27]

At the conclusion of the treaty, the chiefs gave their consent to the treaty with the ceremony that they called "touching the pen," a custom Blatchford described as follows:

> The chiefs came forward to sign the Treaty and also some of the other principal men. A list of the names having been previously made out, a person in signing the Treaty would touch the pen of the commissioner's secretary and the latter would than [*sic*] make a cross opposite the Indians name. This the Indians called touching the pen, as is some to make the Treaty more binding would not touch the pen in the secretarys hands. But they must touch it in the father's [treaty commissioner's] hands Himself.[28]

The ceremony of touching the pen followed an earlier practice where the chief "signed" the treaty documents by drawing their clan symbol next to their names as they were rendered by the treaty secretary. This practice more clearly reflected the decision-making process of the Algonquians, since, in reality, chiefs were signing not for themselves but for members of their patrilineal groups. American negotiators had little, if any, understanding as to this dynamic and saw the chiefs as representatives of political structures such as "tribes" or "nations," which, in fact, did not exist in any real political sense.

Of course, the chiefs could not read the treaty and only knew its contents as they had been explained orally through interpreters. The writing on paper was to them a mysterious and magical phenomena that gave the treaty a kind of supernatural sanction. This aspect of Indian understanding was expressed by Hole in the Day (the younger) in a conversation he had with George

Manypenny, commissioner of Indian affairs. In a rare moment of candor, Manypenny remarked to Hole in the Day that if Indians could not read or write agreements that they signed, they were in danger of being cheated. To this, Hole in the Day replied that while this was true, "where persons [the Indians] have faith in the paper, it is as good and valid as if they could read it."[29] In this sense, for the Algonquians, the written treaty document itself became a talisman of supernatural significance.

Treaty Protocol

As the mutually negotiated treaty procedure evolved over time, a fairly well-established order of negotiation developed, at least when negotiations took place in Indian country. The indigenous elements were less prominent when discussions were held in Washington, D.C., or in other urban areas. At the risk of some repetition, the following is the informal order for the negotiation of most nineteenth-century treaties.

The entrance. Great ceremony—including the display of flags and banners, firing of guns, music, parading in formation, and the wearing of ceremonial regalia—characterized the entrance of delegations to the treaty. Though mainly an Indian element, American delegations participated in the entrance ceremonials and often added to it.

Greeting ceremonies. The ceremonies of greeting featured prayers by an Indian shaman for clear skies (which symbolized success), purification of the treaty ground by smudging with the smoke of sweetgrass and sage, tobacco offerings by way of pipe smoke, and the exchange of gifts. Dances by the Indian delegations were sometimes part of the greeting ceremonies.

Introductory session. The first meeting of the Indians and American delegations featured introductory speeches by the chiefs. In these speeches, the chiefs recited their accomplishments, such as their participation in prior treaties as well as their war exploits. They also usually indicated which band they represented and described the country in which they resided. This was followed by a speech by the U.S. treaty commissioner, who extended a greeting from the Great Father and explained why he had called his Indian children together, that is, the objectives the government hoped to achieve by the treaty. Here, the commissioner carefully explained the benefits the Great Father thought would accrue to the assembled bands. Normally, the negotiations were then adjourned for several days to permit the Indians to discuss the proposition among themselves.

The reply. In their reply, Indian chiefs or speakers would address the specific objectives of the treaty, either accepting various propositions or rejecting them on behalf of their bands. Since Indians almost never agreed among themselves at this point, additional out-of-session negotiations were usually necessary. The treaty commissioner often made another presentation, in which he agreed to some of the new proposals made by the chiefs and rejected others. The formal negotiations were then again adjourned for several days. During this time, the government usually sent mixed bloods, traders who held the confidence of the Indian people, and interpreters to negotiate with recalcitrant chiefs individually. Depending on the depth of disagreement, the treaty commissioner might call for more public meetings to continue debate.

Statement of understanding. When it seemed to the treaty commissioner that he had reached the best agreement possible and would get the consensus of the chiefs, a treaty document was prepared by the secretary and was read and explained through interpreters to the assembled Indians. Often, various chiefs would then comment on the proposed treaty, stating either support or objections to some of its provisions. Once the treaty was written, it was very unlikely that the treaty commissioner would approve further changes.

Touching the pen. The signing ceremony included a community-by-community delegation coming forward from each band and chiefs placing a mark after their name as it was phonetically rendered by the treaty secretary. At this point, some chiefs made short comments, either positive or negative, about the agreement. Some complained, for example, about the way the negotiations were conducted, that the commissioner rushed the discussions, or that the interpreters were not competent.

Closing ceremonies. After the signing, delegations departed rapidly, because local food resources were usually consumed and because important provisioning chores waited at home. This hurry did not preclude blessings and ceremonies to provide safe travel. Sometimes, traders and missionaries took advantage of large gatherings of Indians to conduct their business before the bands scattered. At other times, the government took advantage of the gathering to make annuity payments under former treaties.

With minor variations, this treaty protocol was common to treaty making with Indians during the nineteenth century. On occasions when Indians were called to Washington or other urban areas for treaty making, there were many distractions. Delegations were entertained and treated to lavish banquets. In turn, locals were entertained by seeing "wild Indians" from the hinterlands. In some cases, a circuslike atmosphere invaded the treaty process. After the invention of photography in the 1850s, a photographic record was sometimes made of Indian delegations who visited Washington on official business. These form an invaluable archive.[30]

Not all treaty negotiations resulted in successful treaties. In most cases, this was because the draft treaty did not meet the approval of the U.S. Senate or the Indian Office; in other cases, Indians would not ratify changes proposed by the Senate. Given the enormous gulf that separated the ways the Americans and the Algonquians of the Great Lakes region understood the world around them and how they each saw the future of their people, it is quite incredible that they were able to peacefully resolve their differences by treaty at all. The extent to which these treaty agreements were fair or just is another story, discussed in the next chapter.

CHAPTER 5

Treaties and American Law

The unique place of native people in American society has been a matter of frequent controversy since the early days of the Republic. Consequently, U.S. courts have adjudicated and continue to adjudicate cases involving Indians as individuals as well as the tribes to which they belong. The outcome of such cases rests on interpretation of the laws, executive orders, and treaties that have been expressly designed to regulate the affairs of Indian tribes and the relationship between native and nonnative peoples. As a result of the adjudication of the various instruments of Indian law, the federal courts have evolved a great deal of legal precedent that has itself become an important part of U.S. Indian policy. For example, in the case *Worcester v. Georgia,*[1] John Marshall, chief justice of the Supreme Court, laid out the historical and political rationale that underlies the legal assumptions that have since governed the relationship between the American state and Indian tribes. One of the most fundamental assumptions of this relationship is the ideal of duel sovereignty, in which the legal relationship between the tribes and the United States is an exclusive one. Further, the rights that flow from this special relationship are also exclusive to tribes and Indian citizens.

In regions of the United States with large Indian populations and considerable tribal land, such as the upper Great Lakes region, the non-Indian population is well aware of the fact that tribal members have some legal rights that are exclusive. Treaty-based hunting and fishing that is regulated by the tribe rather than by state authority is one example. Frequently, treaty-based rights are judged to be "unfair" by non-Indians because treaties, in fact, give Indian citizens "special privileges." Without reference to the history of the treaties or their unique place in American law, Indian rights seem to be in sharp conflict with the generally held constitutional guarantee of equal protection under the law. However, for Indian people who have seen their land base eroded, the loss of traditional culture, and their economic and social position in American society continually marginalized, it is often difficult to understand exactly what special advantages have been forthcoming.

Exclusive legal rights are important to Indian people from historical, cultural, and political perspectives. By the early years of the twentieth century, few Indians had seen, let alone read, the contents of the treaties that had been negotiated by their grandfathers and great-grandfathers. Oral history, however, held a special place for the promises that Indian people believed (though not always accurately) to be recorded in the treaties. Consequently, treaties took on a mythological importance in which they represented a viable link to previous generations and, in this way, provided one of the vehicles that helped to define their Indianness as well as to unite their economically depressed and politically fragmented communities. Likewise, the tradition of the promises contained in the treaties seemed to point the way to a brighter future where the contents of the treaties would again be revealed and their Indian rights under them affirmed.

Following World War II, many tribes of the Great Lakes region—now more coherently organized under the Wheeler-Howard Act of 1934 and with new, if meager, resources—began to hire lawyers and historians to investigate the old treaties. Consequently, in the late 1960s and early 1970s, many American tribes began to challenge the status quo in court. From these cases, there emerged an entirely new understanding about the place of native people in American society. Perhaps there was no place where this societal and political revolution was so rapid and so fundamental as in the upper Great Lakes country. Understanding what and how these changes occurred requires a review of the basic foundations of treaty law.

Foundations

In the case *Cherokee Nation v. Georgia,* John Marshall, chief justice of the U.S. Supreme Court, remarked on the unique relationship between the United States and its native tribes,[2] a relationship he described as perhaps unlike that of any other two people (i.e., societies) on earth. The federal-tribal relationship is based on broad but not unlimited federal constitutional powers over Indian affairs, often described as "plenary power."[3] As Felix Cohen notes, the relationship is also distinguished by a special trust obligation requiring the United States to adhere strictly to a fiduciary standard in its dealings with Indians. Although classified as sovereign nations, Indian tribes do not have the same power of sovereignty accorded to foreign nations. Tribes are, instead, empowered with the status of "domestic dependent nations."[4] As Cohen observes, the relationship that requires the trust obligation of the United States to adhere strictly to a fiduciary standard when dealing with the domestic sovereigns creates an inherent tension between this special trust status and the broad federal authority to regulate Indian affairs. This tension has produced a unique body of law.[5]

The plenary power of the federal government in regulating Indian affairs is drawn from three different clauses of the U.S. Constitution: the Indian commerce clause; the property clause, which is used to regulate reservation lands; and the treaty clause. In the decision handed down in *Worcester v. Georgia,* treaties are defined as "a compact formed between two nations or communities having the right of self-government." To give force to a treaty, "each party shall possess the same attributes of sovereignty." Thus, the only requisites of treaty making are that each of the contracting parties shall possess the right of self-government and the power to perform the stipulations of the treaty.[6] As long as tribes exercise the right of self-government, treaties and laws concerning them remain in force.[7] The status of a tribe as a domestic sovereign neither divests it of the right of self-government nor destroys its capacity to enter into treaties. Cohen explains that the treaty clause was more dominant during the early years of Indian affairs and that the Indian Office was housed in the War Department during the first several decades of its existence because Indian affairs were then more closely related to military and foreign policy than a subject of domestic or municipal law.[8]

The Presumptions of Treaty Making

As we have seen, the supremacy clause of the U.S. Constitution gives Indian treaties the force of federal law. In this sense, they represent not only a contract between the United States and the tribal signatories but a legal succession of the signatory tribes. Rights and obligations codified by the treaty can be extinguished or modified in two ways. The first is by inconsistent articles in subsequent treaties with the same tribe, and the second is by an act of Congress.[9] It is, in fact, quite common for former treaties to be changed by later ones. This was especially true during the tenure of George Manypenney as commissioner of Indian affairs in the mid-nineteenth century. In addition to other objectives, Manypenney saw treaty making as an opportunity to simplify and consolidate the government's obligations as they had been incurred in prior treaties.

After the demise of treaty making with native tribes in 1871, Indian affairs were regulated by laws passed by Congress as well as by executive orders. It is an important judicial principle that treaties can only be abrogated or modified by an act of Congress and then only by a very explicit provision.[10] Under this doctrine, Congress must show a "clear and plain intention to abrogate treaty rights."[11] This strict requirement is based in part on the fact that in addition to being ratified by the U.S. Senate, treaties were also, of necessity, approved by the Indian parties to the treaty agreement.

The Reserved Rights Doctrine

Another important principle of treaty interpretation is the reserved rights doctrine. Under this doctrine, a treaty does not represent a grant of rights *to* Indian tribes but is instead a grant of rights *from* Indians.[12] Further, if rights are not specifically granted to the United States by a treaty, the rights remain as a reservation of rights not granted.[13] The reserved rights doctrine laid out in the case *United States v. Winans* is not widely understood by the American public, which generally regards treaties as documents that contain special rights granted to Indian tribes by the United States, rather than the other way around.[14]

The reserved rights doctrine gives rise to another especially common misunderstanding about who is entitled to exercise rights set forth in an Indian treaty. This issue was decided by *Whitefoot v. United States* and followed by *United States v. Washington.*[15] In these cases, the Supreme Court found that treaty rights were vested in the tribes and not in individual Indians. Accordingly, rights reserved by treaty may be exercised by individual Indians as members of a tribe. It is the tribe that determines its membership, regulates its resources, and licenses their use. It is also, therefore, the tribe that has standing to bring suit regarding treaty issues; plaintiffs, however, have standing as individuals.[16]

The Canons of Treaty Construction

As we have seen, it is fashionable in some circles to argue that Indian rights, particularly treaty rights, are unfair, either because treaties are old or because they advantage a minority over the majority. Despite these opinions, the U.S. government has developed a respectable body of law designed to protect the rights of citizens of aboriginal dissent. As a key measure in this effort, our federal courts have propagated a set of rules for the interpretation of Indian treaties. These rules, or "canons," of treaty construction are designed to balance the historical inequities surrounding the conditions under which the original treaties were negotiated. If these conditions were not addressed, Indian tribes would be severely disadvantaged in treaty interpretation. In truth, to say that Indian treaties were "negotiated" is a euphemism. It would be more accurate to say that the scope and content of most treaties were dictated by the United States for its own benefit.

Over the nearly two centuries that treaty issues have been litigated in the federal courts, three basic canons of treaty construction have been generated and incorporated as precedent in treaty interpretation. These include admonitions that the treaty should be construed liberally in favor of the Indian parties, that doubtful expression and ambiguous meaning should be interpreted by ordinary usage rather than modern technical terminology, and that treaties must be interpreted as their Indian signers would have understood their terms.

First, treaties are to be construed liberally in favor of the Indians. In 1898, a Minnesota property dispute, *Jones v. Meehan,* reached the U.S. Supreme Court. This case involved the chain of ownership of land originally allotted by a treaty of October 2, 1863, to an Indian chief of the Red Lake Band of Ojibwe. In consideration of the facts, Mr. Justice Gray included the following reminder in his opinion for the Court:

> . . . negotiations for the treaty are conducted, on the part of the United States, an enlightened and powerful nation, by representatives skilled in diplomacy, masters of a written language, understanding the modes and forms of creating the various technical estates known to their law, assisted by an interpreter employed by themselves; that the treaty is drawn up by them in their own language; that the Indians on the other hand, are a weak and dependent people, who have no written language and are wholly unfamiliar with all the forms of legal expression, and whose only knowledge of the terms in which the treaty is framed is that imparted to them by the interpreter employed by the United States; and that the treaty must therefore be construed, not according to the technical meaning of its words to learned lawyers, but in the sense they would naturally be understood by the Indians.[17]

This eloquent insight followed Justice McLean's observations as part of an opinion given in 1832 in *Worcester v. Georgia,* when he said, "The language used in treaties with Indians should never be construed to their prejudice. To contend that the word 'allotted' in reference to land guaranteed to the Indians in certain treaties, indicates a favor conferred, rather than a right acknowledged, would, it would seem to me, do an injustice to the understanding of the parties. How the words of the treaty are understood by the unlettered people, rather than their critical meaning should form the rule of construction."[18] Thus, the precedent that requires treaty agreements to be construed liberally flows from the immense power of the written word and the advantages gained by the complete control of its use.

Second, doubtful expression and ambiguous meaning is to be resolved in favor of the Indians. The power of language and use of writing also lies at the heart of the canon concerning doubtful or ambiguous expression. In 1907, the United States successfully brought suit to restrain a number of individuals from constructing dams on the Milk River of Montana that were preventing water from reaching the Fort Belknap Indian Reservation. Subsequently, when Henry Winters and other appealants sued to lift the injunction, Mr. Justice McKenna, in his opinion for the Court, made the following observation:

> By a rule of interpretation of agreements and treaties with the Indians, ambiguities occurring will be resolved from the standpoint of the Indians. And the rule should certainly be applied to determine between two inferences, one of which would support the purpose of the agreement and the other impair or defeat it. On account of their relations to the government it cannot be supposed that the Indians were alert to exclude by formal words every inference which might militate against or defeat the declared purpose of themselves and the government, even if it could be supposed that they had the intelligence to foresee the "double sense" which might sometime be urged against them.[19]

When a question related to the right of the state of Arizona to extend its taxing jurisdiction to the Navajo Reservation was at issue in the case *McClanahan v. Arizona State Tax Commission* in 1973, Justice Marshall bluntly and succinctly addressed the rule of doubtful expression: "Doubtful expressions are to be resolved in favor of the weak and defenseless people who are wards of the nation, dependent upon its protection and good faith."[20] The cannon of doubtful expression has been adopted in many cases. Some of the most notable include *Alaska Pacific Fisheries Co. v. United States, Choctaw Nation v. Oklahoma,* and *Worchester v. Georgia.*[21]

Third, treaties are to be understood as Indians understood them. The most complex and difficult canon of treaty construction involves the initial understandings that inform the meaning of a treaty at the time it was written. The fact that treaties are to be interpreted by the courts as their Indian signers would have understood the agreement goes beyond linguistic considerations and contractual vagaries to include the closely held cultural beliefs and values that shaped the way the Indian signers understood a treaty agreement.

In the *United States v. Winans* litigation, which involved the Yakima Nation's right to fish at the usual and accustomed places along the Columbia River as was reserved in the Treaty of 1859, Justice McKenna delivered the opinion of the Court: "As we have said we will construe a treaty with the Indians as that unlettered people understood it, and as justice and reason demand, in all cases where power is exerted by the strong over those to whom they owe care and protection and counterpoise the inequality by superior justice which looks only at the substance of the right, without regard to technical rules. How the treaty in question was understood may be gathered from the circumstances."[22] In a case in which the Choctaw Nation sued to recover money due under the Treaty of 1866, the Supreme Court referred to the duty to interpret treaties as they had been understood by the Indian signatories. Mr. Justice Murphy observed, "Especially it is true in interpreting treaties and agreements with the Indians; they are to be construed, so far as possible, in the sense in which the Indians understood them, and in a spirit which generously recognizes the full obligation of this nation to protect the interest of dependent people."[23] Another application of this rule is found in *Choctaw Nation v. Oklahoma,* a dispute over the ownership of the bottomlands of the Arkansas River. Mr. Justice Marshall delivered the opinion of the Court: "More important is the fact that these treaties are not to be considered as exercises in ordinary conveyancing. The Indian nation did not seek out the United States and agree upon an exchange of lands in an arm's length transaction. Rather, treaties were imposed upon them and they had no choice but consent. As a consequence, this Court has often held that treaties with the Indians must be interpreted as they would have understood them."[24]

The "circumstances" mentioned by Justice McKenna as the basis for determining how Indians understood treaties generally refers to the historical facts related to the negotiations of the treaty. As discussed in earlier chapters, since Indians were seldom participants in creating the historical documents that formed the basis of the archival record, it is necessary to determine the facts by insight into the unique cultural variables that would account for Indian understanding. These variables are the lens through which the words of the historic documents must be read by modern interpreters of the meaning of a treaty. Certainly, this is a broad and liberal mandate, but the courts have also issued limitations. Again citing Justice Murphy, we are warned, "But even Indian treaties cannot be rewritten or expanded beyond their clear terms to remedy a claimed injustice or to achieve the asserted understanding of the parties."[25] We are thus to be mindful that Indian treaties are legal as well as historic documents. Their fair reading requires attention to both contexts.

Clearly, the canons of treaty construction as well as the assumptions of Indian sovereignty, the limitations on abrogation of treaties, and the reserved rights doctrine are all legal mechanisms that recognize the inherent power differential in the negotiation and formulation of Indian treaties. Given the immense advantages that accrued to the United States in its treaty transactions with Indians, U.S. courts have wisely and justly devised rules for the resolution of modern treaty conflicts. These rules recognize and try to neutralize historic power discrepancies. Beyond fairness, no less is required of a nation that has long claimed a fiduciary responsibility for its domestic dependent Indian nations.[26]

As gratifying as the role and policies of our courts may be to those who have come to understand the historic and cultural circumstances of Indian treaty making, the litigation of treaty issues is difficult. First, treaty litigation is a protracted and very expensive proposition, often beyond the financial means of tribes. In addition, it is often very difficult for the tribes in treaty cases to gain the support of the Department of Justice and the Solicitor's Office of the Department of Interior, which is necessary to acquire litigation support funds from the federal government. Finally, even given the advantages built into the interpretation of treaties by the courts, revisiting the historic events and cultural circumstances, which are oftentimes 175 years into the past and the subject of few written records, is very difficult. Not the least of the challenges is the need to convince lawyers and judges, who are trained to read contracts on their face, that historic documents often tell us something very different than what would appear to be apparent from the "plain meaning" of their English words.

PART 2

Usufructuary Litigation

Since most of the tribes of the upper Great Lakes region were never removed from their aboriginal territory, their treaties of land cession frequently contain a provision that permits them to hunt, fish, and gather over the ceded territory. Such usufruct provisions are usually the first to be litigated. This is the case because such rights have both subsistence and commercial value and, perhaps of even more importance in the modern day and age, because the use of natural resources is closely tied to the spiritual and psychological aspects of both tribal and ethnic identity. Many native people see hunting, fishing, and the gathering of wild resources not only as part of their Indianness but as a religious responsibility to ensure the maintenance and regeneration of the natural world.

The historic pattern of resource use in the upper Great Lakes region is fairly consistent. Usufruct rights were insisted on in treaties by the Indians for the simple reason that, at the time of the treaties, the Indians depended on what they could hunt, fish, and gather for their subsistence, clothing, shelter, and many tools and implements. Importantly, Indian-produced food, fur, and handicrafts were also of critical importance to the early non-Indian economies of the region. In this sense, the maintenance of Indian usufruct was also valuable to the general economic well-being of the region. During the last quarter of the nineteenth century, Indians hunted, fished, and gathered under authority of their treaties without molestation by either settlers or state authorities. In many northern Indian communities, dependency on natural resources was critical to day-to-day survival until as late as the 1940s. During the early twentieth century, however, Indians' hunting, fishing, and gathering ran afoul of state laws, which were first instituted in the 1890s and became more common thereafter. The reason state conservation laws were enacted to begin with had little, if anything, to do with Indian practices; instead, they were enacted to bring an end to the vast overharvest of fish and game by non-Indian commercial fishermen and hunters.

During the first decades of the twentieth century, Indian harvesters were targeted for arrest by state game wardens, who confiscated their guns, traps, and nets. These harvesters were prosecuted in state courts that imposed fines beyond the ability of most Indians to pay. Thus, the providers for Indian families were sentenced to jail time and divested of their tools of production while their wives and children went hungry. Indian hunters and fishermen protested that they need not obey state conservation laws because their treaties with the United States superseded the laws of the states. The state courts in which their cases were heard disagreed with this contention, on the grounds that the state held the prerogative to manage and regulate its game and fish populations and that those who harvested them did so as a privilege granted by the state.[1] Regrettably, the federal Office of Indian Affairs agreed with this interpretation of the law and urged Indians to obey the laws of their states while hunting and fishing. Without the support of the federal government, Indians stood alone for many years against the power of the state. Of necessity and with the unwavering belief in the power of their treaties, Indian people continued to contest the law by harvesting natural resources surreptitiously. This state of affairs remained the status quo until the 1970s, when two criminal prosecutions of Indian fishermen in state courts in Michigan produced unexpected results. At this time, the Michigan Supreme Court recognized the continued existence of treaty-guaranteed fishing rights in the Michigan waters of the Great Lakes.[2]

Encouraged by this development in the 1970s, the tribes that were the successors in interest to the Michigan Treaty of 1836 fought for a civil resolution to the validity of their treaty guarantee to usufruct rights. The United States eventually intervened in this case on the part of the tribes, and in 1979, the U.S. District Court for the Western District of Michigan ruled in favor of the tribes.[3] This case, *United States v. Michigan,* permitted treaty-based fishing on the open waters of the Great Lakes, which had been ceded to the United States by the Treaty of Washington in 1836. It also had the important effect of encouraging tribes in neighboring states to seek clarification of their own treaty rights in the federal courts.

The next test cases for hunting and fishing rights involved the Treaty of St. Peter's in 1837 and the Treaty of La Pointe in 1842, which together ceded to the United States lands that now composed the western part of Michigan's Upper Peninsula, the northern third of the state of Wisconsin, and the eastern part of central Minnesota. The 1837 treaty stated that "the privilege of hunting, fishing, and gathering wild rice upon the lands, the rivers and the lakes included in the territory ceded, is guaranteed to the Indians during the pleasure of the president of the United States." Article 2 of the 1842 treaty states, "The Indians stipulate for the right of hunting on the ceded territory with the other privileges of occupancy until required to remove by the president of the United States."[4]

To permanently confirm these rights, five bands of Wisconsin Chippewa who were successors in interest to the two treaties—Lac du Flambeau, Lac Courte Oreilles, Bad River, Red Cliff, and St. Croix bands of Lake Superior Chippewa—filed a lawsuit in the U.S. District Court for the Western District of Wisconsin. This case, *Lac Courte Oreilles v. Voigt,* was the first Indian claim to the right to hunt, fish, and gather—that is, for the use of inland resources—over the ceded territory in the upper Great Lakes.[5] In 1986, the court upheld the tribes' claim, but the first attempts by the Chippewa to exercise the right were met by resistance of so-called sportsmen, and great civil unrest ensued.[6] Eventually, non-Indian citizens came to tolerate the court's ruling, and the tribe continues to peacefully exercise a treaty right free of state control to this day. In fact, it should be said that the tribes—individually as well as through their collective organization for environmental support, the Great Lakes Indian Fish and Wildlife Commission—are today welcome partners to the states of Minnesota, Wisconsin, and Michigan in pursuing their common goal of managing wildlife populations for the future.

The *Lac Courte Oreilles* decision created a problem in the area of Minnesota that had been ceded by the Treaty of 1837. While it was possible for the members of Wisconsin Chippewa bands to hunt and fish in this area of Minnesota, the local Ojibwe, the Mille Lacs band of Chippewa, who were parties to the same treaty, had no guarantees from the state of Minnesota that their fishermen, hunters, and gatherers could work under the protection of the 1837 treaty. Consequently, the Mille Lacs Band sued in the U.S. District Court for Minnesota to settle their right to harvest game and fish and other wild resources under the 1837 treaty. This case was decided in favor of the bands in 1994.[7] Subsequently, the state appealed the trial court's decision to the Eighth Circuit Court of Appeals, which then upheld the district court's decision. The U.S. Supreme Court agreed to hear an appeal by the state of Minnesota and, in 1999, returned a decision favorable to the band.[8]

Despite hard-fought successes in establishing treaty-based hunting and fishing rights in the ceded territories that now form parts of Wisconsin and Minnesota, the Odawa and Ojibwe tribes, including the Bay Mills Indian Community, parties to the Treaty of 1836 in Michigan, had still not established their inland usufructuary rights in the federal courts. They had won the right to fish under the treaty in the ceded waters of the Great Lakes, but their right to use inland waters and land areas was still in dispute by the state of Michigan. Michigan conservation officers often turned a blind eye to Indians harvesting inland resources in the years after the *United States v. Michigan* decision, because the tribes of the 1836 cession had all developed their own conservation codes, licensing systems, and enforcement mechanisms. This stand-off was unsatisfactory, however, to both the tribes and the state, and all parties wanted the issue formally resolved.

In 2003, the state of Michigan filed a lawsuit in federal court to restrain tribal hunters and fishermen from pursuing inland resources under the 1836 treaty. After a prodigious round of briefings and the depositions of numerous expert witnesses, the tribes and the state of Michigan embarked on several years of negotiation to try to settle the lawsuit. These discussions ultimately produced an agreement by which the state recognized the usufruct guarantee of the 1836 treaty, and the tribes agreed to certain limitations on the places in which they would pursue these rights as well as to some specific management objectives. The negotiated agreement was formalized as a consent decree that was issued by the U.S. District Court for the Western District of Michigan in late 2007.

The chapters in this part of this book provide historic and legal details for all the treaty struggles mentioned here.

CHAPTER 6

The Treaties of 1836 and 1855

During the late eighteenth and early nineteenth centuries, having just fought two costly wars with the British Empire, the new U.S. government found itself potentially rich in land and resources but deeply in debt. The obvious solution seemed to be to purchase land cheaply from Indian tribes and to sell it to American settlers from the eastern seaboard as well as to foreign immigrants. Land was to be acquired by treaty agreements, but in many instances, individuals and land companies usurped Indian land. In some cases, settlers took up residence as squatters, and in others, they purchased land from eastern land speculators who had improperly obtained title to the land. This was certainly the case in the Ohio country in the years preceding and following the Revolutionary War. The result was a series of Indian wars, which pitted the administration of George Washington against a broad-based but loose coalition of tribes, including Ottawa and Chippewa of Michigan. These groups sent delegations of warriors south to fight American troops.[1] After several numbing defeats at the hands of the combined tribes in earlier campaigns, General Anthony Wayne, though not defeating the Indian coalition at the Battle of Fallen Timbers, did convince them of the folly of a war of attrition with the United States, and he managed to bring the tribes to the treaty table at Greenville, Ohio, in 1795.

The Treaty of Greenville

The Treaty of Greenville was negotiated by military men in the aftermath of bloody conflict. General Anthony Wayne, who styled himself as the "war chief of the thirteen fires," negotiated for the United States, while the war chiefs of the Wyandot, Delaware, Shawnee, Ottawa, Chippewa, Potawatomi, Miami, Kickapoo, and Illinois tribes negotiated for the Indian side.[2] The Treaty of Greenville is important to treaty making in general because, as the first treaty in which the Old Northwest tribes were directly affected, it both set the tone, general form, and content of and influenced the expectations for many subsequent treaties, including the Treaty of 1836.

The Treaty of Greenville is, first, a treaty of peace and friendship that professed to end hostilities between the Old Northwest tribes and the United States and to regulate trade and other future relations. The treaty also incorporated a large land cession through which the tribes agreed to give up the southern third of Ohio as well as certain strategic positions throughout the Great Lakes region, including specific locations where French and British military posts had already been established. Among the cessions were Mackinac Island and reserves on both the south and north shores of the Straits of Mackinac, as well as Bois Blanc Island in the Straits of Mackinac, the latter given by the Chippewa as a gift of friendship to the United States.

The United States, which apparently considered itself the conqueror of all the Indian land of the Great Lakes region, agreed to relinquish (with several small exceptions) future claims to the land and waters of this vast region. The United States agreed to protect the right of the tribes to the quiet enjoyment of these lands, where they could hunt, plant, and dwell for "so long as they please."[3] The tribes agreed, however, that if they should ever wish to sell the land, the United States would be the sole purchaser. In exchange for the relinquishment of land and pledges of peace, the United States agreed that it would annually provide the various tribes who were parties to the treaties with goods worth twenty thousand dollars. Both the Chippewa and Ottawa were, by separate provisions, entitled to one thousand dollars' worth of goods.

Article V of the Greenville Treaty guaranteed the tribes the quiet enjoyment of their land, but in recognition of the fact that American settlers had long ago begun the practice of settling illegally on unceded Indian land, the United States vowed to protect the tribes from white intruders. This pledge was the quid pro quo for tribal recognition of the fiduciary responsibility of the United States for their welfare. Thus, we find the following in Article V: "[T]he United States will protect all the said Indian tribes in the quite enjoyment of their lands against all citizens of the United States, and against all other white persons who intrude upon the same [Indian land]. And the said Indian tribes again acknowledge themselves to be under the protection of the said United States and no other power whatever."[4]

Articles VI and VII of the Greenville Treaty provide the details of two arrangements that put U.S. trust responsibility to the tribes into practical operation. By Article VI, if a U.S. citizen or other white person presumed to settle on Indian land, the tribe was empowered to "drive off the settler, or punish him in such manner as they shall think fit." Likewise, the United States pledged to "break up" such settlements and to "remove and punish the settlers" in order to "effect that protection of the Indian lands herein before stipulated."[5] Recognizing, however, that both the United States and the Indian tribes desired trade and commerce, Article VIII provided that no person would be permitted to reside in an Indian town or camp as a trader who was not licensed by the Indian superintendent or other person appointed by the president. By this article and by a series of trade and intercourse acts approved by Congress in 1783, 1786, 1790, 1802, 1834, and subsequently, the United States sought to regulate the activities of non-Indian persons within Indian country.[6] In those days, "Indian country" was defined as land not ceded to the United States but within its borders. Non-Indians needed to obtain licenses if they wished to trade, operate mills and blacksmith shops, or perform other activities in Indian country. However, these persons were not considered to be settlers who were banned from Indian country under Article VI of the Greenville Treaty.

Among other specifics of the treaty, which provided for the maintenance of peaceful relationships between the tribes and the American government as well as for the welfare of both American and Indian people, are two provisions related to hunting, fishing, and gathering. The first is in Article V, which recognizes the tribes' right of occupation as well as the right to hunt, fish, and gather in the unceded sovereign territory of the tribes, with their right to live on and enjoy the land. Article VII of the treaty reserved to tribes who were party to the treaty the "liberty to hunt within the territory and lands which they have now ceded to the United States, without hindrance or molestation, so long as they demean themselves peacefully, and offer no injury to people of the United States."[7]

Importantly, the Treaty of Greenville did not terminate the Indians' usufructuary right on the land they ceded. To the contrary, Article VII acknowledges the tribes' right to use the ceded land with the sole restriction that they should "demean themselves peaceably and offer no injury to the people of the United States."[8] The "people of the United States" refers to American citizens who might now enter the newly ceded territory as settlers.

Thus, the foremost principle that governed the agreement between the Great Lakes and Ohio valley tribes and the United States was the right to hunt, fish, and gather, as a fundamental right by which the tribes could make a living from the land. The United States in no way restricted the right of the Indians to pursue fish and game on ceded land as long as their activities did not injure U.S. citizens. The Greenville Treaty was the first of the several treaties that the Michigan tribes would ultimately conclude with the United States, and it was the treaty under which the Ottawa and Chippewa of northern Michigan conducted their usufructuary rights until the Treaty of 1836. Thus, in 1836 the Ottawa and Chippewa would have understood that hunting, fishing, and gathering rights could be reserved on ceded land as long as they did not interfere with American activities on the land.

The Treaty of Greenville was signed by a large number of Ottawa chiefs representing communities from both the Straits of Mackinac and the western end of Lake Erie. Likewise, Chippewa chiefs who signed the treaty included Nahshogashe, a Chippewa from the Lake Superior region, and Keenoshameek from Cross Village. A delegation of about twenty of the Straits of Mackinac area Ottawa is known to have attended the Greenville Treaty.[9]

Early Treaties of Cession and Peace

Chiefs representing the Ottawa and Chippewa tribes signed treaties with the United States in 1807, 1808, 1816, and 1817 that ceded land in southern Michigan, northern Ohio, Indiana, and Illinois to the United States.[10] In all of these cases, the agreements were with the Ottawa of Sandusky Bay and southern Lake Michigan and with various eastern or Mississauga Ojibwa. These groups are socially and politically distinct from the northern Ottawa and the Lake Superior Chippewa.

The one exception to this pattern is the Treaty of Springwells, negotiated at the conclusion of the War of 1812, between William Henry Harrison, Duncan McArthur, and John Graham for the United States and representatives of all of the Great Lakes and Ohio Valley tribes. The treaty, which was signed on September 8, 1815, pledged peace with the Ottawa, Chippewa, and Potawatomi bands that had been allied with Great Britain. This included both the northern Ottawa and Chippewa. By Article 4 of the Treaty of Springwells, the United States agreed to "renew and confirm the treaty of Greenville."[11] The treaty was signed by Kemenechagon and Karbenequane, both Ottawas from Mackinac, and by a large number of Chippewa chiefs.

By the Treaty of Detroit in 1807, the Treaty of the Rapids of the Miami in 1817, the Treaty of Saginaw in 1819, and the Treaty of Chicago in 1821, the southern Ottawa, Chippewa, and Potawatomi ceded to the United States most of southern Michigan south of the Grand River and east of its headwaters and a line running northeast to Thunder Bay on Lake Huron, that is, about two-thirds of southern Michigan.[12] In the case of each of these major land cession treaties, the resident tribes retained the right to hunt, fish, and gather, with the proviso that the right would continue as long as the land remained the property of the United States. In each case, the Ottawa, Chippewa, Wyandot, and Potawatomi retained usufructuary rights on the land ceded. The 1817, 1819, and 1821 treaties were negotiated by Lewis Cass and specifically reaffirmed the hunting and gathering privileges of the Treaty of Greenville. In the case of the 1819 and 1821 treaties, Cass added the language that the right pertained "while it [the land] continued the property of the United States."[13]

The Treaties of June 16 and July 6, 1820

The first treaty between the United States and the northern Michigan tribes subsequent to the Treaty of Greenville was written between the Chippewa bands along the St. Marys River and territorial governor Lewis Cass, acting for the United States. After threats from both parties that included an armed standoff between U.S. troops and the St. Marys River Chippewa, who were fierce British partisans during the War of 1812, the short treaty agreement was concluded at Sault Ste. Marie on June 16, 1820. The treaty ceded a sixteen square mile tract of land on the St. Marys River near the outlet of Lake Superior, for which the Chippewa received "a quantity of goods in full satisfaction."[14] Since the river afforded Chippewa bands distributed over a substantial area access to whitefish from the rapids and adjacent spawning grounds, the United States guaranteed a perpetual right to fishing at the locality. This provision is Article 3 of the treaty from June 16, which reads as follows:

> The United States will secure to the Indians a perpetual right of fishing at the Falls of St. Marys, and also a place of encampment upon the tract hereby ceded, convenient to the fishing ground, which place shall not interfere with the defences of any military work which may be erected, nor with any private rights.[15]

The last clause was necessary for two reasons. First, the purpose of the cession was to acquire land for the construction of an American fort, which would command the St. Marys River and the entrance in and out of Lake Superior. Second, Governor Cass knew that several private claims had already been established along the St. Marys River, dating to the French and British occupations of this strategic locale. Thus, the condition that Indian encampment not interfere with private rights had reference to land occupied by residents such as John Johnston, Jean Nolin, John Sayre, Charles Ermatinger, Lyman and Truman Warren, John Drew and Janette Cadotte, and James Doty.[16] At least James Doty and the family of John Johnston were present and instrumental in the successful conclusion of the treaty agreement.[17]

In early July 1820, Jedidiah Morse and Mackinac Indian agent George Boyd negotiated a treaty in the name of Governor Cass at L'Arbre Croche, an Ottawa settlement on the extreme northwest coast of lower Michigan. By the treaty from July 6, the northern Ottawa and Chippewa ceded to the United States St. Martin's Island, which Henry Schoolcraft had determined in June to be valuable for its deposits of gypsum.[18] For this cession, the Ottawa and Chippewa received a "quantity of goods."[19]

As matters stood entering the decade of the 1830s, the northern Ottawa and Chippewa of Michigan had signed four treaties of cession with the United States. The first, the Treaty of Greenville, assured them the unlimited right to hunt, fish, and gather on territory they ceded to the United States as long as they did not harm U.S. citizens. It also guaranteed unrestricted rights to the enjoyment of the lands they occupied. The second treaty, concluded at Springwells, confirmed the force and effect of the Treaty of Greenville. The subsequent two treaties, negotiated in the summer of 1820, were for small land cessions, but in the Treaty of Sault Ste. Marie, the Chippewa sought and received official assurance from the United States that their right to perpetual use of the fishery at the rapids of the St. Marys would be recognized. As in the Treaty of Greenville, the guarantee provided by the United States was conditioned solely by their own behavior; the Chippewa could continue to camp at the rapids for fishing as long as they did not interfere with the citizens who occupied lots on the south bank of the river.[20] See map 1.

Early Competition for Natural Resources

The Indians' understanding of their rights to resource use seems to have originated in large part from distinctions made in the Treaty of Greenville. This treaty guaranteed the Indians both the quiet enjoyment of their unceded land and the use of resources and occupancy of ceded land. While the latter was conditioned by their own good behavior, the treaty did not link ownership of ceded land and usufruct. Instead, it used the practical definitions of the American frontier, where there were vast tracts of vacant land. On the lands ceded by the Indians, there were small and very scattered parcels of settled land that was cleared and being used for farms and domiciles. Of the remaining unsettled land, some had been obtained in large blocks by land speculators, while other parts were still held by the government. In practice, both Indians and non-Indian frontiersmen used resources of the unsettled land, that is, lands that were not occupied, regardless of ownership.

The situation on unceded land was different and showed that Indians on the Michigan frontier were aware of their rights under the Treaty of Greenville. Specifically, they understood that American settlements and non-Indian resource procurement were prohibited.[21] The desire of Agent Schoolcraft and others to open unceded land in northern Michigan to non-Indian resource extractors would play a role in bringing about the Treaty of 1836.

As early as 1824, Indians complained to Agent Boyd that residents around Fort Mackinac were cutting wood from unceded land.[22] Similar complaints were made in 1833, when the Ottawas charged that whites were cutting wood from Indian land for steamboat fuel.[23] In 1834 Henry Schoolcraft received Indian complaints that a government lightship crew was cutting wood on Waugoshance Point west of the Straits of Mackinac and that steamboat wood had been extensively cut on the Manitou Islands and at Sleeping Bear.[24] The chiefs demanded payment for these depredations.

In 1830 Agent Schoolcraft had written to Secretary Lewis Cass about the problems of regulating fishing by non-Indians in Lake Superior, which was entirely within Indian country. In this case, fish were superabundant and an essential winter food source for both Indians and non-Indians in the area. Even though he believed Indians would give their consent, Schoolcraft was concerned, since the Indian Trade and Intercourse Act did not permit non-Indians to fish in Indian country.

> On the 16th instant I granted a permit to Samuel Ashman, to fish and take provisions & goods to cut the necessary wood and tim-

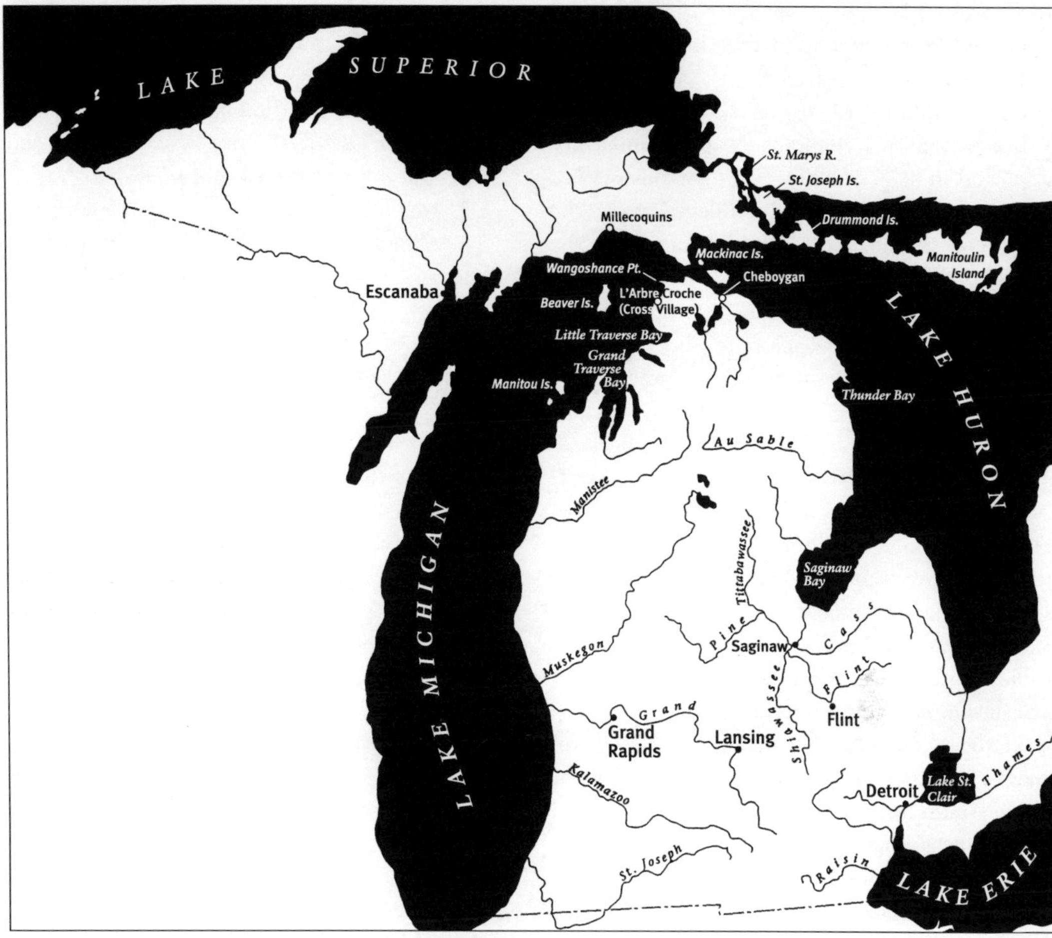

Map 1. Some place-names and locations of northern Michigan

ber in the Indian country of Lake Superior, the consent of the Chippewas being necessary to give validity to the permit, so far as relates to wood & timber. I took a bond with one [illegible word] in the amount of $500 conditioned for the observance of the laws regulating trade & intercourse with the Indian tribes so far as these laws are applicable.

I had the honor to write to you some years ago on this subject, & to report my proceedings in relation to it, since which, no attempts at fishing in the lake have been made. This season the plan has been revived, and with it the embarrassments under which the department labours. It is scarcely necessary to observe that the laws respecting trade, do not contemplate the necessity of citizens entering the Indian country, for any other purpose, except trading for furs & peltries, & their provisions are directed to guard against an abuse of this privilege. Licenses may be granted to trade, & to purchase certain articles and passports may be granted, special permits may be given under certain instructions. But it seems equally clear, that licenses for no other purposes, can be granted, & that no person is authorized to visit the Indian country, except under a view of the laws and regulations.

The inconvenience that would however, accrue to citizens by excluding them from the privilege of fishing in the Indian country, (where the Indians themselves offer no objection) are of a nature that will readily occur. And I am of opinion, that if congress would pass a law allowing Indian Agents to grant permits to fish for the season & cut wood & timber necessary thereto, in the Indian country, that advantages would result both to themselves & to the Indians. No ardent spirits should be permitted for this trade, and bonds should be exacted for an observance of the prohibition of ardent spirits, & conditioned that merchandize & provisions employed in it, are employed in the business of fishing. It would be advisable to leave the amount of the bond discretionary with the President. Perhaps the law should limit the bond not to exceed $1800. I have therefore drafted & herewith enclose a bill to meet the case; and that it might meet it, & no more.[25]

Clearly, Schoolcraft appreciated the Indians' absolute and exclusive right to the fishery on unceded Indian land and his responsibility to protect it. He also understood that his authority to permit resource use by non-Indians was limited by the Trade and Intercourse Act and that non-Indians who were permitted to use resources in Indian country were not settlers, since settlers were not permitted on unceded land.

The greatest controversy over natural resources in northern Michigan in the years prior to the Treaty of 1836 occurred in 1832–33 and also involved fishing. Elbert Herring, the commissioner of Indian affairs, wrote to Agent Henry Schoolcraft on December 27, 1832, forwarding a request from Mackinac traders Edward Biddle, John Drew, and William Sylvester for permits to give them exclusive rights to fish for whitefish and trout at the spawning grounds off Millecoquins and Epoufette on the north shore of Lake Michigan. Although Schoolcraft had not issued permits for the fall season by June 1833, he wrote to the commissioner suggesting that the boundary of the military cession at Mackinac made in the Greenville Treaty should be surveyed so that he could determine if Indian title had been extinguished in the Millecoquins-Epoufette area. If so, this would permit Biddle and Drew as well as other American citizens to fish within the cession. Item 13 of Article 3 of the Greenville Treaty described the Mackinac cession.

> The post of Michillimackinac [*sic*], and all the land on the island, on which that post stands, and the main land adjacent, of which the Indian title has been extinguished by gifts or grants to the French or English governments; and a piece of land on the main to the north of the island, to measure six miles on Lake Huron, or the strait between lakes Huron and Michigan, and to extend three miles back from the water of the lake or strait, and also the island DeBois Blanc, being a extra and voluntary gift of the Chippewa nation.[26]

The fishing sites that were the subject of the Biddle and Drew petition were at the head of Lake Michigan and clearly far to the west of the Greenville cession at Mackinac.

Biddle and Drew wrote again to Schoolcraft on June 13, 1833, saying that their only interest in asking for an exclusive right was so that other competing fishermen could not simply take over the improvements they had made at the fishing site.[27] They had also, as they reported, taken the opportunity to obtain permission to fish exclusively at the site from "Chief" Nabanoi, who was residing at Millecoquins. Word of this arrangement was apparently received by other local Indians who were outraged at the idea that the government would deprive them and "poor whites" from fishing on unceded land and water. George Johnston reported to Schoolcraft that over one hundred Ottawa from L'Arbre Croche under the leadership of Chiefs Apakosigan and Mahconseweamence arrived at Mackinac expressly to contest this suggested arrangement. The chiefs said that Nabanoi was of spurious origin and had no right to make any agreement with Biddle and Drew. They informed Johnston that they were fully aware that the traders were to blame and asked that the president not approve the traders' request. As they put it, they "trusted that their great Father would not allow this to take place."[28]

Schoolcraft relied on the newly expanded Trade and Intercourse Act of June 30, 1834, to resolve the controversy. In September 1834 he issued a notice announcing that the Greenville cession at Mackinac had been surveyed and that it would henceforth cease to be regarded as Indian country. The remaining territory, which included the proposed fishing sites, would be regarded as part of Indian country, and therefore the trade and intercourse laws would be in force. In part, the notice circulated by Agent Schoolcraft declared,

> Licenses to trade will be granted at this office, [Michilimackinac Indian Agency on Mack-

inac Island] under the usual regulations for all the country north of White River and Thunder Bay River of the Peninsula of Michigan. Permits to cut wood and saw logs will only be granted hereafter, on the payment of a fixed money compensation to the Indians, which will be stated at the office. All existing permits for these objects, are hereby revoked.

Hunting and trapping by white men is strictly prohibited by law, as well as the residence of Boatmen and Clerks in the Indian country, after expiration of their licenses. Provisions are inserted in the laws forbidding the formation of settlements on Indian lands, or any occupancy which is designed to originate a claim to title [under the Preemption Act]. Instructions have recently been received declaring that no permission will hereafter be given for building Saw Mills on Indian Lands.[29]

In the Indian Trade and Intercourse Act of 1834 and in Agent Schoolcraft's circular, which made notice of the act, it is clear that settlement and resource extraction were distinct categories of land use. Those permitted to enter Indian country to "trade," "cut wood," and "saw logs" were not settlers and could not become settlers; they were temporary residents with no usufructuary rights except as separately and specifically permitted by license.

Clearly, the northern Michigan Ottawa and Chippewa had good knowledge of the Greenville Treaty and their rights under its terms. Speeches, actions, and petitions of the Chippewa and Ottawa chiefs in the few years immediately preceding the Treaty of 1836 indicate that the tribes were aware of their sovereign status in dealing with the United States. This fact was explicitly stated by Pabamatabi when he explained, "Some of the men are yet living who were at the treaty [Greenville]. And we have been told by our old men of the terms of it."[30] Among others, Pabamatabi was referring to Keenoshameek, who signed both the Treaty of Greenville and the 1836 treaty. The chiefs also indicated their awareness that they had exclusive rights to the resources on unceded territory and that these resources had economic value for both themselves and the United States. Finally, their actions clearly indicate that the chiefs and the Ottawa and Chippewa people understood the obligations of the United States under the Treaty of Greenville and trusted in the goodwill, generosity, and power of the Great Father to oversee and protect their welfare.

Michigan Ecology and Geography

In the Great Lakes states, a sharp ecological transition zone transects the basins of Lakes Huron, Michigan, and Superior. To the north of these great water bodies are the relatively sterile conifer-dominated forests of the Canadian Biotic Province, with its distinctive fauna such as moose, caribou, and lynx. To the south of the lakes lay the huge deciduous forests of the eastern United States, dominated by oak-hickory forests with deer, bear, elk, and many distinctive small animals. This is known as the Carolinian Biotic Province.[31] Between these two provinces is a transition community referred to as the Great Lakes Forest or the Carolinian-Canadian ecotone. The flora and fauna in this place is a mixture of the species that form the two larger provinces that border it.[32] The northern border to the Carolinian biotic zone is very distinct across the southern peninsula of Michigan, as it roughly follows the Port Huron glacial moraine from Standish in the east to Clare in the center part of the state and Reed City in the west. From the vicinity of Reed City, the ecological transition zone leads north, paralleling the east coast of Lake Michigan from Traverse City to the Straits of Mackinac.[33]

This ecological transition line also marks the northern extent of agricultural crop production, because the area to the north, the Great Lakes Forest that covers the northern Lower Peninsula and the Upper Peninsula, receives less than 140 frost-free growing days per year.[34] With such a short season, agricultural commodities like corn and soybeans and truck crops cannot be produced with assurance. For this reason, open farmland is an infrequent feature of the northern Michigan landscape. In fact, the land that composes the vast majority of the country ceded by the Treaty of 1836 remains, to this day, forested with pine, maple, spruce, fir, birch, poplar, hemlock, and oak.[35] As one travels north in Michigan, the climate is less moderate, and the boreal elements of the fauna and flora are more pervasive. The growing season is, however, only one of the factors that discourage crop production in northern Michigan. The soil itself, derived from glacial till, is composed largely of sand and gravel that has not benefited from substantial topsoil development. Thus, the soil is thin, subject to leaching, and, in many places, deficient in the nutrients essential for crop production.[36]

In the nineteenth century, government officials in Michigan, Wisconsin, and Minnesota hoped that agrarian settlement would extend farther north, but they were also aware of the low agricultural potential of the region. Schoolcraft, in particular, was an avid gardener and had lived in northern Michigan and observed the pitiful efforts of Indians and others to grow corn and other crops. He must have known that this part of the state would never be supported by farming.

At the time of the Treaty of 1836, the geography of northern Michigan was still poorly known. No surveyors had ever worked in the region; so maps were based on the observations of explorers, fur traders, and those licensed to work in the area by the Indian Office. The best map, used by Schoolcraft to plot the limits of the 1836 cession and its reservations, was produced and published by H. S. Tanner in 1836 (map 2). Although this map represents a relatively accurate depiction of the settled part of southern Michigan, the Straits of Mackinac, and the Sault Ste. Marie area, the remaining portions are inaccurate and out of proportion. For example, on the Tanner map, the interior portion of Grand Traverse Bay, a prominent landmark, is shown running east-west rather than north-south.

In 1826 special Indian agent Samuel Morse wrote that the eastern shore of Lake Michigan, "extending into the interior as far as the dividing ridge, consists of sandhills crowned with a few stunted trees"[37]—a description that can only be described as imaginary. In 1836 Michigan governor S. T. Mason described the Upper Peninsula as "the sterile region on the shores of Lake Superior, destined by soil and climate to remain forever a wilderness."[38] This view was stated even more forcefully by the *Detroit Daily Free Press* on March 17, 1836, which described the Upper Peninsula as "the region of perpetual snows—the *ultima Thule* of our national domain on the North."[39] On the verge of Michigan statehood, U.S. senator-elect Lucius Lyon voiced the sentiments of many Michigan citizens when he declared that the merits of northern Michigan were that "we can raise our own Indians in all time to come and supply ourselves now and then with a little bear meat for delicacy."[40] After northern Michigan had been surveyed and was better known, the appraisals of its agricultural prospects did not improve. The famous advocate of Western bounty and settlement, Horace Greeley, wrote in an 1859 edition of the *New York Tribune* that Michigan north country was "cold and uninteresting to the cultivator, diversified by vast swamps, sterile, gravelly knolls and dense forests."[41] This was an accurate description.

Any hopes for rapid development in the north were crushed by the financial panic of 1837, which was in part fueled by unsecured land speculation. With widespread failure of state-chartered banks, the sale of public land in the United States fell from twenty million acres in 1836 to three and a half million acres two years later.[42] At the same time, however, a great deal of pressure was coming to bear for the opening of the north country to lumbering and mining. Thanks in large degree to the writing of Henry Schoolcraft following his expedition to explore the source of the Mississippi River in 1832, the public was well aware of the riches of the Lake Superior region.[43] Thus, at the time of the Ottawa and Chippewa cession of 1836 and the Chippewa cessions in Wisconsin and Minnesota of 1837 and 1842, which together made most of the timber and mineral resources of northern Michigan and Wisconsin available to American citizens, government officials such as Lewis Cass, Governor Mason, Senator Lyon, and Indian agent Henry Schoolcraft knew that this area would not be needed for agricultural purposes at any time in the immediate future, if ever. Anxious, however, to acquire rights to natural resources, they were willing to obtain the cessions while permitting the Indians who were thinly scattered over this immense region to remain and to continue to pursue their seasonal rounds by hunting, fishing, and gathering over the ceded territory.

Events Leading to the Treaty of 1836

As the international fur market declined, fur traders put increased pressure on Indian trappers

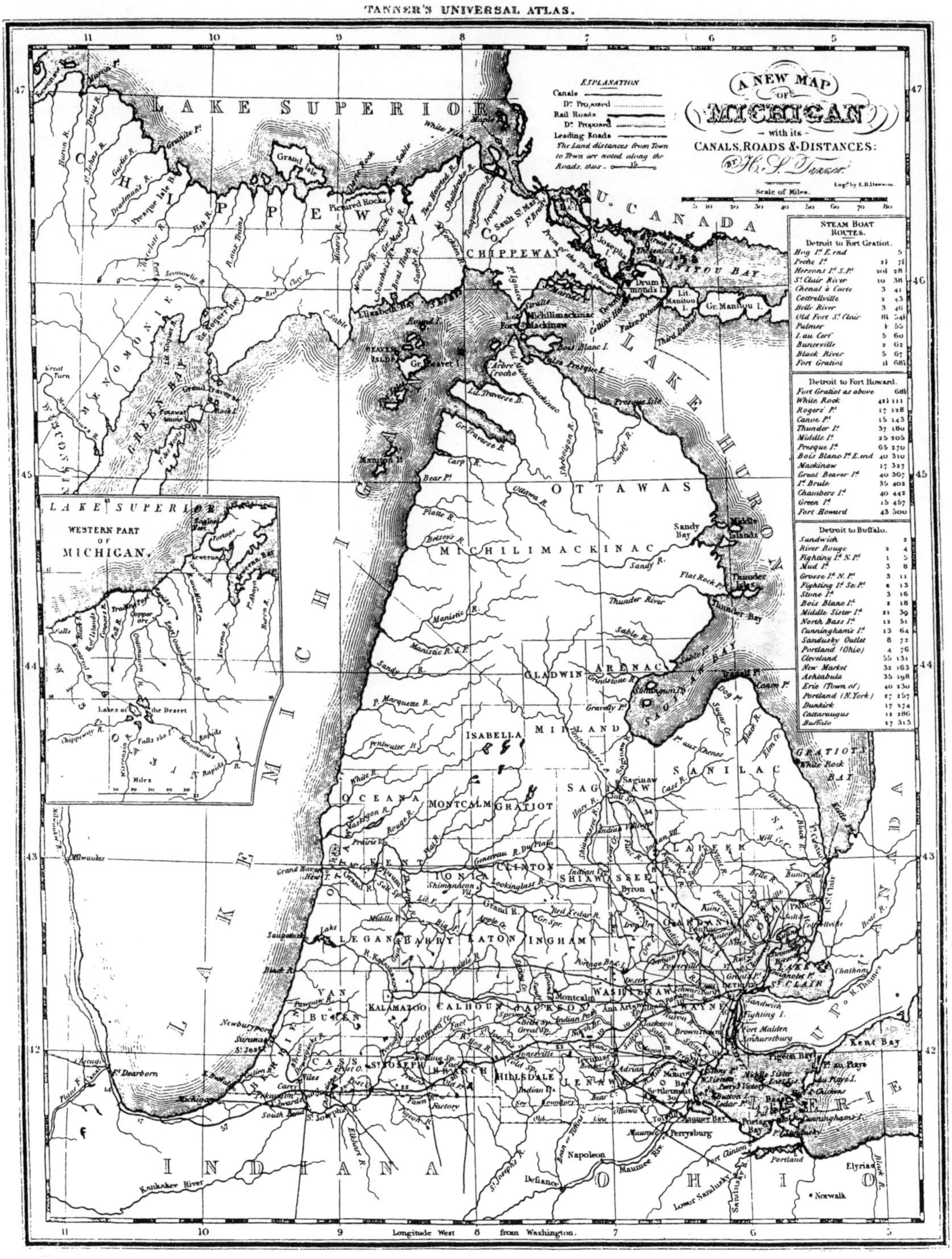

Map 2. A new map of Michigan by H. S. Tanner (1836)

not only to produce more fur but also to repay the debts that had accrued under their liberal credit policies. It must be appreciated that the traders were not remote from their Indian creditors. Indeed, most resided in or near the Indian communities, and most were married to Indian women and had children who were socially classified as Indian. The traders were thus often the in-laws to the chiefs and family heads who were central to Chippewa and Ottawa decision making. In this way, the traders, who often acted as translators, advisers, and cultural middlemen between Indian and non-Indian society, had an immense capacity to influence Ottawa and Chippewa political processes.

It is also important to recognize the role of the Indian affairs bureaucracy in American frontier life and economy. In fact, during at least the early half of the nineteenth century, the activities of Indian agencies, with their offices, blacksmith shops, trading stores, agricultural and mechanical aid programs, and system of government school support, were a core element in American presence on the Michigan frontier. Beyond this, however, was the fact that the Mackinac Indian Agency played an important role in the frontier economy. Not only did the government contract for buildings, equipment, supplies, Indian gifts, and foodstuffs, but it also produced a large number of relatively well-paid jobs for agents, subagents, blacksmiths, mechanics, teachers, farmers, and translators.[44]

Undoubtedly, an even greater impact on the economy resulted from Indian treaties.[45] These were usually the only real source of hard cash on the early nineteenth-century Great Lakes frontier. Treaty money came from two major sources: (1) debt fund provisions incorporated into treaties to pay the debts of individual Indians and (2) the annuity payments that were made each year for land cessions. Although annuity payments were paid to Indian heads of families on a per capita basis, the great majority of these payments soon passed into the hands of the traders, who attended the annuity payments in swarms. The traders either claimed additional debts or offered trade goods in exchange for the gold and silver coinage.

Given these realities of frontier life, it is necessary to understand Indian treaties as relatively rare events, which were regarded as enormous financial opportunities by non-Indians. From this perspective, the provisions of treaties reflect not just Indian objectives but those of private enterprise as well. The latter considerations were often incorporated into treaties with little input from the Indian parties.

At the direction of territorial governor S. T. Mason, Kintzing Pritchette visited the Grand River Ottawa in early 1836 and, among other matters, reported on the relationship between the trader debt system and pressure for land cession.

> They resort to the traders who supply their wants and gratify their increased propensity for dress and finery. As the risk of the trader is great, and his returns in some degree dependent upon a future treaty, the profits demanded are exorbitant. The prices of the most ordinary articles are doubled to the Indians. A few years exercise of this system plunges the tribe in irretrievable debt and the claims of the trader, part real, part artificial are enormous. The effect of all which is to make them entirely dependent upon these men for supply of their wants. They become absolutely under their control and they dictate entirely in the sale of their lands.[46]

In the case of the 1836 treaty, it is clear that the traders, as individuals and as representatives of large fur enterprises, had enormous financial interest in the outcome of the treaty negotiations. Beyond collecting cash in repayment of claimed debts, the traders hoped to pressure the chiefs to request land grants or payments in lieu of land grants for their mixed-blood children. In the end, few individuals profited more from the treaty than Henry Schoolcraft himself.

Indian Politics

In the initial political jockeying prior to the Treaty of 1836, three distinct Indian factions emerged. First, there were the Chippewa of the eastern Upper Peninsula, who were under the strong influence of Henry Schoolcraft and his mixed-blood brothers-in-law George and William Johnston. This faction agreed to land cessions as a means of securing a blacksmith shop and other benefits as well as reservations and usufructuary rights. Second, there were the Grand River Ottawa, who did not want the Chippewa to be included in any treaty to which they were party and who did not want to sell any land to the United States. Finally, there were the Little Traverse Ottawa, who took an intermediate position, with the intention of selling a small amount of marginal land to pay debts but retaining as much of their estate and political integrity as possible. No Indian faction favored removal to the West.

For at least five or six years prior to 1836, the L'Arbre Croche Ottawa had been appealing to Agent Schoolcraft for leave to send a delegation to Washington to discuss their affairs with the president. These requests were either not answered or refused.[47] The northern Ottawa at Little Traverse Bay in 1834 seemed to have come up with the idea of selling some of their land to the United States to repay debts that traders claimed to be owed them.[48] At that time, neither territorial governor George Porter nor Lewis Cass, secretary of war—each well acquainted with the progress of settlement in the Michigan Territory—believed that the United States had any reason whatsoever to acquire land in northern Michigan.[49] Governor Porter said that such a cession would at present be "folly as their lands are not required."[50] In this statement, the governor was no doubt thinking of all the abundant agricultural land in southern Michigan that had been surveyed and offered for sale at $1.25 per acre but had not yet sold.

By 1834 pressure on the Indians by the traders for a land cession was becoming very intense. The Ottawa of Grand Traverse Bay and the Grand River held a meeting in the early summer at Grand Rapids, and both groups determined not to sell any land to the United States.[51] While some authors have claimed that the pressure for land cession north of the Grand River was the result of the need to acquire land for American settlement, this is patently false.[52] There was plenty of unsold farmland in southern Michigan at the time of the Treaty of 1836. The real reason, apparent at the time, was the desire of the traders to collect money through the treaty-making process. With the help of their sympathizers in government service and the desire of government officials to acquire access to natural resources, they were able to overcome strong Indian opposition to the cession. The role of Agent Henry Schoolcraft in the complicity to force the 1836 treaty cannot be overstated. Not only was Schoolcraft the superintendent for the Mackinac Agency and sole U.S. commissioner for the 1836 treaty, but he was also the major individual beneficiary of the treaty's trader debt provision as well as other articles of the treaty that directly provided employment and other benefits to his in-laws.[53]

Although the Ottawa had agreed among themselves that they did not want to part with any land, the northern Ottawa came up with a scheme in early 1834 to raise funds by selling some marginal land in order to raise the forty thousand dollars they believed they owed their traders. Schoolcraft reports that he was approached by a delegation from Little Traverse Bay led by Assiginac (Blackbird) that proposed selling Drummond Island to the United States. Drummond Island, sometimes called Assiginac's Island, was abandoned when Assiginac's band moved to Little Traverse, and it was therefore no longer used by the Ottawa.[54] In November 1835 Schoolcraft wrote to the commissioner of Indian affairs, Elbert Herring, recommending the Drummond Island purchase.[55]

In the meantime, the Ottawa, determined to pursue this idea directly with Washington, applied to Schoolcraft for permission to send a delegation to discuss the proposed cession and other matters with the president and the secretary of war.[56] The Ottawas, in order to sweeten their proposal to sell some land while forestalling a larger cession, offered to sell the Manitou Islands, which were seldom used, and a portion of the north shore of Lake Michigan. The latter was generally regarded as Chippewa territory, but the Ottawa said they claimed it by "the right of conquest."[57]

The political maneuvering of the bands during the period leading up to the treaty shows that the Ottawa's and Chippewa's primary objective was to sell as little land as possible to the United States in order to raise cash. They also wanted the right to hunt, fish, and gather on the land they ceded as well as some basic services. The Indians also desperately needed access to blacksmiths and a shop for repairing weapons, traps, iron implements, and cooking vessels.

Like the French and British before them, the

Americans had always operated a blacksmith shop at Mackinac to incur the favor of the Ottawa and Chippewa.[58] In 1835, however, the government decided that it would only operate such shops if they were required by treaty stipulation. In fact, the blacksmith shop and its services were also a mechanism of political manipulation. For example, in the summer of 1834, Subagent Audrain at Sault Ste. Marie informed Indians who threatened to move to the British side of the St. Marys River that they would no longer be able to use the American shop.[59]

When Agent Schoolcraft announced the closing of the blacksmith shop at the end of December 1834, there was an outpouring of regret from both the Ottawa and Chippewa, who, while acknowledging that the United States had no obligation to maintain the shop, stated their dependence on the services and wondered how they would survive without them.[60] Chief Pabamatabi of L'Arbre Croche reminded President Jackson that the Indian people of northern Michigan had had the services of a shop in the times of the French and British kings as well as under the American flag. As he put it, "We so highly appreciate the value of the shop, that we do not know how to live without it. A great part of the implements we use in hunting and cooking are made twice valuable to us by being mended."[61] Pabamatabi recounted details of some of the events that transpired at Greenville.

> It is forty winters since we first saw the Americans. When we first shook hands with you and smoked the pipe of peace with you, at Greenville General Wayne the Chief who led your soldiers drew lines across our lands, and they were agreed to. He took also a piece of land around each of the forts. You have reminded us that Old Mackinac was among the grants. And requested us to be present to see the lines run, we have not forgotten the grant. Some of the men are yet living who were at the treaty. And we have been told by our old men of the terms of it. The lines were to be drawn three miles each way from the fort. We will send men to go with the survey. And we have but one request to make. It is when the lines are run, the white men will keep within them. And we will promise not to go over them. If any wood is cut upon our land hereafter we should be paid for it, and we authorize you to take care of our land. And to grant the necessary papers permitting the cutting wood and hay. It is now valuable to you. You could not live on the Island [Mackinac] without wine and means ample. We would not ask remuneration. But we are impoverished in many ways. And we therefore ask of you that the shop may be kept open.[62]

Schoolcraft quickly understood that he could use the shop closing to help convince the tribes to cede their land, by presenting a treaty-supported shop as an important potential benefit of successful negotiations. To cover his own involvement, he asked Major Cobbs at Fort Brady in Sault Ste. Marie to arrange to "receive an offer" from the Indians to sell a portion of their land, for which the shop could "then probably come in as one of the equivalents."[63] In another letter, in November 1835, he told Cobbs, "Should the Indians of the Sault, feel willing to part with any portion of their lands, for a moderate consideration, I should be pleased to be apprized of it. I think it important to a good understanding with them that they should have a shop at St. Marys, and will cheerfully cooperate with you, in any measures you may suggest, to procure its establishment."[64] While Schoolcraft used the issue of the blacksmith shop to promote land cession, it is clear, by the basic nature of blacksmith services, that neither the Indians nor Schoolcraft expected that the hunters, fishers, and gatherers who supported the economy of northern Michigan would be removing from the state.

In late August 1835 Commissioner Herring told Schoolcraft that the government had not contemplated such land purchases but that Schoolcraft should inquire about the details and also find out if the Indians were willing to sell land north of the Grand River.[65] As a result of his inquiries, the Ottawa repeated their long-standing request to be able to send a delegation to discuss the situation directly with the president. Schoolcraft recommended that the request be approved, but he suggested that it was too late in the season to select a proper delegation.[66] In late October he wrote to Commissioner Herring that an unauthorized Ottawa delegation was headed to Washington from Little Traverse Bay under the guidance of a young, educated mixed blood named Augustin Hamlin.

By November Schoolcraft reported back to Herring that he had inquired about the Indians' desire to sell land in western and northern Michigan. Schoolcraft's letter betrays his willingness to distort the Indian opposition to land cession while extolling the virtues of mineral wealth and strategic resources of the region, in order to influence the government in Washington in favor of acquiring the land. Schoolcraft started by stating that there was not unanimity among the Indians on the question of a land cession. In fact, they had agreed among themselves not to sell land. Worse yet, he told Herring that he had favorable replies from the "eastern, middle, and northwestern portions of the country." This was incorrect, since certain bands had agreed not to sell any land, and others had agreed to sell only small parcels. Even here, however, Schoolcraft said that a cession must be conditioned on the government providing "liberal considerations, with reservations, and a defined right of hunting on the lands sold," as well as the designation of a future place of permanent residence. Schoolcraft noted the objections of the L'Arbre Croche Indians—that is, the Little Traverse Ottawa—but attributed their opposition to ignorance and tried to diminish their importance by saying that they only occupy "a limited portion of the country."[67]

In late November Schoolcraft's brother-in-law William Johnston, a mixed-blood trader, answered Schoolcraft's inquiry about the Chippewa's willingness to cede land in the northern peninsula. Johnston's letter is one of the most direct statements from Indians relative to their expectations of the guarantee they would insist on at the forthcoming treaty negotiation.

> In compliance with your instructions dated the 7th inst., I proceeded to the Sault Ste. Maries, And at which place I met the two Chiefs [Iaubawandick or Waishkey and Shawono] I stated to them the purpose of my visit, and inquired of them on what conditions they would be willing to cede Drummond Island, or any other portion of their lands. They answered in behalf of their young men, that they were willing to cede their lands to the United States on reasonable terms, the terms to be left to the discretion of the Agent appointed by government; with this provision, they, to have a full right to hunt, on the ceded lands, as long as they were unoccupied, and to make such reservations as they should think proper.
>
> I then proceeded to the foot of Sugar Island, where Ocunogeeged, one of the claimants to the above named island resides. He and his young men also perfectly coincide in opinion, with the above named Chiefs.[68]

In this statement, we see that the Indian understanding of the usufructuary right was tied to the condition of land use, that is, their right to hunt, fish, and gather on unoccupied land. It had nothing whatsoever to do with the legalities of land title.

In the late fall, Schoolcraft himself set out for New York and Washington with several purposes in mind. One of these was to lobby for the governorship of the newly created Wisconsin Territory, and another was to lobby Congress for passage of a special bill to provide compensation to the Johnston family for Indian trade debts owed to his deceased father-in-law, John Johnston.[69] Another important reason was that he was aware that an Ottawa delegation had gone to Washington to discuss land sales, and he wished to be part of such discussions. When Schoolcraft arrived in Washington in December, he was told that the secretary of war, Lewis Cass, had decided to assemble a full Ottawa-Chippewa delegation in order to negotiate a treaty that would cede the remaining Indian land in northern Michigan.

For their part, and despite some difference of opinion among the bands on how to achieve their goals, the Ottawa and Chippewa were in harmony concerning what they hoped to accomplish as a result of the forthcoming treaty. These general goals distilled into a series of interlocking objectives, which the Ottawa and Chippewa chiefs realized they needed to achieve as either concessions or benefits from the United States in exchange for a land cession. These objectives, stated succinctly, were as follows:

1. To pay their debts to the fur traders
2. To obtain financial awards or land grants for mixed-blood relatives
3. To gain access to government services, principally blacksmith shops and schools

4. To acquire land reserves in order to protect their villages, burial grounds, and gardening, sugaring, and orchard sites
5. To secure the right to support themselves by hunting, fishing, trapping, and gathering that provided them food, clothing, shelter, and trade commodities

These objectives were clearly interrelated. For example, they could not live as hunters and gatherers on small reservations, because these small land areas did not have nearly enough resources to support their population. They could not hunt and trap at all without the cooperation of traders, many of whom were also their mixed-blood relatives. Finally, they needed blacksmith shops to repair the guns and traps on which their livelihood depended.[70]

Organization of the Indian Delegation

Secretary Cass decided to appoint Henry Schoolcraft, superintendent of the Michigan Indian Superintendency, to be the sole U.S. commissioner for the proposed land cession treaty in Michigan. Schoolcraft soon remarked on the importance—and difficulty—of obtaining a representative delegation.[71] The major problem was that by December the Ottawa and Chippewa were configured in small family hunting parties scattered across the interior of Michigan.

Both Cass and Schoolcraft realized that the cession of land was an emotional and contentious issue among Indians.[72] Perhaps for this reason, Cass supplied Schoolcraft with a document called a "power of sale" and ordered him to get the signatures of the Ottawa and Chippewa chiefs and headmen on the document before they came to Washington. Schoolcraft described the purpose of this document as a means to give "efficacy" to the delegation.[73] Schoolcraft duly sent the power of sale to John Clitz, commander at Fort Mackinac, who was to try to obtain the signatures of Indians around the Straits of Mackinac. William Johnston was to do the same for the Ottawa of western lower Michigan. Both reported difficulty in collecting the signatures.[74] On December 29, 1835, Captain Clitz forwarded to Schoolcraft a copy of the power of sale signed by thirty-two chiefs and headmen.[75] Schoolcraft did not report receiving this power of sale from Clitz until March 23, 1836, when he had practically concluded the treaty negotiations.[76] Among its other provisions for sale of the land, this document states "the privilege of hunting upon the land and residing upon it, until it is surveyed and sold by the government to be secured."[77] There is no record as to if or how the document was explained to the Indians. As we shall see, this language is much different than that which ultimately described the reservation of usufruct rights in Article 13 of the 1836 treaty.

Schoolcraft went about notifying, collecting, and transporting the chiefs to Washington by enlisting the help of American Fur Company traders, such as John Drew, Rix Robinson, and John Holliday. Both the traders and Commissioner Schoolcraft tried to manipulate the composition of the delegation to enhance their chances of perfecting the treaty. Influential Michigan U.S. senator-elect and land speculator Lucius Lyon, who was to attend the treaty negotiation, wrote to both Rix Robinson and John Drew in late December to urge that they personally select chiefs to represent the various bands and "at the same time to effect a treaty with them for the whole peninsula if possible." He added that if the treaty were to be made, arrangements would be forthcoming to "pay the just debts that the Indians may be owing to the whites."[78] Both Robinson and Drew had heavy claims against the Ottawa and Chippewa and therefore strong motivation for wanting the treaty to succeed. They also had such strong influence with the tribes that Charles Trowbridge of Detroit wrote to Schoolcraft expressing the opinion that a treaty could not be concluded without the influence of these men.[79]

Perhaps the most blatant attempt to influence the treaty delegation was made by Schoolcraft himself. On December 29, 1835, he wrote to his wife, Jane (Johnston), from Washington, telling her of his appointment as treaty commissioner. Since she was in Sault Ste. Marie, Schoolcraft asked her to enlist her brother, William Johnston, as well as Captain Clitz at Fort Brady, to round up a delegation to represent the Chippewa of the eastern Lake Superior region. He asked them to send no Catholic Indians, since he would have enough of them. Here he made reference to the Little Traverse Ottawa, whom he knew opposed any large-scale land sale. The Indians whom he wished to exclude from the Sault delegation were the Catholic members of Oshawano's band, whom he felt might concur with their brethren from Little Traverse Bay. He also indicated that he wanted the Sault Ste. Marie band to be well represented, "so they can get their just rights." In part, this was a reference to earlier attempts by the Ottawa to sell Chippewa land north of the Straits of Mackinac.[80]

To this end, William Johnston did very well, since the delegates who ultimately represented the Chippewa from the eastern Upper Peninsula area included his relatives Waishkey, or Jawbawadic (Young Caribou Buck), the ceremonial name of Waishkey, and his son Waubojeeg (White Fisher).[81] This selection was protested vigorously by Kawgaosh, speaker of the Sault Ste. Marie crane clan. He correctly claimed that Waishkey and his son were of the *addik,* or caribou, totem from western Lake Superior and were not legitimate speakers for people who resided at Sault Ste. Marie. Members of the crane clan, like the Catholic chief Oshawano, traditionally spoke for the Chippewa residing at the Sault. James Schoolcraft, Henry's brother, heard this complaint and told Kawgaosh that he would forward it to the Great Father. On hearing of the episode, Henry Schoolcraft described it as a "somewhat amusing account."[82]

The news of the quick and unexpected treaty negotiations passed like "an electric shock" through the trading community at Mackinac. William Johnston reported that the gossip was full of discussion of "claims, by losses and through ties of blood."[83] In other words, other claimants feared that the Johnston claim and that of the American Fur Company had been assured by the improper selection of chiefs. At least, William Johnston hoped this to be the case. In the same letter, he told Schoolcraft that "Whaiskee and his son [Waubojeeg] are very willing to go [to Washington] . . . You will find from the enclosed that they are willing to allow my mother [Susan Johnston, the Chippewa widow of trader John Johnston and Henry Schoolcraft's mother-in-law] something for her claim as well as others; also the other chiefs who compose the delegation consented to it."[84]

Another ploy used by Cass and Schoolcraft to influence the outcome of the treaty was to hold negotiations in Washington in midwinter. Thus, a small delegation of Ottawa and Chippewa, isolated from the advice and counsel of their kinsmen, could easily be impressed by the power of Americans. Most especially, they were in a position where they could be lobbied and pressured by the traders. The Grand River bands who opposed selling any land sent a petition to that effect to President Jackson. Although Schoolcraft said that the treaty was to be held in Washington as a matter of "economy," the traders knew different. William Brewster, American Fur Company agent at Detroit, explained to his superior Ramsey Crooks in New York,

> I have had some conversations with Mr. R. [Rix Robinson] on the subject of the contemplated treaty and have given my views in relations to the whole matter and have got his notions right in some respects where they were wrong. I have convinced Mr. R. that it would result decidedly better for the interest of just claims against the Indians (such as ours) and for the Indians themselves to have the treaty held at Washington for reasons if held in the country, false claims will always be presented to large amounts and so managed that many of them will be allowed to the exclusion of just claims. I have advised Mr. R. to impress on the minds of the Chiefs the fact that they will be able to effect a better treaty at Washington than at home and also to have them make up their minds fully to sell their country, as the government will have it. I have also suggested to Mr. R. that it would be proper to have the Indians well trained in what they are to ask the government before they arrive at Washington.[85]

Thus, with common purpose, the American Fur Company and the U.S. government conspired to minimize opposition to the treaty by influencing the selection of Indian delegates to the treaty convention and to disadvantage them as to the place, time, and manner in which the treaty would be negotiated.

Negotiation of the Treaty

During the month of March 1836, small groups of Michigan chiefs, in the company of Robert

Stuart, Rix Robinson, John Drew, and other traders, continued to arrive in the nation's capital. These events were duly reported to American Fur Company executive Ramsey Crooks in New York by Mary Holliday, who accompanied her father, John, a fur trader, to Washington, where he was to be the official interpreter for the treaty.[86] On Monday, March 14, the Indian delegation met with President Andrew Jackson and Secretary Cass, at which time the president "received them handsomely."[87]

On Tuesday, March 15, Schoolcraft convened the treaty negotiations at the Masonic Hall. Besides Commissioner Schoolcraft, the American delegation consisted of John Hulbert (Schoolcraft's brother-in-law), acting as treaty secretary, and John Holliday, acting as official interpreter. Twenty-five chiefs represented bands centered at Sault Ste. Marie, the Straits of Mackinac, L'Arbre Croche (Little Traverse Bay), Grand Traverse Bay, the Muskegon River, and the Grand River. Most were Ottawa, and the largest delegations were from L'Arbre Croche and the Grand River. No doubt many of the conductors were also present, including, at least, Rix Robinson, John Drew, Henry LaVake, William Lasley, Leonard Slater (Grand Rapids missionary), and the Moran brothers.

Although none of the Ottawa or Chippewa chiefs spoke English, a great many of the non-Indian observers spoke the Ottawa or Chippewa language with various degrees of fluency. The chiefs could probably count on an honest translation from Augustin Hamlin, the mixed-blood confidant of the northern Ottawa. Although available historical documents leave no comment on the competency of translation offered by Mr. Holliday, we can be sure that the task of translating between English and Algonquian was extremely difficult. Even assuming a high level of competency and complete honestly, there are often no Algonquian words to adequately convey English concepts, and the reverse is also often true.

Schoolcraft's opening statement to the chiefs closely reflected the instructions he had received from Secretary Cass.[88] He stated that the object of the treaty was to buy land. He related the recent history of offers by the Ottawa and Chippewa to sell various small parcels but said that, out of fairness and justice, the president wanted to deal with the whole tribe, not individual bands or communities. He noted the presence of the Chippewa and told the chiefs that the president would offer to buy their land because it was worthless to them and because the Great Father would do well by the Chippewa by purchasing it. The United States, he said, would pay liberally for the land and provide for reservations in common, but not to individuals, either red or white. Likewise, mixed bloods would not get land but could get money in lieu of land. Trader debts would be paid through a special commission to be appointed following the treaty. As to the question of the future residence and conditions of the tribes, Schoolcraft gave them assurances that they would be provided with reservations and hunting privileges so that they could continue to reside and support themselves in Michigan.

> No objection will be made if you deem it imperative, to your fixing on proper and limited reservations to be held in common; but the President judges it best, that no reservations should be made to individuals. Your relations, [mixed bloods] who could be entitled to such reservations, will be compensated for their value, in money. The usual privileges of residing and hunting on the lands sold till they are wanted will be granted.[89]

Following this statement, the council was adjourned until Friday, March 18, so that the chiefs could discuss and respond to Schoolcraft's proposal.

The session on March 18 opened with a traditional blessing in the form of a pipe ceremony. The chief speaker, Mukudaybenasi (Blackbird), stated that the chiefs were upset by the president's refusal to allow reservations for mixed bloods or whites. The Grand River valley chief, Megisinini (Power Shell Man), supported this view and complained about the presence of the Chippewa. He was in favor of reservations but had no intention of selling any land. Apokisigan (Smoking Mixture), of L'Arbre Croche, also spoke in favor of reservations, while his fellow chief, Blackbird, speaking for all the Ottawas, opposed any land sale.

Schoolcraft now turned up the pressure on the Ottawa. While it was good, he said, that they were interested in the welfare of the mixed bloods and their friends, the Great Father would probably not listen to them again in the future on the subject of land sales. He told the Chippewa that the Great Father would make them an offer for their land the next time they met. He chided the Ottawa, saying they should also sell their land so "that when they went home, they would not feel ashamed at seeing their Chippewa brothers, in possession of many goods, and much money and themselves entirely destitute and very poor."[90]

The Ottawa confidant Augustin Hamlin requested the privilege to speak and did so in English. In a poignant plea to Schoolcraft, he said that the chiefs were being hounded unmercifully by the traders, so that the words they spoke were "not their words, not their feelings of their hearts but the words of white men who wanted reservations, and have dictated to them what to say."[91] Hamlin asked that the chiefs be permitted to confer in privacy. Schoolcraft granted his request.

The council next met on Wednesday, March 23. In the meantime, as Mary Holliday reports, the Ottawa delegation visited Schoolcraft and agreed to sell their land provided they were able to make reservations.[92] The L'Arbre Croche chief Apokisigan officially agreed to sell Ottawa land in exchange for two reservations in northwestern lower Michigan. This was agreed to by Megisinini on behalf of the Grand River Ottawa, who also insisted that any treaty be examined for them by their friend and trader Rix Robinson. Schoolcraft now offered one hundred thousand acres for reservations, to be located by the chiefs.

On the next day, Thursday, March 24, speakers for each of the major bands accepted the reservation offer. Most asked that their traders approve the treaty before the chiefs signed it. On Monday, March 28, the treaty was presented to the chiefs, who signed it on behalf of their respective bands.

The official record of the treaty is not very informative. When compared to the complex detail of the treaty, it is obvious that the official treaty journal does not describe much of the substance of negotiation. Presumably, these details were worked out behind closed doors or simply presented as a *fait accompli* by Schoolcraft. Because the resulting treaty called for an independent commission to assess trade debt claims, the treaty was not entirely pleasing to the traders, but they believed it was the best they could do under the circumstances and that the three hundred thousand dollars set aside to cover debts would cover the costs.[93] By the standards of the day, this trader debt provision was enormous.

The treaty itself ceded 13,706,957 acres to the United States (see map 3) in exchange for cash annuities, goods, and services, including blacksmith shops, money for a mission, agricultural implements, livestock, and medicine.[94] According to Articles 2 and 3, reservations for the Ottawa and Chippewa of the Lower Peninsula and the Chippewa of the Upper Peninsula were to be held in common by the bands that occupied them and could only be sold to the United States. Article 13 of the treaty provided that the "Indians stipulate for the right of hunting on the lands ceded, with the other usual privileges of occupancy, until the land is required for settlement."[95]

The treaty provided arrangements intended to facilitate the Ottawa and Chippewa removal to west of the Mississippi River if they chose to go, including provisions to explore for new lands, pay for abandoned improvements, and assist the Indians in making the transition. These provisions are typically found in the many removal treaties that were written with Indians in the rich agricultural regions of the Midwest and Southeast, but this was not a removal treaty. The central provision of the Indian Removal Act was a *voluntary* agreement between the United States and an Indian tribe to exchange land in the organized states and territories east of the Mississippi River for lands west of the river. In the case of the 1836 treaty, no such agreement was made; removal was left entirely at the discretion of the Ottawa and Chippewa.[96]

Article 7 provided for the employment of blacksmiths, mechanics, and farmers, as well as for construction of a dormitory on Mackinac Island. The remainder of the treaty is an extraordinary giveaway to traders and other claimants. Article 5 empowered the payment of $300,000 to the traders in satisfaction of "just debts" against the Indians. Article 9 provided $48,148 for mixed-blood claims, including the claims of many who attended the treaty, including Rix Robinson, Leonard Slater, John Drew, John Holiday, Augustin Hamlin, William Lasley, Henry LaVake, the Moran brothers, and several others.

In addition, Article 6 provided another $150,000 for mixed bloods in lieu of reservations. The children of almost all of the traders would receive money from this fund. Finally, all 135 chiefs and headmen of the Ottawa and Chippewa themselves received a combined total of $30,000 dollars in payments according to a schedule attached to the treaty. Annuities also went to two aged chiefs, and all expenses for travel and lodging were paid by the United States.

Shortly following the ratification of the 1836 treaty, John Edmonds was appointed to examine the mixed-blood claims and to join with Schoolcraft and Henry Whiting to distribute annuities and to evaluate and pay trader debt claims. These commissioners were to consult with the chiefs on the validity of various trade debts that were to be raised in open council. Ultimately, a total of $220,954.57 was paid out in debt claims. Although Schoolcraft said he did not act on the claims of his relatives, they certainly fared well: his brothers-in-law William Johnston, George Johnston, and John Hulbert received $10,521.54, $3,000.00, and $3,493.93, respectively; his mother-in-law Susan Johnston received $7,820.00; the Johnston estate received $32,463.72; and James Schoolcraft, Henry's brother, received $2,286.42.[97] Thus, a total of $56,889.61, or about 25 percent, went to Schoolcraft's relatives. Schoolcraft, acting as agent for the Johnston estate, collected most of the money allotted to his in-laws. Most of this he invested and lost in failed real estate ventures.[98] Other treaty participants were also substantial beneficiaries of the trader debt provision. Rix Robinson collected $22,989.38, Robert Stuart received $17,723.91, and Biddle and Drew received $46,653.51. All of these men were upset because of the great discrepancy between the amount they were paid and the amount they claimed was owed to them.[99] Many of these same men also received large amounts of money under the mixed-blood provision. For example, Rix Robinson was paid $23,040 on behalf of his mixed-blood descendants. Schoolcraft's own wife and children received $1,812.50 as mixed-blood claimants.[100]

On the same day the treaty was signed, Schoolcraft transmitted it to Secretary Cass, who transmitted it to the Senate on April 1 for ratification.[101] Schoolcraft wrote to his wife, Jane, that the treaty secured great advantages to the "unfortunate race" that were her mother's people. "Rejoice with me," he said. "The day of their prosperity has been long delayed, but has finally reached them, in their lowest state of poverty, when their game is almost gone, and the country is shorn of all its advantages for the hunter state."[102] In his personal journal for March 28, 1836, the date of the treaty, Schoolcraft wrote, "This cession was obtained on the principle of making limited reserves for the principal villages, and granting the mass of Indian population the right to live on and occupy any portion of the lands until it is *actually* required for settlement" (emphasis added).[103]

As far as the Ottawa and Chippewa were concerned, they had achieved all they could reasonably hope for in the 1836 treaty. They had satisfied their debts to the traders and met the obligations they felt toward their mixed-blood relatives. Twenty years of annuity payments would enable them to obtain tools, clothing, and other manufactured commodities on the American market. In addition, they had obtained services from the government, including education for their children, blacksmith shops, and practical instruction in Western agriculture and in how to mend their metal tools and firearms. Perhaps most important, they had acquired permanent homes in Michigan in the form of reservations. The right to make a living from the land and to continue to participate in the American economy had been likewise secured to them through the right they reserved in the treaty to hunt, fish, and gather on the newly ceded territory.

One of the important concepts that is somewhat obscure today but was patently obvious to both Indians and non-Indians in 1836 was the relationship between the usufruct provision of Article 13 of the 1836 treaty and the ability of the Ottawa and Chippewa to inhabit their reservations. As hunters and gatherers, a huge amount of land—millions of acres—was necessary to support their population of perhaps five thousand people. It would have been impossible for this number of people to live from the four hundred thousand acres set aside for reservations. The reservations were chosen to protect a variety of resources: summer village sites, gardening spots, orchards, burial grounds, access to offshore fisheries, sugar bushes, and other features of the landscape. Reservations were not set

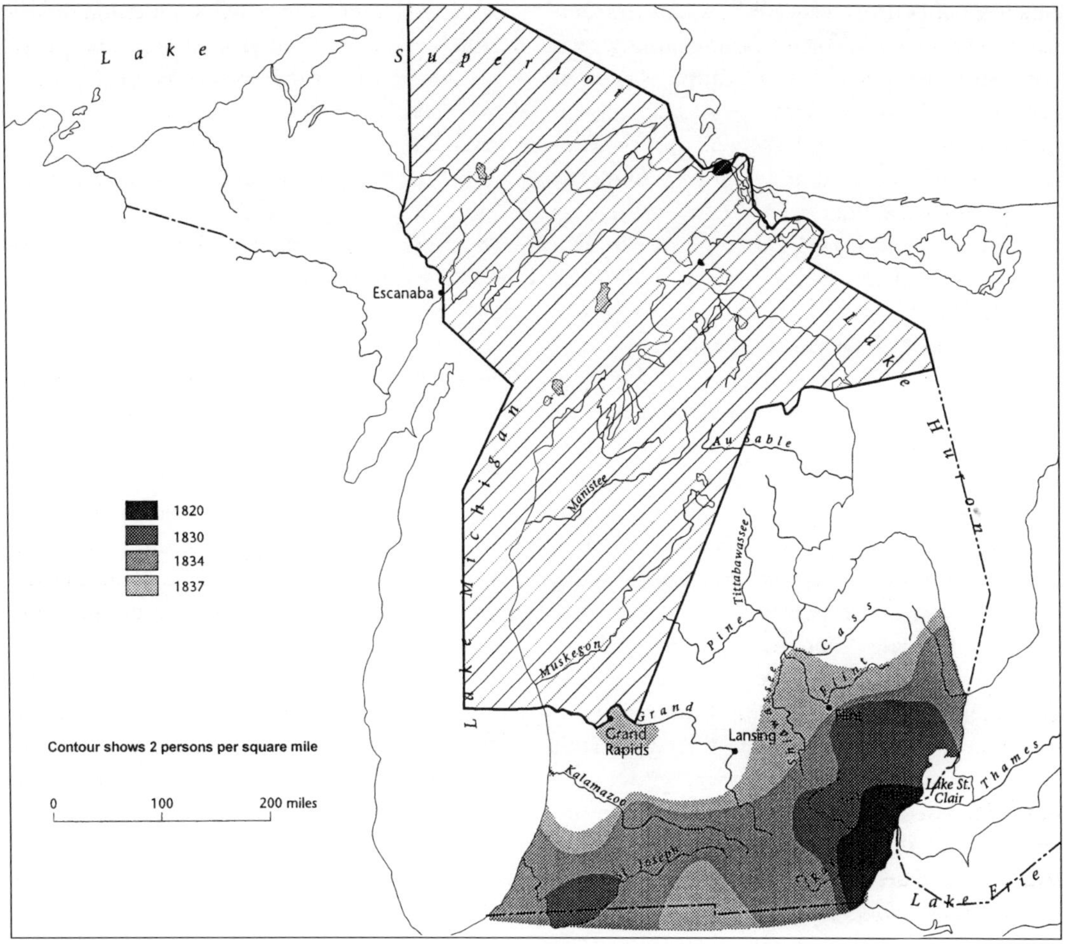

Map 3. Advance of American population in Michigan, 1820–37, and the cession of 1836

aside, or ever intended, fully to support the Ottawa and Chippewa people. For these important economic purposes, the Ottawa and Chippewa depended on the right to use the ceded territory. For this reason, Article 13 was the key to all of the other provisions of the treaty, a point Schoolcraft acknowledged on the day the treaty was signed as well as on subsequent occasions.[104]

Senate Amendments to the Treaty

When the Ottawa and Chippewa chiefs again saw the treaty, they were truly shocked by the amendments made in the U.S. Senate. Although the major reason they agreed to the treaty was because it provided them with reservations of land and the right to hunt, fish, and gather on the ceded territory, the Senate had limited the reservations to a five-year period. Specifically, the Senate inserted clauses in Articles 2 and 3 that describe the reservations to be assigned "for a term of five years from the date of the ratification of this treaty, and no longer unless the United States shall grant them permission to remain on said lands for a longer period."[105] Thus, without permission, the Indians could be forced to vacate reservations in 1841. To encourage the tribes to adopt the removal option in the treaty, the Senate included an amendment that would provide them with an additional two hundred thousand dollars for agreeing to this change in the status of their reserves, to be paid when the reservations were surrendered. In Article 5, the Senate permitted the tribes to retain the balance of the three hundred thousand dollars in the trader debt fund after debts were paid. In other amendments, the Senate permitted the missionary society to recoup funds used to build the mission at Grand Rapids, and in Article 8, they foreclosed the possibility of the tribe's removing to Minnesota. If they removed, it would be "southwest of the Missouri River."[106]

Schoolcraft now set out to gain Indian ratification of these changes. Again, he put out word to the traders to bring the chiefs together on July 10, 1836, at Mackinac Island. Rix Robinson wrote from the Grand River that vague reports had been circulating among the Indians about the amendments, but that he had reassured them and believed that if the affairs were properly managed there would be no problem in getting assent to them.[107] Such "proper management" of the affair had been arranged by Cass and Schoolcraft. Cass wrote to Senator White, chair of the Senate Committee on Indian Affairs, telling him of the importance of giving the Indians annuity provisions from the 1836 treaty as an inducement to agreeing to the Senate amendments. Cass was particularly concerned that the signing bonus of $150,000 provided in goods and provisions by the seventh section of Article 4 be made immediately available. He therefore requested that the regular procurement policy be set aside to permit speedier delivery of the goods to Mackinac in time for the forthcoming amendment conference.[108]

In all, some four thousand Ottawa, Chippewa, and non-Indian treaty claimants visited Mackinac for the discussion of the Senate amendments and for what could be the final ratification of the 1836 treaty. Although there was strong opposition to the five-year limit on the reservations, the chiefs were finally convinced to sign.[109] In forwarding the assent of the Ottawa and Chippewa to the five-year reservation provision added by the Senate, Schoolcraft told Secretary Cass that to obtain approval, it was necessary for him to emphasize the practical operation of the usufruct provision of Article 13.

> The cession of the reservations at the expiration of five years, has been strenuously opposed by a part of the Chiefs, but was finally yielded, on a consideration of *the practical operation* of the provision, contained in the 13th Article of the Treaty, which secures to them *indefinitely*, the right of hunting on the land ceded, with the other usual privileges of occupancy, until the land is required for settlement.[110] (emphasis added)

Thus, despite the enormous inducement to accept the Senate's modifications in the form of annuities and presents that were accumulated on the treaty grounds, it was the guarantee of Article 13, which permitted the Indians to use the resources of the land "indefinitely,"[111] that was the key to their consent to the Senate changes to the treaty.

Schoolcraft's explanation of how he induced the Ottawa and Chippewa chiefs to endorse the five-year limit on the reservation reveals not only the importance the chiefs placed on the usufructuary provision but also how Schoolcraft himself must have understood its operation and must have explained it to the reluctant tribal leaders. First, in Schoolcraft's mind, there was no necessary connection between the five-year limitation on the reservations and the usufructuary right of Article 13. This is why he indicated that the treaty secured to them the rights of Article 13 "indefinitely." To put this concept another way: when the reservations expired, the Indians would still retain the right to hunt, fish, and gather over the ceded territory until it was required for settlement. This is part of what Schoolcraft described as the "practical operation" of Article 13.

In a petition to President Andrew Jackson written in November 1836, in which the Ottawa and Chippewa chiefs made many complaints concerning the distribution of "half-breed" funds under the 1836 treaty, the chiefs questioned the benefit of the cession to the United States: "What is the benefit to be derived by the acquisition of Indian lands at this day to the mass of the community, when you have hundreds of millions of waste [lands] that shall require generation on generations to populate?"[112] Clearly, the Indians understood what Schoolcraft knew: the land ceded was not conducive to agriculture, the United States now owned millions of acres of land that would probably not be taken up by farmers, and this land would be available for Indian occupation and hunting into the foreseeable future. These facts, the practical operation of Article 13, induced the chiefs to accept the Senate amendments, since it gave them a viable alternative to life on the short-lived reservations or removing west of the Mississippi.

Trouble on the Grand

At the time of the 1836 treaty, most of the rich agricultural land immediately south of the Grand River, the southern boundary of the cession under that treaty, was owned in large blocks by eastern investors. While they waited for the price of the land to rise above $1.25 per acre (the price at which they had purchased it from the government), little land was available on the lower Grand for purchase by immigrant farmers. When news of the treaty reached potential purchasers of small tracts, who knew that good land just north of the Grand River would soon be coming on the market, the temptation to cross the river and establish preemption claims became irresistible. No general preemption rights act was passed by Congress until 1841, but by passing a series of acts giving preemption to squatters, Congress encouraged the practice. By crossing the Grand River and improving land now in the public domain but not yet on the market, settlers hoped they would have the first right to purchase land when it was offered for sale.

Unfortunately for these settlers, the best lands in this case happened to be those already improved by the Ottawa. Many of the Grand River bands had cleared land, planted crops and orchards, and built log homes under the tutelage of missionaries prior to the treaty and land survey in the area. As settlers laid claim to Ottawa improvements and land customarily occupied by the Ottawa, such as maple groves and fishing places, tremendous conflicts ensued not only with the Ottawa but also between potential preemptors.[113] The land north of the Grand River was not surveyed and put on the market until the late summer of 1839.

John McDonell and John Clark, who had been appointed to assess the value of Indian improvements under Article 8 of the 1836 treaty, visited the Grand River valley in June 1837. The Ottawa chiefs complained about their treatment at the hands of squatters, and their complaints were confirmed by McDonell and Clark.

> They complained to the undersigned [Clark and McDonell] of the ill treatment they had received from the whites, in taking forcible possession of their homes and premises, and fraudulently and falsely impressing them with the belief, "*that inasmuch as they had sold their lands by Treaty to the Government all their right and title had ceased and that they must surrender possession whenever a white man approached.*" It is proper here to mention that a number of white persons, have not only possessed themselves of the Indian houses, and property, but have by *squatting* obtained the possession of many valuable points on the Indian purchase.[114]

The American preemptors claimed that the Ottawa had no right to occupancy, since they were obligated under the 1836 treaty to remove to their reservation. At the very least, they said, the Indians did not have an *exclusive* right to occupy lands ceded in 1836, since it was now unsold public land.[115] The preemptors counterclaimed that Indians were pulling down fences and buildings raised on the land the preemptors occupied.[116]

Michigan senator and land speculator Lucius Lyon advised settlers that such preemption claims violated the provision of the 1836 treaty, which required, under Article 8, that Indian improvements be appraised and compensated by the government. Senator Lyon suggested, nonetheless, that preemptor claimants form squatter associations to fight the sale of land to others once it was surveyed and put on the market.[117] In January 1837 Superintendent Schoolcraft wrote to the commissioner of Indian affairs, Carey Harris, enclosing a letter from the Reverend Slater, an Indian missionary, regarding the situation on the Grand River. Slater believed non-Indian efforts to take possession of Indian improvements would not abate unless the government upheld the Indian right to hold these improvements until they were appraised and paid for under Article 8 of the treaty.[118] In response, Harris encouraged Schoolcraft to induce the Indians to remove, but Harris also stated that until the appraisals were completed, no preemptionist could take possession of Indian improvements.[119]

Other knowledgeable citizens of the Grand River valley realized that in addition to Indian rights under Article 8, Indians also had rights under Article 13. They wrote Schoolcraft seeking his views concerning these rights. This prompted Schoolcraft to write his view of the affairs on the Grand River. First, he acknowledged that even though the problem might soon be solved by government appraisal of Indian improvements and the removal of the Grand River Ottawa to a northern reservation established by the 1836 treaty, the principle involved in the controversy was an important one. This was so, he said, because the practical operation of the treaty would cause the issue to be raised in the future.[120] The issue that Schoolcraft raised did not involve the Indians' rights under Article 8 but their right of occupancy under Article 13.

In response, Commissioner Harris decided to ask U.S. attorney general B. F. Butler for his opinion about the rights of the Ottawa under Article 13 of the 1836 treaty. The request was forwarded through the secretary of war, Joel Poinsett.[121] On April 20, 1837, Butler replied,

> In answer to the questions proposed in the letter of the Commissioner of Indian Affairs, and referred to me by your communication of the 23d ultimo, I have the honor to inform you that in my opinion, the thirteenth article of the treaty of March 1836, with the Ottawa and Chippewa Indians, by which "the Indians stipulate for the right of *hunting* on the lands ceded, with the *other usual privileges of occupancy,* until the land is required for *settlement*"—must be regarded as reserving the *use* of the ceded lands, for all the purposes of Indian occupancy as it existed prior to the treaty, until such lands shall have been actually disposed of to individuals, by the United States. Such disposition may be made by sale under the general laws or by special grants, or in any other way that Congress may direct, and whenever an *actual disposition* of any particular tract shall be made, the usufructuary right of the Indians will cease as to such tract. In the meantime however, that right cannot lawfully be interrupted by the Government still less by any citizen of the United States.[122]

Butler's opinion essentially addressed two questions. The first dealt with the nature of the "right of hunting" and the "other usual privileges of occupancy" on the lands ceded. In his opinion, he follows Lewis Cass's view that such guarantees in Indian treaties reserved all of the privileges of Indian occupancy, as they existed prior to the treaty.[123] The second question dealt with the limiting clause "until the land is required for settlement." Here, Butler says that settlement requires the disposal of land to *individuals* by public sale or other means. In the context of the practical problem that required the opinion to begin with—that is, the conflict between preemptionists seeking to establish claims to land in the public domain and Indians who had made improvements to those lands—the attorney general sided with the Indians, expressing the view that Indian rights remained in effect while the land remained in the public domain. Butler's reference to disposition to individuals reflects his understanding of "settlement" as set forth in another opinion involving the preemption acts. As explained in that opinion, settlement requires actual improvement to the land by individuals, such as clearing, fencing, and farming.[124]

In his opinion, Butler did not consider the fact that, for the most part, the cession was not agricultural land, would not be purchased by small farmers, and, consequently, would never be occupied by the kind of settlers he was apparently thinking about in writing his opinion. Henry Schoolcraft did understand this fact, and when he explained the "practical operation" of the right to the Ottawa and Chippewa, he told them they could expect to exercise their right for many years to come. In fact, Schoolcraft used the word *indefinitely* because he did not think the cession would be settled in the usual sense. Consequently, this is exactly how Schoolcraft explained the situation to the Ottawa and Chippewa and exactly how they understood the stipulation described in Article 13.

The thirteenth article of the 1836 treaty states that "the Indians stipulate for the right of hunting on the lands ceded with the other privileges of occupancy, until the land is required for settlement."[125] According to Henry Schoolcraft, without this guarantee, the Ottawa and Chippewa would not have agreed to the cession of land that now composes about one-third of the state of Michigan.[126] This article was so important to the tribes because it not only assured their ability to feed themselves and to operationalize reservation life but, at the same time, enabled them to use the harvest of natural resources as a way to participate in the American economy.

By 1836 the Ottawa and Chippewa people had been engaged in commercial exchange with Euro-Americans for nearly two hundred years. This was the method by which the Indians obtained most of their clothing, essentially all of their tools and implements, and especially the firearms on which they were dependent for subsistence. The Ottawa and Chippewa were not, however, just fur trappers. For many generations, they supplied the Euro-American communities of the Upper Great Lakes region with food in the form of fish, game, and gathered products, as well as many manufactured items, such as fur robes, clothing, moccasins, firewood, medicines, tanning bark, building material, canoes, cordage, glue, bags, mats, boxes, spoons, and dozens of other handicraft items. By 1836 they were also producing huge amounts of maple sugar and salted whitefish and lake trout for the American domestic market. In fact, the salt and barrels they requested and received under the sixth provision of Article 4 of the 1836 treaty were used to support their participation in the emergent commercial fishery of the region. These activities were favorable not just to the Ottawa and Chippewa but to the non-Indian population of the region as well. In fact, without Indian production of natural resources, the economy of the Great Lakes region would have ground to a dramatic halt.

These practical considerations aside, it is necessary to examine the wording of the thirteenth article in detail in order to ascertain exactly what the Ottawa and Chippewa reserved and how their guarantee was limited. For these purposes, it is useful to dissect the article in several ways. First, given the huge cultural and linguistic gulf that existed at the time of the treaty between the Ottawa and Chippewa, on the one hand, and the Euro-Americans, on the other, it is necessary to ask how both parties likely understood the article. It is especially important to understand how Henry Schoolcraft, as the drafter and chief negotiator of the treaty, understood its terms, since it was he who explained the meaning of Article 13 to the chiefs. Among the questions to be examined in the latter context are what is meant by the phrase "right of hunting," what constitutes the "usual privileges of occupancy," and, finally, what is meant by the clause "until the land is required for settlement."

It would seem that the answers to these questions are much more complex in contemporary Euro-American context than in the Indian understanding. The reason is because the former considerations involve legal concepts and definitions and because it would seem apparent from the writings of Schoolcraft and his contemporaries that they were themselves in the process of inventing and rethinking these very ideas. It is also apparent that the practical aspect of Indian resource use was being worked out through the conflicts that arose both before the treaty and later, as a result of its provisions.

American Understanding of Article 13

In many ways, Henry Schoolcraft and his contemporaries at the time of the 1836 treaty had exactly the same idea about the terms "the right of hunting" and "the other usual privileges of occupancy" as did the Ottawa and Chippewa. In practical terms—that is, those worked out over the experience of many generations of Euro-American and Indian interaction—this meant that the Indians could move over the landscape following their seasonal rounds and, in so doing, harvest all the fauna, flora, and other resources necessary to sustain their life and economy. As previously mentioned, these were not activities that non-Indians merely tolerated; they were activities vital to the general economy and therefore strongly promoted. Writing about the nature of Indian treaties and their guarantees, Schoolcraft's mentor Lewis Cass noted,

> These are not questions of technical construction, to be settled by subtle arguments like too many of those in our own municipal law, but questions of fair and liberal interpretation, depending on the established rights and duties of the parties, and on their obvious intentions, deduced from circumstances in which they were placed. These reservations and guaranties, whichever they may be, were designed to secure to the Indians their preexisting rights, as they had enjoyed and we had ac-

> knowledged them; to secure to them the possession of their lands; that right of occupancy, which is compatible with their habits and pursuits, and with our immediate jurisdiction and ultimate domain.[127]

It was, of course, Cass's last caveat—how to assure the compatibility of Indian habits and pursuits with American jurisdiction—that raised a practical problem for Henry Schoolcraft. This problem was made more difficult because, as Cass also pointed out, the American system of private ownership of land was utterly foreign in the context of native tradition. Schoolcraft would ultimately evoke the concept of "settlement" to help reconcile Indian use with American jurisdiction.[128]

For Cass, the treaty-making process as well as its underlying assumptions codified the fiduciary relationship between the tribes and the United States. Cass acknowledged the fiction of the assumptions of sovereign equality between the Indian tribes and the American state as well as the logical conundrum of acquiring title to land from people who did not recognize title as a concept. As Cass put it, by quoting John Adams, "[Indian tenure] is not like our tenures; they have no idea of a title to the soil itself. It is overrun by them, rather than inhabited."[129] Remarking on the rights secured to Indians in the course of treaty making, Cass explained, "When we find the words 'lands' 'territory' 'hunting grounds' &c. used in these instruments [treaties], as descriptions of interests reserved or guaranteed to the Indians, the extent of their operation must be ascertained by the principles previously or contemporaneously regulating the intercourse between them and us."[130]

At this point, it is worth reviewing the way that the treaties of cession that preceded the 1836 treaty dealt with the need and desire of the Indians to hunt over the lands ceded. All of the earlier treaties that ceded large amounts of Michigan land located to the south and east of the 1836 cession provided protection for Indian usufruct. Article VII of the Treaty of Greenville in 1795 set the tone for such guarantees with the provision that "the tribes of Indians, parties to this treaty, shall be at liberty to hunt within the territory and lands which they have now ceded, without hindrance or molestation, as long as they demean themselves peacefully, and offer no injury to the people of the United States."[131] In 1807 territorial governor William Hull negotiated a treaty with the several tribes of southwestern Michigan by which, under Article V, they were guaranteed usufructuary privileges: "It is further agreed and stipulated that the said Indian Nations shall enjoy the privilege of hunting and fishing on the lands ceded as aforesaid as long as they remain the property of the United States."[132] In this formulation, Governor Hull apparently appreciated the potential conflict that could derive from the Greenville guarantee of Indian use and the rights of private property owners.

Perhaps for this reason, Michigan territorial governor Lewis Cass later adopted hybrid phraseology in guaranteeing usufruct to the tribes in treaties he negotiated that ceded most of the rest of southern and eastern Michigan. These were the Treaty of the Miami Rapids in 1817,[133] the Treaty of Saginaw in 1819,[134] and the Treaty of Chicago in 1821.[135] In each case, Governor Cass included the clause "the stipulation contained in the Treaty of Greenville, relative to the right of the Indians to hunt upon the land ceded, while it continues to be the property of the United States, shall apply to this treaty."[136] In terms of the practical operation of this terminology, Indians could hunt over the land ceded, free of hindrance or molestation, as long as they did not bother or do injury to the people of the United States, unless the land was sold by the United States, thus becoming private property.

The Cass terminology that had been in use for years prior to the 1836 treaty was, of course, available to Schoolcraft. If it had been his intention to limit the usufructuary guarantee under Article 13 of the treaty, he could have easily done so by using the Cass wording that would seem to terminate Indian usufruct on the ceded territory when it became private property. In fact, this was the wording in the power of sale that Cass had insisted that Schoolcraft circulate prior to the negotiation of the 1836 treaty.[137] We know from the treaty journal that Schoolcraft had even received a signed copy of the power of sale from the Mackinac area chiefs while he was negotiating the 1836 treaty. The power of sale stated "the privileges of hunting upon the land, and residing upon it, until it is surveyed and sold by the government, to be secured."[138]

It is abundantly clear that Commissioner Schoolcraft rejected this wording and the concept behind it, in favor of securing the usufruct privileges found in Article 13 of the treaty with the phrase "until the land is required for settlement." Why did he do so? First and most obvious, Schoolcraft did not want to unduly limit the very hunting, fishing, and trapping activities on which the economy of northern Michigan depended. Second, he knew that the Ottawa and Chippewa needed as much land available as possible to support themselves, particularly if they were to be concentrated on reservations. Finally, Schoolcraft knew that northern Michigan would develop not as an agricultural region but as a region supported by lumbering, fishing, and mining, and he saw little, if any, conflict between these extractive industries and Indian usufruct.

Thus, Schoolcraft found a practical way to avoid the conflict between private landownership and Indian usufruct, by using the concept of settlement. Schoolcraft was accustomed to the distinction between usufruct and settlement, because this distinction is embodied in the Trade and Intercourse Act of 1834, which he administered as an Indian agent. In that case, licensed traders, teachers, blacksmiths, millers, and lighthouse keepers could enter and reside in Indian country in order to practice their trade, but they were not considered settlers. In addition, they could be permitted use of natural resources, such as fish, game, hay, and firewood. These usufruct activities were also not considered settlement. Similarly, the definition of settler under the preemption acts required making improvements to the land on the part of individuals. Persons engaged only in lumbering or mining activities were not settlers under provisions of the preemption acts. To qualify as a settler, a person must personally make the improvements to the land necessary to establish a preemption claim.

According, then, to the normal usage of the day, settled land was improved and occupied by a settler and, in nearly all cases, was also private land. Conversely, unimproved and unoccupied land was, by definition, unsettled. Unimproved and unoccupied land could be public land that was unsold land within the public domain or could be sold land that was not improved and occupied by its owner and therefore not settled. As Schoolcraft wrote to Commissioner Harris, he expected that the area ceded in the 1836 treaty was "uninviting to agriculturalists, and would be chiefly valuable for lumber and mill privileges, and to these tracts the Indians adverted, as places of temporary residence."[139] Schoolcraft, like others who were familiar with the cession, did not believe northern Michigan land would be "settled" (in the sense then in use) for a very long time. Grand Traverse Bay missionary Rev. Peter Dougherty wrote to Superintendent Robert Stuart in 1842 that he had learned from government surveyors and the Indians themselves that the cession contained much wasteland and little good land that would invite a farming population. Dougherty did not believe that it would be demanded for rapid settlement by white people.[140] A petition sent to President Andrew Jackson, attributed to the Chippewa chiefs in November 1836, wondered why the United States needed the ceded land at all. They questioned its benefit to the people of the United States "when you have hundreds of millions of waste [lands] that shall require generation on generation to populate?"[141] Of course, any use of the land for lumbering or lumber mills or mining in the post-treaty era would mean that the land had to be privately owned. Schoolcraft's dilemma in writing the treaty was that he did not want to make private but unsettled land off limits to the Ottawa and Chippewa. Rather, by using the term *settlement,* open, uninhabited, unsettled land would be available for Indian use and occupancy whether or not it was in public or private ownership. In this way, Schoolcraft satisfied the Ottawa and Chippewa as well as fur traders and businessmen of the ceded territory.

Schoolcraft did not seem to have always had a completely clear view of the operation of the wording of Article 13. In fact, many of his explanations of the article seem to be inconsistent. On the one hand, he once explained to American settlers that private ownership would lead to the gradual extermination of the Indian usufruct right, but on the other, he explained to the Indian chiefs that they could hunt, fish, and gather over land that was not settled.[142] He seemed to have also neglected to explain to the Ottawa and Chippewa that much of the nonsettled land, the very land that they would in fact use for many generations, may be in private ownership even though it was not settled.

In a letter he wrote to Commissioner Harris in February 27, 1837, almost a year after negotiating the treaty, Schoolcraft considered preemption problems in the Grand River valley. He made explicit his dual modes of understanding.

> The main question, in the cession made by the Indians at Washington, may be said, in great measure, to have turned, on the right stipulated to be secured to them, to hunt upon, and occupy the lands, ceded, until they were required for settlement. I caused the operation of this provision to be carefully explained to them, stating that as fast as the lands were surveyed and sold, and thus converted into private property, this right would cease. But that it would continue to be enjoyed by them, on all portions of the territory ceded, not surveyed and sold. It was believed, from the best information then extant, that portions of the large and imperfectly explored territory ceded, were uninviting to agriculturalists, and would be chiefly valuable for lumber and mill privileges, and to these tracts, the Indians adverted, as places of temporary residence. The same view of the gradual extinction of this right, was urged upon their consideration, at the council held at Michilimackinac for obtaining their assent to the Senate's proposition to modify the tenure of their reservations from reservations in perpetuity, to reservations for five years. And with the same effect. Their assent, was given. In the course of these negotiations, the bearing of this stipulation, was fully discussed, and the Indians, appeared to set a high value, upon it, and resisted the idea of a general cession of the lands without it. I employed the term "settlement" in its ordinary meaning, to denote the act or state of being settled, and as answering, as nearly as the terms of the two languages would permit, to the tenor of my agreement with them.[143]

In Schoolcraft's view as explained in this letter, the usufructury right was linked to private property, and the conversion of land to private property would gradually extinguish the right to occupy and hunt upon the land.[144] Schoolcraft also expressed this view to three Kent County residents who inquired of Indian occupancy in the Grand River valley as a result of the treaty: "In the meantime, I have no hesitancy in expressing my *private opinion* that the right secured to the Indians by the 13th article of the treaty, applies to the lands, while they remain the property of the United States, and ceases the moment any part of it becomes private property" (emphasis added).[145]

Schoolcraft's "private opinion" about the operation of the usufruct guarantee under Article 13, expressed nearly a year after the treaty was signed, is not in accord with the language in the treaty or his early explanation of the treaty. In his diary entry for March 28, 1836, the day the treaty was signed, Schoolcraft wrote that the Indian usufruct rights would continue on "any portion of the lands until it is actually required for settlement."[146] He repeated this idea in his report on the outcome of the treaty negotiation to Secretary Cass and made no reference to the sale of land extinguishing the right.[147] Had Schoolcraft meant to permanently end Indian occupancy and hunting privileges on the land ceded when it was surveyed and sold, he had the precedent and means to say so in drafting Article 13, but he did not. In his comments on the Indians' assent to the Senate amendments in July 1836, Schoolcraft wrote that the "practical operation of the treaty would preserve the Indian usufructury right indefinitely." Again, he made no mention of the sale of land terminating the right. Even in his letter to Harris of February 27, 1837, Schoolcraft says that he "employed the term 'settlement' in its ordinary meaning, to denote the act or state of being settled."

In review, the original treaty as negotiated by the chiefs and Schoolcraft called for the cession of millions of acres of land in exchange for permanent reservations, access to the ceded territory for usufructuary purposes, annuities, and services. In reviewing the treaty, the Senate ratified it but limited the reservations to five years. The chiefs, in turn, ratified this change on the strength of Schoolcraft's assurance of what Schoolcraft described as the practical operation of Article 13; that is, they could hunt indefinitely on ceded land unless it was settled. The Senate amendments and the chiefs' ratification of them had the effect of strengthening, rather than weakening, the importance of the usufruct guarantee of Article 13. This is what Schoolcraft noted in his annual reports to the commissioner of Indian affairs in 1837 and 1839. In the latter report, he relates that the chiefs decided to give up on trying to colonize the five-year reservations.

> This measure [surrender of the reservations as required by the Senate], when it came under discussion in their councils, induced the Indians to throw themselves upon the usufructuary right to the ceded territory, secured to them by the 13th article of the treaty, and they subsequently gave up the idea of concentrating on the reserves, as it was foreseen the time would expire before they could derive permanent benefit from them.[148]

In his annual report for the year 1837, Schoolcraft said, "Their reservations [under the 1836 treaty] will expire in 1841, after which, they will possess no further right to a residence on the lands, but the conditional usufructuary right contained in the 13th article."[149] This is an important remark for two reasons. First, it links the Ottawa and Chippewa right of occupation to their right to hunt, fish, and gather. Second, it reveals Schoolcraft's belief that the right of both occupation and hunting was indefinite in time; the right to occupy and use the ceded territory was thus to be limited only by settlement, that is, the actual occupation of the land by non-Indians. It is important to emphasize that Schoolcraft did not employ the concept that the usufruct right of Article 13 would cease as soon as the land was surveyed and sold. This idea does not appear in the treaty language. In reality, the only restriction on Indian usufruct found in Article 13 is simply that resources could not be taken from land actually occupied by private landholders.

What the Indians Understood

Perhaps the best statement of what the chiefs expected from the impending treaty was passed along to Schoolcraft by his brother-in-law William Johnston, who spoke the Ojibwe language fluently. On his interview with three Upper Peninsula chiefs, Johnston reported,

> They answered in behalf of their young men, that they were willing to cede their lands to the United States on reasonable terms, the terms to be left to the discretion of the Agent appointed by government; with this provision, they, to have a full right to hunt, on the ceded lands, as long as they were unoccupied, and to make such reservations, as they should think proper.[150]

Like all of the native people of the forested regions of eastern North America, the Ottawa and Chippewa had no concept of the private ownership of land.[151] In fact, at the time of contact with Europeans, they had only a poorly developed idea of the exclusive use of any kind of property. They did recognize personal property (e.g., in the form of charms or amulets of significance to a particular person) and the product of individual labor (e.g., the blueberries one had picked). Certainly, they understood the idea of territories and the natural boundary markers that set them apart. By the time of the 1836 treaty, there may even have been a few individuals, perhaps some of those living in close contact with missionaries on the Grand River or at Mackinac or Sault Ste. Marie, who actually had some understanding of the Euro-American concepts of private landownership. In 1836 such Indian people would have been the rare exception. To the vast majority of the Ottawa and Chippewa, the idea of an individual actually owning land and having exclusive access to it would have been nonsensical. To the Indians, the accepted view was that the earth was a living, spiritual entity that provided for the welfare of all humans—Grandmother Earth.

Superintendent Henry Schoolcraft did recognize that explaining the idea that settlers would have exclusive rights to the land would be difficult, if not impossible. He did appreciate that the concept of private landownership was so foreign to the Indians that the Algonquian languages lacked the specific vocabulary to adequately discuss the idea. In his previously cited letter to Commissioner Harris, Schoolcraft explained how he had struggled, with limited success, to explain the idea: "I employed the term 'settlement' in its ordinary meaning, to denote the act or state of being settled, and as answering, as nearly as the terms of the two languages would permit, to the tenor of my agreement with them."[152]

Irrespective of Schoolcraft's own technical

understanding of private landownership and its importance for Article 13, his letter to Commissioner Harris explains what he told the Ottawa and Chippewa Article 13 meant. First, we must recall that in the context of both the Washington negotiations and the council leading to the approval of the Senate amendments at Mackinac, where the stipulation of Article 13 was explained to them, the complex ideas of one culture were being conveyed to the Ottawa and Chippewa through interpreters whose facility with the Algonquian dialects is largely unknown. Even assuming perfect fluency, which is doubtful, Schoolcraft's caveats that the "tenor" of the right was explained to them "as nearly as the terms of the two languages would permit" indicate that the cultural divide did not permit an entirely satisfactory understanding.

Even if Schoolcraft had been trying to express the idea of private landownership in this and other instances, he employed the practical concepts of "occupation" and "settlement." As he explains, "I employed the term 'settlement' in its ordinary meaning, to denote the act or state of being settled." This was the only sense in which the term could have had any reality for the Ottawa or Chippewa. If, in practical operation, the Indians could actually see that the land was settled—that is, occupied by a family that had, perhaps, built a home, cleared the land, and put up fences—then they had the means to know that the land was indeed settled and likewise that they could not use it for the usual privileges of occupancy. Obviously, the Indians had no means to go to the local federal land office and examine property records. Just as obviously, in the context of trackless forests, they would have had no way to know whether or not a large block of land held by a land speculator or a lumber company was private property. As Schoolcraft knew and likely explained to them, if you see settlers, then the land is settled—this was the "ordinary meaning" of settlement. As he observed in his memoirs on the day he concluded the 1836 treaty, the Indian population has "the right to live on and occupy any portion of the lands until it was *actually* required for settlement" (emphasis added).[153] As he told them in the course of the treaty negotiations, "the usual privilege of residing and hunting on the land sold [ceded] till they are wanted will be granted."[154]

In reality, this was the same concept that the Ottawa and Chippewa were accustomed to by the Treaty of Greenville, under which they enjoyed their own lands until they were ceded by the 1836 treaty. They were entitled, under the protection of the United States, to the unmolested use of the resources of the territory ceded, as long as they demeaned themselves peacefully and did not do damage to the citizens of the United States. This is exactly how the Ottawa and Chippewa did, in fact, exercise their usufructuary rights under Article 13, and as far as it is known, they did so without an objection from settlers or the state authority until near the end of the nineteenth century.

What the Indians knew was that by the terms of the 1836 treaty, they had reserved the right to range over the land as they had done before the treaty and to do so for all of the purposes that were part of their accustomed practices. They understood that this right would be indefinite and that it was limited by settlement in the practical sense. If the land was being used by individual settlers in such a way that these uses would conflict with their own, then they must not interfere.

As can be expected in the case of any major piece of new legislation or a new treaty, the 1836 treaty raised many questions concerning its practical operation. Some of the substance depended on formal interpretation by government officials, while other matters were left to local authorities. In yet other cases, outcomes seemed to emerge from conflicting practice. It is important to remember that just as the United States had an Indian policy that it tried to advance through treaty drafting and interpretation, so the Ottawa and Chippewa parties to the 1836 treaty had their own political agenda. In its broadest terms, the agenda of the Ottawa and Chippewa was to resist change, to maintain their cultural integrity and independence, and, above all, to remain on their native land.

Almost exactly ten months after the 1836 treaty, Michigan was admitted to the Union as the twenty-sixth state. At the time of the state's admission, counties had been formed in the southern half of the Lower Peninsula, that is, south from the mouth of the Grand River, east to the Saginaw River valley, and then east across Michigan's thumb. In this organized region, territorial roads linked Detroit with Saginaw, Port

Huron, Fort Meigs (Toledo), Grand Rapids, St. Joseph, and Chicago.

Because of the Panic of 1837, the period from 1838 to 1842 was one of population stagnation and stalled investment in land and infrastructure. Although all of the Lower Peninsula of Michigan was surveyed and offered for sale by 1843, land sales were very slow between 1838 and 1842. This was particularly true in the northern portions of the Lower Peninsula and all of the Upper Peninsula, where accurate maps were not yet available.[155] While the mineral and timber wealth of northern Michigan was known at the time of the 1836 treaty and certainly was a major reason why the government wanted to acquire these lands, American citizens did not begin to exploit those resources in earnest until the second half of the century.

American Indian policy in Michigan at the time of the 1836 treaty and in the years of Henry Schoolcraft's tenure as agent and superintendent of the Mackinac Agency (1822–41) was guided far more by opportunism than by political objective. Although the 1836 treaty did not require removal, the commissioners of Indian affairs of that era—namely, Carey Harris (1836–38) and T. Hartley Crawford (1838–45)—were both advocates of Andrew Jackson's Indian removal policy. Henry Schoolcraft, who negotiated the treaty and oversaw its formative operation, was often vague and inconsistent in his conduct of Indian affairs. Although Agent Schoolcraft took his responsibility to protect the interests of his Indian charges seriously, he was also very enthusiastic about the development of mineral and other resources of the 1836 cession, believing such development to be consistent with Indian occupancy. He was willing to seek financial resources for Indians of the agency, but he also displayed a sharp interest in using government funds for political patronage, particularly in the interest of his own family.[156] Schoolcraft often touted the civilizing objectives of the government and promoted educational, agrarian, and Christianization efforts, yet he remained mired in nineteenth-century racism, believing that Indians were intellectually, psychologically, and culturally inferior to the white race in every regard. In coping with these two basically irreconcilable beliefs, Schoolcraft, like many of his generation, became both paternalistic and patronizing to Indian people. Rather than affording them respect as individuals, Schoolcraft worked to destroy their culture and to defeat their objective of remaining in their ancestral homeland as a free and independent people.

The daily existence of the Ottawa and Chippewa living in the 1836 cession probably changed very little as a result of the treaty. An exception to this, of course, must be made for the Ottawa of the Grand River, who were immediately overwhelmed by the American settlers expropriating Indian improvements on the north side of the river even before the treaty was ratified. Farther north, annuity payments and goods provided by the treaty improved the effectiveness of Indians who were heavily involved in producing furs, fish, and maple sugar for the American market.[157] The combined effect of treaty funds, treaty gift provisions, and the services of blacksmiths meant that the Ottawa and Chippewa had greater access to netting material, salt and barrels for marketing fish, iron kettles for making sugar, and a great variety of American tools used in working wood and metal. The repair of spears, guns, and traps at government shops also improved efficiency for Indians who produced fur and hides. The 4,872 Indians who Agent Schoolcraft counted in his 1838 census of the 1836 treaty area continued to pursue their traditional seasonal rounds throughout the cession.[158] In these activities, they seldom encountered non-Indians, since most of the Americans in Michigan's north country were located in a few coastal settlements.

By 1839 there were ten schools for Indian children scattered among the Indian communities of western and northern Michigan.[159] These were supported under the terms of the 1836 treaty and were operated by various Christian churches. Besides the schools, the government also operated blacksmith shops at Sault Ste. Marie, Mackinac, and Manistee, to repair guns, traps, kettles, and agricultural equipment, and it supported farmers at several locations, to teach agricultural methods.

Exploring West

Because the 1836 treaty offered an inducement of two hundred thousand dollars for the surrender of their reservations and because the government was offering a land grant and other benefits in the West, it was the expectation of some government officials that the Ottawa and Chippewa would soon leave the state. Those who believed that they would readily emigrate badly underestimated the determination of the Indians to remain in their homeland. The result was that history played out a scenario that was not at all expected by the administrators or senators who advocated Indian removal.

That the Ottawa and Chippewa opposed removal was apparent to many people in Michigan from the beginning. For example, in 1838 Schoolcraft wrote to Commissioner Harris that "as the country ceded by them is large and they are strongly attached by custom particularly to their mode of subsistence, in part, on the lake fish, and of traveling in canoes, it is not expected that they will feel a general wish to emigrate immediately."[160] In the following spring, James Schoolcraft, Henry's brother, was appointed to assemble an Indian exploring party to inspect land south of the Missouri River as a possible final destination of the Ottawa and Chippewa.[161] Following Henry Schoolcraft's instructions to collect a Chippewa delegation, subagent James Ord at Sault Ste. Marie reported that the Chippewa flatly refused to participate, claiming that there was nothing in the treaty that obligated them to remove west of the Mississippi.[162]

Despite the reluctance of the tribes, twenty-four Indian delegates were eventually assembled for an exploring party. These men represented the Grand River bands, the northern Ottawa, and the Manistee bands, along with some Chippewas from Mackinac.[163] The composition of the exploring party betrays the Ottawa's strategy in this matter. With the exception of one Grand River chief, Megisinini, and Kewayqwaskum of Manistee, the entire delegation consisted of young men who had little, if any, decision-making responsibility. The Ottawa leadership knew that if the exploring party was forced to make a decision about the land, that decision could be called into question later. Henry Schoolcraft was aware of this problem and tried to enhance the prestige of the party by falsely describing the delegation as a "full and respectable, one comprising both nations."[164] The Ottawa missionary Rev. Isaac McCoy, who was already colonizing Indians from elsewhere in Michigan along the Osage River, agreed to help sell the exploring party on western lands. Henry Schoolcraft wrote to McCoy, urging, "It is very desirable that, after viewing the country, they should come to some decision, *before their return*."[165] This is because Schoolcraft knew beforehand that the Ottawa and Chippewa chiefs absolutely opposed removal.

Schoolcraft's letter to McCoy further indicates that the 1836 treaty was not a removal treaty in the classic sense. In this letter, Schoolcraft poses a number of practical questions related to potential removal of the Ottawa and Chippewa.

> The quantity of land to be given to them, will also be a question to be decided. Should each head of a family emigrating have a section? Should the Ottawas be located separately from the Chippewas? Are individuals to have patents for their lands, or will the government patent a body to each tribe, to be under the management, as to its occupancy and division, of the Chiefs? I throw out these suggestions for your consideration, as the treaty is silent on the subject.[166]

As discussed previously, these are precisely the kinds of issues that are specifically resolved in the text of actual removal treaties. Overriding the treaty particulars, however, was the basic fact that the Indian Removal Act of 1830 required that the consent of the Indians be obtained if they were to be removed to land west of the Mississippi.[167] No such agreement was ever reached with the Ottawa and Chippewa of the 1836 treaty.

In his report on the outcome of the exploring party, James Schoolcraft stated that Megisinini accepted land at the forks of the Osage for the two nations.[168] Likewise, McCoy told Henry Schoolcraft that a spokesman for the delegation had said, "We are well pleased with the country which we have seen. It is good—much better than we had expected to see. We thank the President for giving us so good a country, and we do unanimously accept of it as ours."[169] At a subsequent council meeting at Mackinac, the Ottawa and Chippewa chiefs told Schoolcraft that they would not remove and that the exploratory party had no authority to accept land in their behalf. At Henry Schoolcraft's urging, the chiefs did agree, however, to accept a larger piece of land between the Osage and Konza Rivers.[170] The chiefs understood this as a gift of land unrelated to the removal issue, and in 1855 the United States came to see the logic of this position and to agree with it.

The Five-Year Reservations

Once the treaty was proclaimed on May 27, 1836, the Ottawa and Chippewa of the cession were in a precarious position. When the ceded territory became part of the state of Michigan, the government claimed that the Trade and Intercourse Act of 1834 ceased to protect Indians and their property.[171] Since Indians were not citizens, they were not protected by Michigan law, but in the view of Superintendent Schoolcraft, they were subject to it. Under Article 13 of the treaty, Indians had a right to freely use the resources of the portions of the cession that were not "settled," but they had no rights otherwise. The only exception was the several large reservations that were to be chosen by the chiefs under the terms of Articles 2 and 3 of the treaty. As unceded land, it was still "Indian country"; however, the treaty limited the reservations to five years unless "the United States shall grant them permission to remain on the lands for a longer period."[172]

In July 1837 Commissioner Harris was trying to make arrangement to have the reservations surveyed and marked.[173] Even though the matter was already urgent because of timber and property trespass on the proposed reserves, Schoolcraft did not like the idea of spending money on a project of such short duration.[174] Because survey of the irregular-shaped reservations chosen by the chiefs would interfere with the orderly running of north-south, east-west section lines as part of the general land survey, it was determined to run the ordinary survey lines through the proposed reservations.[175] Of course, this action made the chiefs exceedingly wary of the ultimate intent of the United States.[176]

By November 1840 Schoolcraft requested that the reservations stipulated in the 1836 treaty be plotted on the government's survey maps. In some cases, such as at Manistee and Grand Traverse, the reservations were listed by township and range and ordered withdrawn from sale.[177] The actual survey, however, had still not been completed by May 1841, the time when the reservations were to be surrendered unless permission to remain was granted. This was true despite the protestations of the chiefs and non-Indian residents.[178]

The main apparent difficulty in surveying the reservations was Henry Schoolcraft, who questioned his duty to survey them at all. In 1840, however, he was finally instructed to do so by T. Hartley Crawford, commissioner of Indian affairs.[179] Schoolcraft, as well as the many missionaries, teachers, and government employees who were providing services on the reservations, knew the Indians would not make a substantial labor investment or progress toward "civilization" as long as they knew the government could dispossess them from the reservations. After May 1841, the date for the termination of five-year reservations, the Indians believed a removal order was imminent.[180]

At the time of the 1836 treaty and especially after the Senate chose to limit the reservations to a five-year tenure, an unanticipated possibility became apparent to Schoolcraft. What if, at the end of the five-year period, the Ottawa and Chippewa simply surrendered the reservations (which only a relatively small number of them occupied at any rate) and lived on the ceded land? This is where they had always lived and where they had a right to live and make a living under the terms of the 1836 treaty.

When the five year reservation lapsed in 1841, Schoolcraft reminded Commissioner Crawford that the Ottawa and Chippewa were not obliged to remove from Michigan and strenuously resisted any attempt to discuss the subject. Moreover, under the thirteenth article of the 1836 treaty they were free to wander from unsettled place to unsettled place in the ceded territory.[181] After all, this is exactly the kind of arrangement Robert Stuart, Schoolcraft's successor as the superintendent of the Mackinac Agency, made with the Chippewa of the western portion of the Upper Peninsula when he bought their land in 1842.[182]

Ottawa and Chippewa Strategy

Although the Ottawa and Chippewa had not agreed to remove west and had no intention of doing so, they feared that they might nonetheless be forcefully removed by the United States. As a result, the various Ottawa and Chippewa factions developed several separate strategies to avoid that fate. The first and least popular strategy among the Indians was to remove somewhere else first. The most obvious destination was Manitoulin Island, across the Canadian border, where the British were trying to colonize Great Lakes Indians. This was an attractive alternative for a few northern Ottawa who had relatives and gardens at Manitoulin as well as in the northwest Lower Peninsula.[183] Although the Ottawa held out the threat of mass migration to Canada in order to try to manipulate U.S. policy, few Ottawa ever actually immigrated to Canada, and most of those who did soon returned to Michigan.[184]

Short of immigration, the Ottawa and Chippewa did their best to push for the United States to extend the reservations beyond the five-year period. They also urged Schoolcraft to complete the surveys of the reservations and to expel preemptionists and trespassers.[185] Some of the Ottawa communities and particularly the Christianized communities along the Grand River and the northwestern coast of lower Michigan developed a sophisticated strategy that enlisted missionaries, mixed bloods, and American citizens to write petitions and to otherwise lobby for the tribes in Congress. Some of these thus mobilized advanced attacks on Schoolcraft for mismanagement of Indian affairs in his superintendency.[186]

By far the most effective strategy, however, was to convince Americans that there was no need to remove the Ottawa and Chippewa, because they were rapidly becoming "civilized"; that is, they were learning English, converting to Christianity, adopting American dress and housing styles, and, especially, taking up European-style agriculture on land they had purchased by pooling annuity funds. The Ottawa and Chippewa, it was argued, should become citizens of Michigan and remain where they were.[187] Whether it was the result of some of these emerging strategies or because of bureaucratic ineptitude, the government made no decision on removing the Ottawa and Chippewa from the reservations by the five-year deadline of May 1841, tacitly permitting them to remain.

Schoolcraft's attempts to promote the removal of Michigan Indians to the West earned the resentment of the Ottawa and Chippewa as well as their many supporters. Requests were circulated to investigate Schoolcraft's handling of the agency's finances and particularly the Johnston estate claims. There were also other issues of family patronage. On top of this controversy came the presidential election of 1840, in which the Whig Party candidate, William H. Harrison, was elected. In April 1841 Schoolcraft, a Democrat, was removed from office because of his partisan position in the election. Robert Stuart, formerly of the American Fur Company at Mackinac, was appointed, with the support of John Astor and other influential friends, to replace Schoolcraft as superintendent in September 1841.[188]

Events Preceding the 1855 Treaty

Not only were the Indians and local citizenry of northern Michigan anxious for resolution of the unsettled nature of Ottawa and Chippewa affairs under the 1836 treaty, but this also became a priority of the state of Michigan. In 1851 the legislature approved the following resolution:

> Whereas the Constitution of the State of Michigan gives unto all civilized persons of Indian descent equal rights and privileges with the white inhabitants of said state, and whereas by the adoption of said clause in the constitution [of 1850], the people of this state have evinced a just and humane desire to see the Indian who now inhabit Michigan raised from a state of semi-barbarism to one of enlightenment and have, by it, removed one great barrier that has hither to prevented the consummation of this philanthropic object and where the Ottawa and Chippewa Indians residing amongst us are a civil, well disposed, peaceable and orderly people, and have during the few past years made great advancement in agricultural and mechanics arts, and a large portion of them ardently desire to remain in Michigan to become civilized and share with us in our social political and religious privileges.
>
> Therefore be it enacted by the senate and house of representatives of the State of Michi-

gan, that we do hereby request the Government of the United States to make such arrangements for said Indians as they may desire for their permanent location in the northern part of this state under such provision in regard to schools, churches, agricultural and mechanic arts as will the best promote their present and future wellfare [*sic*] and adjust all matters of right and equity that may now be in dispute between said Indians and said government, in a spirit of just liberality. Resolved further that the Governor be and he is hereby requested to forward a copy of the forgoing preamble and joint resolution to the President of the U.S. to the Hon the Sec. of the home department to the Commissioner of Indian affairs and to each of our representatives in congress.

This joint resolution shall take effect immediately, April 1, 1851.[189]

The Ottawa and Chippewa continued to be plagued with rumors that they would be required to remove to the West or would be removed by force to the West.[190] Some of these rumors were the result of an inspection tour of a government delegation headed by Elias Murray that was sent by Luke Lea, commissioner of Indian affairs, to check on the condition of the Ottawa and Chippewa.[191] Kanapima (Augustin Hamlin) wrote a warning to the northern Ottawa chiefs that the delegation was promoting removal and reminded them that the removal provision of the 1836 treaty was entirely permissive.[192]

Besides the question of removal that was the central concern of the Indians, another set of problems plagued both the government and the tribes. The government's difficulties came out very clearly in the report of the Murray fact-finding mission. Murray reported that the Ottawa and Chippewa lived in over sixty small communities scattered over three hundred lineal miles between the Grand River valley and Lake Superior. There were no roads in the vast area, thus necessitating water travel on the lakes and rivers.[193] In his annual report for 1853, Agent Henry Gilbert noted that he was compelled to travel over two thousand miles to visit and to pay annuities to the various bands. Many, he said, were savages and pagans with no permanent location and "preserving many of the peculiarities of their race."[194] These he contrasted to other bands who had flourishing churches and schools and who were exercising the rights of suffrage under the Michigan Constitution since they had abandoned "their tribal state."[195] The government's concern was that the dispersed settlement and subsistence rounds of the Ottawa and Chippewa did not permit the expedient delivery of services that would promote civilizing influences. Another concern of the government involved the bonus of two hundred thousand dollars set up by Section 6 of Article 4 of the 1836 treaty. This fund was included to induce the chiefs to agree to the five-year limitation on the reservations and was to be payable when the reservations were surrendered. Interest on this money was paid annually to the Indians. By 1851, ten years after the term initially set for the reservations had expired, Congress was seriously considering suspending these interest payments.[196]

For their part, the Ottawa and Chippewa had many concerns besides the threat of removal. First, they were confused about payment of benefits under the 1836 treaty and desperately wanted an accounting on school and agricultural expenditures, the balance of the debt fund, and the interest on the reservation fund. In addition, many chiefs believed that the money expended on education and farming was being squandered by the government with little benefit to their people. Some chiefs wanted more control over hiring teachers, farmers, and blacksmiths.[197] The timing of annuity payments was another sore point. Often the government required the Indians to assemble in the late summer and fall to collect these payments, which interfered greatly with the fall fishing season and fall hunts, not to mention the harvest of gardens. Besides these important details, the bands of Chippewa and Ottawa were upset at being forced to deal with the United States in concert.[198] They resented Schoolcraft's deliberate integration of their affairs in 1836, and these problems continued to fester to the point that the bands wanted the relationship severed.

In view of this dissatisfaction, public opinion began to solidify around the idea that something needed to be done about the Ottawa-Chippewa problem. On April 7, 1852, the U.S. Senate approved a motion to instruct the Committee on Indian Affairs to inquire into arrangements to settle all questions arising under the 1836 treaty relative to occupancy of the land reserves and the consideration paid for the cession and to make an appropriation for the permanent settlement of the Ottawa and Chippewa.[199] The desperate plight of the Michigan Ottawa and Chippewa ultimately led to the treaties of July 31 and August 2, 1855.[200] Both treaties were negotiated at Detroit by George Manypenny, commissioner of Indian affairs, and Michigan Indian agent Henry Gilbert, as treaty commissioners for the United States.[201] Both treaties attempted to resolve Michigan Indian problems by concentrating Indians on a few large reservations.[202]

George Manypenny and the Reservation Policy

By the early 1850s, a bold new Indian policy emerged that was based on the idea that Indians could be collected on reservations in their home territories, where they would be taught the skills of civilization. Charles Mix, chief clerk of the Indian Office, and George Manypenny, commissioner of Indian affairs from 1853 to 1857, were its chief architects. The new policy was embodied, in varying degrees, in the fifty-two treaties Manypenny promoted during his tenure as commissioner. Although Manypenny's treaties dealt with substantially different kinds of problems, they also showed remarkable similarity in philosophy, as well as in format and phraseology. Manypenny treaties were often innovative and experimental, showing, over time, an evolution of method to achieve core objectives.

As a reformer, Manypenny believed the assimilation goal could be achieved by education. Indians, in his view, were fully capable of learning, and he believed they could be prepared rather quickly for life in civilized society. To accomplish this, it was necessary to teach them English, mathematics, domestic skills, modern agriculture and husbandry, and the value of toil, thrift, private property, and the Christian faith—preferably of a Protestant denomination. Manypenny knew that these and other values of civilized life were not part of native tradition, and he knew that everyday life on the American frontier offered powerful competition to his civilization objectives. Illicit traders cheated Indians and made prostitutes of Indian women. Real estate sharks had dozens of schemes to separate Indians from their land, and whiskey peddlers were quick to addict Indians and take advantage of their desire for alcohol.[203] Given these conditions, Manypenny believed that Indians must be protected vigorously during the period they were learning to fend for themselves.

The reservation system of the 1850s attempted to accommodate Indian desires to remain on their traditional lands, and it attempted to promote federal assimilation objectives while also protecting Indian interests. When George Manypenny succeeded Luke Lea as commissioner in 1853, he moved rapidly to negotiate a large number of treaties that put a reservation system in place all across the country as a means of promoting Indian civilization efforts. One of the primary factors that led Manypenny and his fellow reformers to implement the reservation system was that the Trade and Intercourse Act of 1834 had proven to be inadequate to protect the person and property of the Indians.[204] By their concentration on reservations, the Indians could be protected during the period while they were mastering the arts and skills of civilization. Manypenny believed this process could proceed quite rapidly.

Prior to his appointment as commissioner of Indian affairs in 1853, George Manypenny was an Ohio businessman and politician who owed his appointment to political patronage in the Franklin Pierce administration.[205] Although a skilled businessman and administrator, he had no experience with Indians when he assumed office. By the 1850s, many of the eastern tribes were quite sophisticated in keeping track of claims due under former treaties. Indians were often aware of the schedule for the payment of annuities under former treaties that sometimes called for the United States to pay in perpetuity. Manypenny was concerned about these obligations and, as a businessman, saw the advantage of consolidating money claims in subsequent treaties.

Most of the treaty negotiations in which Manypenny was personally involved were held in Washington. Federal authorities fully appreciated the great advantage Washington held in controlling the number of Indian negotiators and isolating the chiefs from the advice of families and local influence. Likewise, tribal delegations could be impressed with the affluence and power of the Great Father and the numbers and accomplishments of whites. Manypenny learned this lesson early when he sent Henry Gilbert to La Pointe on Lake Superior in 1854 to negotiate with the Chippewa. Thousands of Indians appeared, creating an expensive provisioning problem, not to mention controversy among Indian factions and pressure from special interest groups. For this reason, Manypenny seldom left Washington to negotiate, a notable exception being the three treaties he and Henry Gilbert negotiated with Michigan Indians at Detroit during the summer of 1855.

Manypenny often negotiated treaties in rapid-fire order. For example, he personally negotiated seven treaties between May 6 and June 5, 1854, and he concluded the three Michigan treaties during a ten-day period in the summer of 1855.[206] One reason his treaties could be arranged so quickly is that the form and language of many of their provisions are nearly identical. This observation extends to many of the treaties negotiated by other treaty commissioners working under Manypenny's supervision during his tenure as commissioner. The rapidity with which treaties were sometimes negotiated raises the question of how much actual negotiation took place. In many cases, it appears that Indians often accepted the substance and language as it was presented. In some cases, it is doubtful if they comprehended the terminology and concepts involved, given the cultural and linguistic barriers that separated nineteenth-century Americans from native peoples.

In his November 1855 report as commissioner of Indian affairs, Manypenny specifically commented on the reservations made in the treaties of July 31 and August 2, 1855: "By them the Indians are to have assigned permanent homes, to be hereafter confirmed to them, in small tracts, in severalty. Such guards and restrictions are thrown around their lands and limited annuities as cannot fail, if faithfully regarded and respected, to place them in comfortable and independent circumstances."[207] Likewise, in support of his reservation policy, Manypenny said that all non-Indians who settled on ceded lands should be made to understand "that the tribes are to be protected and remain undisturbed within the limits of their reservations, and that this policy will be inflexibly adhered to by the government."[208] This position was also held by Manypenny's successors J. W. Denver and Charles Mix. Commissioner Denver went so far as to insist that "no white person should be permitted to obtain any kind of possession or foothold within the limits of reservations, nor even to enter them, except in the employ or by permission of the government, and none should be employed except such as would be actually necessary for the instruction of Indians."[209]

An important part of the reservation policy was the allotment process. Except in rare cases, the reservations were partitioned so that land was held by individual tribal members. Individual landownership, it was believed, would teach Indians the value of toil and pride in individual achievement. To protect the interests of Indian allottees in their land and to prevent their land from falling into the hands of whites as a result of fraud or sale, the Manypenny treaties usually contained a mechanism to prevent alienation of allotments. By the time of the 1855 treaties at Detroit, Michigan Indians were well aware of their vulnerability if they did not have "strong" title to the land, that is, a patent or deed.[210]

It was with these understandings of Indians and of the objectives of U.S. Indian policy that George Manypenny and his Michigan agent Henry Gilbert approached the difficult problems facing Michigan Indians in 1855. The practical details of the forthcoming Ottawa-Chippewa Treaty of 1855 were incorporated in a letter written by Agent Henry Gilbert to Manypenny in early March. Gilbert recommended reservations, allotment of land, agricultural investments, and the creation of an educational trust fund with the two hundred thousand dollars provided by the Senate in 1836 for the surrender of their reservations.[211]

In April 1855 Gilbert again wrote Manypenny, urging rapid action. His concern was in finding large blocks of land for allotment that were completely free of white settlers.[212] Although there were hundreds of thousands of acres of totally vacant land in the interior of the Michigan peninsulas, Indians and settlers were now competing for coastal land. Both groups preferred the coasts because, since there were no inland roads, all transportation was by water. In addition, the coasts had the advantage of excellent fishing as well as a more moderate climate. For the Ottawa and Chippewa, the Great Lakes coasts had always been the site of their summer villages, sugar groves, burial places, and fishing stations, and they strongly preferred to acquire land in these locations. On April 10, 1855, the commissioner of the General Land Office, in anticipation of a new treaty, withdrew land in Emmet and Charlevoix counties for a large reservation.[213] Consequently, Commissioner Manypenny wrote to the secretary of the interior, Robert McClelland, recommending a new treaty.[214] This request was rapidly approved, and Manypenny responded by listing the problems that were outstanding as a result of the 1836 treaty.[215] Ultimately, land was withdrawn in other regions of the 1836 cession to accommodate Indian interest under the 1855 treaty.

In his letter to Secretary McClelland, Manypenny proposed settling all matters with the Ottawa and Chippewa that are now "in an unsettled condition" and "making proper arrangements for their permanent residence in that state." He explained the problem of the two hundred thousand dollars to be paid as a bonus upon surrender of the reservations, as well as the Ottawa and Chippewa claim to lands west of the Mississippi, which he believed should be paid as an equitable claim. In addition, Manypenny recommended that the Ottawa and Chippewa be allotted land in severalty.[216] Pursuant to a general letter of instruction, Agent Henry Gilbert arranged to assemble the appropriate chiefs at the city of Detroit in late July 1855 for the purpose of negotiating a new treaty.[217]

Negotiations of the 1855 Treaty

Finally, by late July 1855, the long anticipated treaty to remedy the problems of the 1836 treaty and to create permanent homes for the Ottawa and Chippewa was convened in the city of Detroit. George Manypenny, commissioner of Indian affairs, and Michigan agent Henry Gilbert were appointed as treaty commissioners for the United States. I. L. Chipman and Richard Smith were appointed as official secretaries, and the official interpreters were John Johnston, Augustin Hamlin, George Johnston, John Godfroy, and Louis Cadotte.[218] In fact, Cadotte, Hamlin, and John Johnston did most of the official interpreting.[219] These men were all of mixed descent and competent in both English and either the Ottawa or Chippewa dialects.

The Indian delegations were represented by fifty-four chiefs: twelve representing the Sault Ste. Marie Chippewa bands, seven representing the Mackinac bands, nine from the Little Traverse Ottawa, nine from the Grand Traverse Ottawa, and seventeen representing the Grand River bands. Most of the negotiating for the Indian side was done by Assagon, an Ottawa from Cheboygan. Assagon was not a chief and did not sign the treaty; among the Ottawa, Assagon was well known as an *ogamagigido,* or speaker. Assagon seems to have been sophisticated about the ways of non-Indians. The Grand River Ottawa chief Paybahmesay, Chief Wasson from Little Traverse, and Chief Waubojeeg of the Sault Ste. Marie bands were active in negotiations, as were several others who played more subdued roles.

The negotiations were held over a seven-day period between Wednesday, July 25, and Tuesday, July 31, when the treaty was signed. Unlike many other treaty journals, including the one that resulted from the 1836 treaty, the journal for the 1855 treaty seems relatively complete. This is true at least to the extent that it focuses on the different bargaining positions of the two sides. It is clear from the journal that the United States was determined to implement the provisions of the new reservation policy, and it is equally clear that the Ottawa and Chippewa came to Detroit prepared to ask specific questions related to their relations with the United States. The resulting treaty is no doubt a product of give-and-take on the part of both the chiefs and the treaty commissioners.

Newspaper accounts indicate something of the atmosphere surrounding the treaty negotiations. We know, for example, that some of the chiefs had to be clothed so as not to offend the sensibilities of the metropolitan population. We know also that the weather in late July 1855 was extremely hot and humid, which caused considerable discomfort for the northern Michigan chiefs. Besides the Ottawa and Chippewa, the Saginaw Chippewa chiefs had also been summoned to Detroit for a new treaty. The combined appearance of nearly one hundred members of these delegations in the city caused quite a stir among the curious who flocked to observe the assembled Indians.[220] A reporter for the *De-*

troit Daily Free Press noted that the speeches of the chiefs were clever and laced with wit. The Sault chief Waubojeeg seems to have attracted particular attention for his intelligent comments and for his banter with the crowd of American spectators.[221] The proceedings even drew a visit from aged general Lewis Cass, who addressed the Indian delegates briefly on Friday morning, July 27.[222]

At the outset of negotiations, Commissioner Manypenny set an atmosphere of largesse on the part of the Great Father and the United States when he told the chiefs, "We feel that we [the United States] may say with truth that we are in a position of impartiality. We are seeking no lands—*nothing from you*" (emphasis added).[223] Thus, the United States asked the Ottawa and Chippewa to believe that it would act in their best interest and would require them to surrender nothing in exchange for the settlement of their money claims and the land required for permanent Michigan homes. Assagon replied for the assembled chiefs, saying, "Father, we are like children rejoiced to see their parent." In further describing the relationship between the Ottawa and Chippewa and the United States, he observed,

> Father, your arm is strong and you are a great Chief. We know that, and we wish you to be interested for us. For ourselves, we do not wish, or hope, what is not our due, and we rely upon you, our father, for what is ours. We want no more. It is our only desire that you will act for us and tell us what to do. We are like parents placing money in the hands of their children. We are now acting for our children.[224]

The Ottawa and Chippewa proceeded to enumerate their financial grievances against the United States under the 1836 treaty. Manypenny divided these into legal claims—for example, a claim for annuities past due or interest payments specified in the treaty—and equitable claims. By the latter, he meant claims the United States was not legally bound to pay but would be inclined to pay from fairness. An example of such would be money promised for subsistence and provisioning under the removal provision of the 1836 treaty. Even though they did not choose to remove, the chiefs believed that these funds were due to them as part of the payment for the original land cession. After a series of explanations, Gilbert was able to resolve all the monetary claims made by the chiefs. The main item of remaining business was to create permanent homes.

Well prior to the treaty, Manypenny had requested and received land withdrawals from the federal land office for the purpose of reserving land for allotments. According to provisions of the treaty, individual Indians were to select land from within these reservations. Heads of households were to receive eighty acres, while single people over twenty-one and orphans would receive forty acres. These parcels were to be selected within five years, and the land would be patented thereafter. For the period of another five years, Indians were permitted to privately purchase lands on the reserves. After that time, the unsold land could be open for public purchase. Despite Manypenny's wishes, the treaty also included a trader debt provision of forty thousand dollars. Other money payments to the Ottawa and Chippewa amounted to $538,400 that was used to provide per capita annuities and agricultural, domestic, and educational benefits.

Article 3 of the treaty is a general release clause that was typical of many of the fifty-two treaties negotiated during the Manypenny era.[225] The article states that the money grants and payments provided for in the treaty are in lieu of all legal and equitable treaty claims against the United States for "land, money, or other thing" guaranteed by stipulation of former treaties. An exception was made in the case of the treaty from June 16, 1820, which reserved the right of fishing and encampment at the falls of the St. Marys River to the Sault Ste. Marie Chippewa.

Obviously, the Ottawa and Chippewa chiefs who negotiated the 1836 treaty were well aware of the obligations of the United States under former treaties. The Grand River Ottawa were parties to several other treaties beyond the Treaty of Greenville and the 1836 treaty and accordingly received a special annuity of thirty-five thousand dollars for ten years in lieu of permanent annuities promised in former treaties. Likewise, at the time of the 1855 treaty, the northern Ottawa and Chippewa claimed that they were owed minor payment as a result of former treaties. Manypenny assumed that Ottawa and Chippewa affairs under the former treaties had been settled in 1836.[226] The intent of Article 5 was to resolve money claims, particularly those that tied the government to perpetual annuities.[227] The 1836 treaty required the government to provide things that it no longer wanted to provide, including books in the Indian languages, agricultural implements, cattle, mechanical tools, tobacco, fish barrels, and salt. At the time of the 1855 treaty, the government was still obliged to provide these goods.

The question may be raised as to whether or not the release clause applies to hunting, fishing, and gathering provisions of Article 13 of the 1836 treaty. This is not the case. First, it is important to note that the treaty journal makes no reference to these rights. Inasmuch as the Ottawa and Chippewa depended on the 1836 usufruct provision to feed their families and engage in commerce at the time of the 1855 treaty, any request to surrender these rights would have been met by a furor of discussion. In fact, Manypenny told the Ottawa and Chippewa that the United States wanted nothing from them in the course of the treaty negotiations.[228] Second, hunting, fishing, and gathering rights were not inconsistent with the allotment and civilization objectives espoused by Manypenny in his reservation policy. While it is true that Manypenny looked forward to a day when Indians retired from the chase to become educated, Christian farmers who were citizens of the state, this was not the case in 1855 and would not be so for a long time into the future. In many areas of the 1836 cession, the climate and poor soils defeated this idealistic goal. At the time of the 1855 treaty, Manypenny, the Indians, and certainly the local merchants all knew that the Ottawa and Chippewa would have to continue to live under the 1836 treaty rights of hunting, fishing, and gathering or they would starve. Perhaps this reality is why Manypenny sometimes actually placed hunting and fishing right provisions in allotment treaties if they were not already guaranteed. The Treaty of La Pointe negotiated by Henry Gilbert in 1854 is an example.[229]

The exception for claims under the 1820 treaty that provided for a place of encampment and fishing at the falls of the St. Marys River might perhaps be taken to indicate that this single usufruct provision under former treaties was preserved to the exclusion of others. Actually, however, the 1820 treaty, which dealt nearly exclusively with these fishing rights, was in fact an unresolved legal and equitable claim specific to the Sault Ste. Marie Chippewa. As Manypenny knew, the place of encampment had been illegally destroyed in 1850 by the construction of the St. Marys ship canal, which also damaged the fishery. In fact, on August 2, 1855, two days after the signing of the July 31 treaty, Manypenny reconvened the Sault Ste. Marie Chippewa in Detroit and negotiated a treaty that released the United States of its obligation under the 1820 treaty, in exchange for money damages.[230] Thus, the reason for including the exception for the 1820 treaty in Article 3 of the 1855 treaty was so the money claim for destruction of the encampment and fishery, which was specific to the Sault Ste. Marie bands alone, would not be included in the payments to the other bands.

It thus seems apparent that the government did not ask the Ottawa and Chippewa to relinquish their usufructuary rights under the 1836 treaty and that neither the tribes nor the United States believed that this was the case. Indeed, for the next five decades, the Ottawa and Chippewa continued to pursue their rights to hunt, fish, and gather without any known protest or even comment by any government official. When, in the twentieth century, the state of Michigan began to complain that such activities were contrary to its newly enacted game and fish laws, the Ottawa and Chippewa strongly asserted their rights under the 1836 treaty.

One other provision of the 1855 treaty deserves further comment, since its meaning is not apparent from a casual reading. Article 5 says in part, "The tribal organization of said Ottawa and Chippewa Indians except insofar as may be necessary for the purpose of carrying into effect the provisions of this agreement, is hereby dissolved." Further, it states that "no general convention of the Indians shall be called," it being the intention of the government to deal with local bands who were "immediately interested in the question involved." Did this article mean that the Ottawa and Chippewa tribes would cease to exist? Setting aside the question of the propriety of the United States action in dissolving the government of a sovereign with which it had just signed a treaty, this was not the government's intent.

Returning to the journal of the negotiation of the 1855 treaty, we see that both the Ottawa and Chippewa bands were very uncomfortable with the artificial political amalgamation created in 1836 by Henry Schoolcraft when he merged the political interests of disparate independent bands for the convenience of the United States. In fact, we can recall that Schoolcraft tried to shame the Ottawa into agreeing to sell their lands at the 1836 treaty negotiations, by pointing out the fine gifts the Chippewa would receive for their cooperation. At the negotiations in 1855, Sault Ste. Marie chief Waubojeeg told Manypenny, "At the treaty of '36 our fathers were in partnership with the Ottawas but now the partnership is finished and we who come from the foot of Lake Superior wish to do our business for ourselves."[231] Later in the negotiations, he returned to this point: "I told you when I first came that I wanted to be separated from the Ottawas and you have not answered me. We have sat here and heard you talk to the Ottawas while you paid no attention to us."[232] In answer, Manypenny explained, "Under the provisions of this treaty [1855] you will get your share of the money. The very case you suggested is met in the treaty. You are separated as you desire. This treaty you and the Ottawas must sign together because the old treaty of '36 was made in that way. But here we have followed your suggestion and provide that the money shall be paid to different bands and that no general council shall be called."[233] Thus, Manypenny was dissolving "the tribal *organization* of the Ottawa and Chippewa Indians" (emphasis added to note the singular usage).[234] Wisely, he had decided to return to the band-level organizations that were central to Ottawa and Chippewa interest and decision making.

After the Treaty

Immediately following the treaty, Manypenny forwarded a copy with a letter of transmittal to the acting commissioner of Indian affairs, Charles Mix.[235] Mix, Manypenny, and Gilbert devoted much time and concern in the late months of 1855 to trying to assure that adequate land required by the treaty was available for the Ottawa and Chippewa.[236] The most desirable land was, of course, that land closest to the Great Lakes, some of which had already been sold to non-Indians. Agent William Richmond wrote to Manypenny for the Grand River chief Nebawnaygezhick, pointing out that lakeshore land was important to the Indians because permanent locations would contain opportunities to combine planting with fishing and sugar production.[237]

Along with the separate treaties negotiated with the Sault Ste. Marie and Saginaw Chippewa on August 2, 1855, the treaty from July 31, 1855, was forwarded to the president and the Senate for their concurrence in January 1856.[238] In February the Senate amended the July 31 treaty to include a trader debt provision, with the rationale that it would "prevent lawsuits."[239]

CHAPTER 7

United States v. Michigan, Western District of Michigan, Case No. M26-73 C.A.

Bruce R. Greene
The Law Office of Bruce R. Greene & Associates, LCC, Boulder, Colorado

United States v. Michigan was filed in 1973 in the U.S. District Court for the Western District of Michigan, in Grand Rapids. Although I was responsible for the litigation for ten years, I did not become involved until the spring of 1975, so my understanding of the origins of the lawsuit are secondhand, although nonetheless reliably based on information received from persons knowledgeable in the subject at the time. The U.S. attorney for that district at the time the lawsuit was filed was John P. Milanowski. He served in that role from 1969 through 1974, having been appointed by President Richard M. Nixon. Prior to his appointment, he had been an administrative aide to then House representative Gerald R. Ford.

Milanowski was a Grand Rapids product, having been born there and graduated from Central Catholic High School in that city. By reputation, he was a kind, empathetic man, strongly influenced by his religion and the Catholic schools he attended. He was especially interested in the Chippewa and Ottawa Indian communities located throughout his district. Indeed, one of the apocryphal stories about Milanowski was that when he visited the Bay Mills Indian Community on Lake Superior, not far from Sault Ste. Marie, he would pass out shiny new pennies to the Indian children as a gesture of friendship and compassion. I am told that the Indians at Bay Mills were impressed with Milanowski because he actually visited their reservation, something most U.S. attorneys do not do. He was empathetic regarding the fishing struggles of Bay Mills members and was kind to the children of the community.

While visiting Bay Mills, Milanowski no doubt heard an earful from a prominent citizen of the community—Big Abe LeBlanc. Big Abe was a legend at Bay Mills. As his nickname indicates, he was a bear of a man. He stood about 6 feet and 4 or 5 inches tall, weighed around three hundred pounds (more or less), had a commanding presence, and spoke with a booming voice. Let's just say Big Abe was bigger than life. From time to time, Big Abe held elected positions within the Bay Mills Indian Community. However, even when he held no official office, he nonetheless was a prominent member of the community, with a great deal of influence and power. He was first and foremost an Indian fisherman, who struggled, along with other Bay Mills fishermen, to make a living from the Great Lakes fishery resource. His principal obstacle to successfully prosecuting his fishery enterprise was the state of Michigan, the Michigan Department of Natural Resources (MDNR), and MDNR's conservation officers. In the early 1970s, Big Abe set his gill nets in Whitefish Bay, adjacent to the Bay Mills Indian Community's reservation. The MDNR, having been previously notified by Big Abe in order to set up a test case, seized and confiscated Big Abe's nets because the use of gill nets was not permitted under state law. Big Abe, of course, contended he had a right to fish much of Michigan's Great Lakes waters and that state prohibitions against the use of gill nets had no application to him or any other Bay Mills members.

Big Abe argued that the right to fish commercially with gill nets in the Great Lakes was rooted in a treaty entered into between the United States and the Ottawa and Chippewa Indians residing in western lower Michigan and the eastern end of the Upper Peninsula of Michigan. The Treaty of Washington, entered into on March 28, 1836, was the basis for his claim. Under that treaty, the Indians ceded a vast amount of land to the United States but retained a small number of parcels reserved from the cession and scattered throughout the ceded territory. Generally, these parcels, which were reservations, were located along the Great Lakes shore, at the mouths of rivers or adjacent to other well-known and productive fishing areas. In exchange for the land cession, the Indians received certain annuities and other goods and services, such as blacksmiths located in the Indians' territory and barrels and salt to be used to preserve and ship fish. Other than the reference to fish barrels and salt, the treaty was silent with respect to the Indians' right to commercially harvest fish from the Great Lakes. However, Article 13 provided that "[t]he Indians stipulate for the right of hunting on the lands ceded, with the other usual privileges of occupancy, until the land is required for settlement."

The Indians contended that the treaty's silence with respect to the Great Lakes fishery meant that they had kept that right and not relinquished it during the treaty transaction. The law supported that claim, since treaties of cession must be construed strictly and narrowly; anything not explicitly conveyed by the Indians under the treaty was considered to still be the property of the Indians. Thus, if the treaty was silent regarding the right to fish in the Great Lakes, two possible inferences could be drawn. The first was that the right to fish in the Great Lakes passed to the United States, along with the land cession, even though there was no mention of the right under the grant in the treaty. The second was that the right stayed with the grantor (i.e., the Indians), precisely because it was not specifically mentioned as a part of the grant of lands to the United States. In addition to this theory, the court also construed Article 13 to mean that the right to hunt also included the right to trap, fish, and gather and that the right to fish encompassed subsistence as well as commercial harvests. The court reasoned that the limitation in Article 13—"till the land is required for settlement"—did not affect the right to fish commercially in the Great Lakes because they could not be settled.

Why was the state trying to ban gill nets? That was, after all, the nub of the conflict between the state and the Indians. The answer is rooted in the history of the Great Lakes fishery and the effort of leaders in the MDNR in the 1960s to improve the fishery and the economy of the state all at the same time, notwithstanding any federal treaty rights enjoyed by the tribes. The Great Lakes was a very productive commercial fishery in the nineteenth century and into the early part of the twentieth. Technological changes in the industry, such as the use of microfilament gill nets, the development of the steam engine, and, later, the use of gasoline-powered motors for boats, allowed the fishery to expand greatly. The most productive commercial species were whitefish and lake trout. The industry used gill nets, primarily, to prosecute the harvest.

The use of gill nets was favored by fishermen because they are an efficient and effective fishing device. A gill net fishery could be operated with a relatively small amount of gear—a skiff of sixteen to twenty feet, a motor for the boat, and several boxes of gill nets. One-man operations were common, although more capital could be devoted to the fishery in the form of gill net tugs, which required several men to operate. As the harvest of fish showed significant increases during that period, more and more fishermen were attracted to the industry, and fishing pressure continued to increase. The increased harvest began to stress the fish stocks.

Environmental factors began impacting the resource as well. For example, as Michigan and other states adjacent to the Great Lakes became more industrialized, more discharge of pollutants occurred in the lakes. In the 1930s, the current version of the Welland Canal, which connected Lakes Ontario and Erie, was completed, thereby facilitating ship transportation of goods and raw materials on the Great Lakes and opening all of the Great Lakes to the Atlantic Ocean through the St. Lawrence Seaway. But this progress also brought new, environmental problems, this time through the inadvertent introduction of the sea lamprey into the Great Lakes.

The sea lamprey is a parasitic, eel-like fish that attaches itself to the wall of a host fish and subsists off the host until it is exhausted as a source of food and subsequently dies. The sea lamprey prefers fatty fish as its host, which meant that lake trout, as opposed to whitefish, were more vulnerable to it. From the 1930s and forward, lake trout stocks declined as the instances of sea lamprey wounds increased. In the 1950s, the federal government, in cooperation with the Great Lakes Fishery Commission, an international body, began their efforts to control sea lampreys by applying lampricide to various inland stream habitats where the lamprey were known to reproduce. That effort has been helpful, but the lampreys remain a problem in the Great Lakes even today.

By the early 1960s, all of these problems—pollutant discharges into the Great Lakes, overfishing by commercial operators, and the introduction of nonindigenous species to the Great Lakes—left the commercial fishing industry in difficult straits. The condition of the fishery and the ecological imbalance in the Great Lakes were dramatically revealed to the public by the massive alewife die-off during that period. The alewife, another nonindigenous species introduced into the Great Lakes, was forage food for the predatory lake trout. But as lake trout stocks were reduced due to sea lamprey attacks, the alewife population exploded. A massive die-off of alewives along the shores of Lake Michigan, along with their attendant odor, brought home to the average citizen that there indeed was a problem in the Great Lakes.

In the mid-1960s, under the leadership of Howard A. Tanner and Wayne H. Tody, officials within the MDNR, the state of Michigan decided to shift courses and make an enormous change to the Great Lakes fishery. The commercial fishery was in decline and disarray for the reasons explained. The ecological balance in the Great Lakes had been significantly altered, as evidenced by the alewife die-off. The Michigan economy was no longer benefiting from the commercial exploitation of the resource. In 1966, Tanner and Tody caused the first planting of salmon stocks from the Pacific Northwest. This marked a significant turning point in how the fishery would be managed. No longer was the goal of the state to restore the commercial industry. Rather, the goal now was to devote the fishery to recreational users—sport fishermen—who would positively impact the economy. Lake trout, an important species for commercial fishermen, was now deemed to be a sport fish. The Great Lakes was hopefully to become a recreational playground for the greater Midwest population. Anglers were going to buy fishing licenses from the state, gasoline from local stations, and fishing boats and gear from Michigan retailers, and they were anticipated to spend money at restaurants and hotels and the like. The alewife problem would also be solved, since alewives would now be forage for the introduced salmon, as well as the lake trout resource. Toward this end, the MDNR began an effort to eliminate the use of gill nets, which it claimed was an indiscriminate lethal fishing device. A more discriminating fishing device, according to the MDNR, was the trap net.

A gill net resembles a tennis net. It is usually around one hundred feet long and has floats attached to the top of the net and weights at the bottom. By adjusting the floats and weights, the net can be fished at most any depth. Gangs of nets can be attached to each other, resulting in a long line of gill nets extending hundreds of feet in length. A gill net fishery can be prosecuted with a small, open boat, by one man. Trap nets, in contrast, require a substantial capital investment in a trap net boat, plus nets and related gear. The trap net is stationary, quite large, and expensive to purchase. The net uses a series of leaders to direct fish into it and contains a series of traps or pots from which the fish, once entering, cannot escape. Eventually, the fish move through the net into the final pot, where they swim unimpeded until retrieved by the fishermen. A trap net boat requires a crew of three to four persons to operate it. The net is "fished" by sliding the boat under the net, through the use of winches, until the trap is exposed. Fish can be scooped out of the trap, with unwanted or protected species being returned live to the water. The MDNR insisted that this gear be used by commercial fishermen in order to protect lake trout. However, throughout the history of the litigation and beyond, lake trout, although heavily planted in the Great Lakes, had become a put, grow, and take fishery. Thus, virtually no natural reproduction was occurring in the lakes, either from hatchery-grown and planted lake trout or from remnant stocks of native lake trout. While some natural reproduction is occurring today, lake trout in the Great Lakes is not a self-sustaining species.

This, then, was the setting for the conflict between the state of Michigan and the Ottawa and Chippewa tribes, which are the modern-day political successors in interest to the Indian signatories to the 1836 Treaty of Washington. In the early 1970s, the Chippewa and Ottawa Indians were suffering in Michigan. Although Bay Mills had been recognized by the United States as an Indian tribe continuously since treaty times, it was not until 1972 and 1980, respectively, that the Sault Ste. Marie Tribe of Chippewa Indians and the Grand Traverse Band of Ottawa and Chippewa Indians were recognized. Although both tribes had a long history with the United States, there was an equally long period of time, from the end of the nineteenth century until the 1970s, when the United States did not politically recognize these tribes. As a result, the tribes had little resources. Their governments were fledgling and in disarray, and unemployment was staggering. Fishing had always been a part of the Indians' culture and identity, but being a fisherman in those days meant you were doing it in violation of state law, under a federal right that the state refused to accept, and prior to the *United States v. Michigan* litigation that confirmed the existence of the right.

The first significant legal conflict between the state and the treaty tribes concerned the state's effort to prosecute Big Abe LeBlanc for fishing with gill nets in Whitefish Bay. This case worked its way to the Michigan Supreme Court in 1975. I, along with Kathryn Tierney, a young lawyer at Bay Mills sponsored by the Catholic charity Campaign for Human Development, briefed, argued, and won Big Abe's case. The Michigan Supreme Court agreed that Big Abe had a right to use gill nets in Whitefish Bay under the 1836 treaty.[1]

In the meantime, while Big Abe's case was working its way through the Michigan criminal justice system, John Milanowski filed *United States v. Michigan* in 1973. Although such a lawsuit could not be initiated today without prior approval from the U.S. attorney general in Washington, D.C., that was not required in 1973. U.S. attorneys in their various districts were authorized to initiate civil litigation in the name of the United States at that time. Had the case needed approval from Washington, it is unclear whether it would have been filed at all.

After the *LeBlanc* decision from the Michigan Supreme Court, it was still necessary to prosecute the case in federal court before Judge Noel P. Fox, primarily because *LeBlanc* was a state criminal case. Although the Michigan Supreme Court agreed that Big Abe could fish under his federal treaty right and could not be prosecuted for violating state law, that ruling technically applied only to him and only to fishing in Whitefish Bay. The federal litigation allowed the court to define the full nature and extent of the right, the details of where the right pertained in the Great Lakes (an area hundreds of times larger than just Whitefish Bay), and the exact nature of the state's and the tribes' authority to regulate treaty tribe members in the exercise of the right. In the absence of the federal litigation, it would have been necessary to assert the right as a defense to a myriad of state criminal proceedings as they arose out of criminal citations issued to treaty tribe members fishing throughout the ceded waters under the 1836 treaty. After the decision in federal court, that was no longer necessary.

The tribes' theory for the litigation was straightforward. A treaty was a conveyance or grant of land from the Indians to the United States. Grants are to be construed narrowly. Thus, if the treaty was silent with respect to the Indians' right to fish commercially in the Great Lakes, the law presumes that the Indians retained that right and did not cede it to the United States along with the cession of their aboriginal territory. The Indians also argued that the meaning of Article 13 of the treaty included the right to fish commercially in the Great Lakes. The tribes had to show, however, that they in fact enjoyed the use of the fishery resource, that the fishery provided a substantial amount of their food resources, and that they would likely not have survived without the right to fish in the Great Lakes. In other words, the Indians had to show their historic dependence on the fishery resource in order to demonstrate that it was a right they enjoyed prior to entering into the treaty. To establish those facts, the tribes and the United States retained expert witnesses—anthropologists/archaeologists and ethnohistorians—to explain to the court the facts and circumstances surrounding the treaty transaction in 1836. Treaties are often ambiguous and require explanation in order to discern the Indians' understanding of what was being accomplished through the treaty transaction. Indeed, there is ample law requiring courts to construe treaties consistent with the Indians' understanding and to resolve ambiguities in their favor.[2] These cases rely on the fact that there was always disproportionate bargaining power between the United States and the Indian treaty signatories, in part because the treaties were drafted by the representatives of the United States, who were literate and understood the meaning and nuances of words used in the treaty better than the Indians. After all, the Indians came from an oral, not a literate, tradition.

The state's view of the 1836 treaty was different, of course. The state's principal expert was a historian who specialized in the history of labor unions but also had studied the life and times of Henry Rowe Schoolcraft, the U.S. treaty commissioner who led the treaty negotiations with the tribes in 1836. His views were not accepted by the court, primarily because his knowledge of Schoolcraft allowed him to opine about the motives of the United States but were not particularly helpful in attempting to understand the meaning of the transaction to the Indians. The state seized on one article in the treaty that related to the potential removal of the Ottawa and Chippewa from Michigan to Minnesota. The removal policy of the United States, near and dear to the heart of President Andrew Jackson, was in effect from about 1820 to 1840.[3] Under that policy, Indians in the east were physically removed to lands in the west, ahead of advancing non-Indian settlement. As U.S. citizens systematically settled the country from east to west, the policy had to be abandoned. Although the 1836 treaty did not require removal, as some treaties in the south did, it nonetheless referred to removal as a possibility if the Indians wanted to move, and it authorized an official scouting party to visit Minnesota, where it was contemplated they might wind up. The state seized on this provision and coupled it with a mental intent requirement that was unknown in the law and unsupported by the cases. The state contended that the Indians had to have intended to reserve the fishing right at the time of the treaty and that this was not possible since they were shortly going to be living in Minnesota.

After a four-week trial that occurred over the course of one year in 1978, Judge Noel P. Fox issued a mammoth opinion, covering more than one hundred pages (two columns per page) in the official court reporter, upholding the treaty right and rejecting the state's contentions.[4] The court concluded that the Indians did in fact enjoy the right to fish commercially in the Great Lakes with gill nets and that the state lacked authority to regulate the Indians in the exercise of that right because the tribes, which are governments, were already regulating the exercise of the right by their members. The decision was a blockbuster when it was issued. There had been supportive case law regarding treaty interpretation prior to the Fox decision, but nothing in the modern era except for a similar case in the state of Washington that was decided in the early 1970s.[5] However, the Washington case involved a different set of treaties and contained much more explicit language regarding the fishing right. The so-called Stevens treaties at issue in *United States v. Washington* contained language reserving "the right of taking fish, at all usual and accustomed grounds and stations . . . in common with all citizens of the territory."[6] Thus, *United States v. Michigan* went farther to uphold a treaty right than the Washington case, because the 1836 treaty was comparatively silent about the right.

The aftermath of the treaty litigation in Michigan has been life-altering. While there remains an Indian commercial harvest, there is very little, if any, non-Indian commercial harvest in Michigan's Great Lakes waters. In effect, the commercial harvest was shifted from non-Indians to the tribes' fishermen. Since the Fox decision, the treaty tribes have developed significant in-house capacity to regulate the fishery. The tribes have their own biologists and technicians who monitor the fishery and determine the condition of the stocks. They also employ conservation officers to patrol the Great Lakes and oversee the activities of tribal fishermen to be certain they comply with applicable tribal fishing regulations. Finally, the tribes have courts that hear cases regarding violations of tribal regulations.

When *United States v. Michigan* was filed, the discord and animosity between the state and the tribes was palpable. Neither lawyers nor biologists for the tribes and the state could carry on a civil conversation. More than thirty years later, the state and the tribes generally work well together as they jointly manage the Great Lakes fishery resource. Of course, there are always opportunities for disagreements and misunderstandings, but there is generally increasing respect shown from and to both sides. The effect of the litigation has been to bring more resources to the Great Lakes. The tribal governments have been strengthened due to the added responsibility of regulating their fishermen and managing the fishery resource, albeit on a shared basis, and the relationship between the tribes and the state has slowly improved as the various governments learn to work together with a common goal of protecting and enhancing the Great Lakes fishery resource.

Prelude: Great Lakes Fishing Rights

In 1973, the United States filed a lawsuit in the U.S. District Court for the Western District of Michigan against the state of Michigan entitled *United States v. Michigan.* The United States sued on behalf of itself and the Bay Mills Indian Community "to protect the tribe's rights to fish in certain waters of the Great Lakes" and to enjoin state interference with those rights.[1] Bay Mills and the Sault Ste. Marie Tribe of Chippewa Indians intervened as plaintiffs.

After a trial, the district court held that the tribes retained "the right . . . to fish in the waters of the Great Lakes and connecting waters ceded by the Treaty of 1836."[2] Article 13 of the 1836 treaty provided, "The Indians stipulate for the right of hunting on the lands ceded, together with the other usual privileges of occupancy, until the land is required for settlement." The court held that the limiting condition in Article 13—until the land is required for settlement—"was not intended to affect Indian fishing," since it "is not possible to 'settle' the Great Lakes."[3]

Following the district court's ruling, the Grand Traverse Band of Ottawa and Chippewa Indians, whose status as a federally recognized Indian tribe had been reaffirmed recently by the Bureau of Indian Affairs, intervened as an additional plaintiff to participate in future proceedings in the case. On appeal, the Sixth Circuit Court of Appeals affirmed that the "treaty-guaranteed fishing rights preserved to the Indians in the 1836 Treaty . . . continue to the present day as federally created and federally protected rights."[4] However, the court held that the state could regulate Indian fishing under certain circumstances and remanded the case to the district court for further proceedings regarding the permissible scope of state regulation.

In 1983, Bay Mills, Sault Tribe, and Grand Traverse filed a motion to allocate the Great Lakes fishery between themselves and the state. The court allowed various non-Indian sport and commercial fishing organizations to participate in the proceedings as *amici curiae.* In March 1985, after lengthy negotiations, all parties and most amici signed an agreement for entry of a consent decree that would be effective for fifteen years. The court adopted the decree in May 1985.[5]

In 1994, Congress reaffirmed the status of the Little River Band of Ottawa Indians and the Little Traverse Bay Bands of Odawa Indians as federally recognized Indian tribes. In 1998 and 1999, respectively, Little River and Little Traverse intervened as plaintiffs in *United States v. Michigan* to participate in future proceedings in the case, especially renegotiation of the 1985 decree. In 2000, after lengthy negotiations involving the United States, the five tribes, the state, and amici curiae, the court entered a twenty-year consent decree providing for the regulation, allocation, and management of the Great Lakes fishery.

CHAPTER 8

United States v. Michigan, Western District of Michigan, Case No. M26-73 C.A.

Marc Slonim
Ziontz, Chestnut, Varnell, Berley and Slonim, Seattle, Washington

The Inland Phase of the Case

Following the district court's 1979 decision affirming their Great Lakes fishing rights, the tribes began to adopt formal regulations authorizing their members to exercise reserved hunting, fishing, trapping, and gathering rights in certain inland areas ceded in the Treaty of 1836. Although the tribes' regulations were similar in many respects to Michigan fish and game laws, there were some differences in seasons and bag limits, and the tribes did not require their members to obtain Michigan licenses or otherwise comply with Michigan fish and game laws when exercising their reserved rights. The exercise of inland rights was of vital importance to the tribes in their efforts to maintain their traditions, culture, and identity as Indian people. Along with the Great Lakes fishery, inland hunting, fishing, trapping, and gathering had been the economic mainstay of the tribes in the nineteenth century and well into the twentieth, and these activities remained central to their religious and cultural traditions at the turn of the twenty-first century.

On September 17, 2003, the state defendants filed a motion in *United States v. Michigan* for leave to file a counterclaim against the tribes. In their motion, the defendants asserted, "The parties . . . have . . . a good-faith dispute over the existence of *any* Treaty-reserved usufructuary rights under the 1836 Treaty of Washington apart from the Great Lakes and connecting waters." Noting that all of the tribes had adopted tribal codes authorizing their members to engage in inland hunting and fishing activities, the defendants asserted that they "deny such usufructuary rights exist except for on any federal lands that have *never* passed out of federal control and on which the exercise of those rights is not inconsistent with the purpose for federal ownership" (emphasis added). According to the state defendants, all other lands ceded in the 1836 treaty had been "required for settlement" within the meaning of Article 13.

Upon receipt of the defendants' motion, the tribes initiated a series of consultations among themselves, with the United States, and with the state defendants, to determine how to respond. The tribes were particularly interested in knowing whether the state defendants would agree to a schedule of case management that would afford the tribes a reasonable opportunity to prepare their case on the merits. After receiving assurances on this and other matters, the tribes stipulated that the defendants' motion could be granted, and the counterclaim was filed in November 2003. In January 2004, the tribes filed a joint reply to the counterclaim, in which they elected not to assert sovereign immunity but, instead, to defend against the counterclaim on the merits. The tribes' joint reply admitted that they had adopted tribal codes authorizing their members to exercise Article 13 rights on certain inland lands and waters, but it denied that the treaty right was limited to federal lands that have never passed out of federal control.

The tribes' reply did not seek affirmative relief but simply requested that the district court enter judgment against the defendants and in favor of the tribes on the counterclaim. Thus, the counterclaim and the tribes' joint reply framed a single threshold issue arising from the tribes' exercise of inland hunting and fishing rights under the 1836 treaty: whether such rights are limited to federal lands that have never passed out of federal control. The United States agreed with the tribes' position and filed a supplemental complaint so that this issue could be resolved as to all parties.

The Tribes' Theory of the Case

In addition to large portions of Lakes Michigan, Huron, and Superior, the Ottawa and Chippewa ceded some 13,700,000 acres of inland lands and waters to the United States in the Treaty of 1836. When the state filed its counterclaim in late 2003, the ceded territory contained millions of acres of forests—many embraced in the state and national forest systems—as well as other undeveloped lands and innumerable navigable lakes and streams. Many of these lands had once been disposed of by the federal government, typically in large land grants to railroads or internal improvement companies. The lands were then transferred to timber companies and logged in the latter part of the nineteenth or early part of the twentieth centuries. There was no market for most of these lands after they were logged, and they were ultimately reacquired by the state or federal government as forest lands or held by timber companies as commercial forest land. The United States and the tribes did not believe these lands or the navigable lakes and streams embraced within the 1836 cession had been required for settlement within the meaning of Article 13 of the treaty.

The state's theory of the case was premised on the notion that whenever the federal government disposed of land—no matter to whom and no matter for what purpose—the land was ipso facto required for settlement. In contrast, the United States and the tribes held the theory that only lands actually used for settlement were "required for settlement" within the meaning of the treaty. The United States and the tribes believed that both parties to the treaty—the United States, on one hand, and the Ottawa and Chippewa, on the other—would have understood the treaty in this way.

To develop their case, the tribes retained a number of expert witnesses. The experts were asked to address the following matters.

Ecology of the 1836 cession. The ecology of the 1836 cession formed an important backdrop to the case. As a result of climate and soil conditions, much of the cession was not suitable for agricultural development, the principal form of settlement activity envisioned in the 1830s. To the contrary, large portions of the cession were valuable primarily for their timber, minerals, fish, and wildlife. The activities associated with these resources—hunting, trapping, fishing, logging, and mining—were not, by themselves, considered "settlement" activities at the time of the treaty.

Ottawa and the Chippewa band structure, use and importance of natural resources, attachment to the land and band territories, and land use concepts. These topics presented another critical component of the tribes' case. Although the various Ottawa and Chippewa bands within the 1836 cession confronted different circumstances and had different motivations in approaching the treaty—differences that were deliberately exploited by American treaty makers—they were united in a common desire to remain in their Michigan homeland and to secure access to natural resources that were essential to their subsistence, culture, and economy. Moreover, their own territorial and land use concepts would be central to their understanding of Article 13. They were familiar with "settlement" and could observe it on the ground, as immigrants arrived to build cabins or houses and develop farms and towns; it was not measured by the filing of paper titles in distant land offices or by massive land grants to railroads and internal improvement companies.

The fur trade. The fur trade was the most important forum for interaction between the Ottawa and Chippewa and European Americans during the period leading up to the treaty, and the relations between Indians and traders—familial, personal, and commercial—would be central to the treaty-making process. The traders sought (and obtained) enormous profits from the treaty, but they also had an interest in securing the ability of the Ottawa and Chippewa to remain in Michigan and to continue to harvest and supply natural resources to traders and settlers alike.

Prior Indian treaties. Since 1789, the United States had entered into many treaties with Indian tribes that secured the Indians' right to hunt and fish on ceded lands. Several of these treaties also addressed non-Indian settlement. A thorough understanding of these treaties was essential to the tribes' case regarding the 1836 treaty. One of the lessons these earlier treaties taught was that if the United States intended to condition the exercise of Indian usufructuary rights on ceded lands remaining the property of the United States—as the state argued the United States intended to do in the 1836 treaty—it could use explicit language to accomplish this. These prior treaties also showed that even when the United States used such explicit language, it told the Indians that they could continue using the ceded lands until Americans actually settled on the land. This standard—actual settlement—was the most practical and easiest to understand, since it involved observable activities on the land. It was also the standard adopted *expressly* in the 1836 treaty. Finally, it was apparent from earlier treaty provisions regarding non-Indian settlement that the term *settlement* did not embrace such activities as hunting, trapping, fishing, logging, and mining but referred, instead, to the activities of Americans taking up their residence, clearing and plowing fields, and opening farms and building towns on the land.

Indian removal policy. Congress enacted the Indian Removal Act in 1830, which enshrined the policy of attempting to remove Indians from lands east of the Mississippi to the west. For the tribes' purposes in interpreting the 1836 treaty, it was important to understand that the removal policy was not monolithic; it was applied most rigorously—and with the most horrific consequences—on agricultural lands in the southeast and in the Ohio River valley, where the federal government was either unable or unwilling to resist the settlement pressures of non-Indians. In other regions, including northern Michigan, where settlement pressures were either nonexistent or far less severe, federal officials paid lip service to removal but did not seek to force removal over Indian opposition. The Second Seminole War, which broke out in late 1835 on the eve of the negotiation of the 1836 treaty with the Ottawa and Chippewa, was an object lesson in the risks associated with attempting to force Indian removal. These and other factors explored by the tribes' experts help explain why the federal government was willing to include provisions in the 1836 treaty that provided for the long-term occupancy of the Ottawa and Chippewa in their northern Michigan homelands.

Public land laws and the meaning of "settlement." The term *settlement* was not unknown to the law when it was used in the 1836 treaty. In addition to its use in Indian treaties, the term had been used frequently in federal laws prohibiting "settlement" on the public domain and extending preemption rights to actual "settlers." The tribes engaged an expert in the history of federal public lands to research and analyze these laws, the congressional debates leading to their enactment, the regulations promulgated to implement them, and the judicial and administrative decisions interpreting them. The results of this research showed a widespread understanding among senators, congressmen, federal officials, and the courts that "settlement" involved the residential occupation of land and that activities such as hunting, trapping, fishing, logging, and mining did not, by themselves, amount to "settlement."

The "ordinary" meaning of "settlement." In an 1837 letter, Henry Schoolcraft, the sole American commissioner at the 1836 treaty negotiations, wrote that in his discussions with the Ottawa and Chippewa, he had used the term *settlement* in its "ordinary meaning, to denote the act or state of being settled, and as answering, as nearly as the terms of the two languages would permit, to the tenor of my agreement with them." Accordingly, to shed additional light on the meaning of *settlement,* the tribes asked its experts to explore the "ordinary meaning" of the term—how it was defined in dictionaries at the time, how it was used in ordinary discourse, how it was used by Schoolcraft and other officials involved in treaty, and how it might have been translated into Ottawa and Chippewa and understood by the Indians. Their research confirmed that "settlement" was widely understood to involve the residential occupation of land and the conversion of wild land into fields, farms, and towns. Land speculators—who purchased land to hold for future resale—were not "settlers," and neither were hunters, trappers, fishermen, loggers, or miners. This understanding was shared by Indians and non-Indians alike.

Events leading to the treaty. There is a relatively detailed historical record of the events leading to the negotiation of the 1836 treaty in Washington. The tribes asked their experts to explore this record in an effort to shed additional light on the motivations and positions of the Indian and non-Indian parties. This research indicated that, despite a boom in land sales in the period leading up to the treaty, there was little American interest in settlement within the cession. Rather, the principal American interest lay in acquiring access to the timber, fish, and mineral resources of northern Michigan as well as control of strategic locations along the border with British Canada. For their part, the Ottawa and Chippewa were strongly opposed to selling their lands and removing from Michigan. Some bands sought to sell marginal lands to obtain funds to pay trader debts, open schools, and obtain agricultural assistance, and others were willing to cede lands in exchange for the continued operation of blacksmith shops. However, even those who were willing to cede lands insisted on reservations and the right to hunt on ceded lands until they were "occupied." Schoolcraft was able to exploit these divisions in order to trigger negotiations for and ultimately secure an enormous land cession, one from which he and his relatives would benefit both financially and politically. In order to minimize opposition to the cession, he worked actively behind the scenes, along with prominent traders, to manipulate the Indian delegations that would travel to Washington for the treaty negotiations. In addition, he circulated a "power of sale" to be signed by Indians in Michigan authorizing the cession, with the extent of the cession and the amount to be received for it to be determined in Washington. According to the power of sale, the privileges of hunting and residing on the land would be secured "until it is surveyed & sold by the government."

Negotiation of the treaty. The tribes asked their experts to explore the available evidence regarding the actual negotiation of the treaty in Washington. Although the treaty journal is very limited, correspondence from some of the non-Indian participants during and after the negotiations shed light on the proceedings. In the period leading up to the treaty, there were several references to what would become Article 13, each with a somewhat different formulation of the limiting condition. Schoolcraft first used the phrase "until [the land] is required for settlement" in a letter of January 13, 1836, in which he suggested that the Indians could remain on nonagricultural lands for many years. When he opened the treaty negotiations, he stated that the Indians would be permitted to reside and hunt on the ceded lands "till they are wanted." In post-treaty correspondence, Schoolcraft made clear that Article 13 was critical to the Indians' acceptance of the large land cession sought by the United States; it was the central mechanism by which the U.S. desire to acquire the land was reconciled with the Indians' desire to remain in Michigan and secure access to the wide range of natural resources they needed for their subsistence, economy, and culture. The record thus suggested that Schoolcraft carefully crafted the final version of Article 13 to obtain the Indians' assent to the treaty. Given the limited agricultural potential of the cession, preserving the right to hunt and the other usual privileges of occupancy until the land was "required for settlement" offered significant protection to the Indians, protection on which they were invited to rely and did rely in signing the treaty.

Senate amendments to the treaty. In ratifying the treaty, the Senate made a number of amendments, the most important of which was a change in the tenure of the Indians' reservations. In the original treaty, these reservations were permanent. However, following the Senate amendments, the reservations would last only for five years "unless the United States grant them permission to remain on said lands for a longer period." The tribes asked their experts to investigate the Senate amendments and the process by which the Indians gave their assent to them. The historical record revealed that there was strenuous opposition to the change in the tenure of the reservations and that the government resorted to a variety of tactics to overcome that opposition, such as assembling a vast quantity of goods to be distributed to the Indians if they gave their assent. The key, however, was Article 13. To convince the Ottawa and Chippewa to agree to the change in the tenure of the reservations, Schoolcraft assured the Indians that they would be able to remain on their lands under the protections afforded by Article 13. Once again, the Indians were invited to rely and did rely on those protections in agreeing to the treaty.

Removal efforts. In the period following the treaty, the government sought to persuade the Ottawa and Chippewa to remove to lands southwest of the Missouri River. In exploring those efforts, the tribes' experts found that Ottawa and Chippewa opposition to removal, which had been apparent in the period leading up to the treaty, remained firm in the period following the treaty. Notably, Ottawa and Chippewa opposition to removal reflected both an emotional attachment to their Michigan homeland and a commitment to a way of life that entailed hunting, fishing, trapping, and gathering—the very activities that were protected by Article 13 of the treaty.

Practical construction by the parties. In interpreting a treaty, courts will consider the practical construction of the treaty by the parties. Accordingly, the tribes asked their experts to explore the practical construction of Article 13 by the parties to the 1836 treaty. For their part, the Ottawa and Chippewa consistently exercised their rights on unoccupied lands within the cession. The transfer of title to a railroad, internal improvement company, or logging company did not result in the cessation of Indian hunting and fishing, and no one ever suggested it should. On one occasion shortly after the treaty was ratified, the rush of non-Indians seeking to settle on Indian lands north of the Grand River led to a discussion of Article 13 by Schoolcraft and an opinion by the U.S. attorney general. Although their opinions provided some support for the state's interpretation of Article 13—suggesting that the Indians' rights would end as soon as the lands were either surveyed and sold or actually disposed of to individuals—they were expressed in the context of actual settlement activities and did not address the effect of dispositions to railroads, internal improvement companies, or others where settlement never took place. Moreover, there was no evidence that these opinions were ever communicated to the Indians or applied in practice.

Land use within the 1836 cession after the treaty. For these and other reasons, the tribes believed their Article 13 rights were secured unless the land was actually required for settlement. The question then became whether the lands within the cession were required for that purpose. The tribes asked a historian to explore land use within the cession from the time of the treaty to the time of the lawsuit to answer this question. As briefly described earlier, the land use history indicated that many of the lands and waters on which the tribes sought to exercise their Article 13 rights—primarily state and national forest lands, commercial timberlands, and navigable lakes and streams—had never been used for settlement within the meaning of the 1836 treaty and, as a matter of law, *could* not be used for settlement at the time of the litigation.

The Outcome of the Litigation

The United States, the tribes, and the state prepared to litigate the case in 2004 and 2005. The parties collectively identified seventeen expert witnesses and eleven lay witnesses, including tribal elders, resource managers, and leaders. They exchanged tens of thousands of pages of documents, and their experts prepared hundreds of pages of opening and rebuttal reports. Weeks of depositions were conducted in Detroit, Lansing, Traverse City, Chicago, Boulder, and Berkeley. The tribes and the United States successfully resisted motions to intervene by one of the groups that had participated in the Great Lakes phase of the case as an amicus curiae and by several individuals. In a contested motion, the district court refused to permit the state to relitigate its claim that the 1855 Treaty of Detroit abrogated the tribe's Article 13 rights, a claim the court had rejected in the Great Lakes phase of the case. The case was set for trial in January 2006.

In the spring of 2005, the tribes tentatively approached the state about the possibility of settlement. The parties and the amici curiae held an initial meeting to explore settlement options in early July and began settlement discussions in earnest in the fall. The parties made sufficient progress to postpone the January trial date and continued working on settlement in 2006. By October of that year, the parties, with the support of the amici curiae, had completed a detailed agreement in principle, in which they agreed to resolve the case through the submission of a consent decree for the court's consideration. It took another year to draft and finalize the consent decree, which was entered by the court on November 2, 2007.

The Inland Consent Decree recognizes the existence and defines the extent of the tribes' inland Article 13 rights on lands and waters within the 1836 cession, including over 4,500,000 acres of public lands and waters, private lands and waters in the state's commercial forest land program, lands and waters owned by the tribes or their members (or their members' spouses), and other lands and waters open to public hunting and fishing or on which the tribes or their members obtain permission to hunt or fish. Under the decree, it is up to the tribes to regulate their members' exercise of inland Article 13 rights, and state regulation is prohibited.

The decree contains detailed provisions regarding the manner in which such rights may be exercised on various categories of lands and waters, as well as restrictions on commercial harvests, hunting and fishing at particular locations, the use of certain specially regulated fishing methods, and big game hunting. The decree also includes tagging and reporting requirements for certain species and allocates available harvests of elk, bear, and sturgeon. The decree provides for and sets parameters governing gathering on, access to, and the construction of temporary structures on state lands by tribal members. Among other topics, additional provisions of the decree address natural resource assessment activities; restoration, reclamation, and enhancement projects; consultation and exchange of information; and law enforcement and dispute resolution. Unlike the allocation and management decrees for the Great Lakes, the Inland Consent Decree is a permanent decree. As this brief description of the decree makes clear, it went far beyond the limited issue framed in the litigation—whether the inland Article 13 right was limited to lands that had never passed out of federal control—and provided a comprehensive definition of the right and mechanisms to fully implement it.

The parties' ability to resolve these issues by agreement rested in part on the court's prior rulings regarding the Great Lakes fishery and the parties' successful negotiations to implement those rulings. It rested as well on the outcome of treaty hunting, fishing, and gathering litigation in Wisconsin and Minnesota. Apart from their legal significance, the outcome of those cases indicated that Indian treaty rights could be implemented in a manner that protected the core interests of the tribes, protected and enhanced natural resources, and did not significantly disrupt non-Indian harvest opportunities. The parties drew on those lessons in crafting an agreement that permanently secured to the tribes their rights to hunt, fish, trap, and gather under Article 13 of the 1836 treaty.

CHAPTER 9

The Treaties of St. Peters (1837) and La Pointe (1842)

Chippewa and Dakota Hostilities

During the eighteenth and the first third of the nineteenth centuries, warfare between the Chippewa and Dakota dominated events on the far northwestern frontier and particularly the relations between both tribes and the United States. The origin of these hostilities between the Chippewa and Dakota people seems to be associated with Chippewa incursions into the western Lake Superior country during the mid-seventeenth century.[1] Sustained conflict, however, did not begin until the mid-eighteenth century, as the Chippewa expanded south and west of Lake Superior from villages at La Pointe and Fond du Lac. In 1740 they captured Sandy Lake from the Dakota, and a village founded there became the staging ground for assaults against the Mdewakanton Dakota on the Mississippi and lower Minnesota rivers and the Wahpeton Dakota who occupied the middle reaches of the Minnesota. Meanwhile, the Pillager Chippewa established themselves at Leech Lake, and bands formed that were centered at Cass, Winnibigoshish, and Red Lakes and Rainy River (see map 4). These Chippewa pushed west on a wide front against the Sisseton, Yankton, and Yanktonai Dakota who occupied the upper portions of the Minnesota River, the Red River of the North, and the plains to the west.[2]

In the *Atlas of Great Lakes Indian History,* Tanner shows that there were two separate areas of Chippewa-Dakota conflict in 1768. The first was the lower Chippewa River valley between the Flambeau and Mississippi rivers. The other was a broad front from the junction of the Crow Wing and Mississippi rivers north to the Canadian border.[3] By and large, this warfare had little to do with Americans except that it disrupted the Indian trade and missionary efforts. For these reasons, U.S. Indian policy was designed to discourage Chippewa-Dakota warfare in the western Great Lakes region. Since American officials on the scene had very little understanding of the nature of intertribal war or its objectives, they saw it as a consequence of barbarism and territorial aggression.

Unlike war in the context of nation-states, tribal war seldom advanced political objectives. It was, most often, personal, motivated by revenge for past killings and insults. Since there were few mechanisms through which such conflicts could be resolved, tribal war tended to consist of long periods of low intensity but deadly conflict, punctuated by brief periods of truce. During such times of peace, the combatants might trade, feast, and even intermarry.

In the normal case, Chippewa-Dakota war was conducted by small parties of kinsmen going forth from their respective villages to the territory of the enemy, where they laid in wait hoping to ambush even smaller groups. A successful raid was one in which revenge and prestige were obtained by killing an enemy without the war party suffering loss of life. Tribal warfare frequently involved killing, mutilation, rape, looting, and kidnapping. Even though American traders, missionaries, and government agents were neither participants nor victims of the Chippewa-Dakota hostilities, they were shocked and terrified by the way the war was conducted. Typically, while the Chippewa-Dakota war resulted in a very small loss of life on an annual basis, some of the largest pitched battles resulted in a hundred or so casualties. These numbers could, of course, be catastrophic in the context of the small population aggregations found among both Chippewa and Dakota.

Harold Hickerson has made a detailed study of the ethnohistory of the Chippewa-Dakota warfare.[4] He contends that the conflict was a classic one pitting Chippewa hunter-gatherers against Dakota agriculturists. The former were arrayed through the northern boreal forest, the latter on the margins of the prairies to the south and west. Both groups hunted white-tailed deer,

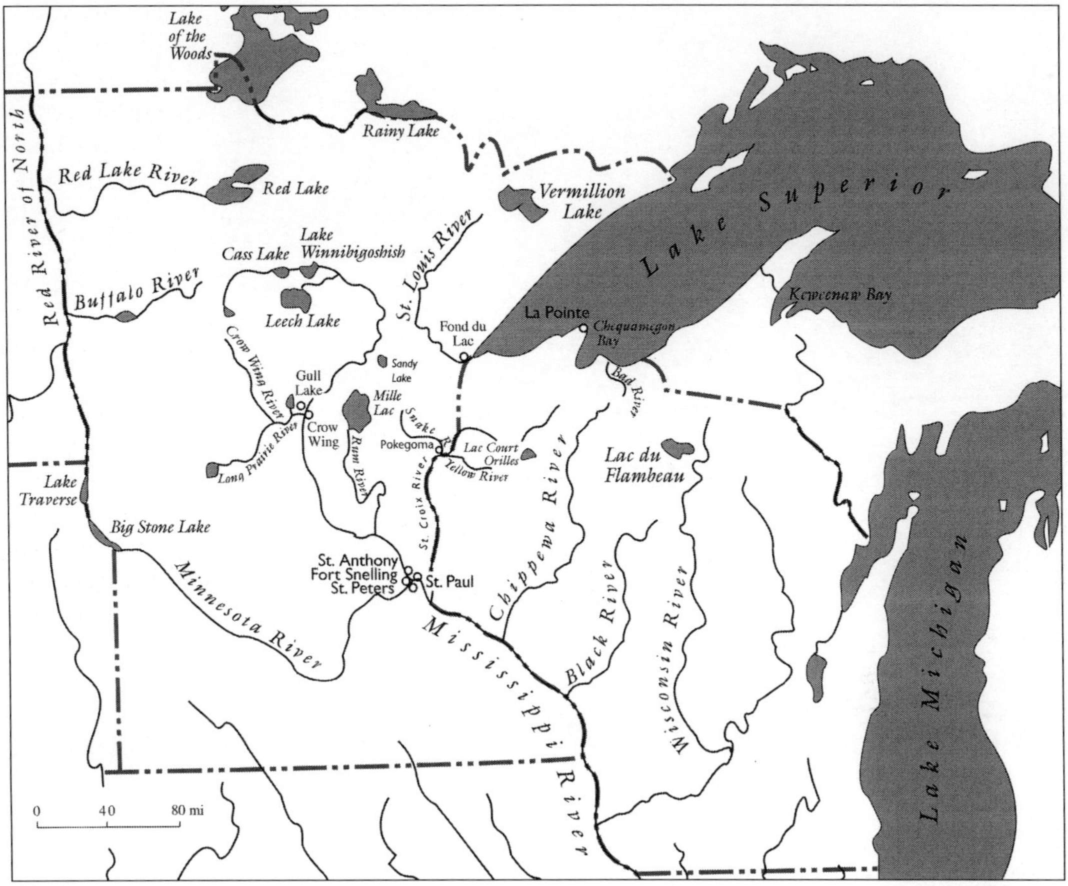

Map 4. Nineteenth-century place-names, Minnesota and Wisconsin, circa 1840

which occurred very abundantly along the ecological transition zone between the forest and the prairies. This transition zone stretched from Lake of the Woods south through western Minnesota, then east through central Minnesota and southern Wisconsin. The ecological transition zone varies in width from fifty to one hundred miles.[5]

Because of the abundance of deer and other animals, both Chippewa and Dakota hunters were drawn to this same narrow band of mixed prairie and woodland. Hunting parties, of course, encountered each other and fought, so that the transition zone was, in effect, a no-man's-land separating the respective tribes. Since it was a dangerous place to be, it received less hunting pressure; game resources increased, and the zone became all the more attractive for the temerarious hunter.

Map 5 shows that the contested zone was traversed by several rivers: the Chippewa, Red Cedar, St. Croix, Rum, and Mississippi. These became war roads for both Chippewa and Dakota war parties crossing into the territory of the other for quick violent raids. Except in the north, where the Pillagers and their allies succeeded in pushing the Dakota west of the Red River, the battle zone was static. The closer to the transition zone a group was, the greater was the danger of attack from opposing groups. Until 1840 the Ojibwe bands living along the St. Croix, Snake, and Rum rivers and those living at Mille Lacs, Leech, and Gull lakes bore the brunt of Dakota raiding.

The Treaty of Prairie du Chien

On August 5, 1825, Commissioners William Clark and Lewis Cass assembled three thousand

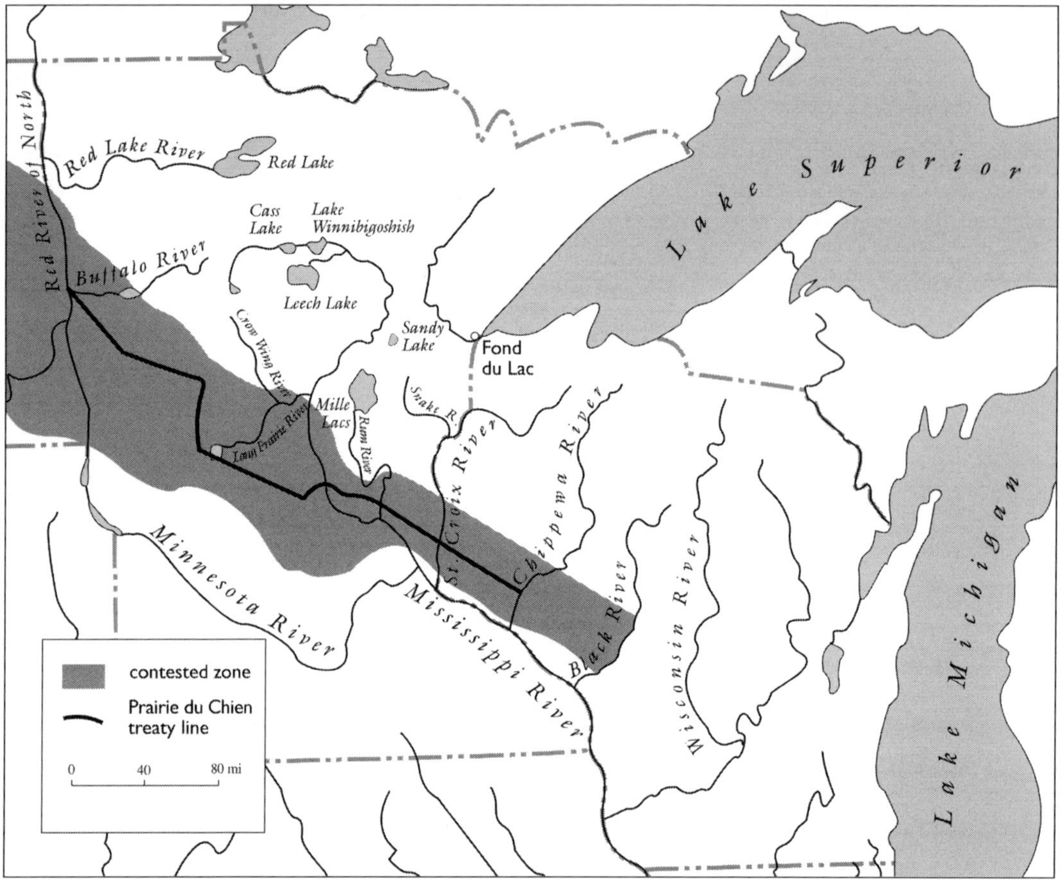

Map 5. Chippewa-Dakota contested territory, 1830–50. (Adapted from Hickerson 1970, map 4.)

Indians at Prairie du Chien at the junction of the Mississippi and Wisconsin rivers, with the object of promoting peace among the tribes of the northwest and establishing boundaries between each tribe.[6] Chiefs representing the Chippewa, Winnebago, Menominee, Dakota, Sac, Fox, Iowa, Ottawa, Potawatomi, and Illinois were represented at the council. Eventually all of the northwestern Chippewa bands were present, including the Mille Lacs, who were represented by Nagonabe (Najwiondabee). Since the United States believed Indian warfare resulted from territorial disputes, the solution seemed to be to get the tribes to define and recognize territories of exclusive use. Thus, the commissioners made the following suggestion: "We therefore propose to you to make peace together and to agree upon fixed boundaries for your country within which each tribe should hunt and over which others shall not pass without their consent."[7]

After two days of difficult negotiation, the Dakota and Chippewa agreed on a boundary line between their respective territorial claims. The line essentially followed the forest-prairie boundary from the Missouri River to the Chippewa River (see map 5). Article 13 of the Treaty of Prairie du Chien reserved tribal sovereignty over resources within each tribal estate but also pledged the right of reciprocal use with permission.

> It is understood by all the tribes, party, hereto, that no tribe shall hunt within the acknowledged limits of any other without their assent, but it being the sole objective of this arrangement to perpetuate a peace among them, and amicable relations being now restored, the chiefs of all the tribes have expressed a determination, cheerfully to allow a reciprocal right of hunting on the lands of one another,

permission being first asked and obtained, as before provided for.[8]

Subsequent to the Prairie du Chien Treaty, the government negotiated the Treaty at Fond du Lac in 1826, in which the Lake Superior Chippewa agreed to the terms of the Prairie du Chien Treaty. In the next year, the Treaty of Butte des Mortes established the southern and eastern boundary between the Chippewa, Menominee, and Winnebago. These three separate, but related, treaties defined the country of each tribe, including the Chippewa.

In retrospect, the Treaty of Prairie du Chien had little effect on intertribal warfare. In fact, the Dakota and Chippewa hardly paused in their well-established cycle of raid and counterraid. In effect, the Prairie du Chien Treaty reaffirmed the ecological boundary already well known to both Dakota and Chippewa. As a practical matter, the contested zone continued to draw hunters from both groups, and they continued to clash, kindling new rounds of blood feuds. The Dakota-Chippewa conflict did not involve Americans; in fact, both the Dakota and Chippewa resented their interference.[9] In 1837 Col. Zachary Taylor wrote to his superior, General Jones, saying that it was a mistake to try to stop Chippewa-Dakota warfare, pointing out that it would be better to allow them to settle their own problems.[10] Even the surveying of the Chippewa-Dakota boundary and the strident urging of peace by government agents had little impact. After a final spasm of fighting between 1838 and 1841, hostile engagements dwindled dramatically, with the final battles fought on the plains west of the Red River in the early 1850s.

The 1826 Treaty of Fond du Lac

The first nine articles of the Prairie du Chien Treaty define the territorial claims of the various tribal parties. By Article 10 the United States agreed to recognize these boundaries as they had been defined. General Clark, commissioner for the Prairie du Chien Treaty, explained to the Indians, "Your Great Father has not sent us here to ask anything of you. We want nothing, not the smallest piece of your land—not a single article of your property. We have come a great way to meet you for your own good and not for our benefit."[11] In directing the drawing of tribal boundaries between the Chippewa and their Dakota, Menominee, Illinois, Potawatomi, and Winnebago neighbors, the secretary of war, Lewis Cass, must have had in mind the partitioning of these Indian land claims for the purpose of future treaty making, since many of the land cessions of the following decades followed the Prairie du Chien "map."

Article 12 of the Prairie du Chien Treaty provided that the Chippewa would be assembled in the Lake Superior country the next summer so that the "objects" and "advantages" of the treaty could be explained to them.[12] The United States included this provision because it was particularly anxious that the Prairie du Chien peace provisions be explained to the Chippewa warriors who may not have been at Prairie du Chien and that the terms of the treaty be reaffirmed by the Lake Superior leaders. Mongozid, Weescoup, Muskoas, and Naubunaygerzhig signed the Prairie du Chien Treaty on behalf of the bands at Fond du Lac, a major staging point for parties raiding into Dakota territory. Since American settlements on the Great Lakes–Mississippi Valley frontier were extremely vulnerable to Chippewa military might, the American government was taking every means to protect its citizens.

When the time came to meet on Lake Superior, the United States took the opportunity to conduct a new treaty with the Chippewa. Michigan territorial governor Lewis Cass and the head of the Indian Office of the War Department, Thomas McKenney, were appointed commissioners for the treaty. In addition to the purpose mandated in 1825, Cass and McKenney were instructed to "impress the Indians in that remote region with some proper conception of our power and by means of its appearance among them to deter them from a repetition of these acts of violence which they have been in the practice of inflicting upon our citizens."[13] The commissioners were also to negotiate for the surrender of four Chippewa men who were accused of murdering American traders at Lake Pepin on the Mississippi. By the latter negotiations, it is clear that the United States believed it proper to deal with the misconduct of Indians as a sovereign affair, that is, as an extradition matter to be negotiated between the United States and the collected bands.

Thomas McKenney made an extensive journal of his travels from Washington to Fond du Lac, including descriptions of the people of Fond du Lac and a journal of the treaty negotiations.[14] After the usual pageantry and ceremony by which both the Chippewa and the United States signaled the official importance of the negotiations, Governor Cass explained to the Chippewa that the Great Father had sent him to inform them that he wished peace between the Chippewa and Dakotas, as they had agreed the previous year. The Great Father, he said, also wished them to give land to the half-breeds for cultivation and to permit Americans to prospect for copper. The mineral wealth and particularly the presence of copper in the Lake Superior country had been known since the days of the French explorers. The Cass expedition of 1820 confirmed this presence, but without a more systematic sampling, it was not possible to ascertain the quantity or extent of the resource. Cass also said that the Great Father would, in exchange, give the Chippewas goods each year as well as a school for their children.[15]

The journal is instructive as to the personal nature of the power relationship between the Great Father and the Chippewa. Although, in 1825, the Chippewa held vast military superiority in the northwest, the United States was confident of its own power. In explaining the importance of peace to the Chippewa, Governor Cass admonished them to refrain from war: "Your young men must obey this peace [Prairie du Chien Treaty] and your Great Father will consider as his enemy, anyone who takes up the tomahawk."[16] Likewise, the commissioners stressed the benefits of peaceful relations with the Great Father and his white children. Colonel McKenney told the Chippewa that the president was mild in peace. Aside from an extended discussion of problems concerning the surrender of the accused murderers of the American traders, the Chippewa were compliant with American requests. As a matter of course, speaker after Chippewa speaker pointed out the utter poverty of their people, expounding on their nakedness, starvation, and misery. While it was true that the decade between 1825 and 1835 was a difficult one for the Chippewa, these laments were likely more symbolic than literal.[17]

The treaty itself is, in fact, couched in personal terms, with the president and Congress giving things to the Chippewa. Article 5 stipulates that, "in consideration of their poverty," an annuity of two thousand dollars would be paid "as the Presidents may direct" and that the payment would continue at "the pleasure of the Congress." In Article 6 money was provided for education that would be expended "under the direction of the Presidents."[18]

For their part, the Chippewa granted the United States the right to prospect for minerals and, at the request of the United States, granted their half-blood relatives land on the St. Marys River in northern Michigan. They also acknowledged the jurisdiction of the United States over the Great Lakes country. Finally, by Article 2 the Chippewa agreed to send a delegation to Green Bay the next year to fix the boundary between themselves and the Menominee.

In the case of most treaties with Indian tribes, if the U.S. Senate chose to amend the treaty presented by the negotiators, the commissioners would be required to reassemble the chiefs and gain their assent to the changes. Perhaps because of the remoteness of the Lake Superior Chippewa, Cass and McKenney sought to eliminate this contingency through Article 7, which specified that Articles 4, 5, and 6 could be rejected by the president and Senate without affecting the validity of the other articles of the treaty. These specific articles covered the allocation of land grants to mixed bloods, the payment of two thousand dollars in annuities, and the payment of funds for education—in short, all the benefits to the Chippewa. Thus, the commissioners wrote the treaty in such a way that the president or Congress could reject all or part of their obligation to pay without impact on the obligations of the Chippewa under the treaty.

At the conclusion of the treaty, Colonel McKenney distributed medals to the chiefs. The medals bore, on one surface, the likeness of the Great Father and, on the other, a pair of hands holding a tomahawk with a pipe bowl attached opposite the blade, a "peace hatchet." These were hung about the necks of the chiefs by ribbons.

There are probably at least three important lessons the Chippewa learned in the course of negotiating the Fond du Lac Treaty. First, their welfare was contingent on the personal goodwill of the Great Father and depended on their willingness to accommodate the Great Father's white children. Second, the United States would deal with them as sovereign equals. Finally, treaty agreements flowed from one to another. This latter conclusion was evident because the 1826 treaty was mandated by the 1825 treaty and, in turn, called for another in 1827. What the Chippewa learned at one treaty was carried by them to the next. Likewise, it would have been their understanding that the Great Father had this same view of his ongoing relationship with his Chippewa children. The treaty arrangements had to be understood in the context of previous treaties.

Since they were on their home ground, ten Fond du Lac chiefs, as well as a large number of headmen, were present and signed the treaty. Included were Shingoop (Balsam), Mongozid (Loon's Foot), and Naubunaygezhig, who had also attended and signed the Treaty of Prairie du Chien. They were joined by seventy-one other Chippewa chiefs who represented thirteen different Lake Superior bands. These included bands from the entire south shore of Lake Superior from St. Marys River to Fond du Lac, as well as the bands from the interior of northern Wisconsin, including those from Lac du Flambeau, Lac Courte Oreilles, Vermilion Lake, Snake River, and the St. Croix River. These bands collectively were later known as the Chippewa of Lake Superior. Bands from Sandy Lake and Rainy Lake represented those later classified among the Chippewa of the Mississippi.

In their separate visits to St. Peters over the next few years, these Chippewa leaders complained to Indian agent Lawrence Taliaferro about a wide variety of problems. Paramount among these was the aggressive behavior of the Dakota. But although they complained about the Dakota, they also claimed that the United States had no jurisdiction over their affairs with this tribe.[19] In hope of fulfilling the peace provisions of the Treaty of Prairie du Chien, the United States began surveying and marking the boundary between the Dakota and Chippewa that was negotiated as part of the treaty. Both the Dakota and the Chippewa tore down the survey monuments because they found straight lines across the landscape offensive.[20]

The Chippewa also complained that pine logs were being cut by white men from their land on the Rum River and at the junction of the Snake and St. Croix rivers.[21] The fact that lumber operations and other activities by non-Indians were encroaching on unceded land was a growing problem for the government. In March 1834 Michigan territorial Indian agent Henry Schoolcraft investigated charges of timber theft and whiskey peddling on the St. Croix River, and in the fall, after the passage of the new Trade and Intercourse Act of June 30, 1834, he issued a circular to attempt to deal with this problem.[22] According to the circular, timber cutting required a permit, to be issued at Mackinac, that specified that compensation be paid to Indians. Further, all trespass by non-Indians was prohibited, as was hunting, fishing, and trapping by whites on Indian land.[23] When the Wisconsin territory was formed in 1837, territorial governor and de facto superintendent of Indian affairs Henry Dodge and American lumber interests lobbied Congress for a new treaty that would provide access to more land and timber resources.

The 1837 Treaty of St. Peters

Pressure from citizens and Wisconsin politicians in the years before 1836 led to a Senate bill authorizing a treaty of cession with the Chippewa that would give U.S. citizens access to valuable pine timber of north-central and western Wisconsin and to that portion of the present state of Minnesota that lies east of the Mississippi River (see map 6). The secretary of war, Lewis Cass, stated this to be the main objective of the proposed treaty but also believed that the land could eventually be sold to American settlers for agricultural purposes. He believed, erroneously, that the proposed purchase was "on the frontier" of the countries of both the Dakota and Chippewa and therefore "very unimportant to either." Cass hoped that the eventual establishment of American settlements along the Mississippi River would help separate the two warring tribes.[24] In the spring of 1837, General W. R. Smith and Wisconsin territorial governor Henry Dodge were appointed as treaty commissioners, and Ver Planck Van Antwerp was appointed as treaty secretary.[25]

The commissioner of Indian affairs, Carey

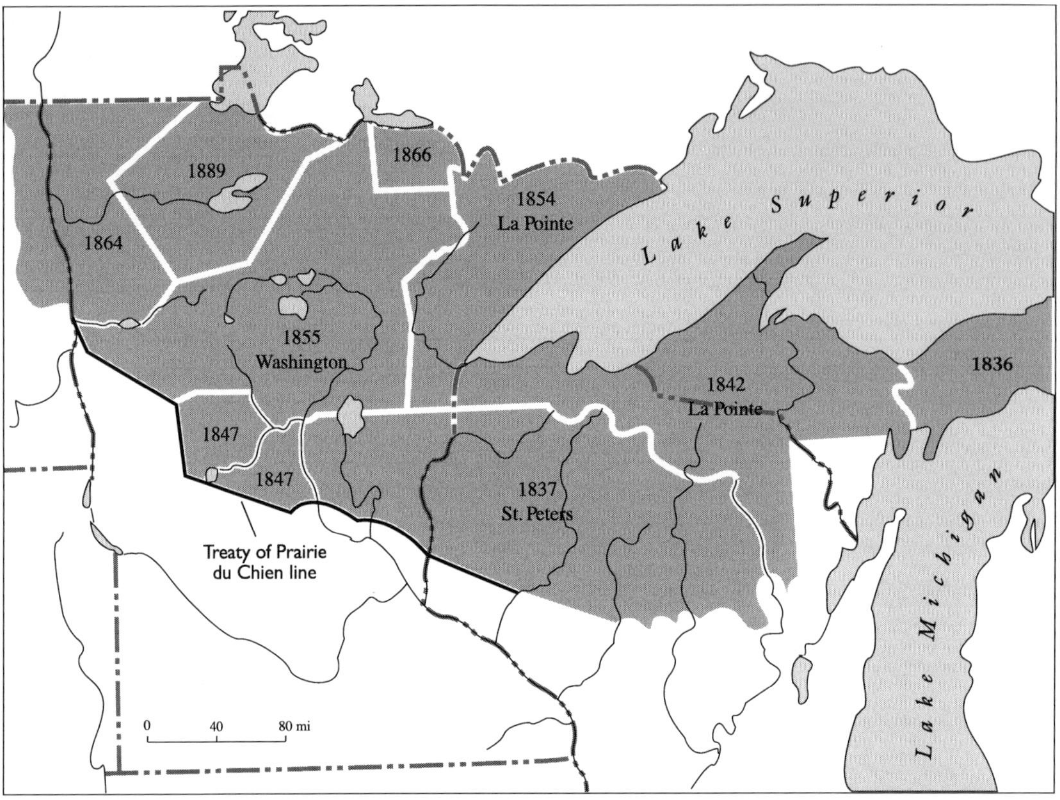

Map 6. Chippewa cessions: Michigan, Minnesota, and Wisconsin

Harris, issued the commissioners instructions reiterating that the main purpose of the treaty was to acquire land "valuable for its pine woods which cover it, but . . . unfit for cultivation." In exchange for the cession, the Indians were to be offered "money, provisions, agricultural and mechanical establishments, education and other means of improvement." These goods and services were "to be delivered at certain points in their own country at the expense of the United States." The commissioners were instructed to provide no reservations for individual Indians, but they could include an article covering trader debts and payment to half-breeds. Finally, they were to impress the Chippewa with the "absolute necessity of refraining from aggression on the Sioux [Dakota] or on our citizens."[26]

One of the other tasks of the commissioners was to try to ascertain if the Chippewa of Wisconsin and Minnesota would accept immigration of the Ottawa and Chippewa from Michigan who had agreed to explore a western removal in treaties concluded in 1836 and 1837. Apparently the western Chippewa refused, since by the fall of 1837, the United States closed out the option of the Michigan Chippewa to remove to the northwest.[27] The attempts to remove eastern Indians were part of a United States Indian policy during the 1830s and early 1840s that was based on the Indian Removal Act of 1830.[28] This act authorized the exchange of lands with Indians residing in any of the eastern states or territories for land west of the Mississippi River. Removal was to be completely permissive, requiring the willing consent of the Indian tribe. The act also included provisions that paid for abandoned improvements in the east and that furnished emigrating Indians with support in moving and in establishing settlements at the location of their new home. Removal treaties contained provisions that met all of these specific requirements of the removal act. Although the treaty to be negotiated at St. Peters was written at the height of the removal era, it is clearly not a removal treaty.

There was no discussion of removal whatsoever during the negotiation of the treaty, and nothing in the treaty itself implies removal. Neither Secretary Cass, Commissioner Harris, nor treaty commissioner Governor Dodge ever suggested removing the Chippewa from the 1837 cession. During the negotiations, the Chippewa were promised that annuities and services would be provided "in their own country," which indicates that the Chippewa expected to remain and to coexist with non-Indians who would enter their territory as a result of the treaty.[29]

In late June 1837, over one thousand Chippewa assembled at Fort Snelling for the purpose of negotiating a treaty with the United States. General Smith, however, did not appear, leaving the treaty business to Governor Dodge and commission secretary Ver Planck Van Antwerp. Apparently, Dodge believed that since none of the Chippewa of the region had yet ceded land and since he was charged with encouraging peace between the Chippewa and the Dakota, he should bring as many Chippewa bands together as possible.[30] Most of the Chippewa, who the United States later categorized as belonging to one of three large groups, that is, the Chippewa of the Mississippi, the Chippewa of Lake Superior, and the Pillager Chippewa, were represented. Specifically, these included at least bands from Leech Lake, Gull Lake and Swan River, Mille Lacs, Sandy Lake, Snake and St. Croix rivers, Fond du Lac, La Pointe, Lac du Flambeau, and Lac Courte Oreilles. As a result, many of the Indians attending the treaty convention did not live on the lands that the United States proposed to buy.

Even though the United States had decided to temporarily delay asking the Chippewa on the south shore of Lake Superior and northern Minnesota to cede their land, Governor Dodge conducted the treaty with the "Chippewa Nation of Indians."[31] He thus created a political amalgam that had no reality for the Chippewa and plagued relations between both the Chippewa and the United States and separate Chippewa bands for years into the future. No doubt, Dodge was well aware of the separate interests of the Chippewa bands but was creating a political entity with whom the United States could deal in the future for land on a piecemeal basis.[32]

The negotiation of the Treaty of St. Peters is recorded in a journal kept by treaty secretary Van Antwerp. As treaty journals go, it is quite complete, reflecting opinions of Indian negotiators as well as those of Governor Dodge. The journal begins by describing several days of preliminary discussion between Dodge and the delegation of Indians who were present on the treaty grounds on July 20. Dodge was frustrated to find that the chiefs were not willing to negotiate until the arrival of the chiefs who would represent the bands of interior Wisconsin. The Pillager chief Aishkebogekoshe (Flat Mouth) explained Chippewa politics and band sovereignty to Dodge.

> My Father, I shall say but little to you at this time. I am called a chief. I am not the chief of the whole nation, but only of my people or tribe. I speak to you now only because I see nobody else ready to do so. I do not wish to take any further steps about what you have proposed to us until the other people arrive who have been expected here. They have not yet come, and to do so before their arrival might be considered an improper interference, and unfair towards them. The residence of my band is outside of the country which you wish to buy from us. After the people who live in that country shall have told you their minds I will speak. If the lands you wish to buy were occupied by my band, I would immediately have given you my opinion. After listening to the people who we are expecting and who will speak to you, I will abide by what they say, and say more to you myself.[33]

The Chippewa from the interior of Wisconsin finally arrived on July 25, permitting full discussion of the business at hand. The Mille Lacs chief Washaskkokone (Muskrat's Liver) made it plain that some of the lands were occupied by the Mille Lacs band. As he told Dodge, "We are talking about the land you have come for. I have tread all over it with my war club in my hand. My ancestors and those of Pagoonakeezhig [Hole in the Day] were the chiefs and protectors of that country and drove the bad Indians (Sioux) away from it."[34]

In explaining his purpose to the chiefs, Governor Dodge stressed again and again that the Great Father wanted the pine timber from the land. After describing the land and showing the chiefs a map of the proposed cession "which the Great Father wishes to purchase for his white children," Dodge told the chiefs, "This country as I am informed is not valuable to you for its game and not suited to the culture of corn, and other agricultural purposes. Your Great Father wishes to purchase your country on the Chippewa and St. Croix for the advantage of its pine timber with which it abounds." Dodge repeated this objective on July 26, telling them that the land was barren of game and worthless for agricultural purposes but that "it abounded in pine timber which the Great Father, the President of the United States wished to buy from them for the use of his white children and that he would give them a fair price for it."[35] In other words, Dodge was saying that the region would not be required for agricultural settlement but was being purchased so the pine trees could be cut. The Chippewa had agreed to a similar offer by the United States at the Treaty of Fond du Lac in 1826. In Article 3 of that treaty, the Chippewa granted the government the "right to search for, and carry away, any metals or minerals from any part of their country." The 1826 grant did not affect land title or jurisdiction.[36]

The chiefs seemed to have no real objection to the central objective of the treaty, but the journal shows that they had four principal negotiating points: retaining the right to gain a living from the land, obtaining just compensation for the cession, sharing treaty benefits with mixed-blood relatives, and gaining the means to pay their debts to traders. The traders, who were, in fact, often mixed-blood relatives as well, were in a position to put immense pressure on the Indians in favor of these concessions. As the Snake River chief Shagobi (Little Six), himself a mixed blood, put it, "But they are afraid to return home, if their traders are not paid. They fear they should not survive the winter without their aid."[37] While the Chippewa were often angry about their treatment by the traders and complained about inflated prices for goods and the fact that the traders used wood, fish, and game without compensation, the Indians were unable to resist their influence.[38]

The treaty journal provides details of the discussion of the terms of the cession. The Chippewa first proposed that the agreement be limited to a term of sixty years, after which time negotiations would be reopened. This seemed reasonable in view of the fact that many of the Chippewa believed they were only selling pine trees on the stump—not land. Governor Dodge, however, insisted that the cession be on the same basis by which the United States obtained cessions from other Indian tribes, that is, in perpetuity. The chiefs then proposed that payments ought also to be made in perpetuity—as "long as the land lasts." Dodge also resisted this suggestion and insisted on a twenty-year annuity schedule. To arrive at a monetary offer, Dodge suggested that the chiefs consult with their agents Bushnell and Vineyard. According to the terms of the treaty, money, goods, blacksmith shops, farmers, seed, tools, provisions, and other treaty benefits were to be paid, provided and established at times and places fixed by the president and the commissioner of Indian affairs.

It was of great importance to the chiefs to win a clear statement of their perpetual right to hunt, fish, and gather in the ceded territory. They explained repeatedly that this right was necessary for their survival and to obtain the support of the traders on whom they depended for guns, powder shot, iron tools, and tailored clothing.[39] Maghegabo insisted, in metaphorical expression, that the Chippewa retain the right to hunt, fish, and gather. As he put it, "Of all the country that we grant you, we wish to hold onto a tree where we get our living and to reserve the streams where we drink the waters that give us life."[40] Flat Mouth stated the same position more directly.

> My father, your children are willing to let you have their lands, but they wish to reserve the privilege of making sugar from the trees and getting a living from the lakes and rivers, as they have done heretofore and of remaining in the country. It is hard to give up the lands. They will remain, and cannot be destroyed—but you may cut down the trees and others will grow up. You know we cannot live deprived of our lakes and rivers. There is some game on the lands yet, and for that reason also, we wish to remain upon them, to get a living. Sometimes we scrape the trees and eat the bark [in times of starvation]. The Great Spirit above, made the Earth and causes it to produce, which enables us to live.[41]

In another speech, Flat Mouth restated this view again: "You know that without the land, and the rivers and lakes we could not live. We hunt and make sugar, and dig roots upon the former, while we fish and obtain rice and drink from the latter."[42] Governor Dodge knew, of course, that this was true, and he offered no resistance to the Chippewa insistence on hunting, fishing, and gathering rights. He replied to Flat Mouth's statement, "My Friends I have listened with great attention, to your chief from Leech Lake. I will make known to your Great Father, your request to be permitted to make sugar, on the lands, and you will be allowed, during his pleasure, to hunt and fish on them. It will probably be many years, before your Great Father will want all these lands for the use of his white children."[43]

Article 5 of the Treaty of St. Peters "guaranteed" the Chippewa "the privilege of hunting, fishing, and gathering the wild rice upon the lands the rivers, and lakes included in the territory ceded . . . during the pleasure of the President of the United States."[44] In Chippewa life, each individual, man, woman, and child made their own decisions; the power of decision making and the authority that goes with it were not assigned to others. Even the most prominent Chippewa chiefs were powerless to make decisions for others. For this reason, they relied on consensus, not authority, in their political life.[45] Given this cultural reality, it is difficult to believe that the Chippewa would have understood that the president could simply and capriciously foreclose on their reserved usufruct. One contemporary individual who knew the Chippewa and understood this point was missionary William Boutwell. Soon after the treaty, he wrote to his superior David Greene that, while he had high regard for Governor Dodge, he believed that "the Indians have no idea of leaving their country while they live—they know nothing of the duration of a man's pleasure."[46]

To the Chippewa, Article 5 meant that they would use all of the resources that were necessary for their support. References in the journal and the treaty itself to "making sugar," "gathering wild rice," and "reserving the oak tree" are categorical references, not strict limitations on what might be harvested. The Chippewa also understood that, to some degree, they would be sharing the resources of the land with non-Indians who would come as the result of the treaty. Given the size of the territory, the purpose of the treaty, and the abundance of resources, the Chippewa did not believe that the newcomers would interfere with their hunting, fishing, and gathering activities. Maghegabo expressed this idea when he told Governor Dodge,

> If I have rightly understood you, we can remain on the lands and hunt here. We have heretofore got our living on them. We hope that your people will not act towards ours, as your forefathers did towards our own [in the War of 1812?] but that you will always treat us kindly, as you do now.[47]

The Chippewa did not understand the phrase "during the pleasure of the President" to mean that they would have to remove from the ceded territory. Had this eventuality been raised at St. Peters, there would certainly have been a huge outcry from the Chippewa, as there was when this possibility was discussed a few years later at the negotiations of the 1842 La Pointe Treaty. At that time, the Chippewa were greatly threatened by the suggestion and repeatedly sought assurances from the government that they would not be removed—at least not for a very long time. The journal of the St. Peters Treaty, the official correspondence of the treaty commissioners, the statements of the Chippewa, and, most important, the treaty itself are silent on removal.

The negotiation of the St. Peters Treaty was attended by language and symbolism intended to create an atmosphere that would lend importance, solemnity, and great weight to the agreement. This was true on both the American and Indian sides. Clearly playing to the Indian concept of diplomatic agreements being a matter of personal honor among chiefs, Dodge cast the discussion of the president of the United States in terms of the Great Father's relationship to his children, both Indian and non-Indian. This relationship was to be guided by wisdom and justice for the welfare of these children and, most of all, in trust. Thus, Dodge explained that in obtaining the land for the benefit of his white children, the Great Father wanted to pay a fair price for the cession—"to give full value, payable in such a manner, as will be most serviceable to your people"—and that "equal justice should be done to all." In another context, Governor Dodge informed the Chippewa, "I tell you this now, that you may not hereafter say I deceived you. Your Great Father has sent me to treat you as his children, to pay you the value of your land and not to deceive you in anything I may do with you, or say to you."[48] Elsewhere, Dodge told the assembled Chippewa that "their Great Father, the President of the United States, would be just toward them."[49] Thus, the Chippewa were invited to rely and did rely on the Great Father to protect their rights.

For the Indians, the treaty was a very important agreement attended by appropriate ritual. Nodin, one of the principal Chippewa speakers, explained to an impatient Governor Dodge that the business of the treaty would take a long time: "My Father, I attended a council at Prairie du Chien [Treaty of Prairie du Chien 1825] which lasted ten days. Some of those now here were then present. This will last longer, as it is one of greater importance."[50] The council opened with "the usual ceremony" which no doubt included a grand entrance, songs, prayers by the shamans, and a pipe ceremony. After this, each band representative rose to introduce himself and to state his authority as a chief.

In Chippewa fashion, most of the formal negotiation was conducted by a peace chief. In this case, Aishkebogekoshe, or Flat Mouth, spoke for the civil chiefs, and a war chief, Maghegabo, spoke for the braves and warriors. Secretary Van Antwerp tells us that Maghegabo, at the occasion of his first formal appearance in council, "came forward in true Indian costume to wit; naked except as to his leggings, breech cloth and flap; his full head of hair ranging loosely upon his shoulders; a sort of crown upon his head made for the occasion and filled with feathers of the Bald Eagle, placed there by the chiefs; and the medals of several of the chiefs hung around his neck. He advanced to the Governor's table with his war flag and planted it there."[51] In typical Chippewa fashion, Maghegabo offered supplication to the Great Father on behalf of all the Chippewa, making it clear he was not speaking personally but was voicing consensus in a formal way: "I have but few words to say, but they are those of the chiefs and are very important. What I am now going to say to you, is a kind of history of our chiefs. The Being that created us, made us naked, but created you and your people with knowledge and power to get a living. Not so with us; we had to cover ourselves with moss and rotten wood; and you must be merciful to us."[52]

When the Treaty of St. Peters was finally signed, Governor Dodge had three copies made: one for the Chippewa, one for the Great Father, and one for himself. Dodge apologized to the Chippewa for not having U.S. flags and presidential medals to pass out to the chiefs, and he promised to deliver them the next year at the first treaty payment. Dodge cautioned the Chippewa not to strike the Dakota who were camped around Fort Snelling, saying that any blow on them would also fall on himself and the Great Father. Thus, the Treaty of St. Peters adjourned with a promise and a warning.

In recommending ratification to Commissioner Harris, Governor Dodge noted that the treaty would help keep the peace, which was being threatened by two hundred lumbermen who were already operating illegally in "Indian country." He went on to state that these trespassers should be removed.[53] Again in midsummer, just after the treaty was ratified, Dodge wrote to Harris with several suggestions so that "the treaty made with them may be carried into effect with good faith by the government."[54] He repeated these ideas in October, when he brought to Commissioner Harris's attention that there were now five hundred lumbermen in the cession. He told Harris, "I deem it a matter of the first importance that the Indians who have heretofore occupied and claimed that country should be satisfied as far as they can be made so to [produce] a friendly understanding between them and the people who are in the occupation of the Pine region building mills, preparing rafts of timber to descent the river and many are making improvements to remain in that country during the next winter. I will do anything in my power to carry into effect the provisions of the treaty."[55]

In February 1839 subagent David Bushnell wrote to Governor Dodge saying that he was well acquainted with the Chippewa and that the general policy of removing Indians west of the Mississippi River could not be applied to "this portion of the Chippewas" because it would not only bring them into closer contact with the Dakota but would "require them to change their habits entirely."[56] Not only was there no talk of removal in the few years after the treaty of 1837 but the federal government, through ex officio superintendent of Indian Affairs for the Wisconsin territory Henry Dodge, seemed dedicated to fairness and to providing services as promised. Dodge believed that such behavior on the part of the United States would promote tranquil relations between the Chippewa and the American citizens occupying the cession.

As in the case of many treaties, the one at St. Peters was followed by a period of confusion, while Indians, their agents, traders, missionaries, and citizens waited to evaluate its practical impact. Other than permitting the influx of lumbermen along the southern fringes of the cession, it had very little initial effect on the lives of the Chippewa. The payment of annuities in the late summer or fall often interfered with the timing of critical rice or fish harvest. When divided per capita, payments were so small that many often did not bother to collect them. The Chippewa continued to hunt and fish for a living and to slip into debt to their traders.[57] Smallpox also struck the Chippewa in the several years following the treaty, with devastating effect.

After an initial scouting report on the condition of the Lake Superior and Mississippi Chippewa by missionary Sherman Hall in 1833, a mission was established at La Pointe under the auspices of the American Board of the Commission of Foreign Missions in Boston.[58] During the 1830s, mission stations were established at various times at Fond du Lac, Bad River, Sandy Lake, Leech Lake, Yellow Lake, and Pokegoma on the Snake River. Missionary efforts encountered great resistance on the part of the Chippewa, who certainly did not meet the high expectations of the missionaries. It is true, however, that the missionaries became important intermediaries between the Chippewa and the United States government, as well as an important source of information about what was happening on the Lake Superior–Mississippi Valley frontier.[59]

During the early 1840s, the Chippewa experienced growing frustration over the 1837 treaty and became increasingly distrustful of motives of the United States. One of the main points of contention was identifying who should be paid treaty annuities. The commissioner of Indian affairs, T. Hartley Crawford, insisted that those Indians who signed the treaty could receive annuities irrespective of whether or not they actually claimed an interest in the land ceded.[60] Governor Dodge, however, argued that annuities should be paid only to those who immediately occupied the land ceded. He said it was deemed proper at the time of the treaty that all of the bands should become parties, "leaving it to the tribe afterward to determine their rights under it."[61]

The 1842 Treaty of La Pointe

Just as access to timber motivated the Treaty of St. Peters in 1837, so the strong desire to mine the mineral wealth of northern Michigan created pressure for a treaty of cession with the Chippewa of the Lake Superior shore (see map 6). In 1842 the new superintendent of the Mackinac Agency and former chief factor of the American Fur Company, Robert Stuart, wrote to the secretary of war, John Spencer, urging that the impending treaty include the balance of the south shore of Lake Superior, that is, from the 1836 cession in Michigan to the mouth of the St. Louis River.[62] In early August, Stuart was appointed as U.S. commissioner for the treaty and received instructions from the commissioner of Indian affairs, T. Hartley Crawford.[63] Stuart was to treat for a cession of seven million acres for an amount not to exceed thirty thousand dollars plus beneficial services and the payment of Indian debts to traders.

Commissioner Crawford suggested that a stipulation be added that would require the Chippewa to remove from the cession. To accomplish this, Stuart was told to include the Chippewa of the Mississippi in the annuity payments for the cession. This would make the unceded land west of Lake Superior "common property," rather than belonging only to those bands who actually lived there.[64] He went on to say that while it was likely that the Chippewa who occupied the ceded territory would not have to remove for a considerable time, the period was uncertain, and they should have the obligation to go when ordered by the president.

Stuart called all of the bands of Chippewa residing on Lake Superior, in the interior of Wisconsin, and as far west as the Mississippi River together at La Pointe in late September. Between three and four thousand Indians representing twenty-three distinct bands arrived at the appointed time. Although no official minutes were kept for the 1842 treaty, an unofficial account was made by Henry Blatchford, the interpreter for the mission at La Pointe, who was also one of the official interpreters at the treaty.[65] In addition, Robert Stuart later reconstructed and recorded several of his speeches at the treaty council, which seem to agree in substantial detail with the record made by Blatchford.[66]

Blatchford records that the bands arrived in fleets of canoes, dressed and painted in their finest regalia. Each brigade was greeted by gunfire from anchored ships, which was answered in return by a fusillade from the Indian canoes. The entrance of Hole in the Day (the elder) and the Gull Lake Chippewa was particularly impressive, as they had built a platform on a bateau on which warriors danced accompanied by war songs sung by Indian musicians. When the bateau landed, "they proceeded to the council ground in truly martial order. The leader at their head bearing the American colors, succeeded by the warriors and these followed by the musicians consisting of drummers and singers and rattlers, that is, men with rattles. These all proceeded in a slow military dance, peculiar to the Indians but difficult to describe."[67]

Stuart opened the council by telling the Chippewa that he had personally talked to the Great Father about them and that the president knew they were poor. Stuart said that the Great Father would therefore purchase the land for their benefit. He pointed out that some of the Chippewa already received treaty benefits while others did not.[68] In this, Stuart was not only trying to induce the Lake Superior bands to sell; he was attempting to deal with hard feelings over annuity payments under the 1837 treaty. As will be recalled, there was confusion over who should rightfully receive annuities under the 1837 treaty, those who signed or only those who occupied the ceded land. Jealousies had already arisen over these benefits, since some of the Chippewa, most notably the Pillagers, were excluded. Further, some chiefs were upset because the United States insisted on making payments under the 1837 treaty only at La Pointe during the late summer or fall. The chiefs complained that this required long, difficult travel that interfered with vital fall hunts and ricing. Following the 1842 treaty, Stuart recommended that annuities and services be paid at La Pointe, L'Anse, Pokegama, and elsewhere in the ceded territory (see map 4).[69]

Stuart specified the land that the United States wanted to buy but also said that the land north of the Fond du Lac River [St. Louis River] to the British line "shall be reserved as a home in common for you all."[70] He declared that annuities would be paid on a per capita basis and would be combined with those due under the St. Peters Treaty [1837] "to all Mississippi and Lake Superior Chippewa, as far up to the Sandy Lake band." This, he said, "would prevent future jealousies and allay the bad feelings which now exist among you and make you like a band of Brothers."[71] Although the collective terms "Chippewa of the Mississippi" and "Chippewa of Lake Superior" were similar to those used by the Chippewa themselves to refer to broad distinctions of geographical and economic residence, and although the terms were used in a similar way by American officials, they did not have political meaning for either the Chippewa or the United States until the Treaty of 1842. By concluding a treaty with the "Chippewa of the Mississippi *and* Lake Superior," Stuart created two large political groups that actually did not exist among the Chippewa, also combining them to form a single treaty entity.[72]

The Removal Provision and Stuart's Assurances

The Blatchford treaty account shows that the Chippewa were very concerned when Stuart raised the prospect of removal. They were much opposed to this idea, and Stuart was only able to get them to agree to sign the treaty by reassuring them of their long-term security on the land. Stuart told the Chippewa, "The great benefit your Father expects to derive from these lands is from the minerals that are on them. Until the lands are wanted, you will be permitted to live on them as you do now."[73] After describing the cession, Stuart told the chiefs,

> You understand these boundaries now don't you? You are to have the privilege of living on your lands to hunt and fish, till your great Father requires you to remove, you understand

he does not want the land now, it is only the minerals he wants. It will be better for you to have the same laws over you than to have the laws of the States. The laws of the United States are to remain over you as at present. I am very glad that some of your chiefs are so wise as to ask and desire it to be so.[74]

In similar language to the 1837 Treaty at St. Peters, Article 2 of the 1842 Treaty of La Pointe stipulated for "the right of hunting on the ceded territory with the other privileges of occupancy."[75] Unlike the Treaty of 1837, however, this treaty stated that the use right would continue until the Chippewa were required to remove by the president. As in the case of the 1837 treaty, the Treaty of 1842 was not a removal treaty in any formal sense. At the time it was negotiated, the Chippewa and, indeed, Commissioner Stuart understood that it would be many years and perhaps generations before the United States might require the Chippewa to remove north of the St. Louis River.[76] In fact, Dodge's emphasis on pine timber and lack of good agricultural land in the 1837 cession, like Stuart's repeated emphasis on the interest of the United States in the minerals and the frequent contention on the part of the U.S. officials that the ceded land was worthless for agriculture, led some Chippewa to believe that they had in fact only sold the pine timber and minerals.

Unlike the negotiators of the 1837 treaty, the Chippewa negotiating in 1842 clearly understood that there was a possibility of future removal. Even so, it was made plain to the Chippewa that any such removal, if it were to occur, would be well into the future. They demanded and received this assurance from Robert Stuart. At the point when the chiefs were filing up to "touch the pen," Chief White Crow balked, saying he was afraid that if he signed, he would be called on to immediately remove. At this point, White Crow asked Stuart for a reservation. Stuart responded that he could not provide a reservation, but he reassured White Crow that "the land would not probably [*sic*] be wanted during his lifetime."[77]

In January 1843 Agent Alfred Brunson at La Pointe wrote to Secretary of War Spencer complaining that the 1842 treaty cheated the Chippewa. Brunson contended that the Chippewa did not receive as much per acre as other tribes, especially considering the commercial value of furs, sugar, rice, fish, and game, which he calculated to be worth $190,000 per year. Brunson also attached letters stating the opinions of several Chippewa chiefs, including Wabijeshi (Marten), listed as head chief at Lac Courte Oreilles. Wabijeshi stated that he was not at St. Peters for the 1837 treaty, so he did not sell his land until the 1842 treaty. The chief said that when he signed the latter treaty, he made a condition "that we should remain on the land, as long as we are peaceable. We have no objections to the white man's working the mines, and the timber and making farms, but we reserve the Birch bark and cedar for canoes, the Rice and the Sugar tree and the privilege of hunting without being disturbed by the whites."[78] Stuart himself confirmed this understanding when he reported to Commissioner Crawford in 1843 that "early removal was not in conformity with the spirit of the treaty."[79]

In later years, when the government did actually attempt to remove the Chippewa, the chiefs made a new round of claims concerning their understanding of the removal discussion, as well as responses from various officials. Addressing an anti-removal petition to the commissioner of Indian affairs in 1851, Chief Buffalo, also a signer of the 1842 treaty, repeated Wabijeshi's understanding. Buffalo explained what Stuart had told him: "Your Great Father," he said, "does not want the land to cultivate but only the minerals on it which he wants. The whites do not wish to come and occupy your country now—until they want it you will be permitted to live and hunt on your lands as before. So far as you may live on land which will be needed by the miners, you will have to remove to one side; but if you are not in the way of the whites, and live on terms of friendship with them, it will be a great while before you will be required to remove. I don't believe you or I will ever see the day when you will be troubled about your lands." Stuart, Buffalo reported, promised that "we and our children after us might be permitted to live on our lands fifty years and even a hundred if we lived on friendly terms with the whites."[80]

In March 1850 subagent John Livermore wrote to Minnesota governor Alexander Ramsey that he tried to soften the blow of their impending removal by an early warning. This tactic seems not to have worked, since Livermore reported that they were "considerably excited" by the news. The chiefs from Bad River told Livermore that "the man who came here to make the treaty [Stuart] told them that they would not probably be required to remove for many years and not until their annuities would have ceased, and probably that they could spend their lives here. This, I am told by those who were present, is true."[81]

Respected citizen Cyrus Mendenhall wrote to the commissioner of Indian affairs on January 6, 1851, stating that he was a witness to the 1842 treaty. He said that Stuart told the Indians that they would be able to occupy the land as long as they behaved well and that Stuart illustrated his point with an analogy. Stuart told the Chippewa, according to Mendenhall, that "the purchase he wished to make was like buying a pack of furs from one of them, paying for it, then handing it back for the Indian's own use."[82] Many non-Indians concurred in this general opinion, as well as the impression given by Stuart that he was interested in acquiring the mineral wealth of the cession and not the land.[83] In later years, even removal agent John Watrous seems to concede that Stuart led the Chippewa to believe they would not be required to remove.[84]

At the La Pointe payment in the fall of 1853, the Chippewa chiefs, now wary of all government intentions and actions, discussed their understanding of the removal provision of the 1842 treaty with Agent Gilbert, who passed on his observations to Commissioner Manypenny.

> The Indians informed me that when the treaty was made, the Commissioner assured them that the clause providing for their removal was only inserted as a mere matter of form. That a compliance with it would never be urged or insisted on by the government and that their annuities would always be paid at La Pointe. The interpreter Mr. Johnson who officiated in that occasion was present with me and collaborated this statement. I saw several other persons who were present at that time and they all concur in saying that without this assurance the Indians would never have signed the treaty. The memory of an Indian is very tenacious. He treasures up everything that is said by a government official and regards his statements and verbal assurances as equally binding upon the government as the formal stipulations of a treaty.[85]

In 1864 the Chippewa chiefs at L'Anse met and recorded in the Chippewa language their own understanding of what transpired at the 1842 treaty. The chiefs agreed that Stuart had asked to buy the minerals, not land, and that they understood that they could remain on the land for a very long time. Recounting the incident between White Crow and Stuart, the chiefs concluded,

> / Midach minawa, gi ajidemigud, gi idud / dach; Anich botch win igo geiabi Nani / -midana dasso bibon gi gadabbetan man / dan Aki, bochke bigo Ningodwak dasso- / -bibon gi gad abitan mandan ki dakim, / Eji dibendaman nongom ebitaman.
>
> / Anich gonima dach win ningoding ki ga- / gi sagassweigowa aw Gimichomissiwa tchi / gagwedjimineg mandan ki dakimiwa / nongom ebitameg.

Ojibwa linguist John Nichols translates this statement as follows:

> Then he [White Crow] was answered back, and told that he any how had the privilege of remaining on the land for fifty years, and even for a hundred years, as he owned and had possession of the land, he has a right to live on it.
>
> But then there may be a time that your Great Father will call you to council and ask you to sell him the land you live on.[86]

This same view was expressed by the Bad River chief Blackbird in 1869, when he contended that the treaty makers sold only the minerals and timber in the treaties of 1842 and 1837.[87]

Hunting, Fishing, and Gathering in the 1837 and 1842 Treaties

In the context of all of the treaties that the United States wrote with Native American tribes, the Treaty of La Pointe in 1842 and the St. Peters Treaty of 1837 are very unusual. First, these may be the only Great Lakes treaties where the major purpose was to acquire specific natural resources. As is made clear by the instructions for both treaties and by the speeches of the respective treaty commissioners, acquiring the land was almost incidental—a necessity to control access to pine timber and minerals. A second unusual feature is that neither treaty makes provisions for the permanent settlement of the Indians who occupied the cessions. In almost every other treaty of cession, a specific homeland was set aside either in a remote place or within the territory ceded. In the case of these two treaties, the assumption was that the Indians would remain as before, scattered throughout the ceded territory. Here, they were to receive annuities and other services and benefits. The facts that the 1842 treaty made provision for payment of annuities on the ceded territory, that the trade and intercourse laws were extended over all of the territory ceded, and that the carpenters provided by the treaty were to circulate among the Indian communities to build houses all confirm this fact.[88] This same conclusion can be reached in regard to the 1837 cession, because annuities and services were also provided on territory ceded in that treaty.[89]

By 1842 the U.S. government had no short- or long-term plan to remove Indians from either the 1837 or 1842 cessions. beyond the vague recognition that the United States might in the far, indefinite future need the land for other purposes. Since neither cession was correctly considered to contain prime agricultural land, American officials at the time had no idea as to why or when, if ever, the land might be required. This is also made abundantly clear by what treaty commissioners Dodge and Stuart told the Indians and by what they themselves wrote after the treaties were concluded. This is why no removal language appears in the 1837 treaty and why the future possibility of removal to unceded land was left at the discretion of the president in the case of the 1842 treaty. It is also why Robert Stuart, notwithstanding this provision of the treaty, was able to reassure the Chippewa of their long-term tenure on the land.

The hunting, fishing, and gathering provisions of both treaties are the nexus of the practical operation of the treaties with the long-term policy objective. In the practical realm, the hunting, fishing, and gathering provisions were of vital necessity to the Indians. They had no other means to feed themselves or to engage in commerce with the non-Indians. If and as long as they remained on the land, these "privileges of occupancy" were a necessity. The Chippewa and the American officials knew that there was no other means of provisioning the Indians. Although it was the idealistic goal of the United States to settle the Chippewa and induce them to take up plow agriculture, all parties concerned in the early part of the nineteenth century knew that the dream of Indian agricultural self-sufficiency was far, far into the future. Surely both Dodge and Stuart thought about the link between Chippewa occupancy and hunting, fishing, and gathering in these terms. As the commissioners explained to the Chippewa and as the Chippewa understood it, hunting, fishing, and gathering was linked to their occupation of the ceded territory. They were assured by the United States that as long as they remained on the land, they would not be impeded from the use of its natural resources.

The 1847 Treaty and Affairs of the 1840s

In contemplation of the eventual removal of the Chippewa from the 1842 cession, treaty commissioner Robert Stuart needed to deal with the problem of a removal destination. To do this, he adopted the fictitious concept of a common "Chippewa Nation" with common interests and common landholdings, which was invented by Henry Dodge for the 1837 treaty. He operationalized this idea by including Chippewa bands who did not reside on the territory ceded in 1842 as parties to the treaty and as recipients of annuity payments. In Stuart's mind this obligated the Chippewa occupying unceded land to the north and west to accept Chippewa from the 1842 cession if they should be required to remove. Article 3 of the treaty makes this explicit by stating that "all the unceded lands, belonging to the Indians of Fond du Lac, Sandy Lake and Mississippi bands, shall be the common property and home of all of the Indians, party to this treaty."[90] In the event of removal, the Lake Superior Chippewa who occupied the 1842 cession would be obliged to move north of the St. Louis River, between the Mississippi River and Lake Superior.

In the years shortly following the 1842 treaty, two practical problems arose with this solution. First, the area west of Lake Superior was very poor country and incapable of supporting further Chippewa populations. Second, this region was discovered to contain vast mineral wealth that was coveted by U.S. citizens. As a result American officials set out to look for an alternative destination if the Chippewa should ever be required to remove. This possibility was given some urgency in 1846, when the president inquired, for no apparent reason, about removing Chippewa from the mining district along the Lake Superior shore.[91] Late in 1846 Henry Dodge, concerned about a removal destination for the Winnebago and Menominee from Wisconsin, asked Agent Hayes to explore the extent of Chippewa land claims west of the Mississippi in Minnesota. Hayes was also instructed to ask resident chiefs if they would be disposed to permit the Chippewa from east of the Mississippi to move to that country, if those Indians decided to sell their lands to the United States.[92] Clearly Dodge was anticipating acquisition of the mineral country at the head of Lake Superior and was seeking a new location if the Wisconsin Chippewa were ever removed from the 1842 cession.

The 1847 Treaty

In 1847 instructions were issued by the commissioner of Indian affairs, William Medill, for a new treaty with the Chippewa to acquire land west of the Mississippi for emigrating Winnebago and Menominee. This document is very instructive regarding U.S. policy toward the Lake Superior and Mississippi Chippewa at the time.[93] Treaty commissioners Isaac Verplank and Charles Mix were to purchase land between the Watab, Long Prairie, and Crow Wing rivers, as well as another parcel between the Long Prairie and Leaf rivers, for an estimated price of about nine cents per acre. In the view of Commissioner Medill, these lands were unused by the Chippewa and therefore of little value to them. The treaty commissioners were told that even after these lands were purchased, it would still leave the Chippewa "a sufficient quantity of lands owned by them west of the Mississippi River for a suitable and comfortable home for all the various bands of those Indians, and, on many accounts it is desirable to concentrate them in this country there; the greater portion it is supposed, now resides east of the Mississippi in Wisconsin. They are widely scattered, lead a roving and unsettled life, and obtain subsistence principally by fishing and hunting."[94]

Medill goes on to say that these Indians only remain in the east by "suffrage" of the United States on account of the 1837 and 1842 treaties. He concludes that because of both future white settlement and the fact that some of the unceded land east of the river contained valuable minerals, it would be ultimately necessary to remove the Chippewa. Since this was so, Medill also believed it "would cost but little more to remove them to the country west of the Mississippi than to the unceded land east [i.e., land designated as a common homeland in the 1842 treaty]." In any case, Medill believed that it was "a matter of comparative indifference to them whether they go west, or to the unceded land east."[95]

Clearly Medill was confused over the obligation of the Chippewa under the treaty of 1837 and knew little about their use and occupancy of the territory west of the Mississippi, little about the nature of the country north of the St. Louis River, and still less about the Chippewa's view of removal. Based on his conclusions, however, Medill decided it was a wise policy to remove the Chippewa from all of their lands east of the Mississippi and to concentrate them west of the river as soon as possible. The treaty commissioners were therefore directed to acquire not only lands west of the river for homes for emigrating Wisconsin Winnebago and Menominee but also the unceded lands north of the 1837 and 1842 cessions to Rainy Lake and the British provinces and from Lake Superior west to Lake Winnibigoshish and then north to the international boundary. Medill also concluded this huge tract of land to be "almost, if not entirely unoccupied by the Indians and therefore valueless to them." Since this was so, Medill concluded that as in the case of the Chippewa lands west of the Mississippi, it would be fair for "the Department to restrict the amount to be given to as small a one as possible."[96] Large annuity payments, Medill believed, "instead of being a benefit, have resulted in positive evil." Large sums that the Indians could do with as they pleased led, according to Commissioner Medill, to "idleness with all its attendant evil of profligacy, intemperance, recklessness and crime."[97] After having lost all incentive to work for subsistence and other necessities, the Indians would then "resort to theft and depredations upon our frontier citizens." This, in turn, has led, he said, to "collisions and bloodshed and in too many instances war by which some of the tribes have almost been exterminated."[98]

Medill then went on to suggest a treaty with concrete removal provisions. The new treaty was to give priority to land for the emigrating Indians. In regard to the land "held in common" west of Lake Superior, Medill admitted that the theory of common property was disputed by some of the bands and that "different bands claim the exclusive title to different portions of it."[99] The treaty commissioners were instructed to glaze over these claims if possible, since "it is very desirable that no questions of this kind be raised, as it is a leading object with the Department to consider the Chippewas and to have them think themselves one United People with possessions and interest in common, especially for the future."[100]

Given this misinformed, paternalistic, and manipulative view of Chippewa-American relations, it is little wonder that the 1847 treaty was a thorough disaster. Actually two treaties were negotiated in 1847. These were the second treaty of Fond du Lac, on August 2, 1847, which ceded the land between the Long Prairie and Crow Wing rivers, and the Treaty of Leech Lake of August 21, 1847, which ceded the land between the Crow Wing and Leaf rivers (see map 4).[101] The first treaty included the Chippewa who, by provisions of the 1842 treaty, were lumped into the geographic groups "Chippewa of Lake Superior" and "Chippewa of the Mississippi." Like the "Chippewa Nation," these groups had little, if any, meaning to the Chippewa, except insofar as they affected their relations with the United States. In this the Fond du Lac bands were classified as Chippewa of Lake Superior. The Leech Lake Treaty was with the Pillager Chippewa who claimed exclusive ownership of the land between the Crow Wing and Leaf rivers and would not permit other Chippewa to participate in the cession.

Both treaties of 1847, as it turned out, were negotiated by Minnesota trader and politician Henry Rice, who replaced the ailing Charles Mix. At the time of the treaties, Rice was an Indian trader on the Mississippi with an interest in the Pierre Chouteau Company, which was in direct competition with the reorganized American Fur Company operating among the Lake Superior Chippewa. During negotiations, the differences between the various Chippewa bands that the United States had tried to suppress since 1837 erupted at the Fond du Lac Treaty. The division occurred between the bands residing on Lake Superior and interior Wisconsin, known as the "Lake Superior bands," and the "Mississippi bands," which in this case effectively meant the Gull Lake bands represented by Hole in the Day (the younger). Since the latter groups used the land to be ceded, they wanted more payment than those further east. Because of the 1842 treaty annuity arrangement, the Lake Superior bands already shared annuities from the cession of their own land with the Mississippi bands, and they believed they should now participate equally in the benefit of the sale of lands used by the Mississippi bands. Rice and Verplank finally settled the problem by negotiating a split in which the Mississippi bands received $63,000 and the Lake Superior bands $17,000 for the new cession. Just as the Pillager and Gull Lake bands stood firm in their own interest, the Fond du Lac, Grand Portage, and Nett Lake bands refused to sell the land between Lake Superior and the Mississippi headwaters.[102] This land was not ceded until the Treaty of La Pointe in 1854.

This new annuity arrangement was vigorously protested by the Lake Superior chiefs and their American Fur Company trading partners, who claimed collusion between the Mississippi band and the Chouteau Company Traders on the Mississippi. In the several years after the treaty of 1847, chiefs and traders alike complained of conflict, collusion, fraud, and improper procedure in the way Rice conducted the treaty.[103] The split in annuities between the Mississippi and Lake Superior Chippewa negotiated by Rice greatly profited the less numerous Mississippi Chippewa and, likewise, the Chouteau Company in which he was a partner.

After the 1847 Treaty

Following the 1847 treaty, there were increasing rumors that the Lake Superior Chippewa would be required to remove.[104] The Chippewa became apprehensive and responded by protesting this possibility and pleading for reservations within the territory they had ceded in 1837 and 1842.[105] Agent James Livermore and the Chippewa missionaries supported the reservation idea.[106] As missionary Sherman Hall put it, "I do not think the government can put the Indians of this region in any spot where they will be really out of the way, and where it would be better for them, than to leave them unmolested in possession of the upper part of this lake, and of the country bordering upon it."[107]

The Fond du Lac chiefs, who still owned and occupied the unceded land west of Lake Superior after the Treaty of Fond du Lac in 1847, realized that the United States was anxious to acquire this territory for its mineral wealth. Accordingly, in late 1848 Shingoop, Mongozid, Nagonabe, and Kitchimeheegun wrote to agent James Hays asking him to send a petition on behalf of the Fond du Lac bands to the Great Father. In good Chippewa custom, they began their petition by pleading their poverty and misery. In this manner, they reminded the Father of his obligation to his children. The chiefs then offered to sell the president the area west of Lake Superior—as they put it, "a certain tract of land in our possession which is valuable; a real mineral country." In this, they were willing to exchange something of great value, but they expected to be rewarded with something of equal benefit in return. Accordingly, the Fond du Lac chiefs suggested that the president provide perpetual annuities: "Father, if you would procure us such a perpetual treaty, this would be the greatest benefit you could bestow on our tribe for which ourselves, and our children and grandchildren would be thankful to you for ever."[108] Just as the chiefs were acting in behalf of their people, they hoped that the Great Father would act toward his children with equal concern.

Beyond all the improprieties embodied in the 1847 treaty and the dissension it created among the Chippewa, the most fundamental problem was that Indian policy was in terrible disarray in the late 1840s. The United States found itself in a dilemma because the old removal policy was dysfunctional, but there was no new way established to accomplish its civilization goals. While the reservation policy that was put in place in the mid-1850s would ultimately suggest a new solution, the government in the late 1840s was still technically geared to remove Indians but had no place to put them. The Minnesota Territory offers a good example. The 1842 treaty mandated the mineral district north of the St. Louis River as the destination of the Chippewa if they were removed from that cession, but five years later the United States wanted it for its minerals. An alternative suggested by Medill, Rice, and others of moving the Chippewa west of the Mississippi conflicted with the desire of the United States to purchase all Chippewa land owned or claimed by them in Minnesota, Wisconsin, or elsewhere.[109] This objective, mandated in the 1847 treaty instructions and repeated in a Senate authorization bill in 1853, made no sense in terms of any policy. It certainly did not make sense in the context of promoting civilization and assimilation objectives. What was the point of removing the Chippewa to a place that the United States was already trying to purchase? If the Chippewa were to be removed from Wisconsin to Minnesota, the motivation had to be something other than the benevolent ideals that had always guided American Indian policy.

A Fur Trade Conspiracy

As historian Rhonda Gilman has pointed out, the fur trade continued to be a very important feature of the economy of the upper Mississippi Valley through most of the nineteenth century.[110] As a business venture, it was characterized by a series of corporate manipulations and reorganizations aimed at eliminating or reducing competition among a dozen or so prominent individuals who financed and organized it. As the nineteenth century progressed, the fur trade companies expanded their enterprise increasingly into banking, real estate, transportation, and retail sales.

At the time of the 1837 treaty, the trade was organized through two business groups within the reorganized American Fur Company. The Western Outfit controlled the country from southern Wisconsin to Iowa from its headquarters at Prairie du Chien. This business was under the leadership of Joseph Ralette, Hercules Dousman, and Henry Sibley. The Northern Outfit operated out of La Pointe under the direction of William Aitken and Lyman Warren. Warren ran the operation at La Pointe, and Aitken managed the Fond du Lac department that extended from Lake Superior to the Red River Valley.[111]

In 1837 there was a great financial crisis in the American economy as a result of unsecured land speculation in the Old Northwest. The traders of both the Northern Outfit and the Western Outfit were saved from financial ruin only by the Chippewa, Sioux, and Winnebago treaties negotiated that year, which provided a huge windfall of $325,000 in the combined payment of Indian trade debts.[112] As the result of the Panic of 1837, the Northern Outfit was reorganized, and both Warren and Aitken were fired and replaced by Dr. Charles Borup, who operated out of La Pointe. Aitken, however, soon returned as the company trader at Sandy Lake.

In 1842 Ramsey Crooks sold the American Fur Company's share in the Western Outfit to the Pierre Chouteau Company of St. Louis. Chouteau now joined Sibley and Dousman in a new arrangement called the Upper Mississippi Outfit, which negotiated a noninterference compact with the Northern Outfit, now owned and operated by Ramsey Crooks under the American Fur Company name. Thus, the American Fur Company still retained control of the Lake Superior and upper Mississippi Valley Chippewa trade. Traders of both outfits haunted the annual treaty payments, where they managed to get the lion's share of annuity money paid to Indians, by offering goods in trade and by collecting debts.

A new wrinkle occurred in the trade in 1846, when Hercules Dousman retired and his place was taken by Bernard Bresbois of Prairie du Chien and a newcomer from Ohio, Henry Rice. Rice managed to ingratiate himself with the Winnebago and, later, the Minnesota Chippewa, so that he was able to manipulate their affairs to his own advantage. Rice rapidly challenged the American Fur Company by claiming to hold a monopoly on the fur trade of the upper Mississippi region, citing an earlier arrangement between Dousman and Aitkin.[113] In 1847 he proceeded to hire away the best traders from Dr. Borup's Northern Outfit of the American Fur Company and to compete with them in the upper Mississippi Valley with goods supplied by himself and Henry Sibley. Rice now organized the Chippewa Outfit, to pursue the fur trade of the northern Mississippi Valley. Pierre Chouteau held a half interest in the Chippewa Outfit as well as the Winnebago and Sioux trades; collectively they were known as the Northern Outfit of the Chouteau Company. In the meantime, the old Northern Outfit of the American Fur Company had been purchased by Borup and continued to operate from La Pointe as the Northern Fur Company.[114] Rice managed to bring Borup's company into the Chippewa Outfit, but during the summer of 1849, Borup replaced Rice and moved the newly consolidated businesses from La Pointe to St. Paul.[115]

By 1849 a consortium of traders, merchants, and politicians was actively promoting St. Paul as the main commercial center of the upper Mississippi Valley. Henry Sibley and Henry Rice were central to this effort, since, as major Indian traders, they both had investments in the Chouteau Company of St. Louis. Between the two, they had already cornered the Sioux, Winnebago, and southern Chippewa trade. Rice and Sibley were also involved in a real estate venture in St. Paul with the brother of Governor Alexander Ramsey.[116] When Sibley went to Washington as the Minnesota territorial delegate in 1849, he was able to establish a working relationship with Thomas Ewing, secretary of the newly created Department of the Interior. Ewing personally managed the office of Indian Affairs and was notorious for authorizing the payment of dubious trader claims.[117] Thus, in 1849 all the pieces were in place to manipulate the Chippewa for private gain. Ambitious trading interest in Minnesota had not just the support of the governor but also that of the secretary of the interior.

Given this situation in the fur business, the anticipation of new treaties of cession, and the possibility of establishing profitable new Indian agencies in Minnesota, Governor Alexander Ramsey, territorial delegate Henry Sibley, Henry Rice, and Dr. Borup all conspired to corner the northwestern fur trade and the Indian business. Their scheme was to promote the removal of all the Chippewa from Wisconsin to the Minnesota Territory. This would not only give them complete control of the fur trade but also provide them with access to money and markets related to supplying annuity goods, jobs, and services for new Indian agencies, schools, farms, and related facilities. As Henry Rice explained to Governor Ramsey,

> They [the Chippewa] should be removed from the ceded land—they should receive their annuities on the Mississippi River [rather than at La Pointe] say at or near Sandy Lake, at which place an agency for the whole tribe should be established. This would better accommodate the whole tribe—and Minnesota would reap the benefit—whereas now their annuities pass via Detroit and not one dollar do our inhabitants get—altho' we are subject to all the annoyances given by those Indians.[118]

In late 1849 Governor Ramsey trumped up phony misbehavior charges against the Chippewa from a list of twelve complaints against Indians that had been drawn up during the summer of 1849. As he well knew, all but one of the twelve offenses were committed by immigrant Winnebago.[119] Despite the fact that these were not committed either by the Chippewa or on the 1837 cession, he told the territorial legislature, "Much complaint is made by settlers about Sauk Rapids, Swan River, etc. of the demoralizing effects of the privilege given the Chippewa, in the Treaty of 1837, to hunt and fish upon the lands ceded by said Treaty"[120] On this flimsy foundation, Governor Ramsey asked the Minnesota Territorial Assembly for a resolution calling on the federal government to remove the Wisconsin Chippewa from the territory that they had ceded as a result of the 1837 and 1842 treaties.[121]

The assembly responded with a joint resolution asking that the privilege of occupancy including hunting, fishing, and gathering be revoked and that the Chippewa of the 1837 and 1842 treaties be required to remove to unceded land in Minnesota. The resolution was forwarded to territorial delegate Henry Sibley, the president of the U. S. Senate, the Speaker of the House of Representatives, and the secretary of the Home Department (interior). Delegate Sibley was specifically directed in the resolution to "urge the necessity of freeing the Territory from the Indian population within its limits, so far as it has been ceded."[122] This procedure is curious in view of the wording of Article 2 of the 1842 treaty, which permits usufruct privileges until the Chippewa were required to remove by the president. It would seem, therefore, that in the case of the 1842 cession, the legislature might have simply appealed to the president to exercise his power under the treaty. Perhaps the reason they chose to concentrate their removal efforts in Congress was because they realized there was no authority for removal of the Chippewa in the 1837 treaty. Only Congress was in a position to accomplish this part of the request.

Thanks to the persistent efforts of both Sibley and Rice in Washington, President Zachary Taylor issued an order on February 6, 1850, canceling usufruct rights guaranteed under the 1837 and 1842 treaties and ordering the removal of the Chippewa from the ceded territory. The text of the order follows:

> The privileges granted temporarily to the Chippewa Indians of the Mississippi by the Fifth Article of the Treaty made with them on the 29th of July 1837, "of hunting and fishing, and gathering the wild rice upon the lands and rivers and the lakes included in the territory ceded" by that treaty to the United States; and the right granted to the Chippewa Indians of the Mississippi and Lake Superior, by the Second Article of the treaty with them of October 4, 1842, of hunting on the territory which they ceded by that treaty, "with the other usual privileges of occupancy until required to remove by the President of the United States," are hereby revoked; and all of the said Indians remaining on the land ceded as aforesaid, are required to remove to their unceded lands.[123]

The wording of the order in respect to the 1837 treaty refers to the privilege granted to the Chippewa of the Mississippi.

The sole purpose of President Taylor's order was to accomplish the removal of the Wisconsin Chippewa. In the case of the 1842 treaty, where usufruct and occupation were linked by Article 2, removal would have eliminated hunting, fishing, and gathering by the Chippewa in the ceded territory. Since the 1837 treaty contained no authorization to remove the Chippewa, cancellation of the usufruct rights contained in Article 5 was intended to force the Chippewa to remove. This was so since they could not live in the ceded territory—or anywhere else for that matter—without the use of the natural resources on which they depended for food. During the next several years, when attempts were made to accomplish removal, no government official ever told the Chippewa they could not hunt, fish, and gather; nor did any official try to stop or suppress Chippewa usufruct activities. On the contrary, the government and especially the merchants who were trying to accomplish removal were encouraging the Chippewa to hunt, fish, and gather, that is, to produce the commodities on which the economic well-being of the traders and the northern economy depended.

At the time of the removal effort, it was no secret to the Chippewa or to the public that Indians were being manipulated for the benefit of outside and private economic interests. For example, the Mille Lac chief Nagonabe, in complaining about the 1847 treaty, wrote to agent John Livermore as follows:

> When our Great Father last year sent the Trader [Henry Rice] from the Mississippi to treat with us for our land, I did not feel happy. I feared that the trader loved our money more than he did us and that he would take greater care of himself than he would either of us or our own Great Father's interest.[124]

The *Lake Superior Journal* laid out the motivation for the Chippewa removal effort very clearly in a story on May 22, 1850.

> The delegate from Minnesota, Mr. Sibley, Mr. Rice, till lately one of his partners in the Choteau branch of the Old American Fur Company and Dr. Borup, present agent of the same company, at St. Paul, could, we doubt not more fully explain these Indian removals than anybody else; but as they would be the last ones to do so, we venture to notice a few features of the scheming system that has been carried on for years in order to make their headquarters the center of attraction, as well for all the money that is paid to the Indians of the Northwest, as for the peltries that are collected by them. This company enjoys an almost perfect monopoly of the trade with the Indians in this region, and it looks as if this monopoly has been secured for some time to come by this plan of removing the Chippewa from Lake Superior.[125]

While the citizens of St. Paul and the other emerging settlements on the Mississippi River may have supported the removal plan, the citizens of Lake Superior utterly opposed it. By 1850 the Chippewa and American settlers along the Lake Superior shore had come to a peaceful and useful accommodation of interests.[126] Praise for the good behavior of the Chippewa came from many quarters in the mid-nineteenth century. La Pointe subagent James Hays said that "the Chippewa as individuals and as a nation are well disposed" and that compared to "almost any civilized community of the same size, there will be found the same aggregate of crime."[127] Those who gave greatest praise to the good behavior of the Chippewa were the American lumbermen, miners, and merchants who were the actual neighbors and business partners of these Indians.

The Chippewa Response

When they heard of the removal order, the Chippewa reacted with shock and disbelief.[128] First, they had no understanding that they could be required to remove under the terms of the 1837 treaty. The 1842 treaty, in their understanding, contained two provisions relating to removal. By Article 6 they agreed to remove if their occupation in the mineral district should interfere with mining efforts. By this they understood they would remove to one side, in order to accommodate mining.[129] Article 2 of the treaty required general removal from the cession when, or if, such removal was required by the president. By this provision the Chippewa understood that they might be required to remove north of the St. Louis River to unceded territory, but only if they misbehaved.[130] Since they had accommodated the interest of Americans in all respects and were living at peace with them both as a tribe and as individuals, they could not believe the Great Father would break his covenant with them. Chief Buffalo wrote to the president to explain their view.

> We have been ready to listen to the words of our Great Father whenever he has spoken to us, and to accede to his wishes. but this time, in the matter of our removal, we are in the dark. We are not satisfied that it is the President that

requires us to remove. We have asked to see the order, and the name of the President affixed to it, but it has not been shown us. We think the order comes only from the agent [John Watrous] and those who advise him and are interested in having us removed.[131]

It bears repeating that notwithstanding the removal provision of the 1842 treaty, the Chippewa residents of the 1837 cession and signatories of the 1837 treaty had never been asked to remove and certainly did not agree to it.

In the fall of 1850, Governor Ramsey and newly appointed removal agent John Watrous developed a secret plan to lure the Chippewa west.[132] They announced a new policy of paying annuities only on unceded territory. The first place of payment was Sandy Lake in Minnesota, where they hoped to entrap the Chippewa by making the payment so late in the fall that the Indians could not return home because the canoe routes would be frozen. This cruel plan proved to be a disaster that cost the lives of four hundred Chippewa men who died of starvation, exposure, and disease before the survivors could return to their Wisconsin homes.[133]

The Sandy Lake tragedy, the opposition of American citizens, the fear of a Chippewa uprising, and the failure of efforts to accomplish removal to date led the acting secretary of the interior, T. Abraham, to suspend the removal entirely in August 1851. In an order transmitted through Luke Lea, the commissioner of Indian affairs, the secretary wrote, "As you request in your letter of 23 inst. You are authorized to instruct agent Watrous to suspend removal of the Chippewa Indians until the final determination of the President upon the subject of your letter of the 3rd June 1851 can be communicated to him."[134] As a matter of fact, the suspension of Chippewa removal was very much in the spirit of the new policy that was emerging in the Indian Office under the direction of Commissioner Lea and chief clerk Charles Mix.[135] In reality, however, Ramsey and Watrous totally ignored the suspension order and continued to plan for and encourage the Chippewa to remove. They also continued their policy of paying annuities on unceded land; in 1851 they paid annuities at the nearest location that had not been ceded, that is, at Fond du Lac.

The Fond du Lac bands, while certainly Chippewa of Lake Superior, were residents of the unceded land north of the St. Louis River and were not subject to the removal order per se, yet they were most certainly impacted by it. Not only did annuity payments bring thousands of their fellow Chippewa to Fond du Lac, putting great stress on local resources, but other Chippewa began to move to Fond du Lac in order to avoid forced removal. Some of this movement was at the encouragement of Agent Watrous, who designated Fond du Lac as a staging area for moving the Chippewa from interior Wisconsin further west. Others may simply have moved to Fond du Lac to avoid removal west of the Mississippi. According to a census made by John Watrous in 1852, the population of the Fond du Lac band had actually doubled since 1847. In all, seven hundred Chippewa now lived at least part of the year at Fond du Lac.[136] In contravention of the 1842 treaty that specified the area north of the St. Louis River as an eventual removal destination, Ramsey and Watrous had decided to remove the Chippewa to the vicinity of Gull Lake, near the Crow Wing trading center on the Mississippi. Steamboat traffic on the river made Crow Wing easy to supply from St. Paul, which was, in turn, supplied from St. Louis. It was, after all, this aspect of the trade that motivated the entire removal effort.[137]

No evidence has been found that President Zachary Taylor's successor, Millard Fillmore, or any other president since him has ever reinstated Chippewa removal. Yet, at the time, Agent Watrous and Governor Ramsey falsely claimed that it had already essentially been accomplished. When the new Democratic administration of Franklin Pierce took office in early 1853, the reign of the Whig politicians in Minnesota was over. Willis Gorman replaced Alexander Ramsey as territorial governor, and John Watrous was removed from office and charged with malfeasance. The new commissioner of Indian affairs, George Manypenny, and Chippewa agent Henry Gilbert both strongly rejected removal as an instrument of Indian policy. It was their belief that the best chance of educating and civilizing the Chippewa was by government programs offered within the confines of reservations set apart from the territories the Chippewa had ceded. This was also the solution that the Chippewa themselves had been urging for over a decade.

Evidence that the failed removal effort had no effect on the understanding of the government relative to the usufruct rights reserved under the 1837 treaty is to be found in the opinion expressed by Minnesota governor Willis Gorman in February 1855. After the construction of a lumbering dam on the upper Rum River in 1849, the Mille Lacs Chippewa, who resided on the 1837 cession, complained that the dam was flooding their wild rice crop. Following several confrontations between the Mille Lacs and lumbermen, including one in which several lumbermen and Chippewa were killed, Governor Gorman, who was ex officio superintendent of Indian affairs for the Minnesota territory, resolved to settle the dispute. Since the dam was located on ceded land that had been purchased by the lumber interest, Gorman determined that, if necessary, he would call in troops from Fort Snelling to protect the lumbermen's "lawful occupation." The Chippewa, he said, had no further "treaty interests in the land except for hunting and fishing."[138] Gorman repeated this same conclusion in June 1855 in a letter to Little Hill.[139]

During the latter half of the nineteenth century, the Chippewa residents of the land ceded under the Treaties of 1837, 1842, and 1847 continued, of necessity, to hunt, fish, and gather over these ceded territories. Except for occasional clashes with lumbermen related to dams on various streams that flooded rice crops and interfered with fish runs, economic life went on as usual. With the advent of Euro-American agricultural settlement after the Civil War, occasional conflicts developed over trespass and competition for game. By and large, however, native people and their new non-Indian neighbors worked out a symbiotic relationship of mutual support in which the Chippewa supplied a wide array of wild food products and handicraft items in exchange for farm products and manufactured goods. By the turn of the twentieth century, however, the unilateral imposition of fish and game laws by the various states increasingly worked hardships on subsistence hunters and gatherers and increasingly forced these activities underground. By the mid-twentieth century, enforcement of state game laws had nearly extinguished Indian subsistence activities except on reservation lands.[140]

CHAPTER 10

Lac Courte Oreilles Band v. Wisconsin, Western District of Wisconsin, Case No. 74-C-313

Kathryn L. Tierney
Bay Mills Indian Community, Brimley, Michigan

> The privilege of hunting, fishing, and gathering the wild rice, upon the lands, the rivers and the lakes included in the territory ceded, is guarantied [*sic*] to the Indians, during the pleasure of the President of the United States.[1]
> (Article 5, Treaty of July 29, 1837)

> The Indians stipulate for the right of hunting on the ceded territory, with the other usual privileges of occupancy, until required to remove by the President of the United States.[2]
> (Article II, Treaty of October 4, 1842)

These promises, contained in land cession treaties between the United States and bands of Chippewa residing in what is now northern Michigan, Wisconsin, and Minnesota, generated two decades of litigation in the federal courts in Wisconsin, concerning the following questions:

- Do the rights reserved by treaty continue to exist?
- If so, what activities are covered by the treaties?
- Can the state regulate tribal member treaty-protected activities?
- Do tribal regulations preempt state regulation of the same activity?

The contemporary controversy began in 1974, caused by the arrests and prosecutions of members of the Lac Courte Oreilles Band of Lake Superior Chippewa Indians in state courts and the imposition of fines and property forfeitures as penalties. The most publicized case involved Fred and Mike Tribble, who were spearing for muskellunge through the ice of a lake adjoining the Lac Courte Oreilles Reservation in Sawyer County. Wisconsin conservation law at the time prohibited even the possession of a spear in that county. The tribe had had enough. Federal court was perceived as the way to stop continued state enforcement of its conservation laws against Lac Courte Oreilles members.

The tribe brought suit on its members' behalf, claiming that the state could not apply its conservation laws to hunting, fishing, trapping, and gathering activities (called "usufructuary activities" by Anglo-Saxon common law) of Lac Courte Oreilles members. The supremacy clause of the U.S. Constitution prevents application of state law, as the right to engage in these activities was guaranteed by the 1837 and 1842 treaties, which are part of the supreme law of the land. The federal court was asked to prohibit the state's employees from enforcing Wisconsin conservation laws against Lac Courte Oreilles members. Named as the primary defendant was Lester Voigt, then secretary of the Wisconsin Department of Natural Resources (DNR). For better or worse, the ensuing litigation over the course of the next sixteen years is commonly called the "*Voigt* case."

Members of Lac Courte Oreilles were confident that the case would be won in federal court, as the oral tradition of the tribe contained many recollections of band chiefs and warriors who attended either or both of the 1837 and 1842 treaty negotiations. All versions contained the understanding that the rights to hunt, fish, trap, and gather would continue to apply to the ceded lands as long as the Indian people lived in the area. Therefore, as the Lac Courte Oreilles band had ensured its continued occupation of its historic and traditional territory by signing a subsequent treaty in 1854,[3] it believed these use rights continued to exist. The Lac Courte Oreilles band was willing to bear the burden of litigation unilaterally, without the participation of the other five tribes in Wisconsin who had also signed the 1837 and 1842 treaties and shared in the rights reserved in them.

Representing the Lac Courte Oreilles in this momentous litigation were two attorneys from the local legal services program, Wisconsin Judicare, Inc., John Wiley and Peter Sferrazza. They engaged in their own historical research, traveling to the regional federal records center in

Chicago to locate historical documents from the period. The documents supported the Lac Courte Oreilles oral tradition about the rights reserved in the 1837 and 1842 treaties and showed that the tribe's leaders in the 1850s demanded assurances through the 1854 treaty that the tribe would always remain on its ancestral lands in northwest Wisconsin.

The case was assigned to Judge James E. Doyle, who consolidated it for decision with two other cases involving the Wisconsin Chippewa bands and the 1837 and 1842 treaties. Both of the other cases were initiated by the United States. The first was filed in 1972, claiming that all sections 16 contained within the initial boundaries established in the 1854 treaty as the Lac Courte Oreilles Reservation are owned by the United States in trust for the tribe; the case was titled *United States v. Ben Ruby and Sons*.[4] The second case was filed in 1976 and was a criminal prosecution of a non-Indian for allegedly trespassing on the Bad River Reservation by hunting there in violation of tribal regulation and in contravention of federal law. The case required the court to determine whether the bed of the Kakagon Slough formed a part of the tribe's reservation, as established under the same 1854 treaty that was at issue in the *Ben Ruby* case. This case was titled *United States v. Bouchard*.[5] None of the three cases involving the 1837, 1842, and 1854 treaties were decided after a trial. All three cases were decided on the submission of historic documents deemed relevant by the litigants and written arguments by the lawyers as to their historic meaning and modern effect.

The Lac Courte Oreilles argued that the rights to hunt, fish, and gather natural resources were guaranteed by the plain language of both the 1837 and the 1842 treaties and had never been relinquished by the tribes and that there was no subsequent act of the United States that abrogated those guarantees. The state argued that whatever rights had been reserved by those treaties were terminated by the removal order issued by President Zachary Taylor in 1850, directing the Chippewa to move to their unsold lands in Minnesota. The state went on to argue that even if the removal order did not completely abrogate the rights to hunt, fish, and gather, the rights were terminated by the creation of permanent land reservations for the Chippewa bands, including Lac Courte Oreilles, by the Treaty of La Pointe in 1854.

Judge Doyle reviewed all the documents submitted by any of the litigants in the consolidated cases and wrote a lengthy opinion in September 1978.[6] In reaching his decision, he carefully noted that the binding rules of interpretation of a treaty with an Indian tribe require that a treaty

> be construed as the Indians would have understood it . . . as disclosed by the practices and customs of the Indians at the time the treaty was negotiated . . . and by the history of the treaty, the negotiations that preceded it and the practical construction given the treaty by the parties.[7]

To carry out this responsibility, Judge Doyle related a detailed chronology of the treaty negotiations in 1837, 1842, and 1854. He discussed the circumstances under which President Taylor issued the 1850 removal order. In reaching his conclusions as to the continued existence of rights to hunt, fish, and gather, Judge Doyle relied on his general training and experience as a judge and on common-law principles of statutory interpretation in order to determine the meaning and intent of the parties to these historic agreements and enactments.

Judge Doyle did not have to determine if usufructuary rights were, in fact, reserved by the 1837 and 1842 treaties. The state conceded that issue. The issue Judge Doyle needed to decide was whether those rights were terminated, or extinguished, by the 1850 removal order and/or the 1854 treaty, as the state contended. Applying the rule of construction that treaties with Indians must be interpreted as the Indians would have understood them, Judge Doyle concluded that the president's authority to require removal was explained in the 1837 and 1842 treaty negotiations to exist only if the Indians misbehaved by harassing white settlers through crop depredations and the like. Since there was no evidence of such misbehavior, the removal order was not authorized by the 1837 and 1842 treaties and therefore invalid and without any force and effect. The usufructuary rights reserved in the two treaties therefore also could not be terminated by the invalid removal order.

Judge Doyle's reliance on the documented historic record for this analysis of the effect of the 1850 removal order was facilitated by the amount of written material on this matter from many sources. All contemporary accounts were in agreement: the Indians understood that they could remain on their ceded lands—and use the natural resources found thereon—as long as they were peaceful. In contrast, no contemporary accounts on the effect of the 1854 treaty on the usufructuary rights reserved in the 1837 and 1842 treaties were part of the record before Judge Doyle. Such accounts simply did not exist. No one—Indian or white—discussed that issue during treaty negotiations, and the treaty itself does not contain any reference to the rights of harvest reserved in the earlier treaties. Judge Doyle relied not on direct documentary evidence but, instead, on his general tools of construction to determine that the Indians must have agreed to give up any right to harvest natural resources on the lands ceded in 1837 and 1842 in return for the establishment of permanent homes/reservations in the 1854 treaty. He reached this conclusion even though there was substantial evidence that the lands continued to be utilized by Indians for harvesting natural resources into the twentieth century. (The judge concluded that this was the lifestyle for whites living in the area as well, so that no inference could be made that Indian people were doing so in reliance on treaty guarantees.)

Lac Courte Oreilles filed notice of appeal with the U.S. Court of Appeals for the Seventh Circuit within twenty days of the issuance of this decision, challenging the court's conclusion as to the meaning and effect of the 1854 treaty. The state also appealed, challenging the court's interpretation of the legality of the 1850 removal order. The case was removed from the active docket of the Seventh Circuit by agreement of Lac Courte Oreilles and the state, in order for the documents contained in the case record to be utilized in yet another case that had since been filed in the federal district court and assigned to Judge Doyle, *State of Wisconsin v. Baker.*[8]

The *Baker* case had initially been filed in state court to seek an injunction against the members of the Lac Courte Oreilles tribal governing body, who sought to regulate the fishing of non-Indians on the lakes of the Lac Courte Oreilles Reservation; the state argued that it had the exclusive right to regulate non-Indian fishing, both on and off the Lac Courte Oreilles Reservation. Nothing happened in the court of appeals while the *Baker* case remained before Judge Doyle awaiting decision. That decision was not reached until October 1981—three years later. In the meantime, the state of Wisconsin continued to apply its conservation laws to Lac Courte Oreilles members (and members of other Chippewa tribes in Wisconsin) when off-reservation.

Judge Doyle determined in *Baker* that title to the Lac Courte Oreilles Reservation's lakes was the determinative factor as to which jurisdiction could regulate non-Indian fishing on that body of water. He concluded that the state held title upon achieving statehood in 1848 (the "equal footing doctrine") and therefore had the right to regulate fishing by non-Indians on the Lac Courte Oreilles Reservation.[9] The tribe appealed that decision.

The Seventh Circuit recognized the common issues of fact and law presented by the *Baker* and *Lac Courte Oreilles* cases, so it ordered in 1981 that they be consolidated for briefing and argument. The arguments were held on the same day before the same three-judge panel. The decisions were issued one day apart, approximately four months after arguments were held. The *Lac Courte Oreilles* decision was issued on January 25, 1983.[10]

The appellate court concurred in Judge Doyle's conclusions as to the legality of the 1850 removal order, but it reversed his decision that the Indians' acceptance of reservations by signing the 1854 treaty abrogated any rights to harvest natural resources outside reservation boundaries. The court refused to find that treaty-reserved rights could be abrogated by inference or implication, holding instead that relevant case law[11] precludes a finding of abrogation in the absence of compelling evidence that such extinguishment was intended by both the United States and the Indians. Cited in support of the legal conclusions and as presenting analogous factual circumstances on the treaties negotiated were *United States v. Michigan* and *People v. LeBlanc* (discussed in chapter 7).

The attorneys involved in crafting the appellate briefs and argument for Lac Courte Oreilles made a tactical decision that was intended to ensure court acceptance of the continued existence of treaty-reserved usufructuary rights. The concession was the acknowledgment that these rights were limited to those lands and waters that were not privately owned. This concession is expressly cited in the opinion in a footnote (no. 14) and is the basis for the court's holding that the rights' exercise is limited to those portions of the ceded land that are not privately owned.

The issuance of this decision was a surprise to the people of Wisconsin, as the press had not reported its status for years. People were taken aback to see headlines announcing the right of Indians to hunt, fish, and gather outside of state control. Lac Courte Oreilles was not immediately prepared to actively regulate its members' off-reservation harvesting activities; it did not have off-reservation regulations or the personnel to enforce them. Of even more immediate concern was that other tribes had also signed the Treaties of 1837 and 1842 and also shared the rights reserved by them; Lac Courte Oreilles asked for a meeting of all the tribes to discuss how to handle the need to regulate and manage off-reservation resources and the future of legal proceedings.

In March 1983, Lac Courte Oreilles hosted a meeting attended by all the tribes who were the legal successors to the bands that signed the 1837 and 1842 treaties. From Wisconsin came the Red Cliff Band of Lake Superior Chippewa Indians, the Bad River Band of Lake Superior Chippewa Indians, the St. Croix Chippewa Indians of Wisconsin, the Lac du Flambeau Band of Lake Superior Chippewa Indians, and the Sokaogon Chippewa Indian Community of the Mole Lake Band of Wisconsin. From Michigan came the Keweenaw Bay Indian Community. From Minnesota came the Mille Lacs Band of Lake Superior Chippewa Indians.

Two matters were of paramount concern. The first was that chaos be avoided through simultaneous prosecution of tribal members throughout the Wisconsin portion of the 1837 and 1842 cession for harvesting in contravention of state law. The tribes soon concluded that it was in their best interests to discuss with the state's representatives how off-reservation harvest by tribal members should be conducted and to agree on harvest seasons, bag limits, and similar measures pending definitive court rulings of those matters. The Wisconsin DNR was receptive to the tribes' offer to meet, and a series of negotiations were held to resolve the number of deer that could be harvested by members, the hunting restrictions members would follow (time, manner, etc.), and where such hunting could occur. This initiative was the impetus for the formation of the Voigt Task Force, comprised of representatives of the eight tribes affected by the Seventh Circuit's decision. The Task Force met as required in order to develop the tribal position on harvest and to negotiate as a group with the state's representatives. The first successful harvest season negotiation was for white-tailed deer in November 1983; admittedly, it was not reached until after Judge Doyle refused to resolve one aspect of the season about which the parties could not agree. As he observed, either there is full agreement on an interim exercise, which is outside court authority to order in the absence of evidentiary hearings, or there is no agreement and no exercise. That conclusion required the tribes and state to work through their differences. Those that could not be resolved, such as the DNR refusal to permit harvest of albino deer, awaited resolution through a trial. Most resource harvest seasons, however, were the subject of stipulation of the state and tribes and resulted in an order of the court from late 1983 to the resource regulation trials that began in 1987 concerning walleye and muskellunge.

The second matter of immediate concern to the tribes was that the case was not over. The state immediately requested rehearing before the entire bench of the Seventh Circuit (termed "rehearing en banc"), arguing that harvesting on land by tribal members could constitute an encumbrance on the land title, which clearly was not the intent of the United States and adversely affected private land ownership. In denying the state's motion for rehearing, the court of appeals revised its January opinion to include in the body of the opinion, as well as in footnote 14, its limitation on exercise to lands that are not privately owned. The state did not give up; it appealed the Seventh Circuit decision to the U.S. Supreme Court, which refused review in October 1983. The only issue determined by the courts at that time, then, was the continued existence of the usufructuary rights. The case was remanded to Judge Doyle for entry of a judgment consistent with the Seventh Circuit's decision; the mandate was received in November 1983.

At the initial hearing before Judge Doyle on November 14, 1983, attorneys for the other five Wisconsin treaty signatory tribes announced their intention to intervene and to participate in any further proceedings. Judge Doyle indicated that such motions would be granted, and he directed the parties to develop a schedule for deciding the remaining issues. In the meantime, he tackled the appellate court's direction to issue a judgment. He directed Lac Courte Oreilles' attorney (myself) and the state's counsel to prepare proposed judgments for his consideration. The judgment he issued in March 1984 resulted in the state's second appeal to the Seventh Circuit. Judge Doyle decreed that treaty rights could be exercised on any land that was publicly owned as of the date on which the revised decision of the appellate court was issued (March 8, 1983). That was not a reasonable construction, the court of appeals concluded. The decision directs the trial court to not establish a bright-line date on which lands available for treaty rights exercise are determined forever; instead, the court is advised to determine the matter in the context of the circumstances as they exist at the time of the treaty rights activity. The appellate court went on to note that some lands, although public, have uses that might not be compatible with certain usufructuary activities, such as hunting. Schools, hospitals, and highways are specifically cited as potentially incompatible with harvesting activities.[12] The question as to the type of land subject to treaty rights exercise continued to arise until issuance of final judgment in 1991.

Contemporaneously with the intervention of each of the Wisconsin treaty signatory tribes as a plaintiff, the scope of the case changed. The tribes sought to include claims for damages against state actors in their official capacity in the complaints filed in 1984, and the state sought to force the United States to join the litigation, arguing that it had claims for negligence in the drafting of the treaties with the Chippewa. The United States claimed sovereign immunity from unconsented suit and did not participate as a party. It was clear that case management required a detailed schedule for further proceedings. The tribes suggested bifurcation into discrete subjects in three phases:

- *Phase I (Declaratory Phase)*—requiring determination as to the nature and scope of the treaty right, meaning what resources can be harvested, using what methods and for what uses
- *Phase II (Regulatory Phase)*—requiring determination of the permissible scope of state regulation and the extent of tribal regulation preempting otherwise applicable state regulation
- *Phase III (Damages Phase)*—requiring determination of damages tribes are entitled to receive for state interference with exercise of treaty harvest rights

Judge Doyle agreed to this structure and scheduled the trial in the declaratory phase for late 1985. The six plaintiff tribes decided to develop a joint litigation strategy, sharing responsibility for witness identification, preparation, and payment. Funds were sought from the Bureau of Indian Affairs for Litigation Support; the first grant, in 1984, was utilized to train tribal judges to adjudicate natural resource cases and to hire and train conservation wardens for each of the six Wisconsin Chippewa tribes. Litigation support from the Bureau of Indian Affairs paid for the services of expert witnesses on the tribes' behalf, as well as for the costs of depositions and transcripts and the travel costs of the tribes' trial attorneys. There was also funding obtained to support the time and travel of tribal representatives (the Voigt Task Force, generally) in negotiating interim season agreements with the Wisconsin DNR.

The trial in the declaratory phase took place in December 1985, being rescheduled due to Judge Doyle's surgery earlier that year removing a portion of his tongue as treatment for oral cancer. Of his condition, he wryly observed from the bench, "It is easier to say an objection is overruled than it is sustained." He refused all offers to reduce the amount of time spent in court each day and listened carefully to the witnesses. Expert witnesses for both the tribes and the state presented testimony on natural resource harvesting by tribal members in the nineteenth century. Post-trial briefs were submitted in the first quarter of 1986, and Judge Doyle issued his decision in February 1987.[13] At the time the decision was issued, he was hospitalized for treatment of his cancer, which returned in late 1986.

Simply put, the decision held that tribal members utilized every animal, plant, and fish in the ceded territory for food, clothing, shelter, and medicine or for participation in the white commercial economy. The methods authorized for harvest are those employed both traditionally and as they may have been enhanced through technological improvement. Tribal members sold these items in the nineteenth century and can do so today. The last element of this decision was a determination that allocation of harvest could be sought if circumstances warranted it and that the measure for tribal share was the amount necessary to provide the Indians with a livelihood, or a moderate living.

Very soon thereafter, Judge Doyle passed away, and the case was transferred to Judge Barbara Crabb. Her first decisions dealt with preparatory matters leading up to the regulatory phase, such as whether or not sporting groups had the right to intervene in the case. Her answer was no, as the sport harvesters' interests were adequately represented by the state's defendants.[14]

An essential component for initiation of the regulatory phase was the determination of the applicable legal standard for permissible state regulation in order to achieve conservation and/or health and safety objectives. Up until this point, case law was quite clear and pervasive that state regulation for conservation purposes had to (1) be reasonable and necessary for those purposes, (2) be the least restrictive alternative available to accomplish conservation, (3) be necessarily applied to Indian harvesters in order to achieve conservation, and (4) not discriminate against Indians.[15] Judge Crabb extended this standard to health and safety regulations, declaring that such regulations may apply when reasonable and necessary to prevent or ameliorate a substantial risk to the public health or safety and do not discriminate against Indians.[16]

The last legal element that required decision prior to engaging in the analysis of appropriate state regulations as contemplated by the regulatory phase was an inquiry as to whether the moderate living guaranteed to the Indians from natural resources imposes an upward ceiling on the amount of resources subject to harvest by tribal members. As Judge Crabb observed, this was the second attempt by the state to establish an allocation between treaty and nontreaty harvesters, which it argued would have to be implemented through regulations of both. Trial on this issue was conducted in 1988, with the tribes presenting the only expert witness, a natural resource economist who established a value to the moderate living standard and quantified the value of all natural resources harvested by tribal members. His conclusion was that even if all Chippewa households were limited to the amount required to purchase necessities only, the financial value of all natural resources would be less than that number. In other words, the moderate living standard was not a ceiling; and the standard imposes no practical limit on harvest by tribal members.[17]

The stage was finally set for the regulatory phase. The first trial in this phase was limited to walleye and muskellunge, which comprised a significant area of contention between tribal fishers and the state. State fishers objected to the use of spears and nets to harvest them and worried that this efficient gear would result in localized instances of overharvest. Even if overharvest did not occur, there was concern that tourist-based local economies would be adversely impacted by tribal members' fishing. Outside the courtroom, these fears resulted in serious threats to tribal members, who were shot at, run off roads, targets of pipe bombs, and so on. This case study will not address in any detail the civil unrest that was generated by treaty rights exercise, other than to observe that the nature and intensity of antitreaty and anti-Indian protests did impact the position of the litigants in the federal courtroom.

The trials in the regulatory phase were scheduled by Judge Crabb to result in one every ninety days, with the need to schedule discovery, trial, and post-trial activities simultaneously. The state's attorney group grew to five attorneys to handle this workload. The tribes' lawyers selected one of their number to serve as lead for each resource, so that the burden could be more easily carried by all. Trials were scheduled for walleye and muskellunge, deer, bear and furbearers, wild rice, other fish species, plants, and timber. Not all were held, as the litigants were able to settle many of the resource issues. Ultimately, trials were conducted only on walleye and muskellunge, deer, and timber.

The conduct and outcome of the walleye and muskellunge trial set the stage for the other natural resource disputes with the state. The state enacted a separate set of regulations applicable only to harvesting by tribal members according to the treaty. The regulations were meant to meet the conservation standard established in *Lac Courte Oreilles IV.* The tribes simultaneously sought a declaration that the state's regulations were too restrictive and a declaration that tribal regulations were adequate to protect the resource and therefore preempted state regulatory authority. A review of the trial transcript demonstrates that each side was simultaneously seeking to establish the appropriateness of its regulatory scheme and the legal inadequacy of the other side's regulatory scheme. The trial order of witness presentation was hijacked, as tribal witnesses were called adversely by the state as part of its case in chief (which is permitted by the Federal Rules of Civil Procedure). This allowed the state's lawyers to cross-examine tribal expert witnesses (biologists) before the tribes' lawyers could provide their direct testimony. The record became confusing, and the parties became more and more contentious. The decision was a bellwether, as the tribal regulatory capacity was naturally in its neophyte stage, and there was no significant track record of effective tribal regulation that could enhance the credibility of the opinions of tribal resource management on what level of regulation was necessary to protect walleye and muskellunge from potential overharvest. As a result, tribal regulation is permitted when it includes substantive regulations required by the state and approved by the court as necessary to protect the resource. For walleye and muskellunge, most of the regulations and management mechanisms approved by the court are derived from the state's regulatory scheme.[18]

This result occurred in the 1989 deer trial as well, although the grounds for requiring compliance with the state's proposed regulations was then predominantly safety-based, rather than conservation-based. For example, safety concerns prevented hunting with firearms before Labor Day, due to the presence of other people in the woods at the same time.[19] This decision also finally settled the issue of the availability of privately owned land for treaty-based harvesting activities. Judge Crabb proclaimed that the treaty right did not apply to privately owned lands, even if the owner gave consent to harvesting by tribal members. Persons engaged in usufructuary activities on privately owned land had to do so in compliance with Wisconsin law.

The last resource trial in the regulatory phase was conducted in February 1990 and included elements missing from the other trials: (1) inquiry into each tribe's capacity to adjudicate disputes between timber contractors and the landowner relating to contract performance and (2) participation of the Wisconsin County Forests Association as defendant-intervenor, due to the significant ownership of commercial forest property by counties within the 1837 and 1842 cession areas. Permitting the counties' association to intervene resulted in a significant increase in the witness list, cross-examination time, and the number of argument points to the court. The trial was so extended that the court directed the tribes to present only one witness as to tribal government capacity to enact laws related to commercial timber harvest by tribal members and to present only one witness regarding the composition and operation of the Tribal Court. Expert testimony as to the efficacy of tribal enforcement personnel and staffing and of Tribal Court capacity was also permitted. Ultimately, however, the court found that the rights reserved by the treaties did not include commercial timber harvest, which mooted much of the evidence presented at trial.[20]

The damages phase was supposed to be tried thereafter, but Judge Crabb ruled in 1990 that the Eleventh Amendment to the U.S. Constitution provides immunity from money damage claims against state employees acting in their official capacity.[21] The reasoning for this conclusion was mirrored in the U.S. Supreme Court decision of the following year involving the Alaskan Native Village of Noatak.[22] The sovereign immunity barrier of the Eleventh Amendment does not preclude the United States from seeking money damages from the state, so efforts were undertaken by attorneys representing the tribes to bring the United States into the litigation. They were not successful in so doing, and final judgment was entered by Judge Crabb on March 19, 1991.[23]

For most of the pendency of the *Lac Courte Oreilles* litigation, it was the only major treaty rights case in which the United States did not participate as a litigant. Until the very end, on the issue of state liability for money damages suffered by the tribes and their members, the absence of the United States did not impede the tribes in securing the rights they so carefully preserved in 1837 and 1842. However, it is highly unlikely that the tribes would have been able to engage in this protracted litigation without the financial support of the Bureau of Indian Affairs of the Department of the Interior. That support ultimately proved more meaningful in obtaining the favorable decisions of *Lac Courte Oreilles I* through *Lac Courte Oreilles VIII* than having the United States at the counsel table.

It is fair to say that my participation in this case was almost a full-time undertaking from 1983 through the 1990 timber trial. Between the courtroom and the negotiation table, there was very little time for any other legal work. The same must also be said for all the tribal representatives who negotiated with the Wisconsin DNR and sat in the federal courtroom during hearings. To an attorney, this was a professional obligation and privilege to participate in an important case. To the tribes and their members, it was the only way to ensure that the rights reserved by their ancestors were more than words on a paper. That insurance not only fulfilled promises and guarantees made by the United States in its treaties but also enabled the continued viability of a culture based on preserving and protecting Mother Earth.

CHAPTER 11

Mille Lacs Band of Chippewa Indians et al. v. State of Minnesota et al., District of Minnesota, Case No. 4-90-605

Marc Slonim

Ziontz, Chestnut, Varnell, Berley and Slonim, Seattle, Washington

The *Mille Lacs* case involved Chippewa rights to hunt, fish, and gather under the Treaty of 1837.[1] In the treaty, made at Fort Snelling in what was then Wisconsin Territory, Chippewa bands from present-day Wisconsin and Minnesota ceded about 13.6 million acres of land to the United States but retained rights to hunt, fish, and gather in the ceded territory. In particular, Article V of the treaty provided,

> The privilege of hunting, fishing, and gathering the wild rice, upon the lands, the rivers and the lakes included in the territory ceded, is guarantied to the Indians, during the pleasure of the President of the United States.

Wisconsin and Michigan bands retained similar rights in the 1842 Treaty of La Pointe,[2] in which they ceded lands in northern Wisconsin (north of the 1837 cession) and the western portion of Michigan's Upper Peninsula, until "required to remove by the President."

The *Mille Lacs* case involved lands in the Minnesota portion of the territory ceded in 1837. It was a direct successor to *Lac Courte Oreilles v. Voigt,*[3] which involved the rights of Wisconsin Chippewa to hunt, fish, and gather in the Wisconsin portion of the 1837 cession (as well as in the Wisconsin portion of the 1842 cession). In important respects, the *Mille Lacs* case was also a successor to *United States v. Michigan,*[4] involving the rights of Michigan Ottawa and Chippewa to fish in portions of the Great Lakes they ceded to the United States in the 1836 Treaty of Washington and to earlier litigation in the state courts in Michigan and Wisconsin involving the 1836 and 1842 treaties.[5]

Unlike its predecessors, the *Mille Lacs* case ultimately would be decided on the merits by the U.S. Supreme Court. The Supreme Court's decision affirmed the continued existence of Chippewa hunting, fishing, and gathering rights under the 1837 treaty and provided support for similar rights under the 1836 and 1842 treaties. Because of the respect accorded a Supreme Court decision, the *Mille Lacs* case played a pivotal role in the preservation and public acceptance of Indian treaty hunting, fishing, and gathering rights in the upper Midwest.

The *Mille Lacs* case is also significant in light of the development of a successful tribal self-regulatory system and a comanagement regime for highly prized natural resources. I touch on these features of the case in this case study, but the focus here is on the threshold issue of the continued existence of the Mille Lacs band's treaty rights.

Lac Courte Oreilles

It is unlikely there would have been a *Mille Lacs* case but for the 1983 decision by the U.S. Court of Appeals for the Seventh Circuit in the *Lac Courte Oreilles* case. Accordingly, it is appropriate to begin a discussion of the *Mille Lacs* case with a brief summary of the Seventh Circuit's decision in *Lac Courte Oreilles.* A more complete discussion of the *Lac Courte Oreilles* litigation is in chapter 10 in this volume.

The Lac Courte Oreilles band filed suit in the U.S. District Court for the Western District of Wisconsin to prevent Wisconsin officials from interfering with the exercise of its usufructuary rights under the 1837 and 1842 treaties.[6] In response, Wisconsin argued that those rights had been extinguished by an 1850 executive order and an 1854 treaty. In the 1850 executive order, President Zachary Taylor revoked the Chippewa's usufructuary rights under the 1837 and 1842 treaties and ordered them to remove from the ceded territory. In the 1854 treaty, Chippewa bands (including Lac Courte Oreilles) ceded lands in the Arrowhead Region of northeastern

Minnesota and secured reservations there and on the previously ceded lands in northern Wisconsin and the western Upper Peninsula of Michigan.[7]

The case was decided on motions for summary judgment—there was no trial. The district court rejected the state's argument that the 1850 executive order extinguished the Chippewa's treaty rights. On the basis of historical documents provided by the parties, the court found the Chippewa did not understand either treaty to confer unfettered discretion on the president to terminate their usufructuary rights; rather, the president could do so only if the Chippewa misbehaved by harassing white settlers. The court found the Chippewa had not misbehaved, and it therefore concluded that the 1850 order exceeded the president's authority under the treaties and was invalid. However, the district court also found that when they secured permanent reservations in the 1854 treaty, the Chippewa implicitly relinquished their rights to hunt, fish, and gather outside their reservations. The court noted that the 1854 treaty contained a provision reserving hunting and fishing rights in the territory ceded in 1854 but was silent with respect to hunting and fishing rights on the lands previously ceded in 1837 and 1842.

In 1983, the Seventh Circuit reversed the district court's judgment. It agreed with the district court's factual findings and its conclusion regarding the 1850 executive order. However, the Seventh Circuit disagreed with the district court's interpretation of the 1854 treaty. According to the Seventh Circuit, the 1854 treaty could only terminate the Chippewa's usufructuary rights if it expressly referred to termination of those rights or if the circumstances made clear that Congress intended such termination. Because the 1854 treaty made no reference to the usufructuary rights secured in the 1837 and 1842 treaties and because the Seventh Circuit found no clear evidence Congress intended to terminate those rights, it held that they were not abrogated by the 1854 treaty.

The Supreme Court declined to review the Seventh Circuit's decision. The case returned to the district court to determine the nature and extent of the rights retained by the Chippewa and the extent to which the state of Wisconsin could regulate the exercise of those rights. In addition to Lac Courte Oreilles, the other five Chippewa bands in Wisconsin participated in the remand proceedings. Those proceedings would last another eight years and were punctuated by violent and racist protests against the Chippewa as they sought to exercise peacefully the rights their ancestors had secured and to preserve their culture and traditions for future generations. However, after the district court entered final judgment in 1991, no party appealed.

Mille Lacs Band v. Minnesota—Prelude

The western part of the 1837 cession, comprising about three million acres, is located in present-day Minnesota. It is bordered on the west by the Mississippi River and encompasses most of Mille Lacs Lake, one of Minnesota's premier walleye lakes. After the Seventh Circuit's 1983 decision, the Mille Lacs band contacted the Minnesota Department of Natural Resources to discuss implementation of the band's 1837 treaty rights in the Minnesota portion of the ceded territory. Neither the Mille Lacs band nor the state of Minnesota was a party to the *Lac Courte Oreilles* case. However, the Seventh Circuit's decision held that these rights still existed, and the band could see no reason to distinguish its rights in the Minnesota portion of the cession from the rights of the Lac Courte Oreilles band in the Wisconsin portion of the cession.

The state of Minnesota saw things differently. It asserted that the Seventh Circuit's decision regarding the 1850 executive order was incorrect. Because Minnesota is within the jurisdiction of the U.S. Court of Appeals for the Eighth Circuit, the state did not believe it was bound by the Seventh Circuit's decision. In addition, the state claimed that the 1855 Treaty of Washington[8] expressly terminated the Mille Lacs band's usufructuary rights. The 1855 treaty was not in issue in the *Lac Courte Oreilles* case, and its effect on the Chippewa's 1837 treaty rights had not been addressed in that case.

At the time, the Mille Lacs band, like many Chippewa bands in Minnesota, Wisconsin, and Michigan, was impoverished. It had lost most of its reservation lands in timber scandals of the late nineteenth century and had spent decades resisting efforts to remove its members from the Mille Lacs Reservation to the White Earth Reservation. Several band economic development projects on the Mille Lacs Reservation had failed.

However, the Mille Lacs Reservation was also a center of traditional Ojibwe culture, beliefs, and language. The band, led by a visionary Indian leader, Art Gahbow, was intent on preserving its culture and heritage. That heritage included netting fish in Mille Lacs Lake for ceremonial and subsistence purposes, a practice that was outlawed by the state of Minnesota. The band was determined to take whatever action was necessary so that its members could continue to harvest natural resources as their ancestors had done for generations.

With extremely limited financial resources, the band retained attorneys, anthropologists, and ethnohistorians to begin researching its claims. The principal areas of research were (1) the band's use of natural resources at the time of the 1837 treaty and thereafter; (2) the 1837 treaty itself; (3) the 1850 executive order; and (4) the 1855 treaty.

Although the *Lac Courte Oreilles* case already held the 1850 executive order invalid, the band knew the state of Minnesota was intent on relitigating this issue. The band also knew that the *Lac Courte Oreilles* decisions were based on a limited set of historical documents supplied by the parties, with no expert testimony or analysis. The band wanted to determine whether additional evidence and analysis could be obtained regarding the parties' understandings of the 1837 treaty, the actual circumstances leading to the issuance of the 1850 executive order, the manner in which the order was implemented, the Indians' response to the order, and the subsequent history of the order.

The band also needed to compile evidence regarding the 1855 treaty, which was not at issue in *Lac Courte Oreilles*. Here, the band was interested in evidence regarding the circumstances leading to the treaty, the parties' understanding of it (especially a provision in which the signatory bands ceded not only a defined tract of land but all their right, title, and interest to any other lands), and the subsequent history of the treaty.

The band was most interested in giving voice to its ancestors' understandings, motivations, and actions. Most of the historical documents were written in English by non-Indians. The band sought the assistance of anthropologists and ethnohistorians to help bring the Indian side of the story to light.

The Mille Lacs Band Files Suit, and the Parties Attempt to Settle

On August 13, 1990, the Mille Lacs band and four of its members, including Art Gahbow, filed suit against the state of Minnesota and various state officials in the U.S. District Court for the District of Minnesota. The band sought a declaratory judgment that "the privilege of hunting, fishing, and gathering the wild rice upon the lands, the rivers and the lakes included in the territory ceded" in the 1837 treaty, which had been guaranteed to the Indians "during the pleasure of the President," continued to exist.

The band also sought a declaration defining the permissible scope of state regulation of these activities and an injunction prohibiting the state from interfering with its members' exercise of these rights, except as authorized in the court's declaratory judgment. The band did not seek a treaty right of access to private lands, recognizing that the treaty rights could only be exercised on those lands, public and private, to which band members had access under generally applicable law. Nor did the band seek money damages for past violations of its rights.

The state's response raised a host of procedural and substantive defenses. The state claimed that it was immune from suit, that the band had waited too long to bring suit, that the band's claims were foreclosed by prior Indian claims litigation, that the band was required to join the United States and other Indian tribes who could not be joined, and that the case belonged in state, not federal, court. In addition, as expected, the state argued that the band's rights had been terminated by the 1850 executive order and the 1855 treaty.

The band and the state agreed to bifurcate the case into two phases. The first phase would address the state's procedural defenses and (if the band survived those defenses) determine whether the band retained rights under the 1837 treaty, whether those rights extended to private lands, and the general nature of those rights. If the court determined that the band retained rights under the treaty, a second phase would determine the validity of particular state laws regulating those rights.

As the parties began work on the first phase of the case, they also met to discuss settlement possibilities. After several starts and stops, band officials and representatives of the Minnesota Department of Natural Resources reached agreement on a settlement that would recognize but limit the exercise of the band's rights under the 1837 treaty.

The agreement was subject to ratification by band members in a referendum vote and to approval of the Minnesota legislature. Although band members approved the agreement, the legislature did not. Anti-treaty organizations, many with ties to the anti-treaty protestors in Wisconsin, argued strenuously against the settlement and insisted that the case should be decided by the courts.

The Trial

With the legislature's rejection of the settlement, the parties refocused their efforts on litigating the case. The district court had denied motions to intervene by a group of counties and a group of landowners opposed to the band's claims, but the Eighth Circuit reversed those rulings, and the counties and landowners joined the case as full parties in April 1993. In late 1993, the United States successfully moved to intervene in support of the band's claims, and it, too, joined the case as a full party.

The band developed a two-part approach to the first phase of the case. It would seek summary judgment on all of the state's procedural defenses, as well as any related defenses asserted by the counties and landowners, in an attempt to eliminate those defenses from the case before trial. However, it would seek a trial on the merits of the case, so that the district court judge could hear from and evaluate the credibility of the witnesses. The band believed a trial was essential for it to present the Indian side of the story and to create a full record for the district court.

The judge was the chief judge of the U.S. District Court for the District of Minnesota, Diana E. Murphy. On May 13, 1994, she ruled on the parties' motions for summary judgment, rejecting the state's procedural defenses and setting the case for trial on June 13, 1994.[9]

Modeling its case on the successful trial in *United States v. Michigan,* the band assembled a team of experts to help present its case. The experts included anthropologists and ethnohistorians (Charles Cleland, James McClurken, Helen Tanner, and Bruce White), a Chippewa linguist (John Nichols), and a legal historian (Tom Lund). Their direct testimony was largely presented through written reports, in which they presented the results of their research and the bases for their opinions. The experts would summarize their qualifications and their reports at trial and then be subjected to cross-examination. Three band members would also testify: Herman Kegg, Brenda Boyd, and Joseph Dunkley.

The band's case encompassed several major themes, which ran through almost all the testimony:

• The rights secured by the 1837 treaty—of hunting, fishing, and gathering wild rice on the lands, the rivers, and the lakes included in the territory ceded—were of profound spiritual, cultural, and economic importance to the Chippewa at the time of the treaty and remained so throughout the nineteenth century and well into the twentieth. Even by the time the case went to trial in the late twentieth century, the spiritual and cultural importance of hunting, fishing, and gathering and their centrality to Chippewa identity and traditions were undiminished.

• The Chippewa participants in the 1837 treaty were invited to rely and did rely on the good faith of the president of the United States—their "Great Father"—to protect their rights and interests. The English idiom "during the pleasure of the President" was foreign to Ojibwe, and there was no evidence that the Chippewa were told or had any reason to believe that the president could revoke their rights at any time and for any reason.

• There was no discussion of removal during the 1837 treaty council, and there was no provision for the Indians' removal in the treaty. Save for a small number of missionaries, lumbermen, and fur traders, the 13.6-million-acre cession had virtually no non-Indian inhabitants, and neither the government nor the Indians anticipated an influx of white settlers at any time in the foreseeable future. The government's sole interest was in acquiring legal access to pine timber on the land; it saw no need to work out arrangements for the Indians' removal from the land. When the government sought to include a removal provision in the 1842 treaty, the Chippewa refused to sign until they received assurances they would not be removed unless they misbehaved by harassing white settlers.

• The 1850 executive order was not a response to Indian misbehavior or even to non-Indian settlement pressures. Instead, the impetus for the order arose when influential officials in the newly formed Minnesota Territory saw a business opportunity. The government maintained an Indian agency at La Pointe on Lake Superior, and it made annual payments to the Indians under the 1837 and 1842 treaties in specie and goods there. The annuity provisions were purchased in Detroit and shipped to La Pointe through the Great Lakes, and the cash payments often ended up in the hands of Indian traders at La Pointe. If the Indians could be removed from northern Wisconsin to northern Minnesota, the government would need to move the Indian agency to Minnesota, would acquire annuity provisions in St. Louis or St. Paul for shipment up the Mississippi, and would make the payments in Minnesota. All of this promised significant business opportunities for the new territory, in which Indian annuity payments represented one of the few sources of cash and goods on the frontier.

• There never was an attempt to remove the Mille Lacs band from the 1837 cession under the 1850 order. Instead, the entire focus of the government's removal agent was on removing the Wisconsin Chippewa to northern Minnesota. The practical focus of the removal effort confirmed the underlying motivation for the order.

• The Chippewa strenuously opposed the removal order. Chippewa leaders expressed shock at the order and argued there was no basis for it. They insisted that they had been told they would not be removed unless they misbehaved and that they had not misbehaved. Missionaries and other non-Indians agreed with them. Indeed, fur traders, miners, and lumbermen valued the Chippewa's assistance and wanted them to remain.

• To induce the Chippewa to remove, the government's removal agent arranged to have their annuities paid in Sandy Lake, Minnesota, and timed the 1850 payment so that it would not arrive until after winter weather set it, preventing the Chippewa's return to Wisconsin. The plan had disastrous consequences. Hundreds of Chippewa men who had gone to retrieve their annuities died awaiting the payment or on a defiant trip home to Wisconsin. The deaths at Sandy Lake strengthened the Chippewa's resolve not to remove. When government officials in Washington, D.C., realized that it would take troops to enforce the removal order, they first suspended and then abandoned the order altogether. Federal and territorial officials and local lumbermen specifically recognized that the Mille Lacs band retained hunting, fishing, and gathering rights under the 1837 treaty in 1855—five years after the 1850 executive order was issued.

• The local Indian agent excluded the Mille Lacs band from the 1854 treaty. However, when the government summoned the Minnesota Chippewa to make a new treaty in 1855, Mille Lacs leaders insisted they be allowed to participate. In that treaty, negotiated in January and February 1855 in Washington, D.C., the Mille Lacs band joined with other Minnesota Chippewa in ceding lands in northern Minnesota but also secured a permanent reservation in their traditional homeland on the south shore of Mille Lacs Lake within the 1837 cession.

• The circumstances surrounding the 1855 treaty negotiation showed that the Mille Lacs band's leaders selected their reservation to secure important resources critical to the band's seasonal round of hunting, fishing, and gathering and had no intent to relinquish the band's rights to engage in these activities under the 1837 treaty. In the provision of the treaty on which the state of Minnesota was relying, the Chippewa, after ceding a defined tract of land in northern Minnesota, ceded any right, title, and interest to any other lands anywhere. This provision was inserted in the treaty by federal officials after some of the northern Minnesota bands stated they could not precisely define the full extent of their lands claims. The additional clause, phrased in the highly technical language of American land law, was intended to extinguish these ill-defined land claims, not to affect the specific usufructuary rights reserved by the Chippewa in 1837.

The *Mille Lacs* trial began on June 13 and

concluded on July 6, 1994. Judge Murphy issued her decision on August 24, 1994.[10] She made detailed findings of fact regarding the importance of hunting, fishing, and gathering to the Chippewa and the 1837 treaty, 1850 executive order, and 1855 treaty. In addressing the legal issues in the case, she applied established canons of treaty interpretation, which provide that Indian treaties should be construed as they were understood by the Indians and that ambiguous provisions should be construed in favor of the Indians.

Judge Murphy concluded that the 1850 executive order did not revoke the band's 1837 treaty hunting, fishing, and gathering rights on three independent grounds. First, she held that the 1837 treaty did not provide for the removal of the Chippewa from the ceded lands. Thus, in purporting to order the Chippewa to remove, the order exceeded the president's authority and was invalid. Because the revocation portion of the order was merely an incident of the directive to remove, the entire order was invalid. Second, Judge Murphy held that even if the revocation portion of the order could be severed from the removal portion of the order, it, too, was invalid. As the courts held in *Lac Courte Oreilles,* the president could only revoke the Indians' usufructuary rights if the Indians misbehaved by harassing white settlers, and they had not done so. Third, Judge Murphy found that the 1850 order was never intended to apply to the Mille Lacs band, was subsequently suspended as to the Wisconsin bands, and was revoked as to all of the bands when, in 1854 and 1855, they received permanent reservations in the ceded territory.

Judge Murphy also concluded that the 1855 treaty did not revoke the band's 1837 usufructuary rights. She found that the 1855 treaty did not contain an express revocation of those rights and that neither the government nor the Indians intended or understood the treaty to revoke those rights. Judge Murphy then declared the general nature of the band's rights. She held that the rights extended to all natural resources in the ceded territory with the exception of pine timber, could be exercised for commercial as well as ceremonial and subsistence purposes, and were not limited to any particular techniques, methods, devices, or gear. In addition, she held that the state could only regulate the exercise of the band's rights if such regulation was necessary to conserve the resources being harvested or to protect public health or safety and that it could not regulate at all if the band had an effective system of self-regulation.

The state, counties, and landowners wanted to take an immediate appeal from Judge Murphy's decision. The band resisted that course. It felt the resolution of regulatory and management issues in Phase II would be important to demonstrate to the court of appeals that implementation of the band's treaty rights was workable and would not threaten either the natural resources in the cession or nontreaty hunting, fishing, and gathering opportunities. The district court and the court of appeals refused to permit an immediate appeal, and the case proceeded to Phase II. Around the same time, President Clinton appointed Judge Murphy to the Eighth Circuit Court of Appeals, and the case was reassigned to Judge Michael Davis.

Phase II

At the outset of Phase II, the six Wisconsin Chippewa bands intervened in the case so they could exercise their 1837 treaty rights in the Minnesota portion of the cession. On motions for summary judgment, Judge Davis reaffirmed that the Wisconsin bands retained their usufructuary rights under the 1837 treaty and that their rights had not been revoked by the 1850 executive order or the 1854 treaty. In so doing, the court rejected a new argument that, under the "equal footing doctrine," the 1858 act admitting Minnesota to the Union[11] impliedly extinguished the bands' treaty rights. This argument was based on an 1896 Supreme Court decision but had been discredited in many subsequent decisions until it appeared to have been revived by the Tenth Circuit in 1995. In the *Mille Lacs* case, Judge Davis found the argument had no application to the bands' rights under the 1837 treaty.

The Mille Lacs and Wisconsin bands developed a model tribal code and resource management plans to regulate the exercise of their treaty rights. They then engaged in extensive negotiations with the state to address the state's concerns regarding the conservation of the resources and public health and safety. Those negotiations resolved nearly all of the regulatory issues in

Phase II and led to the development of information sharing and resource management protocols between the bands and the state.

During this process, the district court ruled, in a separate case, that the Fond du Lac band also retained usufructuary rights under the 1837 treaty. In that case, which had been filed in 1992, the court held the state could not relitigate its claim that the rights had been revoked by the 1850 executive order, since the state had had a full and fair opportunity to litigate that claim in the *Mille Lacs* case. After that ruling, the *Mille Lacs* and *Fond du Lac* cases were consolidated for resolution of Phase II issues, and the Fond du Lac band adopted the model code and protocols that had been developed in the *Mille Lacs* case.

Phase II presented two other issues. First, the state, counties, and landowners argued that because some of the bands had successful gaming enterprises, they had attained a "moderate living" and should not be entitled to harvest more than a tiny fraction of the available natural resources. In addition, the parties disagreed about the extent to which the bands could exercise their rights on private lands.

Judge Davis resolved all of the Phase II issues without a trial on January 29, 1997.[12] He ruled in favor of the bands on all of the outstanding regulatory issues and rejected the state-county-landowner efforts to limit the bands' harvest, but he accepted the state's position on the private lands issue.

Appeals

The state, the counties, and the landowners appealed almost every aspect of the district court's decisions to the Eighth Circuit Court of Appeals, and the bands filed a cross-appeal with respect to the private lands issue. The court of appeals entered a stay to prevent the bands from exercising their rights pending resolution of the appeals and expedited the appeals.

On August 26, 1997, the court of appeals, in a decision written by Judge Donald Lay, affirmed the district court's decisions in all respects.[13] The court specifically addressed and rejected the state's arguments based on sovereign immunity, the 1850 executive order, the 1854 treaty, the 1855 treaty, prior Indian claims litigation, and the equal footing doctrine. The court also rejected efforts to limit band harvests under the moderate living doctrine and affirmed the lower court's ruling on the private lands issue.

The state, the counties, and the landowners petitioned the U.S. Supreme Court for writs of certiorari. On June 8, 1998, the Supreme Court granted the state's petition, agreeing to review the Eighth Circuit's decision with respect to the 1850 executive order, the 1855 treaty, and the equal footing doctrine. In taking the case, the Supreme Court put at risk not only the bands' rights in the Minnesota portion of the ceded territory but the rights that had been secured in the Wisconsin portion of the ceded territory in the *Lac Courte Oreilles* case.

In briefing and arguing the case in the Supreme Court, the bands relied heavily on the factual record compiled in the district court. They filed separate briefs addressing each of the three issues on which the Court had granted certiorari. The bands emphasized that they had developed a self-regulatory and management system that would protect the resources, and they filed a fourth brief that chronicled the successful implementation of their rights in Wisconsin, notwithstanding violent protests against the exercise of their rights there.

On March 24, 1999, the Supreme Court affirmed the Eighth Circuit's decision.[14] Justice Sandra Day O'Connor wrote the opinion for the five-justice majority. Chief Justice Rehnquist filed an opinion for the four dissenting justices, and Justice Thomas filed a separate dissent on his own.

Justice O'Connor's opinion for the Court contained a detailed discussion of the historical circumstances surrounding the 1837 treaty, the 1850 executive order, and the 1855 treaty, based in large part on the expert reports and testimony presented by the Mille Lacs band during the 1994 trial. Applying the established canons of Indian treaty construction, she concluded that President Taylor lacked authority to issue the 1850 executive order, because the Chippewa had never agreed to remove from the 1837 ceded territory; that neither the government nor the Chippewa intended the 1855 treaty to revoke the band's hunting, fishing, and gathering rights under the 1837 treaty, and that Congress did not intend to revoke those rights when it admitted Minnesota to the Union in 1858.

The decision was a rare victory for Indian tribes in the Supreme Court in the 1990s. According to Indian law scholar David Getches, in the ten Supreme Court terms up to and including the term in which the *Mille Lacs* case was decided, the Supreme Court decided twenty-four cases involving principles of Indian law. Besides *Mille Lacs,* only two other cases were decided in favor of Indian tribes; another was decided partially in favor of a tribe.

The decision conclusively determined that the Chippewa's rights to hunt, fish, and gather under the 1837 treaty continued to exist. The Lac Courte Oreille band's victory in the Seventh Circuit was secured and extended to Minnesota. The Chippewa bands' sovereign authority to regulate their own members' usufructuary activities was recognized and affirmed. More generally, the traditional canons of Indian treaty interpretation were given renewed life, and the attempt to revive the equal footing argument was rejected.

Art Gahbow died before the *Mille Lacs* case went to trial in 1994. On the eve of the Supreme Court's decision, his successor as chief executive of the Mille Lacs band, Marge Anderson, called on band members and nonband members to respect the Supreme Court's decision, no matter what the result. The bands have worked hard in the years since 1999 to implement their rights in a manner that protects natural resources for future generations and is respectful of non-Indian hunters and fishermen with whom they share these resources. At the same time, they have been able to exercise their treaty rights in ways that preserve the traditions of their ancestors and strengthen the identity of current and future generations of Chippewa.

CHAPTER 12

The Menominee and the Coming of Europeans

According to Menominee legend, the Menominee people were created at the mouth of the Minikanisepi (Menominee) River, where the Great Spirit created the first Menominee from a bear. Thus was the origin of the people of the bear (*owasse*) clan or totem. Later the eagle was called to join the bear people, and the Great Spirit created from it the people of the golden eagle (*kineu*) clan.[1] As time passed, these two clans each called other animals to join them, and from these, in turn, were created the people of other Menominee clans. Each episode of creation is identified with specific places in the territory of the Menominee tribe, so that, for example, the wolf clan was created on the Wolf River (Moqwaioosepeome), the dog clan was created at Sturgeon Bay (Nomawiqkito), and the deer clan originated at Shawano Lake.[2] Each of the other dozen or so clans was created in this way from their animal ancestors.

Ultimately the Menominee thought of themselves as belonging to one of several dozen clans, which were, in turn, grouped into two divisions or phratries. These main divisions were the bear and the thunderer, the latter associated with the powerful medicine birds. Thus, for example, the bear phratry consisted of the bear, porcupine, turtle, crane, wolf, otter, sturgeon, and sunfish clans. Members of these clans felt they were more closely related to each other than they were to members of the clans of the thunderer phratry. In marriage, both clans and phratries were exogamous, meaning that a person was required to marry a member of one of the clans grouped into the opposite phratry. Each clan was thought to bring special attributes of strength, courage, skill, and leadership, which together strengthened the whole of the Menominee people. As the Menominee envisioned their realm, it was like a huge wigwam extending north and south with a fire kindled by the thunderers in the middle.[3] When the Menominee traveled their homeland between Bay de Noc and the Milwaukee River and between Lake Michigan and their western hunting grounds, they visited the places of creation, the locale of legend, and they venerated the sites where Nanabush the creator hero performed the feats that gave shape to the natural world. Although the Menominee were called the wild rice people (Manomini) by Euro-Americans (Follies Avoines in French) they referred to themselves by the name *Omanominewak*, which has the same meaning in the Menominee language.

Culturally and linguistically, the Menominee people constitute a subgroup of the Central Algonquian–speaking people who populated the Great Lakes region from the Canadian Shield to the Ohio River. The Central Algonquian languages can be linguistically divided into several subgroups: the Sauk-Fox-Kickapoo; the Illinois-Maimi-Shawanee; the Chippewa-Ottawa-Potawatomi; and the Menominee. The Menominee language is thus a distinct dialect, and while mutually intelligible with other Central Algonquian dialects, it is sufficiently different to render communication difficult. Historically, however, many Menominees also spoke Ojibwa and used it in contact with outsiders; as a result, there are many Ojibwa loanwords in the Menominee language.[4]

The first written description of the Indians living around Green Bay resulted from the visit of Jean Nicolet in 1634.[5] Although his account is confusing as to the exact placement and size of the various tribes west of Lake Michigan, it would appear that the Menominee then occupied the Lake Michigan and Green Bay shore between the Nouquet (i.e., Chippewa) bands in the Bay de Noc area and the Winnebago who occupied the country around and southwest of Lake Winnebago. The Sauk-Fox may have also shared the upper Fox River valley at this time.

After AD 1650, the area west of Lake Michigan became a refuge for many eastern tribes of lower Michigan and southwestern Ontario who were attempting to escape the westward raiding of the Five Nations Iroquois.[6] Potawatomi, Ottawa, Ojibwa, Nipissing, Huron, and other refugee Indians founded villages in the territory of the Menominee and their powerful Winnebago neighbors. This period is documented by the visit of Father Claude Allouez in 1669.[7] Father Allouez established the Mission of St. François Xavier on the Oconto River to attempt the conversion of the Menominee to Christianity.[8] Father Louis Andre moved the mission to the De Pere Rapids on the Fox River in 1671, where he remained until 1684, having fair success in converting some of the Menominee.[9] The French diplomat-trader Nicholas Perrot, who visited Green Bay in 1667, established a fur trade relationship with the local Indians and recognized the strategic importance of Green Bay as a point to control access to a trade with the tribes south of Lake Michigan and west to the Wisconsin and Mississippi River regions. The importance of the Fox River corridor was not lost on the Potawatomi or the Sauk-Fox, who themselves tried to limit and monopolize trade access to more distant tribes.

By the early decades of the eighteenth century, warfare, European disease, and maneuvering for the fur trade had changed the complexion of tribal affairs around Green Bay. The once populous and powerful Winnebago had been vastly reduced in number, the Potawatomi had come to dominate the Lake Michigan shore of Wisconsin, and the Menominee began to expand their tribal domain to the south (see map 7). This expansion was likely motivated by the rich rice and fish resources of the Lake Winnebago basin as well as the desire to be in closer contact with the French trading and mission establishments at the mouth of the Fox River. This was particularly the case after the construction of the French fort of La Baye in 1716.

During the period of the French and Indian War, the Menominee were firm allies of the French. Menominee warriors led by La Motte, Old Carron, La Chat, Konot or Glode Carron, Osawwishkeno (Yellow Bird), and Kachakawasheka (Notch Maker) fought in a great many campaigns against the English and their Iroquois allies, including the defeat of General Braddock near Fort Duquesne, the falls of Fort Oswego and Fort William Henry, and many other engagements.[10] Finally, the Menominee, under the leadership of Charles de Langlade, himself part Menominee, were present in 1759 at the fall of Quebec, which ended the rule of France in Canada.[11] The annual summer war forays to the eastern conflicts in birch bark canoes certainly speaks to the ability of the Menominee as accomplished Great Lakes mariners.[12]

During the era of French control, the Menominee became firmly immersed in the fur trade. They intermarried with the traders and became dependent on manufactured goods, particularly textiles, firearms, iron cutting tools, and copper and brass cooking vessels. To acquire these items, the Menominee not only trapped and hunted fur and hides but also collected other trade commodities, such as wild rice and maple sugar. In addition, the Menominee supplied the French community with manufactured goods, such as bags, baskets, mats, canoes, building materials, gums, resins, cordage, and items of skin clothing, including moccasins and robes.

The period between the fall of Quebec in 1759 and the end of the War of 1812 was dominated by the British and by British trade policy. Locally, the British had very little influence over the Menominee, who continued to live in harmony with the French community at Green Bay. In 1761 a British garrison arrived at Green Bay to occupy Fort La Baye, which was rebuilt and renamed Fort Edward Augustus. The Menominee requested presents of the British as reparations for the many chiefs and warriors they had lost in the decades of warfare with these former enemies. In 1763 the Menominee took no part in the Pontiac uprising against the British, but the British did abandon Fort Augustus. Despite repeated requests by the Menominee, the British never again regarrisoned Green Bay.

The Menominee eventually became British partisans and, in the Revolutionary War era, joined British-sponsored expeditions against the Americans in the Illinois country and in the recapture of Fort Mackinac. This alliance continued with the outbreak of the War of 1812, when Menominee warriors under the leadership of Chakauchokama, or "Old King," and Tomah fought alongside British troops. In this warfare, Old King entrusted Tomah with the care of his young grandson Oshkosh (Bear's Claw), who, with the future great orator of the Menominee tribe Kauskkaunonaive (Grizzly Bear), apprenticed under Tomah's leadership.

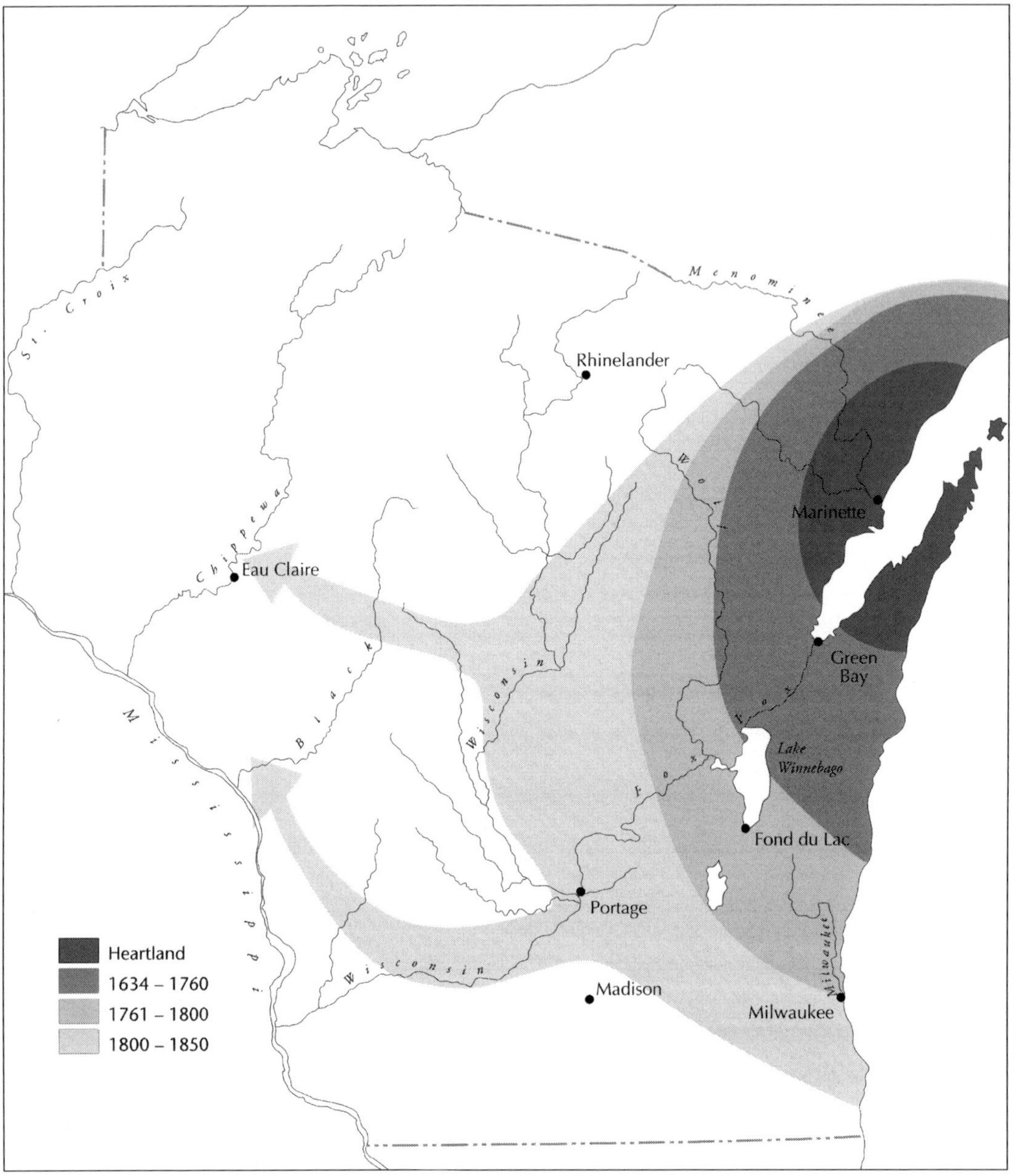

Map 7. Territorial expansion of the Menominee tribe.

At the conclusion of the war, the British were obliged to leave American territory but did so very reluctantly. In 1816 the British withdrew to Drummond Island, where they built a fort and Indian Department establishment that served as a counterpoint to the American fort at Mackinac. From these posts, the competing American and British powers wooed large numbers of Great Lakes Indians each year with presents in exchange for promises of future loyalty.

In their home country, the Menominee continued to expand their tribal domain as Menominee bands ranged farther and farther from the shores of Green Bay and Lake Winnebago. By the beginning of the American period, they occupied the Lake Michigan shore from the Milwaukee River to Bay de Noc and west to the Black River. Winter hunting expeditions took them even farther west, to the valleys of the Chippewa and Mississippi rivers and even beyond.[13]

At the turn of the nineteenth century, little had changed for the Menominee since their first adaptation to the presence of Euro-Americans and the fur trade enterprise. In fact, the Menominee had adopted an economic, social, and political strategy that allowed them to take advantage of new opportunities without requiring radical cultural change. By establishing kin ties with the Green Bay traders and by developing new ways to harvest and market natural resources, they were able to accommodate new technology and market demands within the traditional subsistence cycle. Despite rather major technological change, the Menominee were able to maintain their social, political, and ideological system essentially as it had been since time immemorial.

Principles of Menominee Social and Political Organization

The Menominee, as a people, developed an economy that was uniquely suited to the resources and conditions of the country that is today northeastern Wisconsin. Central to this adaptation are aquatic resources—namely, wild rice and fish, particularly the sturgeon.[14] These and a huge variety of other resources occurred abundantly in the shallow, slow-moving, nutrient-rich, waterways of Green Bay, Lake Winnebago, and the Fox River valley, which were essential to the adaptation of the Menominee. Although the Menominee planted crops of corn, beans, and squash, they did not depend on these foods to the degree of their southern and western neighbors, the Winnebago and Potawatomi. Instead, the Menominee's economic cycle depended on their ability to move between and harvest wild resources as these were seasonally available. Thus, the Menominee spent the warmer seasons of the year gathered in lakeside villages where they planted, collected wild plant foods, and hunted in the surrounding countryside. After wild rice was harvested in the late summer and garden products processed and stored in the fall, the summer villages broke up as individual families went off to hunt and fish during the winter months.

Typically each Menominee family had a separate wintering territory. Here they exploited spawning runs for whitefish and lake trout in the late fall, speared and harpooned sturgeon, and hunted deer, bear, and other game in the upland areas. During the fur trade era, men and women were occupied by trapping and preparing the pelts of fur-bearing species, including principally beaver, otter, muskrat, mink, and martin. Hides of deer, elk, bear, wolf, and the wild cats were also important trade commodities.[15] At the end of the winter hunting cycle, the Menominee gathered in small groups at maple groves where they made huge quantities of maple sugar. While some of the sugar was for their own consumption, most of it found its way into the American market. In 1819–20 the Menominee could obtain $2.50 to $3.50 for a single *mokock,* or bark container, of sugar (approximately forty pounds), while a beaver pelt brought $6.00.[16] When, in the first decades of the nineteenth century, the supply of prime fur-bearing animals decreased from overharvest, less valuable furs, like muskrat, raccoon, and deer hides, came to dominate the trade. These species, particularly deer, were most abundant along the forest-prairie transition of west-central Wisconsin, and it was partially for these reasons that the Menominee expanded their hunting west.[17]

Throughout the economic year, the family was the smallest essential group of cooperating producers. Although economic cooperation of the extended family and multiple family groups occurred during the summer season, the nuclear family was the minimal cooperating group necessary for survival. The Menominee, like other native people of the Great Lakes, were organized as a kin-based society in the sense that every interaction between individuals—be it economic, social, or political—was conditioned by the degree of kin relationship between them. The closer a relationship was, the greater were the expectations of mutual support. This expectation, as well as the difficulties of gaining a living from the landscape, dictated that the Menominee form networks of interrelated and, therefore, cooperating families. These extra familial social organizations were called bands.

Bands were composed of a group of families that occupied the same territory and shared its food resources. Put another way, the territory of a Menominee band contained enough resources to support its members. Normally Menominee bands ranged from 150 to 250 members, or approximately thirty to fifty families. During the winter season, the families of the band would be widely dispersed over the band territory, but during the warm seasons, they would gather in strategically located villages. The band was often named for the locality of the main village or for its leader.

Because the Menominee were patrilineal in kin orientation, children belonged to the father's clan. After marriage, wives lived with the family of the husband. Thus, it might be said that the families of Menominee bands exchanged daughters in marriage. Marriage was, in this sense, a means of creating in-law relationships between the families of the band, since in-law relationships entailed strong obligations for mutual economic and political support. The rule that one must marry a person of a different clan also helped to extend the ties of kinship created by marriage.

Leadership in Menominee society was based on the charisma of individuals who were known to be wise, experienced, and generous. These people were recognized as *okwemaw,* or chiefs, and were seen by the Menominees as fathers who cared for their children. The position of *okwemaw* also tended to be hereditary, in the sense that distinguished chiefs were often succeeded by their sons. Actually, Menominee chiefs had no power and very little authority. Since decision making was on the basis of individual choice and consensus, each individual made independent decisions. As a result, one of the most important abilities of a Menominee leader was consensus building, which, of necessity, was accomplished by proven leadership and oratorical skill. The prominent chiefs of Menominee history—Tomah, Konot, and Oshkosh, to name a few—all apprenticed under prominent chiefs and proved themselves in the arenas of war or diplomacy.

While the family was the smallest economic unit of Menominee society, the band was the largest political entity. The chiefs of particular bands consulted with leaders of component families, called headmen, to make decisions that affected the band. The larger a decision was, the wider and deeper was the consultation. While the Menominee certainly recognized their kinship, both real and fictive, to other Menominee bands and knew of their shared attributes of language and culture, bands were not politically cooperating units. In the nineteenth century and earlier, there was no such political entity as the "Menominee tribe" except insofar as such distinctions were made by outsiders. In most cases, references to the "Menominee tribe" or "Menominee nation" were ethnic, rather than political. When the "Menominee chiefs"—that is, the chiefs of Menominee bands—signed a treaty, they did so in behalf of their band, not a more inclusive polity.

Among the Menominee, there were, however, political positions that superseded the band. These were functional and did not pertain to authority. Thus, talented war chiefs might, for example, gain fame and prestige beyond the band. Likewise, mythology provided a superstructure of clan descent that had with it a recognized political division of labor. Thus, the head of the *owasse,* or bear, phratry provided the head, or paramount, civil chief, while other clans or other supergroupings of clans provided chiefs with specialized duties, such as speakers, war leaders, heralds, hosts, camp police, and keepers of various sacred paraphernalia.[18] The longtime civil chief of the Menominee, Oshkosh, held that position by virtue of his being the hereditary leader of the *owasse*—that is, the original, or bear, clan and the other clans of the *owasse* phratry. While a position of great prestige and a necessary element of diplomatic discourse, the head, or paramount, civil chief of the Menominee had no more real authority than the head of any other Menominee band. This system of clan-based political position did crosscut the band divisions of Menominee society, and while not of much importance in decision making, it did help to create political solidarity among Menominee bands.

Throughout the treaty period and thereafter until the first decades of the twentieth century, the Menominee remained a very traditional people. This occurred not only due to the strength of their own beliefs but because they were ultimately concentrated on a relatively isolated reservation. Here, despite the influence of their French Canadian relatives, their participation in modern commerce, and the growing success of missionaries and teachers, the Menominee managed to preserve their language, to continue to live from the land, and to observe their unique social and religious customs.

The Early Treaties: 1817–30

Sometimes, in the course of history, chance plays an important role in political outcomes. This was likely the case during the first years of American-Menominee relations following the War of 1812. During the war, Menominee war parties assisted their British allies in their brief but decisive skirmishing against the Americans at the Straits of Mackinac. In these endeavors, they were ably led by Tomah, who replaced his brother Konot, or Glode Carron, who died in 1804. These were the sons of a French Canadian Green Bay trader named Thomas Carron (Old Carron) and a Menominee woman who was the sister of Waupesepin, war chief of the Milwaukee River band. The other prominent chief of the War of 1812 era was Chakauchokama, or Old King, who was the hereditary chief of the Menominee bear clan. As circumstances played out, by the beginning of American hegemony in 1816, both Tomah and Chakauchokama were old or in poor health.[19]

To put an end to hostility with the United States, the Menominee were summoned to St. Louis in 1817 for their first official dealing with the American government. The Menominee delegation often did not include the two head chiefs whose presence was necessary to finalize any external agreement for the Menominee, and neither of the main Menominee chiefs were among the St. Louis delegation who signed the 1817 treaty. Tomah died at Mackinac in 1818, and while Old King lived on until 1821, he was very elderly.[20] With Menominee leadership severely lacking, the delegation that met U.S. commissioners William Clark, Ninian Edwards, and Auguste Chouteau had no real official weight among the Menominee. This treaty did have the effect of establishing perpetual peace between the United States and the Menominee tribe. Further, at this time, the Menominee acknowledged themselves to be under the protection of the United States and no other sovereign, and, in turn, the United States specifically claimed exclusive stewardship over and responsibility for the welfare of the Menominee.[21] In this agreement, there is clear continuity with the U.S. Indian policy as it had been articulated by Congress in the Northwest Ordinance of July 13, 1787.

> The utmost good faith shall always be observed towards the Indians, their lands and property shall never be taken from them without their consent; and in their property, rights and liberty, they never shall be invaded or disturbed, unless in just and lawful wars authorized by Congress; but laws founded in justice and humanity shall from time to time be made, for preventing wrongs being done to them, and for preserving peace and friendship with them.[22]

The leadership question was still unresolved when the United States next met with the Menominee in 1825 at Prairie du Chien. The important treaty made there included most of the tribes of the Old Northwest.[23] For its part, the United States hoped to reconfirm its key role in Indian affairs, to suppress intertribal hostility that threatened American settlement, and to assert U.S. sovereignty along its northern border with Britain. One of the devices that treaty commissioners William Clark and Lewis Cass employed toward these ends was to get each tribe to declare its exclusive territorial claims. They naively supposed that each tribe could be confined to its own territory and would ask its neighbor's permission to hunt abroad. At Prairie du Chien, the lack of leadership among the Menominee again confused their relations with the United States. This is clearly seen in Article 8 of the treaty, which includes a general disclaimer: "The representatives of the Menomines [*sic*] not being sufficiently acquainted with their proper boundaries . . ." The article also includes a general description of the land claimed by the Menominee, as "bounded on the north by Chippewa country, on the east by Green Bay and Lake Michigan extending as far south as the Millawaukee [*sic*] river, and on the west they claim to Black river."[24] It was understood that some of this land was also claimed by the Winnebago, the Potawatomi, and particularly the Chippewa. The treaty was not to affect these conflicting claims at present, as these would be unsnarled in the future. Overlapping Chippewa claims were to be settled by a treaty in the following year (the Treaty of Fond du Lac in 1826).[25] As it turned out, the southern Chippewa boundary with the Menominee was not decided on until the Treaty of Butte des Morts in 1827, and the boundary between the Menominee and Winnebago was never formally defined.[26] It was likewise not until the Butte des Morts Treaty that the Menominee leadership problem was resolved by the selection of Oshkosh as head chief.

Although the Treaty of St. Louis in 1817 and the Treaty of Prairie du Chien in 1825 were the first official agreements between the Menominee tribe and the United States, neither treaty had much impact beyond establishing and promoting the peaceful coexistence that has since characterized the relationship between these two proud sovereigns. In a pattern quite different from other Indian tribes, the first attack on Menominee land and threat to Menominee independence came not from the United States but from a group of Christianized and educated New York Indians and their American supporters. Before turning to this episode in Menominee history, however, it is appropriate to summarize the situation of the Menominee tribe in the early 1820s.

The Land of the Menominees, 1820–25

In 1820 the secretary of war, John Calhoun, commissioned Rev. Jedidiah Morse to submit a report on the condition of Native American tribes in the United States. As part of his work, Morse traveled through the Northwest Territory and spent some time at Green Bay collecting information on the Menominee and their neighbors.[27] His report provides excellent baseline information on the Menominee at a time when they were faced with pressure from the New York Indians and their allies to cede land to accommodate the emigration of these eastern Indians.

According to estimates collected by Morse, the Menominee numbered about 3,900 people.[28] These people were distributed from Bay de Noc in the north to Winnebago Lake in the south and from Lake Michigan to the Mississippi.[29] Morse mentioned a village located eight miles above the mouth of the Menominee River where corn, potatoes, pumpkins, and squash were raised. Other villages were placed as "circumstances justify," including along the Fox and Wisconsin rivers.[30] During the summer and part of the fall, they had a village on the east shore of the head of Green Bay where gardens were planted. Across the bay was another village. Morse noted, "In the spring they subsist on sugar and fish; in the summer on fish and game; in the fall on wild rice and corn; and in the winter on fish and game."[31] The fish, he reported, consisted principally of sturgeon and salmon trout (lake trout), in greatest abundance in the bay.

Morse collected more detailed information from local informants John Law (*sic*), Jacques Portier, Laurent Feley, and the Grignor (*sic*) brothers. These men were members of old Green Bay families and, as traders, were well familiar with the Menominee. From these men, Morse learned that the Menominee consisted of six hundred men, nine hundred women, and twenty-four hundred children. These people were distributed in ten villages scattered from "Milwakie" (*sic*) to Prairie du Chien and along the Lake Michigan coast, the Fox Valley, and Lake Winnebago. Morse also learned that over this broad territory, the Menominee claimed use of some land and water exclusively, while in other regions, these were used jointly with the Winnebago, Sac-Fox, Chippewa, and Sioux.[32] The exclusive claim included "the whole of the waters of Green Bay with its islands. On its northwest shores, and on Fox River, they claimed from the entrance of the Menominee River in length one hundred and twenty miles, southwest and northeast; and in breadth sixty miles. On the southeast shore of the Bay and on Fox River, from the River Rouge, or Red River, to the Grand Cockalau [Kaukaulin] a distance of forty-five miles, and twenty-four in breadth."[33]

In 1824 Green Bay Indian agent H. B. Brevoort reported on the location and number of Indians in his agency.[34] According to this document, the Menominee were distributed along the Lake Michigan coast from the Menominee River south to Lake Winnebago and west to the Wisconsin River. In the north and west, Menominee villages contained Chippewa members; in the south, Potawatomi and Winnebago. The approximate location and the sizes of the Menominee villages are shown on map 8. If Brevoort's population figures, given as the numbers of Indian hunters, are converted to a total population by multiplying the number of hunters by five family members, then the Menominee would number less than two thousand. Given larger estimates for 1820 and for 1830, Brevoort's accounting is likely too low.

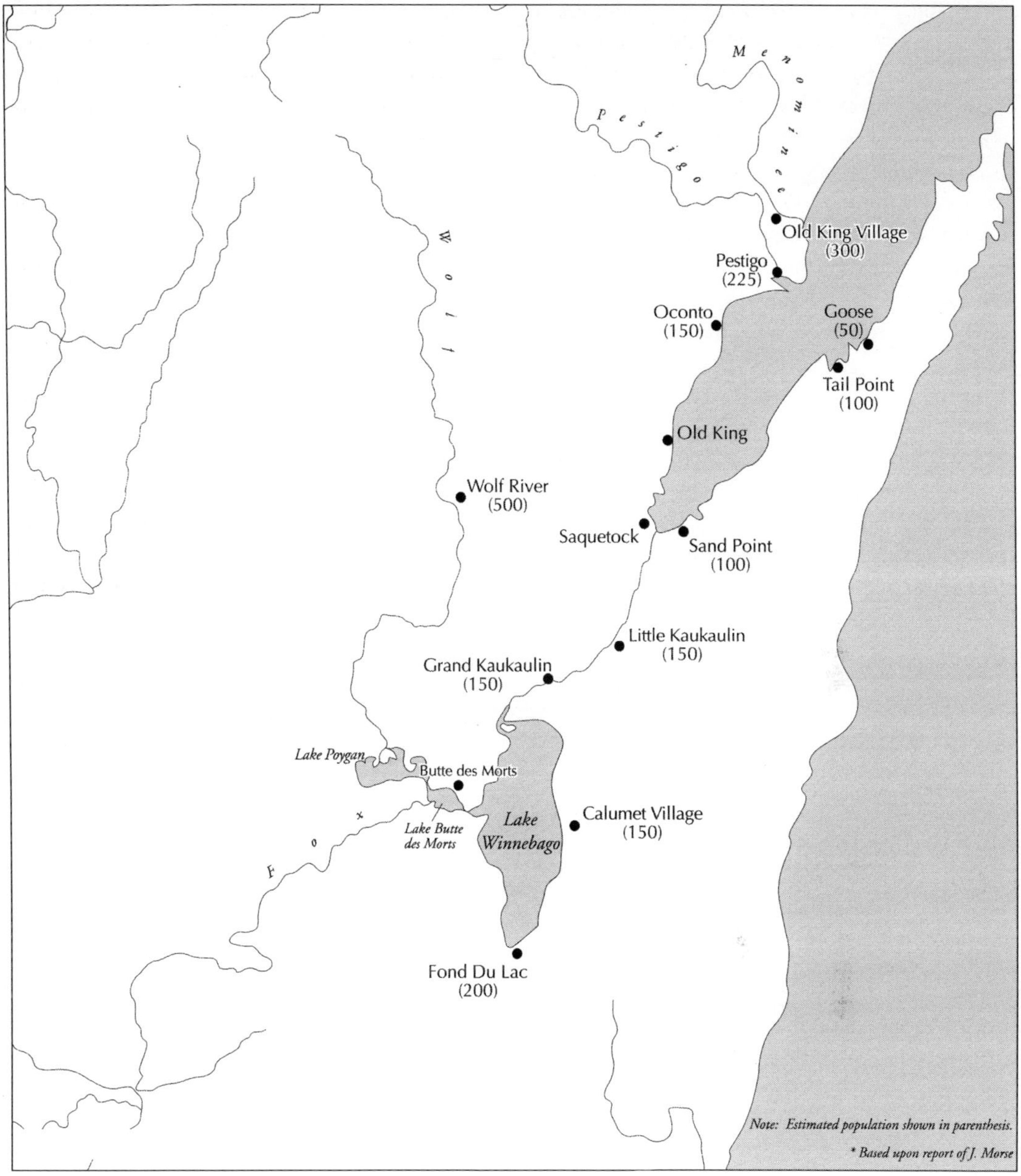

Map 8. Menominee villages in 1820.

The distribution of Menominee villages in 1824 shows a strong orientation toward lakeshore and riverine environments. It also shows an increasing presence of the Menominee in the Lake Winnebago–central Fox Valley region. To some extent, these may reflect the presence of Indian traders at crucial water junctures. In 1823–24 Agent Brevoort approved four traders for eastern Wisconsin: Jacques Porlier at the Wisconsin portage, Samuel Irwin on the headwaters of the Rock River, Dominick Brunetti at Lake Winnebago, and Stanislaus Chappues on the Menominee River.[35]

Morse also gives an account of a meeting with several Menominee chiefs who "were young men with less influence than their predecessors." Specifically three chiefs are named: Maucautaubee, age twenty-two, and Skakautcheokemaw, of about the same age, were the two first chiefs of the Menominee; Iwyematan was the other. These young chiefs were the beginning of a new generation of Menominee leadership. As Morse notes, they were kin to the former head chiefs. Two of the chiefs Morse met, Maucautaubee and Iwyematan (or Iometah), were respectively the son and brother of Tomah. Shortly after Morse's visit, Maucautaubee died, leaving another son, Josette Carron, with the claim to hereditary chieftanship.[36] Skakautcheokemaw was undoubtedly the heir apparent to the position of *okwemaw,* or peace chief, of the powerful bear clan. Following the death of his aged grandfather Chakauchokama (Old King) in 1821, he took the name of Oshkosh (Bear's Claw).[37] After 1821 Oshkosh and Josette Carron became rivals for leadership of the tribe. While Oshkosh represented the traditional element of the tribe, Josette had the support of the mixed-blood, or métis, Menominee. This faction, with its links into the French Canadian population, was a powerful force throughout Menominee history.

The French Canadian community at Green Bay was founded during the French regime at the foot of the bay. This location was, of course, a very strategic location for the fur trade, because it served as the point of entry into the Fox River system, which, in turn, permitted an easy portage to the Wisconsin River and thus to the Mississippi Valley. Large lake canoes carrying fur trade supplies from Montreal and Quebec would be unpacked at Green Bay, rebundled, and consigned to small trading posts scattered throughout the interior of Wisconsin. Not surprisingly, a stable community of traders and their *engagés,* or hired workers, soon developed at this vital crossroads.

Just before the time of Morse's visit, the town of Green Bay was truly a métis community.[38] The people spoke both French and Menominee, lived in small log houses of the French colonial architectural tradition, and dressed in western costume with a mixture of Indian elements. The community was devoutly Catholic, and many of its French Canadian and mixed-blood citizens were literate in both the French and Menominee languages. The French Canadians and Menominee at Green Bay had already been intermarried for at least three generations. As the Menominee chiefs made clear to Morse, "The traders here have been our friends; have raised our children."[39] In addition to their kin relations with the Algonquian tribes, the métis at Green Bay were related to and kept close ties to other Great Lakes métis communities at Grand River, Mackinac, St. Ignace, Sault Ste. Marie, and La Pointe on Lake Superior.

Thanks to the recollections of Augustin Grignon, who was the grandson of Charles de Langlade, one of the original founders of the Green Bay settlement, we have a good firsthand description of the community's history.[40] According to Grignon, the late eighteenth-century Green Bay was composed of seven extended métis families headed by Charles de Langlade, Pierre Grignon, Lagial, Baptist Brunet, Amable Roy, Baptist La Duke, and Joseph Roy. Most, if not all, of these men married Indian women, many of whom were Menominee. In all, the Green Bay community contained fifty-six people.[41] Before the War of 1812, there was a substantial immigration of French Canadians into the community. Among them were Jacques Porlier, Charles Reume, and the American John Lawe, who would each play an important role in the history of the Green Bay region. The new immigrants, likewise, married heavily into the Menominee tribe, and by the time the Americans arrived to build Fort Howard in 1817, there were about 250 people in the Green Bay community.[42]

Morse left the following account of Green Bay in 1820:

> This settlement extends about six miles on both sides of the mouth of Fox River and contains about eighty families. The females are part of the half, and the remainder of the full, aboriginal blood, whose husbands, with few exceptions, are Canadians; some of whom are Indian Traders; others are farmers and indifferent mechanics. If their children are estimated at about five to each family, it would give a total of two hundred and twenty-five, almost in a state of nature. These people, and the Menominees with whom, by the ties of relationship, they are connected, make from the maple tree, about one hundred thousand pounds of sugar annually; and from three to four hundred gallons of molasses [maple syrup]. [43]

Most of the French property holdings beyond those in the community per se were long narrow strips of land that ran perpendicular to the lower Fox River. In 1820 a government commission investigated French land claims at Green Bay, and eventually most of them were surveyed and confirmed by the United States.[44]

A discussion of early Green Bay would not be complete without mention of Fort Howard, which was constructed with the permission of Chief Tomah in 1816 on the west bank near the mouth of the Fox River. The fort was thus just downstream and on the opposite bank from the civilian community. It is important to appreciate that the American military garrison was very large, with an initial population of military personnel and dependents of 673 people.[45] Part of the American establishment included a government Indian trade store run by Major Matthew Irwin, which did not compete well since its goods were more expensive.[46] Immediately following the War of 1812, William Puthuff was appointed Indian agent for Michilimackinac, which had jurisdiction over the Green Bay region. Col. John Bowyer was appointed the first Indian agent at Green Bay in 1816 and served until his death in the winter of 1820–21. Superintendent Puthuff served until 1818, when he was replaced by George Boyd, who served at Mackinac until 1832.

The New York Indians

As white settlement advanced into the rich agricultural regions occupied by the Iroquois tribes of upstate New York, pressure to rid the area of aboriginal inhabitants increased. For many years, the Holland Land Company had held preemption rights to purchase Indian lands, and it began to do so in the last decades of the eighteenth century. One difficulty with this right was that some of the most desirable land was set aside as large Indian reservations, which the Seneca and other tribes refused to sell. The Holland Land Company consequently sold its preemption rights to these reserves in 1810 to Mr. David Ogden and a group of his investors, who proceeded to scheme for a means of extinguishing Indian title to the reserves and removing the Indians from New York.[47] These efforts eventually led to much difficulty for the Menominee in far-off Wisconsin.

During the next decade, the Ogden Land Company hatched a plan to acquire land in the west and to convince the reservation Indians of New York to remove. To this end, they eventually gained the acquiescence of the Office of Indian Affairs and the strong support of local politicians and the Protestant missionaries who ministered to the New York groups. While the traditional people who held the Cattaraugus, Cornplanter, Tonnewanda, and Tuscarora reservations strenuously opposed this real estate swap, several groups of Christianized Indians fell into step. These were, for the most part, educated and relatively affluent segments of the local Iroquoian tribes or Eastern Algonquian–speaking remnants of New England tribes who had sought refuge adjacent to New York Iroquois towns. These latter included the Stockbridge (Mohekunnucks) and the Brothertowns (Munsee) who were residing near the Oneida.

Either by coincidence or design, the same plan was taken up in 1818 by Rev. Eleazer Williams, a quarter-blood Indian Episcopal missionary to the Oneida.[48] Williams, who also claimed to be the last dauphin of France—Louis the Seventeenth—organized a substantial group of Oneida for the purpose of moving west as a Christian, agricultural colony. As a missionary, Jedidiah Morse also seems to have approved of this plan, and in some measure, his commission by the secretary of war to investigate Indian affairs in 1820 was tied in with the desire to move the New York Indians to Green Bay. At any rate, permission was sought for a delegation to visit Green Bay and the Indians in that vicinity. Both permission and financial support for twelve delegates were granted by the government.

The delegation arrived at Green Bay in 1820, and Col. John Bowyer, the Indian agent, acted as a go-between with the Menominee. With their leadership still in disarray, the appearance of these ancient enemies—referred to as *nadoways,* or "great serpents," by the Algonquian tribes—was upsetting. When Morse interviewed the Menominee chiefs just prior to the delegation's visit, they told him, "In regard to the Delegates from the Six Nations, we Menominees have no enemies. We are ready to give them our hand. But in regard to a piece of land to give them, we know not what to say, our Territory is so small."[49] As a matter of fact, the visit of Morse as well as the New York delegation came on the heels of an unofficial treaty negotiated with the Menominee by Agent Bowyer that ceded forty square miles of their best land on each side of the Fox River. This agreement was not signed by the legitimate chiefs, who all strongly opposed it, nor was it approved by the U.S. government. Morse reported that when the Menominee heard that the president and the Senate had rejected this purchase, "the joy expressed . . . was correspondent to the extreme grief and depression, which they had previously felt."[50]

This episode frustrated the plans of the New York Indians in 1820, but they returned the next summer. This time, fourteen delegates representing most of the New York tribes appeared, and an agreement was reached between the Menominee and the New York Indians ceding a five-mile-wide strip of land on each side of the Fox south of and equal in width to the French private claims on the lower Fox. The Menominee were told that the cession did not include the Fox River because the water "was for both."[51] Clearly, in these negotiations, the Menominee were at an enormous disadvantage compared to the educated and worldlier New York Indians, who were better able to manipulate the situation to their own advantage. The Menominee agreed to receive a payment of two thousand dollars for this land, with five hundred to be paid immediately and the remaining fifteen hundred to be paid the following year. This agreement was not signed by the young chiefs, and the signing headmen and warriors later denied knowing its contents.[52]

Despite growing opposition by the Indians in New York against removal, Williams and the Ogden Land Company, with the support of the federal government, kept the idea alive and returned in 1822 to bargain for more land. Although the Menominee received the payment of fifteen hundred dollars due on the previous year's agreement, they at first refused further cessions. In fact, the Winnebago who were also at the council left the treaty ground. Finally the Menominee headmen, with the two young chiefs absent, agreed to give the New York Indians a right in common to all of their lands. The formal written agreement specified that the Menominee ceded "all the right, title, interest, and claim" to the whole of the Menominee country but reserved "the free permission and privilege of occupying and residing upon the lands herein ceded, in common with them—the Stockbridge, Oneida, Tuscarora, St. Regis, and Munsee nations; *provided nevertheless,* That they, the Menominee nation, shall not in any manner infringe upon any settlement or improvements whatever, which may be in any manner made by the said Stockbridge, Oneida, Turcarora, St. Regis, or Munsee nations."[53] For this cession, the Menominee were to be paid three thousand dollars in goods.

This agreement, as well as the associated discussions, was likely beyond the understanding of the relatively unsophisticated and leaderless Menominee. It might be concluded, however, that this first experience of treaty negotiations conditioned the way the Menominee regarded the relationship between landownership and land use in later treaties. Here we see the Menominee being told they had sold "all right, title, interest and claim" to their country, on the one hand, while, on the other, they reserved the "free permission and privilege of occupying and residing upon the land" in common with the purchasers. The Menominee may not have been able to understand the meaning of title, but they certainly knew they could occupy and make a living from the land. In later protests, they stressed that they were trying to accommodate the Great Father and their New York brethren by providing a place where the latter could live and hunt.

The Menominee had no intention of handing over their tribal estate to another tribe, let alone for an outrageous, small amount of money and goods.[54] Nonetheless, on March 13, 1823, President Monroe "approved" this intertribal agreement with the proviso that the land cession be limited to that made in 1821 plus land lying between Sturgeon Bay, Green Bay, and the Fox River.[55] It might be mentioned in passing that purchase of Indian land was the sole prerogative of the United States under Section 12 of the Trade and Intercourse Act of 1802.[56]

Thanks to their métis and French Canadian relatives at Green Bay, the Menominees soon came to realize they had been swindled, and they sought to invalidate the agreement. In the meantime, small parties of Stockbridge and Munsee immigrants began to arrive and to settle along the east side of the Fox River. They were joined in 1823 by

Oneida, who moved to Duck Creek in 1825. In June 1824 Indian agent Henry Brevoort and Judge James Doty wrote a petition to President John Quincy Adams that stated the Menominee case against the 1822 agreement.[57] This petition was signed by fifteen Menominee leaders, including Oshkosh and Josette Carron, the contending but legitimate Menominee chiefs. This problem was foremost in the minds of the Menominee when they were called to Butte des Morts in 1827 to continue the discussions started at Prairie du Chien in 1825 about their territorial claims.

The Treaty of Butte des Morts, 1827

The Treaty of Butte des Morts was held pursuant to Article 2 of the Treaty of Fond du Lac held at the western end of Lake Superior in 1826.[58] Both of these treaties were in fact legacies of the uncompleted process of defining tribal land claims begun at Prairie du Chien in 1825, which could not be completed on that occasion due to the absence of the major Menominee chiefs.[59] Thus, the main purpose of the Treaty of Butte des Morts was to define a boundary line between the Menominee and the Chippewa and Winnebago. As events transpired, the Winnebago portion of the line was not dealt with in this treaty. The eastern and southeastern territorial claims of the Menominee and Chippewa were specifically defined from the Wisconsin River to Bay de Noc (see map 9). The Butte des Morts Treaty did not sort out the overlapping claims of the Menominee, Chippewa, Fox, Sioux, and Winnebago to the huge area of Wisconsin lying west of the upper Wisconsin River and east of the Mississippi.

Article 3 of the treaty also defined the boundary between Menominee lands and those claimed by French and British citizens, which were the private claims defined by the Land Claims Commission of 1820. Two provisos accompanied this article. One, which no doubt reflected the interest of the métis community, stated that the defined boundaries would not have any effect on their private land claims. Likewise, the New York Indians were assured that if the boundary between non-Indian and Menominee claims affected the New York Indians' purchase of 1821–22, the president could change the boundaries to sort it out.[60]

Article 2 of the Butte des Morts Treaty dealt with the difficult relations between the Menominee and Winnebago and the New York Indians in regard to the land cession agreement between the Menominee and the New York Indians. During the negotiation of the Butte des Morts Treaty, the Menominee chiefs, who now included their two most prominent leaders, Oshkosh and Josette Carron, complained vigorously to U.S. commissioners Lewis Cass and Thomas McKenney about these arrangements and denied having agreed to them at all. One of the Menominee chiefs, Komanikin (Big Wave), who was present at the "treaty" by which the New York Indians claimed that the Menominee sold them all their land, addressed the commissioners as follows:

> Father: The New York Indians came to us in great distress and we listened to them. They said, "We are pushed out of our own country and have come here to take you by the hand." We answered, "Since it is our Great Father's pleasure, we are glad to have you with us. We are few and possibly our country may be large enough for all to sit down upon!"[61]

The commissioners asked Komanikin if he signed the paper, and he answered, "We signed it without knowing the contents."[62]

Article 2 concluded by giving the president the power to establish boundaries between the Menominee and the New York Indians based on "the allegations, proofs, and statements, of the respective parties having been entered upon the Journal of the Commissioners."[63] Fearful of the result of this provision, Reverend Williams and the Ogden Land Company likely lobbied friends in the U.S. Senate to attach an amendment to the Treaty of Butte des Morts.[64] In its resolution of confirmation, the Senate inserted the following proviso: "That the said treaty shall not impair or affect any right or claim which the New York Indians or any of them have to the lands or any of the lands mentioned in the said treaty."[65] This proviso had the effect of vastly weakening the provisions of Article 2 of the treaty.

Even though the Menominee had signed the treaty, they refused to accept it with this amendment. From the Menominee's point of view, their actions in 1821–22 had been made with the desire to accommodate the Great Father by taking pity

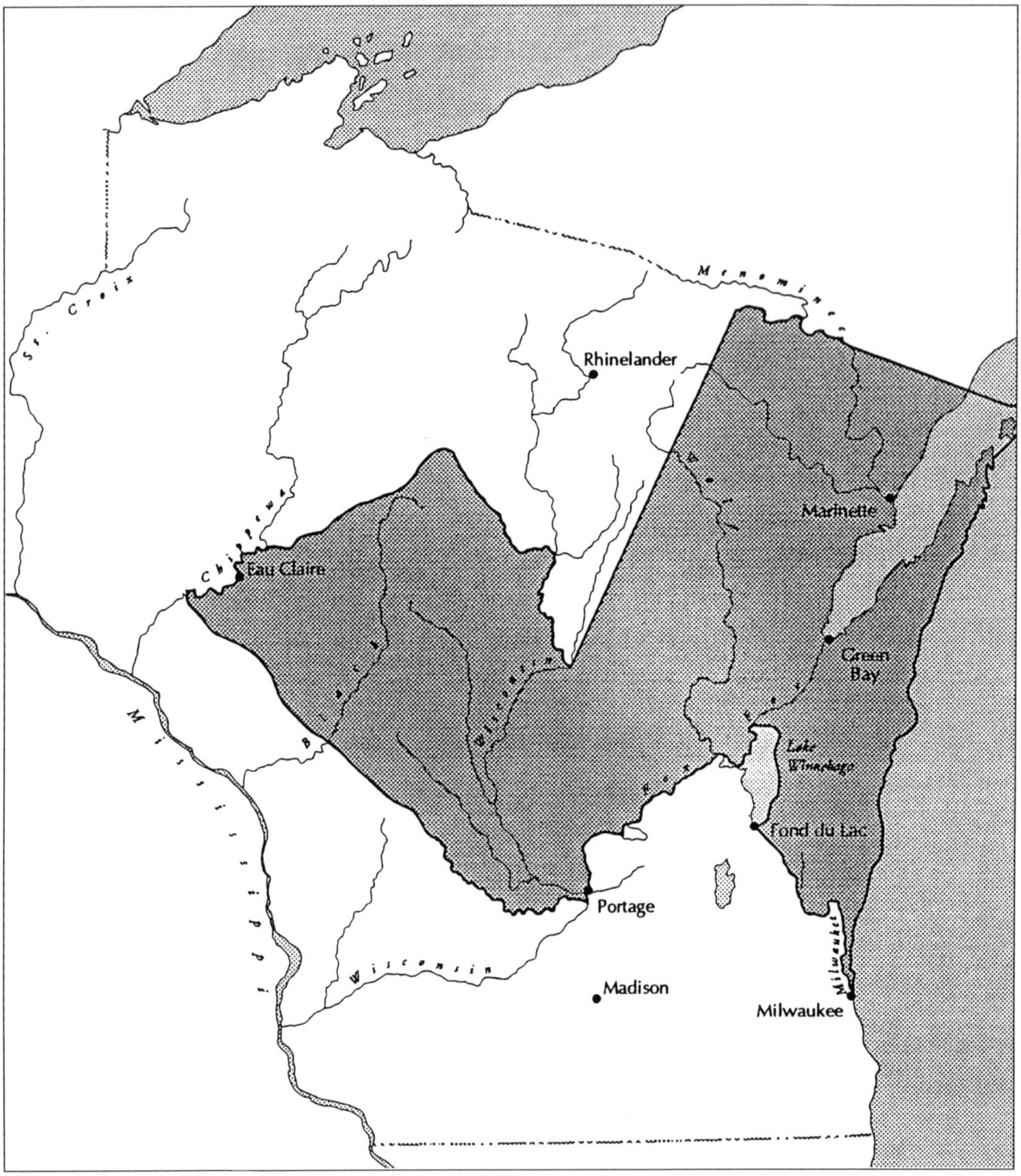

Map 9. Territory claimed by the Menominees in the treaty of 1831.

on the New York Indians, whom they understood to be in need. Their only agreement had been to let the New York Indians "sit down among them."[66] By this they undoubtedly meant that the immigrants would be permitted to reside on Menominee territory and to use its resources. Unlike their more acculturated and educated eastern brethren, the Menominee did not understand the agreement as a real estate deal.

Before the Treaty of Butte des Morts, the Menominee and their allies in the French métis community were so upset by the way the New York Indians and their white supporters had fleeced the Menominee that the government had to warn both parties of the consequences of violence against emigrant New York Indians.[67] After the treaty, the Menominee took a more diplomatic approach in attempting to defeat the 1821–22 agreement. The reason for this change in Menominee tactics was because of the consolidation of Menominee leadership under Chief Oshkosh. Prior to the Butte des Morts Treaty, leadership was divided, with the métis and more progressive Menominee faction following Josette Carron, while the more traditional Menominee followed Oshkosh. As Governor Cass put it, the Menominee were "like a flock of geese without a leader. Some fly one way and some another."[68] At the treaty negotiations, the American commissioners were asked to help resolve this dispute, and they did so by selecting Oshkosh as the paramount chief.[69] Apparently this choice was accepted by the Menominee since Oshkosh was an able and influential Menominee *okwemaw* for many years. Josette Carron continued to serve his people as a distinguished chief until his death in 1831. Although the two men were, to some degree, rivals, each representing legitimate but different points of view in the Menominee community, they were both trained by Josette's father, the great Menominee chief Tomah.

The problem between the New York Indians and the Menominee was simply deferred by the Treaty of Butte des Morts. The New York Indians continued the claim of two tracts of land, and the stiffening Menominee opposition declared that these agreements were not valid. Thomas Ogden not only lobbied Congress to preserve the deals by modifying the treaty but was successful in enlisting Superintendent Thomas McKenney in his effort to remove the New York Indians, particularly the Seneca.[70] Faced with the controversy and lobbying efforts, the Senate took considerable time to ratify the Treaty of Butte des Morts, and it was not proclaimed until late February 1829. Meanwhile, McKenney continued to encourage Ogden that the New York Indians would be removed to Green Bay.[71]

In February 1830 McKenney wrote to the secretary of war, John Eaton, concerning the appointment of a presidential commission under Article 2 of the Treaty of Butte des Morts to study the Green Bay land question. As he saw it, "Whatever tract of Country the Commissioners may esteem it proper to lay off under the direction of the President, will be binding on the Menominie [*sic*] and Winnebago Tribes, and they so understand it. But they will never permit the New York Indians to hold, in their right, the 2,000,000 acres of land which are claimed under the purchases, which it will be seen in the Journal of proceedings [journal of the Treaty of Butte des Morts] the Green Bay Indians, say was never made."[72] Thus, the United States would not confirm the 1821 and 1822 purchases. The government believed that the Menominee were under obligation to accommodate the New York Indians as a provision of the Treaty of Butte des Morts but that the president had the discretion of determining the location and quantity of land that they must forfeit.[73]

Consequently, Secretary Eaton appointed Erastus Root, James McCall, and John Mason as U.S. commissioners to sort out and settle the Green Bay land dispute. The commissioners were instructed to be fair to both resident and emigrant Indian groups, noting that they must remember that "Indian Tribes in a hunter state, (and this is the state of the Winnebago and Menominies,) require large tracts of Country; whilst Tribes whose condition is essentially agricultural, (and this is the condition of the New York Indians) require a less extensive domain."[74] The commission arrived in Green Bay in August and assembled the Menominee and New York Indians. The commission met for eight days in council, but the Menominee, under Oshkosh, would not yield to the claims of the New York Indians and their supporters. The Menominees agreed that the immigrants could stay, but they would not be owners of the soil.[75] With this, the presidential commission gave up. Its only important work was a detailed report on the agricultural potential of the Menominee country.[76]

In early September, the newly appointed Green Bay Indian agent, Col. Samuel C. Stambaugh, arranged for commissioners Mason and McCall to meet at the invitation of the Menominee chiefs. This was an important council in that all the principle chiefs and headmen were present, excepting Josette, who was represented by his adopted father. The chiefs, speaking through Kauskkaunonaive (Grizzly Bear), pleaded with the commissioners and agent Stambaugh for the opportunity to be able to travel to Washington to speak directly to President Jackson. This request was motivated by several important factors.[77]

First, the Menominee trusted the Great Father with their welfare. Not only did they state this explicitly on many occasions, but by the Treaty of Butte des Morts, they had trusted the president with the fate of their most important possession—their land. Agent Stambaugh reinforced this trust and understanding by telling the Menominee, "Brothers, I will write your great father, the President, and tell him what you have said to me. Your great Father loves you as he loves his white children, and always inquires kindly after you."[78] Another important reason had to do with difficulty in communication between the Menominee and U.S. representatives. For example, this particular council was translated from Menominee to French by Charles Grignon and then from French to English by the interpreter Henry Conner. Although Conner acted as Menominee interpreter at Green Bay for at least twelve years, he could not speak the Menominee dialect, having to rely instead on his knowledge of the Chippewa dialect.[79] Perhaps the Menominee hoped that person-to-person communication with the president would improve mutual understanding. Finally, the Menominee wished personally to see the president because they conceived of treaties and other agreements with the United States as personal arrangements between the Great Father and their own chiefs. As Grizzly Bear put it, they wished to go to Washington after their summer rice harvest so "we may see his [the president's] lips move when he speaks and his heart drum."[80]

True to his word, Stambaugh wrote a long letter to President Jackson in which he not only forwarded the chiefs' request for a visit but also laid out the history of their problem with the New York Indians. Agent Stambaugh's own views were solidly in support of the Menominee position. As he told the president, "I believe the Menominee tribe of Indians have been most shamefully deceived both by the agents of the New York Indians and by their own agents and advisors. I believe the New York Indians have been duped and deceived by their own agents, and I am sorry to say the government appears to have participated in the deception."[81] In the fall of 1830, Agent Stambaugh, contrary to the wishes of Michigan territorial governor Lewis Cass, led a delegation of fourteen Menominee chiefs and headmen to Washington. In Detroit the delegation was increased by the addition of John Mason, who was a member of the presidential commission, and Robert Forsyth, the governor's "Indian expert." Eleazer Williams and Oneida chief Daniel Bread, who had shadowed the Menominee delegation to Detroit, were also added to the party by Cass.[82]

As the Menominee delegation made its way to Washington, the dispute at Green Bay was even further from solution. The various claims were as follows:

1. The New York Indians claimed that through agreements with the Menominee and Winnebago in 1821 and 1822, they had purchased 6,720,000 acres, essentially all the Menominee land, for $3,980. This sale was confirmed by President Monroe on March 13, 1823.
2. Although the Menominee vigorously denied this claim, they agreed by Article 2 of the Treaty of Butte des Morts to let the president resolve the matter.
3. The Senate amendment to the Treaty of Butte des Morts was added to preserve but not confirm the New York Indian land claim.
4. Following the latter treaty, the Stockbridge, St. Regis, Tuscarora, Oneida, and Munsee sold a portion of the ceded land to the Brothertown Indians with the understanding that they pay the Menominee $950.
5. Small groups of New York Indian emigrants had established farming communities along the east side of the Fox River and on Duck Creek, and it was anticipated that large numbers of Seneca and other people from the Six Nations tribes would soon come flooding into Menominee country.
6. The presidential commission that was to settle the dispute had been unable to resolve the issue.
7. Through these negotiations on the New York Indian land question, the Menominee were gaining a better understanding of the complexities of the process they were involved with on the part of the New York Indians and the United States. Their experience to date had taught them that land use and landownership were two separable entities.

The 1831 Treaty with the Menominee

Perhaps as a result of the leadership crisis that preceded the Treaty of Buttes des Morts, the Menominee seemed to have developed a clever negotiating strategy that permitted them to slow down and better control the development of formal relations with the United States. They must have learned that if the principal chief did not participate in treaty negotiations, the agreements were not binding on the Menominee people. This strategy was somewhat comparable to the confirming power of the U.S. Senate in the American treaty-making process. The delegation that went to Washington in the fall of 1830 to negotiate a land cession and the resolution of the New York Indian problem did not include the two principal Menominee chiefs, Oshkosh and Josette Carron. The delegation was, however, a powerful one led by the chief speaker of the Menominee, Kauskkaunonaive (Great Speaker; aka Medicine Bear or Grizzly Bear), and by the leaders of the nine principal Menominee bands, including the renowned chiefs Ayamataw (Fish Spawn), Komanikin (Big Wave), Komanikeenoshah (Little Wave), and Ohopashah (Little Whoop).[83]

Besides the festering problem of the New York Indians' claims, the Treaty of 1831 was precipitated by the Menominee's desire to collect treaty benefits. They often complained that not only did they not receive annuity benefits from land cession treaties from the United States as did their neighbors the Potawatomi and Winnebago, but they were also subject to incursions by displaced Potawatomi and Winnebago.[84] The main pressure for land cession, however, came from the mixed bloods and Euro-American traders who hoped to acquire cash from Menominee annuities as repayment of trade debts.

The Menominee delegation, along with the New York Indian observers, arrived in Washington on December 11, 1830. They were soon taken to the White House, where their wish to meet with the Great Father, President Jackson, was satisfied.[85] The president appointed the secretary of war, John Eaton, and the acting Green Bay Indian agent, Col. Samuel Stambaugh, as U.S. commissioners for a treaty with the Menominee. Although the interests of the New York Indians as well as the Ogden Land Company were well represented at the negotiations, the new treaty was to be between the United States and the Menominee tribe.[86] This made the New York interest extremely wary, since Colonel Stambaugh thought the agreements of 1821 and 1822 to be illegal and was known to favor the Menominee side in the dispute.[87]

The treaty negotiations, which took place in January and early February 1831, proceeded on the presumption that the Menominee controlled all the land they claimed. The resulting treaty, which was sometimes referred to as the Stambaugh Treaty, was signed on February 8. It began by describing the country claimed as the exclusive property of the Menominee tribe. The country thus described included all the land between the Menominee and Milwaukee rivers on Lake Michigan west to the Wisconsin River, following the line negotiated between the Menominee and Chippewa by the Treaty of Butte des Morts, then to the Soft Maple and Plume rivers, tributaries of the Chippewa, which in turn flows to the Wisconsin. From the Wisconsin River, the Menominee claimed all the land north of the Fox River and east of Lake Winnebago.[88] This large territory was not all the land or water used by the Menominee but only what they claimed exclusively. They also used and claimed the waters of Lake Michigan north to Bay de Noc, Lake Winnebago, and land as far west as the Mississippi River drainage of western Wisconsin.

After stating their exclusive territorial claim, the treaty moved directly to the problem of the claims of the New York Indians. In the first provision of the treaty, the Menominee stated that "they are under no obligation to recognise [*sic*] any claim of the New York Indians to any portion of their country [and] that they neither sold, nor received any value, for the land claimed by these tribes."[89] Yet they agreed to cede a tract of five hundred thousand acres to the United States for these tribes west of the Fox River. This cession was rectangular in shape, stretching forty miles along a base between the old mill dam on the Fox River near Little Kaukaulin to Oconto Creek on Green Bay. The body of the cession extended inland from northwest to southeast so as to exclude confirmed private claims and the military reserve for Fort Howard (see map 10).

Although the Menominee had steadfastly re-

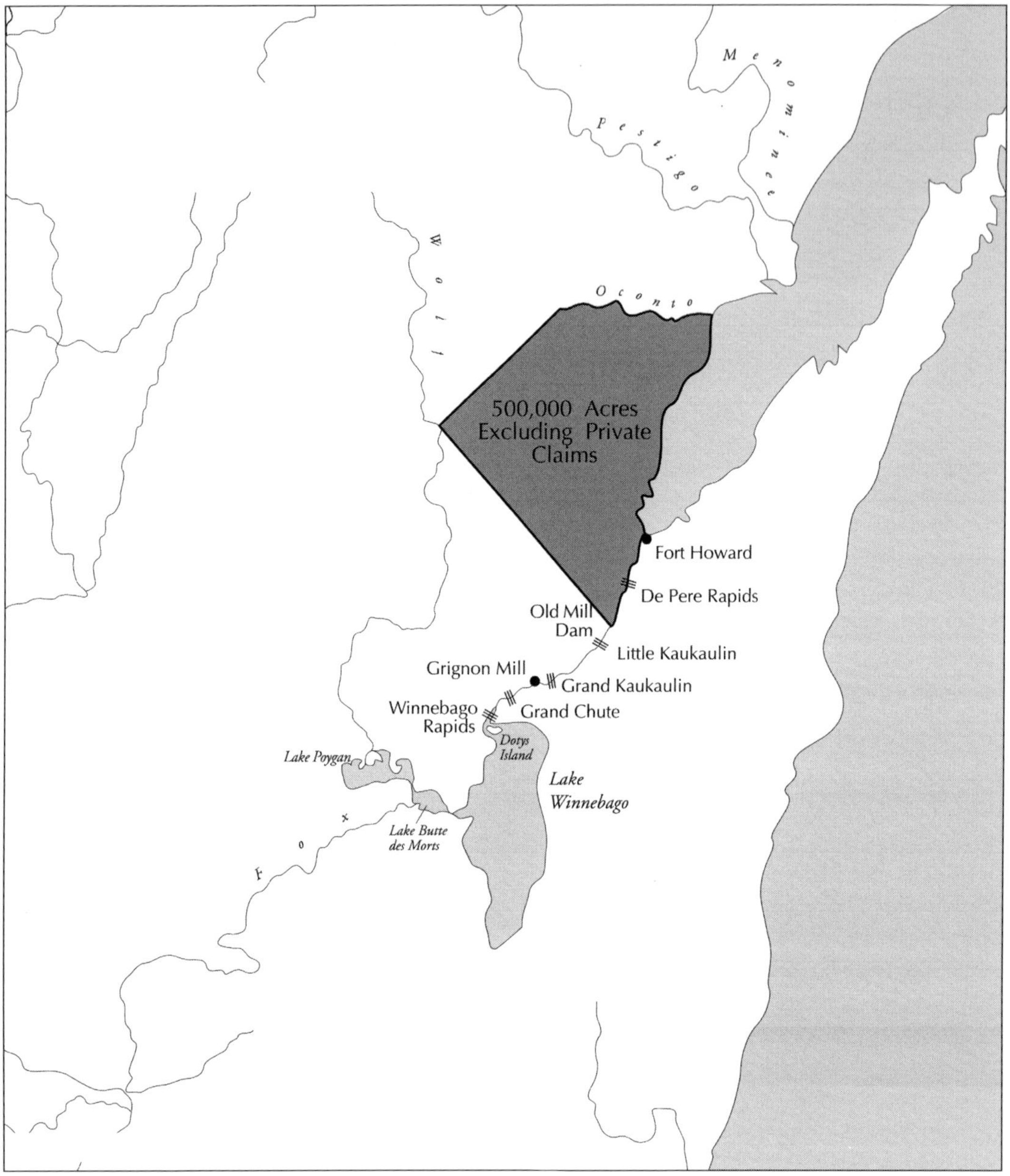

Map 10. Approximate location of the cession for New York Indians described in the original version of the treaty of 1831.

jected the purchase claimed by the New York Indians, and despite the hostility they and their supporters felt toward the New York Indian immigrants, they made land available to them because "the Menomonee [*sic*] tribe of Indians declare themselves the friends and allies of the United States, under whose parental care and protection they desire to continue."[90] In other words, the Menominee made the cession expressly to accommodate the United States. The first section of the treaty makes the appeal explicit: "at the solicitation of their Great Father, the President of the United States, and as evidence of their love and veneration for him,"[91] the Menominee not only agreed to the purchase but also gave their Great Father the power to adjust some of the important details.

The Menominee grant was not open-ended; a

period of three years was given for the New York Indians to take up residence on the cession west of the Fox River. The president was empowered to allot land to immigrants not to exceed one hundred acres per person, and at the end of three years, unoccupied land would revert to the United States. The Menominee also accommodated the interest of the United States in the cession by granting the government the right to cut timber and firewood for the Fort Howard garrison and to build roads across the land ceded for the New York Indians.[92] Thus, just as the United States granted the Menominee special use of the territory ceded for the purpose of hunting, fishing, and gathering, the Menominee granted the United States the right to establish roads and to cut wood on the lands they ceded to the United States to accommodate the New York Indians. Thus, the cessions contained some provisions for ownership and others for use. For these cessions of land and use privilege, the Menominee received twenty thousand dollars.[93]

Next, the Menominee agreed to cede to the United States all of the land between the Milwaukee River and the tip of the Door Peninsula and between Lake Michigan and Lake Winnebago, including the islands of Green Bay and the Fox River (see map 11). In all, this consisted of 2,500,000 acres, which, according to a General Land Office report, did not include the surface of Green Bay.[94] The extent of this grant and its location were, to some degree, conditioned by the Menominee's diminished ability to use its resources. As Agent Stambaugh explained, "The country you have now sold, was of but little use to the Menominies [*sic*] in their present condition; and by the boundary which you have defined on the west side of the Fox River and Green Bay you retain a country large enough for every purpose of farming and hunting."[95] By "present condition," Stambaugh was probably referring to the fact that the Menominee population had been reduced by European diseases.

For this cession, the Menominee were provided with an annuity of six thousand dollars for twelve years and various services. The latter included a blacksmith and gun shop, schools, and agricultural benefits. Since the United States, as a matter of general policy, wished to settle Indian tribes and to gradually transform them from hunters to agriculturists, the Menominee treaty set up an informal "reservation" where agricultural and educational services would be provided. This "farming country," as it was described, was to be located on the west side of the upper Fox River to Winnebago Lake and on the Fox between Winnebago Lake and the mouth of the Wolf River. One of the major reasons the Menominee chose this region was because of the profusion of wild rice that flourished along these waterways.[96]

These provisions for the Menominee and the New York Indians were, to a large degree, open-ended because the exact potential of the immigration of eastern Indians to Wisconsin was unknown. To try to cope with the contingencies, the United States made several general provisions in the 1831 treaty. First, of course, they purchased five hundred thousand acres for this purpose. To try to assure that the immigration would proceed rapidly and equitably, they set a limit of three years and one hundred acres per person. The sixth section of the treaty also required that the New York Indians immediately approve this arrangement; if they refused, the president would direct the immediate expulsion of those New York Indians who had already taken up residence on Menominee land. The real problem, however, was the fact that there were approximately six thousand New York Iroquois alone who could potentially move to Wisconsin.[97] Although Colonel Stambaugh believed that the five hundred thousand acres of land already set apart was sufficient to accommodate the number that might actually immigrate, a question remained as to whether the government was going to move other eastern Indians to the Green Bay region. Stambaugh asked the secretary of war for clarification on this point.

> In my opinion, however, there is one question, which I consider of great importance, which should be settled before the government incurs any more expense on this subject; and that is "*whether the government now intends to establish an Indian colony east of the Mississippi and west of the Lakes; or has it abandoned that idea?*" This plan was introduced by Mr. Calhoun, and afterward, favorably noticed by Mr. Barbour, in able reports of these gentlemen, when occupying the Office

Map 11. Territory ceded by the Menominee in the treaty of 1831.

of Secretary of War [1825–28]. If it is still considered expedient to locate the North Western Indians in this country, the land should be apportioned among the first settlers, with an eye to the ultimate object. The Menominee treaty has a clause providing for this contingency, which gives the United States the power, at any time, of extinguishing the title to this Tribe to all their lands on the west side of the Fox River, and Green Bay, with the exception of the tract set apart for their farming country. There, the government can at once possess itself of at least *four millions of acres,* for the purpose of establishing this colony, exclusive of that already obtained for the New York Tribes.[98]

The clause Stambaugh referred to appears in Section 6 of the treaty, which states that all of the Menominee land incorporated in their claim of exclusive use with the exception of the two cessions made in the 1831 treaty would remain Menominee country. That portion on the west side of the Fox adjoining their farming country (reservation) would remain as a hunting ground for the Menominee unless the United States needed to extinguish Menominee title to accommodate more immigrant eastern Indians than could be settled in the five hundred thousand acres ceded to settle the immigrants. If this were the case, the Menominee agreed to relinquish additional land. This option was based on two propositions: first, that the reason for the cession would be to acquire land to establish an expanded Indian colony; second, that a new treaty would be required to accomplish this end since the land in question was defined as Menominee country.

The Menominee were very aggressive in their defense of their exclusive land use privileges west of the Fox, since it was in this region that they were in competition with the New York Indians and wandering bands of Potawatomi and Winnebago, as well as non-Indian residents. In 1832 the Menominee speaker Kauskkaunonaive complained to Governor Porter that the New York Indians were making sugar on Menominee land and cutting down their maple trees.[99] He also complained that they were killing deer as far west as the Wolf River.[100] "Now my father," he concluded, "I hope it will be as we have told you. And it must be understood that these N.Y. Indians shall not hunt on our Lands. We forbid them to do so—have told them so."[101] It would thus appear that at the time of the 1831 treaty, the Menominee were well acquainted with the idea that landownership and land use were two different but interrelated concepts. Not only had they sold land while retaining use rights in the 1831 treaty, but by the same treaty, they also sold land to the United States for another group of Indians in which they permitted the United States use rights. They may even have concluded that while they had sold land to the United States for the New York Indians, the New York Indians themselves had only limited rights that did not include the privileges of making sugar or hunting animals on the land. In granting the United States the right of making roads and establishing military posts on Menominee land, the tribe was granting a usufruct right to the United States.

In a sense, this arrangement of ownership and use was not much different than the arrangement they had been accustomed to in regard to mill privileges. For at least a decade before the 1831 treaty, the United States had been leasing mill privileges to various U.S. citizens within Menominee territory. In 1831 there were water-powered mills on the Menominee and Fox rivers and Goose Creek. While the Menominee gave their permission for these concessions on the theory that they would benefit from the operation of the mills, they did not understand that the leases conferred the right to use or disrupt their own use of other resources. Chief Renaitenow (the Rain) of the Menominee River band was particularly upset that a grant of mill privileges to Mr. Farnsworth had resulted in a dam across the stream.

> Father, I do not like to have the Menominee River damed [*sic*] up. Is this what our Great Father gave them permission to do? Did he direct this? I ask you, Father is it the words of our great Father that our river should be damed [*sic*] the whole way across? We used to catch plenty of fish [sturgeon], it was our principal means of subsistence. Father I think these men should be satisfied with cutting down all our best timber and saving it up without stopping the fish. I have nothing to say against the grant [of mill privilege]. Our Chiefs gave their permission, sent it to their Great Father. But have these men the right to dam the River so that the fish cannot go up the River? Father did we ever sell all the fish? I have no recollection of doing this. Father this man says he owns all the fish in that River and all the cranberries. We never sold all these. Did we? Father all I wish is that the channel of the river may be left open, so that the fish can go up and down, and that we may catch them as heretofore, to subsist on.[102]

The use of water in general was considered to be different than use of the resources of the land. The Menominee never ceded Lake Michigan, Green Bay, the Fox River, Lake Winnebago, or the Wisconsin River. Although the land adjoining and surrounding these water bodies and their islands were ceded, the Menominee continued to use their resources and to travel these water courses. The United States never complained that the Menominee did not have such rights, for the likely reason that in the nineteenth century, everyone, Indian and non-Indian alike, considered waterways to be free transportation routes and believed the resource of the lakes to be inexhaustible.

It is also clear from the comments of the

chiefs at the final approval of the 1831 treaty that they considered the treaty agreement to be perpetual. This understanding was stated by Kauskkaunonaive: "You now see all the principal men of our nation here. We ask you to take care of our nation, to protect us and to be good to our children after we are dead."[103] As historic events played out in subsequent years, the possible mass immigration of eastern Indians never occurred; therefore the United States never required this land for Indian immigrants and did not exercise the option of concluding a new treaty with the Menominee for this purpose. As a result, it remains, as described and confirmed by the 1831 treaty, a "hunting ground" of the Menominee tribe.[104]

Hunting, fishing, and gathering rights were also the subject of a reserve right on the land ceded to the United States east of the Fox River. Here the Menominee were granted the "liberty" to hunt and fish along "with the same privileges they at present enjoy, until it [the land] be surveyed and offered for sale by the President."[105] This reserve clause has two parts. First is the right of the Menominee to use the resources of the cession—that is, the liberty to hunt, fish, and gather. Since the Menominee depended on fish and game for their subsistence, this right simply assured their continued survival. Likewise, since the economy of the region was centered on the furs and hides produced by the Menominee, the non-Indian population was eager for the Menominee to continue hunting and trapping at an undiminished rate. To pursue these privileges of usufruct, the Menominee had, of necessity, to be assured some privilege of occupancy. This usufructuary privilege was problematic since its application east of the Fox River also had the potential of interfering with other uses associated with the private purchase of the land by non-Indian settlers. This potential conflict between use and ownership was a problem that confounded Indian treaty drafters throughout the treaty-making era. In almost all cases, wording was designed to accommodate Indian use but also to give preference to the rights of private landholders if conflict were to occur. The 1831 treaty is not an exception. Here, as in several other treaties, the land use principles and general understanding established by Article 7 of the Treaty of Greenville in 1795 was used to structure the usufructuary rights of tribes.[106] Simply stated, usufruct was conditioned only by the behavior of the Indians themselves.

Article 6 of the Treaty of 1831 stated the expectation that the Menominee could hunt, fish, and gather "until it [the land included in the cession to the United States] be surveyed and offered for sale by the President; [as long as] they conducted themselves peaceably and orderly. The chiefs and Warriors of the Menomonee [*sic*] nation, acting under the authority and on behalf of their tribe, solemnly pledged themselves to preserve peace and harmony between their people and the Government of the United States forever."[107] In other words, the Menominee could occupy the cession to pursue their usufructuary rights as long as ("forever") they did not interfere or disrupt the use of the land that was implicit in the rights of private ownership. In cases of conflict, usufruct rights would give way in the sense that Indians would have to move on to practice their right on unoccupied land. It was not the intention of the United States to deny the Menominee the use of the land to make a living, nor is there any historical evidence subsequent to the treaty that the U.S. government attempted to deny the Menominee these privileges. The intent of the sixth provision of the treaty was to avoid conflict between Indian land use and non-Indian landownership. At the time of the 1831 treaty and for many years afterward, the cession was devoid of settlers despite having been surveyed and offered for sale. During this time and even when the cession was largely transformed into private property, the Menominee continued to use it. The penalties for bad behavior that were also described in Article 6—namely, the "forfeiture of protection of the United States government" and/or the surrender of their annuities—were never invoked by the government.[108] In other words, the arrangement made in the treaty seems to have worked as planned; the Menominees were able to use the cession with little, if any, disruption to the right of private landowners.

The Treaty of 1831 was signed at the White House on February 9. Unfortunately, Thomas Ogden and Rev. Eleazer Williams, who represented the New York interests, were not satisfied with its provisions.[109] They doubted that the New York Indians could be persuaded to leave their reservations before the three-year limit expired, and they were also concerned that both the quantity and quality of land set apart for their use in Wisconsin was insufficient. Their lobbying efforts against these provisions resulted in the New York congressional delegation threatening to block both the ratification of the treaty in the Senate and Agent Stambaugh's appointment as permanent Indian agent at Green Bay. To save the treaty, the Menominees agreed to supplemental provisions that were signed on February 17, 1831.[110]

These supplementary articles made two modifications of Article 6 of the treaty. The first provision modified the first section of the February 8 agreement by removing the three-year time limit for the settlement of the New York Indians, making the period of settlement at the discretion of the president. Likewise, the president was empowered to apportion land among the immigrant Indians as he saw fit, thus removing the limit of one hundred acres per person. The second amendment canceled a provision of Article 6 of the February 8 agreement that required the removal of unsettled New York Indians from Menominee lands after three years, by making such removals discretionary on the part of the president.[111]

By provisions of Article 6, the treaty was to have immediate effect. The New York Indians and their political supporters, however, still hoped to acquire more Menominee land and used their influence to block Senate ratification during the first session of Congress. In hope of saving the agreement, the treaty commissioners added a stipulation so that the treaty would be binding until the next session of Congress.[112] The president appointed Colonel Stambaugh as temporary Indian agent to Green Bay, since the Senate had held up his regular appointment.

Senate Amendments to the 1831 Treaty

Modification made to the February 17 version of the 1831 treaty by the Senate shows the political influence of the New York Indians or at least the missionary and land interest that sought their removal from New York. When the Senate finally ratified the treaty in its second session, it added provisions that gave two townships of land from the U.S. cession east of Lake Winnebago for the immigrant Stockbridge and Munsee tribes, as well as twenty-five thousand dollars to buy out their improvements west of the Fox. One township was also given to the Brothertown Indian colony, which was also to be paid for relinquishing improvements. The Menominee had no objection to these provisions. They did, however, vigorously object to the Senate's reconfiguration of the reserve of five hundred thousand acres for the New York Indians. The Senate, at the instigation of the New York interest, shifted the whole tract southwest to include two hundred thousand acres of the best Menominee land between the Little Chute and the Grand Kaukaulin (see map 12). Although Agent Stambaugh pointed out the benefits for the Menominee in regaining the fishery and sugar groves in the Oconto Valley on the northeast side of the reserve, the Menominee remained intransigent; they would not permit the New York Indians to deny them the rich riverine resources and valuable village sites of the upper Fox Valley.[113]

Given this impasse, the Senate included a formal conflict resolution procedure as part of the now vastly modified 1831 treaty. George Porter, governor of the territory of Michigan, was to proceed to Green Bay to endeavor to obtain the consent of the Menominee chiefs to the Senate amendments or, failing that, to obtain their assent "to the best practicable terms short of those proposed by the Senate."[114] It was also suggested that Governor Porter obtain the agreement of the New York Indians to any necessary changes. The Menominee did indeed vehemently object to the new proposed location of the reserve for the New York Indians. Besides taking much of the best land on the west side of the Fox, the New York Indian reserve suggested by the Senate would have deprived the Menominee of access to several critical locations. As the Menominee pointed out to Governor Porter, some of them lived upriver and others downriver of the Grand Chute, that is, within the newly proposed southwest corner of the New York Indian reserve (see map 12). In traveling up and down the Fox, it was necessary to portage from the Grand Chute to the head of the Grand Kaukaulin. The portage that was on the west side of the river passed over the confirmed private claim of Augustin Grignon, who ran a trad-

Map 12. Approximate location of the cession for New York Indians proposed as a Senate amendment to the 1831 treaty.

ing establishment at this strategic location. Grignon was a mixed-blood Menominee and one of their principal traders and supporters. By surrendering this section of the Fox River to the New York Indians, the Menominee would have denied themselves access to both the portage and the Grignon trading post.[115] Beyond this, the Treaty of 1831 promised that the United States would build a grist and lumber mill for the Menominee along the Fox River. The Menominee contended that the Grand Chute was the only place the mill could be built. This was probably true, since most of the other good mill sites had already been claimed by French inhabitants or American settlers and confirmed by the United States. In any case, the Menominee would not give up the Grand Chute locality to the New York Indians.[116]

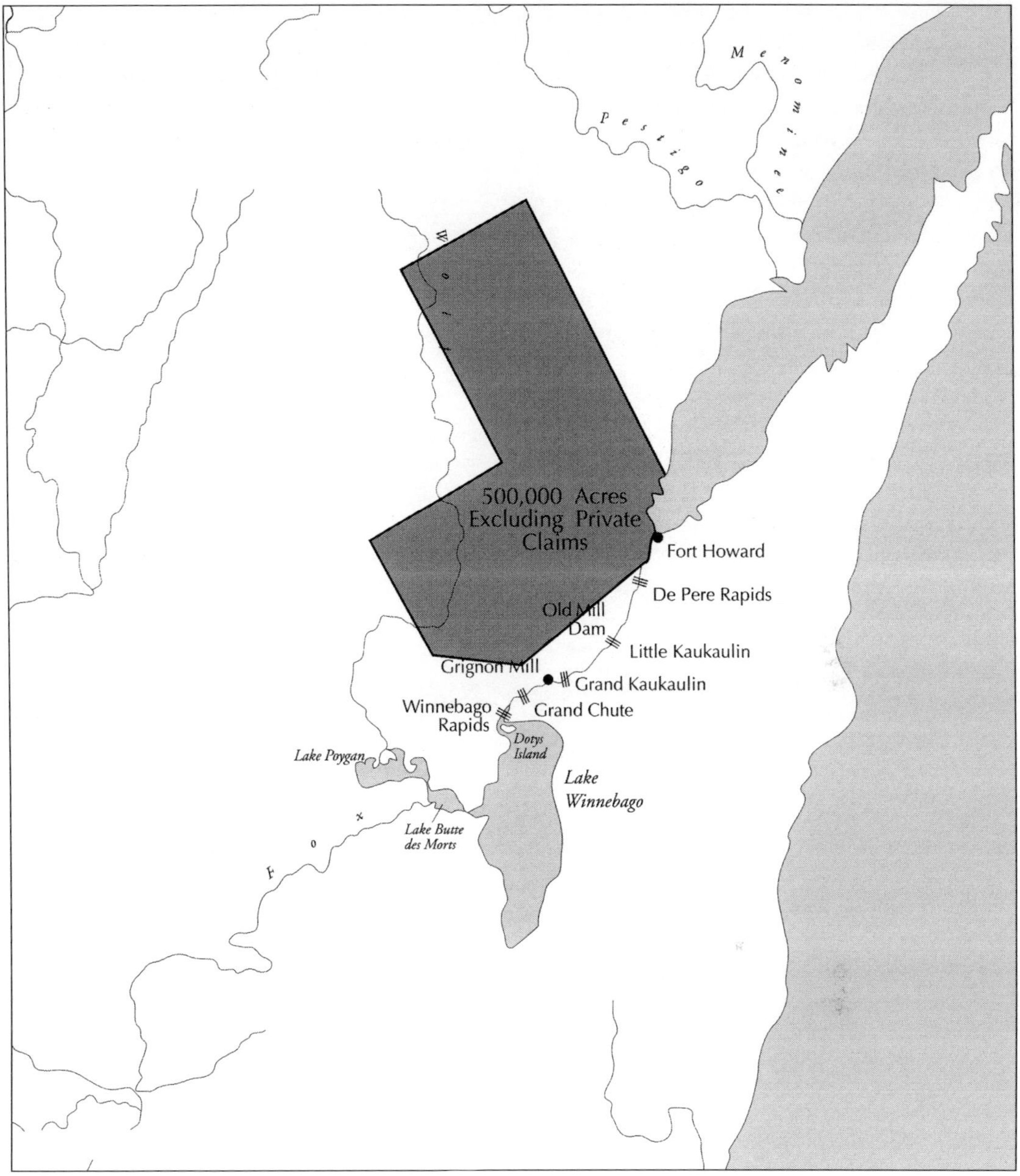

Map 13. Approximate location of the cession for New York Indians in the final version of the 1831 treaty.

After much negotiating, Porter was able to locate a tract of five hundred thousand acres for the New York Indians that extended southwest to the Grand Chute but that also preserved the Fox River corridor to the Menominee by drawing the reservation line three miles inland from the river (see map 13). This seemed to be an excellent compromise, since the New York Indians acquired the superior agricultural lands important to them, while the Menominee maintained access to the aquatic resources of the Fox River as well as the means to travel its length for the purpose of moving through the Fox Valley to Green Bay in pursuit of their subsistence and commercial resources. With this agreement, the Treaty of 1831 was finally concluded. The process of negotiation had taken a year and eight months and was now approved by the principal

Menominee chiefs, including Oshkosh, who had not participated in its negotiation. In an appendix to the treaty, representatives of the Stockbridge, Munsee, and Brothertown also approved the reservation agreement.

The Menominee were never comfortable with ceding land for the New York Indians and only did so with the assurance that the Great Father would treat them fairly. As Agent Stambaugh explained to them, "Your Great Father will not permit the stranger white or red man to cheat you."[117] Kauskkaunonaive, speaking for the Menominee, clearly indicated that the Menominee received this message: "Father [in reference to Agent Stambaugh], we the Menominies [*sic*] look up to you to protect us in our rights, our great Father at Washington, promised last winter, before the great spirit, to take care of his Menominie [*sic*] children, and not permit them to suffer wrong. We feel it in our hearts that he will keep his promise."[118]

In all, the Menominee were resoundingly successful in negotiating their first major treaty with the United States. This is all the more remarkable considering that the chiefs in Washington were subjected to enormous pressure brought to bear by the New York land interests. Among their accomplishments in the 1831 treaty, the Menominee could number the following:

1. They had confirmed their alliance with the United States and their paternal relationship with the Great Father.
2. The United States had recognized their exclusive territorial claim to an extensive tract of land and water in Wisconsin.
3. By the reservation of usufruct rights over their entire area of claim, they had assured their survival and the preservation of their culture.
4. They had resolved their territorial dispute with the New York Indians in a way that had minimal impact on their own tribal domain.
5. They had ceded a relatively small amount of land in order to receive the annuities they regarded as important in the changing economy of the times.

Thus, faced with the prospective claim that they had already ceded all of their territory to the New York Indians—that is, that they had already given up everything—they came out of the 1831 treaty with their cultural and political integrity intact. Not only had they given up very little, but they were gaining political sophistication.

The Early Settlement of Menominee Country, 1828–36

Prior to the establishment of the Wisconsin Territory on July 3, 1836, eastern Wisconsin was part of Brown County of the Michigan Territory. In 1830 there were only 1,154 non-Indians in the Michigan Territory west of Lake Michigan. Of these, 474 were soldiers posted at Fort Howard and Fort Crawford, which left only 680 other, permanent residents.[119] By 1836 this number had doubled, with 2,706 non-Indians residing in Brown County. The inhabitants of Brown County were almost exclusively settled in and around Green Bay, where the old French Canadian families had taken up land claims along the Fox River. In the French fashion, these landholdings were configured as long rectangles with a short side abutting the water. Typically, "ribbon farms" were measured in French acres, or arpents, so that each farm was two to seven arpents wide and eighty arpents deep and thus contained from 100 to 640 English acres. Each claim extended back from the river about two and three-quarter miles. At Green Bay, the strip farms were generally located side by side and stretched from the Green Bay settlement proper down both sides of the Fox for six miles to the vicinity of the Depere Rapids. Besides these claims, there were others on the upper Fox.[120] Land claims by French settlers were inspected by various government commissioners, and most were confirmed in 1821, while others were surveyed and confirmed in 1828.[121]

Most of the non-Indian population of Brown County was thus concentrated on the lower Fox and at the head of Green Bay. The settlement of homes, trading, and drinking establishments located near Fort Howard was called Shantytown. In 1830 the town of Navarino was laid out on the east bank of the Fox, and in 1835 the American Fur Company started the competing town of Astor. These two villages eventually merged to become the town of Green Bay.

The Green Bay community was indeed isolated. Before 1830 there were no roads in Wisconsin, and mail came by trail from Detroit and arrived twice every six months.[122] Although steamers and sailing ships plied the Great Lakes, there were only eleven Great Lakes steamers by 1833, and in 1834 there was only one regularly scheduled line between Buffalo and Chicago.[123] Great Lakes vessels of this period seldom stopped at Green Bay, because of navigational hazards and especially the lack of good docking facilities. Until at least 1836, it took four weeks of difficult travel overland to reach Green Bay from Washington, D.C.[124] In 1830 Congress appropriated funds for a military road linking Green Bay and Chicago, but it was several years before it was completed. This very poor road ran down the east side of the Fox and Lake Winnebago and followed the lake shore south. Another military road was surveyed from Green Bay to Prairie du Chien via Fort Crawford at Portage, Wisconsin, in 1834, but this road was not even nominally complete until 1837.[125] The Fox River system continued to be the main source of transport, but it was unimproved and very difficult to travel due to frequent rapids.[126] While a dam was chartered in 1835 to improve navigation on the Fox, it was not until 1856 that the waterway was finally improved.[127]

All of these difficulties hurt the anticipated commercial development of the Green Bay region, which had seemed so promising during the 1820s. In that day, the economy of the country west of Lake Michigan was centered on the fur trade. The Green Bay traders depended on their extensive kin connections with the Menominee, Chippewa, and Winnebago to control access to furs. To protect these interests as well as the welfare of their Indian relations, Louis, Pierre, and Augustin Grignon, John Lawe, Jacques Porlier, and others from extended Green Bay trading families often interceded in relations between the Menominee and the outside world.

Much of the trade was conducted by government license from the Green Bay settlements and along the Fox River, although licenses were also issued for the Menominee River and on the upper Wisconsin and Wolf rivers. With the failure of the American government's factory trading system in 1821, the American Fur Company brought the Green Bay traders under its control. An 1821 agreement between the Grignon brothers, John Lawe, and Jacques Porlier, with Ramsey Crooks as agent for the American Fur Company, created the Green Bay Company as a copartnership.[128] This new company was able to drive out rivals by obtaining cheap goods through the American Fur Company, which, in theory, would not trade with other interests in the Green Bay region. In reality, however, this partnership was fraught with competition between the traders and the American Fur Company.

The Green Bay Company was never profitable, and its position was not helped when, in the early 1820s, Daniel Whitney, William Dickinson, and Robert Irwin, newly arrived American merchants, set up shop in Shantytown. These merchants were able to undersell the Green Bay–American Fur Company, and the Menominee flocked to Shantytown to trade. For their part, the Green Bay Company tried to keep the Menominee away from the Green Bay settlements so they would trade at their scattered fur posts. In the face of new competition, the Green Bay Company traders also loosened credit to Indians, who as likely as not continued to sell their furs to the Shantytown merchants. As a result, the Grignons, Lawe, and Porlier slipped increasingly into debt to the American Fur Company. Either by default or, more likely, by design, the American Fur Company financially ruined the old Green Bay trading families. In 1823 the Green Bay Company was disbanded, with sixteen thousand dollars in debts. The individual traders continued to trade as agents of the American Fur Company through 1837, and they just as surely continued their slide into debt. As the old traders' fortunes declined, the new American merchants, particularly Daniel Whitney, increasingly turned their attention to the retail trade and became suppliers for immigrants.[129]

By the late 1820s, the old French families began mortgaging land to the American Fur Company to repay the debts of the Green Bay partnership. As profits declined in 1834, John Astor sold his Great Lakes fur interests to Ramsey Crooks, who moved the reformed company increasingly into mercantile and real estate ventures. Part of this enterprise was to acquire land titles for repayment of debts from the Grignon and Lawe families, which was used to plat the speculative town of Astor to compete with Whitney's town of Navarino. Neither of these ventures was an initial success. John Haeger, who studied the historic development of towns along the western shore of Lake Michigan, points out that the success of early towns was directly related to the ability of local developers to attract eastern capital. In 1833 the future town sites of Green Bay, Milwaukee, and Chicago were at the same stage of economic and political development.[130]

The Menominee Treaty of 1831 and the Chicago Treaty of 1833 with the Potawatomi extinguished Indian title to the entire Lake Michigan shore of Wisconsin. The majority of this land was surveyed between 1833 and 1835 and was offered for sale in 1835, when a government land office opened at Green Bay. Despite the sale of 859,318 acres in Wisconsin during the land boom of 1835–36, fourteen and one-half million acres of government land remained for sale in southern Wisconsin.[131] Most of the sales in the Green Bay land office were for land in the region of Chicago or Milwaukee.[132] In 1837 a national financial panic due to unsecured land speculation severely depressed land sales. Aside from the sale of town lots at Astor and Navarino and some land speculation at the future sites of Kewaunee, Manitowoc, and Sheboygan, the land ceded by the Menominee tribe to the United States remained an unknown wilderness until after the middle of the nineteenth century. In the end, John Astor was not willing to commit sufficient capital to make Green Bay competitive with Chicago or Milwaukee, and as a result, Green Bay could take advantage of neither the Wisconsin-Fox waterway nor the agricultural potential of the Fox River valley and its hinterlands.[133]

For the Menominee, these events spelled economic hardship. As the fur trade declined, their French Canadian and métis trade partners not only tightened credit but also passed along a portion of their debt. Thus, increasingly, the Menominee were pressured for repayment of debts from their treaty annuities. With the rise of American trading interests and the development of closer ties with the federal government, the old French Canadian community that had often helped represent Menominee interests progressively lost influence in local and regional affairs.

War and Pestilence

Apart from the solution of their long-standing dispute with the New York Indians and the receipt of much needed annuities as a result of provisions of the 1831 treaty, the decade of the 1830s was a very difficult one for the Menominee people. At the very time the Menominee chiefs were negotiating these treaties, the Menominee were attacked by neighboring tribes. In early 1831 the Menominee complained that the Chippewa had killed two of their women and a young hunter the previous fall. The murdered people were hunting on Menominee land (presumably in western Wisconsin). The Menominee restrained their urge to avenge these deaths as required by custom, not because of fear of the Chippewa, but because they "were only afraid to break one promise to [the Great] Father."[134] This statement seems to be in reference to Article 6 of the 1831 treaty, which had just been agreed on. By this article, the Menominee were granted the right to use the land ceded if they conducted themselves peaceably and orderly.

> The chiefs and Warriors of the Menomonee [*sic*] nation, acting under the authority and on behalf of their tribe, solemnly pledge themselves to preserve peace and harmony between their people and the Government of the United States forever. They neither acknowledge the power nor protection of any other State or people. A departure from this pledge by any portion of their tribe, shall be a forfeiture of the protection of the United States' Government, and their annuities will cease. In thus declaring their friendship for the United States, however, the Menomonee [*sic*] tribe of Indians, having the most implicit confidence in their great father, the President of the United States, desire that he will, as a kind and faithful guardian of their welfare, direct the provisions of this compact to be carried into immediate effect.[135]

The Menominee took this pledge very seriously, and it was very much in keeping with their own understanding of the treaty relationship between themselves and the Great Father. The entire essence of the agreement to the Menominee was that they would be the allies of the United

States and that the United States, through the Great Father, would in return protect their welfare and interests. The lack of response by the Great Father to the killing of their people was therefore very troubling. In April, General Clark, superintendent of Indian affairs at St. Louis, wrote to Secretary of War Eaton expressing this concern.

> I am informed the Menomonees [*sic*] are becoming very uneasy at the apparent indifference of the Government toward their present situation in regard to the murders committed upon their people by the Chippeways. They say they can no longer sit in their lodges with their arms folded and not revenge the murder of their women and young men.[136]

While this problem went unresolved, an even worse event occurred. On the morning of July 31, 1831, a large Sauk and Fox war party attacked a Menominee camp of about forty people on the Mississippi River a mile and a half above Fort Crawford at Prairie du Chien. Twenty-five Menominees, including eight men, six women, and eleven children, were killed. The dead included the entire family of Chief Carron. This tragedy was all the worse since the Menominee had been called to council at Fort Crawford and were camped in the shadow of the fort. In the aftermath, they asked the superintendent, "Our Father, the Chippewa murdered our people last winter, you ask us not to revenge until you could write to our Great Father. We waited and yet, we have not heard from him. When will he answer? Shall we wait till the Chippeway and the Sauk and Foxes kill us all?"[137] In the following months, the United States tried, without success, to seek the surrender of the Sauk-Fox murderers and provided one hundred dollars for clothing for the survivors of the massacre.[138] A pioneer settler, Charles Whittlesey, recollected that this incident became an affair of honor with the United States, since the Menominee were faithful friends of the United States and considered themselves under its protection.[139]

During the summer of 1832, general warfare broke out between the Sauk-Fox and the United States—an episode known as the Black Hawk War. Settlers throughout the Old Northwest were terrified at the prospect of a general Indian uprising. This was particularly true of those collected at Green Bay, since it was rumored that Chief Black Hawk might try to escape eastward to Canada by way of the Fox River valley. Before U.S. regular troops could be summoned to reinforce Fort Howard, General Atkinson, the American field commander, called for two to three hundred Menominee warriors to assemble at Green Bay to protect the settlement. Agent George Boyd reported that no more than 150 warriors could be effectively armed and that the war chief Pawakonem (Big Soldier) had assembled fifty to sixty fighting men.[140] Ultimately two companies of Menominee were formed under the general command of Col. Samuel Stambaugh, with Charles Grignon and George Johnson acting as captains. This Menominee force played a peripheral part in the defeat of the dissent Sauk-Fox by defeating a splinter group of warriors as they retreated down the Wisconsin River.[141] Agent Boyd reported that the Menominee companies had been given high praise by both General Scott and General Atkinson for "their ready appearance in the field in the aid of the United States."[142] The Menominee were certainly doing their part to uphold their allegiance with the United States as well as their pledge to the Great Father.

On top of the disruption of warfare and treaty making that together took up the attention of the Menominee leadership during 1831 and 1832, the Menominees were struck by two disastrous epidemics. During the late summer of 1834, a "species of cholera" swept through the Menominee communities, killing about sixty people. This was probably the same epidemic of "Asiatic cholera" noted by Henry Baird for the following year.[143] An even worse disaster befell the Menominee people in 1834, when smallpox arrived at Green Bay with a shipload of soldiers bound for Fort Howard. The disease rapidly spread through the Menominee population, killing about 625 people, an estimated 25 percent of all the Menominees.[144] As cruel as this epidemic was, it was not the first or the last epidemic of European diseases to decimate the Menominee. The cholera and smallpox plagues of the early 1830s were, however, particularly hard on the political solidarity of the Menominee at a difficult time in their history. Traveling artist George Catlin expressed the general condition in 1834 when he stated, "The Menominies [*sic*] and the Winnebago, are the remnant of a much more numerous and independent tribe, but have been reduced and enervated by the use of whiskey and the ravages of the smallpox."[145]

Besides reducing the absolute numbers of an already small population, warfare and disease had the effect of eliminating individuals who played critical roles in political and spiritual leadership. Although the exact causes of death are not known, the chief Josette Carron died in 1831, and 1834 saw the passing of the great orator and negotiator Kauskkaunonaive (Grizzly Bear).[146] The deaths of these and other leaders created huge problems, since leadership was based on charisma, which was in turn based on the wisdom acquired by years of experience. Further, no sure mechanism existed to replace respected chiefs except as new leaders arose through practice by gaining the esteem of their peers.

Another impact of depopulation was simply on the number of people remaining in families or bands to perform the labor necessary to produce food, clothing, and shelter for the survivors. Since many instances required extrafamilial cooperation, large epidemics often led to the consolidation of extended families and the reformation of band units. In the latter process, territory often had to be abandoned. It was likely with this understanding that Samuel Stambaugh reported that the 1831–32 cession the Menominee made to the United States between the Fox River and Lake Michigan "was of but little use to the Menominies [*sic*] *in their present condition*" (emphasis added).[147] Thus weakened in number and leadership, the Menominee found it increasingly difficult to resist the territorial designs of the United States as well as the occupation of their unceded land by Chippewa, Potawatomi, and Winnebago bands.

A Change in Agents

Green Bay agent Samuel Stambaugh was an outspoken advocate for fair play in the case of the land controversy between the New York Indians and the Menominee. After reporting the blatant manipulation of the Menominee by the more sophisticated Iroquois and witnessing the political power of their supporters on the Washington scene, Stambaugh soon became an outspoken advocate for the Menominee position. These views and the fact that he had alienated the New York congressional delegation cost him his position at Green Bay.

In June 1832 George Boyd, Indian agent on Mackinac Island and brother-in-law of the former president John Quincy Adams, was appointed as agent at Green Bay.[148] As an experienced agent, Boyd came to Green Bay with a specific agenda for Christianizing and educating the Menominee and other pagan Indians attached to his agency. By 1833 he had formed a solid relationship with Reverend Richard Cadle, who ran the local Episcopalian Indian mission, so that treaty money and other funds were transferred through the agency to support Cadle's work.[149] Boyd was not sympathetic to the educational efforts of the Catholic priest Father Mazzuchelli, on the grounds that the Catholics taught dogma along with other school subjects.[150] Boyd's desire to civilize the Menominee faced several obstacles beyond the fact that the Menominee were not enthusiastic about abandoning their own culture and religion. The first was that liquor, although illegal in Indian country, was much used in the Indian trade and was having an increasingly bad effect on the Menominee. Boyd had a difficult time controlling the distribution of alcohol, because the Green Bay settlement was spread over a considerable stretch of the lower Fox River where Indians were encouraged to come to trade.[151] Combined with the problem of the corruption of the Menominee was that if they had any inclinations toward Christianity or acculturation, it was at the behest of their French Canadian relations, who were staunchly Catholic and less than enthusiastic for either Protestantism or the English language.

Like many Americans of the early nineteenth century, George Boyd was imbued with a sense of racial and cultural superiority that led to a negative and paternalistic attitude toward not only Indians but the growing tide of new European immigrants. In this view, cultural, linguistic, and religious heterogeneity had no role in their perceived vision for the American Republic. Thus, Boyd approached the Menominee with a fundamental disregard for Menominee culture and a clear vision for change. During the decade of his tenure at Green Bay (1832–42), he worked diligently to suppress alcohol use, concentrate the Menominee away from non-Indian settlements, and promote literacy, western agriculture, and Protestant Christianity. His views and his attitude often brought him into conflict with the Menominee chiefs, who were very much concerned with controlling their own destiny and maintaining their ancient language, culture, and religious traditions.[152]

By 1834 the Menominee chiefs, particularly Chief Oshkosh, protested the use of their treaty funds for the support of the Episcopalian mission. They were informed, however, that such expenditures were at the discretion of the secretary of war.[153] Oshkosh and Boyd had little respect for each other, and Boyd continued to maneuver to try to get Oshkosh deposed as head chief. When Oshkosh and his brother killed another Indian as an obligation of revenge in 1834, Oshkosh was charged with murder but later released by Judge Doty because the United States had no jurisdiction over conflicts between Indians that took place in Indian country. Agent Boyd disputed Doty's finding and claimed that in return for the judgment, the judge received an Indian deed to an island at the entrance to Lake Winnebago, later known as Doty's island.[154]

In 1834 the Green Bay Agency let contracts for a model farm community at Winnebago Rapids near the juncture of the Fox River and the upper end of Lake Winnebago. Two houses for farmers were to be built, twenty houses for Indians, a house for a teacher, and a school and a blacksmith shop.[155] The two farmers succeeded in clearing, plowing, and planting seventy acres of land, but this experiment in acculturating the Menominee was short lived, ending in April 1837.[156] The Menominee complained vigorously about the fact that they got little benefit from this establishment. As the chiefs put it, "The farmers, and millers, and teachers were kept several years under pay, but the mills never were in condition to do a single hours work, the farmers and teachers rendered no service, nor did we derive *one dollar benefit* from any of the improvements intended for our use."[157] Agent Boyd suggested that a major reason for the failure of the farm experiment was the whiskey that was being sold at a nearby island, the one now owned by Judge Doty.[158]

The Condition of the Menominee in the 1830s

The Treaty of 1831 did little to change the Menominee way of life. Despite the land cessions, they continued to follow their traditional seasonal subsistence rounds and to use the resources and territories that they had used since before the arrival of Euro-Americans. In fact, they were very much encouraged to do so by the Green Bay traders who depended on the product of their labors. The government, for its part, continued to license traders to enter Indian country and engage in commercial relations with the Menominee. In 1832 Agent Boyd issued three licenses to trade at Butte des Morts, three more for Portage, and one license each for Duck Creek, the Menominee River, the upper Wisconsin River, and Neeshotyewayoc at Two Rivers on Lake Michigan.[159]

The Menominee lived over this ancestral territory in at least nineteen villages from the Menominee River in the north to the Milwaukee River in the south and from Lake Michigan to the upper Wisconsin River.[160] Politically, they were organized in eleven bands, each led by a band chief. In 1836 these men included Oshkosh, Ayamataw (Fish Spawn), Komanikin (Big Wave), Komanikeenoshah (Little Wave), Wainesaut, Iskkininew, and Glode Carron.

Menominee population estimates for the early 1830s vary from four thousand to two thousand. It is likely, however, that thirty-five hundred is an accurate figure prior to the smallpox and cholera epidemic, when a 25 percent mortality reduced the overall Menominee population to about twenty-six hundred people. This figure is roughly consistent with a figure of two thousand given by the commissioner of Indian affairs, Carey Harris, in December 1836.[161] In this same document, Harris reported that three-quarters of the Menominee were living on the Oconto and Menominee rivers. He said further that these Menominee had no interest in farming and that the great majority of the others also opposed it.

The Treaty of the Cedars, 1836

The Indian Removal Act was the centerpiece of American Indian policy during the 1830s. This

1830 act permitted the exchange of Indian land within the organized states and territories east of the Mississippi River for land held by the United States west of the Mississippi River. Specific provisions of this act required that the assent of a tribe be obtained before any removal could take place. If a tribe agreed to remove, the United States would aid emigrating Indians, pay for their improvements, protect them in their new homes, and otherwise ensure a successful transition.[162] The idea behind the removal act was to protect Indian people by removing them to a region beyond any corrupting influences of non-Indians, where they could either maintain their own cultures or, more preferably, be transformed into educated, God-fearing farmers. The act not only was unsuccessful for these civilization purposes but resulted in the mass removal of thousands of eastern Indians into conditions of hopelessness, poverty, and despair. The United States, for its part, acquired millions of acres of valuable and productive agricultural land as the result of removal treaties.

Carey Harris, commissioner of Indian affairs from 1836 to 1838, was a protégé and trusted political confidant of the then secretary of war, Lewis Cass, and part of President Andrew Jackson's inner circle. During his tenure as commissioner, Harris was involved in the forcible ejection of the Seminoles, Cherokee, Creek, and Chickasaw from the southeast, as well as the removal of some of the Indian tribes of the Old Northwest. In 1838 he was removed from office for his involvement in a scheme to speculate in Indian allotments in the south.[163] Harris's view of the Menominee situation is revealed in his official report for the year 1837.

> These Indians still retain their wandering habits. The experiment made by the Government in furnishing them farmers, has entirely failed. They raise corn on the Oconte [*sic*], Menominee, and Fox rivers, in small quantities, but depend on the chase, fishing, fowling, and gathering of the wild rice, for their subsistence. They are scattered over a large extent of country, and are well disposed towards the whites. They are, however, entirely under the control of their traders, who will endeavor to control the greater part of their annuities. The remnant of this nation of Indians can only be saved by their removal from the country they now occupy, to the country south of the Missouri river.[164]

The first suggestion of a new treaty with the Menominee after the Treaty of 1831 was made by Green Bay agent George Boyd in 1835, when he notified Commissioner Herring that the Menominee would consider another land cession.[165] This idea, although agreed to by Herring, needed to await a congressional appropriation.[166] In March 1836, Secretary Cass suggested to the president of the Senate, Martin Van Buren, that the government should purchase land in the region of Green Bay and remove the Menominee west.

> From the nature of the country and the progress of settlements west of Lake Michigan the Indians now holding lands in the vicinity of Green Bay can only be considered as temporary residents there. The time will soon come, when circumstances will require them to remove, and it appears to me that it will be much better to purchase out their title now, if they are disposed to sell, and transfer them to the country west of the Mississippi. Their position there would be better in every point of view than it now is, as they would consider their residence permanent, and make their arrangements accordingly.[167]

As the government was soon to find out, the Menominee did not agree with Cass's view. In the Menominee perspective, they not only considered their Wisconsin residence permanent but would not even hear of the prospect of removal.

When Wisconsin became an official territory on July 3, 1836, the new territorial governor, Henry Dodge, also became the superintendent for Indian Affairs of the territory. Dodge was already experienced in Indian affairs in Wisconsin and was an active advocate of removal. Following congressional passage of an appropriations bill for the purpose of removing several eastern tribes, Dodge was appointed as the sole U.S. commissioner to treat with the Menominee for their land in Wisconsin and to remove them west. Making his way to Green Bay, Dodge appointed young Green Bay lawyer Henry Baird as secretary for the treaty and sent word to the

Menominee to meet him at "the Cedars," a promontory along the Fox River just below the Grand Kaukaulin.[168]

Negotiation of the Treaty

Dodge opened the treaty negotiations on August 29, 1836, addressing the assembled Menominee chiefs through mixed-blood interpreters Charles Grignon and William Powell. In opening statements, Dodge explained that he had been sent by the Great Father, the president of the United States, who had "the welfare of all of his red children greatly at heart" and wished to make them "prosperous and happy."[169] Dodge told the Menominee that the Great Father wished to provide them with a country west of the Mississippi where they could live unmolested from the advancing line of white settlement. This country, Dodge said, would be "better adapted to hunting, the culture of farming and the raising of cattle."[170] Here the Menominee could live in peace protected by the Great Father's troops. Dodge proposed to buy all of the Menominee land in Wisconsin, but he told them that if they were not disposed to sell their whole country, they should tell him what they would sell and for how much.[171]

Finally, Dodge called the Menominees' attention to a provision of Article 6 of the Treaty of 1831. In reference to the boundary of the land set apart for the New York Indians, the 1831 treaty stated that the Menominee territory (outside of the land ceded for this purpose) would remain a hunting ground for the Menominee "until the President of the United States shall deem it expedient to extinguish their title. In that case, the Menomonee [*sic*] tribe promise to surrender it immediately, upon being notified of the desire of the Government to possess it. The additional annuity then to be paid to the Menomonee [*sic*] Tribe, to be fixed by the President of the United States."[172] The council was adjourned for the reply of the Menominee, which was given the next morning by Chief Oshkosh.

Oshkosh began with a sharp disagreement with Dodge's reading of the 1831 treaty: "Father we always thought that we owned the land we occupied, but yesterday we heard that our great father had a right to take it when he wanted it. We did no[t] so understand the treaty."[173] He went on to tell Dodge that the chiefs who went to Washington to make the 1831 treaty (neither Oshkosh nor Dodge had been present) agreed to sell land to the east of the Fox but not to the west. Among the chiefs assembled at Cedar Point were Ayamataw (Fish Spawn), Komanikin (Big Wave), Komanikeenoshah (Little Wave), and Shawwannoh (The South), all signers of the 1831 treaty, as well as Charles Grignon and Charles Ellis, who served as interpreters in Washington where the treaty was negotiated.[174] Ayamataw addressed Dodge's contention about the intent of Article 6.

> I am one of the Chiefs who went to Washington accompanied by Charles A. Grignon and Mr. Ellis. Father, when we first saw you here we were very desirous of hearing what you had to say to us. What we heard from our Great Father was altogether different from what we expected to hear from him. Father Messers. Grignon and Ellis were present as interpreters at Washington, and I take the supreme being to witness what I am going to relate in regard to that treaty is nothing but truth. Father I know that you are sent here by our Great father the President and we look upon you in the same way we did upon him when he made the treaty at Washington. Father, it was understood by us that our land on the east side of the Fox river we ceded to our Great Father not no more; nor did we bind ourselves to our Great Father that we should purchase the balance of our land on the west side when he should require it.[175]

The other chiefs who had been at Washington "assented to and confirmed" this understanding.

It is apparent in the foregoing exchange that the Menominee chiefs who negotiated the Treaty of 1831 had a far different understanding of its meaning than did Dodge, who was not present and had only the text to go by. The Menominee understood the language of Article 6 to be an option for the purchase of more Menominee land if it should be needed to accommodate the six thousand or so New York Indians who, by terms of the treaty, could potentially join the Oneida and other eastern Indians on the lands purchased to receive them in Wisconsin. They did not understand it to mean that the president could unilaterally require them to surrender land for other purposes. This was apparently the way Samuel Stambaugh also understood this provision of the 1831 treaty.

The treaty journal of 1831 indicates that on August 31 Oshkosh described the land the Menominee would sell and indicated it on a map that the Menominee prepared. Dodge made no further mention of the 1831 treaty, nor did he even try to get the Menominee to remove from Wisconsin. In exchange for the cession of land, the Menominee asked for a cash annuity for twenty years, provisions each year for the same period (including two hundred pounds of tobacco and thirty barrels of salt), and two blacksmiths. Oshkosh also asked that all the benefits for farming and education under the 1831 treaty, including the salaries of the farmers, millers, and teachers, be included in the annuity payment. Oshkosh told Dodge, "Father, there is only one thing we do not like in this treaty, that is the one thousand dollars a year for a school. We do not want schools. We do not wish our children to read the papers."[176] Dodge also agreed to include a provision for payment of a $99,710 debt to the traders and $80,000 to be divided among mixed-blood persons of Menominee descent.[177]

The governor asked the Menominee to cede a tract of pine timberland on each side of the upper Wisconsin River. The Menominee agreed to this request with the understanding that the Great Father would not permit the river to be dammed, as they "depended upon fishing" and "wanted a passage for their canoes up and down the river."[178] The treaty, which was concluded at Cedar Point and ultimately agreed to by the U.S. Senate, ceded about four million acres north and west of Green Bay and another 184,320 acres on the upper Wisconsin River (see map 14). This included much of the land described as a "hunting ground" in the 1831 treaty and all of the land that was to be the location of the government's farming experiment.[179]

In forwarding the draft of the Treaty of 1836 to Secretary of War Butler in December, Commissioner Harris made the current state of the Menominee clear by citing from the report of special agent Edmund Brush, who visited the Menominee a year earlier.

> Of about 2,000 of the Nation, three fourths live on the Oconto and Menomonee [*sic*] Rivers. The latter take no interest in the farming experiment. The great majority of the others oppose it. All, save the few actually engaged, too indolent to work, and incited by the traders, desire to put an end to it, in the expectation that the money expended for these objects will in that event, be added to their specific annuity.[180]

It is apparent from Commissioner Harris's letter that he had not given up on the removal of the Menominee from Wisconsin.

The 1836 cession is very curious. Of all their landholdings, why would the Menominee cede this particular land? First, it seems apparent that, despite the statement of the treaty journal, the land to be ceded was not chosen by the Menominee. The fact that Oshkosh's description of the boundaries of the cession in the treaty journal are nearly identical to the description in the treaty itself raises suspicion, especially since it contains technical references to boundaries of former treaties. Oshkosh, who was not literate in the English language, would have been unlikely to express the cession in these terms and further would almost certainly not have provided a map, which is a literate document.

Second, one wonders why the Menominee, a hunting, fishing, and gathering people, would cede some of the best territory in their domain for these purposes as well as the part of their estate where as many as three-fourths of the Menominee lived.[181] Why would Governor Dodge and Secretary Cass, who were supposedly acquiring land in advance of American settlement, ask for the Menominee land that was totally unsuited for agriculture? In fact, in 1836 there were fewer than two non-Indians per square mile in the entire cession, and most of it was entirely devoid of white settlers for many, many years.[182] Further, why would Dodge give in so easily to the collapse of the farms, mills, and schools that were the cornerstone of the civilizing objective of U.S. Indian policy?[183]

The answers to these questions seem to come from two directions. First, Dodge and the United States wanted this cession not for agricultural purposes or American settlement but for its natural resources. The Treaty of the Cedars, like the

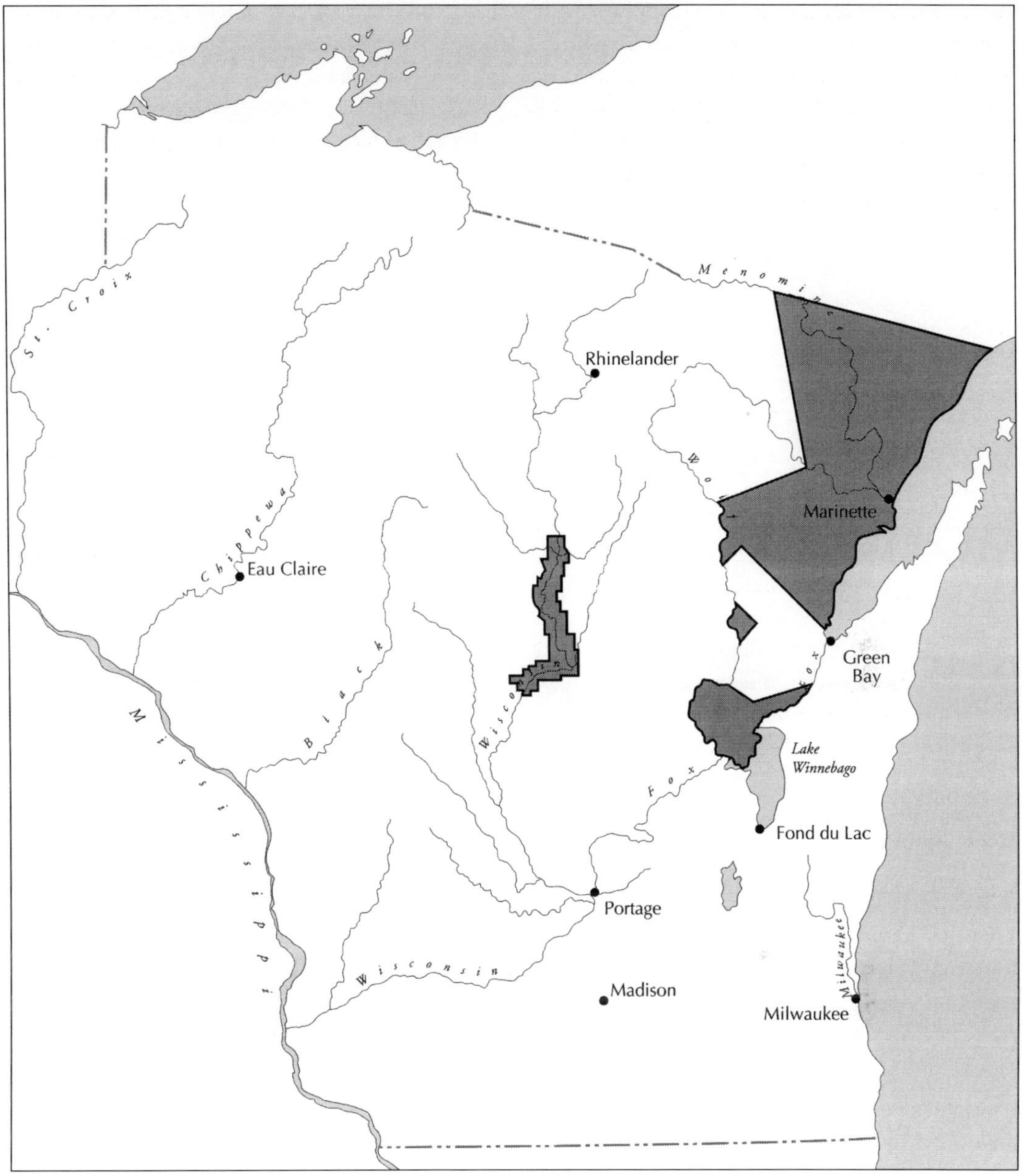

Map 14. Territory ceded by the Menominee in the treaty of 1836.

one Dodge negotiated in the next year with the Chippewa for the cession of north-central Wisconsin, was a lumbermen's treaty. The Menominee treaty of 1836 called for the Menominee to leave the ceded area within a year. The Menominee were called on to do so, and many peacefully complied, but no effort was ever made to enforce this provision. By and large, the activity of the Menominee as hunters and gatherers were not thought by Dodge to be incompatible with lumbering. It is likely for this reason that the 1836 treaty does not discuss usufruct.

The second consideration in explaining the location of the 1836 cession and the way the Menominee were to be accommodated involved the civilization experiments under the 1831 treaty. These had been an abject failure. By specifically releasing the United States from these provisions in the third article, both the government and the Menominee were acknowledging the fact that the Menominee were and wished to remain a hunting people. Further demonstration of this fact is found in the treaty's provision for blacksmith services crucial to the repair of guns and traps, as well as its provision for salt, which was used to preserve whitefish and lake trout for the new American commercial fish markets. In later time, Oshkosh claimed that the only reason the Menominee negotiated the 1836 land cession was to rid themselves of the education and farm expenses of the 1831 treaty.[184] The assumption made by government officials and the Menominee in 1836 was that the Menominee would continue to hunt, fish, and gather over the territory ceded. Within all of the official correspondence, including the treaty journal and the treaty itself, there is not a single mention of the surrender of usufruct rights held by the Menominee.

Another factor in understanding the 1836 treaty lies in the power of mixed bloods and traders in Menominee affairs. In fact, many of the traders were of mixed descent. This was particularly true of the large, extended Grignon family, which had been married into the Menominee tribe for at least three generations by 1836. The 1836 treaty was, above all else, an extremely profitable opportunity for these powerful interests. For example, the Grignons received 45 percent of the nearly one hundred thousand dollars set aside for trader debts, an enormous fortune in 1836. Charles Grignon and William Powell, who were mixed-blood traders and the interpreters for the treaty, received $11,525 and $2,100, respectively, for the trade debt provision of the treaty. Since the trade in furs was becoming less and less profitable by 1836, mixed-blood traders, John Lawe and Jacque Portlier of the American Fur Company, and American independent traders (e.g., William Farnsworth, William Dickson, and the Irwin brothers) all wanted the Menominee to intensify their hunting and trapping activities. If the United States would have urged a cession of hunting, fishing, and gathering rights over the huge piece of land ceded in 1836, it would have completely bankrupted the Green Bay economy. These nationally powerful fur interests would have mounted a huge protest even if the Menominee did not.

The Treaty of the Cedars provided the United States with 4,284,320 acres of valuable timberland and left the Menominee with the means to support themselves from the land as they had done in the past. The traders, trading companies, and mixed-blood Menominee likewise received cash payments under the debt and mixed-blood provisions and were relatively satisfied with the treaty. This huge influx of cash into the local economy was about the only source of hard money during the years between 1837 and 1842, when the American economy was suffering a disastrous recession.

The Fight to Remove the Menominee (1836–48) and the Fall of Agent Boyd

During the period between the Treaty of 1836 and the Treaty of 1848, the Menominee were faced with a series of assaults on their political integrity as a people and consequently on their culture itself. The focus of this struggle, though certainly multidimensional, was their removal from Wisconsin to country west of the Mississippi River. One of the major goals of the federal government in negotiating the Menominee Treaty of 1836 was to seek their removal west. It was soon apparent to Dodge that this objective could not be accomplished, if for no other reason than the fact that the Menominee would not give their agreement to remove, which was required by the Indian Removal Act. Any attempt to remove the Menominee met with stiff resistance from the Green Bay trading interests, who were not only largely the mixed-blood or spousal relatives of the Menominee but also very influential in Menominee politics, as exemplified by the very large and extremely influential Grignon family.[185] The last thing traders wanted was for the Menominee, their fur trade partners and customers for manufactured goods, to leave Wisconsin. The economic welfare of the traders and the Menominee had historically been tightly linked and remained so during the first half of the nineteenth century.

At the time of the 1836 treaty, the traders' economic interest and the Menominee goal of resisting acculturation fit neatly together. For example, the Menominee believed the farms, churches, and schools that were paid for by Menominee funds under the Treaty of 1831 were little more than an eleemosynary for the farmers, millers, and teachers employed by the government. Not only did the Menominee, particularly Oshkosh, believe they received little benefit from the funds used to support the "civilization establishment," but they did not agree with its purpose—namely, to promote English literacy, teach western agriculture, and Christianity. For their part, the traders were interested in putting as much hard cash as possible into the hands of the Menominee, because these dollars would rapidly flow to their own pockets. Thus, in 1836 Oshkosh, with the encouragement of the traders, successfully shut off funds to the civilization experiments at Winnebago Rapids (the farming country). The seventy-six thousand dollars allowed for these purposes was to be invested in stock, with the interest payment added to the annuity.[186]

The Menominee-trader alliance soon came into direct conflict with government policy and with the objectives of Agent George Boyd at Green Bay, an ardent believer in civilizing Indians. During the period leading up to the 1836 treaty, Boyd believed the Menominee could be Christianized and educated in their own country through Christian missionaries who were supervised and financially supported through the government. With the defeat of these efforts in the 1836 treaty, Boyd became an advocate of Menominee removal, now subscribing to the theory that the Menominee could only be civilized if they could be separated from the influence of their traders and mixed-blood relatives.[187]

This view put Boyd on a collision course with both the Menominee and their supporters. When he paid annuities in 1837 in goods rather than in silver, as specified in the treaty, the Menominee bitterly complained and said they would take no annuities rather than accept the worthless goods supplied by the government. Payment in goods was, of course, antithetical to the interest of the traders, who, after all, sold goods. Among these trade goods was whiskey, which Boyd knew was more easily purchased with coin than trade articles. When Boyd had the Menominee complaints against the government's annuity payment practices printed and published, he incurred the wrath of his own superiors.[188]

Although a conscientious administrator of Indian affairs, George Boyd was a slipshod bookkeeper who had his accounts called into question on several occasions.[189] In the late 1830s Boyd fell into an increasingly difficult financial situation. In 1836 the reorganization of the Wisconsin Indian establishment reduced his position to that of a subagent at half his former salary.[190] On top of this problem, the financial panic of 1837 wreaked havoc with Boyd's speculative investment in land set aside for a Wisconsin town site. Finally, Boyd was accused by the politically powerful traders of commingling personal and government funds. These charges were investigated by the Treasury Department, and Boyd was found to owe $7,256 to the government. Faced with these pressures, George Boyd retired as subagent at Green Bay on March 1, 1842.[191]

It is not surprising that Boyd was replaced by George Lawe, son of Green Bay trader John Lawe and his Menominee wife. Lawe's appointment was made by the new superintendent of the Michigan Agency, Robert Stuart, who was himself the former chief factor of the American Fur Company at Mackinac. When Boyd reported on the condition and location of the Menominee tribe near the end of his long regime at Green Bay, his tone reflects his total dissatisfaction with the state of affairs.

> Since their treaty of 1836, they [2,500 men, women, children, and half-breeds] have in a great measure ceased to labor or to hunt—but look to their annuity alone for a support—They are completely under the control of their traders—those above Green Bay, being guided and directed by the Grignons—and those living below the Bay by Mr. Lawe. The present moment should be seized to purchase their remaining lands, and to move them West of the Mississippi. Wisconsin will not fill up with Settlers from the East, so long as these Indians are retained within her bosom, and they will continue to go from bad to worse, so long as their Traders are their Chiefs, and their head men nothing. Five or Six Traders made the Treaty of 1836, and I can designate half that number who shall sell the balance of their lands tomorrow. If their Agent [George Boyd] had been a plaint [*sic*] tool in the hands of the Grignons no vile slander originating with them for sordid purposes, and unknown to the Indian (with the exception perhaps of the head chief, Oshkosh, the greatest scoundrel in the Nation) would ever have reached the War

Department against him as the Documents forwarded to meet these slanders to the Indian Department in 1839 will establish & prove to any unprejudiced mind.

These Indians are divided into eight bands living on the Wolf, Wisconsin, Menominee, Oconto and Payshetigo Rivers, Shawanoe Lake, Big and Little Bay des Noquest, and the Grand Cacalin.[192]

Condition of the Menominee in the Early 1840s

The first household-by-household census of the Menominee tribe was taken in 1842 by subagent George Lawe. This census counted 2,464 Menominee who were living in nine bands, including Oshkosh's band of 411 on Lake Butte des Morts; Shononiew's band of 167 on the Wolf River; Ianmetau's band of 288 at the Grand Kaukaulin and Little Chute; Little Wave's band of 406 people residing on the east shore of Lake Winnebago, led by Wahnehunnah; Waukechon's band of 202 at Lake Shawano; a band of 258 living at Green Bay and along its shores, led by Mawbawzo; Chemebowme's band of 154 on the Oconto River; Shauwanopenessee's band of 154 on the Peshtigo River; and Wawnawco's band of 265 on the Menominee River.[193] Besides these Menominee, the Menominee villages contained an assortment of mixed bloods of Menominee and French, American, Chippewa, Potawatomi, and Winnebago descent. In addition, there were Chippewa, Ottawa, Potawatomi, and Winnebago spouses of Menominee people. After the Winnebago and Potawatomi of southern Wisconsin ceded their land to the United States in the early 1830s, many members of these tribes moved north onto Menominee land or land the Menominee had ceded to the United States. In 1845 the Menominee were still complaining vigorously that the Winnebago were continuing to plant, hunt, fish, and make sugar on their land.[194]

In his report for 1843, George Lawe concluded that about half of the Menominee had honored the government's request that they remove to their unceded territory, which, after the Treaty of 1836, included about eight to ten million acres between the Wolf and Wisconsin rivers and then northeast to the Chippewa River.

> The whole tribe is of an erratic and roving disposition, gaining a precarious subsistence from the chase and trapping and fishing . . .
>
> . . . Notwithstanding the attempts made to civilize the Menominies [*sic*], they still retain their primitive habits and customs—living in lodges made of mats or the bark of trees, and depending upon the chase, fishing, and boiled rice for support. They consider labor degrading, and all performed among them is done by females.[195]

Indeed, one of the most persistent complaints against the United States was that annuity payments were often held in the late summer and fall, when the Menominee were engaged in the collection of rice, garden products, and the fall deer hunt. This conflict was potentially disastrous, since the Menominee depended on both natural resources and annuity money for their survival.

The year 1842 was a productive one, as George Lawe reported.

> The only land cultivated by this tribe is small patches dug up with the hoe by the women, for raising corn, pumpkins, and beans. The crops this year are very good. The wild rice has also yielded very abundantly. In the spring of the year, they make large quantities of maple sugar, which they sell to the traders. Their success during the preceding year in hunting and trapping was unusually good. The value of the furs disposed of would, I think, exceed forty thousand dollars.[196]

In late February the pioneer settler Increase Lapham made a trip from Milwaukee to Green Bay. On reaching the upper Rock River and Fond du Lac, he met about one hundred Menominee who were likely from Little Wave's band, which frequented the west and south sides of Lake Winnebago. Lapham found these Indians living on venison and fish and preparing to make maple sugar.[197] The latter activity accounts for this large congregation of Menominee in the late winter.

In 1846 all of the Menominee except the three hundred who had settled at the Catholic mission on the south shore of Lake Poygan remained hunters and gathers.[198] Green Bay and its rivers continued to be the home of four of the nine Menominee bands, while others made an annual trek to the fisheries and rice beds of Lake Winnebago, Green Bay, and Lake Michigan.[199] These visits to collect resources from their former band territories in the 1831 and 1836 cessions became longer after many of the Menominee moved to their unceded land at the request of the government in 1844 and 1845.[200] Subagent Albert Ellis reported,

> The greater share of them [the Menominee] are hunters, living exclusively by the chase and the fisheries; for the last they resort to Green Bay, and the rivers falling into it, where they take at all seasons of the year, but especially in winter, large quantities (beyond their own consumption) of *trout* and *sturgeon.* When the Menominies [*sic*] shall leave the shores of Green Bay, the sturgeon fisheries will cease—none but the Indians being able to endure the cold and fatigue of taking them.[201]

Ellis's remark that the Indians took trout and sturgeon beyond their own consumption indicates their participation in the commercial market for salt fish, especially lake trout, which was barreled and sold to wholesalers for shipment to eastern population centers.[202] The trout were undoubtedly taken in gill nets during the fall, while the sturgeon were taken with spears and harpoons from offshore ice ledges during the deep winter.[203]

Following the collapse of the civilization experiment set up in the Treaty of 1831 and withdrawn at the insistence of the Menominee chiefs in the Treaty of 1836, the only attempt to teach the Menominee Christianity, English, and agriculture was at the Catholic mission station at Lake Poygan. Here Father F. J. Bonduel had gathered three hundred Menominee in a village of sixty-two log houses. Schools were operated for both boys and girls in the English language. This Christian group had also cleared some farmland and was raising potatoes and corn.[204] Unfortunately the Lake Poygan site was low, wet, and without running water, not only unhealthy, but largely unsuited for agriculture. Reverend Bonduel and his Menominee were anxious to move the mission to a more suitable locality but were reluctant to make the required improvements without a reservation that would guarantee their tenure. A reservation, it was suggested, would "ensure permanency to the possession of their improvements" and provide an inducement for the Menominee to devote more labor toward these ends.[205] A new treaty would be necessary to make a reservation.

Conflict with American Settlers

One of their agents who knew them well described the Menominee as a "brave and patient people, the firm friends of the government," who "rely with abiding confidence on its justice and magnanimity."[206] Unlike the Sioux or Sac-Fox, the Menominee never made war on the United States after the defeat of the British in the War of 1812. Unlike the Winnebago or Chippewa, the Menominee never threatened the use of military force against the United States or its citizens. To the contrary, when called on, the Menominee, like good children of the Great Father, heeded the call to arms of the government, by sending warriors to fight in all of the engagements of the nineteenth century from the Black Hawk War to the American Civil War. American officials consistently praised the behavior of the Menominee and their loyalty to the United States.[207]

This does not mean, however, that the relationship between the Menominee and American settlers was entirely harmonious. As American immigrants began to enter Menominee territory, there were occasional conflicts. These occurred because settlers often entered unceded land and also because the Menominee were still using the resources of ceded land by virtue of the usufructuary rights preserved in the Treaty of 1831.

Conflicts that arose in Menominee country between the Indians and U.S. citizens were the result of three principal causes: expropriation of Menominee resources, drunkenness, and cultural misunderstandings. Alcoholism has taken a heavy toll on the Menominee throughout their history, but particularly during the fur trading era. Liquor was introduced as a trade commodity because the Menominee had little will to resist it.[208] Traders, although aware of its illegality in Indian country and its destructive impact, nonetheless used it as a means to induce the Menominee to part with their annuity money. For example, subagent George Lawe reported that during the annuity payment of 1843 on the Wolf River, there were fifty to one hundred barrels of whiskey within two hundred yards of the Indian camp.[209] He was powerless to take action, because the whiskey traders were on private land. Such activity led to complaints about Menominee behavior, particularly around the Green Bay settlement.

After the negotiation of the 1836 treaty and prior to its ratification by the U.S. Senate, lumbermen began to enter the cession to cut timber from Menominee land as well as to build mills and dwellings.[210] This caused consternation for both the Menominee and the government. The United States was legally bound to evict these squatters whom it knew were trying to establish preemption rights to the land, but it was reluctant to do so because rapid ratification of the 1836 treaty was anticipated. Officials feared, however, that should the treaty not be approved by the Senate, troops would then be needed to forcefully evict squatters. In the meantime, the Menominee and the U.S. government continued to resist these incursions.[211]

By far the greatest number of conflicts between the Menominee and American citizens involved charges of theft, trespass, and the killing of domestic animals, made by American farmers who took up residence on land the Menominee had sold to the United States. These activities often led to claims for Menominee "depredations." In such cases, government regulations required the agent to investigate claims against the Indians, submit documentation in the form of interrogatories of claimants as well as Indians, and make personal recommendations as to the justice of the claim. If the commissioner of Indian affairs was convinced of the legitimacy of the claim, funds would then be deducted from the annuity owed the tribe and paid directly to the claimant for damages.[212]

In actuality, most of the claims made for Menominee depredations were for the killing of domestic animals that settlers permitted free range in the forest. As was the custom of the day, fields, rather than animals, were fenced in, the presumption being that the resources of the countryside were free for the taking unless they were fenced or posted. Thus, Menominee finding pigs or cows wandering free in the woods killed them for food as they would a bear or elk. The Menominee apparently had trouble understanding that a free-ranging animal was someone's "property."[213] As the Menominee gradually began to reside more on their unceded land, contact between themselves and American settlers decreased, and with this came a decrease in the number of depredations reported.

Charges of Menominee depredations against U.S. citizens were also used for political purposes and therefore exaggerated. For example, in the annual report to the commissioner of Indian affairs for 1845, Governor Dodge, who was anxious to remove the Menominee from Wisconsin, reported that the Menominee were troublesome and were annoying citizens along the Fox River "by committing depredations on their stock and other property."[214] In another section of the same report, Green Bay agent Albert Ellis says that since he instituted rules the previous year that required settlers to offer proof of money claims against the Menominee, "to the present time, I have but one report for depredations, and that of a trifling nature."[215]

Governor Dodge, as well as the federal officials who oversaw the Indian Office in the War Department, never gave up on the idea of removing the Indians from Wisconsin. In the case of the Menominee, however, they were up against the resistance of not only the Menominee themselves but also their influential mixed-blood relations as well as the politically powerful fur trade interests. The Treaty of 1836 was a defeat for the removal interest, but Governor Dodge and Green Bay subagents Boyd and Ellis continued to agitate for Menominee removal. Their reports alternatively argued for removal on the basis that the Menominee were troublesome to the settlers, that Indian culture was doomed to fall before the onslaught of civilization, that Menominee land was needed for agricultural settlement, and that removal was the only way to keep the Menominee from destroying themselves with whiskey. Until 1845 the Menominee and their traders were able to maintain the status quo, but in that year President James Polk appointed William Medill as commissioner of Indian affairs. Medill was arrogant and paternalistic in his dealings with Indians. To Medill, Indians were "ignorant, degraded, lazy and possessed of no worthwhile cultural traits."[216] With Medill in control, the fate of the Menominee seemed sealed.

Prelude to the Treaty of Lake Poygan (Powawhaykonnay), 1848

In her volume on the early history of Wisconsin, Alice Smith observes that "the governor of the territory was also the superintendent of Indian affairs. In the transitional era of the 1830s, when title to the greater part of the present Wisconsin passed into the possession of the United States, the Indian superintendency required about as much attention as the executive duties."[217] Smith goes on to say that "the President, the Congress, the Secretary of War, the Commissioner of Indian Affairs, the commanding officers of military posts, and the appointed agents and subagents each had a finger in the conduct of Indian matters."[218] Though responsible for coordinating the efforts of others not wholly subordinate to him relating to Indian matters, the governor represented all of the people of the territory. Obviously these interests were in sharp conflict.

Territorial governor Henry Dodge, who resumed the governorship in May 1845 after a four-year hiatus, clearly favored the interests of the non-Indians. In his annual report to the commissioner of Indian affairs for 1846, Dodge recommended a treaty to purchase the remaining Menominee land in Wisconsin at the earliest practical time: "I deem that measure of the first importance to the future growth and prosperity of the northern portion of this territory."[219] In his report of the next year, he described the removal of the Menominee west of the Mississippi as a "humane policy."[220]

Actually, forces had been at work for some years before 1848 to assure Menominee removal. Well before any proposition for removal had been made to the Menominee, Congress had appropriated money and negotiated a land cession with the Chippewa to relocate the Menominee between the Crow Wing and Long Leaf rivers in the Minnesota Territory. This treaty was concluded at Fond du Lac on August 2, 1847.[221]

Commissioner Medill and Governor Dodge realized that negotiating a treaty that would purchase all of the remaining Menominee land in Wisconsin and removing them west would not be easy. It was clear that besides their own strong resistance to these objectives, the Menominee held close counsel with their traders as well as their mixed-blood relatives who acted as intermediaries between themselves and outside interests. The traders, of course, wanted the Menominee to remain in Wisconsin, and both Henry Dodge and Green Bay agent Albert Ellis reported that the traders would try to block any treaty that did not contain funds to pay Menominee trade debts.[222] This was particularly problematic because the Senate had passed a resolution forbidding this practice.[223] Dodge suggested that it would be necessary to hold any treaty negotiations in Washington in order to isolate the Menominee from the influence of the traders and mixed bloods.[224] This technique of separating Indian chiefs from the advice of their kin networks during negotiations was an effective intimidation technique, since they depended on consensus in decision making. By late 1846 Medill told Dodge that they should postpone a Menominee treaty until they could get Congress to change its policy on debt provisions.[225]

Another problem of considerable proportion was the extent of the Menominee's land claim. The Menominee had a long-standing claim to their hunting territory through central and western Wisconsin to the Mississippi River.[226] Most of this land was confirmed by the Treaty of 1831. By 1847 the United States, though aware of these expansive Menominee claims, had received cessions for these lands in separate treaties from the Chippewa and Winnebago. It was, of course, in the interest of the United States to deal with a single tribe and to thereby ignore the customary joint use arrangements that members of many tribes had agreed on. If possible, the United States wished to avoid paying for the same land twice (see map 15). Yet as far as the Menominee were concerned, their claim to the western Wisconsin hunting grounds was as sound as that of any other tribe.[227]

The Menominee used land in central and western Wisconsin as a hunting ground because

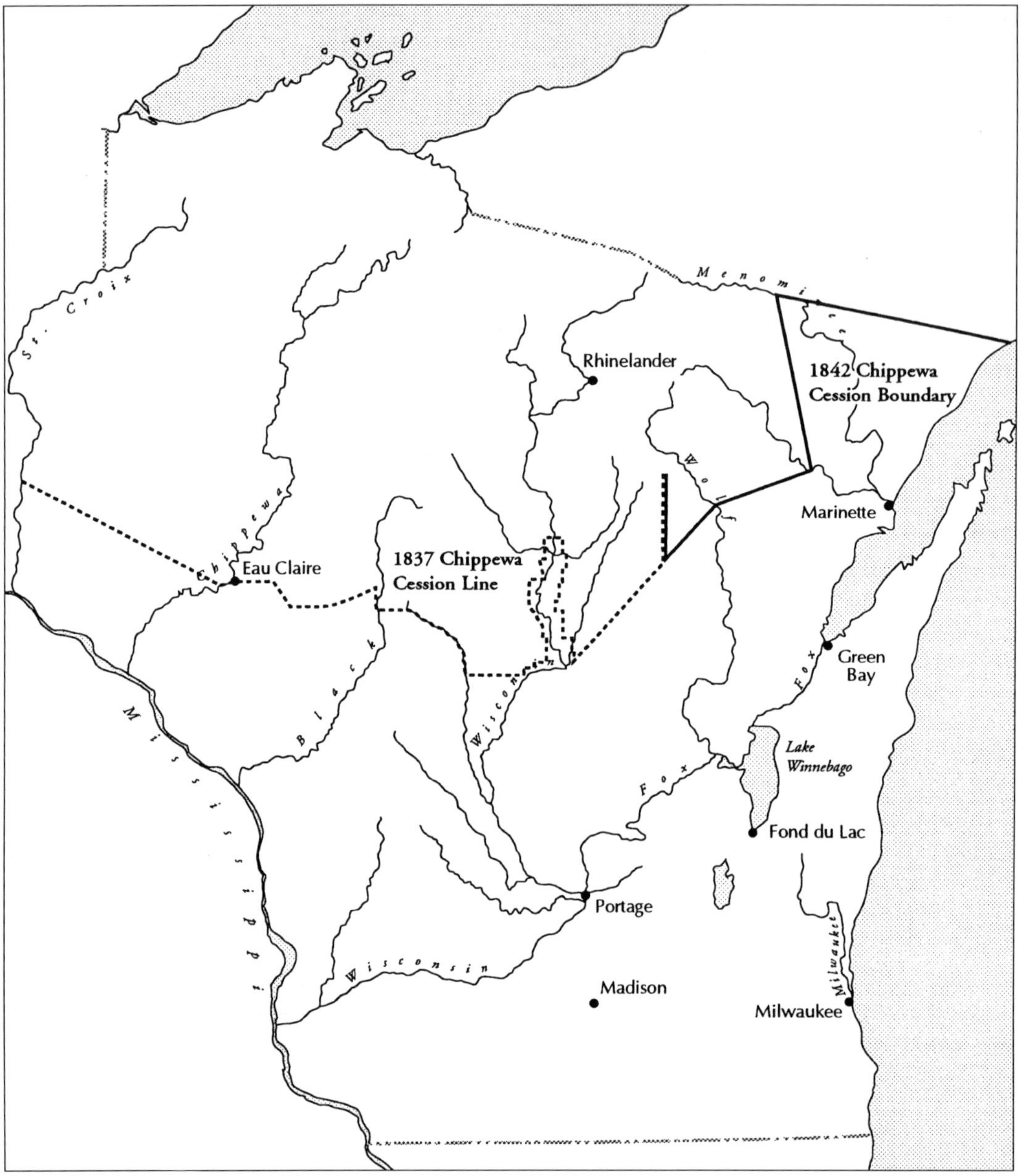

Map 15. Boundaries of the Chippewa cessions of 1837 and 1842.

it was an ecological transition zone between the northern hardwood forest and the southern prairies. This was part of the land they claimed as a hunting ground in the 1831 treaty. This ecotone was rich in game, particularly deer, which was the mainstay of Indian winter subsistence. The Chippewa, who resided in the forests of the north, and the Siouan tribes, among them the Winnebago, who occupied the more open country to the south and west, both exploited the ecotone and had for generations been locked in warfare over this rich hunting territory.[228] The Menominee, who were on relatively friendly terms with both the Chippewa and the Winnebago, were able to use the ecotone more frequently and safely than either the Chippewa or Siouan groups who were in hostile competition for its resources. Thus, the Menominee were in a position to concentrate their winter hunting north and west on the Wisconsin River, through the middle reaches of the Black, Chippewa, and St. Croix river valleys, to the upper Mississippi and even to the prairies beyond.[229]

This territory was difficult for the Menominee to define. Perhaps because of the overlapping nature of their western claims, the Menominee were reluctant to sort out the boundaries between themselves and the Chippewa and Winnebago at the Treaty of Prairie du Chien in 1825. In 1827 the Treaty of Butte des Morts was held specifically to resolve this problem, but only the Chippewa-Menominee boundary between the headwaters of the Menominee River and Plover Portage on the upper Wisconsin was resolved. A true line was never negotiated to sort out the claims of the Menominee, Winnebago, and Chippewa in western Wisconsin. In the Treaty of 1831, the Menominee claimed land west to the Chippewa River. After the Chippewa ceded much of this land in 1837, the Menominee still believed their own claim valid and were upset when public surveys were commenced in this region on land they had not sold.[230] Governor Dodge was well acquainted with the Menominee claim and knew that they occupied this land in common with the Chippewa.[231] At the time of the Treaty of 1848, the Menominee said they still owned about eight million acres in Wisconsin.[232]

Those who conspired to acquire the remaining Menominee land in Wisconsin and remove the Menominee west had a difficult dilemma on their hands. They did not have a removal destination for the Menominee and did not know how to deal with the influence of the traders and mixed bloods who opposed the impending removal efforts. Ramsey Crooks, hoping to recover American Fur Company claims, suggested applying political pressure to repeal the Senate resolution barring debt provisions. He also suggested two men to be appointed as commissioners to conduct the treaty: Henry Dodge, who had successfully included a large debt provision when he acted as commissioner for the 1836 treaty of Cedar Point; and U.S. representative M. L. Martin from Green Bay, because he "understand[s] the business."[233]

In July 1848 Governor Dodge and the Wisconsin congressional delegation wrote the House of Representatives urging a Menominee treaty, suggesting that it be held in Washington to avoid pressure from "interested persons."[234] The delegation contended that trespass on private land by Menominee threatened "friendly relations" with the Menominee.[235] Commissioner Medill, who was not friendly to trader interests, would not support lifting the debt provision ban but was anxious to proceed with the treaty.[236] Since only two thousand dollars had been appropriated to hold the treaty, there was not enough money to follow Dodge's suggestion of taking the Menominee chiefs to Washington.[237] Green Bay subagent Albert Ellis suggested a plan to effect a treaty with the Menominee without alerting the traders.

> On the whole, were I to venture any counsel, it would be that your Excellency [Dodge] should appear, (perhaps rather unexpectedly to the traders and whites) at the approaching annuity payment, empowered, and prepared to submit the Menominees a proposition for the purchase of their country, to which they would be compelled to reply before the malign influence could organize itself to [illegible word] the government.[238]

During August 1847 Medill sent General Isaac Verplank to Minnesota, where, with Indian trader Henry Rice, he negotiated two treaties of cession with the Chippewa.[239] This land was obtained expressly as destinations for the Winnebago and Menominee, who Medill was anxious to remove from Wisconsin. Given Medill's poor understanding of the Chippewa, Rice's part in a trader conspiracy to corner the Indian trade in Minnesota, and the questionable tactics used by Verplank in negotiating, these treaties plagued relations between the United States and the Chippewa for years.

Medill now diverted Verplank to Green Bay, where, with Dodge, he hoped to negotiate for the Menominee removal. Verplank, however, became ill and never traveled beyond Milwaukee. From there he wrote to Medill advising that the treaty be postponed until the fur trade interest had a chance to lobby for repeal of the trader debt resolution.[240] Medill concurred and postponed negotiations with the Menominee until the following summer.[241]

In the end, Medill opted to take Ellis's strategic advice. On September 9, 1848, Medill wrote Ellis to delay assembling the Menominee for annuity payments because a duly authorized treaty commissioner would appear to negotiate with the Menominee. The letter does not reveal the identity of the commissioner.[242] Ellis, who was instructed to cooperate with the mysterious commissioner, was no doubt shocked when, in early October, Commissioner Medill himself appeared to negotiate with the Menominee.

Negotiations at Lake Poygan

Despite subagent Albert Ellis's glowing appraisal of the Lake Poygan Treaty to his superior, William Medill, and despite the commissioner's own favorable view of the agreement, this treaty was one of the worst shams in the history of treaty making between the United States and any American Indian tribe.[243] The 1848 treaty was negotiated by deceit and intimidation. While couched in terms that seem to promote the interest of the Menominee, the chiefs were forced to sign a treaty whose every real benefit was for the United States and its citizens. The 1848 treaty was soundly criticized by the Menominee, who never accepted its provisions, and by the supporters of the Menominee in Wisconsin. Eventually, when the government realized the extent of the fraud perpetrated by Commissioner Medill, the United States itself repudiated the central provisions of the 1848 treaty.

One of the difficulties in reconstructing what happened at Lake Poygan is the fact that Commissioner Medill did not follow proper protocol and prepare a journal of the negotiations. Several years after the treaty, the Menominee's attorney R. W. Thompson pointed out the significance of the absence of a treaty journal. Without a journal, he argued, it was not possible to reconstruct the intentions of the Menominee during the negotiations, since as a people without a written tradition, they could make no written record of their own. A journal would have provided a means to ascertain the wishes and understanding of the Menominees at a later time when problems involving interpretation of the treaty arose.[244]

As it is, there is a great deal of sworn testimony available by witnesses to the treaty negotiations. It was collected by Thompson to support the claims of the Menominee. In essence, witnesses said that the speeches of Medill at "Councils were filled with threats and menaces toward said Indians."[245] Subagents Bruce and Ellis, however, both wrote that charges against Medill were gratuitous and malicious.[246]

According to sworn statements, Medill told the chiefs that they had no real title to the land they were being asked to cede and that this land already belonged to the United States. He said that

> the United States only allowed them to occupy the [lands] temporarily, for the purposes of hunting and fishing and that they were liable to be removed at any time, by the United States, whether a treaty was effected at that time or not and that they would be removed unless they did sell the land; that the present was the last time they would be called upon by said United States to treat for the sale of the said lands.[247]

This is apparently a reference to the provision of the 1831 treaty that could be read to permit the president to acquire unceded land by giving notice. Medill's statement that they were only on the land temporarily for the purpose of hunting and fishing indicates his understanding that the usufruct rights reserved west of the Fox in the 1831 treaty survived the Treaty of 1836.

Medill went on to tell the Menominee that the land in question was under the jurisdiction of the state of Wisconsin and that the United States had no power to protect them in possession of their land.[248] The implications of this were obvious to the Menominee, since American squatters were already pouring onto their unceded land. Nonetheless, Medill made the threat explicit by saying that it amounted to an absolute certainty that if sale of the land was not effected at this treaty, non-Indians would overrun and settle Menominee land within the year and dispossess them of their homes.[249] Further, Medill told them that if they did not sell the land, the United States would take possession of it and drive the Menominee from the country; he warned that he "should not be surprised if on his return to Washington and no treaty was effected, the president should issue an order to have the lands surveyed immediately and brought into market."[250] At this announcement, the chiefs tried to show

Medill copies of the 1831 and 1836 treaties as proof to the contrary, but he would not discuss them.[251] It seems evident that the Menominee must have believed that the 1831 and 1836 treaties provided them with an exclusive claim to their unceded land, the right to occupy it and to freely use its resources.

Faced with what they perceived as a *fait accompli,* the Menominee made the best of an impossible situation and signed the Treaty of Lake Poygan. Oshkosh told Medill that the hearts of the chiefs and their people "were bloated with grief" at the effect of the treaty.[252] To his fellow chiefs, he said, "My friends we cannot do otherwise, we are forced into it."[253] Chief Shonene later commented that "the Commissioner last fall spoke to us as his children, and in fact did speak to us as we do little children to amuse them. After he had effected his purposes, he told us that he would go home with a smile on his face."[254] There were few smiles in Menominee country.

The 1848 Treaty

As far as the United States was concerned, the 1848 treaty was a straightforward treaty of cession and removal. It begins by the agreement that the "peace and friendship now so happily subsisting between the government and the people of the United States and the Menomonee [*sic*] Indians shall be perpetual."[255] By Article 2 the Menominee agreed to cede all of their land in Wisconsin. This was accomplished by the phrase that the Menominee "agree to cede, and do hereby cede, sell, and relinquish to the United States all their lands in the State of Wisconsin wherever situated."[256] Article 3 provided the Menominee with a tract of six hundred thousand acres of land in Minnesota for a future home. These lands were to be held "as Indian lands are held," that is, as the common property of its members.[257]

In consideration for the Menominee concessions, the United States agreed to pay $350,000 for a variety of purposes. Thirty thousand dollars was to be provided to the chiefs "to enable them to arrange and settle the affairs of their tribe preparatory to their removal."[258] Another forty thousand dollars was to be distributed to the mixed-blood relatives of the Menominee. Article 4 also contained an allocation of twenty thousand dollars to cover the costs of removal. Fifteen thousand dollars was to be spent on civilization projects: a manual labor school, a gristmill and sawmill, and other improvements. A millwright's salary was also included for a nine-year period, as was money to build and operate blacksmith shops. The balance of two hundred thousand dollars was to be paid as annuities over a ten-year period.[259]

By Article 6 the United States agreed to pay the expense of a Menominee delegation "to explore and examine their new country."[260] While the exploration and preparation to remove were underway, the Menominee, by provision of Article 8, were permitted to remain for two years "and until the President shall notify them that the same are wanted."[261] This meant the president could extend their residency in Wisconsin.

The treaty was signed by Commissioner Medill and all of the Menominee chiefs on October 18, 1848, and was ratified by the Senate on January 23, 1849, and signed by President James Polk. The 1848 treaty was not, however, written in the certain terms found in many removal treaties; that is, it did not have a specific date for the removal to take place. The removal destination in Minnesota was first to be explored by the Menominee, and the president was authorized to extend the Menominee's tenure in Wisconsin if they so desired it. Thus, while the Menominee agreed to remove from Wisconsin, the nature of the treaty was tenuous in this regard, and the Menominee had a different view of their obligations under the 1848 treaty than did the United States. It was not long before controversies arose between the Menominee and the United States over the effect and intent of the treaty. One argument centered on how much land had been ceded, and another had to do with the timing and conditions of removal.[262]

The Land Controversy

It was known well in advance of negotiating the Treaty of 1848 that the Menominee claimed extensive lands in western Wisconsin.[263] These lands were claimed at the time of the 1831 treaty (see map 9). As the United States well knew, however, some of this land had been ceded by the Winnebago in 1832 and 1837, and substantial areas had been ceded by the Chippewa in 1837 and 1842 (see map 15).[264] William Medill, not wishing to purchase the same land twice, asked the attorney general to give an opinion as to the extent and quantity of land owned by the Menominee. This opinion, which was rendered on September 13, 1848, was based on a map submitted by the government as well as previous treaties.[265] The attorney general determined that the Menominee owned 3,023,800 acres. Although this amount was far less than the eight million acres the Menominee claimed to own or the ten million acres estimated by subagent Albert Ellis, it was the amount of land Medill was instructed to purchase.[266] The price he was to pay was the same as the cost per acre paid by the government for land purchased by the 1836 treaty of Cedar Point, twelve years earlier: 18.9 cents per acre.[267]

When Medill arrived in Wisconsin, before he negotiated with the Menominee, he discovered an error on the map used by the attorney general. Correcting the map error would have increased the attorney general's estimate of the quantity of land belonging to the Menominee to about four million acres, but Medill did not correct the error.[268] In 1853 a Senate committee studied the 1848 cession, and it was determined that the United States actually acquired 5,230,240 acres by the Treaty of 1848 (see map 16).[269] This amount of land does not include another 2,488,320 acres the Menominee claimed west of the Black River, which was the western boundary of the 1848 cession. This was land already ceded by the Winnebago and Chippewa.

In fairness to Medill, he did point out the map error in his annual report for 1848 and in a letter to the secretary of war.[270] This warning gave the Senate time to adjust the quantity of land ceded by the treaty as well as the price paid to the Menominee. Since the Senate made no such amendment, the United States acquired 5,230,240 acres of Menominee land for $350,000 dollars by the 1848 treaty. This payment, according to Medill's own accounting, was less than half the amount paid per acre in the 1836 treaty.[271]

The Menominees pointed to the discrepancies in the amount of land they claimed as opposed to the land they sold under the provision of the 1848 treaty that ceded "all their lands in the State of Wisconsin *wherever situated.*"[272] This catchall phraseology was used by Medill precisely to gloss over the larger and ill-defined Menominee claim. The United States had, of course, already purchased some of this land from the Chippewa and Winnebago. The Menominee claimed that the amount of land they actually ceded by the 1848 treaty was greater than the 3,023,800 acres calculated by the government and that the price per acre was not equal to that paid in the 1836 treaty as authorized in the treaty instructions. According to the Menominee, if they ceded all their Wisconsin land, they had ceded 7,718,560 acres, and the United States, in addition to the money provided in the 1848 treaty, still owed them $1,083,807.[273]

The Menominee hired an attorney, R. W. Thompson, to pursue these claims, which he did by preparing a memorial that was sent to the secretary of the interior, A. H. H. Stuart, on October 11, 1850.[274] Since the Indian Office had been transferred from the War Department to the Department of the Interior in 1849, the secretary of the interior now supervised Indian affairs.

By the second article of the 1848 treaty, the Menominee tribe agreed to "hereby cede, sell, and relinquish to the United States all their lands in the State of Wisconsin wherever situated."[275] This terminology was entirely related to their *lands*. In all of the documentary records relating to the treaty, there is no statement nor implication that rights of usufruct were relinquished by this clause. In fact, the treaty permitted the Menominee to remain in Wisconsin for at least two years and longer, if permitted by the president. During this time, it was certainly assumed that the Menominee would continue to feed themselves from the natural resources of the land. Had the United States intended otherwise, it could have written a treaty with them similar to the Winnebago Treaty of 1846.[276] This treaty was a companion treaty to the Menominee Treaty of 1848 in that both were intended to remove Indians from Wisconsin and to place them on neighboring tracts obtained from the Minnesota Chippewa. By the terms of both treaties, the Winnebago and Menominee agreed to cede and sell all their land wherever situated. The Winnebago, however, were also asked to cede "all right, title, interest, claim, and privilege, to all lands, wherever situated, now or heretofore

Map 16. Territory ceded by the treaty of 1848 as understood by the United States.

occupied or claimed by said Indians."[277] The Winnebago agreed to remove within one year. By Article 4 of the treaty, the Winnebago also surrendered their usufruct rights to the United States for a consideration of forty thousand dollars. No such surrender of interest, claim, or privilege is to be found in the Menominee treaty conducted two years later under the hand of the same commissioner of Indian affairs. Had this been the intent, he would certainly have compensated the Menominee for the relinquishment by adding such a clause to Article 4 of the 1848 treaty.

Exploration of the Minnesota Lands

The next formal council with the Menominee following the 1848 treaty negotiations took place on July 25, 1849. On that occasion it became apparent that the Menominee and the United States had different views of what had been agreed to at Lake Poygan the previous summer. Chief Oshkosh complained that the Menominee had neither a copy of the treaty nor the treaty journal (which, of course, did not exist). Apparently Agent Bruce had a printed copy of the treaty that the Menominee would not accept as that to which they had agreed. Chief Josette Carron stated, "We would like to have a copy of all that was said, when the Treaty was made [the journal], so that we could refer to it. It is the custom of the whites when they make a contract to put it in writing—This [the treaty] looks like a mere verbal contract."[278] He also told Bruce, "I did not know that the white men had so many different ways of expressing themselves, and am astonished. As an Indian I have but one way of *speaking—my tongue is not forked."[279] In a footnote marked with an asterisk on the original document, the interpreter stated that this "is an allusion to the printed copy of the Treaty not being what they understood it to be when they signed it."[280]

The immediate problem, in addition to the question of how much land had been ceded, was a confusion over what the Menominee had agreed to under the removal provision of the treaty. The United States seems to have surmised that the Menominee agreed to an unconditional removal to the Crow Wing region of Minnesota within two years unless permitted to remain longer by the president. The Menominee may have believed, however, that the removal agreement, which they also believed they had been forced to accept, was much more open-ended. For example, Chief Shonene said, "We requested the privilege of remaining upon our lands for eight years. He [Medill] said he could not promise this, but that no one should molest us for two years . . . [and] that the President might probably allow us to remain longer perhaps for eight years."[281]

One consistent element of the Menominee understanding was that the treaty did not require them to remove to a country of which they did not approve.[282] This understanding is best articulated by Charles Geisey, who attended the 1848 treaty negotiations. Mr. Geisey remembers "that the Head Chief Oshkosh made the remark that he would assent to the Treaty provided that their Great Father would bear the expense of a good outfit for a delegation of young warriors to visit and inspect their new country and that if not satisfied with the same that they were to be at liberty to crawfish, translated backout from the Treaty. To this proposition Mr. Medill . . . using the same term said if they did not like the new country they could crawfish."[283] Mr. Geisey also states that he was surprised when he saw a copy of the treaty that had no provision giving the Menominee "a choice of land or repition [*sic*] of [the] treaty."[284] The treaty, he further says, "was read without much comment and was not explained in time to the Chiefs to enable them to detect the substitution of new conditions in their full force."[285]

After accusations of Menominee foot-dragging and numerous organizational problems with the leadership of the expedition to explore the Minnesota country, the expedition set out in early June 1850.[286] By that time, Colonel Childs (who was originally to lead the party), Secretary Ewing, Commissioner Orlando Brown, and Minnesota trader Henry Rice were all urging the forceful removal of the Menominee. Missionary Bonduel was also mounting an active campaign to exempt the five hundred members of the Catholic band at Lake Poygan from the removal effort.[287]

The exploratory party, consisting mostly of young men who were not in decision-making positions, returned in August 1850. They reported that the new country contained lots of fish but not much wild rice or game.[288] William Powell, who accompanied the party as an interpreter, reported that he saw one deer and only a few tracks of a larger game.[289] Once returned, the Menominee decided they did not like the Minnesota land and that they would reject it, opting instead to remain in Wisconsin.[290]

The Wolf River Treaty of 1854

By the later 1830s, it was evident to many, both within and outside of government, that the removal policy initiated in the late 1820s and implemented in the early 1830s was a failure. Not only had its "civilization" objectives failed to materialize, but the lands west of the Mississippi River to which Indians were to be removed were in high demand by American settlers. In the waning years of the removal era, government officials tended to blame the failures of the Indian civilization efforts on what they believed were the innate faults of the Indian character—laziness, stubbornness, and lack of intelligence.[291] These faults, they believed, kept the Indians in a state of barbarism, wandering the forest in search of game rather than settling and becoming educated, Christian farmers.

By the late 1840s there were still a few attempts to remove eastern Indians, but these efforts were not instigated to benefit Indian people. They were little more than thinly veiled attempts to clear the eastern states in advance of American settlement. At the same time, a new cadre of officials in the Indian Department—led by the very able, longtime clerk Charles Mix, Commissioner T. Hartley Crawford, and eventually Commissioner George Manypenny—came to believe that the failure of the civilization efforts under removal were the fault not of the Indians but of government policy.[292] These men believed that if Indians could be located on reservations within their own territories and if they could be protected in these areas, then schools, missions, and agricultural establishments would be successful. In order to teach Indians the value of private property, resourcefulness, and hard labor, it was decided that the reservations should be allotted to individual Indians, that is, that each family should have its own farm deeded in fee simple.[293]

During the tenure of Commissioner George Manypenny (1853–57), fifty-two treaties were written with Indian tribes that incorporated these principles. In Wisconsin this new philosophy of Indian policy was not put into practice until the early 1850s. As it was applied, the new policy had only a peripheral effect on the Menominee, but the reservation policy did contribute to the demise of efforts to force their removal to Minnesota under the terms of the Treaty of 1848.

Condition of the Menominee in the Late 1840s

In the period immediately following the 1848 treaty, the Menominee were in a state of confusion. Owing to the successes of the Catholic missionary at Lake Poygan, they were now seriously factionalized into Christian and "pagan" elements.[294] The Christian Menominee were strongly supported by Father Bonduel and the old French Canadian mixed-blood trading families. Those Menominee who chose a more traditional lifestyle, which included about two thousand of the twenty-five hundred Menominees in 1850, found it increasingly difficult to influence the American power structure. The traditional bands were divided into two groups: the lake bands, who continued to inhabit the shore of Green Bay and its rivers; and the interior bands, which occupied the territory between the Wolf and Black rivers.[295] During the summer of 1849, cholera struck the lake bands, killing at least twenty-two people.[296]

The traditional Menominee bands continued to gain a living as they had always done by hunting, fishing, and gathering wild rice. Even the Catholic bands at Lake Poygan depended on hunted and gathered food to supplement their agricultural production. For example, in 1849 the Christian bands at Lake Poygan grew four thousand bushels of corn, one thousand bushels of potatoes, twenty bushels of wheat, and twenty bushels of barley, but they also collected two hundred bushels of wild rice and one thousand bushels of cranberries and made thirty-five thousand pounds of sugar.[297]

The pressures attendant to the payment of the mixed-blood and trader debt funds provided by the 1848 treaty created great tension in the Menominee community, as traders and their supporters pressured various chiefs for their support of specific private claims. Despite hardships and divisive forces, the Menominee were absolutely united on two major issues: (1) that they had been defrauded and cheated by the 1848 treaty and (2) that they were determined to remain in Wisconsin.

The Quest to Remain in Wisconsin

By the terms of the 1848 treaty, the Menominee were to remove to Minnesota within a two-year period, that is, by October 1850, unless the president permitted them to remain longer. Article 8 of the treaty permitted them to remain "during the period of two years from the date hereof, and until the President shall notify them that the same [ceded lands] are wanted."[298] At the request of Chief Oshkosh, the president did in fact grant the Menominee an extension until the spring of 1851. Supporters of the Menominee then began to agitate for a change in the government's insistence on their removal, and the president extended the Menominee's tenure once again. It seems likely that the petitions of Wisconsin citizens influenced the president's decision. The new extension in 1851 allowed the Menominee to stay until June 1852 on the condition that they not interfere with the public land survey that was then being conducted on the land ceded in the 1848 treaty. The Menominee were also reminded that they were still subject to removal at the discretion of the president, but in early 1852, the Menominee were granted yet another presidential extension until October 1, 1852.[299]

Other events now began to work in the Menominee favor. First, Governor Dodge, who was instrumental in advancing the removal effort, was elected as one of Wisconsin's first senators when Wisconsin became a state in July 1848. These duties took his attention away from Indian problems. When the Whig Party elected Zachary Taylor in November 1848, the Democratic hold on Indian affairs shifted in favor of a Whig-dominated patronage system, which soon returned George Lawe to the Green Bay Indian Agency. Lawe was, of course, much more sympathetic to the Menominee's desire to remain in Wisconsin, since he himself was of partial Menominee descent.[300]

The Menominee's attorney Richard Thompson was a convincing writer who kept a steady stream of petitions and briefs flowing between Green Bay and the corridors of power in Washington. Thompson used the precedent of law as well as the writing of the Swiss jurist Vattel, an expert in international treaty law, to argue the Menominee case. Beyond documenting the details of the land transactions of 1848, Thompson argued that the gross discrepancy in power and enormous practical advantage that accrued to the United States in dealing with the Menominee in 1848 mitigated against any unilateral resolution of the problems that ensued. As Thompson argued the Menominee case, it was both the moral and legal responsibility of the U.S. government to deal fairly with the Menominee tribe as their true sovereign. In his view and in theirs, the only way to right the fraud and inequities of the 1848 treaty was by negotiating a new one.[301]

In the meantime, American settlers in Wisconsin began to appreciate the plight of the Menominee. They, too, sent petitions to Washington in favor of permitting the Menominee to remain. These petitions, which were signed by four hundred of Wisconsin's residents, suggested that the Menominee might settle permanently on the headwaters of the Wolf, Wisconsin, and Menominee rivers.[302] Here, out of the path of non-Indian agricultural settlement, they would be relatively isolated in a country that could also support their way of life.[303]

At the same time the settlers of Wisconsin were assessing the impact of the 1848 treaty in the context of its basic fairness and personal impact on their Menominee neighbors, the government was trying to sort out and evaluate the legal and equitable claims made by the Menominee.[304] In his annual report of 1851, the commissioner of Indian affairs, Luke Lea, who was an appointee of the new Whig government, presented a long and detailed analysis of the 1848 treaty. After consideration of Thompson's arguments, Lea came as close as the propriety of official Washington permitted in admitting the flaws of the 1848 treaty.[305]

It seemed to Lea that the language of the treaty in which the Menominee ceded "all their lands in Wisconsin wherever situated" was precise and definitive, so that short of declaring the treaty fraudulent, the only argument had to do with the quantity of land ceded and the price paid. In a letter to Lea, Wisconsin representative James Doty called the wording "wherever situated" a "nominal cession."[306] The Menominee no doubt wondered why Medill had not bothered to determine the extent of the Menominee claim and to describe it by metes and bounds as had been done in all their former treaties. Commissioner Lea finally concluded that apart from the land claimed by the Menominee and ceded by other tribes, the government owed the Menominee $221,840 for the land actually ceded. He pointed out, however, that it was hardly fair to buy valuable farmland in 1848 for the same price paid in 1836 for timberland.[307] This is essentially the same conclusion reached in 1853 by Senator Walker of Wisconsin in his report to the Committee on Indian Affairs.[308]

In January 1851 U.S. representative from Wisconsin and former territorial governor James Doty wrote to Luke Lea suggesting a new treaty with the Menominee.

> Allow me therefore to urge upon yourself, and upon the Department, the absolute necessity of forming a new commission to treat with these Indians, to settle definitively and justly all pending questions between them and the U.S. and for a relinquishment of all claim to the country which they insist (and we all know) was not actually ceded by them in their former treaties.[309]

In March 1851 outgoing agent William Bruce wrote to Luke Lea forwarding the suggestion made by the Menominee that they be permitted to permanently settle in northern Wisconsin.[310] In July the newly appointed superintendent of Indian affairs for Wisconsin, Captain Elias Murray, asked interpreter William Powell to present this idea to the Menominee. When he did so, they reacted with enthusiasm.[311] William Powell was then sent north to find a potential location for the Menominee. In company with Chiefs La Motte, Oshkishhenayniew, and Waukechon, Powell inspected the country north of the falls of the Wolf River. Among its other attractions, Powell reported, "We also found a number of cedar and tamarack swamps where are many signs of Bears, deer, and other games, the Lakes abound with fish, and wild Ducks. The Chiefs are highly pleased with this Country and say they hope the President will give it to them for a home, where they can leave [*sic*] in peace from their enemies."[312]

In the fall of 1852, Superintendent Murray forwarded a request by the president to the Menominee chiefs asking them to remove to the Wolf River country.[313] This they agreed to do, and in that November, annuities were paid at the falls of the Wolf River. Although the winter was extremely hard for the Menominee people, the chiefs expressed their satisfaction with this arrangement.[314]

On the first day of February 1853, the Wisconsin legislature did its part to resolve the Menominee problem by passing the following resolution:

> That the assent of the State of Wisconsin is hereby given to the Menominee Nation of Indians to remain on the tract of land set apart for them by the President of the United States on the Wolf, and Oconto Rivers, and upon which they now reside, the same being within the State of Wisconsin aforesaid, and described as follows, to wit:—Commencing at the South east corner of township twenty eight, north, range nineteen; running thence west thirty miles, thence north eighteen miles, thence east thirty miles, thence south eighteen miles to the place of beginning.[315]

In July the government ordered this land withdrawn for public sale for the benefit of the Menominee.[316] It now only remained to conclude a treaty with the Menominee chiefs.

The Wolf River Treaty

Superintendent Francis Huebschmann was appointed commissioner for a new Menominee treaty and elected to hold it in the Menominee country. The treaty, which was negotiated between Huebschmann and the Menominee chiefs, is described in the preamble as being "supplementary and amendatory" to the Treaty of 1848.[317] This language was necessary because the new treaty had two objectives, both of which flowed from the earlier agreement. The United States wanted, first, to correct an injustice of the 1848 land cession and, second, to exchange the six hundred thousand acres of Minnesota land given to the Menominee in that treaty for the new Wisconsin reservation. Thus, in Article 1 the Menominee ceded their Minnesota land to the United States, while in Article 2 the United States gave the Menominee 276,480 acres in Wisconsin (see map 17).[318] Article 4 of the treaty provided payment to the Menominee, "consideration of the difference in extent between the lands hereby ceded to the United States, and the lands given in exchange, and for . . . the difference in quantity of lands supposed by them to have been ceded in the treaty of eighteenth of October, eighteen hundred and forty eight, and what was actually

Map 17. Menominee Reservation, 1854.

ceded."[319] The payment was $242,686, to be paid as an annuity. The Menominee were also provided with a school, mills, and blacksmith shops.

The Wolf River Treaty, which was agreed to by all of the chiefs and headmen of the Menominee tribe, is an unusual one in the context of the Manypenny era, most notably because the reservation was not allotted to individuals.[320] Article 2 states that the land given as a home for the Menominees is "to be held as Indian lands are held."[321] By this terminology, it was meant that the land would be held in common by the tribe rather than allotted to individuals in severalty. Such an unusual provision was necessary for two reasons. First, the Treaty of 1848 provided land in common to the Menominee tribe. Second, the Treaty of Wolf River was a land exchange, as made explicit in the last paragraph of the preamble of the treaty. Thus, with the blessing of the legislature of the state of Wisconsin, the federal government provided the Menominee with the same tenure to the land that they were given in Minnesota by the Treaty of 1848.

Like the Treaties of 1848 and 1836, the Treaty of 1854 is silent on the usufruct provision reserved in the Treaty of 1831. While it was the general hope of the federal government and the citizens of Wisconsin that the Menominee would move to and eventually remain on the new reservation, this was not required or, in fact, expected. The two thousand or so Menominee who depended on the chase at the time of the Wolf River Treaty could not possibly make a living within the boundary of the reservation. Of necessity and choice, they continued to hunt, fish, and gather over much of the territory they had ceded in former treaties. Even in the strictest application of Manypenny's allotment policy, it was recognized that northern reservations simply could not support the people who were assigned to them. This was particularly true of reservations like the Menominee Reservation, which was selected for its natural resources, not its agricultural potential. For this reason, a treaty negotiated under Manypenny's supervision in Wisconsin and Minnesota in 1854 reserved usufruct over the ceded territory while at the same time creating reservations.[322] In the decades following the Wolf River Treaty, most of the Menominee people did move to their reservation. They also continued to leave the reservation to hunt, fish, and gather, as they had been assured they could in the Treaty of 1831.

CHAPTER 13

Menominee Indian Tribe of Wisconsin v. Thompson, Western District of Wisconsin, Case Nos. 96-3596 and 96-3985

Bruce R. Greene

Law Offices of Bruce R. Greene & Associates, LLC, Boulder, Colorado

Presently, the Menominee people occupy lands in northeastern Wisconsin set aside for them under their sacred Wolf River Treaty of 1854.[1] With the exception of carving out a portion of the reservation for the Stockbridge-Munsee tribe in 1856, the reservation boundary for the Menominee has remained relatively unchanged since the 1854 treaty, and it encloses more than two hundred thousand acres of land. On the ground, the boundary of the reservation is readily apparent, even to the untrained eye. The reservation is surrounded by farmland, all cleared, plowed, and tilled. In stark contrast, the reservation is a dense forest—indeed, an island of forest in an otherwise vast, open, endless, flat series of agricultural fields. Entering the reservation is like disappearing into a Hobbit forest. The canopy is lush and in places creates a veritable tunnel over the top of the two two-lane roads traversing the reservation.

The 1854 treaty was the last of four treaties negotiated between the Menominee and the United States, which led to the tribe's present-day location. Aboriginally, the tribe occupied a much larger portion of northeastern Wisconsin. Although their heartland was in and around present-day Green Bay and the Door Peninsula, they hunted, fished, trapped, and gathered in a much larger area, including all around Lake Winnebago, areas as far west as Eau Claire and as far north as the present-day boundary line between Wisconsin and the Upper Peninsula of Michigan.

Beginning in 1831, the tribe began ceding its aboriginal territory, piece by piece. The first cession occurred in an 1831 treaty.[2] The tribe ceded the area from the tip of the Door Peninsula down to just north of Milwaukee and west to the east side of the Fox River and the east shore of Lake Winnebago. Later, in 1836, the tribe ceded lands on the west side of Green Bay, stretching north to the state boundary with Michigan, as well as lands in the interior of Wisconsin, along the Wisconsin River.[3] Under the third treaty, the Treaty of 1848,[4] the tribe ceded all other lands in the state to which it claimed ownership. There are many troublesome issues surrounding the negotiation of the 1848 treaty, which are addressed by Professor Cleland in his report in chapter 12 about the Menominee people and the treaties they negotiated. Suffice it to say that the Menominee refer to this as "the fraudulent treaty," primarily because the Indians were misled by the treaty commissioners and did not even know the amount of land they were ceding or the land's location when they entered into this treaty of cession.

Under the 1831 treaty, the Menominee specifically reserved rights to hunt, fish, trap, and gather—the usual usufructuary rights—but according to the treaty language, the use rights were specifically conditional. We know this from reading the literal words of the treaty. For example, according to Article 6, on lands on the east side of the Fox River, the tribe was "at liberty to hunt and fish on the lands they have now ceded . . . with the same privileges they at present enjoy, until it be surveyed and offered for sale by the President, they conducting themselves peaceably and orderly." As to the lands on the west side of the Fox River, the tribe's hunting and fishing rights were reserved to them "until the president of the United States, shall deem it expedient to extinguish their title."

In the mid-1990s, I was asked by the then chairman of the tribe, Glenn Miller, to look into these treaties and try to determine whether the Menominee had continuous use rights that extended far beyond the reservation set aside for the tribe under the 1854 Treaty of Wolf River. Chairman Miller, a young and charismatic leader, whose life was suddenly cut short at an early age by a rare, aggressive, and deadly fungal lung infection called blastomycocis, knew the history of his people, knew their dependence on subsistence hunting and fishing, and believed that the tribe had never relinquished those off-reservation usufructuary rights. I was asked to undertake this task, along with Jim Jannetta, another experienced treaty litigator, precisely because both Jim and I had handled similar litigation for other tribes in the upper Great Lakes. We were guided by our past experiences and knowledge of the law and knew that we needed to commission experts to prepare reports explaining the facts and circumstances surrounding each of the treaty transactions.

Fortunately, the law regarding how treaties are to be interpreted is clear. Treaties are contracts, although different from contracts or agreements between private parties. Treaties are specialized contracts between sovereign entities. Because of the special relationship between Indian tribes and the United States, the Supreme Court has developed rules, called "canons of construction," that apply to treaty interpretation. The special relationship between the federal government and Indian tribes is akin to a wardship or trust relationship. The United States, as the conquering sovereign, acts as a trustee for the benefit of Indian tribes. The bargaining power in treaty transactions tipped disproportionately in favor of the United States.[5] It was the United States that typically sought the treaty transaction, not the Indians.[6] The treaties themselves were all written in English by the U.S. treaty commissioners. The subtleties of the English language typically escaped the Indians, who came from an oral, as opposed to literate, tradition.[7] They were not skilled in reading, writing, or even speaking the English language.[8] A venerable canon of construction requires that treaties be interpreted as the Indians would have understood them and that any doubtful expressions in treaties must be resolved in the Indians' favor.[9] These principles have been repeatedly sanctioned by the Supreme Court for almost two hundred years.[10]

With these canons in mind, the question is, what is the nature of the process associated with determining the Indians' understanding of a treaty transaction? It is far easier to discern the U.S. understanding of a treaty. First, one can read the treaty language and get some understanding of the non-Indian commissioners' purpose for a treaty. In addition, treaties are typically associated with a long series of communications on the U.S. side between the on-the-ground U.S. treaty negotiators and their superiors in Washington, D.C. Thus, typically, there will be correspondence to and from Washington, D.C., outlining the goals and objectives of the United States in connection with the treaty transaction. During treaty times, the Bureau of Indian Affairs, within the Department of the Interior, issued annual reports describing the condition of the tribes, their lifestyle, their seasonal rounds, and other pertinent information about them. Historical accounts of the tribes and reports by various religious leaders in the area of the tribes are often available as well. Thus, it is not terribly difficult to understand the motives, goals, and objectives of the United States and its representatives when consummating treaty transactions.

The same cannot be said of the Indians, for reasons already described. There is no written record from the Indians' side, no equivalent trail of correspondence between Indian leaders at home and their representatives at the treaty negotiations. Indeed, the leaders of the tribe or tribes negotiating a treaty are often on-site during the actual negotiations, as opposed to subordinates of the leaders of the United States in Washington, D.C. Sometimes, but not always, there are treaty minutes, which help provide depth and understanding of the transaction from the tribal side. But even treaty minutes, if they were kept, require interpretation in order to glean the Indians' understanding.

The tribes, once determining to assert their treaty rights, typically retain expert anthropologists, historians, and especially ethnohistorians, to explain their motivations for entering into a treaty and to give life to an otherwise sanitary document, at least from the Indians' perspective. It is not possible to discern the Indians' motivations for entering into a treaty without understanding their lifestyle, their subsistence habits, how they interacted with the advancing population of non-Indians, the nature and extent of the emerging non-Indian commercial environment, the activities and motivation of various church representatives bent on "saving" the Indians, and the like. In addition to ethnohistorians and anthropologists, tribes often retain linguists expert in the language of the tribe entering into the treaty. English words, especially legal terms, do not readily translate into the various languages of the affected tribes. Once reports are prepared and discovery is complete, a trial is required to hear the experts explain their reports and what they believe the Indians' understanding of the treaty transaction(s) to be. Typically, the views of the experts will conflict, and it is necessary for the court in a bench trial to decide which opinions are more credible and reliable. Indeed, this is the matrix used for treaty rights litigation. As I explain, the district court deviated from this norm and instead decided that a trial was not necessary in order to construe the treaties central to the Menominee claims.

The Legal Proceedings Associated with the Menominee Claims

The Menominee tribe filed suit in the U.S. District Court for the Western District of Wisconsin in 1995, naming the governor and various state officials as defendants. The gist of the Menominee claims was that notwithstanding their land cessions contained in the Treaties of 1831, 1836, and 1848, they reserved off-reservation use rights to hunt, fish, trap, and gather throughout the ceded territory, subject to regulation of that right by the Menominee tribe. The use rights reserved under the 1831 treaty were never subsequently abrogated in the 1848 treaty, according to the Menominee. The state defendants moved to dismiss the lawsuit on a variety of procedural grounds. Normally, a motion to dismiss a lawsuit of this character is very difficult to sustain, since the court must conclude that there is no basis for any form of relief based on the facts alleged by the tribe. The court acknowledged that cases of this nature are rarely disposed of without a trial or a well-developed record supporting a motion for summary judgment, and on that basis, it denied the state's motion to dismiss. Then, seven months later, without explanation or any additional proceedings in the district court, the court simply changed its mind and dismissed the tribe's case, and the court of appeals affirmed.[11]

To reach its conclusion that the tribe had no usufructuary off-reservation rights, the district court had to make the following conclusions. First, it had to construe the meaning of the language reserving the right to hunt and fish on the east side of the Fox River "with the same privileges they at present enjoy, until it be surveyed and offered for sale by the president; they conducting themselves peaceably and orderly." The district court concluded that the use rights were gone as soon as the land was offered for sale, which was in 1834. It reached this conclusion without any examination of the Menominee understanding of the treaty transaction, as well as the manner in which the Menominee exercised its subsistence rights in the area. Nothing changed for the Menominee after the 1831 treaty was concluded. Surveying and offering land for sale had little or no meaning to the Menominee. Indeed, as long as the land was unoccupied, it was available to the Menominee to exercise their subsistence rights. Furthermore, open and unoccupied land was not only available to the Indians for hunting and fishing; it was also available to non-Indian settlers for the same purpose. The Menominee retained an expert in early American natural resource laws who stated that conclusion in his report. The court ignored that report, along with all the other expert reports the tribe had produced. What was the meaning to the Menominee about the phrase conditioning their use rights to their peaceable and orderly conduct? What sort of meaning might that have had to the Menominee? How would that have been explained to the Menominee during the treaty negotiations? The district court did not care or even begin to allow the tribe to explain how that might have been communicated to and perceived by the Menominee treaty negotiators.

Second, the district court had to construe the meaning of the tribe's reserved use rights on the west side of the Fox River. Those rights were reserved to the tribe "until the President of the United States, shall deem it expedient to extinguish their title." What might the word *expedient* mean to the Menominee? How would that word have been "translated" into the Menominee language? The word *translation* itself has a wholly different meaning to the Menominee than that term normally has to an English speaker. Words in English do not technically translate into the Menominee language, because there are rarely equivalent words between the two languages. That would have been explained to the district court as well, had the court been willing to listen to the testimony of the tribe's linguistics expert. Notwithstanding the lack of direct correlation between the Menominee language and the English language, the concept of "expediency" could probably have been explained in some manner. The district court did not care. To make matters even worse, the court of appeals concluded that the Indians' understanding of the word *expedient* was "irrelevant."[12] According to the district court and the court of appeals, the tribe's usufructuary rights were merged with the tribe's title to lands. Once the title was gone, the use rights were extinguished, according to both courts. But one of the tribe's experts explained in his report that the reserved use rights were not interests in lands at all. Rather, they were qualified immunities from state law and regulation. Under that analysis, the use right was not attached to land title, and as land title was extinguished, the use right was unaffected. The district court was not interested in that explanation and refused, once again, to consider or even acknowledge the tribe's expert reports.

The court of appeals compared the language in the 1831 treaty to the language in a treaty with the Chippewa, construed in *Lac Courte Oreilles Band of Lake Superior Chippewa Indians v. Voigt.*[13] In *Voigt,* the Chippewa reserved usufructuary rights "during the pleasure of the President."[14] There was a lengthy trial in *Voigt* in order to discern the Chippewas' understanding of that phrase. But according to the district court, a trial was unnecessary to understand the Menominees' understanding of "until the President shall deem it expedient to extinguish their title"; all one needed to do to understand the meaning of the treaty was to read it. Are we to assume that is what the Menominee did at the time of the treaty? Did they simply read the phrase and understand that title to land and usufructuary rights were inextricably intertwined and that as one was lost, so was the other? I am both flabbergasted by the court's reasoning (or lack thereof) and unable to explain how that conclusion could be reached in the face of the overwhelming authority requiring courts to examine all of the facts and circumstances surrounding a treaty transaction in order to discern the Indians' understanding. Remember the Supreme Court's oft-repeated admonition that treaties "must therefore be construed, not according to the technical meaning of its words to learned lawyers, but in the sense in which they would be naturally understood by the Indians."[15]

The third step in the district court's rush to judgment required it to construe the 1848 treaty under which the Menominee ceded any and all remaining lands to which it claimed title in Wisconsin. Title to land and use rights were inextricably tied, according to the district court. Thus, again according to the district court, the Menominee, unbeknownst to them, lost their use rights in the areas ceded in the 1831 and 1836 treaties when they ceded what remained of their aboriginal title to *other and different* lands in the 1848 treaty. But the 1848 treaty had language of removal in it. Under that treaty, the Menominee exchanged whatever remaining lands they claimed in Wisconsin for six hundred thousand acres of land in Minnesota. The district court and court of appeals reasoned that the Menominee would not have reserved a use right in lands in Wisconsin if they were going to live hundreds of miles away in Minnesota. This brilliant reasoning is unimpeachable, one would think. However, the Menominee were unalterably opposed to leaving their aboriginal homeland in Wisconsin. In fact, they never left Wisconsin, because the state sanctioned their remaining in Wisconsin and the president never forced them to remove. By 1848, the removal policy championed by Andrew Jackson was losing its steam. Officially, the policy began in 1830 and was all but over by 1840. It was not a uniformly applied policy and, of course, became less and less effective as a tool for dealing with the Indians as the westward movement of non-Indian society progressed. As non-Indians moved west, there was less and less available land to which the Indians might be removed. Because the Menominee were unalterably opposed to removal and did not remove, how were they to subsist in Wisconsin? How could the courts conclude that although the Menominee were going to remain in Wisconsin, they were not going to have any basis to survive? The courts concluded that the Menominee ceded all remaining lands in Wisconsin in 1848 and that use rights were tied to title. For the courts, this was the end of the story and the end of the Menominee use rights.

The fourth and final piece of the puzzle was the 1854 treaty under which the present-day Menominee Reservation was set aside as a permanent home for the Menominee. This time, the district court decided to pay lip service to the Indians' understanding of the treaty. Apparently, Oshkosh, a Menominee leader, was reported, in the 1853 annual report of the commissioner of Indian affairs, to have inquired whether he would be granted permission to leave the area of the 1854 reserve (not yet officially withdrawn as the Menominee Reservation) in order to gather wild rice. The district court said, without embarrassment, "It seems unlikely that if the Menominee believed that they had retained usufructuary rights throughout the ceded lands, they would have asked permission to exercise such rights."[16] That statement leaves this author almost speechless. What was the context of Oshkosh's statement? Might it have something to do with the Menominee's precarious position in Wisconsin based on their treaty history in general and the 1848 treaty in particular, under which there was a possibility that they might be removed to Minnesota? Context meant nothing to the district court or the court of appeals. The district court had the audacity to rely on one document, from thousands of others neither considered nor explained, in order to buttress its already spurious conclusion that the tribe has no valid use rights in their ceded territory. If I were part of the district court, I would have been embarrassed by this conclusion.

Another case involving a neighboring tribe in Minnesota went to the Supreme Court at about this same time. In *Minnesota v. Mille Lacs Band of Chippewa Indians*,[17] the issue concerned the survivability of use rights on lands ceded by the tribe under an 1837 treaty in which the use rights were "guarantied to the Indians during the pleasure of the President."[18] Later, in 1850, President Zachary Taylor signed an executive order purporting to revoke those rights. Then, in 1855, one of the tribal bands party to the 1837 treaty entered into another treaty with the United States that "fully and entirely" relinquished and conveyed to the United States "any and all right, title, and interest, of whatsoever nature the same be, which they may now have in, and to any other lands in the Territory of Minnesota or elsewhere."[19] Based on an extensive record developed at trial explaining the historical background of the treaties and the understanding of the Indians to those transactions, the lower courts concluded and the Supreme Court affirmed that the 1837 treaty rights were neither interests in land nor dependent on title to lands and that the rights were extinguished by neither the 1850 executive order or the 1855 treaty. Interpreting the 1855 treaty language or the 1850 executive order shorn of their historical context and of evidence of the understanding of the parties, which was the approach taken by the district court in the Menominee litigation, could well have led to a different—and wrong—result. The similarity between the two cases, particularly the similarity between the language at issue in *Mille Lacs* and the language in the Menominee 1848 treaty, is striking. Had the district court allowed the Menominee to follow the traditional rules governing treaty interpretation and proceed through trial in order to develop a proper record, it seems likely the district court could have reached a different conclusion.

Conclusion

The Menominee tribe suffered an enormous miscarriage of justice at the hands of U.S. district judge Babara B. Crabb. How can this be explained? Unfortunately, one can only conjecture about her motives and mind-set. Judge Crabb, now on senior status, enjoys a stellar reputation for intellect and fairness. How, then, can one explain her immediate and unrelenting hostility toward this lawsuit? Is it possible that once completing the *Voigt* litigation, which lasted almost twenty years in the Western District of Wisconsin, she was unwilling to allow the Menominee the same opportunity afforded the Chippewa? Is it possible she felt that she could not face another protracted series of trials similar to the ones she presided over in the *Voigt* litigation? No one will ever know. It does seem clear in retrospect, however, that she was not about to afford the Menominee the normal process required in cases of this nature. Only a very impatient judge could have disposed of a case of this nature without any facts, just as the tribe's expert reports were being finalized pursuant to the court's pretrial schedule—and then ignore them as she concluded that the Menominee had lost all of their off-reservation use rights. There is no way of fixing that now, of course, because the district court's conclusion, affirmed by the court of appeals, is final and may not be litigated again, under the black-letter doctrine of res judicata. There is no way to fix the harm dealt to the Menominee as the result of an impatient judge, who seemed to have her mind made up simply by reading the treaties at issue, devoid of any meaningful historical context.

PART 3

Reservation Issues

Unlike the Western part of the United States, where many Indian reservations were created by the General Allotment Act passed by Congress in 1887, most of the existing reservations in the East were created by treaties written in the 1850s and 1860s. By the 1840s it was clear to the federal government that the strategy of removing Indians to the west of the Mississippi River so that they could be colonized and civilized was a failure. Commissioner of Indian affairs George Manypenny (1853–57) and chief clerk of the Indian Office Charles Mix reasoned that Indians could better be acculturated on reservations within their own native territories. These reservations would be created by treaty so that they would have strong boundaries and could be defended against invasion by avaricious frontiersmen while the Indians were being educated and Christianized.

A major cornerstone of Manypenny's reservation policy, as well as the later General Allotment Act, was that reservations would be partitioned, giving each family a farm that would eventually be held in fee simple; that is, it could be freely sold by the allottee. This was referred to as "allotment in severalty." Presumably allotment would teach Indians the value of individual property and the pleasure of hard physical labor, while at the same time providing them with the means to become self-supporting in the American economy. In this way, allotment would eventually get the government out of the Indian business.

The allotment provisions of Commissioner Manypenny's treaties were written in different ways, but in general, parcels of forty to eighty acres were to be selected by adult members of the tribe and heads of households. These parcels were certified by a nonnegotiable certificate and, after a specific time, by deeds in fee simple. During a specified waiting period, the certificate or preliminary deed contained a restriction against alienation of the allotment. Once the final deed was issued, however, on the presumption that the deed holder had become competent to manage his or her own affairs, the allotment could be freely sold by the allottee or the allottee's heirs.

In the northern Great Lakes region, where the majority of eastern allotted reservations were located, thin soil and a short growing season precluded the kind of farming Manypenny envisioned. As a result, allotments were of little value to Indian families, who, of necessity, continued to make a living by following the seasonal round and, on occasion, by temporary wage labor. By long tradition, the Ojibwe and Odawa (Ottawa) people of the region were fishermen and hunters for whom gardening was a supplemental enterprise conducted by women. In fact, these Indian people of the region had no reason to try to improve or to live on their allotments.

Sadly, Manypenny's reservation and allotment system, though well-intentioned, was a complete and total disaster. This was true because while the northern allotments were worthless for farming, they turned out to be valuable for their standing timber. Accordingly, during the last two decades of the nineteenth century and the first decade of the twentieth century, buyers for lumber companies plundered Great Lakes Indian reservations. Indians, unfamiliar with Western property and ownership concepts and unable to read contracts, were easy prey for powerful lumber companies. If all else failed, the companies lobbied Congress to permit the sale of reservation land. Once the lumber was cut, land speculators followed and acquired most of the land held by lumber interests. Failing such sales, most lumber companies simply did not pay taxes on the cutover land, so that it reverted to public ownership. By the 1930s Indians actually owned only a few small parcels out of the thousands and thousands of acres that once constituted their reservation homelands. At the same time, the general market was glutted by surplus land.

With only two exceptions, by the late twentieth century, the reservations of northern Michigan, Wisconsin, and Minnesota consisted of a checkerboard of ownership made up of non-Indian fee land, Indian fee land, tribally owned land, and federal trust land. Non-Indian fee land constituted by far the largest part of most reservations. The exceptions are the Menominee Reservation in Wisconsin and the Red Lake Reservation in Minnesota. Since neither was ever allotted, both remain today as monolithic blocks of tribal land.

Given the divided ownership of the northern reservations, the question soon arose as to what land actually constituted any particular Indian reservation. Non-Indian owners and the various states insisted that the reservation was composed of the small portion of land still owned by individual Indians, as well as tribal and federal trust land. The tribes, however, insisted with equal vigor that the reservation consisted of all the land within the exterior boundaries of the reserve, or, in other words, the reservation as it was described by the treaty that created it. For them, the reservation existed in the original form irrespective of who currently owned the land within the boundaries.

The reason why the status of the reservation boundaries is frequently litigated is to settle the conflicting jurisdictions of the local and state authorities, on the one hand, and tribal and federal authority, on the other. As Indian legal scholar Felix Cohen tells us, tribes maintain substantial sovereignty over their members and their territories, and Indians and tribes are consequently included within the scope of federal statutes.[1] Whether a federal statute applies to Indians or tribes depends on the intent of Congress, as statuses are territorially confined to Indian country (reservations) or topically applicable only to Indians.[2] Because tribes maintain substantial sovereignty over their members and territories, the Supreme Court requires that the intent of Congress to invade tribal sovereignty be clearly expressed.[3] When federal statutes conflict with particular Indian rights under a treaty or other statutes, the Supreme Court has supplied three rules of construction: (1) repeal by implication is not favored, (2) specific laws prevail over more general ones, and (3) as in the case of treaties, doubts or ambiguities in statutes must be construed in favor of the Indians.

As a practical matter, jurisdiction over land that is within the original boundaries of an Indian reservation is virtually beyond the reach of state or local authority. This status provides substantial tax advantages and the potential for the tribes to regulate the natural resources of the reservation by imposing federal air and water standards and to institute tribal zoning. There are, however, exceptions related to the applicability of tribal jurisdiction. For example, in 1953 an act of Congress authorized five and, later, six states to accept jurisdictions over crimes and many civil matters of reservation land. This act, Public Law (PL) 280, offered these six states the option of asserting jurisdiction over Indian country within their boundaries.[4] In the upper Great Lakes region, Minnesota, except for the Red Lake Reservation, and Wisconsin, except for the Menominee Reservation, are PL 280 states.

In normal course, the sovereignty of the tribe and its power as a government are strongly expressed on reservation lands. The two most important provisions of the federal criminal code relating to federal jurisdiction and the prosecution of Indians in Indian country are the Indian Country Crime Act and the Indian Major Crimes Act.[5] In non-PL 280 states, such as Michigan, the state lacks jurisdiction to arrest, try, or punish Indians on an Indian reservation absent the consent of Congress.[6] To a very limited degree, tribes may regulate the activities of non-Indians on the land within an Indian reservation. Such regulation is permitted where those activities by non-Indians threaten to have a direct effect on the political integrity, economic security, or health or welfare of the tribe.[7]

A legal question that arises in cases of checkerboard reservations is whether or not the reservation has been diminished in size or even entirely disestablished. To show either case, it must be demonstrated that Congress specifically expressed such an objective by formal action. In a boundary case involving the Stockbridge-Munsee Reservation, described in chapters 16 and 17, the court found the reservation had been diminished by specific congressional action.

The reservation issues discussed in this volume deal most often with the boundaries of reservation land, that is, the question of what constitutes the reservation. The first upper Great Lakes case to take on the boundary issue was initiated by the Keweenaw Bay Indian Community. Although their reservation in northern Michigan was created by the Treaty of La Pointe in 1854, the state insisted on enforcing its traffic laws against Indians on U.S. Route 41, a highway that crosses the Keweenaw Bay Reservation. The tribe contended that only tribal police and tribal courts had the authority to arrest and charge Indians on the reservation. State authorities challenged the authority of the tribe, claiming that the reservation had been greatly diminished and subsequently constituted only those lands actually owned by Indians or held in trust for them by the federal government. In 1988 the tribe filed suit in the U.S. District Court for the Western District of Michigan, which found in 1991 that the Keweenaw Bay Indian Reservation was composed of all the land within the external boundaries described by the Treaty of 1854. Similar cases were filed thereafter by the Saginaw Chippewa tribe, the Mille Lacs Band of Ojibwe Indians, and the Stockbridge-Munsee Tribe of Wisconsin. The details of these cases are provided in the chapters that follow.

Many other issues arise here and will continue to arise following territorial claims. One example included here is a case brought by the Keweenaw Bay Indian Community related to the authority of the state of Michigan to levy ad valorem property taxes on property holdings of tribal members on their reservation. This case was filed in the U.S. District Court for the Western District of Michigan and was decided in favor of the community in 2005.[8] This landmark decision ruled that Keweenaw Bay Reservation was created by the Treaty of 1854 as a permanent homeland for the community. As the court pointed out, the effect of property taxation by the state of Michigan was to potentially and in fact diminish the size of a federal Indian reservation through the sale of Indian lands on tax liens. The future is certain to bring more lawsuits that will test the authority of the tribes to regulate the reservations as well as to define the limits of state jurisdiction.

CHAPTER 14

The Boundary of the Keweenaw Bay Reservation

As we have seen in chapter 9, the Treaty of 1842 was negotiated by Robert Stuart with the Lake Superior Ojibwe. This treaty was important in the litigation of *Lac Courte Oreilles Band v. Wisconsin* as well as *Mille Lacs v. Minnesota,* both inland usufruct cases. It, like the Treaty of 1854, also negotiated at La Pointe, is central to *Keweenaw Bay Indian Community v. Michigan* (see chapter 15), a reservation boundary case, as well as later litigation regarding the right of the state to levy property tax on reservation land, *Keweenaw Bay Indian Community v. Naftaly* (see chapter 22).

The first of these treaties, that of 1842, was a cession of Indian lands on the south shore of Lake Superior that left the Ojibwe bands of the region homeless. The second, the 1854 treaty, tried to rectify this problem by creating reservations for the bands in the ceded territory. The case under discussion here examines the historic circumstances under which the Keweenaw Bay Reservation was created, how the reservation was partitioned through allotment, and why the external boundaries persisted irrespective of the change of landownership within the boundaries.

The Ojibwe Bands of Keweenaw Bay

Ojibwe origin mythology, which is in large part shared with the Odawa (Ottawa) and Potawatomi who speak mutually intelligible dialects of the same Algonquian language, tells of a migration from the east coast to the western Great Lakes and beyond. This oral tradition is, in part, borne out by French historical records of the seventeenth century that document a continued westward expansion of the Ojibwe along the shores of Lake Superior. West of the lake, the Ojibwe advanced against the Dakota (Sioux) people, who they eventually pushed west of the Mississippi.[1]

Soon after Ojibwe bands settled along the south shore of Lake Superior in the late seventeenth century, they began to move into the hinterlands of northern Wisconsin. These people developed a very different economic adaptation than their lakeshore relatives. Those who lived on the lake were primarily dependent on a deepwater gill net fishery in Lake Superior. During the warm seasons of the year, they remained in large lakeshore villages. There they fished; planted small gardens of corn, beans, and squash; and hunted in the adjacent highlands for moose, bear, and smaller game. The Ojibwe bands that occupied the interior settled during the summer on inland lakes, such as Lac du Flambeau, Lac Courte Oreilles, or Lac Vieux Desert, where they fished and collected wild rice or planted gardens. In the fall, these villages broke up as families traveled south to the Wisconsin River valley to hunt deer. During the winter, they slowly hunted their way back north to their summer village sites.[2] The French recognized these adaptations in labeling the two Ojibwe groups as the *gens de lac* (people of the lake) and the *gens de terre* (people of the land). The seasonal movements of the Ojibwe are referred to as a "seasonal round" since, as with all hunters and gatherers, the Ojibwe needed to move from resource to resource as they became available with the season.

During the late seventeenth through mid-nineteenth centuries, the Ojibwe were heavily involved in the fur trade with French, British, and ultimately American partners. Although the Ojibwe readily adopted European manufactured goods, such as iron kettles, knives and axes, firearms, glass beads, and especially woven fabrics, and although these items rapidly replaced functional equivalents made of native materials, cultural change in other realms was slow. At the time American explorers, missionaries, and traders began to enter the Lake Superior basin during the first half of the nineteenth century, the Ojibwe were following nearly the same cultural practices as they had since antiquity.[3] While it is true that such items as firearms, iron implements, liquor, and blankets were ubiquitous among them and that a small number had converted to Catholicism under the guidance of French priests, the vast majority spoke only Ojibwe (although some also spoke French), followed the seasonal round, dressed in a mixture of traditional skin as well as textile woven clothing, and lived in dome-shaped wigwams. They traveled by bark canoes or on snowshoes, practiced band and clan exogamy and patrilineal marriage (sometimes plural), made decisions by consensus, had an economy based on reciprocal gift exchange, and believed strongly in the power of the spirits who shared their world.[4]

One of the major cornerstones of emerging U.S. policy in the first half of the nineteenth century in the poorly known Great Lakes region of the Old Northwest was to encourage the loyalty of the Indian tribes to the United States and to promote peaceful relations between the Ojibwe and Dakota west of Lake Superior. Toward this end, Indian agencies were established at Mackinac in Michigan and at Fort Snelling in Minnesota. The Mackinac Agency was established in 1815, and its offices were on Mackinac Island and at Sault Ste. Marie. The latter, a subagency, had responsibility for the Lake Superior Chippewa.[5] In those days, the western end of Lake Superior was very remote, and even as late as the 1840s, it often took fifteen months for a letter from Washington to reach La Pointe on Chequanmegon Bay.[6]

In 1826 George Johnston was stationed at La Pointe as a subagent of the Sault subagency. Johnston was the half-Ojibwe brother-in-law of Henry Schoolcraft, the agent at Mackinac. The Mackinac Agency and Sault subagency were consolidated in 1832, and Henry Schoolcraft was appointed as agent. Schoolcraft served in this capacity until 1836, when he became superintendent of the newly formed Michigan Indian Superintendency, which absorbed the old Mackinac Agency. In 1841 Schoolcraft was replaced by Robert Stuart. At that time, David Bushnell was appointed as a subagent at La Pointe. In 1851 the La Pointe subagency became an agency on its own.[7]

The influence of the United States on the south shore of Lake Superior and in the daily lives of the Ojibwe people was weak but growing during the first third of the nineteenth century. As the United States began to establish formal treaty relationships with the Ojibwe bands of the region, the mutual obligations created by the treaties forced more sustained and intense contact.

The Ojibwe community that was established at the head of the long, relatively narrow bay of Lake Superior, which lies to the east of the Keweenaw Peninsula, was composed of several distinct bands. This locality was at first referred to as L'Anse-Keweenaw, combining the French word *lance,* for the "point," with the Ojibwe word *kiwedeonan,* or "detour." Both were applied separately and together to the peninsula as well as the bay. Today, *Keweenaw* is used for the bay and peninsula, and *L'Anse* is the name of the modern town at the end of the bay. During the nineteenth century, *L'Anse* was used to describe both the town and the Ojibwe bands that were centered nearby.[8] The bands were drawn to the locality by its excellent fishery but also to be near the trading houses and missions that were established to cater to Indians. In this way, the L'Anse community was much like other Ojibwe multiband settlements that grew up at Bad River, La Pointe on Madeline Island in Chequanmegon Bay, and Fond du Lac on the western Lake Superior shore. The whitefish and lake trout that were so abundant in these localities made the lakeshore settlements more secure and stable than Ojibwe communities in the interior.[9] Rev. John Pitezel, the Methodist missionary at L'Anse, summed up the importance of fish to his parishioners in 1852: "One means of subsistence must be from the nature of things fishing. Lake Superior abounds with the finest fish. As long as they reside about the lake, this occupation must be to them what the farm is to the farmer or the trade is to the mechanic."[10]

During the early decades of the nineteenth century and even earlier, traders also took advantage of the abundant fishery to establish fur posts at these same localities. The fur posts were mostly managed by métis, people of half-French and half-Ojibwe descent. Métis formed their own distinct communities, and the large métis community at La Pointe, 150 miles west of Keweenaw Bay, was an important trade and administrative center for Indian affairs. Métis spoke French and Ojibwe, took French names, wore a mixture of European and native clothing, lived in log homes, and were devout Catholics. They were also very influential in Indian affairs, since they were often middlemen between the Ojibwe and the United States, serving as advisers to their Indian in-laws as well as translators; sometimes they took advantage of this relationship to the detriment of the Ojibwe.[11] During the first two decades of the nineteenth century, métis and American traders were licensed to operate trading houses at Grand Island, Keweenaw Bay, Ontonagon, Fond du Lac, and La Pointe on Madeline Island.

These posts were under the supervision of John and William Holliday, Peter Crebassa, Louis Nolin, Jean Dubay, Michael Cadotte, Charles Clothier, and William Aitkin.[12] John Holliday, Peter Barbeau, George Burket, and Peter Crebassa all lived at L'Anse and operated trading houses during the mid-1820s through the 1840s. When the Schoolcraft expedition to discover the source of the Mississippi River passed down Keweenaw Bay in 1832, it was reported that there was a village of 140 people at the foot of the bay.[13] It was composed of 112 Ojibwe and twenty-eight métis, including a few licensed traders.

In 1834 John Holliday of the American Fur Company, who had a trading house at L'Anse, invited John Sunday, a Methodist preacher and a Mississauga Ojibwe from the Toronto (York) area of Ontario, to establish a mission at L'Anse. With the assistance of other Ojibwe Methodist ministers, such as George Copway, Peter Marksman, and John Taunchey, the church assigned, in succession, D. M. Chandler, William Brockway, and John Pitezel to preach at this mission during the next decades.[14] The Methodist church, school, and parsonage and the homes of its converts were located on the east side of the bay, near the modern village of L'Anse.

In 1843 Peter Crebassa, who was then the American Fur Company agent at L'Anse and a Roman Catholic, invited Reverend Frederick Baraga to establish a mission.[15] Father Baraga soon arrived at Keweenaw Bay to serve the Catholic congregation. He eventually built a church, a school, and thirty log homes for his Indian parishioners on the west side of Keweenaw Bay, three miles from the Methodist mission and near the modern village of Baraga. Although the Indian Office was not happy with what they considered to be a "competing" mission establishment being located at Keweenaw Bay, efforts to Christianize the Ojibwe seemed to proceed in relative harmony.[16]

The Methodist mission struggled in its early years but managed to attract a few converts.[17] Following the Treaty of 1842, which ceded the land that is now the western part of Michigan's Upper Peninsula, the government selected L'Anse as one of the sites that would receive government services under the treaty. Soon thereafter a carpenter and blacksmith shop were built adjacent to the Methodist mission, and a government farm was located close by.[18]

Certainly the missions and the government services drew Indians to the L'Anse area, creating a more permanent population. Although the population fluctuated between winter lows and summer highs, reflecting the availability of food, the increased use of garden products as well as the abundance of fish provided the basis for a higher and relatively sustained population. By 1843 the Ojibwe population had more than doubled from the time of Schoolcraft's visit in 1832. Now 304 Indian people were gathered at Keweenaw Bay, including the two mission communities and a non-Christian band.[19] A census in 1847 confirms that this new population level was relatively stable, since 261 Ojibwe were counted.[20]

There appear to have been substantial shifts in the leadership among the Christian Indians at L'Anse during this period, apparently because Christian Indians were no longer content with their traditional band leaders. In effect, two new bands were formed from the Protestant and Catholic converts. Two of the younger L'Anse chiefs, Shawanodin (Southwind) and Okimase (Young Chief), were converted to Methodism by John Sunday. Upon baptism, they were given the names John Southwind and David King, respectively.[21] By the mid-1840s, David King, John Southwind, and the Indian preacher Peter Marksman were declaring themselves to be chiefs of the Methodist band. Although a Methodist, King often spoke for all of the collected L'Anse bands. Of the three Methodist chiefs, only Peter Marksman was literate in the English language. Marksman was appointed as speaker, or *ogamagigido*, for the Methodist band in 1842.[22] As a speaker, Marksman spoke for the chiefs on public occasions but was not a chief in the political sense. He was listed as a headman when he signed the 1854 treaty, which created the L'Anse Indian Reservation.

On the Catholic side of the bay, the Indian community was represented by Awseneece (Small Stones) and Nawtawmegezhick (First Sky). The traditional chief of at least some of the Catholic converts was a preteen boy, Kesewaaush (Little Eagle), who was under the tutelage of Reverend Baraga and at times was probably represented by Charles Binnayshi (Bird). None of these men was able to read or write the English language, as indicated by the fact that they signed documents with an X.

The greater L'Anse Ojibwe community included interior bands of non-Christians who visited L'Anse in the summer to see relatives and avail themselves of the blacksmith shop. These bands came from Lac Vieux Desert, Ontonagon, and other interior localities. As time went on, their connections to L'Anse grew stronger, until one of the Lac Vieux Desert bands and some of the Ontonagon people joined the L'Anse community, shortly before and after the 1854 treaty.[23] The chiefs at Ontonagon during this period were Okundekun (Buoy) and Keeshketawwug (Cut Ear), both nonliterate in English and non-Christian. The Lac Vieux Desert people were led by Maydwayawshi and Poshquaygin (Leather). Neither spoke English, but Poshquaygin converted to Methodism.

By 1849 the Methodist community was composed of ninety Indians, of which sixty-one belonged to the church.[24] At the same time, the Catholic congregation numbered about 125 Ojibwe.[25] The annual report of the commissioner of Indian affairs for 1851 reports three hundred Indians and mixed bloods living at L'Anse. In other words, by the midpoint of the nineteenth century, the L'Anse community was composed of approximately one-third Methodists, one-third Catholics, and one-third followers of traditional beliefs. In 1850 Indians had 676 acres of land, which either was owned by them or had been purchased for them. They owned sixty-five boats and had caught and preserved seventeen hundred barrels of salt fish for market and for their own use. The Christian Indians lived in sixty-four log houses, owned forty-one cattle, and had stored thirty-five hundred barrels of potatoes.[26] As will be shown later, the fact that they occupied some privately purchased land was a powerful argument against their removal from the area.[27]

These statistics do not tell the whole story. The Indians of the Catholic mission at L'Anse followed their traditional work patterns and labored collectively to chop firewood and to plant and harvest gardens.[28] By sharing labor and the things it produced, the Ojibwe knew their efforts would benefit the whole community rather than a few industrious individuals. Further, a large part of the crop production was done either by the government farmer or in close cooperation with him. The farmer, John Beedon, sometimes treated the crop as his personal property. For example, in 1849 he sold the entire Indian harvest to the captain of the American Fur Company vessel when it visited L'Anse.[29] It was very difficult for the mission Indians to support livestock, because of the lack of hay to feed the animals through the long winter.

The two Indian missions operated under completely different philosophies. While Catholic homilies were given in the Ojibwe language by priests who had mastered its complexities, Methodist missionaries preached in English with translations. Methodist efforts were directed toward socializing Ojibwe converts by teaching English and encouraging the adoption of American customs. The use of English given names and Anglicized surnames was also encouraged. For example, Magozid became Edward Loonsfoot, his surname being a literal translation of the Ojibwe. Usually in the case of the Catholic community, Ojibwe names were retained as surnames. The names of Joseph Aishquaygezhick and John Battise Kawmetighyosh are examples of this practice, but often no given name was used at all. Among the non-Christian bands, Ojibwe names were used to the exclusion of English names; however, French given names occasionally appear, especially in the case of métis.[30] Many of the L'Anse Indians maintained multiple identities appropriate for the different circumstances in which they found themselves.

There was also a small non-Indian community on the bay, the village of L'Anse. According to the

1850 federal census, the village was composed of 126 residents. Essentially all of the non-Indian residents were either white or métis and had either Indian or métis wives. Among the L'Anse residents in 1850 were B. F. Rathbun, government blacksmith; George Berkett, government farmer; John Beedon, government farmer; Rufus Crane and Nelson Barnum, Methodist clergymen; and Peter Crebassa and Ransom Sheldon, both merchants. Besides these men, the community consisted of métis and foreign immigrants who listed such occupations as fishermen, coopers, blacksmiths, sailors, miners, and masons.

It should be observed that by the early 1850s, the L'Anse community was a very dynamic one in many different respects. As we have seen, it was by and large an Ojibwe community with some small numbers of mixed-blood métis and non-Indians attached to it. The concerns of the community were Indian concerns not only because the Ojibwe were the center of the region's economy but also because the Ojibwe were practically the sole focus of the federal government's presence on this far frontier of the United States.

As was discussed in chapter 9, by the 1850s the Lake Superior Ojibwe had reached several treaty agreements with the United States that profoundly affected their circumstances. For example, they had ceded their land by treaties in 1837 and 1842, but these treaties provided no reservations of land for their own use. They continued to make a living as hunters, trappers, fishermen, and gatherers on the land they had ceded. Payment for the land cessions came in the form of per capita cash payments and government services, which at L'Anse included a school, a demonstration farm, and a blacksmith shop. In addition, both the Catholic and Methodist churches provided important services to the Indians at L'Anse.

Although the Indians made only very limited progress in learning the methods of Western agriculture, their children did attend school, and progress was reported in both education and religious instruction. Although the missionaries listed many conversions to Christianity, it is an open question as to how these converts might have interfaced Christian teachings with their traditional animistic beliefs.

Treaty payments in the form of silver coins provided one of the few sources of hard currency on the frontier. In the usual case, the annuity payments were quickly expropriated by traders who claimed unpaid debts on the part of their Indian trading partners. Nonetheless, some of this money was undoubtedly used for other purposes. Collusion between traders and Agent Watrous during the 1852 annuity payment at Fond du Lac resulted in a substantial amount of money and supplies being directed to the traders. The government blacksmith at Fond du Lac, William VanTassell, provided a sworn statement concerning the first payment of cash annuities since 1849, which took place in January 1852 at Fond du Lac.

> William E. VanTassell. September 12, 1855. Sworn says, I was at Fond du Lac at the cash annuity payment in Jan 1852 I witnessed the payment, was Indian blacksmith there—was in the payroom—helped count the money. There were two doors on opposite sides of the room. At one door the Indians came in thro' one but out at the other door. At the door of exit just outside the door C. H. Beaulieu was located with a table and papers and some silver change. As the Indians passed out of the door they were stopped by Beaulieu and his assistants and compelled to settle their accounts. Beaulieu took the money. I frequently heard him say on taking the money now we are square. The account is all settled. All the Fond du Lac Bands were served on this way. These Indians were paid $10 each. The La Pointe bands and Interior bands were paid the 2d day after. They rec. $8 each. I saw one woman paid $80 as the share of herself and children. It was paid to her in gold. She put it in her blanket. Beaulieu took it away from her and gave her some silver in change. Don't know how much. It was not much. She held it in her hand.
>
> The same woman came to me the next day to borrow money and said they took all her money but $3.00. She was a widow woman with a large family of children. I knew her well. Sometimes the Indians would try to go on to the same door they came in and the agent Watrous would not permit them. The woman I spoke of was a very poor woman

> and the traders were not in the habit of crediting her. Beaulieu was acting for the Northern fur Co. This company was not in the habit of doing a credit business so I understood. Had heard the clerk say so. The clerk was J. B. Landy. He was not clerk for the company at the time of the payment. He was there doing business for himself. Had left the Co. a few months before. He was there outside trying to collect money for himself. A good deal of money was paid on powers of attorney. Orders purporting to be signed by Indians authorizing the holder to draw their money. They were handed in by Nettleton and Julius Antoin who were there and the money on them was handed by the agent to said Beaulieu. Benj. Roy and Vincent Roy were on the inside—V. Roy was clerk for Austinian, Benj. Roy was acting for Nettleton. I judged at the time there was two or three thousand dollars paid on such order.
>
> From what I saw, I think the traders received the greater portion of the money paid the first day to the Fond du Lac Bands. The Indians carried away but very little.[31]

It should not be forgotten that the L'Anse Ojibwe were members of the much larger Lake Superior Ojibwe community. They were linked by cultural traditions and beliefs to the other Lake Superior bands that were their political partners in treaty arrangements with the United States. As we have seen, the Lake Superior Ojibwe community consists of both lakeshore and interior bands. The former included those centered at L'Anse, Bad River, La Pointe, and Fond du Lac on the south shore of Lake Superior. In the interior were many small, scattered bands, being principally centered at Lac Vieux Desert, Lac du Flambeau, Mole and Post lakes, and Lac Courte Oreilles. The interior people had little contact with Americans and were more traditional than the lakeshore groups, which were exposed to American travelers since they lived on the main east-west transportation route along the lakes. Although it is true that the lakeshore bands were generally more sophisticated in dealing with Americans, they were intermarried with and closely attached to the Ojibwe of the interior. This connection can be seen in the close relationship between the L'Anse and Lac Vieux Desert bands.

As presently will be discussed, the early 1850s brought events that consolidated and sharply focused the political interests of the Lake Superior Ojibwe. During this time, the United States made a serious attempt to remove the Lake Superior Ojibwe people from their traditional territories in Michigan and Wisconsin to northeast Minnesota. These actions caused the Ojibwe incredible hardship and generated among them a fierce determination to resist removal by any means necessary. Thus, the early 1850s was dominated by removal paranoia, not only among the Ojibwe, but on the part of their agents and missionaries as well.

For their part, the Ojibwe feared removal and struggled to avoid it. Antiremoval feeling was based on the strong attachment they had for the communities and territories in which they lived. They knew the resources of these areas well and were not inclined to leave their fishing grounds, sugar maple groves, and hunting territories, let alone their homes, their gardens, and the graves of their relatives. Importantly, they were also familiar with the area where the government wished to settle them, that is, in the "common country" of the Ojibwe. This area of northeast Minnesota was very poor in resources and composed of conifer swamps and muskeg. It was already the territory of the Fond du Lac and Grand Portage bands and could support no more population. To move to this place, they knew, would result in slow starvation.

The Ojibwe and their non-Indian supporters adopted several strategies to stave off removal. The first was to try to convince the government that they were well on their way to becoming civilized and Christian citizens whose good progress would only be retarded by removal. This was a particularly effective argument for the L'Anse bands because it was articulated for them by their agents, clergymen, and traders. Another strategy—one that could only be employed at L'Anse, since the land for this area was already surveyed and offered for sale—was to acquire title to land. In fact, land was purchased on the Indians' behalf by missionaries and others as a means of providing security and to safeguard their permanence in an otherwise unstable and fearful time. More will be said about the private purchase of land later in this chapter.

Earliest Treaties with Lake Superior Ojibwe

Following the War of 1812, the United States slowly started to exert its hegemony over that part of the Old Northwest that now constitutes the states of Michigan, Wisconsin, and Minnesota. Of special concern to Michigan territorial governor and later secretary of war Lewis Cass was the fact that the Indian tribes on the northern border with Canada were still loyal to the British. They renewed this relationship each year by streaming to British Indian Department posts at Fort Drummond and Manitoulin Island to receive presents. The United States countered by distributing presents to the same tribes at Fort Mackinac. In addition, Governor Cass led an exploratory party to the south shore of Lake Superior in 1820 for the purpose of showing the flag and obtaining the fidelity of the Ojibwe.

The first formal relations between the Old Northwest tribes and the United States came by means of three treaties of peace and friendship. These included the Treaty of Prairie du Chien in 1825, the Treaty of Fond du Lac in 1826, and the Treaty of Butte des Morts in 1827.[32] Although there is scant evidence that any chiefs from the Keweenaw Bay bands signed these treaties, chiefs from the nearby Ontonagon community certainly did, and it is clear that all of the Lake Superior Ojibwe were included.

The most important of the early treaties is the one negotiated at Prairie du Chien in 1825. This treaty included the Sac and Fox, Menominee, Ioway, Dakota (Sioux), Winnebago, and portions of the Ottawa, Ojibwe, and Potawatomi. The U.S. treaty commissioners Lewis Cass and William Clark had three basic objectives in mind in order to assert American control over the tribes: establishing peace in the region between the tribes and the United States, stopping the ongoing warfare between the Ojibwe and the Dakota (Sioux), and sorting out the often competing territorial claims of the various tribes. Although the treaty did not stop Ojibwe-Dakota raiding or resolve all the territorial issues, it was otherwise successful. Toward the end of the treaty negotiations, it occurred to the treaty commissioners that the Lake Superior Ojibwe, the group most involved in raiding against the Dakota, were not well represented at Prairie du Chien. It was resolved, therefore, to gather the Lake Superior Ojibwe during the following summer at Fond du Lac at the head of Lake Superior for the purpose of asking them to ratify the Prairie du Chien peace accord.

Lewis Cass, along with the head of the Indian Office in the War Department, Thomas McKenney, did indeed appear the following August to meet the Ojibwe of Lake Superior as well as those from the upper Mississippi Valley.[33] In due course, the Ojibwe did ratify the peace agreement reached at Prairie du Chien, as well as recognizing the "authority and jurisdiction of the United States" while they disclaimed "all connections with foreign powers."[34] The treaty also provided a location for a settlement of French-Indian mixed bloods, or métis, near Sault Ste. Marie and permitted the United States "the right to search for and carry away any metals or minerals from any part of the country."[35]

One boundary issue remained unsolved by the Prairie du Chien Treaty, namely, the southern boundary of the Ojibwe country that separated the Ojibwe from the Winnebago and the Menominee. This issue could not be addressed in the absence of the latter tribes that were not represented at Fond du Lac. As a result, another treaty session was scheduled for Green Bay for the following summer. Two of the signers of the 1826 treaty, Binnayshi (Bird) and Keeshketawwug (Cut Ear), were listed among the twelve Ontonagon chiefs who signed the treaty. However, on the Treaty of La Pointe in 1842, both are listed as chiefs from Keweenaw Bay. In August 1827 the Lake Superior Ojibwe, along with those representing the Menominee and Winnebago (Ho-Chunk) tribes, met with Lewis Cass at Butte des Morts on the Fox River near Green Bay. Within a few days, the chiefs agreed on a boundary line that separated their various tribal claims.

During the late 1820s, there was a great deal of discussion in the United States about the advisability of removing eastern Indians west of the Mississippi River. Some suggested this was necessary because Indians were, by nature, hunters and warriors who would never be able to master the arts of civilization and consequently assimilate into American society. According to this view, the sensible course was to settle eastern tribes west of the Mississippi, that is, beyond the settled frontier of the United States. Others, mostly missionaries and eastern intellectuals, argued that Indians could be brought to Christ, could learn to read and write English, and could settle down as productive, self-sufficient farmers. The problem, however, as these reformers saw it, was that Indians could not be civilized where they were exposed to numerous unscrupulous traders and whiskey peddlers who thwarted educational efforts. Thus, they, too, argued that the trans-Mississippi west offered the ideal place for Indian colonies, where they could be educated and acculturated far from the evil influence of bad white men.[36]

These two polar philosophies that supported the same solution resulted in the passage of the Indian Removal Act in the spring of 1830.[37] The Indian Removal Act permitted Indian tribes that resided in the settled states and territories east of the Mississippi River to voluntarily exchange their land for new lands in the west. A clear benefit of the removal policy to the United States was that the government acquired millions of acres of fertile land that could be sold to immigrant farmers.

During the 1830s, many of the tribes that inhabited the rich farmland of the southeastern and midwestern states were, in fact, removed. In most cases, these removals were less than voluntary. In the far north, however, where the land and climate were not conducive to agriculture and where the United States was more interested in access to the timber and mineral resources, Indian removal did not occur. Indian occupation there was seen as compatible with resource extraction. Although much has been said about the Treaties of 1837 and 1842 in the previous chapters, they are recapped in brief in the following section because they were also important to reservation cases.

The Natural Resource Treaties

The United States was not insistent on removal where Indians occupied cold and remote areas with poor soil, like the country of the Ojibwe. The United States was, nonetheless, interested in acquiring the vast timber, mineral, and fishing resources found within the Ojibwe homeland. The first major land cession of the Lake Superior Ojibwe, although they did not originally understand it to be such, was the result of the Treaty of St. Peters. This treaty was negotiated by Wisconsin territorial governor Henry Dodge and the "Chippewa Nation of Indians," who met at the confluence of the St. Peters River (Minnesota River) and the Mississippi River in July 1837.[38] This treaty, like the one later negotiated at La Pointe in 1842, was motivated by pressure from American citizens who were eager to acquire access to natural resources in Ojibwe territory. In the case of the 1837 treaty, the principal resource was pine timber.

By the terms of the 1837 St. Peters Treaty, the Ojibwe ceded the north-central part of Wisconsin and central Minnesota. In exchange, the United States agreed to pay the Ojibwe annuities for twenty years, along with services, such as blacksmith shops and instruction in farming, and various other provisions. Seventy thousand dollars was also made available to be applied to Indian trade debts. The privilege of hunting over the ceded territory was guaranteed at the pleasure of the president.[39]

The 1837 treaty, although negotiated during the removal era, was not a removal treaty. Not only was the subject of removal never raised with the Ojibwe, but the treaty also assumes that the Ojibwe occupants would not only live as before but would now also exist harmoniously with the American citizens who would be entering their territory to harvest timber.[40] Soon after the treaty was signed, a controversy arose as to which bands of the "Chippewa Nation of Indians" would receive its benefits. Some supposed that all the bands that signed the treaty would profit, but Governor Dodge, the de facto Indian superintendent of the territory, decided that payments would only be made to the bands that actually occupied the ceded land. Since none of the lakeshore Ojibwe actually lived on these lands, they received no benefits from the 1837 treaty.[41]

In 1842 the United States again approached the Lake Superior Ojibwe for a land cession. Robert Stuart, who had replaced Henry Schoolcraft as the superintendent of the Mackinac Indian Superintendency and was the former chief factor of the American Fur Company at Mackinac, was the U.S. commissioner for this new treaty. This treaty was entirely motivated by the desire of U.S. citizens to gain access to the copper and iron deposits of northern Michigan. It would directly impact the Ojibwe at Keweenaw Bay, who lived within the mining district.[42] As in the case of the 1837 treaty, the United States amalgamated disparate bands of Ojibwe into an otherwise politically meaningless entity called "the Chippewa Indians of the Mississippi *and* Lake Superior" (emphasis added).[43] This strategy was devised in the event that the United States might want to remove the Ojibwe from the cession to unceded Ojibwe lands in northeastern Minnesota in the future.[44]

Even though Article II of the 1842 treaty provided that the Indians would have "the right of hunting on the ceded territory, with the other usual privileges of occupancy, until required to remove by the President of the United States," Commissioner Stuart assured the Ojibwe that it would be many years before the United States wanted their land, if ever.[45] The annuity payments, services, and trader debt provision as well as payments to métis relatives were provided as compensation for the cession. Unlike the 1837 treaty, these benefits were made available to all the Ojibwe who signed the treaty, a provision that was unpopular with the Keweenaw Bay Ojibwe, who did not share in annuities from the 1837 treaty cession.

The removal language of the 1842 treaty did not make this treaty a removal treaty under the provisions of the removal act, since the chiefs who signed the treaty never agreed to removal or to any of the other kinds of removal arrangements that are specified in the language of the act. These include, among other removal arrangements, a date certain for removal, payment for improvements, and a description of the place of resettlement.[46] The removal language of the 1842 treaty did, however, create a good deal of anxiety among those bands that occupied the ceded land. As in the case of the 1837 treaty, no reservations were made for Indians, as it was assumed they would continue to follow their seasonal rounds as they hunted, fished, and gathered over the land that they had just ceded. To protect the Ojibwe from Americans that they would now encounter, the 1842 treaty extended the trade and intercourse laws of the United States over their interactions with non-Indians within the cession. After the treaty was ratified, the ceded land became part of the state of Michigan and the territory of Wisconsin.[47] The government paid treaty annuities and provided services at various places in the ceded territory, including L'Anse, so that the Ojibwe would be able to provision themselves and continue to generate the furs, maple sugar, and other Indian-produced commodities that formed the basis of the economy of the Great Lakes region.[48]

In addition to the signers from other bands, the 1842 treaty was signed by four chiefs, two each from the closely related communities of "Ance" and "Ontonagon." Binnayshi and Guckwesonsish (Keweezaisish) signed for the L'Anse band, and Okundekun (Buoy) and Keeshketawwug (Cut Ear) signed for the Ontonagon bands. All four of these men also signed the Fond du Lac Treaty of 1826, but all were listed as representatives of the Ontonagon bands. Agent Alfred Brunson's annual report for 1843 includes a census that lists Mitshekabenase (Michikapenayshe, or Big Bird) as chief at L'Anse and Okundekun as chief at Ontonagon. The census lists 304 people at L'Anse and 87 at Ontonagon.[49]

Twenty-two years after the 1842 treaty, a group of Ojibwe elders met at Bad River and prepared a bilingual petition in Ojibwe and English that set forth the Ojibwe understanding of their treaty history.[50] The petition evidences their belief that they had, by the terms of the 1837 treaty, sold the pine trees and not the land on which they grew. Likewise, in the case of the 1842 treaty, they understood that it was only the minerals that had been sold. The written journals of both treaties provide evidence that such an interpretation is plausible. In each case, the commissioners stressed again and again that the land being purchased was not suitable for agriculture and therefore would not be wanted for American settlement for a long time in the future. As the commissioners told them, the United States wanted the timber and minerals, not the land.[51] Beyond this, it is unlikely that the Ojibwe in 1842 had any understanding of the American system of land tenure, which provided for exclusive individual ownership of the soil. In this, they were no different from tribal people all over the world who found themselves in the path of the establishment of capitalism as it expanded from western Europe starting in the seventeenth century. In effect, the Great Lakes Ojibwe were seeing their traditional system of communal land use being rapidly replaced by a system that privatized land. This new system transformed the land that they conceived as a living entity into a commodity. Now the land could be divided, leased, bought, and sold. Such a transformation required that the land be partitioned by an invisible grid, a system developed much earlier by Europeans to navigate the oceans. Apart from not understanding the details of land survey, the whole concept of private ownership of land would have seemed nonsensical to the Ojibwe. Indeed, it would have been antithetical to their way of life, which was based on cooperative use of the land's resources to promote group survival.

As governor of the huge Michigan Territory and later as secretary of war, Lewis Cass oversaw a large number of Indian land cession treaties. Cass knew the northern Ojibwe well and understood the clash of land tenure systems. Writing in 1830 on U.S. Indian policy, he noted the irony of the United States negotiating land cession treaties with people who had no concept of landownership to begin with. Cass made the point by quoting from an argument presented before the Supreme Court.

> The nature of the title, by which the Indians held their lands, is not easily reconciled to the principles by which the tenures of their description of property are regulated among civilized nations. Mr. Adams [perhaps John Q. Adams], in the argument of the cause of Fletcher and Peck, before the Supreme Court, describes it as "mere occupancy for the purpose of hunting. It is not like our tenures; they [the Indians] have no idea of a title to the soil itself. It is overrun by them, rather than inhabited."[52]

The Treaty of 1847

In late July 1847, U.S. commissioners Isaac Verplank and Henry Rice met with chiefs representing both the Lake Superior and Mississippi Ojibwe at Fond du Lac. The purpose of this treaty was to obtain a land cession west of the Mississippi River in Minnesota.[53] This cession, like the one obtained from the Pillager Ojibwe several weeks later, was to provide land to accommodate emigrating Menominee and Winnebago that the government hoped to remove from Wisconsin. The Ojibwe bands that actually claimed the land the United States wanted to purchase in the 1847 treaty were part of the Mississippi division, but both the Lake Superior and Mississippi Ojibwe were represented, since the earlier strategy of commingling their affairs continued. The problems and antagonisms this created continued as well. In fact, the United States was only beginning to appreciate the real complexities of the Ojibwe land tenure system.[54] It was now known that the common territory fiction created by Henry Dodge and Robert Stuart in earlier treaties was not tenable. Notwithstanding this fact, the commissioner of Indian affairs, William Medill, instructed Verplank and Rice to encourage the Ojibwe "to think [of] themselves [as] one united people, with possessions and interests in common, especially for the future."[55]

Faced with great dissatisfaction over this very issue, the commissioners negotiated a split annuity, so that the Mississippi Ojibwe, who occupied the ceded land, got sixty-three thousand dollars for the cession, while the Lake Superior bands received only seventeen thousand. Considering that the annuity payments for the much larger 1842 cession occupied by the Lake Superior bands had been evenly divided with the Mississippi Ojibwe, the Lake Superior bands felt cheated by this treaty. In fact, many chiefs refused to sign it, and the powerful trading families also renounced it, since it contained no trader debt provisions.[56] The treaty did provide that métis who resided among the Ojibwe would henceforth share in treaty annuities. This feature seemed unfair to full bloods, who knew that small annuity payments would now be stretched even further.

The 1847 treaty was signed by fifty-nine chiefs representing two dozen Ojibwe bands, including Keeshretowno (Keeshketawwug) of Ontonagon as well as David King, Peter Marksman, Matakosega, and Assurcens (Assinines) of L'Anse. King and Marksman were listed as chiefs, the others as warriors. Beyond exacerbating an already tense relationship between the Lake Superior and Mississippi Ojibwe bands, the 1847 treaty set the tone for later efforts to remove the Lake Superior Ojibwe to Minnesota.

Removal Anxiety and Early Land Purchase

As early as 1845, there were murmurings in Washington about invoking the provision of the 1842 treaty that permitted the president to cancel Ojibwe hunting and fishing rights and require them to remove from the mineral district in Michigan. Apparently the impetus for this suggestion was the supposition that the Ojibwe would be hostile to miners entering their territory. The Indian Office did not support the removal suggestion, because they believed that the Ojibwe would peacefully receive their new neighbors.[57] The Indian Office was also fully aware of the fact that the politically powerful fur trade interest of Michigan and Wisconsin would certainly protest any removal effort.

Nonetheless, the 1840s saw a sharp increase in anxiety among the Lake Superior Ojibwe, for the very important reason that they had no secure land base. The 1837 and 1842 land cession treaties had provided no reservations and thus left the Ojibwe to continue to live in their former territory without their own land.[58] By May 1848, the general land survey had been run and certified, and the land at the end of Keweenaw Bay was placed on the market. The Catholic chiefs led by Assinines wrote to the commissioner of Indian affairs, William Richmond, asking if their small village would be sold during the coming summer. They also reminded him that Father Baraga was holding the land "by preemption" and intended to buy it when it came on the market.[59] That fall, the Ojibwe chiefs of all the Lake Superior bands hired an attorney, who wrote to the president asking that a nontransferable deed in the name of the head chief of each band, including the L'Anse, Lac Vieux Desert, and Ontonagon bands, be issued to provide a permanent home for each of these groups.[60]

As he promised his parishioners, Father Baraga began purchasing land for them in 1849, when he bought 182 acres, including the lots that contained their homes.[61] In the meantime, Peter Barbeau, a L'Anse trader, wrote to Commissioner Richmond asking if the agent could withhold annuity money to buy land for the Indians. Richmond replied that such a tactic was not permissible but that the Indians could pool their funds for their joint benefit and that the land could be "deeded to the Governor of the state in trust for certain Indians naming the band of which so and so is the chief."[62] Commissioner Richmond also suggested that it would be possible to deed the land to one person and then subdivide it among others in proportion to their contribution with a deed made out to each one.[63]

This strategy of deeding in common was followed by thirty-one Methodist members of the Lac Vieux Desert band who purchased eighty-five acres on August 28, 1853. The money for this purchase was given to Peter Marksman, the Indian preacher who visited the Sault Ste. Marie land office as an agent for the band. The land was deeded to chief Poshquaygin and to headman Adam Nungo, who died a year or two later. However, when those who had contributed to buy this land asked Marksman some years later to have the deed changed to name each individual, Marksman objected.[64] This same group also purchased another seventy-one acres that was held for them by Reverend Dubois. Money for this purchase was borrowed partly from Father Baraga and partly from their agent, Andrew Fitch. In the case of the latter purchase, the band wished the deed to be made out to each of its members and delivered to Curtis Ojininin. This information was later communicated for the Indians through Peter Crebassa.

> We the undersigned Indians of Le vieu Desert will explain to you a few words concerning our Chief Pashkwekin. About five years ago we give him some money to buy land with and the money was given to Peter Marksman, and he bought us the land at the land office at the Sault and the deed was in the name of Pashkwekin and Adam Nongo. Now these several years we ask our Chief to give us each individual our deeds but he won't do it and he don't want to do it. Several other things we done for him and more we do for him. More is Worth. He acts very mean about us. There was 85 acres and 45 hundred land bought between Pashkwekin and Adam Nongo.
>
> And about the money we let you have to

> buy the land of Mr. Dubois we wished you if you please to fixed so that we can get each individual get a deed that every Indian that furnished money. We don't want have our chief again to have it only in is [*sic*] name. We have all our confidence in you. We know you will do . . . for your red children.
>
> [names of 31 Indians follow, also the following note]
>
> To Rev. Mr. Curtis [no date]
>
> This band of Indians of Pashkwekin Band have borrowed of the Priest on the other side the money of eighty-four dollars the Amount and balance of purchase of Mr. Fitch bought the land of Mr. Dubois. And Pashkwekin is gone deliver you the money. And the band wished you to have the deed made out in the name of all the names that . . . of the paper I made out for them and the deed send it to my care and I shall delivered to Curtis Ojininin the man that join the Church lately perhaps Pashkwekin will tell some other way in delivering the money to you. Please explain this to Mr. Fitch . . . P. Crebassa.[65]

The worry of the Lake Superior Ojibwe as well as their missionaries and agents was that they might be required to remove to unceded Ojibwe land in Minnesota. This fear was well founded, since a conspiracy was developing for just such a removal effort. The motivation for the removal had nothing to do with the federal government's removal policy—which was, at any rate, all but dead by the mid-1840s—or with the welfare of the Ojibwe people. The removal effort was instead an attempt by Minnesota Whig politicians and the fur trade companies on the Mississippi to advantage the territory of Minnesota and its merchants.[66] The object was thus not so much to remove Indians *from* a place as to remove them *to* Minnesota.

At the urging of Minnesota territorial governor Alexander Ramsey, territorial senator Henry Rice, and the Minnesota fur cartel, President Zachary Taylor issued an executive order on February 6, 1850, that cancelled the usufruct rights granted by the Treaties of 1837 and 1842 and ordered the removal of the Ojibwe from the territory ceded by these treaties (see map 6 in chapter 9).[67] Despite an outcry against the removal effort on the part of the Ojibwe, their missionaries, citizens in Michigan and Wisconsin, and the Indian Office employees, John Watrous was appointed as a special government agent for removal.[68]

An attempt to lure the Lake Superior Ojibwe west by making their annuity payments at Sandy Lake on the Mississippi River in the month of December resulted in one of the most deadly tragedies in the history of Indian relations. During the fall of 1850, the Lake Superior Ojibwe were forced to go to Sandy Lake and wait for their payment. Unfortunately, Agent Watrous did not make the payment until after heavy snow and ice had closed the canoe routes and trails back to Wisconsin and Michigan. Disease, exposure, and starvation at Sandy Lake and on the way home killed four hundred Ojibwe men, almost 12 percent of the entire Lake Superior Ojibwe population. James Clifton, who wrote about this incident, called their trip home a "death march."[69]

The L'Anse Ojibwe were to some extent isolated from the direct effects of these removal attempts, if not the psychological trauma associated with it. For one thing, the fact that they had two substantial mission establishments as well as a government demonstration farm and blacksmith shop meant that their missionaries and government workers could intercede on their behalf.[70] In addition, because they had either purchased some land or had land purchased for them by missionaries, the L'Anse community was on a different footing than the totally landless interior bands. Finally, most important, their situation permitted them to argue that unlike their brethren, they were Christian and civilized Indians.[71] Despite the fact that this was true of only the missionized L'Anse people, it was undoubtedly an effective argument.

The public scandal following the Sandy Lake affair stiffened resistance to the Ojibwe removal effort, and on August 25, 1851, the secretary of the interior ordered the suspension of the removal order.[72] The order was never reinstated, and although an informal and much-diminished removal effort continued until 1852, the Ojibwe simply refused to be removed. In one of the final acts of the removal effort, Alexander Ramsey,

Minnesota territorial governor and chief advocate of the Ojibwe removal, used his discretionary power as superintendent of Indian affairs for the Minnesota Territory, where the removal effort was based, to exempt the L'Anse community from removal, and he agreed that their annuities would henceforth be paid at Keweenaw Bay.[73] Presumably, this concession was granted because it would considerably diminish the overall opposition to the removal that the L'Anse community was able to generate.

The Reservation Policy

A decade before the midpoint of the nineteenth century, the policy of removing eastern Indians to land west of the Mississippi was dying a natural death. Western removal was problematic from the start, since even by the time the Indian Removal Act was passed in 1830, the trans-Mississippi was already filling rapidly with American settlers. Further, Indians adapted to the eastern forest environment were less than anxious to live on the plains and prairies. Likewise, native people who already lived in the West were not anxious for competition from eastern tribes who were being relocated into their territories. Most important, the Indian colonies, which were formed to teach Christianity and the arts of civilization to removed Indians, were not very successful. This latter fact caused many observers to blame the failure of Indians to achieve "civilized lifestyles" on innate weaknesses in the Indian character and intellect.[74]

Fortunately, a new set of ideas was taking form in the Indian Office, which incidentally was transferred from the War Department to the newly organized Department of the Interior in 1849. Charles Mix, chief clerk of the Indian Office, and George Manypenny, who served as commissioner of Indian affairs between 1853 and 1857, espoused the theory that the lack of progress in Indian acculturation was due not to any fault in the Indian character but to a poorly conceived and executed Indian policy on the part of the government.[75] Manypenny reasoned that if Indians could be protected in their own country from the abuses of marauding traders and whiskey peddlers by the establishment of permanent and secure reservations, they could be successfully acculturated. Commissioner Manypenny stated his position in an 1856 report.

> I also desire again to urge all that I have presented in former reports, as well as in this one, with reference to the obnoxious and fatal policy of removing Indian tribes, and the absolute necessity of fixed habitations and permanent homes as indispensable to their preservation, domestication and civilization. To preserve the small reservations already made, and hereafter to be made, by tribes who have or may resolve to settle down and till the land, and to preserve to all Indians their annuities, I again urgently recommend such penal and other legislation as may be required to effect these objects. But any measure of protection short of this will fail to guard the Indians against the artful schemes of those bad men who, under more or less specious pretences, desire to obtain either their lands or their money, or both.[76]

In the 1857 report of the commissioner of Indian affairs, Manypenny's successor, Commissioner James Denver, explained that the reservations would have secure exterior boundaries and would give missionaries and teachers the chance to work effectively. These boundaries would be marked, and the agents would have authority to secure them against intruders.

> No white person should be permitted to obtain any kind of possession or foothold within the limits of the reservations, nor even to enter them, except in the employ or by permission of the government, and none should be employed except such as would be actually necessary for the instruction of the Indians. Power should be conferred on the agents to eject summarily all intruders from the reservations. They should also be clothed with executive and judicial authority in matters pertaining to their agencies, and appeals from their decision be allowed to the superintendents, and thence to the department.[77]

In order to teach Indians the value of private property and hard labor, it was envisioned that each Indian family would receive a forty- or eighty-acre farm on the reservation. This process, referred to as "allotment in severalty," would eventually result in a reservation community composed of small, independent and self-sufficient farmers. Commissioner Denver provided a statement of the reservation policy in his 1857 report.

> With large reservations of fertile and desirable land, entirely disproportioned to their wants for occupancy and support, it will be impossible, when surrounded by a dense white population, to protect them from constant disturbance, intrusion and spoliation by those on whom the obligations of law and justice rest but lightly . . . Their reservations should be restricted so as to contain only sufficient land to afford them a comfortable support by actual cultivation, and should be properly divided and assigned to them, with the obligation to remain upon and cultivate the same. The title should remain in the tribe, with the power reserved to the government, when any of them become sufficiently intelligent, sober and industrious, to grant them patents for the lands so assigned to them, but leaseable or alienable only to members of the tribe, until they become so far advanced as to be fitted for the enjoyment of all the rights and privileges of citizens of the United States.[78]

While the acculturation process was taking shape at the hands of teachers, missionaries, and government agents, Indian property would be protected by restrictions against alienation of the allotments. As it was envisioned, Indian allottees would eventually receive a patent in fee when the government was sure that the landowners could read and write well enough to protect their own interests.

The reservation policy was given effect by means of fifty-two treaties that Manypenny and his associates promoted during his term as commissioner. It is doubtful if many of the concepts incorporated in Manypenny's treaties were actually understood by the Indian parties, given the enormous linguistic and cultural gulf that separated native from American societies. Concepts like private landownership and citizenship or details of land division and alienation would have been a mystery to all but a tiny handful of Indians.

The Origins of Allotment

Prior to the Treaty of 1854, land was occasionally provided to individuals as a provision of Indian treaties, but 1854 marked the inception of providing land allotments to individual Indians as an instrument of U.S. policy. The earliest grants, usually made by Indians from land they had not yet ceded, were made to such persons as influential chiefs, the mixed-blood children of traders, resident missionaries, teachers, or physicians as a reward for service to the tribe.[79] The practice of making such grants was, however, officially discouraged by the mid-1830s.

The first treaty to provide land in severalty to Indians was negotiated by Commissioner Manypenny with the Otto and Missouri tribes on March 15, 1854. A copy of this treaty was sent to Henry Gilbert and David Herrington as one of several informational items supplied by Commissioner Manypenny prior to negotiations of the La Pointe Treaty of 1854. Gilbert was told, "These documents may be useful as affording you indications of the views of the Department and of such provisions as it may be desirable to have incorporated in a treaty."[80] The Otto-Missouri Treaty gave the president the discretion to survey the reserve into lots so that heads of various-sized families and single persons over twenty-one years of age would receive appropriate-sized allotments. When all had received land, the residue would be sold for the benefit of the tribe. The president could then issue patents for the allotted lands to individuals, with the condition that the land was not to be alienated or leased for longer than two years. Accordingly the treaty allotments were to "be exempt from levy, sale, or forfeiture." The latter provision was to continue in force until a state constitution was formed, and the legislature of the state was permitted to remove this restriction. To accomplish this, however, the new state would need the specific consent of Congress.[81]

Between the Otto-Missouri Treaty in March 1854 and the La Pointe Treaty in late September, Manypenny negotiated ten other treaties; seven of these also contained allotment provisions. Keeping in mind that these treaties covered a wide range of cultural and environmental situations, the allotment measures were general and often very similar or identical from one treaty to another. This is the result of the fact that while the theory of allotment was well articulated, the methods and problems of actually making allotments were more or less left to trial and error. Generally the allotment process called for the subdivision of the land into parcels in conformity with the ongoing general land survey. The president was then given the discretion to allot these parcels according to some prescribed formula that often varied from case to case. The president might then issue fee patents with appropriate restrictions. Following the language of the Otto-Missouri Treaty, treaties with both the Omaha and Miami tribes that created reservations in the territory of Missouri anticipated the eventual formation of a state as well as a possible role for the state in taxation of Indian land.[82] When a state was formed, the legislature could initiate a process to remove restrictions on taxation, but again only with the expressed consent of Congress.

Three other treaties, those with the Iowa, Sauk-Fox, and Kickapoo tribes, were all negotiated within a three-day period and all contained the identical allotment language.[83] The land would be surveyed at the tribe's expense, a sufficient but unspecified quantity of land would be given to each person, and a patent would be issued, with whatever safeguards against alienation Congress wished to impose. A treaty with the Kaskaskia and Peoria tribes in Illinois called for the survey of allotments in conformity with the usual legal subdivisions and for awarding 160 acres of land per capita. Patents were to be issued subject to such restrictions respecting leases and alienation as the president and Congress may proscribe.[84] This treaty also had a surplus land provision by which land left over after the selection of allotments would be offered at public sale for the benefit of the tribe.

Prelude to the 1854 Treaty

It had been a long-standing policy of the United States to try to acquire all Indian land east of the Mississippi River. By the midpoint of the nineteenth century, the largest unceded parcel lay between Lake Superior and the upper Mississippi Valley, in what is today the northeastern portion of the state of Minnesota. This was the so-called common country of the Ojibwe, as defined by the Treaty of 1842. This land was low, swampy, and covered with conifer forest. It was relatively sterile and was used as a hunting and trapping territory by the Fond du Lac, Grand Portage, and Bois Forte Ojibwe bands. It did, however, hold a strong appeal for the United States, as it was known to contain mineral wealth, especially iron and copper.[85] When treaty commissioners were appointed to try to acquire land for emigrating eastern Indians in 1847, Congress instructed them to try to buy the Minnesota mineral district as well. However, since the Ojibwe objected to selling this land during negotiation of the 1847 treaty, the matter was dropped.[86] In 1851 reports of mineral prospectors trespassing on Indian land again raised talk of another purchase attempt by means of a new treaty.[87]

The Ojibwe of Lake Superior were also interested in a new round of treaty negotiations, for the simple purpose of securing permanent homes for themselves within their native territory. They were particularly anxious to acquire reservations given the recent and traumatic removal episode that continued on until 1852. Agent Henry Gilbert of the Michigan Indian Agency wrote to Commissioner Manypenny in December 1853 reporting on his talks with the Lake Superior Ojibwe.

> First and chief of all is the order heretofore made for their removal. This is the great terror of their lives and I hazard nothing in saying that they will sooner submit to extermination than comply with it. They look with fear and distrust upon every Government officer that goes among them and indeed so sensitive are they upon this point that many of them came this year [to La Pointe in 1853] to the payment with great reluctance and anxious foreboding lest the notice of payment should prove a ruse to get them together in order the more easily to effect their removal.[88]

In the spring of 1854, a bill was introduced in Congress that authorized "the extinguishment of the title of the Chippewa Indians to the lands owned and claimed by them in the Territory of Minnesota, and the State of Wisconsin, and for their domestication and civilization."[89] This bill, HR 293, was concurrently introduced in the Senate and was reported out of the Committee on Indian Affairs after a great deal of discussion. The debate that arose was not concerned with the substance of the bill so much as the relative power of Congress and the executive branch in treaty making. Some lawmakers were apparently concerned that the specific provisions of HR 293 would impinge on the president's treaty-making discretion under the Constitution.[90] Although the bill passed the House of Representatives, it was tabled by the Senate toward the end of the first session of the Thirty-third Congress.

In the meantime, Commissioner Manypenny, who was aware of the bill but was determined to obtain a cession of the mineral district quickly, as well as to provide reservations for the Lake Superior Ojibwe, saw an opportunity to negotiate while the Ojibwe were assembled at La Pointe for annuity payments under former treaties during the fall of 1854. He also, no doubt, anticipated the passage of HR 293, which had been reintroduced in the second session. The bill, however, did not pass Congress until December 19, 1854, after the negotiation of the treaty.[91] The text of the authorization act is as follows:

> Be it enacted by the Senate and House of Representatives of the United States of America in Congress assembled, That the President be, and he is hereby, authorized to cause negotiations to be entered into with the Chippewa Indians, for the extinguishment of their title to all the lands owned and claimed by them in the Territory of Minnesota and State of Wisconsin, which treaties shall contain the following provisions, and such others as may be requisite and proper to carry the same into effect:
>
> First. Granting to each head of a family, in fee simple, a reservation of eighty acres of land, to be selected in the territory ceded, so soon as surveys shall be completed, by those entitled, which said reservations shall be patented by the President of the United States, and the patent therefor shall expressly declare that the said lands shall not be alienated or leased by the reservees, or their heirs and legal representatives, until otherwise ordered by Congress, and no change of location shall be made without the assent of the President of the United States.
>
> Second. The annuities to which said Indians are entitled, under existing treaties, with the consent of said Indians, together with such as may be allowed them for the cession, or cessions, under the provisions of this act, shall be equally distributed and paid them at their villages, or settlements, within the limits of the ceded territory; but the President shall be invested with power to cause said annuities to be commuted, from time to time, for such articles of goods, provisions, stock, cattle, implements of agriculture, the clearing and fencing of land, and the erection of buildings and other improvements, as in his discretion, will conduce most to promote their comfort, civilization, and permanent welfare.
>
> Third. All the benefits and privileges granted to said Indians shall be extended to and enjoyed by the mixed bloods belonging to or connected with the tribe, and who shall permanently reside on the ceded lands.
>
> Fourth. The laws of the United States and the Territory of Minnesota shall be extended over the Chippewa territory in Minnesota whenever the same may be ceded, and the same shall cease to be "Indian country," except that the lands reserved to said Indians, or other property owned by them, shall be exempt from taxation and execution; and that the act passed thirtieth June, eighteen hundred and thirty-four, "to regulate trade and intercourse with the Indian tribes," etc., be inoperative over the said ceded territory, except the twentieth section, which prohibits the introduction and sale of spirituous liquors to Indians.
>
> Fifth. The President shall have power to prescribe and enforce such rules and regulations, not inconsistent with the foregoing provisions, as he may deem necessary for the effectual execution of the purposes of this act, which said rules and regulations shall be annually reported to Congress.
>
> Sec. 2. *And be it further enacted,* That, for the purpose of defraying the expenses of said negotiations, the sum of ten thousand dollars be, and the same is hereby, appropriated out of any money in the treasury not otherwise appropriated.
>
> Approved, December 19, 1854.[92]

It is apparent that many elements of the new reservation and civilization policy of George Manypenny are incorporated in this bill. Besides the land cession, the bill provides for allotments in fee simple with safeguards against alienation, including the fact that Indian lands and property were to be exempt from taxation and execution. None of these lands could be alienated by allottees or their heirs unless specifically ordered by Congress. In the strongest possible terms, Congress was encouraging the president to create permanent homelands for the Lake Superior Ojibwe. Quite simply, the reservations to be created were the quid pro quo by which the United States was to acquire the fabulously rich iron ore deposits that we know today as the Mesabi and Vermillion iron ranges.[93]

In August 1854 Commissioner Manypenny sent Henry Gilbert, the agent of the Michigan Indian Superintendency, and David Herriman, Indian agent at Crow Wing, Minnesota, several letters that directed them to try to negotiate a new treaty at the fall annuity payment at La Pointe.[94] Gilbert was instructed to keep the intention to negotiate a treaty as quiet as possible, for fear of attracting non-Indian opposition. Manypenny knew that the desired cession would require making land reservations, and he expressed the view that one large reservation would be best because of the efficiency it would provide for supplying services and oversight.[95] Herriman, who was to bring the Ojibwe of the Mississippi, was warned that a treaty required a full delegation.[96]

Manypenny was aware that the Lake Superior and Mississippi Ojibwe were hostile to each other, due to previous treaty provisions that commingled their separate interests. He also knew that third parties would try to manipulate the treaty to include a large trader debt provision and benefits for mixed bloods. Given these problems, he described his instructions as "conditional." Accordingly he instructed Gilbert to pay half a million dollars for the land in exchange for nearly a quarter of a million acres of previously ceded land being made available for reservations. Manypenny included three documents with his instructions: a map of lands claimed by the Ojibwe, a congressional resolution passed in 1847 to treat for purchase of the Minnesota mineral district, and a copy of the treaty that he had recently negotiated with the Otto and Missouri tribes.[97] The latter was a suggested model for how Gilbert and Herriman might set up the allotment of land, since, as Manypenny said, it was in the government's interest "to give them a small tract as a permanent home, with such means of support and mental and moral improvement as may be of great advantage to them."[98] A few days later, Manypenny sent Gilbert a follow-up letter in which he stated that while one or a few land reserves was preferable, it was likely that the Lake Superior bands would insist on smaller reserves located in their separate territories. This, he said, was permissible, but Gilbert was to name "all of them by bands which select a reservation."[99] See map 18.

Gilbert and Herriman did negotiate a new treaty in September when they met the Lake Superior Ojibwe and the delegations from the Mississippi bands at La Pointe.[100] There is no official journal of the negotiations, but Gilbert wrote to Manypenny on October 17, 1854, forwarding the treaty and describing the difficult circumstances of its negotiation.[101] Not only did four thousand Indians appear at La Pointe, but they were accompanied by interested mixed bloods, traders, and "claim agents" from St. Paul who were trying to influence the treaty by manipulating various Indian factions. Gilbert reported that the Mississippi Ojibwe would sell no land and would not even meet with the Lake Superior chiefs in council. As a condition of the sale of the mineral district, the Lake Superior chiefs insisted on making small, local reservations as well as having a trader debt provision. They also held out for land reservations for two hundred mixed-blood families.[102]

As negotiated, the La Pointe Treaty of 1854 ceded land actually claimed and used by the Lake Superior Ojibwe but designated as the common property of both the Lake Superior and Mississippi Ojibwe by the Treaties of 1837 and 1842. Gilbert and Herriman did manage to sever the combined interest of these two groups by getting the Mississippi Ojibwe to agree to the cession as long as the Lake Superior chiefs would agree to forego future claims to other Ojibwe land in Minnesota. Thus, the western boundary of the cession became the boundary line between the two Ojibwe groups.

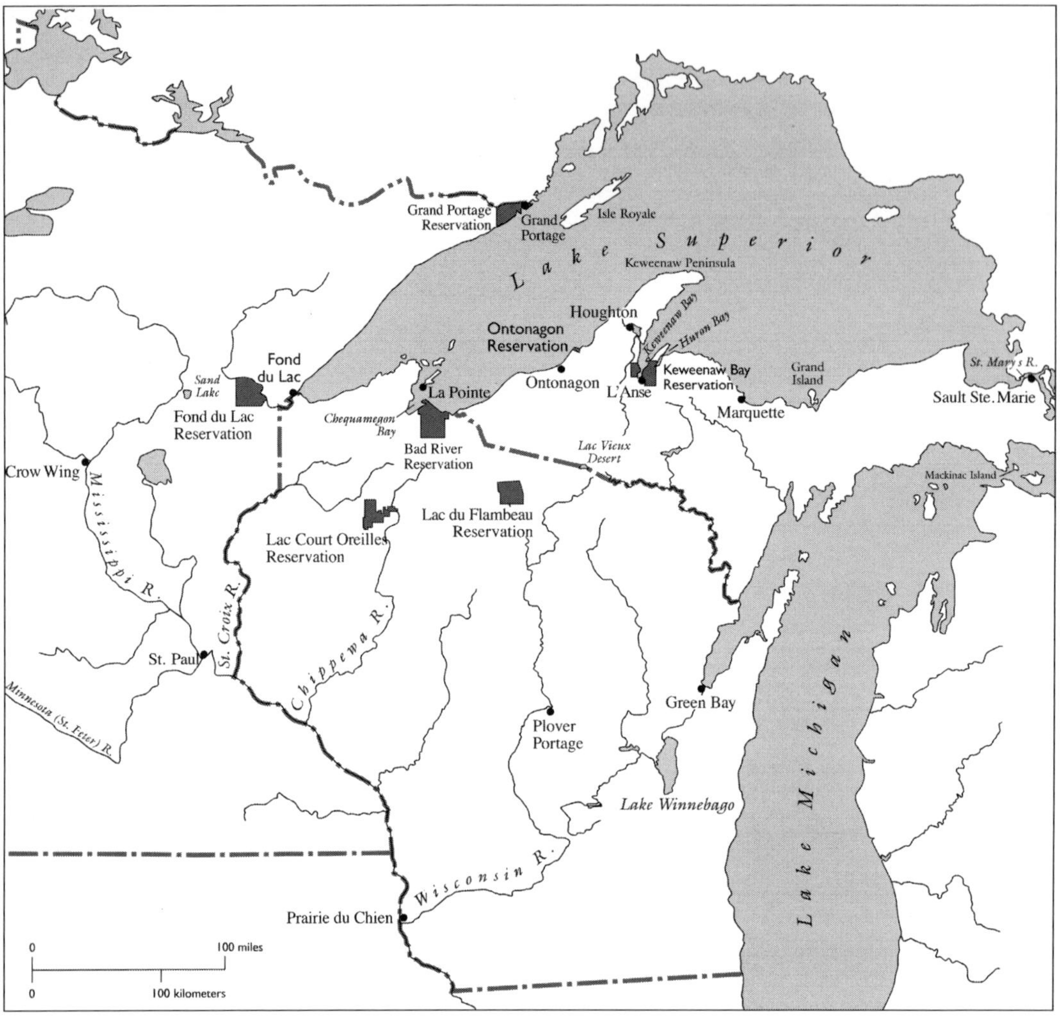

Map 18. Some place-names of the Lake Superior region

The 1854 Treaty

Article 1 of the 1854 treaty describes the cession of land that today constitutes the northeastern part of the state of Minnesota. At the time of the treaty, this part of this region was actually used by families belonging to the Fond du Lac, Grand Portage, and Bois Forte Ojibwe bands, all of which were classified as Lake Superior Ojibwe. In the Treaties of 1837 and 1842, U.S. treaty commissioners had defined the area ceded in 1854 as the "common country" of the Ojibwe, thus including both the Ojibwe of Lake Superior and those of the Mississippi. The purpose of this "common country" terminology was to create a place to which Ojibwe people from Michigan and Wisconsin could be moved in the future if it was ever decided to move them west.

In the second part of Article 1, the ownership of the lands to be ceded—the former "common country"—had to be resolved. This was done by having the Ojibwe of the Mississippi, who did not occupy the lands to be ceded, agree to forfeit their payment, while having the Ojibwe of Lake Superior, who did receive payment, agree to surrender future claims to any land west of the cession. The latter lands were those actually occupied by the Ojibwe of the Mississippi.

Article 2 of the treaty created, through six subsections, reservations for each of six Lake Superior Ojibwe bands. The first subsection of Ar-

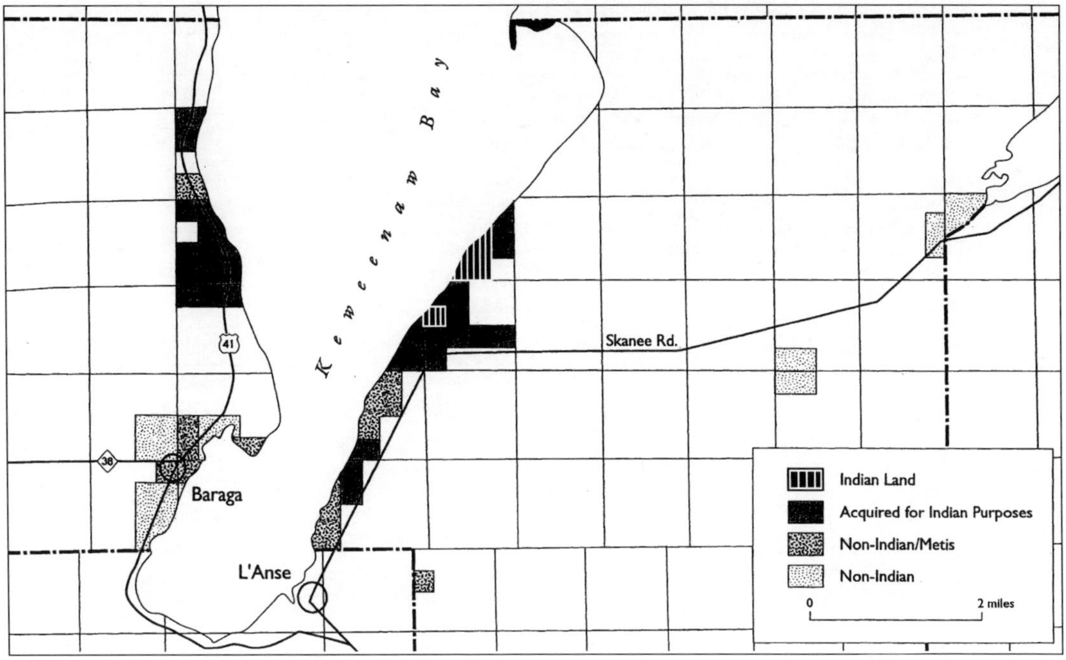

Map 19. Map of land sold prior to the treaty of 1854

ticle 2 created the L'Anse and Lac Vieux Desert Indian Reservation.

> Article 2. The United States agree to set apart and withhold from sale, for the use of the Chippewas of Lake Superior, the following described tracts of land, viz:
>
> 1st. For the L'Anse and Vieux De Sert bands, all the unsold lands in the following townships in the State of Michigan: Township fifty-one north range thirty-three west; township fifty-one north range thirty-two west; the east half of township fifty north range thirty-three west; the west half of township fifty north range thirty-two west, and all of township fifty-one north range thirty-one west, lying west of Huron Bay.[103]

Unlike the cases of the other five reservations, which were described by metes and bounds, the L'Anse and Lac Vieux Desert Indian Reservation was described by township and range designations. This is because the area around the end of Keweenaw Bay had already been surveyed as part of the general land survey. It was also the only area where land was already for sale; in fact, land at the foot of the bay had been on the market since the summer of 1846. See map 19. It is also worth noting that the treaty combined the L'Anse bands with those from Lac Vieux Desert. The latter group normally resided along the Michigan-Wisconsin border about fifty miles south of Keweenaw Bay, and some of the families of the two groups were undoubtedly related by marriage.

Because it was known at the time of the 1854 treaty that some of the land within the townships described in the treaty as an Indian reservation had already been sold, the treaty specified that the L'Anse and Lac Vieux Desert Indian Reservation would be created from the "unsold land" of these townships.[104] Table 2 shows that 2,388.79 acres had been sold prior to the date of the treaty, namely, September 30, 1854.

The sold land can be described in terms of the nature of the private ownership as well as of its owners. Nearly a third of the total sold land, 726.79 acres, was owned by non-Indians who had no real ties to the Indian community. Only two of these owners, Oscar Foote and Cyrus Pennock, actually resided on their land. By 1855, however, Pennock had sold his land to John Southwind, one of the chiefs of the L'Anse Methodist band. Oscar Foote was a baker and

TABLE 2. Land Sold Prior to the Treaty of 1854

Name	Occupation	Ethnic Ties	Acres
Clement March	Nonresident/speculator	White	229.24
Columbus Douglass	Nonresident/businessman	White	160.0
Ransom Sheldon	Nonresident/businessman	White	189.80
Oscar Foote	Resident/baker	White	124.35
John Billinghast	Nonresident	White	23.40
Land owned by nonmembers of Indian community:			726.79
Percentage of total = 31.0%			
	Non-Indian/Métis		
Name	Occupation	Ethnic Ties	Acres
Adolph Nolan	Trader	Indian wife—métis	45.15
James Bendry	Ship owner/business	Indian wife—white	143.80
Francis LaClair	Fisherman/trader	Indian wives–métis	45.30
Peter Crebessa	Trader	Indian wife—métis	74.65
Gilbert Miller	Hunter	Indian wife—métis	5.50
N. Magnent	Trader	Indian wife—métis	4.0
John Hotley	Carpenter	Indian wife—métis	35.8
George Burkett	Agency farmer	Indian wife—métis	52.8
Edward St. Arneau	Sailor	Indian wife—métis	13.0
John Holliday	Trader	Indian wife—métis	7.0
Augustus Bashman	Carpenter	Indian wife—métis	2.0
Land owned by associates of Indian community:			429.00
Percentage of total = 18%			
	Acquired for Indian Purposes		
Name	Occupation	Ethnic Ties	Acres
Frederick Baraga	Missionary	White	497.05
William Brockway	Missionary	White	165.95
Benjamin Rathbun	Agency blacksmith	White	179.45
Abel Hall	Agency farmer	White—Indian wife	122.25
John Beedon	Agency farmer	White	7.0
Robert Dubois	Missionary	White	71.60
Land acquired for Indians:			1,043.30
Percentage of total = 44%			
	Indian Land		
Name	Occupation	Ethnic Ties	Acres
Poshquaygin and Adam Nungo	Chiefs	Indian	85.45
David King	Chief	Indian	73.25
Owned by Indians: Percentage of total = 7%			158.70
Total land sold = 2,388.79 acres			

later the register of deeds for Baraga County and was most likely the man that the chiefs mentioned in their 1864 petition when they recalled, in their complaint to Commissioner Manypenny in 1855, that there was a white man living on their reservation.[105] A second group of private landowners were the métis and white men who had Indian wives and were, therefore, actually members of the Indian community. The federal censuses of 1850 and 1860 list the children of these marriages as "Indian," and many of the same families are today enrolled members of the Keweenaw Bay Indian Community. These men had purchased 429 acres, about 18 percent of the sold land. The next and largest percentage of sold land, 1,043.30 acres, or 44 percent, was owned by men who were temporarily holding land for Indians. Most of this land was located adjacent to the Catholic or Methodist missions and was already incorporated into the missions.

It should be recalled here that both the Lake Superior Ojibwe and their missionaries were dealing with the threat of removal in the few years preceding the 1854 treaty. Both knew that little effort would be made toward construction of houses or the clearing of land for agriculture as long as their work could be forfeited by forced removal to new lands in Minnesota or elsewhere. To provide for their security and to encourage cultural change, Father Baraga of the Catholic mission and Methodist clergymen, such as Reverend Brockway and Robert Dubois, as well as employees attached to the local Indian agency, such as Abel Hall and Benjamin Rathbun, acquired land for Indians. This was the land where the Indians actually had their villages along the lakeshore and around their mission communities.

Both Father Baraga and Benjamin Rathbun, the government blacksmith at L'Anse, made claims for reimbursement for the purchase of this land under the debt provision of the 1854 treaty. This provision was meant to cover the just debts of the Indians. Baraga asked for three hundred dollars to cover the purchase of three hundred acres of land in 1849. Part of this amount included the lots where he had built thirty houses for his parishioners.[106] The Rathbun claim was for one thousand dollars for 124 acres of land, which was described in the claim as being held for the Indians and encompassing a portion of their village at L'Anse.[107] At the time the claims were registered in 1855, both Agent Gilbert and Commissioner Manypenny believed the Baraga and Rathbun claims to be just, but since the purpose of the treaty's claim provision was to "settle the just debts" of *individual* Indians, they did not believe that such land claims would qualify.[108] It was decided to try to find another mechanism by which the government could acquire these lands for the L'Anse Ojibwe. Perhaps, it was suggested, claims could be made later and paid from any surplus in the debt fund.

In July 1863 Reverend Frederick Baraga, now bishop, deeded his land at the Catholic mission to Edward Assinines and thirty-seven named Indians for $150.[109] The Rathbun holdings, as well as those owned by Hall and Reverend Dubois, followed a somewhat more circuitous route into Indian ownership. Since Rathbun died soon after the treaty, the land went to his widow. Fortunately, there was an understanding that the Indian Office had promised to buy the Rathbun land as well as that held by Abel Hall and Reverend Dubois. Mrs. Rathbun deeded her land to Agent Fitch in 1857, and shortly thereafter Fitch deeded it to individual Indians in ten-acre parcels.[110]

The land purchased by Abel Hall remained his property until the first decade of the twentieth century, when he died. In fact, Hall continued to buy up land on the reservation for years and permitted Indian families to reside on it. When he died, the Hall properties were sold individually to their Indian occupants. Land owned by Reverend Dubois was purchased in 1858 by Agent Andrew Fitch with eighty-four dollars that Chief Poshquaygin borrowed from the Catholic priest. By 1860 this land, which lies adjacent to a large parcel owned by Poshquaygin and Adam Nungo, was combined with the larger piece.

The final category of sold land was actually purchased under the name of Indian chiefs for the benefit of their band and included seventy-three acres owned by David King. These purchases were made during the era of the removal threat and were each to some extent instigated and financially supported by non-Indians. Indian-owned land consisted of 158.70 acres, or 7 percent of the total sold land. Poshquagin was chief of one of the Lac Vieux Desert bands, and Adam Nungo was a subchief. Both men were Methodist converts and had joined the mission community. Funds for the purchase of these lands were accumulated by individual donations of Poshquaygin and Adam Nungo plus thirty-one other contributors.[111] Presumably, these funds came from annuity payments made per capita under the 1842 treaty. The collected funds were entrusted to Peter Marksman, who purchased the land at the Sault Ste. Marie federal land office and had it deeded to Poshquagin and Adam Nungo in trust for the band. Apparently in 1858 all of the Indian contributors wanted Marksman to have the deed corrected to show all of their names, but Marksman refused.[112]

The seventh subsection of Article 2 of the 1854 treaty states that "mixed bloods, belonging to the Chippewas of Lake Superior, shall be entitled to eighty acres of land, to be selected by them under the direction of the President."[113] The government subsequently decided that mixed-blood selections must be made outside of the reservations, where they could be selected from among public domain lands.

Article 3 dealt with the creation of allotments: "The United States will define the boundaries of the reserved tracts [reservations], whenever it may be necessary, by actual survey, and the President may, from time to time, at his discretion, cause the whole to be surveyed, and may assign to each head of family or single person over twenty-one years of age, eighty acres of land for his or their separate use; and he may, at his discretion, as fast as the occupants [allottees] become capable of transacting their own affairs, issue patents therefor to such occupants, with such restrictions of the power of alienation as he may see fit to impose."[114] Presumably, such restriction was based on the ability to speak, read, and write the English language and to understand the American monetary system. The treaty does not say how restrictions on the patents would be removed, but we can reasonably assume that this would occur under the president's rule-making power.

To initiate the allotment process described by Article 3, the president could survey the reservations to create allottable tracts eighty acres in size. In other words, sections one-mile square would be divided again into quarters, with each allottee receiving one-half of the quarter, or one-eighth of a section. The phrase "the president may from time to time, at his discretion, cause the whole to be surveyed" implies that the allotment process was to be ongoing.[115] The result of this wording would be that Indian allotments would eventually take up all of the land within the exterior boundaries of the reservation.

Article 4 specifies the payments that would be received by the Ojibwe for the land cession. Briefly stated, the United States agreed to pay five thousand dollars in coin and eight thousand dollars in goods annually for twenty years. In addition, tools, implements, and livestock would be provided to encourage agriculture, although the treaty also provided one hundred rifles, ammunition, and five hundred beaver traps to support traditional subsistence practices and the fur economy. In order to repair iron tools and make new ones, the government agreed to provide a blacksmith and a smithy at each reservation.

In a controversial provision also found in Article 4, the United States provided the "sum of ninety thousand dollars, as the chiefs in open council may direct, to enable them to meet their present just engagements."[116] In effect, this was a government payout to the fur companies and their agents. In his report to Commissioner Manypenny after negotiating the treaty, Henry Gilbert described this provision of the treaty as an "embarrassment" but noted that the Indians, doubtlessly at the bidding of their creditors, insisted on its inclusion in the treaty document.[117]

One of the main reasons that the Ojibwe would have needed to leave their reservations was to visit blacksmith shops provided as benefits of former treaties. Apprehensive as they were of leaving their reservations, the Ojibwe insisted that blacksmith shops be provided on each of their reservations. The government agreed to this by Article 5.

Article 6 prohibited the practice of traders forcing Indians to surrender annuity payments for the payments of individual debts. This was a standard practice of the day because traders customarily attended annuity payments and literally collected for debts as soon as payments were received by the Indian debtor. The sale of spirituous liquors on either reservations or the ceded territory was prohibited by Article 7. This ban could, however, be lifted by the president. In Article 8 the Ojibwe of Lake Superior and the Ojibwe of the Mississippi agreed to a split of the annuities due under former treaties, such that the Lake Superior people who actually lived on the land ceded would receive two-thirds, while the Mississippi Ojibwe would receive the rest.

By Article 9 the United States agreed to audit the payments due under former treaties, in order to determine if there were any equitable arrears. If so, these were to be paid forthwith. This provision was particularly important to the L'Anse Ojibwe, because they had not attended payments for three years during the failed removal efforts of the early 1850s. They were anxious to receive these payments.

Since some missionaries, a few teachers, and other government employees were currently living on and had made improvements to the lands that were to become Indian reservations under terms of the 1854 treaty, these people were permitted by Article 10 to buy up to one-quarter of a section of land that would incorporate any improvements they may have made. Thus, Article 10 was a de facto preemption provision that bestowed the right to purchase land on those who had served the Indian communities. In permitting agency personnel and missionaries to obtain 160 acres of land—twice as much as Indians—the treaty framers were likely recognizing that much of this land would actually be held for Indian benefit, as, for example, the Catholic and Methodist holdings at L'Anse.

Article 11 was of particular importance to the Lake Superior Ojibwe. In part it provided that "all annuity payments to the Chippewas of Lake Superior, shall hereafter be paid at L'Anse, La Pointe, Grand Portage, and on the St. Louis River [Fond du Lac]; and the Indians shall not be required to remove from the homes hereby set apart for them."[118] This article was requested by the Ojibwe as a direct outcome of the fear they felt as a result of the Sandy Lake affair in the fall of 1851, when the government lured the Lake Superior Ojibwe west to receive their annuity payments. This action resulted in hundreds of deaths by disease and starvation when the Wisconsin Ojibwe were trapped by winter ice. Article 11 solemnly guarantees that the signatory band would never, for any reason, be required involuntarily to leave or give up their reservations created by the treaty.

Article 12 of the treaty deals with the special circumstances of the Bois Forte band, which is the most northern and western of the Lake Superior Ojibwe. Article 13 is a standard provision of Manypenny treaties that confirms the effective date of the treaty.

In 1860 the secretary of the interior, Jacob Thompson, summed up the government's policy toward Indians during the last several years. First, he divided Indians into two classes: those who had treaty relations with the United States and those who did not. Treaty Indians were again divided into two classes. The first classification consisted of treaties of peace and amity, but without governmental recognition of title to any particular tract of land. The second classification consisted of those with whom title to particular tracts of country was recognized and whose undisturbed possession of those tracts was guaranteed. This subclass was again divided into two more types: those who held their lands in common, whether in fee or by the usual Indian title, and those whose lands were held in severalty by the individual members of the tribe. Thompson went on to observe, "There is yet a further distinction to be made between those cases where the several reservations [allotments to individuals] are in a compact body, surrounded by a well-defined exterior boundary, constituting them a tribal reservation, over which the intercourse laws could be enforced, and those in which the individual reservations [allotments] are scattered among the white settlements, and subjected to the operation of the laws of the state or territory in which they are situated."[119]

The critical distinction Secretary Thompson made between two later kinds of reservations created by treaty is appropriate to the present discussion. A simple treaty mechanism created this difference, that is, a surplus land provision that opened nonallotted land, or so-called surplus land, to public sale and thus guaranteed that allotments would be "scattered among the white settlements." No surplus land provision is found in the 1854 treaty, thereby indicating that the government and the Ojibwe were trying to and did create a "tribal reservation" with a strong exterior boundary and the allotments in a compact body. No subsequent act of Congress or executive order has altered the major provisions of the 1854 treaty. The Keweenaw Bay Reservation remains as it was created in 1854, that is, four adjacent townships of land surrounded by an exterior boundary.

CHAPTER 15

Keweenaw Bay Indian Community v. Michigan, Western District of Michigan, Case No. 784 F. Supp. 418, 427

Bruce R. Greene
The Law Office of Bruce R. Greene & Associates, LLC, Boulder, Colorado

The Keweenaw Bay Indian Community is a small tribe of Lake Superior Chippewa Indians located at the base of Keweenaw Bay, Michigan, on the south shore of Lake Superior. The Keweenaw Bay Indian Community is a federally recognized Indian tribe, with a venerable treaty history with the United States. Tribal headquarters are located in Baraga, Michigan, on the west side of Keweenaw Bay, although tribal members also reside on the east side of the bay, in and near the town of L'Anse.

For many, many years, prior to the successful conclusion of the litigation described in this chapter, the reservation boundary at the Keweenaw Bay Indian Community was uncertain. The genesis of the problem was rooted in the 1854 Treaty of La Pointe,[1] which created the tribe's reservation. Article II of that treaty provided in pertinent part that "the United States agree to set apart and withhold from sale, for the use of the Chippewa of Lake Superior, the following-described tracts of land, viz: 1st. For the L'Anse and Vieux De Sert bands, *all of the unsold lands in the following townships* in the State of Michigan [approximately three townships were identified]" (emphasis added). The issue in the litigation was whether the reservation boundary followed the township lines referred to in the treaty or merely encircled unsold parcels of land within those townships, creating a so-called checkerboard reservation.

Predecessors in interest to the modern-day Keweenaw Bay Indian Community signed two treaties with the United States, one in 1842 and the second in 1854. Under the Treaty of 1842,[2] signed on October 4, the Chippewas in the western half of Michigan's Upper Peninsula, along with Chippewa Indians residing in northern Wisconsin, conveyed their aboriginal territory to the United States. Underlying the ceded territory were vast and valuable mineral deposits, primarily copper and iron ore, which the United States wanted to exploit. The Indians' occupation of those lands, the United States feared, would interfere with any mineral exploitation. Thus, the desire to extract the minerals from that area became the driving force behind the 1842 treaty.

Although Article III of the 1842 treaty contained language contemplating the removal of the Keweenaw Bay band to the western area of the Mississippi Chippewa in Minnesota, it was thought at the time that if removal was in fact required, it would not take place for many years in the future. Article VI of the 1842 treaty provided for the removal of the Chippewa from the mineral district, at the pleasure of the president. This provision appeared to reinforce the notion that removal to the west, to the area of the Mississippi Chippewa, was less likely because mineral extraction could occur notwithstanding the presence of the Indians. Thus, mineral extraction could occur either because the Keweenaw Bay Chippewa did not reside where the minerals were located or because, if they did, they could be removed from the mineral district and still remain within their aboriginal territory. Indeed, the 1842 treaty also contained typical provisions, found in many other treaties, whereby the Indians received annuities, goods, and services from the United States, including blacksmiths, carpenter shops, and schools. The provision of these goods and services was antithetical to the removal of the Indians to the west, since none of these goods and services would be needed in Michigan if the Chippewa were to be relocated to the area of the Mississippi Chippewa.

The second treaty with the predecessors of the Keweenaw Bay Indian Community, the Treaty of La Pointe, was entered into in 1854.[3] This treaty set aside six different reservations for Chippewa residing in the 1842 area of cession. The reservations were located in northern Michigan and Wisconsin. While many treaties of this era contained cession language followed by land reserves withheld from the cession, the 1842 treaty and the 1854 treaty accomplished the same end but in two separate treaties. Thus, the cession language was contained in the earlier treaty, while the creation of the reservations within the area of cession for the Chippewa was found in the later treaty. The reservation for the Keweenaw Bay Indian Community was the easternmost created under the 1854 treaty. The language in the treaty creating the reservation provided that "all of the unsold lands" in approximately three named townships was to be set aside as a reservation for them.

Modernly, uncertainty regarding the location of the reservation boundary created law enforcement problems for the tribe, the state, and the federal government. Notwithstanding numerous exceptions not pertinent here, states generally do not have jurisdiction within reservation boundaries. For example, if an Indian commits a major crime[4] within the exterior boundary of a reservation, only the federal government may prosecute him or her for the alleged offense, even if the alleged offense was committed on so-called fee lands within that reservation boundary. Most Indian reservations contain some fee lands within the reservation boundary. The fee lands are owned sometimes by non-Indians, sometimes by individual Indians, and sometimes by the tribe itself. Irrespective of the status of the landownership, if the land where the alleged criminal offense occurred is located within the exterior boundary of the reservation, it is "Indian country,"[5] and the federal government has exclusive jurisdiction to prosecute the Indian perpetrator.

If the Keweenaw Bay Indian Community reservation boundary followed the township lines specified in the 1854 treaty, there would be no issue regarding which entity had jurisdiction to prosecute a criminal offense. Picture, however, the situation of the boundary of a checkerboard reservation: instead of a reservation boundary following the township lines, only lands owned by the tribe in trust would constitute the tribe's reservation. Thus, the reservation boundary would be those lines that encircle each parcel of trust land owned by the tribe. All fee lands, irrespective of the owner, would be excluded from the reservation of the tribe. Some of those "reservation" parcels might be contiguous, but many would not. There is a substantial amount of fee lands within the townships identified in the 1854 treaty, including the towns of L'Anse and Baraga, where there are numerous non-Indian businesses and residences. A law enforcement officer driving within the townships identified in the treaty would need a plat book showing current ownership of each parcel of land in order to determine whether the state, the tribe, or the federal government had jurisdiction over an alleged criminal offense. Land that was "sold" at the time of the treaty but subsequently reacquired by the tribe and placed into trust probably would not be a part of the "reservation." Similar problems arise in the civil context as well. For example, Indian tribes have some civil regulatory authority over lands within their reservation boundaries, such as zoning authority. If the reservation boundary did not follow the township lines, the tribe's civil regulatory authority would only pertain to tribally owned trust land that was "unsold" in 1854, since each such parcel would constitute the tribe's reservation.

In 1988, the tribe filed suit against the state of Michigan in the U.S. District Court for the Western District of Michigan, seeking a declaration that the tribe's reservation boundary follows the township lines identified in the treaty. The state's position, described by the court as "rather straightforward,"[6] was based on what it characterized as the plain meaning of the treaty. Thus, the state contended that all the government gave to the tribe under the 1854 treaty were those lands that were unsold at the time of the treaty. That would have excluded fee lands owned by non-Indians, as well as lands that had passed to the state by operation of law prior to the treaty. These would be swamplands, canal lands, and school lands.[7] Boundary, according to the state, was of no special interest or concern of the Indians, since the reservation was only temporary. Thus, the state's view was that the 1854 treaty authorized the allotment of lands to tribal members. When the land was fully allotted, the treaty was fully executed. The treaty was, according to the state, "a form of self-executing land distribution."[8]

The tribe's position was that the lawsuit was fundamentally a treaty interpretation case. In other words, to understand whether the boundary line followed the township lines, it was necessary to understand the treaty, what it was trying to accomplish, the intentions of the parties (i.e., the United States and the Indians), and most important, the Indians' understanding of what was transpiring as a result of the treaty. A treaty, after all, is a public contract between sovereigns. To discern the meaning of the contract, it is necessary to understand the interests and motives of the parties. In addition, certain rules of treaty interpretation must be followed. For example, the treaty must be construed consistent with the Indians' understanding, and ambiguities in the treaty must be resolved in the Indians' favor.[9]

With those rules in mind, the court conducted an eight-day bench trial. Witnesses included two anthropologists/ethnohistorians for the tribe and one such expert for the state, in addition to the testimony of tribal officials and members. Based on that testimony, the court made extensive findings of fact.

The court found that the earliest historic records reflect that there has always been a band of Lake Superior Chippewa Indians living in and around Keweenaw Bay. The Indians subsisted consistent with their traditional lifestyle and engaged in their traditional rounds of hunting and trapping in the winter and fishing in the spring, summer, and fall. In 1832, the American Fur Company established a post at Keweenaw Bay, where it conducted its usual business of supplying goods to the Indians and buying fish from them. The earliest demographic statistics show that in 1832 the population at Keweenaw Bay consisted of 140 people, 112 of whom were Indians and 28 of whom were métis (French Canadian voyagers who intermarried with the Indians). By 1850, about 640 Indians lived there, constituting 80 percent of the population. In 1833, Methodist missionaries arrived, followed by Catholic missionaries in 1842. Permanent churches, schools, and houses were built, and the missionaries worked with the Indians to "civilize" them by, among other things, urging them to wear the clothes of the white men. As discussed, the 1842 treaty was motivated by the U.S. desire to exploit the mineral estate. Since that was not where the Indians from Keweenaw Bay resided, the Chippewa were advised that their lifestyle would be unchanged after the treaty was concluded. The Indians were greatly frightened by the possibility of removal. Indeed, Henry C. Gilbert, the Indian agent who later negotiated the 1854 treaty, reported in one document that removal was "the great terror of their [the Indians'] lives and I hazard nothing in saying they will sooner submit to extermination than comply with it."[10] Beginning in 1845, the land in that area of Michigan was being surveyed. Completion of surveying in that area meant that land sales would be facilitated, and such sales signified more non-Indian settlers might move to the area. The Indians feared such settlement was the precursor to removal. Indeed, in 1850, the president issued a removal order, which was rescinded a year later.

The court understood why specific townships were used to identify the Keweenaw Bay Indian Community reservation, while the other reservations created under the 1854 treaty were described by metes and bounds or in even more general terms in some circumstances, such as a parcel of land of a specified size with the boundaries to be located at a later date. Surveying the United States was a long process, which began in the east and moved westward. At the time of the 1854 treaty, the area around Keweenaw Bay was as far west as the survey had proceeded in the upper Great Lakes region. Indeed, little was known about the geography of areas to the west. Without a survey, the best description available was by metes and bounds. However, in the case of the westernmost reservations under the treaty for the Lac Courte Oreilles and the Lac du Flambeau Bands of Lake Superior Chippewa Indians, so little was known about the territory that even description by metes and bounds was not possible. There was nothing in the treaty or the documents supporting the treaty to suggest that Keweenaw Bay Indian Community's reservation was to be treated differently than the reservations set aside for the other Lake Superior Chippewa simply because it was described by townships rather than metes and bounds. Thus, there was no particular significance to the use of the unsold lands within specified townships other than the fact that the survey of the area made that description possible.

The court also found that although there were some patented parcels within the townships described in the 1854 treaty, most of them were occupied by Indian residences, with the land having been purchased by the Indians or the Catholic and Methodist missionaries. According to the court, "It defies common sense to conclude that Indians would seek a treaty to create a permanent home for themselves and exclude the Indian villages and the property upon which many of their own residences were located."[11] Indeed, there were approximately 60,000 acres of land within the townships described in the treaty, of which 2,600 acres were sold at the time of the treaty. All but 970 acres of the 2,600 acres were lands not being used for the benefit of the Indians. The 970 acres were held in seven parcels, and land speculators who did not reside on them owned six of those. Thus, according to the court, from the Indians' perspective, "they would have been 'on notice' of but one unaffiliated white landowner within the townships which formed their reservation."[12] With respect to school lands, canal lands, and swamplands, the Indians would not have been aware of their title. Indeed, they were undeveloped and unoccupied, further supporting the Indians' understanding that they were a part of their reservation.

After hearing all the testimony, the court concluded that the boundary of the reservation was understood by the Indians and intended by the United States to follow the township lines described in the treaty. Although the sold lands within that boundary were not available for allotment by the Indians, there was no logical reason or explanation for excluding those lands from the reservation. If they were excluded, a checkerboard reservation would have been created, which was not the intention of any of the parties to the 1854 treaty.

The successful conclusion of this litigation has been of great importance to the tribe. No longer is there uncertainty about the location of the boundary. Criminal law enforcement is substantially easier and more efficient as a result of this litigation, and the tribe, as well as the state, understands the territorial extent of the tribe's authority.

CHAPTER 16

Factionalism and Removal: The Stockbridge and Munsee, 1830–56

During the dark years of the American Revolution, the Indian tribes of northern New York sent their warriors on a series of devastating raids against the American colonial settlements of the Mohawk Valley and northeastern Pennsylvania. Only the Mohican—Christianized, English-speaking Algonquian Indians of the Hudson River Valley—and the Oneida, one of the tribes of the Iroquois League, stood beside the colonists. Perhaps as a reward for their faith in the American cause, the new government of the United States helped both of these tribes acquire land in Wisconsin during the early nineteenth century. Although the story of their immigration to Wisconsin is complex, it suffices to say that by a treaty with the Menominee tribe in 1831, the Mohican, who consisted of members of the Stockbridge and Munsee tribes, received a reservation of two townships on the east side of Lake Winnebago (see map 20), while the Oneida received land west of the Fox River.

Development of the Removal Policy

Following the difficult years of the American Revolution and the War of 1812, the United States found itself with a vastly depleted treasury, a weak central government, and a population reluctant to suffer the burden of taxation. The apparent solution to raising much-needed hard currency was for the government to convert its enormous existing and potential land reserves into cash by selling the land to pioneer settlers; these yeoman farmers would clear the land and convert the wilderness to productive farms. Having recently pushed the national borders west to the Mississippi and, by the Louisiana Purchase of 1803, far to the unexplored west, the United States had practically limitless land resources.

In the years after the election of President Andrew Jackson (1829–37), continued American settlement in the trans-Allegheny west brought conflict between the tribes that held extensive tracts of productive agricultural land and American settlers. A solution to this problem seemed to be treaties with the tribes for a voluntary exchange of their eastern land reserves for land west of the Mississippi River. Not only would this free more land for sale to non-Indian settlers, but it would, in the perspective of many eastern reformers and liberals, provide the opportunity to form Indian colonies in the west where Indians could be taught the arts of civilization in an atmosphere that was free of the corrupting influence of traders and whiskey peddlers. After considerable public debate, on May 28, 1830, Congress passed the Indian Removal Act. Under this legislation, the president was empowered "to exchange any or all such districts, so to be laid off and described, with any tribe or nation of Indians now residing within the limits of any of the states or territories, and with which the United States having existing treaties, for the whole or any part or portion of the territory claimed and occupied by such tribe or nation."[1]

By the terms of the Indian Removal Act, a proper removal treaty required a precise description of the land to be relinquished and that to be acquired by the tribe, a purchase price, assistance in removal, a date certain for removal, aid in establishing new settlements, a provision for appraisal and payment for improvements in the territory ceded, and arrangements for payment of existing and future annuities at the removal destination. During the 1830s, numerous removal treaties were negotiated between the United States and the southeastern and midwestern tribes. Unfortunately, many of the removals, particularly in the southeast, which involved the Cherokee and the other "civilized" tribes, became blatantly coercive.[2]

The pressure to remove the eastern tribes was not primarily driven by forces bent on the benevolent objectives of bringing Indians to a civilized state. Instead, the very pattern of removal

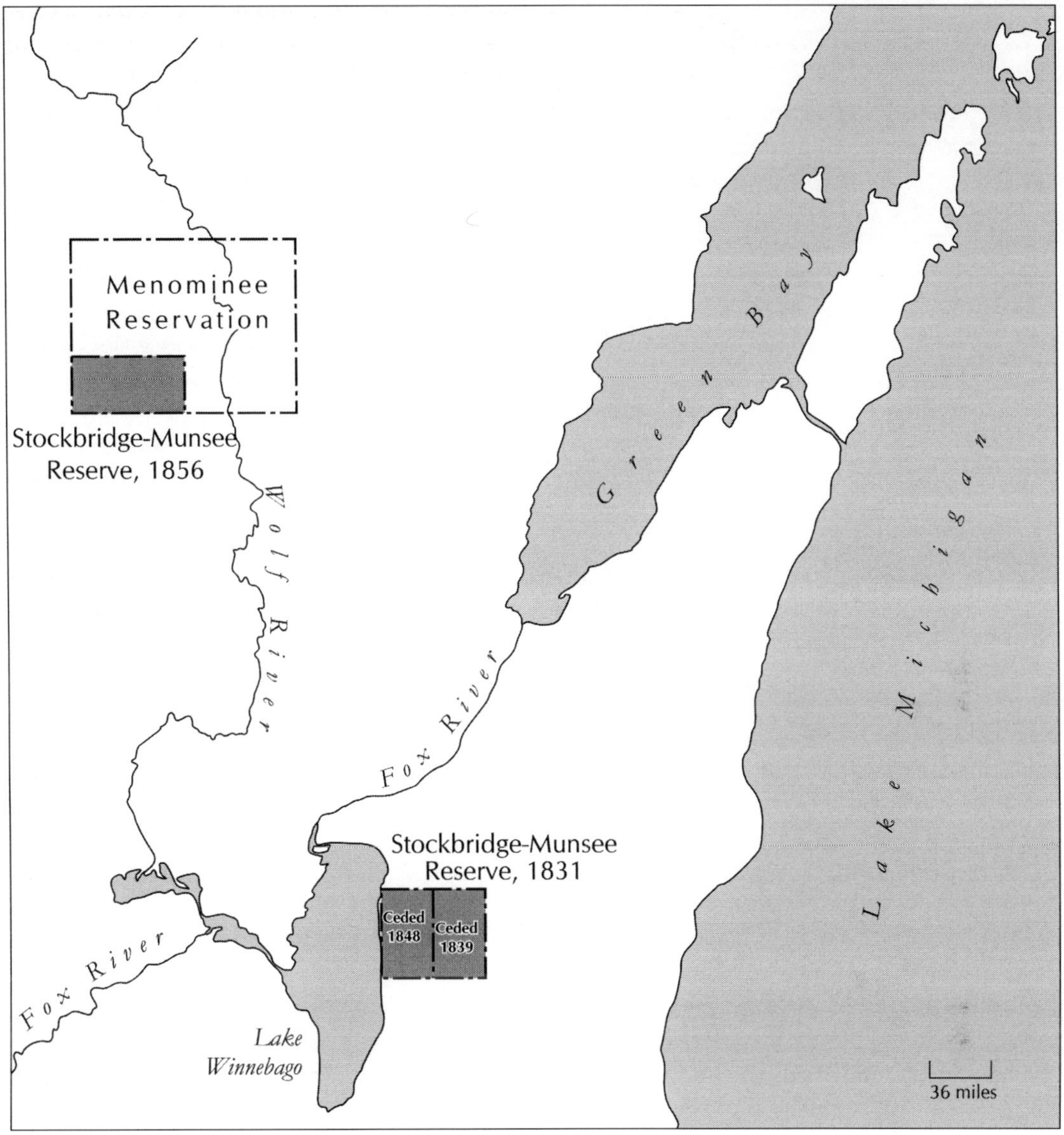

Map 20. Location of Stockbridge-Munsee reserves created by treaties of 1831 and 1856

demonstrates that those tribes that held the most productive agricultural land were those who received the greatest and most irresistible pressure to remove. This desirable agricultural land was quickly taken up by pioneer immigrants during the land boom of the mid-1830s. The agricultural tribes of northern Illinois, Indiana, and southern Michigan and Wisconsin—for example, the Potawatomi, Ho-Chunk (Winnebago), Miami, and related groups—signed removal treaties and were sometimes removed by force.[3] Examples include treaties with the Seneca in 1831,[4] the Shawnee also in 1831,[5] the Potawatomi in 1833,[6] and the Winnebago in 1832.[7]

To the north, however, where the rich midwestern prairie land met the Great Lakes forest, the growing season was much shorter, and the soil was thin and poor. Here the demand for farmland to accommodate immigrant settlers was much reduced, and the Indian removal effort lost its intensity. The United States wrote quasi removal treaties with several northern tribes, such as the Ottawa and Chippewa in 1836,[8] the Chippewa in 1842,[9] and the Stockbridge in 1848.[10] In these cases, removal was voluntary, on an indefinite timetable, and to places to be eventually determined by exploring parties.

Even farther to the north, it became clear that the main value of the land was not as farmland but for its timber and mineral resources. Here no real conflict with Indians was anticipated, since the extraction of resources and Indian occupancy would not conflict in any serious way. Indian treaties in this region contain very weak or no removal provisions at all. Examples include the Chippewa Treaty of 1837[11] and the Menominee Treaty of 1848.[12]

To Remove or Not: Indian Strategy

Since the earliest years of the American Republic, the cornerstone of its Indian policy has been to ultimately acculturate native people so that they could be brought into the mainstream of American society. American political leaders from Jefferson onward fostered the ideal that the government must treat Indians with fairness. This is clear from the first comprehensive statement of American Indian policy found in the words of the Northwest Ordinance, proclaimed in 1787, which observed in part that

> the utmost good faith shall always be observed towards Indians; their lands and property shall never be taken from them without their consent; and in their property rights and liberty, they never shall be invaded or disturbed unless in just and lawful wars authorized by Congress; but laws founded in justice and humanity shall from time to time be made, for preventing wrong being done to them and for preserving peace and friendship with them.[13]

This simple statement of goodwill and responsibility has underlain America's relationship with native people throughout the history of the country.

Bringing "civilization" to people with vastly different cultures, languages, ethics, morals, and domestic economics was a much more difficult task in practice. It required not only destroying indigenous ideals but, further, substituting those deemed compatible with American social norms. As American reformers saw it, Indians must ultimately pass from a tribal state to a civilized one. By this they meant that Christianity must replace paganism, modern agriculture must supersede the chase, and settled life must supplant a wandering mode of existence. Indians had to be taught the English language, to read and write, and to appreciate the sanctity of private property and the inherent value of physical toil. The rule of democratic principles must replace the egalitarianism of tribal politics, and the precepts of capitalism and mercantilism must prevail over the indigenous economy, with its strictures against producing surplus and hoarding wealth. This was indeed a challenging and often discouraging task for the teachers, agents, and clerics who faced the job. Adopting new ways created factionalism within families, as well as within and between Indian groups. The most troubling of these was confusion between cultural practice, on the one hand, and ethnic identity, on the other.

Such factionalism was noted among the Stockbridge and Munsee by Agent Boyd in 1838, when he warned of a division between the fully acculturated members under the leadership of the missionary Rev. Cutting Marsh and those "who wish to remain tribal and remove west."[14] It is difficult to assess the depth or source of the original split in the Stockbridge and Munsee group, but such divisions were common, if not universal, among Indian tribes who were subject to intense pressure to acculturate. Depending on perspective, Indian people at the time saw vastly different futures. Some opted for change, others for clinging to ancient traditions. In each case, the common goal was to maintain a sense of Indian identity and political viability.

Indian groups often touted their advances toward civilization, because they knew that if they were perceived by the government as civilized, they would have access to more benefits than if they were perceived as unrepentant "barbarians." In the case of the Stockbridge and Munsee, it seems evident that the majority sensed that their best hope of maintaining the integrity of their community at Stockbridge was to identify with the American citizens who were taking up farms in Wisconsin in increasing numbers. This did not mean that they repudiated their identity as Stockbridge or Munsee, but they did not believe there was a future in promoting their Indian identity given the tenor of the times.

During the 1830s, the government was actively trying to remove Indians west. Many eastern tribes who occupied good agricultural land and made their living as farmers were loathe to move to the arid land in the west, where they would be surrounded by "wild" Indians who were hostile to eastern intruders.[15] The "citizen" faction of the Stockbridge and Munsee was one of these groups. These people hoped to maintain their land at Lake Winnebago, to become citizens of the Wisconsin territory, and to exercise the rights of citizenship in a democratic society.

Another survival strategy common at the time was to embrace an Indian identity and to rely on the largesse of the Great Father. After all, Indian people had been conditioned to this course since the earliest inception of American Indian policy. Some of the Stockbridge and Munsee saw this option as the best avenue to maintain their identity and to assure their survival. For these individuals of the so-called Indian Party, the prospect of treaty annuities, support for economic ventures, and the promise of good agricultural land on the remote frontiers of the United States seemed the better course.

It was not unusual among native groups for just this kind of difference of opinion to lead to factionalism, and it can be seen as a major feature of the history of such Great Lakes groups as the Ottawa, Potawatomi, and Stockbridge and Munsee. In the latter case, the division was both bitter and long lasting, for the simple reason that both factions were able to find and to cultivate political support from outside of the tribe. In most cases, the interest of outside groups was, however, detrimental to the ends the Stockbridge and Munsee factions hoped to achieve.

The Stockbridge Factionalism and American Law

All things considered, the Stockbridge and Munsee seemed to be more sophisticated in dealing with the federal government than most Native American groups of the early nineteenth century. They were both conversant in the English language and Christians, as well as affluent enough to be able to send delegations to Washington on a frequent basis. In fact, James Oberly titled his recent book on the history of the Stockbridge and Munsee *A Nation of Statesmen*.[16] These delegations and emissaries represented their various interests, not only to the Indian Office but also to Congress. This situation, in addition to the aid of their non-Indian allies in the church and government, sharpened factional competition and led to a complex series of congressional acts and treaties that confused and complicated tribal affairs during the first half of the nineteenth century.

The Stockbridge and Munsee prospered on the two township reserves on Lake Winnebago until 1843. The soil was excellent, and these skilled farmers were soon prosperous. Unfortunately, the Treaty of 1831, which created the reserve, did not make provision to survey and allot the land, which was soon subject to encroachment of settlers who began buying and leasing land from individual tribal members.

To settle this problem, Albert Gallup was sent to Stockbridge to negotiate a new treaty. The first article of the Treaty of 1839 ceded the eastern half of the reserve, leaving the western township as the new reservation (see map 20).[17] By the second article, a census roll was prepared and appended to the treaty, listing all those heads of families who wished to immigrate west of the Mississippi. The list indicates that eighty men, women, and children had a desire to head west. These people were members of the Indian Party, who were paid $8,767.75 as full compensation for their interest in the ceded land. Members of the Citizen Party, those who would remain on the unceded township, were paid $10,392.95 for their share of the land ceded. Article 6 of the 1839 treaty provided for an exploratory party to go west to find suitable land for the emigrants and to pay expenses for this enterprise. A final article made arrangements to adjust money claims that existed between emigrants and those who would remain.

This was a hopelessly unspecific treaty that contained omissions that only exacerbated the problem of the Stockbridge and Munsee. For example, the treaty did not provide for any firm destination for the emigrant faction, did not make citizens of the Stockbridge and Munsee who remained, and did not allot the remaining township to individuals. In the year following the treaty, 174 Stockbridge, Munsee, and Delaware removed from Stockbridge to Missouri without government assistance.[18] More followed, until it was estimated that only 276 people remained at Stockbridge in 1844.[19] Matters did not improve under the 1839 treaty, and the Citizen Party continued to lobby Congress for land allotments. Apparently, many of those who had immigrated were also dissatisfied because no permanent reserve land had been found in the west. Most of the emigrating Indian Party eventually returned to the Wisconsin reservation.[20]

The Acts of 1843 and 1846

As a result of congressional lobbying by the "Citizen" Stockbridge, Congress passed a new act on March 3, 1843. This inept piece of legislation was called "An Act for the Relief of the Stockbridge Tribe of Indians in the Territory of Wisconsin."[21] Under this act, the township of land comprising their reservation was to be surveyed and allotted to individual Stockbridge and Munsee who remained at Stockbridge on Lake Winnebago. All were to have the rights of citizenship. The Indian Party correctly perceived that they would be giving up their position as wards of the government and also, by the operation of citizenship, their only protection against alienation of the land.[22]

Members of the Indian Party flatly refused to be governed by the Act of 1843 and actively lobbied Congress for its repeal. The act made the day-to-day affairs at Stockbridge worse and hardened the factionalism within the tribe. Another unfortunate outcome of the 1843 act was that since the act contained no safeguards against alienation of the land, many Stockbridge sold their new allotments to non-Indians, creating a checkerboard of Indian and non-Indian ownership on the reserve land.

Under intense lobbying by representatives of the Indian Party, Congress again stepped in during 1846 with another act, called "An Act to Repeal the Act of March 3, 1843," which was approved on August 6. Section 1 repealed the 1843 act and restored the Stockbridge tribe to its "ancient form of government." Presumably, this meant that they would be governed by traditional sachems and counselors rather than elected ones.[23]

The 1846 act instituted an enrollment of all Stockbridge and Munsee who wished to become citizens. After this enrollment, the township composing the reservation would be divided into two parts, with half to go to the Citizen Party and half to the Indian Party. The Indian Party land was to be held in common, and the Citizen Party portion was to be subdivided into allotments and patented to each recipient. All previous patents to any piece of land would be void. Thereafter, allottees were not to receive benefits from future treaties.

In the year after the 1846 act, the annual report of the commissioner of Indian affairs pointed out that serious flaws in the act made it totally impracticable. The report concurred with Wisconsin governor Henry Dodge that the only solution to the Stockbridge and Munsee situation was "to completely buy out the reservation."[24] The first problem was that since many Stockbridge had sold allotted land to non-Indians after the 1843 act and since Citizen Party members had taken allotment all across the township, there was no longer the possibility of a good or equitable basis for the division of the reservation.[25] Citizen Party members did not accept the act and refused to register for citizenship, because they claimed they were already citizens.[26] From their point of view, the interests in the reservation by members of the Indian Party had been bought out by the 1843 act. In comparison, the Indian Party believed that the 1846 act made them all Stockbridge Indians again and that they were all, therefore, entitled to an interest in the remaining land. It was now up to the Indian Office to try to straighten out the mess at Stockbridge, and it did so by sending Green Bay subagent Albert G. Ellis and Wisconsin lawyer Morgan L. Martin to negotiate a new treaty. This treaty was concluded at Stockbridge on November 24, 1848.[27]

The Treaty of 1848

After a long preamble detailing the failure of congressional legislation, Article 1 of the Treaty of 1848 again repealed the Act of 1843. Presumably, this provision wiped out the citizenship lists and all the allotments made as a result of that act. By Article 1 the Stockbridge acknowledged the guardianship of the United States in the same manner as other Indian tribes. Article 2 called for a census of the tribe so that any remaining question about who was a member of the tribe would be forever concluded.

In Article 3 the Stockbridge and Munsee tribe ceded to the United States its interest in the township of land on Lake Winnebago. Article 4 called for the survey of allotments issued to "Citizen Indians" under the 1843 act and the issuance of patents to these parcels. The remaining or unpatented land would be sold by the United States. For this land cession, the tribe would be paid $16,500. An additional sum was to be paid to the tribe for improvements made on the ceded land.

Article 7 called for the removal of the tribe to lands that would be acquired for them in the immediate future west of the Mississippi. In the meantime, they could occupy the reservation for one year. By Article 8 the United States agreed to pay the expense of immigration. A stock fund was created in Article 9 by the investment of $16,500 to be paid to "the rising generation," that is, young people who were not old enough to benefit from immediate payments for land and improvements ceded by the present treaty.

A supplemental article to the treaty relinquished older claims to money and land made by the Stockbridge and Munsee tribe under former treaties for the sum of twenty-five thousand dollars. The United States also promised to provide two townships of land west of the Mississippi River for a permanent home within two years.

The treaty was signed by twenty-seven men who were the sachems, counselors, and headmen of the Stockbridge and Munsee tribe. Interestingly, fourteen, or more than half, signed with a mark rather than a signature, indicating that they were not literate in the English language. To the Treaty of 1848 was appended several lists, including the census of the tribe, totaling 177 members.

Regrettably, the 1848 treaty did not resolve the problems of the Stockbridge and Munsee tribe. Irrespective of the 1848 treaty, members of the Citizen Party continued to claim rights under the Act of 1843 and to reject the Act of 1846, while the Indian Party believed that the Act of 1843 had wronged them and that the Act of 1846 had restored their interests. Meanwhile, following the 1848 cession, white settlers crowded on to the newly ceded land, usurping Indian farmsteads, until they soon outnumbered the 360 Stockbridge and Munsee on their reserve lands three to one.[28] The provision of the treaty requiring the government to find western land within two years was not carried out. Trapped at Stockbridge without land or means of making a livelihood, the Stockbridge and Munsee were forced to spend the money they received as payment under the treaty just to survive, and the once prosperous farmers were soon homeless and destitute.[29]

The Acts of 1843 and 1846, as well as the Treaty of 1848, contained removal provisions but were not removal instruments in the sense that their main purpose was to acquire Indian land for white settlement. All of these actions by the government were attempts to accommodate one or both of the Stockbridge and Munsee factions, each of which was pursuing different political strategies in the hope of retaining their identity and political viability in the face of a rapidly changing social and political landscape. In the end, the Stockbridge and Munsee were not removed but, for a variety of reasons, were permitted to remain in Wisconsin. Not least among these reasons was a sharp shift in government policy away from the objectives of the old removal policy of the 1830s.

The Treaty with the Stockbridge and Munsee from February 5, 1856

Finally, after his third year as commissioner of Indian affairs, George Manypenny turned his attention to the crisis on the former Stockbridge and Munsee Reservation. By that point in his career, Manypenny had written nearly fifty treaties with Indian tribes and had developed his reservation policy to a fine degree. On January 6, 1856, he wrote to Francis Huebschmann, superintendent of the Northern Superintendency, notifying him that he was to be the commissioner for the United States to negotiate a new treaty with the Stockbridge.

Manypenny first told Huebschmann that he had personally met with the secretary of the interior, Robert McClelland, on the Stockbridge situation and was issuing Huebschmann instructions pursuant with that meeting.[30] In typical style, Manypenny gave detailed instructions that reflected his knowledge of the problems faced by the Stockbridge and Munsee as well as his own policy objectives. First, he focused the new treaty on the affairs of the Stockbridge and Munsee who were party to the Treaty of 1839, that is, those who held the Lake Winnebago Reservation. In this manner, he hoped to finesse the factionalism that resulted from the Acts of 1843 and 1846. He told Huebschmann that the new treaty was necessary "not because of any pecuniary interest of the United States . . . but because the peace and welfare of the Indians require it."[31]

Second, he told Huebschmann that it would be very important to the goals of the treaty for the government to "use all its efforts to put a stop to further population dispersions and if possible to unite and settle those Indians together"[32]—in other words, to find a permanent home for the Stockbridge and Munsee from which they would not be removed. To accomplish this, Manypenny wanted to provide a reservation where all factions could settle together. While he acknowledged that common justice required the recognition of the right of some individuals to receive a patent and remain at Stockbridge, he advised Huebschmann to notify the Stockbridge and Munsee that they should abandon all hopes of remaining on their former reservation lands. Finally, Manypenny authorized Huebschmann to try to buy land from the Menominees to accommodate the Stockbridge and Munsee within the state of Wisconsin.

Huebschmann, a German immigrant and medical doctor, was very thorough in his dealing with the Stockbridge and Munsee. The treaty he negotiated was detailed and in conformity with Manypenny's specific instructions as well as Manypenny's reservation policy in general.

The Treaty of 1856 was signed on February 5 and ratified on April 18.[33] It commences with a long preamble that details the treaty and legislative history of the tribe. Importantly, the preamble is anchored on the Treaty of 1839, whose purpose was to settle all of the Stockbridge and Munsee in Wisconsin wherever they were presently located, that is, in Wisconsin, New York, and Canada or west of the Mississippi. This goal was restated for the Treaty of 1856, which was to encompass all of those Stockbridge and Munsee who wished to remain under the care of the government.

Article 1 of the treaty required all of the Stockbridge and Munsee who were parties to the 1839 treaty to jointly and severally cede and relinquish to the United States all their rights in and title to the lands on Lake Winnebago as well as to land they had been offered as a removal destination in Minnesota in 1848. It also discharged the United States from money claims under former treaties. By Article 2 the United States agreed to provide land in Wisconsin near the southern boundary of the Menominee Reservation sufficient to allot each family as well as immigrant Stockbridge and Munsee with forty- and eighty-acre parcels. Money was also provided to aid in removal to the new Wisconsin reservation as well as to help them get settled in farming enterprises, to build a suitable infrastructure, and to pay outstanding debts.

Article 3 required the United States to rapidly survey the new reservation, setting out quarter sections. This article also specified that the tribe itself would assign allotments, under the supervision of the superintendent of the Northern Superintendency, so that each head of family, single person over twenty-one years of age, and orphan child would receive a share. Since Indians had often complained that Manypenny's allotment treaties did not make provision for children who were not of age or for those yet unborn, this treaty promised to reserve sufficient land for the "rising generation."

Article 3 also contained an alienation provision that required the issuance of land certificates, followed in ten years by a patent, provided that the tribal council approved. The patent would not be restricted, so that the land could be sold by the patentee. Article 3 also contained an heirship provision that guaranteed that land could be left to children or other assigns. In cases where persons holding land had no heirs, the land would return to the tribe and could be reassigned with the issuance of new certificates.

Article 4 directed that one-fourth of the money provided for improvements be used for public infrastructure, roads, schoolhouses, and the like. By Article 5 a census was to be taken of all tribal members for the purpose of determining who should be eligible for payments and allotments under the treaty. In recognition that the Stockbridge and Munsee who resided in other places would be eligible to take land allotments on the new reservation, those negotiating the treaty were asked to accept them as "brethren." Such people were, however, required to emigrate to the new reservation within a two-year period.

As typical of many Manypenny treaties, Articles 7 through 12 dealt with funding education and developing road systems and with local issues related to removal and resettlement. Articles 13 through 17 tackled the complexities of land sale and landholdings at the old Lake Winnebago Reservation. By Article 13 the secretary of the interior was empowered to examine sales made by the Stockbridge under the Act of 1843, to determine their legality, and to issue patents to the owners where justified. Where such title was not valid but the lots had been ceded by the Treaty of 1848, these parcels would be sold, and the Indian owners would be paid for their land and improvements.

Article 16 permitted Stockbridge and Munsee Indians who held title to lots at Stockbridge to sever tribal relations and to enjoy the "privileges granted to persons of Indian descent by the State of Wisconsin."[34] A list of twenty-five people wishing such patents was appended. Where any of the provisions of the present treaty were in conflict with the treaties of 1839 or 1848, these former treaty stipulations were abrogated by action of Article 17.

The Treaty of 1856 was signed by Francis Huebschmann for the United States and 122 sachems, counselors, and delegates of the Stockbridge and Munsee tribe. Among the signatories were representatives from New York as well as Wisconsin. Also attached were censuses of 414 people claiming membership as Stockbridge and Munsee and a roll of 43 people who wished to remain at Stockbridge as "citizens."

Analysis of the 1856 Treaty

Simply stated, the goals of the 1856 treaty were to settle the outstanding problems of the Stockbridge and Munsee people; to unite them as a single, unified tribe; and to provide a permanent homeland for them and their progeny. These goals were all consistent with more general ends that Manypenny promoted, that is, to civilize and assimilate Indians into American society. First, their affairs needed to be put in order by providing just the kind of help, encouragement, and protection designed into the Treaty of 1856.

The first and most formidable problem was to resolve their affairs at the Lake Winnebago Reservation, which were largely the result of what Manypenny called "ill-advised legislation on the part of Congress."[35] Manypenny obviously had in mind *all* of the Stockbridge and Munsee, wherever they were located. Writing to John Quinney and Ziba Peter in 1852, Manypenny declared that the only reason he would recommend the negotiation of a new treaty to begin with was "to bring together and unite in harmony as one people, at some suitable location, all members of the Stockbridge and Munsee tribes, wherever situated."[36] This is, undoubtedly, one of the reasons why the amount of land provided for the new reservation was doubled from what was occupied on Lake Winnebago. Potentially enough land was needed for Stockbridge and Munsee from New York, Ontario, Missouri, and Wisconsin and for the rising generation. Further, since the Stockbridge and Munsee were farmers, Article 2 of the treaty promised that one-half of the land of the new reservation would be arable.

Much of the Treaty of 1856 is devoted to resolving debts and land affairs on the old reservation. Reluctantly, Manypenny and Huebschmann allowed a few landed and independent Stockbridge to remain near the town of Stockbridge. But it was obviously their ultimate objective to assimilate Indians, and these few Stockbridge and Munsee seemed ready to look after their own affairs.

The next matter was to provide a new reservation. Huebschmann had been suggesting a Wisconsin location for some time, and this destination seemed to meet the agreement of the Stockbridge and Munsee.[37] Ongoing discussions of a land cession with the Menominee ultimately produced a two-township parcel that was not only different from the one promised during the negotiation of the 1856 treaty but much poorer in terms of agricultural potential.

By the time the 1856 treaty was negotiated, Manypenny had the experience of working out the troublesome aspects of his allotment system.

The problems of land alienation, although not solved, had been addressed in earlier treaties by creating a nonnegotiable certificate, which was issued to allottees and, after a period of time, would be replaced by a patent in fee simple that was also sometimes temporally restricted. In the case of the Stockbridge-Munsee Treaty, two restrictions were put in force. First, after waiting ten years, a certificate holder could receive a patent only with the concurrence of the tribal council and then only when the president of the United States determined it was in the best interest of the certificate holder. If both conditions were met, an assignable patent in fee simple would be issued to the certificate holder. Given the record of fraudulent land loss on the former Stockbridge Reservation, the judgment of both Manypenny and Huebschmann was that the Stockbridge and Munsee needed to be protected from non-Indian speculators within the confines of their new reservation.

There were, in fact, a number of ways that Manypenny had designed reservation systems to achieve his assimilation objectives. When he believed an Indian tribe was on the verge of being capable of protecting their own interest, he set aside a temporary reservation. Within this kind of reserve, he gave individuals of the tribe a period of time to choose allotments and to make private purchases of land. After the expiration of a sufficient restricted period, the unselected or unpurchased land—that is, the "surplus land"—was returned to the government land office for public sale. In such a case, the Indian allotments would be scattered among the holdings of non-Indians. The treaty with the Ottawa and Chippewa of Michigan in 1855 was constructed in this manner.[38]

The treaty Manypenny concluded with the Chippewa of Lake Superior in 1854 shows an alternative construction, where he intended to create a permanent reservation with clear and immutable boundaries.[39] Here allotments were made to heads of families and to single people, with no excess land provision; it was the intention to allot land within the reservation until it was all taken up. In that case the exterior reservation boundary would be permanent.

In the case of the Stockbridge and Munsee Reservation created by the 1856 treaty, it is evident that the United States intended to provide a permanent reservation that would eventually be entirely allotted. The initial allottees would be people emigrating from Stockbridge, plus those expected to come from other Stockbridge and Munsee communities outside of Wisconsin. Land not taken up immediately would be reserved for young people and those not yet born. As it was stated in the treaty in Article 3, the reserve would contain "sufficient land . . . for the rising generation."[40] For evidence that the phrase "rising generation" was understood to indicate that land would be held for allotment to future generations, one can turn to the instructions given to the jury in a case involving timber fraud on the Stockbridge and Munsee Reservation, *U.S. v. Jesse Wybro,* heard by the U.S. District Court for the Eastern District of Wisconsin in 1870. Here Judge Drummond noted, "They [the Stockbridge tribe] are very particular to have this allotment made under the direction of the Superintendent of Indian Affairs [in reference to George Manypenny and the Treaty of 1856] because a portion of the land is to be set off for the young and rising generation."[41] Other documents also clearly indicate that this is the interpretation given to the phrase "rising generation" by the Stockbridge and Munsee. In a petition to agent M. M. Davis, the Indian Party reminded him that "there are also quite a number of the rising generation who have arrived at the age to entitle them to lots, as provided in the treaty, who have not yet selected or made any interest."[42] Thus, the intention of the United States in 1856 was to create a permanent, two-township reservation with definable boundaries that would forever be the estate of the Stockbridge and Munsee tribe. If the intent was otherwise, Manypenny could certainly have ordered that a surplus land provision be included in the treaty.

Although the Treaty of 1856 seems to have met the expectations of most of the Stockbridge and Munsee, it was not supported by all of them. Under Indian Party leader Austin E. Quinney, approximately sixty-seven individuals, or one-fifth of the Stockbridge and Munsee, did not sign the treaty.[43] This faction was unwilling to agree to the provision of the treaty that repealed the Act of 1846. In the view of the Indian Party, the 1846 act terminated the tribal relations of that faction of the tribe that had accepted citizenship as well as allotments at Lake Winnebago and

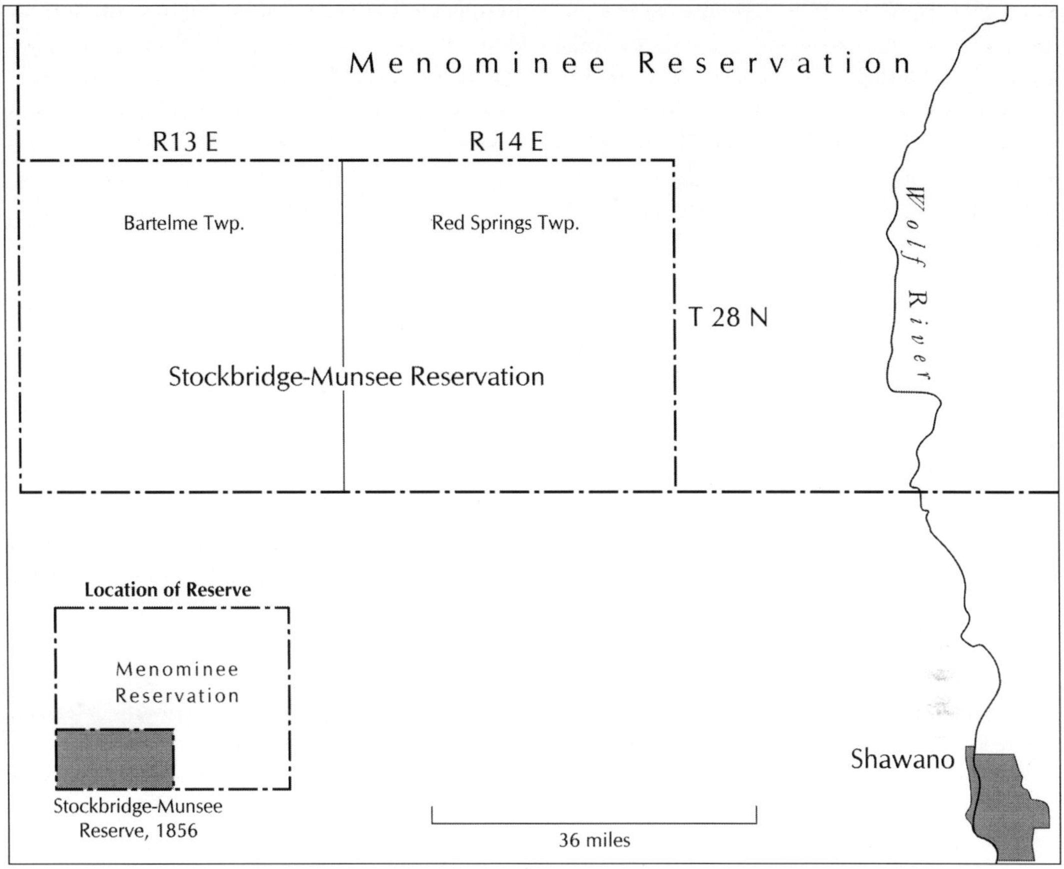

Map 21. The Stockbridge-Munsee Reservation as created by the treaty of 1856

their share of the money for sale of half of the reservation under the 1843 act. These people were generally referred to as "Old Citizens." This issue continued to factionalize the Stockbridge and Munsee for years to come.

The conclusion that the purpose of the 1856 treaty was for the United States to provide a permanent reservation of two townships of land for the Stockbridge and Munsee was affirmed nine years later by the secretary of the interior (map 21). At that time, the state of Wisconsin claimed the sixteenth section in each township that composed the Menominee and the Stockbridge and Munsee reservations. Normally, on the date of admission to the union, the United States granted these sections from the public domain lands to each state for the support of public education. The secretary asked the commissioner of the General Land Office, J. M. Edmunds, to investigate Wisconsin's claim. After a thorough review of the treaty history of the two reservations, Edmunds concluded that the twelve townships of land that had composed the original Menominee Reservation were given by the United States to the Menominee as a permanent homeland with the concurrence of the state of Wisconsin. No restrictions were imposed on the land granted by the treaty that created the reservation in 1854.[44] Moreover, the reservation, by terms of the treaty, provided this land as a direct exchange for over twenty-seven townships of land that had been given to the Menominee in Minnesota.

The Menominee thereafter ceded two of the twelve sections of this land to the United States expressly to provide a homeland for the Stockbridge and Munsee in 1856. Of this grant made by the 1856 treaty, Edmunds concluded, "For though ceded to the United States, the cession was for a specific purpose [the Stockbridge and Munsee Reservation] and therefore could not be reached by any other grant."[45] The secretary of interior, James Harlan, concurred with this opinion and concluded in a letter to the commissioner of Indian affairs that the Menominee, Stockbridge, and Munsee Indians "are entitled to the quiet and undisturbed possession of land included within the reservations. Should any attempt to be made to oust them the agent should promptly report the fact to your office [the Office of the Commissioner of Indian Affairs] in order that you may authorize such legal measures as will secure, if necessary the judicial recognition and enforcement of their rights."[46] The Treaty of 1856 was to be the last treaty agreement between the United States and the Stockbridge and Munsee tribe.

The Road to Assimilation

Understandably, the federal government was distracted from Indian affairs during the Civil War years and in the years following that conflict, by hostile relations with the tribes of the Great Plains and the southwest. Yet President U. S. Grant (1869–77) and his commissioner of Indian affairs, the Seneca Indian Eli Parker, developed a new policy that continued to the turn of the new century and beyond.[47] Most of Grant's Indian administrators seem to have been driven by public reaction to reports of injustice toward native people and by zealous evangelical Christians with an interest in Indian affairs. Grant's policy hoped to place Indians on reservations where they could be taught the methods of modern agriculture and be economically independent. He espoused humane treatment but also advocated severe punishment for rebellious tribes. Most important, Grant wished to recruit Indian agents of high character and Christian values to the Indian service and to institute a system in which Indian affairs were jointly administered by Christian organizations and the government. As noted by historian Francis Prucha, Grant's so-called peace policy might better have been called the "religious policy."[48]

Indian policy of the era was largely determined by the Indian Peace Commission, appointed by Congress. This body was composed of religious leaders and humanitarians who knew little about the practical affairs of managing the various Indian agencies. Instead, they espoused high-minded principles that had little effect in practice. They believed that Indians must simply embrace civilization, with all of its institutions. It was hoped to blot out ethnic and tribal divisions and to fuse Indians into a homogeneous mass. Tribal practices were to be not only discouraged but punished. Money annuities were seen as corrupting, as were nonagricultural economic pursuits.

The dilemmas faced by postwar assimilationists are illustrated by the ambiguity they felt about Indian participation in the market economy. On the one hand, such participation was a necessary step toward assimilation in the American mainstream; on the other, they saw cash at the disposal of Indians as a source of potential corruption. For example, treaty annuities were thought to promote laziness, and labor on the cash economy would provide the freedom for Indians to buy alcohol and useless luxury goods.

The extractable resources of reservations, such as timber and minerals, were vested not in the tribe but in the United States. Indians were not permitted to profit by harvesting resources from their reservations until the twentieth century and then only with congressional approval. Despite this restriction, widespread fraud resulted in the plundering of reservation land and resources, with little opposition from the government, which was usually unwilling to stand up to the powerful political interests.

Although the Indian Peace Commission turned over the administration of Indian agencies to Protestant churches in order to protect Indians from corruption, the Grant era was one of the most corrupt in the history of Indian affairs in the United States. During the post–Civil War period, mismanagement and fraud in Indian Office procurement, as well as widespread land and timber fraud on reservations, sapped the morale of missionary and education efforts. Under the administrations of Jacob Cox, who resigned as secretary of the interior in 1870, and his successor Columbus Delano, who served until 1875, the Interior Department was stung by one scandal after another. In fact, "Grantism" became a term for fraud and corruption in public office, and the Indian service was one of the most lucrative areas in which politicians and spoilsmen could grow rich.[49]

The decade of the 1870s was probably the low point in American public morals. It was in this period that New York mayor William Tweed and the Tammany Hall Ring looted the city treasury of at least seventy-five million dollars. The Whiskey Ring, a conspiracy of revenue officials led by O. E. Babcock, Grant's private secretary, defrauded the government of internal revenue tax. William Belknap resigned as secretary of war after it was revealed that he had received bribes for the sale of concessions for trading posts in Indian territory.

In the Great Lakes region, timber, land, mining, and railroad interests largely controlled the machinery of government. Many Indian reservations, including all of those in northern Michigan and Wisconsin, suffered timber depredations, allotment by allotment. In some cases, Indian agents colluded with lumber interests; in others, they simply turned their heads. In rare cases, Indian agents brought in a U.S. attorney to try to protect Indian property rights, but even successful prosecutions only resulted in confiscation and small fines. Only the Menominee, who refused to allot their reservation, were able to hold off the lumber thieves, but just barely.

It was also in the post–Civil War era that the entire manner in which the United States conducted Indian affairs changed abruptly. Since the earliest years of the nation, all during the Colonial era, Indian affairs had been managed by treaty, with the assumption that both parties were independent sovereigns. With the development of the concept that tribes represented "dependent wards" of the United States, the sovereignty assumptions of treaty making seemed less tenable. At the same time, the House of Representatives, which was excluded from the treaty-making process by the U.S. Constitution, managed to promote and pass a bill that totally ended all Indian treaty making on March 3, 1871.[50]

Trouble on the Reservation

Six days following the signing of the Stockbridge-Munsee Treaty, the United States concluded a treaty with the Menominee for two townships of land (specifically township 28N and ranges 13E and 14E) for the new Stockbridge and Munsee Reservation (see map 21).[51] These townships were soon discovered to be particularly unfit for farming, since they had poor, sandy soil and a very short growing season. The land was also densely forested with pine and hardwoods.[52]

In 1859 the agent at Green Bay noted in his annual report that the new reservation was so poor in resources that many Stockbridge and Munsee refused to remove from the old reserve on Lake Winnebago and that many who did so soon left for better conditions.[53] Only one-third of those who were eligible, or about 150 people, actually settled on the reservation, and as late as 1870, only between eight hundred and nine hundred acres had been cleared for cultivation.[54] Year after year, crops and gardens planted by Stockbridge and Munsee farmers were either killed by the cold or eaten by swarms of insects. Agent Martin reported in 1866, "If their location had been selected in a fertile region instead of the cold and barren sand hills of their present home, their advancement in agriculture and the arts of civilized life would have been more satisfactory, and far more beneficial to them."[55]

The Stockbridge and Munsee were soon starving, having neither the capacity to feed themselves nor the ability to earn income from crop production. This situation was particularly insidious because they were skilled and once prosperous farmers. Since some would not voluntarily remove to the sterile reservation, the government refused to release the resettlement and education funds promised by the treaty.[56] These funds were particularly needed to make farm fields by clearing timber, which could cost thirty-five dollars for each acre.[57] Conditions on the reservation were growing steadily worse and, in part because of the disruption of the Civil War, little attention was paid to the barrage of complaints made by the Stockbridge and their agents. Despite their own problems, at least fifteen men of the Stockbridge and Munsee tribe served in Wisconsin's volunteer regiments during the war.[58]

After the war, it became evident that there were two apparent solutions to the deplorable problems on the reservation. As might be expected, both factions advocated for separate alternatives. The Indian Party believed a new treaty must be written that would cede the reservation in favor of one with better land in Kansas, in North Dakota, or among the Oneida at Green Bay.[59] The Citizen Party, many of whom had already claimed allotments on the new reservation, opted for a short-term but less disruptive solution. They favored a plan to generate income by cutting and marketing the pine timber that flourished on their reservation. Unfortunately, there were major barriers to both options.

First, suitable new land could not be found for an alternative reservation, the Oneida refused to sell, and finding two whole townships of good agricultural land without non-Indian owners by 1866 was extremely difficult. The problem of cutting timber for profit was even more vexing.[60] In the 1860s and for the rest of the nineteenth century, timber rights on Indian reservations were vested in the United States rather than the tribe. Congress did not even permit the sale of dead and down timber until 1889, and it was not until 1910 that tribes were permitted to cut timber with congressional approval.[61] When Green Bay agent Martin wrote to the Indian Office asking to help relieve the poverty on the reservation by giving permission for the Stockbridge and Munsee to be able to cut and market their timber, Commissioner Lewis Bogy replied, "I may repeat what has often been said, that cutting and disposing of valuable timber from their lands for the purpose of procuring intoxicating liquors and other injurious articles, for the Indian is a crying evil of long standing, and on that has the unqualified disapproval of the office."[62] Lumbering to acquire cash was forbidden.[63]

What the Indian Office would approve was harvesting timber for the purpose of clearing homesteads for farming, but here again there was a major impediment in the case of the Stockbridge and Munsee Reservation. Although the 1856 treaty called for an immediate survey of the new reservation so that it could be allotted in forty- and eighty-acre parcels, the government survey only laid out the section corners.[64] Since the lines for the quarter sections were not run, accurately locating forty- or eighty-acre parcels was impossible. The government, therefore, never approved allotment selections nor issued certificates or patents as required by the stipulation of Article 3 of the 1856 treaty. In view of this situation, U.S. federal judge Drummond ruled, in the *U.S. v. Jesse Wybro* case heard in 1870, that the Stockbridge and Munsee Reservation was held in common by the tribe and, therefore, that its timber was also common property.

The Stockbridge and Munsee—particularly members of the Citizen Party, who badly wanted allotments—had long since taken advantage of provisions of Article 3 of the 1856 treaty that specified the allotment process.[65] The council of the tribe was empowered to make fair and just allotments under the direction of the superintendent of Indian affairs for the Northern Superintendency. Lacking government initiative, the council developed an allotment schedule of its own, so that despite the absence of an accurate method for locating selections and of formal government acknowledgment that they had been made, some individuals did claim to "own" specific parcels.[66] Two-thirds of these parcels were never improved, that is, cleared for farming.[67]

Those who had selected allotments requested certificates and patents, but these requests were in vain. When new agent M. L. Martin took over the Green Bay Agency in 1866, he found no record of allotments ever having been made on the reservation.[68] Agent Martin, like Judge Drummond a few years later, believed that both the land and timber of the reservation were owned in common by the Stockbridge and Munsee tribe. Obviously, as long as the reservation was not officially allotted and the parcels were not patented to individuals, the government could not sanction the sale of pine timber from allotments that were at that time only recognized informally.

In the 1860s the Stockbridge and Munsee Reservation was a place of misery, poverty, and despair. These unbearable conditions produced desperate people who, lacking effective government help, had to take matters into their own hands.[69] While the Citizen Party defied the government and schemed to cut timber from the reservation, the Indian Party plotted to sell the reservation and move on.

Without belaboring the partisan politics of the era, it suffices to say that the minority Indian Party, led by Darius Charles and Jeremiah Slingerland, managed to hold power by arranging fraudulent elections, which gave Charles and Slingerland a veil of legitimacy, despite the fact that the majority Citizen Party had also elected tribal officers.[70] As "tribal delegates," Charles and Slingerland visited Washington on many occasions and for extended periods.[71] They tried to advance the goal of selling the reservation and disenfranchising the "Old Citizens," those Stockbridge and Munsee who had declared themselves citizens and received payment for their land on the Lake Winnebago Reservation. Charles and Slingerland also became very skilled at political manipulation.

The Stockbridge Timber Grab

During the several decades before the turn of the twentieth century, vast amounts of money could be made cutting the virgin pine forests of the Great Lakes. Powerful lumber interests controlled much of the business enterprise of the region, as well as much of the local and statewide politics. Lumber barons were also a force on the national scene.

Typically, producers, be they corporations or local jobbers, would bid on the right to cut stumpage, that is, standing timber. Lumber companies also often bought huge amounts of timberland at the fixed government price of $1.25 an acre. After cutting the pine, they might hold it for speculation or, as often occurred, would simply let the land revert to state ownership rather than pay property taxes. In that day, the public often perceived of logging as a necessary first step in taming the Great Lakes forests for agriculture, rather than as the giant economic enterprise it was in its own right. On timberland like the Stockbridge and Munsee Reservation, 1,736 board feet of lumber could be obtained from each acre. At the going rate of $2.50 per thousand board feet, each acre would produce $4.34. Even considering logging costs, the uncut logs could essentially be produced at no net cost, and the real money was to be made in marketing the saw logs and the lumber they produced. It was estimated that the stumpage alone on the Stockbridge and Munsee Reservation was worth at least $160,000.[72]

Soon after the conclusion of the Civil War, the Stockbridge and Munsee and the Menominee reservations were surrounded by the sawmills of Wolf River and by logging entrepreneurs aggressively seeking ways to get at the virgin pine stands, which had thus far been preserved on the reservations through government policy.[73] One of the largest mill owners was the influential U.S. congressman Philetus Sawyer. A self-made man, a leader among the Wolf River lumbermen, and a respected citizen of Oshkosh, where he eventually made millions as a sawmill owner, Sawyer served as a U.S. representative and, later, a U.S. senator. In 1870 he was running to return to his seat as congressman from Wisconsin's fifth district. As a congressman, he supported the federal sponsorship of public works, especially river and harbor acts and land incentives for railroad construction. In these endeavors, he was supported by his republican colleagues, particularly Governor Lucius Fairchild and Wisconsin senator Timothy O. Howe. Senator Howe's first election to the Senate was due in large part to the efforts and influence of Philetus Sawyer.[74] As colleagues on the Wisconsin congressional delegation, Sawyer and Howe worked closely together for many years.

During his bid for reelection for a fourth term in the summer of 1870, Sawyer was accused by Democrat opponents and in stories in the public press of trying to scuttle several river and harbor improvements in Wisconsin because he favored competitive rail interests, especially for the Northwestern Railway, which would immediately profit lumber interests of the Wolf River valley. Sawyer was also accused of using his official position to grab for himself some of the best pine timber in the Wisconsin woods.[75] This charge had to do with two bills introduced by Sawyer and Senator Howe to gain access to timber on the Menominee and on the Stockbridge and Munsee reservations.

Although the upper Wolf River and its tributaries ran through an area covered by spectacular virgin pine forests, logs from the area were difficult to bring to market because they had to be floated down a stream system that was small and filled with rocks and rapids. In the summer of 1868, Representative Sawyer spent weeks personally investigating this situation with experts and determined to make the "improvements" necessary to float timber from the Wolf River valley to his Oshkosh mill.[76] He procured a charter for what he called the Keshena Improvement Company, which was authorized to make the improvements and to collect tolls on logs run through them. The company was capitalized by one hundred thousand dollars, a large part of which was Sawyer's own money.[77] The resulting system of dams and log sluices opened vast timber resources that Sawyer had been quietly purchasing for very nominal prices.[78] Although Sawyer ultimately made enormous amounts of money in the lumber business, in 1869 two of the best sources of pine remained free of his grasp, namely, those millions of board feet of timber protected by the Department of the Interior because they were growing on Indian reservations. By the beginning of Mr. Sawyer's first term in Congress, he was well aware of the value of the timber on the Stockbridge and Menominee reservations.[79]

As early as March 1866, Oshkosh lumberman E. S. Hammond wrote to Wisconsin senator James R. Doolittle complaining about the lack of access to reservation timber resources and warning about the intention of U.S. representative Philetus Sawyer.

> Dear Sir,
>
> I understand that our member of Congress Mr. Sawyer is making an effort to get the Commissioner [of Indian affairs] to allow Dr. Davis the Indian Agent to sell the pine timber on the Menominee and Stockbridge reservation at private sale or a portion of it—representing among other things that it has been burnt and is going to waste. Whereby said Sawyer expects to make a nice thing.
>
> Two years ago Dr. Davis sold some timber on the said reservation, he advertised for several bids, and it was generally understood among the lumbermen as Davis said himself he would sell nothing but the burnt timber. James Jenkins bought the lumber and within the last two years has cut off from four to five million feet of logs and all green timber.
>
> The plea of burnt timber is all a humbug. The lumbermen on the river [the Wolf] do not feel satisfied to have a few select individuals have that timber for nothing and bring their logs into market in competition with those that have to pay two dollars per thousand feet of timber standing alongside of them.
>
> The fact is that timber is all worth two dollars per thousand feet and would bring that if brought into market and sold at public sale and not have the sale go off on the plea of selling burnt timber only.
>
> If it is necessary to have the lumbermen on this river substantiate the facts set forth in this letter I will do so.
>
> When we Republicans sent Mr. Sawyer to Congress we expected him to look after the interests of the whole district and not give his special attention to a small portion of it.
>
> Respectfully yours[80]

Mr. Sawyer was only one of the many lumbermen and mill owners who coveted the timber of the Stockbridge and Munsee Reservation, but as a U.S. congressman, he was in a position to try to overcome the policy of the Indian Office, which hoped to protect the timber of the reservation as the common resource of the tribe.[81] With the failure of a proposed new Stockbridge treaty in 1868, Sawyer and Howe began to plot other means to get at Indian timber.

In the meantime, some members of the Citizen Party who believed they had private property rights to their allotments began to cut timber or to sell stumpage on their allotment claims.[82] This occasioned strong protest from Indian Party members, who, believing the tribe owned the timber in common, complained in turn to Agent Manley as well as Representative Sawyer about timber theft.[83] Ultimately, such cutting led to several prosecutions and convictions of "Citizen" Stockbridge by the U.S. attorney.[84] More important, however, piecemeal marketing of reservation timber greatly increased the pressure on lumbermen and particularly on Representative Sawyer to do something before this immense resource slipped from their grasp.

Perhaps because he realized that the timber interest would likely get the reservation's standing timber one way or another, Agent Manley began to consider how the timber might be sold with maximum benefit to the tribe as a whole. He first suggested that the pine timber stumpage could simply be bid at public auction with a minimum price per thousand board feet.[85] In fact, several offers had already been forthcoming on this basis.[86]

Another method would have been to sell the

land within the reservation boundaries to lumber interests for the timber at a minimum cost per acre. It was probably expected that land purchased for stumpage would likely revert again to public ownership once the pine timber was stripped away. It was, by the late 1860s, a widely held belief among Indians, the government, and lumbermen alike that the land composing the Stockbridge and Munsee Reservation was totally worthless, except for its pine timber.

The main problem with bidding the land in parcels was that the pine timber was not evenly distributed, and Agent Manley foresaw that reserve land without pine simply would not sell.[87] Thus, the purpose of disposing of the entire reservation so that a new home could be found for the tribe in a place with decent agricultural land would be defeated. An unratified treaty proposed in 1867 that contained this basic proposition was still on the table. If a suitable new location for a reservation had been at hand, the Stockbridge and Munsee, as well as the Indian Office and the Senate, would likely have approved the cession of the two-township reservation.

Attempts were, in fact, still being made by the Indian Party to amend and forward the 1867 draft treaty. Darius Charles and Jeremiah Slingerland, two of the four Stockbridge and Munsee who had been given power of attorney to represent the tribe in the initial 1867–68 negotiations in Washington, returned to their task. Both men spent the winter of 1870 in Washington obstinately working toward passage of the unratified treaty.

There is some confusion over just whom the delegates Charles and Slingerland represented. Although Representative Sawyer later reassured members of the Citizen Party that these two men represented all of the members of the tribe, this was obviously not the case. Both Charles and Slingerland were Indian Party partisans, and both men wrote extensively in support of Indian Party goals and objectives. On February 1, 1870, Agent Manley forwarded a power of attorney from the Indian Party appointing Charles and Slingerland delegates "to effect any treaty and make any provisions for said *party* that they should think beneficial" (emphasis added).[88] Bearing in mind that the Indian Party believed that the majority Citizen Party had no rights whatsoever on the 1856 reservation, this meant that in the view of Indian Party members, Charles and Slingerland could speak for the entire "tribe." Of course, the Citizen Party disagreed and soon after wrote the commissioner of Indian affairs, asking that a delegate or delegates be appointed to represent their wishes.[89] The Citizen Party's suspicion was that Charles and Slingerland were probably "selling them out."[90] As Citizen Party member Stephen Gardner complained to Representative Sawyer, "Slingerland and Darius Charles are in Washington for what purpose I do not know our supposed sachem deny our rights therefore we are left without officers and without law."[91] Thus, Representative Sawyer was well aware that the majority Citizen Party opposed the work of Charles and Slingerland and that the body politic of the Stockbridge and Munsee people was divided into two very hostile factions.[92] Despite this, Sawyer wrote to Citizen Party member Stephen Gardner to reassure him about the work of Charles and Slingerland.

> Mr. Slingerland and Charles are here for the purpose of selling their pine for the benefit of the whole nation that is for the Munsees as well as the Stockbridge. They are also here to get each name's land allotted to him and I think you need have no fears of them as I think they are endeavoring to do what is for the best interest of your whole people and I will do what I can to see that your interests are taken care of.[93]

The Honorable Philetus Sawyer certainly knew that this was not the truth.

When U. S. Grant became president in 1869, he turned to the military for help in administering Indian affairs. He appointed career military officers as agents for most Indian agencies.[94] These men had no experience with administering Indian affairs, and most were rapidly posted from one duty station to another, resulting in poor continuity in any given agency. When Green Bay lawyer M. L. Martin resigned his post at the Green Bay Agency in early April 1869, he was replaced by Lieutenant J. A. Manley, who began work in early August and served until March 1870, when he was transferred to New Mexico. Manley was replaced by Lieutenant W. R. Bourne, who served from April until November 1870. Bourne was then replaced by a civilian, William Richardson, who took up the job in late January 1871 and remained an agent at Green Bay for several years.

Obviously the officers who served the Green Bay Indians during the critical 1869 and 1870 years could hardly have mastered the complex conditions under which they labored. Nonetheless, Manley did a fairly good job, considering the volatile political nature of matters at the Stockbridge and Munsee Reservation in January 1870. Soon after taking office, Manley wrote to seek the advice of Eli Parker, commissioner of Indian affairs.

> Sir,
>
> I have the honor to report that numerous applications are being made to me by members of the Stockbridge tribe for permission to cut and sell pine timber on what they term their allotted lands claiming they have the right to do so.
>
> The allotment of their lands by the government was provided for in the treaty of 1856 but never carried out. Yet certain portions of the reservation has been surveyed out and allotted to individuals on the authority of the Sachems and Counselors of [*sic*] nation.
>
> I do not know which view the Department takes of this matter and it is the object of this letter to solicit instructions.
>
> My advice to the Stockbridges has been that they should dispose of no timber on the reservation as it had all better be sold and the prices it sold for would in a great measure be determined by the amount of pine upon it.
>
> They represent themselves to me as being nearly in a starving condition and say they must do something to provide themselves with food. I told them I would submit their case to your decision and act only upon that, and that all my proceedings in the matter of their allotted lands would be governed by the instructions I received from the Department. I have positively forbidden any one of them to take any timber from land the common property of the Nation.
>
> Very respectfully
> Your obedient servant[95]

It did not take Representative Sawyer long to see that agent Manley's enforcement of the Indian Department's no-cut policy was detrimental to the interest of his lumbermen constituents and himself. On January 7, 1870, he wrote to Commissioner Parker asking that Manley be removed from office for permitting cutting of pine on the Stockbridge and Munsee Reservation.[96] When informed of these charges, Manley denied them, saying that those who accused him were upset not because he was permitting pine to be cut but because he "had the firmness to reject any policy and any impropriety in any party's or parties' interest that my judgment condemned as not being advantageous to the government or the Indians."[97] In mid-February Sawyer sent the secretary of the interior, Jacob Cox, three affidavits from Wisconsin citizens accusing Manley with drinking on the job and encouraging lumbering on the reservation.[98]

Senate Bill 610

In March 1870 Wisconsin senator Timothy Howe, working with Representative Sawyer, proposed Senate Bill 610. Though couched in benevolent terms, the purpose of this bill was to give lumbermen access to the virgin pine timber growing on the Stockbridge and Munsee Reservation. As long as the land remained under control of the Indian Department, its policy prohibited the sale of timber.

Senate Bill 610, introduced in the second session of the Forty-first Congress, was described as a bill "For the relief of the Stockbridge and Munsee Tribe of Indians in the State of Wisconsin."[99] The first section provides for the independent appraisal of the two-township reservation set apart by the Treaty of 1856. The appraisal was to be done in eighty-acre lots, and the appraisal value was to include the value of timber on each parcel at not less than one dollar per thousand board feet. The section also called for appraisal of improvements that might be found on each eighty-acre parcel.

Section 2 ordered the advertisement and sale of the reservation, with the eighty-acre parcels being sold to the highest bidder. Unsold land would be rebid after a period of one year at not less than $1.25 per acre. The secretary of the interior was empowered to reserve from sale eighteen contiguous sections, which were to be allotted to members of the Indian Party. The next section of SB 610 specified that the costs of the act, including the expenses of appraisal and sale as well as the restitution for improvements and debts of sachems and counselors, should be paid from the proceeds of the sale of the land.

Section 4 requires the General Land Office to account for the receipt of sales, which would reflect proceeds minus expenses. Added to this sum would be the value of unsold land in the two townships, valued at sixty cents per acre, as well as six thousand dollars held in trust under the Treaty of 1839. This amount would constitute the entire sum due the Stockbridge and Munsee tribe.

The distribution of proceeds was the subject of Section 5. The money gained by sale of the reservation was to be divided between the Indian and Citizen parties on a per capita basis. That due the Citizen Party was to be equally distributed among them. The portion due the Indian Party, however, was to be invested, and the interest was to be used to provide schools, agricultural services, and other infrastructure. Thirty thousand dollars could be used to secure a new location for the Indian Party and for the costs of removal. Upon removal, the eighteen sections reserved should be sold for the benefit of the Indian Party.

According to Section 6, two rolls would be prepared. The first would show those who wished to sever their tribal relations and become citizens of the United States. The second would include the names of all who wished to "retain their tribal character" and remain under the protection of the United States. Any person who had been enrolled as a "citizen" under the Acts of 1843 or 1846 or their descendants could not be included on either of the new rolls. Section 6 further disenfranchised people enrolled as citizens from any future treaty or law made to benefit the Stockbridge and Munsee tribe. Section 7 declared that the enrolled members of the Indian Party would henceforth constitute the "Stockbridge Tribe of Indians."

Future allotment of the Indian Party reservation was the subject of Section 8. By this section the present or a future reservation was to be divided into forty- and eighty-acre parcels to be assigned to families and individuals. Any female who married out of the tribe was required to relinquish all rights to hold lands, "as if deceased." Finally, Section 9 provides that the United States would hold land allotments in trust for individuals and that surplus lands would be held for the purpose of future allotments.

Senate Bill 610 seems to have been purely a product of Representative Sawyer's negotiations with Indian Party representatives Darius Charles and Jeremiah Slingerland. During the same session of Congress, Senator Howe and Representative Sawyer also proposed Senate Bill 849, which was an attempt to sell the Menominee Reservation. The first three sections of SB 610 and SB 849, those sections that relate to the appraisal of each reservation's sale and recovery of costs, are essentially identical. While SB 849 ends with the simple goal of selling the Menominee Reservation, SB 610 goes on to include the agenda of the Indian Party. The remaining sections of SB 610 incorporate some of the provisions of the unratified treaty of 1868, especially those that permanently split the tribe into two independent factions. SB 610 goes further, however, by completely disenfranchising the Citizen Party, specifically those members who had been separated from the tribe by congressional action in 1843 and 1846 but reunited by the Treaty of 1856.[100] The incorporation of these provisions would never have met the agreement of the majority Citizen Party and is both evidence of Sawyer's collusion with Charles and Slingerland and explanation for the fact that the provisions of SB 610 were not made known in Wisconsin until the bill was a fait accompli.[101]

The Enactment of Senate Bill 610 as the Act of 1871

Senate Bill 610 died in the Forty-first Congress and was reintroduced at the beginning of the Forty-second Congress, in January 1871. Both the Senate and House versions, the latter sponsored by Representative Sawyer, passed on February 6, 1871. Drafts of SB 610 and rumors that it had passed began to circulate on the reservation in late January.[102] Agent Richardson wrote for a copy of the bill in mid-February, describing it as a bill selling the pine land belonging to the Stockbridge and Munsee and to the Memominee.[103] He seems to have had little information about the details.

The fact that the U.S. Indian agent responsible for the affairs of the Stockbridge and Munsee tribe in their day-to-day relationship with the United States was totally ignorant of the provisions of a pending act of Congress that would have a major impact on the tribe speaks volumes about how Indian policy was being conducted. Not only was Agent Richardson kept in the dark, but the entire executive branch of government seems to have been bypassed. With the lack of input or comment by those responsible for the management of Indian affairs, it could hardly be expected that the long-established protocol for assuring fair treatment of the tribe was being observed, and, in fact, it was not.

On March 25, 1871, after SB 610 was received, having passed into law as Bill No. 13, members of the Citizen Party sent a petition of protest to President Grant. A note of transmission, probably attached by Agent Richardson, states that "a large portion" of the Stockbridge and Munsee tribe signed a petition objecting to Bill No. 13 and that the enclosed petition was signed by the leading men.[104] The petition states that Bill No. 13 was the work of one faction of the tribe and was not agreed to by many others, since it violated the terms of the Treaty of 1856 that would have provided allotments on the reservation. The petitioners asked President Grant to protect them from unjust laws that were being enforced on them.[105] Clearly, the majority Citizen Party, who were so severely penalized by the new law, did not agree to it or accept it.

After approval, Bill No. 13 was officially known as the Act of 1871 for the Relief of the Stockbridge and Munsee Tribe of Wisconsin. It was then sent to the president for his signature. President Grant promptly asked the secretary of the interior, Columbus Delano, for his opinion as to whether or not he should give the bill his approval.[106] Five days later, on January 30, the president received a letter from Mr. Delano, which cautiously noted that while he could not advise the president not to approve the bill, some of its provisions were not in full accord with views of the Department of the Interior.[107] While we do not know for sure which provisions of Bill No. 13 the Department of the Interior found objectionable, it is likely that the main problem was with Section 6 of the bill, which disenfranchised fully two-thirds of the Stockbridge and Munsee that were members of the tribe and had rights on the reservation under the Treaty of 1856.

While the president was considering the Sawyer bill, Citizen Party member Stephen Gardner wrote a bitter letter of complaint to the secretary of the interior.

> Will you have the Kindness to hear to my supplication, that I am about to lay before you in this communication. I beg of you to incline your ear to my statement. I have written to Honorable Philetus Sawyer last winter begging of him to secure my home that I have on the Stockbridge and Munsee Reserve he answered my statement and made big promise. I told him that I had been a Soldier in the rebellion don [*sic*] my duty faithfully and was honorably discharged at Washington. I had saved most of all of my money after returning home with hard labor finished me a house costing nearly nine hundred dollars besides making improvements. I told Mr. Sawyer that Slingerland went to Washington for what purpose I did not know when he returned home he did not make no report. After a while we heard he and Major Martin got in a Bill we sent for a copy of the Bill and examined it. I see at once the Bill did not correspond with Sawyer's statement that is the way I understand if the Bill is passed I am ruined. I have lost my home I want to keep my home and become citizen. The time Major Martin was agent he made out a list to see how many wanted to remove as Indians and how many wanted to be citizens. I hesitated to sign because wise men can take advantage so I told Slingerland I wanted to keep my home. He said we must call a council that same evening and see how many want to receive patents on their homestead and how many want to sell out and get all money. I guess he did not present the list of those persons that wanted patents when he returned home I inquired of him if I was going to have patent he said no the Big Men at Washington won't give patents. This was I believe 2 years ago this winter the letter I

wrote to Mr. Sawyer last winter he said he would present my letter to the Indian Bureau. I do not know if he ever did will you present this to our Great Father the President. My last resort rests on your Honor and my Great Father for protection if that Bill is passed as I saw it the Hostile party or so called Indian party will throw me and my family in the road where to go I do not know. I have stated my condition to a gentleman from Boston Mr. Beeslen he see [*sic*] at once Rev. Slingerland is doing wrong he talked to him like a Christian man trying to discard me and a portion of the tribe. Will you by all means answer this I am no schollar [*sic*] as you can see by this letter.

Yours truly[108]

Mr. Gardner was undoubtedly speaking for the majority of the Stockbridge and Munsee tribe. He was prophetic in his appraisal of the impact of the act, which did, by its very provisions, disenfranchise many members of the Stockbridge and Munsee community.

On February 6 the president directed his personal secretary to return the Stockbridge and Munsee bill to the Senate without his signature.[109] It thus de facto became the law of the land. It is not known why President Grant did not sign the bill, but it may be presumed that his failure to approve the bill was not simply a matter of oversight. Soon after Bill No. 13 became law, Representative Sawyer sent a curious letter to Jeremiah Slingerland.

Your letter of the 31st ultimo, was duly received, and I have been waiting for the land bill to be printed to send you a copy. It has only today come from the printers, and I send you herewith. It was delayed at the president, I suppose for further consideration, and as you will see has become a law without his signature, but it goes into force and operation all the same, being now a law of the U.S. I have seen the Secretary of the Interior, about this law and he says it will now be necessary for you to call a council of the tribes and lay this bill or act before them, and have them sanction it in every part, and when they have done so, have it signed by the head men and appended to one of the copies of the law I now send, and then mail it to me and I will lay it before the Secretary of Interior, who cannot take steps in regard to it until he gets the sanction of the tribes.

Don't forget to attach your sanction to a copy of the law.[110]

In this environment, we can understand Secretary Delano's ambivalence about the Act of 1871 and his insistence to Sawyer that he must obtain the concurrence of the Stockbridge and Munsee to this legislation. First, in January and February 1871, it was still government policy to conclude important agreements with Indians by treaty. This was particularly the case where a standing treaty—in this case, the Treaty of 1856—was to be implicitly modified. Secretary Delano, the commissioner of Indian affairs, and President Grant no doubt recognized the Act of 1871 for what it was—timber larceny. It had nothing whatsoever to do with advancing the welfare and improvement of the Stockbridge and Munsee tribe. As far as it is known, no general council was ever held to obtain the tribe's concurrence to the Act of 1871. What is known is that more than half the tribe bitterly opposed the act.

Unlike the acts of Congress passed in both 1843 and 1846 to regulate the affairs of the Stockbridge and Munsee, the Act of 1871 did not expressly repeal or even modify the existing treaty relationships of the tribe. While the act did disenfranchise the Old Citizen Faction, that had been reinstated to tribal affairs by the Treaty of 1856, it otherwise is silent on the features and provisions guaranteed by the treaty. Most important among these was the creation of a permanent two-township reservation homeland for the Stockbridge and Munsee people. Inasmuch as it was not the expressed intent of Congress to abolish the reservation, it should still exist, notwithstanding the fact that the Act of 1871 sold three-quarters of the land within its exterior boundaries. The purpose of the Act of 1871 was to give lumbermen access to the pine timber growing on the reservation, not to change the reservation or even to acquire reservation land, for which there was little or no market as farmland. That Secretary Delano called for a referendum and approval of the Stockbridge and Munsee of the Act of 1871 could well reflect confusion over the manner in which Indian policy was being conducted as well as whose responsibility it was to conduct it at the time. Perhaps in calling for Indian approval, the secretary was also trying to bring a measure of fairness to a law that he knew was motivated by the most corrupt of motives.

The Protesting of the Act of 1871

Nothing improved for the Stockbridge and Munsee following the passage of the Act of 1871. In fact, conditions grew progressively worse as a result of the new law. Three-fourths of the reservation land reserved by the Treaty of 1856 was quickly appraised, advertised, and sold for the pine timber that grew on it. H. R. Wells, who was appointed to create the list of Stockbridge Indians eligible to receive allotments on the unsold reservation land, proved to be both inept and corrupt.[111] His was an impossible task at any rate, because members of the Citizen Party, who had lived on the reservation since the move from the Lake Winnebago Reservation, refused to be displaced by the Act of 1871. Members of the Indian Party pushed vigorously to have Citizen Party members expelled from their reservation homes, and both sides were locked in a bitter and protracted struggle for survival.

The Sawyer-Howe timber and land grab that the Act of 1871 represented seemed to increasingly grate on the sensibilities of the Christian morality that guided U.S. Indian policy until the turn of the century and beyond.[112] Throughout most of the remaining part of the nineteenth century, leaders of the Indian and Citizen parties sent forth a steady stream of letters, complaints, affidavits, and petitions to the government, each extolling the justice of their respective causes. For every argument on one side, there was an equally vociferous argument from the other. Indian Office officials watched in confusion as the Stockbridge and Munsee, their lawyers, and their political allies did battle. Every so often, the Department of Interior sent a new official inspector to study the problem. E. K. Kemble reported in 1877, and William Leeds sent a long analysis the next year; both men agreed on the cause of the problems but totally disagreed about a solution.[113]

As the years went by, people got used to the practical realities of the reservation; the tribe's land base was now just one-quarter of its former amount. It was now commonly being called the "new reservation" or the "current reservation." Numerous maps published by public and private sources erroneously depicted the Stockbridge and Munsee Reservation as the eighteen sections that were not sold by the Act of 1871, rather than the seventy-two sections defined by the treaty with the Menominee in 1856 (see map 22).[114] The Stockbridge and Munsee found that there was little point in fighting for land already sold when the majority of Stockbridge and Munsee were in dire danger of being turned off the allotments on which they had built their homes and farms and on which they had by now lived for over twenty years. Although both parties had to accept the practical operation of the provision of the Act of 1871 that sold their reservation land, the Citizen Party did not accept the act, particularly the enrollment provision that effectively disenfranchised them. For the remaining years of the century and into the next, they continued to argue that the Act of 1871 was without legal or moral foundation.

To put their argument in its simplest construction, the law of 1871, by its provisions and its operation, deprived the Stockbridge and Munsee tribe and the majority of its members of rights guaranteed to them by the negotiated provisions of the Treaty of 1856. In passing the Act of 1871, Congress thus unilaterally sold off reservation land and disenfranchised many of the tribe's members without specific repeal or even modification of the 1856 treaty. A congressional act does not automatically repeal a treaty, but only those provisions expressly modified. The

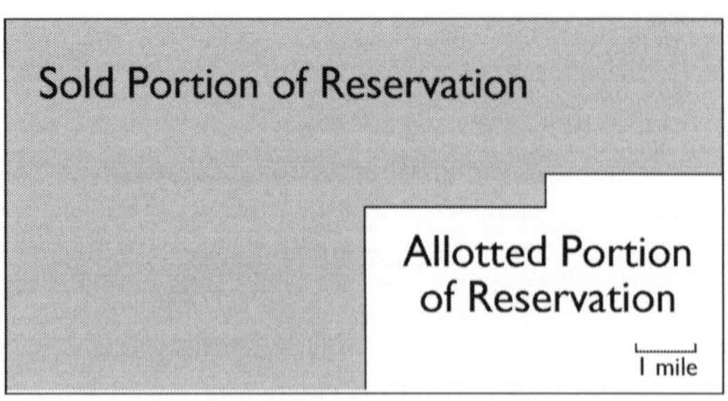

Map 22. Portion of the Stockbridge-Munsee reservation sold pursuant to the act of 1871

Act of 1871, other than in name, contained no lasting benefit for the Stockbridge and Munsee tribe.

The Citizen Party raised the 1856 treaty argument almost immediately after the Act of 1871 was passed. In 1873 John Wilson, an attorney for the Citizen Party, argued that action taken by the commissioner of Indian affairs to sell reservation land under the Act of 1871 "not only works inevitable hardship to the Indians but is in violation of stipulated agreement by the United States with these Indians under the Treaty of 1856; and also that the action contemplated by the Act of Congress aforesaid, will result in injustice to a portion of the tribe by reason of defects in the roll on which a per capita distribution of the funds found to belong to these Indians is to be made."[115] Citizen Party members sent an appeal to their Great Father (President Grant) as parties to the Treaty of 1856. The petitioners prayed "for a decision on the question of the right and title of the sale of land approved under the 3rd section of an act of Congress entitled 'an Act for the Relief of the Stockbridge and Munsee tribe of Indians in the State of Wisconsin' submitted to the President of the United States on 25 January 1871, but to which you did not sign your approval."[116]

In late 1873 Green Bay agent William Richardson, acting as a special agent for enrollment under the 1871 act, made a detailed report on conditions on the Stockbridge and Munsee Reservation to the commissioner of Indian affairs, E. P. Smith. Noting the inconsistencies in the operation of the Treaty of 1856 and the Act of 1871, Richardson concluded,

> If some of the persons whose names are inscribed on the rolls or census of the treaty of 1856 have rights and privileges thereby, why have not all. I have charity to believe that Congress did not examine the treaty of 1856, when the 6th section of the law of 1871 was passed for the relief of the Stockbridge and Munsee Indians. The former is a *guaranty* of lands and rights to each person subscribing to its provisions. The latter in a single sentence *divests* nearly one third of the tribe, of all these lands and rights."[117]

Richardson also pointed out that the Act of 1871 made no specific reference to the treaty provisions that were in force at the time the act was passed. He noted, for example, the explicit statement in the Treaty of 1856 that stipulations of earlier treaties that may be in contravention or in conflict were abrogated and annulled.[118]

The 1871 act disenfranchised a majority of the tribe, the so-called Old Citizens, and the Indian Party demanded their removal from the reservation on the grounds that they were trespassers and could have no legitimate voice in tribal affairs. On many occasions between 1871 and 1893, the government tried to remove the Old Citizens faction of the tribe from the reservation. These actions, in turn, raised protests not only from those to be turned out of their homes and farms but also from their supporters among the citizenry of Wisconsin and their representatives in Congress. Beyond humanitarian concerns, local politicians were afraid that these self-supporting Indian farm families would suddenly become displaced persons dependent for their support or the welfare of Shawano County.[119]

The attempted removal of the so-called Old Citizens—forty people of the ten families who had taken settlement money under the 1848 treaty—created an enormous stress on the reservation and in central Wisconsin.[120] Except for members of the Indian Party and their supporters, Senator Howe and Representative Sawyer, other Wisconsin citizens and the Indian Office perceived the attempted removals under the Act of 1871 as cruel and unfair. Former Green Bay agent Thomas Chase wrote that the Citizen Party had "a perfectly legal and moral claim to an interest in that reservation." Chase refers to the Act of 1871 as an "infamous proceeding," attributing its passage to the desire of the Indian Party for revenge and the desire of Representative Sawyer and his friends "to have a fresh lick at Indian pine."[121]

Still reeling under criticisms for attempts to remove the Citizen Party members, the commissioner of Indian affairs in 1877, E. H. Hayt, sent a special inspector, Edward Kemble, to investigate. Kemble filed a long and detailed report. Among its findings were the following:

> The passage of the law of 1871 was procured by a fraction of the tribe cooperating with outside parties, who desired to effect a sale of a part of the reservation. A delegation of the

faction working in this interest, went to Washington, and the bill was passed without the knowledge or consent of the party opposed to the scheme.[122]

The circumstances under which the law of 1871 was passed and the proceedings had under it were such to justify a belief that misrepresentations and fraud were resorted to by those who urged the passage of the law and had charge of the enrollment under it.[123]

The law of 1871, the passage of which was procured by a fraction of the tribe, aided by interested parties, white and Indian, the proceeding had under the law and the manner in which its provisions were executed, constitute a flagrant wrong against the tribe which ought to be redressed as speedily as practicable.[124]

The setting aside of this treaty [the Treaty of 1856] was an act of bad faith as well as mistaken policy and subsequent legislation has again opened the door to fraud, bitter criticism and the utter ruin of the tribe.[125]

Letters continued to flow from the Stockbridge and Munsee Reservation citing the rights of the Citizen Party to reservation land and resources under the Treaty of 1856.[126] At various times, critical stories were circulated in the popular press about the deplorable situation on the reservation. A letter in the *Appleton Crescent* for April 1, 1874, accused Representative Sawyer, Myron McCord, and others of manipulating the tribal election and praised attempts of Agent Richardson to bring justice to the scene.[127]

An article titled "The Indian Ring" appeared in the *Oshkosh Times* on July 26, 1873, and also in the *Shawano Journal* and the *Appleton Crescent*. This article implicated Representative Sawyer in the sale of the Stockbridge and Munsee Reservation, saying that the details of the activities of the Indian Ring were "too true to need a rehearsal." This article also strongly condemned the government for not protecting the rights of the Stockbridge and Munsee under both law and treaty.[128]

An article in the *Chicago Tribune* of June 29, 1882, reported that Sachem Waunnondos was on his way to Washington to ask for a congressional investigation of the fact that "the tribe has been robbed of three-fourths of its reservation, consisting of some of the finest pine lands in the world, by the pineland ring."[129] The article also reported, "The Indians claim that the treaty [of 1856] with them [in effect] in 1871 was as binding on the government as on themselves and the passage of the act of that year [1871] and the sale of their land in spite of the treaty was a fraud and wrong which the government should modify."[130]

The effects of the Act of 1871 and the circumstances of its enactment were no secret to the citizens of Wisconsin. In 1886 the Wisconsin legislature approved "Memorial No. 7 to Congress," which reads as follows:

The memorial of the legislature of the State of Wisconsin respectfully represents:

That by Act of Congress, passed February 6, 1871, and by the interpretation placed them by government officials, a large part of the Stockbridge and Munsee tribe of Indians, have been excluded from the participation in their tribal fund and the right to occupy their reservation, and have thereby, and by their continuous efforts to regain their property been reduced to the most distressing poverty; and,

That it will place the government of the United States in an unenviable position, to have it known that it has first made a treaty with confiding Indians [Treaty of 1856], giving them permanent homes on a reservation for a consideration, named in the treaty, and has then after the Indians had peaceably possessed their property for many years, suddenly, without previous notice, abrogated the treaty, deprived the Indians of their homes, and has not returned the valuation consideration, the Indians gave in exchange for their share of the reservation; whereas your memoralists ask the speedy passage of bill H.R. 7175, and other measures that will give full relief to the cruelly wronged Indians.[131]

In 1892 J. C. Adams, an educated member of the Stockbridge tribe who was also a lawyer, prepared a petition on behalf of a group of Stockbridge and Munsee at the request of the commissioner of Indian affairs. The petition was a detailed review of the legislative and treaty history of the tribe, with appropriate documents and reports appended. Adams pointed out that the Treaty of 1856 was a treaty of consolidation that was to provide a permanent home for all Stockbridge and Munsee wherever they were located. This treaty also released and discharged the United States from obligation under all former laws and treaties. In exchange for valuable consideration, each Stockbridge and Munsee was to get a tract of land for which they would receive a patent after ten years. Adams showed how various provisions of the Act of 1871 violated stipulations of the Treaty of 1856 without repealing it in whole or part. Finally he concluded that the lands of the Stockbridge and Munsee "have been sold by the government in violation of the pledge of the treaty."[132]

Certainly the Christian reformers of the 1870s were anxious to acculturate and assimilate native people. They were willing to encourage this end to the point of creating both incentives for cultural change and punishments for those who insisted on retaining traditional values. Those in the Indian Office, who had worked to advance the Indian policy of the day, could not have condoned the object of the Act of 1871, which stripped Stockbridge of the majority of their land base and left them with no viable option for supporting themselves in the future. To be sure, the Stockbridge and Munsee received a small financial payout for the sold portion of their reservation, but this money was soon spent for day-to-day subsistence. With these funds gone or inaccessible, the Stockbridge and Munsee were destitute and without prospects. The Act of 1871 did not further acculturation or assimilation. In fact, it did not further Indian policy in any way. The Act of 1871 had nothing whatsoever to do with the welfare or well-being of the Stockbridge and Munsee.

Retrospect on the Act of 1871

The Act of 1871 had a major impact on the course of the history of the Stockbridge and Munsee people, yet it evolved and was passed in secrecy and with ulterior motives. The protocols of treaty making, which had been developed since before the birth of the United States, were discarded in its passage, and with them went any pretext of fairness. In preparing the Act of 1871, there were no negotiations with representative tribal leaders, no explanation of the contents or effect of the provisions of the bill, and no chance for Stockbridge or Munsee leaders to express their approval or disapproval before or after the act became law. In other words, the sale of three-quarters of their reservation and the disenfranchisement of many members of the tribe occurred without their knowledge or a chance for them to object.

Beyond this travesty, neither was the executive branch of government a participant in the preparation and approval of the act. Agent Richardson seems to have been in the dark about the bill's contents. Likewise, the secretary of the interior and the commissioner of Indian affairs apparently had no opportunity to comment on the bill until it went to the president for his approval. On that occasion, they noted its inconsistencies with the policies of the Department of the Interior. For his part, President Grant did not give his sanction to the bill.

Why would Congress pass a bill of this nature and in this way? The answer is that they were deceived by Representative Sawyer, Senator Howe, and two lobbyists from the Indian Party into thinking that this bill was written for the purpose of relieving poverty by selling land to raise cash for starving Indians and to provide allotments for family farms. This bill was in fact entirely motivated to gain access to valuable pine timber and for partisan revenge against the Old Citizen faction of the Citizen Party. Even so, was it Congress's intent to vastly reduce the size of the reservation and its configuration by provision or operation of law?

The Act of 1871 does not expressly modify the Treaty of 1856; it does not even mention it. By 1871 the government of the United States—more specifically, the executive branch—had abundant experience, through the Office of Indian Affairs, the Executive Office, and the U.S. Senate, in acquiring Indian land and changing boundaries of Indian reservations. The House of Representatives certainly understood land transaction and how to accomplish relinquishments. Indian treaties and agreements of the era offer abundant examples, including the treaty with the Chippewa on February 22, 1855 ("Chippewa Indians hereby cede, sell, and convey to the United States all their rights, title, and interest in and to . . ."); the treaty with the Sioux from April 19, 1858 ("cede and relinquish to the United States all lands now owned, possessed, or claimed by them"); the treaty with the Chippewa from October 2, 1863 ("cede, sell, and convey to the United States"); and the treaty with the Sauk and Fox from February 18, 1867 ("cede to the United States a full and complete title to the land").

By 1871 the section lines on the Stockbridge and Munsee Reservation had been run; if Congress had intended to lay out a new reservation or, in fact, designate the land to be allotted in severalty, it could have done so precisely and easily. The fact of the matter is that Congress did not elicit the proper legal wording or precise description because it had absolutely no intention of diminishing the Stockbridge and Munsee Reservation by the Act of 1871. It did intend to sell at least 34,560 acres of land within the reserve, and this objective was accomplished. It is hard to believe that Congress, with a large number of experienced lawyers among them, would assume that real estate objectives would occur by chance and especially that treaty relationships with an Indian tribe would be radically altered by simple implication. The Act of 1871 was not carefully designed, but it was deliberately written to profit lumber interests. It was simply not an act intended to advance Indian policy objectives or to benefit the majority of the Stockbridge and Munsee people.

Too Little Too Late: Attempts to Amend the Act of 1871

During the twenty-five years following the Act of 1871, at least fifteen bills were introduced in Congress to try to fix the situation on the Stockbridge and Munsee Reservation by amending the Act of 1871. In fact, during that period, Congress did pass acts in 1893 and 1906 that would modify conditions on the reservation. The Stockbridge and Munsee at this time consisted of 519 people who lived on the approximately 11,520 acres that constituted the unsold portion of their original reserve, that is, the part saved for allotment.[133] See map 22. Most made their living by small-scale farming in the summer and by lumbering in the winter. Much of the latter activity was illegal, but the government acknowledged it was impossible to stop.[134] Although there were many allotment claims, 65 percent of the land in the eighteen sections was still technically held in common, since the government had issued few patents. In all, 7,520 acres remained unallotted, and most of this was covered by valuable timber.[135] The country north and west, or the sold portion of the reservation, was now composed of abandoned, cutover land dotted with pine stumps and an impenetrable tangle of slash and emergent underbrush. Very few non-Indian settlers had gained a foothold in this country.[136]

Congress's first attempt to rectify the problems created by the Act of 1871 came in 1879 and 1880, when bills were introduced that would have reincorporated the disenfranchised Citizen Party faction by recognizing the 1856 treaty as the membership baseline.[137] These did not pass, despite the support of various special agents sent out to access the situation by the Indian Office. In 1884 and 1887 new bills were introduced in both houses of Congress that would have reinstated the Citizen Party but, by various schemes, would have also divided the reservation among claimants, sold any surplus land, and divided the tribal fund per capita; thus the government hoped to reduce reliance on federal support.[138] This notion was very much in the tenor of the times and part of the thinking that led Congress to pass the General Allotment Act in 1887. Neither of these proposed Stockbridge and Munsee bills passed, nor did those introduced in 1900.[139]

Stockbridge provides a good example of the conflict between the concepts of the treatment of dependent Indian wards under the General Allotment Act and the rights of allotted Indians under treaties. At least some of the Stockbridge and Munsee were made citizens as early as 1843. How, they wondered, could those citizens now be made citizens again so many years later. Certainly, if the opportunity came up, they, like their neighbors the Oneida, would also have claimed the treaty right to hunt and fish within the bounds of the reservation. The Stockbridge and Munsee quickly rejected the notion of being allotted under the General Allotment Act as suggested by special inspector William Parsons in November 1887. They argued that many were already citizens and that the Act of 1871 already contained an allotment provision that was in force.[140]

Nonetheless, once they were finally allotted after the turn of the century, troubling questions arose. Were they citizens? Were they liable for criminal prosecution by the state of Wisconsin for a crime on their reservation?[141] Did they have to pay taxes like Indians that were allotted under the General Allotment Act?[142] Would the government continue to support their school?[143] The Office of Indian Affairs weighed in on one of these issues in 1901 by posting a policy circular to its agents. As to the question of agents being empowered to issue arrest warrants, the government declared that agents could issue warrants where Indians lived within the boundaries of an Indian reservation over which the United States had control as it did over Indian country. In cases where lands had been allotted and the surplus thrown open to settlement (as in the case of the General Allotment Act reservations), reservations ceased to be Indian country, and the agent had to relinquish control to the laws of the state or territory.[144]

The question of the specific case at Stockbridge and Munsee remained problematic since the 1871 act opened three-quarters of the reservation land to non-Indian purchase. The U.S. attorney for Wisconsin, E. J. Henning, who was prosecuting the *State v. Gardner* case, wrote to the commissioner of Indian affairs, F. H. Abbott, for an answer. After reviewing the treaty and legislative history of the Stockbridge and Munsee up until 1910, Commissioner Abbott concluded his letter in part with the following observations:

> Knowing the history of the Stockbridge and Munsee Indians, their affiliations and habits of life, the Office is inclined to the opinion that the defendant was a citizen of the United States by virtue of the provisions of the act of 1887 after the passage of the act of the Congress of 1893, supra.
>
> (3) The Crimes Act of 1885, supra, grants jurisdiction for the crime of rape committed "within the limits of any Indian reservation" under the same provisions of law as if committed within a place "within the exclusive jurisdiction of the United States." *In this connection attention is called to the fact that the Office knows of no act of the Congress which has in any wise changed the limits of the Stockbridge and Munsee reservation, that is to say, the two townships of land set aside for the Stockbridge and Munsee Indians.* Where the limits of a reservation have been disturbed, as by opening the lands to settlement or otherwise, as has often been authorized by the Congress, the limits of a reservation may be said to have been destroyed, but in the case at bar no such fact exists. In the case of the *United States v. Kiya* (126 Fed. Rep. 879), a case involving the crime of rape, it was said that:
>
> > There is no question that the offense charged in this action was in fact committed within the limits of an Indian reservation, for the simple allotment of lands in severalty does not abrogate the reservation.
>
> Attention is invited to the decision in the case of the *United States v. Sutton* (215 US 291), which refers to and comments to a certain extent upon the decision in the case of the *United States v. Celestine* (id. 278).
>
> > From these decisions the inference is drawn that the mere fact of making allotments does not militate against the continued existence of an Indian reservation, and that an Indian reservation continues to exist after allotment, unless the reservation is duly opened by act of the Congress or an administrative act, as in the case of a reservation created by Executive Order whereon allotments have been made and the surplus lands returned to the public domain by Executive Order.
>
> Referring specifically to the closing paragraphs of your letter, the records of the Office show:
>
> 1. That the lands described in the plea of abatement have been patented in fee, that is to say, the patents therefor are dated April 4, 1910, being made under the act of 1906, supra.
> 2. Taking into consideration the decisions of the Supreme Court of the United States in the several cases cited, *it would appear that the Stockbridge and*

> *Munsee Reservation, although allotted—except as before noted—remains intact, because (a) it has not been opened by act of the Congress, and (b) the limits thereof have not been changed by administrative action.*
>
> If it be decided that at the time the offense was committed the place was "within the limits of an Indian reservation," the offense appears to come within the act of 1885, irrespective of the personal status of the Indian allottee, provided the act of 1885 applies to Indian reservations in Wisconsin.
>
> The Act of the Congress of March 3, 1847 (9 Stat. L., 178), admitting Wisconsin to statehood, makes no reservation of exclusive jurisdiction on the part of the United States over the lands of Indian tribes within the limits of the State.
>
> In this connection attention is invited to the decision of the Supreme Court of the State of Wisconsin in the case of the *State v. Doxtater* (47 Wis. 278), wherein it was held that the criminal laws of the State apply to the Indians on their reservations within the State, and that the original jurisdiction generally extends over such reservations. Doxtater was convicted of the crime of adultery committed on the Oneida Reservation.
>
> While the State courts have decided that they have jurisdiction over crimes within the State of Wisconsin, it does not follow that the jurisdiction is exclusive; it may be concurrent with the jurisdiction exercised by the Federal courts.
>
> In the opinion of the Office, it would be of great importance to have the question of jurisdiction in criminal cases in the State of Wisconsin decided by the Federal courts.[145] (emphasis added)

Conceding that the Act of 1871 did make land within the Stockbridge and Munsee Reservation available for purchase and that this land was sold, Commissioner Abbott made the important distinction that this action did not diminish the reservation in the same sense as the sale of surplus land under the General Allotment Act. In the latter case, once the surplus land was restored to market, Section 5 of the act provided that the tribe would release the surplus land "in conformity with the treaty or statute under which such reservation is held."[146] Commissioner Abbott correctly concluded that the Act of 1871 did not make any such provision in regard to the sold part of the Stockbridge and Munsee Reservation and that it therefore remained part of the reservation as originally created.

The Acts of 1893 and 1906

The constant introductions of bills relating to the Stockbridge and Munsee Reservation problem created no consensus either in Washington or on the reservation among the Stockbridge and Munsee themselves. Nonetheless, Congress eventually managed two acts, the first passing on March 3, 1893.[147] This act quite simply affirmed the Treaty of 1856.

In a preamble to the Act of 1893, Congress noted that the problem to be solved originated from the "interpretation placed by government officials" on the tribe under the 1856 treaty concerning participating in tribal funds and the right to occupy the reservation. This was a disingenuous description, since the interpretation blamed on government officials came from a literal reading of the 1871 act approved by Congress itself. By Article 1 of the new law, the full rights of those declared members of the Stockbridge and Munsee tribe under the 1856 treaty were restored. In Article 2 the secretary of the interior was instructed to create a roll listing all tribal members and their progeny under operation of the new law.[148] C. C. Painter was appointed to make the required enrollment, and he apparently did an excellent job; in an extremely rare show of unanimity, sixty-six members of both the Indian and Citizens parties sent forward a petition expressing satisfaction with his work.[149]

Unfortunately, one vital ingredient was missing from the Act of 1893—a mechanism for the per capita distribution of tribal trust funds. This problem was not solved until Congress passed another act on May 18, 1916, a full twenty-three years later.[150] In the meantime, twenty-nine allotments were patented under the authority of the Act of 1893. These were issued on February 27, 1897.[151] There continued to be dissatisfaction among the Stockbridge and Munsee because of the lack of a mechanism to distribute the tribal trust funds, and a bill was introduced in Congress in 1904 to accomplish this end. The bill, SB 385, had the support of the commissioner of Indian affairs, the secretary of the interior, and, not surprisingly, "local businessmen in Shawano," but it did not pass.[152]

On June 21, 1906, Congress passed an act that it hoped would settle all of the problems at the Stockbridge and Munsee community by allotting every qualified individual and expending their entire trust fund to do it.[153] The act provides for the allotment of all unallotted members as they are defined in the Act of 1893. If the unsold portion of the reservation—that is, the eighteen sections—was not sufficient for this allotment, then several mechanisms were suggested to assure complete allotment. First, the secretary of the interior was authorized to offer tribal members money at the rate of two dollars per acre in lieu of land. If additional land was still required, the secretary was authorized to purchase what was needed in excess. The bill suggested possible sources: Menominee land, private land from individuals or corporations, or "unappropriated public land."[154] The last source seems particularly appropriate, since to the north and west of the eighteen sections (i.e., on the sold portion of the reservation), there was an abundance of unappropriated public land. Finally, $75,988.60, the entire tribal trust fund, was authorized to be released from the U.S. Treasury to pay the costs incurred by the act.[155]

By September 1907 the entire eighteen sections of the reservation available for allotment had been selected for allotments under provisions of the Treaty of 1856, the Act of 1871, or the Act of 1906. The new allotments had not been made formally as of yet, because a new concern had emerged. A very serious problem had come to the attention of government officials—land fraud. The Act of 1906 contained no alienation provision, and it was apparent that many Stockbridge and Munsee were not capable of protecting new allotments against the unscrupulous land agents, or real estate sharks, of the day. Other members of the tribe wanted to obtain allotments simply for the purpose of selling them for cash.[156] With this problem in mind, the Indian Office continued to delay in approving the new schedule of allotments.[157]

Fraud was a concern to the sachems as well. In June 1910 they wrote to President Taft warning that they would be subjected to schemes of land fraud and would surely suffer land loss.[158] This warning was prophetic. The allotment schedule was approved on June 3, 1909, and fee patents were issued to allottees on April 4, 1910. The land was now taxable by local and state jurisdiction and was held in unrestricted fashion by individual members of the Stockbridge and Munsee tribe. Within a matter of only a few years, there was virtually no land in Indian ownership within the eighteen sections where the allotments had been made.

CHAPTER 17

State of Wisconsin v. Stockbridge-Munsee Community and Robert Chicks, Eastern District of Wisconsin, Case No. 98-C-0871

Brian Pierson
Godfrey and Kahn, Milwaukee, Wisconsin

Background

By a treaty with the United States in February 1856, the Stockbridge-Munsee Community[1] exchanged its remaining lands on Lake Winnebago for a new reservation, a rectangular tract comprising two townships, known today as Bartelme and Red Springs (forty-six thousand acres), in Shawano County, about 80 miles to the north. The treaty included provisions for allotment, and while allotment was not carried out for another fifty years, members chose to make their homes in the southeastern quadrant of the reservation, the southern half of the town of Red Springs. The western half of the reservation, the modern town of Bartelme, was used, but not occupied, by tribal members.

In 1871, as a result of a bitter feud between the tribe's "Indian Party" and "Citizen Party," timber interests procured an act of Congress ordering the sale of three-quarters of the reservation. Only the southeastern quadrant, comprising 11,500 acres, remained. In 1906, Congress enacted a law ordering that fee patents be issued to tribal members for the remaining land. By 1934, many members remained in Red Springs, but ownership of the land had passed entirely from their hands.

Stockbridge-Munsee was among the first tribes to seek reorganization under the Indian Reorganization Act of 1934 (IRA).[2] On March 19, 1937, the secretary of the interior placed into trust and declared "reservation" approximately 1,049.88 acres of "cutover" land in the town of Bartelme, within the 1856 boundaries. The tribe was formally reorganized under the IRA when its constitution was approved by the Department of the Interior on November 18, 1937.

On April 15, 1938, by Executive Order 7868, approximately 13,077 acres within the boundaries of the tribe's 1856 reservation were purchased for the tribe's benefit by the secretary of agriculture and placed under the jurisdiction of the secretary of the interior for the tribe's exclusive use. The land was not, however, formally placed in trust for the tribe. In 1948, a second proclamation added approximately twelve hundred acres to the 1937 proclamation lands. By an act of Congress in 1972, the 13,077 acres purchased in 1938 were placed in trust for the tribe and declared reservation. Most tribal members relocated to Bartelme after the tribe's reorganization, and Bartelme remains the geographical focus of the tribe today.

Settlement patterns and the accidents of the IRA reorganization process explain the tribe's tenacity in fighting for the 1856 boundary. While the 1856 reservation comprised two townships, tribal members settled only in the southeastern quadrant of the reservation, the lower half of Red Springs. Even after tribal members had lost their property through acts of Congress and sales to non-Indians, they continued to live in Red Springs. Their schools, churches, and cemeteries were in Red Springs. Many members still live in Red Springs. Only if the 1856 boundary survives intact is this land, so closely associated with 150 years of tribal history, legally part of "the reservation."

Events Leading to the Filing of the Lawsuit

In 1991, Stockbridge tribal member Bert Davids was cited by Wisconsin game wardens for fishing on upper Gresham Pond without a fishing license. The pond is located within the boundaries of the reservation established pursuant to the Treaty of 1856 but outside the tracts of land placed in trust for the tribe after its reorganization in 1937 under the Indian Reorganization Act. If Davids was within reservation boundaries, the state conceded, he had the right to hunt and fish free of state regulation.

Davids's case eventually made its way to the Wisconsin Supreme Court, which held in *State v.*

Davids[3] that the tribe's 1856 reservation had effectively been disestablished. The tribe supported Davids's defense but did not intervene as a party and could not be bound by the decision under principles of *res judicata*. State officials were now bound by the *Davids* decision, but the tribe would wait for an opportunity to take the matter to federal court. Although, according to conventional wisdom, hunting, fishing, and cultural issues, not gaming, furnish the most sympathetic facts for Indian law cases, a gaming-related dispute precipitated the federal boundary case before the "ideal" case could be built.

Under its 1992 gaming compact with the state, the tribe was authorized to conduct Class III gaming "on tribally-owned land or land held in trust by the United States on behalf of the tribe, but only on such lands within the exterior boundaries of the tribal reservation." Since 1992, the tribe had operated North Star Casino and Bingo on tribal trust land in the town of Bartelme, near Bowler, Wisconsin. In an effort to diversify its economy, the tribe purchased Pine Hills Golf Course and Supper Club (hereinafter "Pine Hills") in 1993. In December 1995, the tribe conveyed the property to the United States in trust for the tribe.

Pine Hills lies in the northern half of the town of Red Springs, which had been sold under the 1871 act of Congress. Under the Indian Gaming Regulatory Act (IGRA),[4] gaming is permitted on "Indian lands," which include "all lands within the limits of any Indian reservation" and land held in trust. With respect to lands acquired after the passage of IGRA in 1988, however, the consent of the state governor is required when land is taken into trust for gaming purposes.[5] The tribe had not followed this process when it purchased Pine Hills. Class III gaming was legal, therefore, only if Pine Hills lies within the limits of the tribe's reservation.

The tribe placed slot machines in Pine Hills on August 28, 1998. The state filed an action in the U.S. District Court for the Eastern District of Wisconsin on September 3, 1998, seeking a preliminary injunction against Class III gaming at Pine Hills pending trial, a permanent injunction, and a declaratory judgment that the 1856 reservation no longer existed. The litigation battle over the Stockbridge reservation boundary had begun.

Legal Context

Cases concerning Indian reservation boundaries are not uncommon. The U.S. Supreme Court has decided seven such cases in the modern era, and the legal principles that control, while awkward to apply, are well established. According to diminishment law theory, only Congress can diminish a reservation: "Once a block of land is set aside for an Indian reservation, and *no matter what happens to the title of individual plots within the area,* the entire block retains its reservation status until Congress *explicitly* indicates otherwise" (emphasis added).[6] The four-part test established to determine whether a diminishment has occurred, however, clearly provides otherwise.

The most-cited formulation of the test derives from the Supreme Court's decision in *Solem v. Bartlett:*

1. "The most probative evidence of congressional intent is the statutory language used to open the Indian lands. *Explicit* reference to cession or other language evidencing the *present and total surrender of all tribal interests* strongly suggests that Congress meant to divest from the reservation all unallotted opened lands" (emphasis added).[7]
2. "Explicit language of cession and unconditional compensation are not prerequisites for a finding of diminishment. When events surrounding the passage of a surplus land act—particularly the manner in which the transaction was negotiated with the tribes involved and the tenor of legislative reports presented to Congress—*unequivocally* reveal a widely-held, contemporaneous understanding that the affected reservation would shrink as a result of the proposed legislation, we have been willing to infer that Congress shared the understanding that its action would diminish the reservation . . ." (emphasis added).[8]
3. "*To a lesser extent,* we have also looked to events that occurred after the passage of a surplus land act to decipher Congress' intentions. Congress' own

treatment of the affected areas, particularly in the years *immediately* following the opening, has some evidentiary value, as does the manner in which the Bureau of Indian Affairs and local judicial authorities dealt with unallotted, open lands" (emphasis added).[9]

4. "On a more pragmatic level, we have recognized that who actually moved into opened reservation lands is also relevant to deciding whether a surplus land act diminished a reservation. Where non-Indian settlers *flooded* into the opened portion of a reservation and the area has *long since lost its Indian character,* we have acknowledged that *de facto,* if not *de jure,* diminishment may have occurred" (emphasis added).[10]

Notwithstanding the four-part test, the *Solem* Court cautioned that "when both an act and its legislative history fail to provide *substantial and compelling* evidence of a congressional intention to diminish Indian lands, we are bound by our traditional solicitude for the Indian tribes to rule that diminishment did not take place and that the old reservation boundaries survived the opening" (emphasis added).[11] Applying these legal principles, the Court found in *Solem* that Congress did not diminish the Cheyenne Sioux Reservation when it passed the Cheyenne River Act in 1908.

While the *Solem* decision seemed to set the bar high for states alleging diminishment of reservations, it proved to be the high-water mark for pro-tribe diminishment decisions. In the only two post-*Solem* diminishment cases, *Hagen v. Utah*[12] and *South Dakota v. Yankton Sioux Tribe,*[13] the Court found that acts of Congress had diminished the Ute and Yankton Sioux reservations, respectively.

The Parties' Legal Positions

The state and tribe both acknowledged that the four-part *Solem* test provided the analytical framework that would determine whether the 1856 reservation boundaries had been diminished. The parties applied the elements of the *Solem* test separately to the fifty-four sections of land sold under the 1871 act of Congress and to the remaining eighteen sections of the reservation patented to tribal members under the 1906 act of Congress. The 1871 act (1) provided for the appraisal and sale at auction, in eighty-acre lots, of fifty-four out of the seventy-two sections comprising the reservation; (2) authorized the secretary of the interior to reserve eighteen sections of the reservation for tribal members to continue to reside on and provided that the tribe could remain on the reserved lands or relocate to another reservation; (3) ordered the preparation of an Indian Party roll, composed of tribal members wishing to maintain their Indian status, and a Citizen Party roll, composed of those who wished to sever their tribal ties; (4) authorized the commissioner of Indian Affairs to appoint an agent to make the rolls and authorized the agent to exclude from both rolls anyone who had derived certain benefits from previous treaties and congressional acts; (5) provided that enrollment on the Citizen roll would be held as a full surrender and relinquishment by the Citizen Party of all claims derived from tribal membership; (6) provided that the money raised from the sale was to be divided between the Indian Party and Citizen Party members, with the Citizen Party members receiving their shares in cash and the Indian Party portion being deposited in a trust account in Washington, D.C.; and (7) provided for the allotment of unsold reservation lands to members of the Indian Party in 40- or 80-acre parcels, depending on family status.

The Indian Party members elected to reserve the southeastern quadrant of the reservation, the southern half of the town of Red Springs, where they already resided. The Indian Party colluded with federal agents in drawing up the Indian Party and Citizen Party rolls, with the result that many of the Indian Party's longtime political enemies were left off both rolls and disenfranchised entirely. This resulted in repeated attempts by the disenrolled, henceforth known as the Old Citizens Party, to procure remedial legislation. Their efforts culminated in an 1893 act of Congress reenfranchising those excluded from the rolls made under the 1871 act and restoring their rights to share in tribal funds and lands pursuant to the provisions of the 1871 act. This proved impractical because there was too little land to provide allotments for the members wishing to receive them. In 1906, Congress passed a law ordering the patenting of the land in fee simple and cash payment in lieu of land for those who did not receive allotments. The patents were issued in 1910.

The state's argument that Congress intended to diminish the reservation by fifty-four sections when it passed the 1871 act cited the complete alienation of these lands by the tribe, the compensation received by the tribe for the land sold, and extensive documentation reflecting the understanding of federal, state, and tribal officials that the fifty-four sections sold were no longer subject to federal or tribal jurisdiction or part of the reservation. With respect to the 1906 act, the state principally argued that after the patents were issued in 1910, there remained no land in federal trust status subject to federal oversight; that extensive documentation reflected an understanding among federal, state, and tribal members that the tribe and its reservation had ceased to exist; that two federal court cases decided in 1911 and 1915 had both concluded that the reservation had been dissolved; and that federal officials handling the tribe's application for reorganization under the IRA during the 1930s determined that the tribe was without a reservation. The state pointed out that proclamations that certain lands within the 1856 boundaries were "reservation lands," by the Department of the Interior in 1948 and by Congress in 1972, would have been unnecessary if the 1856 reservation had not previously been disestablished.

The Tribe's Strategy

The documentary record was overwhelmingly favorable to the state. Virtually all parties—state, federal, and tribal—seemed to largely concede the demise of the 1856 reservation after 1910. The tribe's strategy was to do everything possible to undermine the weight of this material while insisting on the primacy of the text of the congressional acts and the absence from them of certain language deemed by the U.S. Supreme Court in *Solem* to be indicative of an intent to diminish.

On the one hand, the tribe highlighted ambiguities in the historical record, offered alternative interpretations whenever possible, and attacked the state's documentary case by adducing all available countervailing evidence. The tribe emphasized in particular a letter written in 1911 by Frederic Abbott, the assistant commissioner of Indian affairs, explicitly stating that the reservation survived both acts of Congress. On the other hand, the tribe argued that the numerous statements by state, federal, and tribal officials that seemed to acknowledge the reservation's disestablishment were, in any event, hardly relevant. Far from reflecting the intent of Congress, they merely reflected the allotment era's common understanding and expectation that tribes and reservations were on an inevitable path to extinction. Reliance on this sort of evidence, the tribe contended, would contradict the Supreme Court's warning that such assumptions and expectations were insufficient to support a finding of diminishment.

The tribe insisted that the language used by Congress, not subsequent understandings by others, provided the most relevant evidence of congressional intent. According to *Solem,* congressional intent to diminish must be "explicit," "unequivocal," or "substantial and compelling." In *Solem,* the Court's preferred linguistic indicia of legislative intent to diminish were certain phrasings in treaties and congressional acts, such as "hereby cede, sell, and relinquish all right, title, and interest." The tribe vigorously and repeatedly emphasized the absence of these phrasings from the 1871 and 1906 acts. The Court's demand for clear expressions of congressional intent to diminish in *Solem,* the tribe argued, should be understood in light of the Court's acknowledgment that the policy of allotment and assimilation has been repudiated. In light of that repudiation, an insistence on clear language was not a sophistic distraction but a matter of historical justice.

To bolster its "historical justice" argument, the tribe also stressed the fraudulent aspects of the 1871 congressional act. These included the collusion between Indian Party members and Wisconsin congressman and lumber baron Philetus Sawyer, the concealment of the legislation from certain Citizen Party members and the local Indian agent, the Indian Party's subsequent use of the enrollment process to expel large numbers of Citizen Party members, and Congress's recognition of the these circumstances at the time it enacted a remedial law in 1893.

Both the tribe and the state took a "no stone unturned" approach to the case, hiring multiple expert witnesses and performing extensive research on tribal history, congressional records, and the records of the Office of Indian Affairs and its successor agency, the Bureau of Indian Affairs.

The fourth prong of the four-part Solem test, whether a reservation has lost its "Indian character" and consequently undergone a "de facto diminishment," though not the major battleground of the case, was nonetheless the focus of much attention. In addition to documenting the tribe's continuing presence within the 1856 boundaries, the tribe's experts interviewed tribal elders and mapped historical uses of forest and other lands for hunting, fishing, and gathering activities.

The Course of Litigation

Upon filing, the case was assigned to magistrate judge Patricia Gorence. The state immediately moved for a preliminary injunction requiring the tribe to cease Class III gaming activities at Pine Hills. A three-day hearing was held on October 28–30, 1998. The state's witnesses included Dr. James Clifton, a well-known scholar in the field of Indian treaties, Fred Kafura, a local activist opposed to tribal jurisdiction, a local deputy sheriff, and the corporation counsel for Shawano County. The tribe's witnesses included Sheila Powless, a tribal land and enrollment officer, and Dr. James Oberly, a historian. By an order dated October 4, 1999, nearly a year after the hearing, the court granted the state's motion for a preliminary injunction barring gaming at Pine Hills pending final judgment, as reported at 67 F. Supp. 2d 990.[14] The parties proceeded with their historical research in preparation with the case.

The state's suit, as originally filed, could not result in a final clarification of the reservation boundaries because a determination whether the 1871 act diminished the reservation boundaries would not address the issue whether the eighteen sections of land in the southern half of Red Springs, which were reserved under the 1871 act but patented under the 1906 act, were still within reservation boundaries. Both sides recognized that the boundary litigation would involve an enormous amount of historical research, effort, and expense. Therefore, the tribe and the state agreed to "create" a separate issue involving the status of the southern half of Red Springs, so that its status could also be determined by the litigation.

It is well established in Indian law that a state has no authority to tax Indians residing on their reservations on their reservation-source income. Many Stockbridge members living in Red Springs worked at the casino but chose not to have state income tax withheld from their wages. The state was aware of this circumstance. In order to raise the issue of the status of southern Red Springs, therefore, the tribe brought a counterclaim on April 28, 2000, seeking a declaratory judgment that the 1856 boundaries of the reservation remain intact and an injunction barring the state from taxing tribal members residing within the 1856 boundaries on income earned within those boundaries.

The parties agreed that pending final resolution of the boundary issue, the tribe would withhold from the wages of affected tribal members and hold in escrow an amount equal to state income tax withholding. The state would desist from any enforcement action (stipulation of March 2000, recitals A–D). The court accepted the parties' stipulation by an order dated April 12, 2000.

In its preliminary injunction briefs and at the October 1998 preliminary hearing, the state relied primarily on James Clifton for expert testimony. The court took a full ten months after the post-hearing briefs were filed to issue its preliminary injunction in September 1999. It was then expected that summary judgment proceedings or possibly a trial would be held in the fall of 2000. Dr. Clifton died in the summer of 2000, however, pushing back the briefing schedule for nearly a year, as the state retained two additional experts, Dr. Lawrence Kelly and Alan Newell. To supplement Dr. Oberly's testimony, the tribe retained Dr. Charles Cleland, an eminent historian of the Great Lakes tribes and a treaty litigation veteran. All of the expert witnesses were deposed at length.

Ultimately, the parties agreed that the case was largely based on historical documents and could be decided on summary judgment affidavits and briefs. Because of the vast scope of the case, Judge Gorence permitted briefing that was unusually extensive. The tribe filed its summary judgment motion, a fifty-four-page brief, and thirty-one pages of proposed findings of fact on March 1, 2002. The state responded with its sixty-page brief and fifty-one pages of proposed findings on May 1, 2002. The tribe replied with another fifty-six-page brief and an eighty-two-page response to the state's proposed findings.

A major development occurred on June 2, 2002, when the U.S. Department of Justice, after two years of urging by the tribe, filed a fifty-two-page amicus curiae brief taking the tribe's side. The court permitted the state and the tribe to respond. On July 31, 2002, the state filed a fifty-two-page surreply. The briefing ended with the tribe's modest, ten-page surrebuttal on August 16, 2002.

Although the briefing was formally complete on August 16, 2002, the case was not yet ready for the court's consideration. The historical documentation submitted by the parties took up some twelve feet of shelf space. The parties had previously agreed to assist the court by submitting a set of "core" documents that the court could use for easy reference. These documents, consisting of the records actually cited in the briefs, comprising two large volumes, were assembled in October. After the core documents were assembled and numbered, revised versions of the briefs and proposed findings of fact were prepared using the new document numbers.

Outcome of the Case

On September 30, 2004, Judge Gorence handed down her 147-page decision in the state's favor, holding that the 1856 reservation was diminished in 1871 when Congress ordered the sale of fifty-four sections and was disestablished when the remaining eighteen sections were distributed to tribal members in fee simple pursuant to the 1906 act. The court was persuaded largely by the extensive documentary evidence that supported the state's case, the federal court decisions in 1911 and 1915 holding that the reservation was dissolved, statements to that effect by federal officials implementing the acts, the determination of the Office of Indian Affairs during the 1930s that the 1856 reservation had been disestablished, and the 1972 congressional declaration that certain lands within the 1856 boundaries were now (but presumably not before 1972) "reservation lands." Judge Gorence's decision is reported as *State v. Stockbridge-Munsee Community and Chicks.*[15]

The tribe filed an appeal from Judge Gorence's decision to the Seventh Circuit Court of Appeals in Chicago. Shortly after the appeal was filed, the tribe and the state agreed to stay the appeal while the parties pursued unsuccessful settlement discussions. On January 20, 2009, the court affirmed Judge Gorence's summary judgment in the state's favor, 554 F.3d 657 (7th cir. 2009). The court's nine-page decision was not a significant contribution to reservation diminishment jurisprudence.

Significance of the Case

For the tribe, the significance of Judge Gorence's ruling is threefold. First, it means that lands that the tribe has purchased or will purchase in fee simple within the 1856 boundaries do not have "Indian country" status until placed into trust. As a consequence, they are subject to state zoning laws and other regulation in the absence of an agreement with the state. Second, tribal members living on fee land within the 1856 boundaries are liable for state income tax. Finally, on an emotion level, tribal members had to accept that the sites in Red Springs where so much of the tribe's history unfolded after 1856 and where their parents and grandparents lived, worked, worshipped, went to school, hunted, fished, gathered and lay buried, were not "the reservation," except to the extent they could be reacquired and placed into trust.

The significance of the decision for federal Indian law is modest. The district court acknowledged that the tribe presented "well-crafted and researched briefs . . . along with their detailed documentary support." The tribe's argument was supported by the controlling legal test to the extent that Congress did not, in either the 1871 act or 1906 act, employ language the U.S. Supreme Court had considered most indicative of an intent to diminish. This circumstance, together with the doctrine that doubtful cases should result in a finding of no diminishment, certainly could have supported a favorable decision for the tribe. It is also true, however, that no court has ever held that a reservation has survived congressional acts causing 100 percent of the reservation to be patented in fee simple, without a single acre remaining in trust status. To the extent that another tribe should contend for its treaty-established reservation in the face of similar congressional acts, the Stockbridge decision is a negative decision. Such cases are likely to be very rare. The vast majority of diminishment cases will afford tribal litigants ample grounds for distinguishing the Stockbridge decision based on the historical record.

The Treaty of 1855

CHAPTER 18

The Ethnohistory of the Mille Lacs Reservation Boundary

The main objectives of the United States in the treaty it made with the Chippewa on February 22, 1855, was to acquire land in northern Minnesota and, pursuant to the policies of George Manypenny, the commissioner of Indian affairs, to settle the Chippewa on reservations where they could be exposed to civilizing influences as well as protected from unscrupulous traders and whiskey peddlers. The Chippewa, particularly the Mille Lacs bands, were also anxious to acquire permanent and protected homes. By 1855 lumbermen were already having an impact on the Mille Lacs people, because a dam they built in order to float logs down the Rum River was backing up water and destroying the rice crop on which the Indians depended for their subsistence.

During the negotiations, the Mille Lacs bands were represented by the chiefs of four bands: Pedudence (Muskrat's Liver), Menomenkeshin (Rice Maker), Kaygwaydash (The Attempter), and Shobaushkum (He That Passes under Everything). These were seasoned political leaders who were familiar with the treaty negotiation process. It was the young Gull Lake Chippewa chief Hole-in-the-Day, however, who was selected to do most of the negotiating for the Chippewa at the Treaty of 1855. Although Hole-in-the-Day may have understood some English, he could not converse in the language.[1] When it came time to discuss their reservations, Commissioner Manypenny instructed the Indians to confer among themselves and to define the boundaries of the reservations they desired.[2]

Two of the Mille Lacs chiefs actually marked out the boundary of the proposed reserve on a map supplied by the commissioner.[3] Of all eight reservations created by the treaty, only in the case of the Mille Lacs Reservation was the land described by the township and range designators of the United States land survey system. In other cases, simple descriptions by metes and bounds were made in anticipation of actual survey at a later date. This was, of course, due to the fact that the general land survey had already been extended to the Mille Lacs area as a result of the lumbering frontier. Specifically, Article 2 of the 1855 treaty reads in part, "There shall be, and hereby is, reserved and set apart, a sufficient quantity of land for the permanent homes of the said Indians; the lands so reserved and set apart, to be in separate tracts as follows, viz: For the Mississippi bands of Chippewa Indians: The first to embrace the following fractional townships, viz: forty-two north, of range twenty-five west; forty-two north, of range twenty-six west; and forty-two and forty-three north of range twenty-seven west; and also the three islands in the southern part of Mille Lac."[4] Although the 1855 treaty reserved the right for the United States to survey and allot the land within the four fractional townships to Mille Lacs Indians and to build roads across reservation land, its exterior boundaries remain today as they were described in 1855. See map 23.

The Mille Lacs chiefs made an excellent choice in the selection of the reservation. The designated townships provided access to the lake and adjoining marshes, where the Chippewa could secure the rice and fish that were their two most dependable resources, as well as waterfowl, muskrat, beaver, and a host of useful plants. Higher ground surrounding the lake supported maple groves where they made sugar, gardening sites, and shelter for deer, bear, and a wide variety of other plant and animal species the Mille Lacs relied on for their subsistence as well as trade. These reservation resources, coupled with their reserved right to hunt over the territory they ceded in the Treaty of 1837, made their future seem secure. In fact, the country around Mille Lacs Lake was so productive for hunters and gatherers that the other Chippewa of the Mississippi bands began to suggest it as a removal destination.[5]

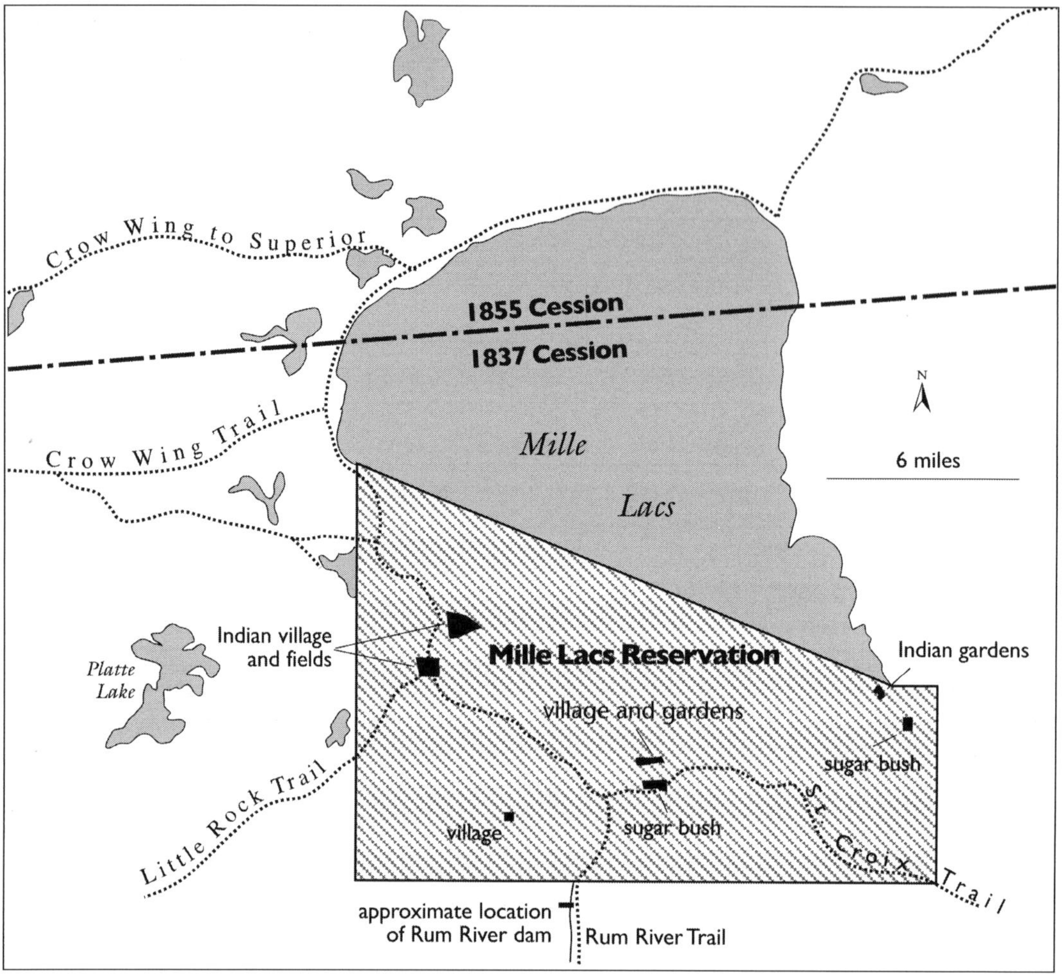

Map 23. Location of Mille Lacs reservation and Indian settlements 1855. (After Trygg 1966.)

Under the classificatory scheme outlined by Jacob Thompson, secretary of the interior, in 1860, it is clear that the Mille Lacs Reservation is an example of a "tribal reservation" where the intention was to provide allotments in a compact body with a well-defined exterior boundary, over which the intercourse laws could be enforced. In fact, Article 7 of the Treaty of 1855 does extend the intercourse laws over the reservation.

The Post-1855 Treaty Period

During the last half of the nineteenth century, many ploys were used to get the Mille Lacs Chippewa off the land they had reserved by the Treaty of 1855. These involved the worst kind of deceit, fraud, and outright theft. The Chippewa understood that what was happening to them was not what had been promised in their treaties, but they were almost powerless in the situation. Since the Chippewa were not citizens of the United States or the state of Minnesota, they were not protected by the law except for the nonintercourse statutes that regulated trade and resource use in Indian country. Beyond that, the Mille Lacs people had no standing as individuals in the federal or state courts. Their only recourse was to appeal to their personal relationship with the Great Father with whom they had signed treaties. The frequent appeals of the chiefs to go to Washington to see the president were almost always rebuffed by local Indian agents.

During the 1850s and 1860s, the Mille Lacs people were repeatedly swept by epidemics of smallpox, syphilis, and other introduced diseases. These ravages left their numbers depleted and their labor pool diminished. The latter situation can be devastating to hunters and gatherers, who typically have a low ratio of producers to consumers to begin with. Another problem that made their lives difficult was that their Indian agents at Crow Wing, like those at many other Indian agencies of the period, were corrupt. These men enriched themselves by selling the annuity goods meant for Indians to others, by padding annuity rolls to steal money from the tribes, and by taking kickbacks from fees charged to issue licenses for Indian traders. The traders, in turn, passed the increased cost of goods on to the Indian customers. Further, all of the protests of the chiefs fell on deaf ears, even though the transgressions of the agency were well documented by Minnesota Bishop Henry Whipple in letters to Presidents Buchanan and Lincoln as well as Senator Henry Rice.[6]

Finally, in 1862 the Santee Dakota could stand no more corruption. They revolted and destroyed the Redwood agency and, in the process, killed more than eight hundred settlers in the Minnesota River valley.[7] Heightened threats of violence spread as Hole-in-the-Day as well as some of the other Mississippi Chippewa chiefs raised a war party of several hundred warriors with the announced intention of killing all of the whites in the upper Mississippi Valley. Terrified American settlers were soon streaming into Fort Ripley near Crow Wing, where a standoff ensued between the Chippewa warriors and the U.S. military.[8]

The Mille Lacs chiefs promised by Article 9 of the Treaty of 1855 to conduct themselves peacefully and to not commit depredations or wrong upon citizens of the United States. The Mille Lacs took this pledge very seriously. Indeed, they went so far as to send a large group of warriors under Chief Shagobi to Fort Ripley in 1862 to help the American soldiers protect the refugees.[9]

In the midst of the ensuring standoff, the commissioner of Indian affairs, William Dole, along with former governor Alexander Ramsey and Senator Henry Rice, appeared at Fort Ripley and diffused the situation by meeting Hole-in-the-Day's demands. These officials, as well as the settlers, were extremely appreciative of help from the Mille Lacs. Commissioner Dole met with chiefs Moseomannay, Menomenkeshin, and Shobaushkum and promised them the friendship and support of the United States. It was not long before the Mille Lacs chiefs had occasion to remind Dole of his promise.[10]

Early Attempts to Concentrate the Chippewa, 1863–64

Just a year after the United States promised the Mille Lacs Chippewa that it would safeguard their interests, serious attempts were made to remove the Mississippi Chippewa bands, including the Mille Lacs, from their reservations. The idea behind this removal was to clear them off the valuable timberland they occupied at Mille Lacs and to curtail their use of other areas of southern Minnesota, so that these areas would be available to frontier farmers and lumber merchants. The removal was justified by the idea that such a move was good for the Indians, since they could be concentrated for the purpose of turning them into individual landowners and self-sufficient farmers. As the nature of the plan would ultimately show, however, the driving force behind the idea was not really a genuine desire to better the conditions of the Chippewa but sheer greed. To put it simply, as long as the land around Mille Lacs Lake was a federal Indian reservation, federal law prohibited the harvest of standing timber, and it was thus off-limits to timber merchants.[11] For most Americans on the Great Lakes frontier, this was just another example of Indian savages standing in the path of civilization.

In 1863 former Minnesota senator, Minnesota politician, and Indian trader Henry Rice started a campaign to remove the southern Chippewa, including the Mille Lacs bands, to the northern part of the state. Rice was well known to the Indians from his trading days, and the Chippewa referred to him as "White Rice." When serving as a senator, he had appeared at the 1855 treaty negotiations to urge the Chippewa to sign.[12] On that occasion and in later times, Rice styled himself as a "friend to the Indians," and the chiefs accepted him in this role, placing their trust in his advice.[13]

In fact, Rice was no friend of the Indians. His interest instead was in advancing the settlement of Minnesota and his own financial interests.

Rice and his compatriots in Minnesota politics and business seemed to believe that what was good for the local economy was also good for the Indians. In late 1862 a plan was hatched to concentrate the Mississippi Chippewa—consisting of the Gull Lake, Rabbit Lake, Rice Lake, Pokegama Lake, and Sandy Lake bands, along with the Mille Lacs bands—on a large reservation around Leech, Cass, and Winnibigoshish lakes. The Chippewa chiefs objected and suggested instead that they might better join the Mille Lacs on an expanded reservation that would surround Mille Lacs Lake.[14] This idea was rejected for the reason that it was contrary to the idea that initially motivated the proposed removal.

In 1863 the Chippewa of the Mississippi were called to Washington to approve a new treaty. Article 1 of this treaty with the Chippewa of the Mississippi and the Pillager and Lake Winnibigoshish bands required the cessions of all of the reservations created by the Treaty of 1855. Article 2 of the treaty created the new reservation that was to serve as the removal destination and new home for the Chippewa of the Mississippi. The 1863 treaty was based on the same philosophy that motivated the earlier, Manypenny treaties; the thing that was different is that it called for removal from their traditional territories. Surely the 1863 treaty was one of the worst and most bizarre treaties ever concluded between the United States and an Indian group. Henry Rice boasted that he had written every word of the treaty, accepting no input from either whites or Indians, and that he had allowed no changes during its negotiation—although he did lament that the U.S. Senate had made certain ill-advised modifications.[15] While Rice was pleased with his own efforts, the Chippewa were not.

Unlike Rice, the Chippewa knew the country around Leech, Cass, and Winnibigoshish lakes proposed for the Chippewa agricultural colony that was described in the treaty. The chiefs knew this land to be marshy, conifer muskeg. Not only was it unfit for farming, but there was not enough dry land to allot to all of the Indians involved in the proposed removal. It was also a sterile country for hunters and gatherers, one that could not support any more Indians than already lived there. Chief Shobaushkum referred to the area around the new reservation as "a country of starvation."[16] It is little wonder the Mille Lacs refused to remove to such a place and had absolutely no intention to do so.

When Shobaushkum died early in 1890, Henry Whipple eulogized him in a newspaper article that relates Shobaushkum's encounter with an agent sent by the government to talk to the Mille Lacs people about removing to the Leech-Cass-Winnibigoshish Reservation. Trying to impress Shobaushkum, the agent, bragging of his own honesty and wisdom, told Shobaushkum that the "winds of fifty-five years had blown through his hair and turned it grey." Shobaushkum replied that "the winds of fifty-five years had also blown through his own hair and silvered it but it had not blown his brain away."[17]

So why did the Mille Lacs sign the 1863 treaty? They did so for two reasons. The first was that they were party to the 1855 treaty, where, by Article 1, they received an equitable interest in all of the reservations created for the Chippewa of the Mississippi. Thus, as Shobaushkum explained to E. P. Smith, commissioner of Indian affairs, "We signed the paper [the Treaty of 1863] because we were asked to sign with the other Indians who were signing the paper for their land, and we did sign the paper giving our land away because the others wanted us to sign with them."[18]

The second reason the Mille Lacs chiefs signed was because they believed that the treaty did not affect their right to live at Mille Lacs. This belief flowed from a proviso in Article 12 of the treaty that "owing to the heretofore good conduct of the Mille Lacs Indians, they shall not be compelled to remove so long as they shall not in any way interfere with or in any manner molest the persons or property of the whites."[19] This was their reward, what they alone of all the Mississippi Chippewa bands received from a grateful U.S. government for their action to protect American citizens during the Indian uprisings of 1862. There were many subsequent records to indicate that their interpretation of the 1863 treaty was clear and consistent over the years. Ultimately, the author of the treaty, Henry Rice, absolutely confirmed the interpretation of the Mille Lacs chiefs.

Soon after the chiefs returned home from negotiating the new treaty in 1867, they wrote to the secretary of the Indian Department about their understanding of the 1863 treaty: "We have remembered the words of our great father that he said to us six years ago when we went down to Washington, if we would behave ourselves as we had done before that we should be let alone on the land we had before occupied for a hundred years or a *thousand* years or as long as we not commit any *depredations.* It is because we *behave ourselves* is the reason why we are so differently treated from other Bands."[20] In the spring of 1870, Joseph Roberts visited Mille Lacs and talked to the chiefs. He reported that the chiefs "are strictly opposed to leaving the reservation. They are now just as much opposed to leave the reservation as they were in the year 1866, when I was sent by Gen. Coarse, to find out if they were willing to leave at that time. They claim the right under the Treaty of 1863 or 4, that they should be allowed to remain at that reservation of the country they occupied before, for four hundred years, providing they would commit no depredations, *which they claim they did not.*"[21] In 1880 the Mille Lacs chiefs petitioned their Great Father President Rutherford B. Hayes:

> In the summer of 1862 when other Indians made war on the whites, we stood by them and offered to fight with them against our own people.
>
> For our kindness our Great Father in Washington [President Abraham Lincoln] and the great and good men with him who ruled this great nation made us a promise that we should inherit our home on the beautiful and to us lovely Mille Lac forever; or so long as we behaved ourselves well towards our white neighbors.[22]

A story in the *Minneapolis Tribune* on July 18, 1883, reported that a delegation of four Mille Lacs chiefs visited Governor Hubbard. Chief Moseomannay, who was a signer of the 1863 treaty, is quoted as saying, "At the time [1863] the Indians were given to understand that they should, as long as they were peaceful towards the whites, occupy the reservation forever."[23] Given this understanding of the 1863–64 treaties and the alternative of moving to a desolate northern reservation where they would face sure starvation, it is little wonder that the right to remain on the Mille Lacs Reservation was appealing.[24]

Soon after the treaty was negotiated, when it was suggested that the Mille Lacs bands might be required to remove from their reservation, the chiefs sent a message to their Great Father President Lincoln, by way of Bishop Henry Whipple, that they did not wish to remove but instead wished "to stick with the treaty of last winter and further that we will be friendly to the whites as long as we live." They also told the president that they wanted the treaty "carried out to the letter."[25] This language hardly sounds like they believed that the 1863 treaty would rip them from the security of their homeland afforded within the reservation boundary created for them in 1855 and send them to "the land of starvation." The Mille Lacs bands did not believe the Treaty of 1863 or the nearly identical companion treaty approved in 1864 required them to do anything at all except to not molest the persons or the property of the whites. Certainly they did not believe that these treaties disrupted their tenure on the Mille Lacs Reservation. This is why they embraced them.

The Chippewa, like other tribal people on the North American continent, were born and raised within a nonliterate tradition. Their intertribal agreements, like their history, were entirely oral. The Chippewa were very skilled not only in verbal expression but especially at hearing and remembering what was said on official occasions. Since they could not read the English language, a written document that emerged from treaty negotiations with Euro-Americans was regarded by the Indians more as a magical talisman that symbolized the real agreement, which was the oral one. The Gull Lake chief Hole-in-the Day once expressed this view during the negotiations of the Treaty of 1855. When Commissioner Manypenny cautioned that the Chippewa might be cheated with documents they could not read, Hole-in-the-Day replied that while this was true, "where persons have faith in the paper, it is as good and valid as if they could read it." When Manypenny warned against this view, Hole-in-the-Day replied, "Our people must have faith in somebody or they cannot trust anybody."[26]

The Chippewa, as well as other Great Lakes

tribes, also thought of treaties more as agreements made between men, not governments. This is why, from the earliest time of interaction with Europeans, the tribes saw agreements concerning war, peace, and trade as personal agreements between the chiefs representing Indian groups and the Great Father, the president. In Chippewa society, a chief was like a father, a wise and respected leader whose people followed out of trust. It was assumed that the Great Father was equally concerned with the welfare of his followers. Likewise, in Chippewa custom, they often cast themselves as supplicants symbolized as "children" of the Great Father. Thus, the Great Father became a protector who would demonstrate his wealth, wisdom, and generosity by providing goods and services to his red children as he did for his white children. On the nineteenth-century American frontier, Indian people were becoming increasingly economically dependent and politically powerless. They were in need of the support of the Great Father, whom they implicitly trusted to look after their interests.

The Chippewa seldom understood government bureaucracy, the operation of American law, conflicting interests among officials, or the division of power within the American government. They certainly did not understand how, of all the things talked about and decided on in the course of a treaty negotiation, it was only the few things that were written down that really seemed to count. In February 1875 Shobaushkum and a delegation of Mille Lacs chiefs met in Washington with the commissioner of Indian affairs, E. P. Smith, who had formerly been their agent. The chiefs reminded Smith about the promise President Lincoln had made to them about the occupation of their reservation. Their conversation illustrates the difficulty of working between the understandings of two distinct cultural traditions.

> SHOBAUSHKUNG: We signed the paper [the Treaty of 1863] because we were asked to sign with the other Indians who were signing the paper for their land, and we did sign the paper giving our land away because the others wanted us to sign with them.
>
> COMMISSIONER: That is not here [in the treaty]. That was something that was spoken and it went away when they swept the room out in the morning.
>
> SHOBAUSHKUNG: Well we do not understand. It is very strange to us that whenever anything is done before us we think it is all right; but [we are] misled after getting out of the office something more was added of which we knew nothing.
>
> COMMISSIONER: Yes, that is the trouble you and [I] are in and I have no doubt there is a good deal of truth in what you say, but I cannot help it.
>
> SHOBAUSHKUNG: How was it that these things were added to the treaty? Can it be changed in our favor?
>
> COMMISSIONER: It cannot be changed now except by Congress. They could do it.
>
> SHOBAUSHKUNG: Yes, it is true that Congress could change it because the Great Spirit is near to them with power.
>
> COMMISSIONER: No, that is not it. The Great Spirit is no nearer a congressman than a Mille Lacs Indian.
>
> SHOBAUSHKUNG: Yes, whenever we express ourselves between us the Great Spirit hears our words. He is looking at us. The Great Spirit has placed us where we are and he has made us poor as we are, and has made us to live on what is on the earth that he has placed before us. We have been living on what has been before we were placed there by the Great Spirit.[27]

In this exchange, the Chippewa are saying first that they never understood that they were giving up their rights on the Mille Lacs Reservation by the 1863–64 treaties. They agreed to the cession because they believed they should sign with the other bands; because they trusted the promises of Rice, Dole, and Lincoln; and because of the assurances of the proviso of Article 12 of the treaty. The question that the Chippewa must have asked themselves is how, if they retained the privilege of occupying the land and living on it, would it be claimed that they had given it away? How, they wondered, could land promised for their use be invaded by those eager to cut timber and their maple sugar groves, to steal their garden plots, and to build dams that flooded out their rice crops? In their traditional system of land use, the resources of one band could not be used by people of other bands without permission. Yet they did acknowledge that they signed the treaty "with the other Indians *who were signing the paper for their land*" (emphasis added).[28] As signers of the Treaty of 1855 that created all of the reservations for all of the Chippewa bands, the Mille Lacs chiefs believed they had an obligation to sign off on the surrender of those reservations. They did not believe they were signing a paper that would restrict their occupation and use of the Mille Lacs Reservation. The chiefs believed that they had reserved the right to occupy the reservation as long as they remained at peace with the whites and that the Great Father was bound by the agreement to protect this right.

In October 1889 the two men who actually knew all the complexities of the negotiation of the 1863 treaty met for a final time, when Henry Rice and Shobaushkum met on the shore of Mille Lacs Lake to negotiate the fate of the Mille Lacs bands under the Nelson Act. This time there was a secretary to record their conversation. On that occasion, twenty-five years after the fact, Henry Rice finally admitted for the first time that the interpretation given by the chiefs was correct. As he declared, "The time has come when I am able to tell you all he [Joseph Roberts] said, all I have said to you, all the chiefs told you—who were there and made the treaty is correct; that the understanding of the chiefs as to the treaty was right. Here is the acknowledgement of the government that you were right, that you have not forfeited your right to occupy *the reservation*" (emphasis added).[29]

This startling and long-belated admission by their "friend" must have been bittersweet. Although the unwavering belief of the chiefs as to the meaning of the 1863–64 treaties was vindicated, the misery and hardship of land loss due to Henry Rice's silence were hard to accept. At least they could take comfort in the fact that despite these encroachments, the government continued to recognize their right of occupancy and the existence of the reservation.

Fighting for the Reservation, 1867–89

By early in 1867, the government realized that the Chippewa were correct about the character of the land around the Leech, Cass, and Winnebigoshish lakes. It was not fit for agricultural allotments. Besides, it was also clear that the Mississippi Chippewa had no intention to remove to the new reservation, particularly since the government's obligation to prepare land for agriculture as a condition of removal, as stated in Article 12 of the treaty, had not been fulfilled.

A new treaty with the Chippewa of the Mississippi was negotiated in 1867 that ceded back to the government a portion of the land that composed the reservations created by the 1863–64 treaties.[30] A principal provision of the new treaty was the creation of a reservation of thirty-six townships at White Earth to accommodate all of the Mississippi Chippewa. It was hoped that added inducements such as schools, homes, health care, annuity payments, and agricultural equipment and training would rapidly draw the Chippewa to White Earth. It should be noted, however, that there was no provision in the new treaty calling for the removal of Indians to the new reservation, nor did any of its provisions affect the Mille Lacs people's right of occupancy granted to them under the 1863–64 treaties.

The Mississippi Chippewa chiefs were only home from negotiating the new treaty for a few months when they wrote to the commissioner of Indian affairs repudiating the 1867 treaty and asking him to meet them in council at Fort Ripley: "We as a tribe of Chippewa of [the] Mississippi are opposed to the Treaty made last winter with some of our people, who held no authority from us to make such a treaty. We consider the recent treaties made are not binding upon our people and we will never consent to remove to the new proposed reservation [White Earth]. We will *die first* in our old homes before we will ever consent to such removal."[31] This petition was signed by five principal Mille Lacs chiefs: Kaygwaydash and Menogeshick (Fine Day), who both signed the 1867 treaty, and three signers of the 1863 treaty, including Menomenkeshin (Rice Maker), Pedudence (Muskrat's Liver), and Tedawkaymosay (The Pacer). This was a major representation of chiefs; in fact, at least seven of the ten Mississippi Chippewa chiefs who signed the Treaty of 1867 also signed this petition that opposed the treaty.[32]

The treaty immediately set off a new and

more vigorous round of requests for the removal of the Mille Lacs bands. To the disappointment of the government and timber speculators, the Mille Lacs showed no intention of going anywhere and, with the help of missionaries and other Minnesota friends, reminded officials in Washington and in St. Paul that they were under no obligation to go to White Earth.[33] The timber interests responded, in turn, with false claims that the Mille Lacs had been misbehaving, in hope of providing grounds for compelling their removal under terms of the 1863–64 treaties.[34] The Mille Lacs chiefs not only disputed such claims but repeatedly appealed for approval to visit Washington so they could lay their concerns before the Great Father, who they believed would not go back on the promises he had made to them when they negotiated the Treaty of 1863.[35]

The post–Civil War period did not bring peace to the Mille Lacs. Although the reservation had some good agricultural land, it also had some of the best pine timberland in Minnesota.[36] It was this resource that really fueled the desire to remove the Indians. With the Indians gone, the federal government would no longer be obliged to protect their right of occupancy and could put the reservation land on the open market, and the lumber barons would have access to the timber. On no less than three occasions between 1870 and 1884, the government approved land entries of the reservation and then canceled or suspended them.[37] Each time this occurred, it produced legal entanglements and depletion of the reservation's resources, as settlers cut maple groves, confiscated garden spots, cut hay, and threatened the rice crop with dams.[38] Needless to say, these unwelcome intrusions greatly heightened the anxiety of the Mille Lacs people.

Even though the United States made many attempts to persuade the Mille Lacs to remove during the decades of the 1870s and 1880s, the federal government agreed with the chiefs concerning their right of occupancy on the reservation. In 1882 the secretary of the interior, Samuel J. Kirkwood, ordered a thorough study of the problems on the Mille Lacs Reservation that had resulted from claims for reservation land made by non-Indians during the previous two decades as well as problems of land fraud on the reservation.[39] This work was undertaken by the commissioner of Indian affairs, Hiram Price, whose report concludes that the Mille Lacs had ceded their land in 1863 but that the treaty of that year did not require them to remove from their reservation, since they had not molested the persons or property of the whites, either within or beyond the bounds of the reservation. He also concluded that the fact that the government had extended the general land survey to the reservation and had, in fact, allowed settlers and lumber interests to make land entries did not affect the rights of occupancy of the Mille Lacs Indians.[40] Moreover, Price pointed out that the United States had protected the Chippewa Indians' rights of occupancy since the Mille Lacs had refused to remove and had given no cause for the United States to require an end to their tenure to the reservation. This, of course, was precisely how the Mille Lacs people understood the situation and how they understood the meaning and substance of the 1863–64 treaties. In late 1882 the Mille Lacs chiefs sent a petition to the Office of Indian Affairs that made clear in the starkest possible terms their unwillingness to move from Mille Lacs: "We are not willing to leave our land we want to stay where we are we had as soon the government would send and kill us all as to have to leave our home."[41]

During the decades of the 1870s and 1880s, there were approximately one thousand Mille Lacs Indians living for at least part of the year on the reservation. U.S. Indian inspector George M. Chapman, who visited the reservation in 1882 and issued a report on conditions, said that the reservation was bounded by township lines and comprised about sixty-five thousand acres. The Mille Lacs Indians, he reported, were organized into ten bands under the leadership of various traditional chiefs and had no fixed habitations, going from place to place hunting, fishing, and gathering wild rice.[42] They lived in wigwams made of bent poles covered with bark or rush mats. Chapman remarked that although Shobaushkum had a hewn log house, he preferred a wigwam, while the cabin stood vacant. There were no villagers per se, as the wigwams were dispersed along the shore of the lake. Chapman noted that the Chippewa planted small gardens but that only a little less than nine acres were cultivated in total and that only seven acres were fenced. He also noted that whiskey sellers were constant visitors to the reservation and that drunkenness and poverty were common.[43]

One point made very obvious from Chapman's report is that the Mille Lacs bands were totally dependent on natural resources to support themselves. This fact is central, in many ways, to the arguments that were used to try to persuade or force them to remove to White Earth. Making a living by hunting and gathering requires both great mobility and a large area from which to extract food. This is because resources are scattered and not always dependable in any given place. Thus, the Mille Lacs had to move between sites where resources might be found. As rich as the reservation was, it could not provide nearly enough food and other resources to support the people who lived there. This is why the usufruct provision of the 1837 treaty that permitted the Chippewa to forage across the ceded territory was so important in the post-treaty era—in fact, it permitted them to survive *on* their reservation by foraging *off* their reservation.[44]

As the ceded territory started to attract settlers after the Civil War, Mille Lacs hunters and gatherers complained that they had to compete for deer and other game with frontier farmers, who also relied to some extent on these resources.[45] Likewise, the settlers complained about the Mille Lacs hunters, who, they said, were destroying and frightening the game and, they believed, should be confined to their reservations. Apparently, game was not the only thing being frightened by the Indians. Swedish immigrant settlers, who were not used to seeing free-roaming Indians, were terrified by the appearance of Mille Lacs families on their subsistence rounds.[46] The Swedes circulated stories of Indian depredations that, on investigation, were seldom verified.[47] Conversely, persons and property of Indians on the reservation were not protected from incursions of American citizens who sought to provoke them to violence by confiscating their resources. In fact, the Mille Lacs Chippewa were congenial, kind, and generous people—as others among their white neighbors testified.[48] These were characteristics that were strongly reinforced in Chippewa culture, since they were values that the Chippewa relied on to foster the interpersonal and interfamily cooperation that hunters and gatherers required to survive.

From their point of view, the Mille Lacs people knew how to make a living from nature and regarded it as a secure way of life that had been given to them by the creator. As Shobaushkum and the other chiefs told the commissioner of Indian affairs in 1877, "We are perfectly satisfied to live where we are. We have some good land for farming purposes. We also have fish in the lakes, wild rice and game in abundance. And we make plenty of sugar. We have lived so far without the assistance of our Great Father and if we did not intend to live a different life, we would not ask any assistance now."[49] The Mille Lacs people did not know how to farm, and they did not trust farming as a means of their own support. Undoubtedly, they had observed the efforts of American farmers and were probably not impressed with the immense amount of hard labor it took to clear fields in order to produce what, to them, would have been a diet of unfamiliar grains and vegetables. They had, likewise, not been very successful with efforts to keep domestic animals, because they were not around to feed them during the winter, since that was the time when they were dispersed for hunting and sugar making. Finally, they knew of the experiences of their few relatives who had gone to White Earth, where the people faced famine after insects wiped out their crops several years in a row.

The Mille Lacs people were stuck in a very difficult position. They did not know how to practice Euro-American agriculture, and although they knew it was the expectation of the Great Father that they learn these skills, they found it impossible to abruptly change their mode of subsistence; both agriculture and hunting and gathering were all-or-nothing propositions.[50] This is so because hunting and gathering required mobility while agriculture required a sedentary existence.

In the winter of 1883–84 and again the next year, conditions took a bad turn for the Mille Lacs people. Because of a dam built by lumbermen to increase the flow of water in the Rum River, their vital rice crop was flooded and failed.[51] On top of this, there was no tracking snow for deer hunting, and the state of Minnesota tried to limit the deer kill by instituting a fifteen-day hunting season.[52] About all the Mille Lacs had to eat were fish and potatoes. Minnesota governor L. R. Hubbard complained about the condition of the people, "The loss of their rice crop partially of their hay [marsh hay] which used to bring the Indians some money from lumbermen, and of their usual crop of cranberries which also afforded some income, and the non-payment of their annuities were known to me, and they are facts calculated to produce scarcity, want, suffering, and if the elements were unfavorable or traders refused to trust to unusual amounts [of credit], actual starvation."[53]

During this period of crisis, the Mille Lacs got no help from their agent, who did not visit them for a period of fifteen months and skipped payment of their annuities.[54] Although many observers, in and out of government, were sympathetic to the plight of the Mille Lacs people, vigorous complaints about the poverty and hardship became just another reason to justify removing them to White Earth—for their own good. Those who really knew the Mille Lacs Indians, however, stressed that they knew how to weather such shortages, and the chiefs were as resolute as ever in their refusal to give up their right of residence on the reservation.[55]

The necessities of making a living from natural resources meant that the Mille Lacs had to leave the reservation to get the food they needed to survive. They were aware that hunting and gathering off the reservation was a right they reserved in the Treaty of 1837. They also believed that their rights to harvest resources and to live in possession of their homes and garden plots on the reservation were secured to them by the 1863–64 treaties. They knew the distinction between being on and off the Mille Lacs Reservation, and they knew the location of the exterior boundaries exactly. What is more, the boundaries of the reservation were also known to non-Indians of the region, who recognized that, like the Mille Lacs people, they had different rights off the reservation than they did within its boundaries. This knowledge on the part of the Mille Lacs chiefs, as well as a history of their harassment both on and off the reservation, was the basis of their extensive discussions of on- and off-reservation problems with commissioners sent to negotiate the Nelson Act of 1889.[56]

On the eve of the Nelson Act, the position of the Mille Lacs bands relative to their reservation was firm. In 1886 a congressionally authorized delegation circulated among the Minnesota Chippewa, trying to get them to subscribe to an agreement to remove to White Earth. They met staunch resistance at Mille Lacs.

> The Indians were assembled on the west shore of the lake [Mille Lacs] at the Rum River outlet on the 9th day of October. They were made fully acquainted with the action taken by the White Earth and other Indians, and the agreement was carefully read and explained to them, article by article. Every possible argument was used to influence their minds in favor of the movement, but they stubbornly refused to accept the propositions. They denied that they had ever ceded their reservation to the United States, and declared that they would never consent to remove therefrom. It was apparent from the beginning that they had come into council pledged to refuse all overtures conditioned upon their removal. They would not listen to advice nor to entreaty, and we became convinced that no possible inducement would be sufficient to change their minds. That they had been tampered with before our arrival was clearly evident. They had received their lessons from the outside and had committed them to heart. They charged the Government with bad faith on all former occasions, and were impatient to close the council. Their refusal is absolute and unqualified.[57]

A year later, the Mille Lacs chiefs sent a communication to President Grover Cleveland that said in part,

> We are told that we ceded our reservation at Mille Lacs to the United States in 1863 and that we now only have the right to occupy it during good behavior. We never intentionally ceded all our lands at Mille Lacs to the United States; we never intended to go away from our home at Mille Lacs but if our Great Father shall decide that we have ceded them away and that we still have only the right of possession left we think our Great Father is willing to let us have some lands and as it will make but little difference to him where they are, and a great deal of difference to us, we would respectfully ask you to let us remain at

Mille Lacs and give us in severalty, the lands on this reservation.[58]

The Nelson Act and the Mille Lacs Reservation

In January 1889 Congress made a new effort to consolidate the affairs of all of the Minnesota Chippewa. Collectively, these consisted of the three bands of the Lake Superior Chippewa that resided in Minnesota, including the Fond du Lac, Grand Portage, and Bois Forte bands, each with its own reservations; the Red Lake and Pembina bands occupying land in northern Minnesota; and the Pillager, Lake Winnibigoshish, and Mississippi Chippewa bands. The latter included the Mille Lacs bands as well as bands residing at Gull, Sandy, Pokegama, Rabbit, and Rice lakes. It was hoped that at least some of these groups could be convinced to remove to either Red Lake or the reservation at White Earth.

The Nelson Act, named for its sponsor Representative Knute Nelson, provided for the negotiation with the Minnesota Chippewa for the written relinquishment of their title to all of their reservations except the White Earth and Red Lake reservations.[59] Pursuant to a provision of the act, the president appointed three commissioners to council with the various Chippewa bands on this proposal and to report as required by the act. According to a notice circulated by the Department of Interior, the act was to provide lands in severalty on the Red Lake or White Earth to Indians "residing and belonging on" the Leech Lake, Cass Lake, Lake Winnebigoshish, White Oak Point, Mille Lacs, Fond du Lac, Bois Fort, Deer Creek, and Grand Portage reservations.[60] Besides land allotments, the Nelson Act provided generous payments and government service at White Earth that was hoped to induce the Indians to remove. Section 3 of the act also provided an alternative to removal; that is, Indians of each reservation could elect to take allotments on the reservation where they resided at the time of the negotiation.[61]

The commission appointed to negotiate with the Chippewa included Rev. Martin Marty of South Dakota, Henry Rice of Minnesota, and Joseph B. Whiting of Wisconsin. In early October 1889, Henry Rice and J. B. Whiting appeared at Mille Lacs to negotiate the terms of the Nelson Act. In their report, the commissioners described the Mille Lacs people as "intelligent, cleanly, and well behaved, and with a good reputation among the neighboring whites. White men unfortunately have been permitted to rob them of their pine, and for years to settle upon their agricultural lands, to great injury and fear of the Indians. Squatters are now settling upon this reservation."[62]

Chiefs Shobaushkum, Wahweyaycum, Mahungance, Aaygwonay, Puggwonaygeshik, Nezeegum, Mahgekewis, Nahbahnayaush, and Moseomannay represented the people of the Mille Lacs bands. A record of the discussions between the commissioners and the chiefs over the period of several days provides insights into the mood and tactics of the negotiations. It is obvious from the transcripts that Henry Rice presented a highly optimistic vision of the future of the Mille Lacs people under the provisions of the Nelson Act. For the most part, the chiefs set aside the polite and acquiescent behavior usually reserved for occasions of formal importance, in favor of tough and thorough questioning of the commissioners. The document in which the Mille Lacs Indians agreed to accept the terms of the Nelson Act is informative in its description of the unique position of the bands of that reservation: "We the undersigned, being male adult Indians over eighteen years of age of the Mille Lacs band of Chippewa of the Mississippi, occupying and belonging to the Mille Lacs Reservation under and by virtue of a clause in the twelve articles of the treaty of May 7, 1864" (13 Stat. 693).[63] This distinction was important because the Mille Lacs, unlike the other Chippewa of the Mississippi bands, were clearly regarded by the government as "occupying and belonging to" a federal Indian reservation.

The council began with Commissioner Whiting greeting the chiefs and complimenting them on their good behavior while acknowledging their services in 1862: "I know too, that in years gone by you were friendly and rendered important service to your great father's government. Your services, your faithfulness to your Great Father in times when the white people were in peril have not been forgotten."[64] After further assurances that the process of negotiation of the Nelson Act would be fully opened to them,

Henry Rice made the astounding announcement that the Mille Lacs chiefs' long-held position regarding their right to occupy their reservation under the Treaty of 1863 had indeed been correct. Rice had been silent on this matter for over twenty-five years, and because of his unwillingness to support the chiefs' contention, the Mille Lacs people had suffered enormously.[65] Rice went on to explain that the Nelson Act was not like an ordinary treaty, since they would lose "no rights under the old treaties," and the United States "would do our best to have those old matters settled equitably as soon as possible."[66]

On the third meeting between the chiefs and the commissioners, Henry Rice produced a map of the Minnesota reservations. Upon examining the map, Mozeomannay pointed out that the boundaries of the Mille Lacs Reservation were in error, since they omitted a piece of land at some distance from where the lines were shown. Rice conceded that a mistake could have been made in 1855, when the boundaries of the reserve were first set up. Shobaushkum noted, however, that the government had cleared and plowed a portion of this property at the expense of the Indians and that the improved parcel was now in the possession of a non-Indian. Rice responded that it was now too late to correct the error.[67] From this exchange, it is apparent that the chiefs had exact knowledge of the boundaries of their reservation and were concerned about the future consequence of the location of the reservation lines. No one suggested that the lines drawn in 1855 would be changed by the Nelson Act.

Over the period of the negotiations, Rice and Whiting patiently answered all the questions posed by the chiefs and, in so doing, painted a rosy picture of the future. As Rice told them, "It is not the intention of the government to pull out your teeth and then tell you to eat tough meat."[68] The Mille Lacs were to be allotted ample farmland on the reservation that would assure their support for generations to come. The government would protect their interests and would provide them with schools, health care, a mill and blacksmith shop, and missionaries. As Rice put it, "It will be the same as a village is among white people, where they go and do business."[69]

In order to carry out the allotment provision of the Nelson Act, land within Minnesota Indian reservations was to be classified as "agricultural land" or "pineland." Indians were only able to make their allotment selections from the agricultural lands; after such selections were recorded, the pinelands and surplus, or nonallotted agricultural lands, would be offered for sale to U.S. citizens by public notice. A government circular issued on March 5, 1890, stated in part,

> All persons are, therefore, thereby warned not to go upon any of the lands within the limits of the reservations [Red Lake, Leech Lake, Cass Lake Lake Winnebigoshish, White Oak Point, Mille Lacs, Fond du Lac, Boise Fort, Deer Creek, and Grand Portage] as heretofore existing for any purpose or with any intent whatsoever. No settlement or other rights can be secured upon said lands, and all persons found unlawfully thereon will be dealt with as trespassers and intruders.[70]

Unfortunately, settlers paid no attention to this warning, and many flooded onto the reservations—particularly the Mille Lacs Reservation.

Before the Mille Lacs chiefs gave their assent to the Nelson Act, the very aged Chief Shobaushkum, perhaps now leery of Rice's promises, directly inquired about Rice's authority to commit the United States to the agreement: "I wish you to understand that the words you are brought are in my heart, and I accept what you have told me. Although I understand you thoroughly, I want you to answer me this question: where do you take these words from who sent you here to utter these words you have spoken? Will you please answer me the last question?" Commissioner Rice replied, "We come direct from the great Father, from no one else."[71] The chiefs were satisfied, and Chief Mahungance, speaking for the Mille Lacs people, told the commissioners,

> I have understood everything you have put before us for consideration. You say that whomever wishes to go to White Earth shall be allowed to do so. We make known to you that as the government speaks so kindly, and you have uttered the words of the law [the Nelson Act] stating that an Indian can take his allotment on the reservation where he resides, we make known to you that we wish to

> take our allotments on this reservation and not to be removed to White Earth.[72]

Under the terms of their agreement to the provisions of the Nelson Act, the Mille Lacs people surrendered their right of occupation to the reservation reserved by the twelfth article of the Treaty of 1864. The *quid pro quo* for this surrender was that they would be able to take allotments on the reservation. While the Mille Lacs people held the right of occupancy, reservation land could not be entered by settlers or lumbermen. As Henry Rice explained this point to T. J. Morgan, commissioner of Indian affairs,

> Upon this Reservation there are now probably one hundred squatters. Some of them took the gardens the Indians had made, and built thereon, appropriating to their own use the fields which the Indians had broken and cultivated with much labor, and without assistance from anyone.
>
> It is claimed by the Indians that a patent could not have been *legally* issued upon any land embraced in the Reservation, consequently no authority has or can be given to dispossess them of any part of it without their consent. As many of the settlers have only board shanties without other improvements, they can leave at any time without serious loss. In the interest of justice this subject cannot be too rigidly examined, or at too early a period.[73]

The exchange between the chiefs and the commissioners recorded in the Nelson Act journal leaves no doubt that the Mille Lacs people were offered and accepted a future that secured their right to remain on the Mille Lacs Reservation. Neither is there any doubt that the Mille Lacs chiefs and people understood that they were exchanging their right to occupy the reservation in common for the right to take land in severalty and thus secure their tenure on the reservation. This being the case, there is, likewise, no doubt that the Mille Lacs chiefs and their people as well as Congress intended for the Mille Lacs Reservation to continue to exist. In fact, the existence of the exterior boundaries was necessary to carry out the provision of the Nelson Act.

As a starting point, the Nelson Act, like the Treaties of 1863, 1864, and 1867, does not in any way annul or modify the boundaries of the reservation created by the Treaty of 1855. Before, during, and after the passage and negotiation of the Nelson Act, it was assumed that the 1855 boundaries would exist into the future. The reason, of course, was that the boundaries of the Mille Lacs Reservation were necessary for implementing the act. Because the act held open the possibility that at least some of the Indians would take their allotments on the reservation, the remaining land had to be held open for that purpose.[74] The Mille Lacs people would not be permitted to make selections from the public domain off the reservation, although Rice informed them they were welcome to buy land there just as they could on the reservation if they had the means.[75]

In discussing the land available to them, it was explained that the reservation land was divided into agricultural land and pineland and that they could make allotment choices on vacant agricultural land on the reservation. Chief Mahungance described to the commissioners how whites were "making themselves masters of the meadows *inside our reservation*" (emphasis added).[76] He also asked who would deal with off-reservation lumber dams that were flooding out rice crops on the reservation.[77] Henry Rice replied that problems of this kind would be referred in the future to various state or federal authorities for solution. He did not say that the reservation would cease to exist.

Finally and most conclusively, on the afternoon of October 2, 1889, Henry Rice told the assembled chiefs and people of the Mille Lacs bands that the Nelson Act "was a proposition coming from the Great Council [Congress] and the President, and not like an ordinary treaty—they had lost no rights under the old treaties and that we would do our best to have those old matters settled equitably as soon as possible."[78] "The acceptance of this act will not affect these old matters at all or weaken your chances of hereafter obtaining your dues," he explained, "but, on the contrary, leave you in a stronger position than before."[79] In other words, the commissioners assigned with the responsibility to carry out the provisions of the Nelson Act understood that the Mille Lacs were giving up their right to occupy reservation land in common in exchange for allotments in severalty, but they did not believe that the terms of the act changed or dissolved the exterior boundaries of the 1855 reservation. This is also how the United States government understood the Nelson Act, and it was certainly how the Mille Lacs chiefs and people understood the act. In fact, it was with this understanding and with the assurances of the commissioners that the chiefs agreed to the act.

In July 1890, just eighteen months after it enacted the Nelson Act and certainly at a time when that act was still fresh in the collective conscious of the senators and representatives, Congress passed a bill called "An Act Granting Right of Way to Little Falls, Mille Lacs, and Lake Superior Railroad across the Mille Lacs Indian Reservation." This act granted land for a right-of-way, spur lines, stations, machine shops, and other facilities "within the limits of the reservation."[80] Certainly, Congress could not have intended the Nelson Act to terminate or diminish the external boundaries of the Mille Lacs Reservation.

CHAPTER 19

County of Mille Lacs v. Melanie Benjamin et al., District of Minnesota, Case No. 02-CV-407

Marc Slonim
Ziontz, Chestnut, Varnell, Berley and Slonim, Seattle, Washington

This case was, in a sense, a sequel to the lawsuit undertaken by the Mille Lacs Band of Chippewa Indians to enforce its hunting, fishing, and gathering rights under the Treaty of 1837, a case that is treated in chapter 11 in this volume. In the wake of the U.S. Supreme Court's 1999 decision upholding the band's treaty hunting, fishing, and gathering rights, rumors began to spread that the band was threatening to prosecute, regulate, and tax non-Indians within the band's reservation. The band's opponents, including Mille Lacs County, argued that the band's belief that its reservation continued to exist was a grave threat to non-Indians living within the reservation. They claimed that, contrary to the band's position, the reservation had been disestablished and no longer existed.

To set the context for this case, I first outline the history of the Mille Lacs Reservation. I then discuss the circumstances giving rise to the county's lawsuit and the positions of the parties in the case. I follow that discussion with a description of the legal framework in which cases concerning reservation disestablishment are decided. Finally, I discuss the band's strategy for responding to the lawsuit and the outcome of the case.

The Mille Lacs Indian Reservation

The 1855 Treaty

In an 1855 treaty,[1] the Mississippi, Pillager, and Lake Winnibigoshish bands of Chippewa Indians ceded lands to the United States in the northern part of the Minnesota territory while reserving several tracts of land for their permanent homes. The treaty helped pave the way for Minnesota's admission to the Union as a state in 1858. The Mille Lacs band was classified as a Mississippi band and selected the first tract reserved for the Mississippi bands in the treaty. The tract embraced four fractional townships on the southern and southwestern shores of Mille Lacs Lake as well as three islands in the lake. The band's principal villages, wild rice lakes, meadows, and other valuable resources were located within the tract.

The 1863 and 1864 Treaties

In 1862 there was a violent Dakota uprising in Minnesota. The Mille Lacs band came to the defense of white settlers at Fort Ripley and persuaded other Chippewa bands not to join the uprising. In 1863 the United States, responding to local political pressures fueled by the Dakota uprising, demanded that the Mississippi bands cede their 1855 reservations and remove to a more northerly location. The Mille Lacs band resolutely refused to yield its reservation. After the intercession of Minnesota senator Henry Rice, a treaty was made in which the Mississippi bands collectively ceded their 1855 reservations and agreed to move north.[2] However, Article 12 of the treaty provided that, "owing to [its] good conduct," the Mille Lacs band would not be required to remove from its "present reservation" as long as it did not "molest the persons or property of the whites." The 1863 treaty was replaced by an 1864 treaty, which retained these provisions.[3]

The Mille Lacs Reservation contained valuable stands of white pine timber. Powerful timber interests, including Amherst Wilder and future Minnesota senator Dwight Sabin, sought access to the timber. Initially, federal officials, including the attorney general and the secretary of the interior, protected the band's right to occupy its reservation under the 1864 treaty, refusing to permit non-Indian land entries and evicting squatters. However, Sabin and Wilder persuaded a successor secretary, Zachariah Chandler, to open the reservation to land entries. Their agents descended on the local land office and, using soldiers' additional homestead entries, laid claim to thousands of acres of reservation timberlands. Secretary Chandler's successor, Carl Schurz, canceled these entries and prohibited further entries within the reservation. But Secretary Schurz's successor, Henry Teller, reinstated the Sabin-Wilder entries, and the land office began to issue patents. Then Congress itself intervened. The act of July 4, 1884, provided that lands within the reservation "shall not be patented or disposed of in any manner until further legislation by Congress."[4]

The Nelson Allotment Act

By the latter part of the nineteenth century, there was tremendous pressure to make lands and other resources within Indian reservations available to non-Indians. In addition, some reformers believed it would be beneficial if, instead of communal ownership, Indians owned their lands individually. These factors as well as a multitude of local circumstances led to the negotiation of agreements with tribes and the enactment of legislation that provided for the allotment of Indian reservations to tribal members and for the opening and sale of "surplus" lands to non-Indians.

The most dramatic consequence of the allotment policy was the loss of Indian landholdings: in 1887, when the General Allotment Act was passed, Indians held 138 million acres of land; less than fifty years later, when the allotment policy was abandoned, only 48 million acres were left in Indian hands.[5] In addition, allotment-era agreements and legislation would lead to disputes in the twentieth century over whether the affected reservations had been "diminished" or "disestablished." The issue would be whether the opened areas remained part of their respective reservations, allowing the federal government and the tribes to exercise a measure of jurisdiction over them (especially as the tribes or their members reacquired some of the opened lands from non-Indians), or whether these areas had been removed from the reservations and were subject to plenary state jurisdiction.

Congress enacted the Nelson Allotment Act in 1889.[6] Named for Minnesota congressman Knute Nelson, the act established a commission to negotiate with the Chippewa Indians in Minnesota for the cession and relinquishment of their existing reservations, except for the portions of the White Earth and Red Lake reservations that were needed to make allotments to the Indians. In reporting the bill that would become the Nelson Act, the House Committee on Indian Affairs listed the existing reservations, including the 61,014-acre "Mille Lac Reservation."[7] The committee proposed that all of the Indians "on the small outlying and scattered reservations should be removed to and colonized upon the White Earth Reservation, where allotments should be made to them."[8] The bill was amended on the House floor to allow the Indians to remain and take allotments on their existing reservations, rather than remove to White Earth. This provision accommodated the demands of the Chippewa Indians at Leech Lake, Mille Lacs, and other "outlying" reservations, who had refused to accept earlier proposals to move to White Earth. It would prove critical to their acceptance of the Nelson Act.

When the bill reached the Senate, Senator Sabin added a new provision stating that the provisions of the bill did not authorize the sale or disposal of any tract on which there was a "subsisting valid preemption or homestead entry." According to Sabin's provision, "any such entry shall be proceeded with under the regulations and decisions in force as of the date of its allowance, and if found regular and valid patents shall issue thereon."[9] The purpose of this provision was to protect and secure patents on the Sabin-Wilder land entries in the Mille Lacs Reservation, the only reservation in which there were any such preexisting entries.

In explaining the bil! on the Senate floor, Senator Henry Dawes, the chairman of the Senate Committee on Indian Affairs and the author of the 1887 General Allotment Act, stated that the Chippewa occupied a number of reservations in Minnesota and that the greatest value of all the reservations, except White Earth, was in the pine timber, which had become of immense value. According to Dawes, the purpose of the bill was "to get some method to dispose of the pine timber upon these reservations for the benefit of the Indians—in other words, to capitalize it."[10] The act provided that the net proceeds from the sale of timberlands and agricultural lands "not allotted under this Act nor reserved for the future use of the Indians" would be placed in the U.S. Treasury as a permanent fund for the benefit of the Chippewa. Expenditures could be made for such purposes as establishing and maintaining a system of free schools in their midst and for their benefit.

The president appointed three men to the Chippewa Commission to seek the agreement of the Chippewa to the terms of the Nelson Act. One of the commissioners was Henry Rice, who had been instrumental in making the 1863 treaty. The secretary of the interior, John Oberly, prepared written instructions for the commission. He included the Mille Lacs Reservation among the reservations subject to the act, and he stated that the Mille Lacs Indians retained their right to occupy the reservation.

When the commission met with the Mille Lacs band, Commissioner Rice referred to the attempts by squatters and timber magnates to gain access to the reservation.

> I wish to refer to an old matter that has given you a great deal of trouble. That is the treaty made at Washington some twenty-five years ago. I was there, and know all about it. It was a wise treaty, and if it had been properly carried out you would have escaped all the trouble that has befallen you. Men who cared more for themselves than they did for you thought they had found a hole in it, and that they would take advantage of that and deprive you of your rights. They knew that the Government was engaged in a great war which occupied all its time. They thought that under the circumstances they would be able to drive you from this reservation . . . The time has come when I am able to tell you that . . . all the chiefs told you who were there and made the treaty is correct; that the understanding of the chiefs as to the treaty was right. Here is the acknowledgement of the Government that you were right, that "you have not forfeited your right to occupy the reservation."[11]

Commissioner Rice then stated that the commission had come to explain a proposition from Congress and that the Indians' acceptance of it would not affect their rights under the old treaties at all but would leave them in a "stronger position than before" to remain on the reservation.[12]

After the act was explained to them, band members confirmed that they wanted to take their allotments on the Mille Lacs Reservation and not remove to White Earth. Commissioner Rice confirmed that they could do so.[13] Band members also asked about white people who had taken land on the reservation; they wanted to know whether those people would go away soon and whether the Indians would have "any more difficulties relative to our land and our possessions here, and our rights."[14] Rice responded that he did not think "any more will come upon your reservation, and perhaps some who are merely visiting you will leave." Concerning others who had papers, he said their cases would be looked into and that "whatever is right will be done."[15]

During the discussions, the commission produced a map of the reservation and discussed the rights of band members on and off the reservation.[16] There was no suggestion that the band's acceptance of the Nelson Act would affect the boundaries of the reservation. In accepting the act, band members believed that it was "a settlement of all our past difficulties" and that it would allow them to "stay here forever" and receive "allotments here."[17]

The agreement prepared by the commission and approved by the band stated that the Indians "occupying and belonging to the Mille Lacs Reservation under and by virtue of a clause in the twelfth article of the treaty of May 7, 1864," accepted the Nelson Act "and each and all of the provisions thereof."[18] This included the act's provision allowing band members to take allotments on their own reservation, which had formed the basis for their agreement. The agreement also included a provision in which the band "relinquish[ed]" its rights of occupancy on the Mille Lacs Reservation under the 1864 treaty.[19] This provision was necessary so that lands not needed for allotments or reserved for the future use of the Indians could be sold (or "capitalized," to use Senator Dawes's term) for their benefit.

The Chippewa Commission prepared a report of its negotiations and the agreements it made on each of the Chippewa reservations. The commission stated that the provisions of the 1864 treaty "affirmed the belief that [the Mille Lacs Chippewa] were not only permanently located, but had sole occupancy of the reservation." The report stated, "[The] Interior Department now holds that: 'the Mille Lacs Indians have never forfeited their right of occupancy and still reside on the reservation.'"[20] The commission added that lumber syndicates had been permitted to "rob [the Indians] of their pine," that some whites "had the shameless audacity to take from the Indians land the latter had, with much labor and perseverance, put into cultivation," and that "squatters [were] now settling upon this reservation, and the interests of the Indians ignored." The commission believed there were some "well intentioned but misled" whites who had settled on "the Mille Lacs Reservation," and it urged that their right to remain be resolved as quickly as possible. It made no suggestion, however, that such claims would affect the band's right to allotments or the reservation's status.[21] Finally, the commission noted that "the various bands decided to take their allotments on their respective reservations"; that wherever the commission went, the Indians expressed a desire that lands be set aside for government buildings; and that the Indians requested that a tract of pinelands on each reservation be reserved for the common use of the Indians of that reservation. The commission endorsed these requests.[22]

The secretary of the interior transmitted the commission's report and the agreements to President Harrison. In so doing, the secretary confirmed the good conduct of the Mille Lacs band and expressed the hope that the Nelson Act would provide a basis for resolving the difficulties it had confronted on its reservation. In approving the agreements, the president noted that the Indians had expressed a general desire to take their allotments on their existing reservations.

Subsequent History

Government officials failed to make allotments to the Mille Lacs band as required by the Nelson Act. Instead, "the whole political machinery of the State seems to have set to work to force the Mille Lacs Indians off their homes."[23] The Interior Department issued conflicting opinions in January 1891 and April 1892; the first suggested that the reservation was open to public entry and settlement, and the latter held that it was not. In 1893, to protect "settlers" who allegedly relied on the first opinion, Congress confirmed entries "within the Mille Lacs Indian Reservation" made between the dates of the two opinions.[24] In 1896 the Interior Department recognized that band members remained entitled to allotments on the reservation, but non-Indian settlers continued to move onto the reservation. In 1898 Congress confirmed their entries, making "public lands formerly within the Mille Lacs Indian Reservation" available for entry under the public land laws and reserving lands for an Indian burial ground.[25]

In 1900 the secretary of the interior ruled that, notwithstanding the 1893 and 1898 resolutions, the Indians could not be displaced from lands they actually occupied on the reservation. To acquire reservation lands, settlers fraudulently claimed that lands occupied by Indians were unoccupied and, upon receiving patents from the government, forced the Indians off lands they had occupied for generations. The Mille Lacs County sheriff ejected band members from their homes and burned down their dwellings. In a 1902 act, Congress offered compensation to band members for their improvements "on the Mille Lac Indian Reservation" if they would agree to remove from the reservation, but it also provided that band members who acquired title to land "within said Mille Lac Reservation" could remain on "said reservation." Band members agreed to the terms of the 1902 act after being assured that they would be paid for their improvements before being required to remove and that they could use the payments to purchase lands and remain on the reservation.

Some band members left the reservation under the 1902 act, but others remained, and many who left soon returned. In 1909, Congress authorized the band to sue for losses sustained by the opening of the reservation to public settlement.[26] The government defended on the grounds that the reservation had been ceded in the 1863 and 1864 treaties and that public settlement was authorized by the 1893 and 1898 resolutions.

The Court of Claims rejected these defenses, holding that the 1863 and 1864 treaties "reserved to the [Mille Lacs band] the Mille Lacs Reservation."[27] On appeal, the Supreme Court held (1) that the Nelson Act resolved a controversy that had arisen over the meaning of the 1863 and 1864 treaties, by accepting the band's understanding of the Treaties while permitting (in the Sabin proviso) bona fide entries on the reservation to be patented; (2) that the band's relinquishment of its right of occupancy under the Nelson Act was subject to express trusts created in the Nelson

Act; (3) that the 1893 and 1898 resolutions exceeded Congress's authority to manage Indian affairs and were doubtless based on a misapprehension of the true relation of the government to the lands; and (4) that all of the new entries allowed on the reservation in the period after the Nelson Act were unlawful.[28] The case was remanded to the Court of Claims to determine the damages from the wrongful disposition of those lands, which comprised over half the reservation.

Congress appropriated moneys from the Nelson Act fund to acquire lands for allotments to Mille Lacs band members in 1914,[29] and the allotments were made in the 1920s. The federal government then opened a school for and provided other services to band members on the reservation. The continued existence of the reservation has since been recognized and acted on in federal and state legislative, judicial, and administrative actions. The band's continuing presence on the reservation, where it maintains its seat of government, a major commercial complex, housing, schools, a health clinic, and cultural facilities, is comparable to that of other Indian tribes on other Indian reservations in Minnesota in terms of landownership, population, and other demographic characteristics.

In 1991, the Minneapolis field solicitor in the U.S. Department of the Interior concluded that Congress had neither disestablished nor diminished the Mille Lacs Reservation. The opinion was based on and is consistent with federal and state court decisions that determined the effect of the Nelson Act on other Chippewa reservations in Minnesota. Those cases hold consistently that the Nelson Act did not disestablish those reservations on which allotments were to be made to the Indians; only those portions of the Red Lake and White Earth reservations that were ceded outright, with no provision for allotment, were disestablished. Other federal officials who considered the issue concurred with the field solicitor's determination. However, beginning in the mid-1990s, some state and county officials began to challenge the continued existence of the reservation.

The County's Lawsuit

As noted earlier, in the wake of the U.S. Supreme Court's 1999 decision upholding the Mille Lacs band's treaty hunting, fishing, and gathering rights, rumors began to spread that the band was threatening to prosecute, regulate, and tax non-Indians within its reservation. In January 2000, the Mille Lacs county attorney found that "widespread misinformation" about these matters was creating civic unrest and a public safety risk.[30] Concerned that county residents were being "intimidated or pressured . . . to participate in political activity currently underway regarding these issues," the county attorney undertook to advise the Mille Lacs County Board of Commissioners "regarding the general legal ability of the Mille Lacs Band to affect the daily living situation of non-Indian County residents."

The county attorney reported that the band had not sought to tax or to regulate any businesses other than those that chose to do business with the band. She stated that, with one exception, she was "unaware of the Mille Lacs Band ever attempting to exercise any other civil or regulatory jurisdiction, including attempted taxation, regarding any non-Indian in Mille Lacs County." Based on her analysis of the band's legal authority, the county attorney concluded that even if the 1855 reservation continued to exist, the band could not tax, zone, or prosecute non-Indians within its boundaries.

Despite this advice, the county board demanded that the band forever disclaim the continued existence of its reservation. The county and the band entered into negotiations and were able to agree on the administration of zoning and other laws within the reservation. In general, these agreements would have recognized the band's regulatory authority over its own members and lands, while preserving state and county authority over non-Indians. However, the band was unwilling to disclaim the existence of its reservation. As outlined earlier, the band's ancestors had struggled for decades against overwhelming odds to remain on the reservation—persevering even when the county sheriff burned down their homes in the late nineteenth and early twentieth centuries—and the continued existence of the reservation remained central to the existence and identity of the band.

When the band refused to disclaim the existence of the reservation, the county board terminated negotiations, retained outside counsel, and filed suit in the U.S. District Court for the District of Minnesota. The county sued the band's elected leaders, including its chief executive, Melanie Benjamin, seeking a judicial declaration that the 1855 Mille Lacs Reservation had been disestablished. A local bank intervened, seeking the same relief. The county and the bank argued that the reservation had been disestablished by the 1864 treaty and the Nelson Act.

The band defendants asserted both "jurisdictional" and "merits" defenses. Article 3 of the U.S. Constitution limits the "judicial power" of the United States to determining "cases and controversies." Accordingly, to bring suit in federal court, a plaintiff must establish the existence of a "case" or "controversy." This requires, among other things, that the plaintiff demonstrate it has been injured by the challenged action of the defendant. In this case, the band defendants asserted they had done nothing to injure the county or the bank. Unless the county or the bank could establish they had been injured, the lawsuit would be dismissed on jurisdictional grounds.

The parties engaged in written discovery and took depositions of band, county, and bank officials to explore this issue. The band defendants then filed a motion for summary judgment, asserting that there was no evidence to support the county's and the bank's claims of injury. The district court heard oral argument on this motion and took it under advisement.

In the meantime, the case was proceeding on the merits. The band vigorously disputed the claim that its reservation had been disestablished. To facilitate understanding of the band's defense, I next describe the legal framework governing this issue.

Legal Framework

To the extent that the argument made by the county and the bank rested on the 1864 treaty, it was subject to familiar rules of treaty interpretation. To interpret an Indian treaty, courts begin with the language of the treaty but "look beyond the written words to the larger context that frames the Treaty, including 'the history of the treaty, the negotiations, and the practical construction adopted by the parties.'"[31] Insight into how the Indian signatories understood the treaty "is especially helpful . . . because [courts] interpret Indian treaties to give effect to the terms as the Indians themselves would have understood them."[32] Moreover, "Indian treaties are to be interpreted liberally in favor of the Indians . . . and . . . any ambiguities are to be resolved in their favor."[33]

To the extent that the argument made by the county and the bank rested on the Nelson Allotment Act, it was subject to the legal framework articulated in a series of Supreme Court cases involving the interpretation of allotment-era legislation. The most important principle is that only Congress can alter the terms of an Indian treaty by diminishing an Indian reservation, and its intent to do so must be clear and plain.[34] The disestablishment of an Indian reservation does not result merely from the disposition of lands within its boundaries: once a block of land is set aside for an Indian reservation, no matter what happens to the title of individual plots within the area, the entire block retains its reservation status until Congress explicitly indicates otherwise.[35]

Some surplus land acts diminished reservations, and others did not. For example, in two cases, the Supreme Court held that acts declaring surplus land "subject to settlement, entry, and purchase," without more, did not evince a congressional intent to diminish the reservations.[36] In another case, the Court did not read as language of cession a phrase authorizing the secretary of the interior to "sell and dispose" surplus lands belonging to a tribe.[37] In contrast, an act adopting a negotiated agreement providing for the total surrender of tribal claims in exchange for a fixed payment bore the hallmarks of congressional intent to diminish a reservation.[38] Thus, the "effect of any given surplus land Act depends on the language of the Act and the circumstances underlying its passage."[39] In the absence of "explicit language of cession and unconditional compensation," the events surrounding the passage of the act—"particularly the manner in which the transaction was negotiated with the tribes involved and the tenor of the legislative Reports presented to Congress"—are considered to determine whether there was a "widely held, contemporaneous understanding that the affected reservation would shrink as a result of the proposed legislation."[40]

Post-enactment events, such as "Congress'

own treatment of the affected areas, particularly in the years immediately following the opening," may also be considered but are of "lesser" significance.[41] Where an opened part of a reservation lost its Indian character as non-Indian settlers flooded into the area, de facto diminishment may have occurred.[42] Such subsequent demographic history provides an additional clue as to what Congress expected would happen once land on a particular reservation was opened to non-Indians, but it "is the least compelling factor for a simple reason: Every surplus land Act necessarily resulted in a surge of non-Indian settlement and degraded the Indian character of the reservation, yet [the Supreme Court has] repeatedly stated that not every surplus land Act diminished the affected reservation."[43] Ultimately, congressional intent to disestablish a reservation must be clearly established: "When both an Act and its legislative history fail to provide substantial and compelling evidence of a congressional intention to diminish Indian lands, [the courts] are bound by [their] traditional solicitude for the Indian tribes to rule that diminishment did not take place and that the old reservation boundaries survived the opening."[44]

The Band's Strategy

To defend the continued existence of their reservation, the band defendants believed it was essential to present the history of the establishment of the reservation in 1855 and the events leading to and surrounding the 1863 and 1864 treaties, the Nelson Act, and the government's failure to make allotments to band members in the 1890s. Moreover, in presenting this history, the band wanted to present its ancestors' perspective as well as that of non-Indian actors. Accordingly, as in its 1837 treaty rights case, the band retained historians, anthropologists, and ethnohistorians to research and prepare expert reports and to present testimony regarding the history of the reservation and the band's understanding of the relevant treaties and agreements.

As briefly outlined earlier, the results of the experts' research indicated that the treaties and the band's agreement to the Nelson Act were neither intended by the government nor understood by the band to diminish or disestablish the Mille Lacs Reservation. To the contrary, they were intended to protect the band's right to occupy the reservation and secure its ability to remain there forever. In addition, the experts' research indicated that the subsequent history of the reservation did not reflect what Congress expected to happen but was the product of the wholesale violation of the band's rights under the Nelson Act. Despite these violations, enormous pressures to remove, and the torching of its homes, the band persevered on the reservation and maintained its homeland there. The band believed that if it could effectively communicate this history, the court would affirm the continued existence of its reservation.

The Outcome

While the district court was preparing its ruling on the band defendants' jurisdictional defenses, the county and the bank filed motions for summary judgment on the merits. The band defendants began drafting briefs and assembling their expert reports and historical documents to respond to the motions. However, about a week before the band defendants' response was due, the district court granted their motion to dismiss the case on the grounds that the county and the bank lacked standing.

The district court ruled that the band defendants had done nothing to injure the county or the bank and, therefore, that it had no jurisdiction to decide the case on the merits. The county and the bank appealed to the U.S. Court of Appeals for the Eighth Circuit, but it affirmed the district court's decision. They then filed petitions for writs of certiorari in the U.S. Supreme Court, but those, too, were denied. Accordingly, the case came to an end without a decision on the merits.

From the band's perspective, an important principle had been affirmed: absent a concrete dispute, the fundamental rights of an Indian tribe could not be challenged in court by those hostile to Indian rights. Moreover, in preparing to defend the continued existence of its reservation, the band had acquired a greater understanding of the history of its reservation and the struggles of its ancestors. That understanding strengthened its resolve to protect its reservation in the future and to occupy it forever.

CHAPTER 20

The Treaties of Detroit (August 2, 1855) and Saginaw (October 18, 1864)

Prelude: The Chippewa Treaties of 1836, 1837, and 1838

In 1831 Lewis Cass, governor of the Michigan Territory, moved to Washington to become secretary of war, and his protégée Henry R. Schoolcraft was appointed superintendent of the Mackinac Indian Agency. By 1835 Michigan was approaching statehood, and it was anticipated by some politicians that more land would be needed to accommodate new settlers. Cass and Schoolcraft hoped to acquire Indian land and, at the same time, drastically reduce the number of Indians on Michigan's peninsulas.[1]

In March 1836 Schoolcraft negotiated the Treaty of Washington with the Ottawa and Chippewa of western lower Michigan and the eastern Upper Peninsula.[2] As originally negotiated, the treaty ceded thirteen million acres in exchange for money payment of about eight hundred thousand dollars as well as services, including the services of teachers, blacksmiths, farmers, mechanics, and physicians. The Ottawa and Chippewa reserved substantial but scattered land reserves and retained the privilege of hunting over the ceded territory. When the treaty was considered by the U.S. Senate, a clause was added that limited occupation of the reserves to five years, after which time the Ottawa and Chippewa were expected to voluntarily remove to new lands west of the Mississippi. The Ottawa and Chippewa were called together at Mackinac Island in 1837, where they reluctantly agreed to this provision but utterly refused to leave their Michigan reserves.

In the eastern part of lower Michigan, the Saginaw, Black River, and Swan Creek bands had selected reserves under the 1807 and 1819 treaties very wisely (see map 24). As whites became more familiar with the territory, they found that much of the choice lands, such as river mouths, fords, road junctions, and other strategic locations, had already been reserved. The fact that the modern cities of Saginaw, Port Huron, Bay City, Flint, and other smaller towns are located on or close to these reserves demonstrates this point.

Cass and Schoolcraft decided to treat with the Black River, Swan Creek, and Saginaw Chippewa bands for the cession of these prime reserve lands. Once ceded, the reserves were to be surveyed and sold for the benefit of the Chippewa. The other major objective was to require the Chippewa to remove from the state.[3]

By the Treaty of May 22, 1836, the Black River and Swan Creek Chippewa bands ceded the four reserves made in the Treaty of 1807. As payment, the Chippewa accepted the proceeds of the sale of the reserve lands as well as thirteen sections of land in the west.[4] A similar treaty was negotiated with the Saginaw Chippewa bands on May 24, 1836, but that treaty was never ratified by the Senate.

In January 1837, Schoolcraft tried again to negotiate a cession from the Saginaw Chippewa, and on January 14, 1837, a treaty was concluded that immediately ceded all but the AuGrais and Rifle River land reserves made under the 1819 treaty.[5] Ceded reserve lands were to be sold on the open market to provide annuities and specified benefits for the tribe. By Article 6 of the 1837 treaty, the Saginaw Chippewa agreed to "remove from the State of Michigan, as soon as a proper location can be obtained." The treaty also provided for an exploratory party to be sent west to find land in unceded territory west of Lake Superior.[6] Before ratification by the Senate, the commissioner of Indian affairs, Carey Harris, ordered Schoolcraft to make several changes: (1) to reduce the proposed payments, (2) to exclude the option of lands west of Lake Superior, and (3) to not bind the United States to give land in more than one place.[7] These changes were incorporated into the final treaty.

Apparently, land speculators conspired to drive down the price per acre paid for the re-

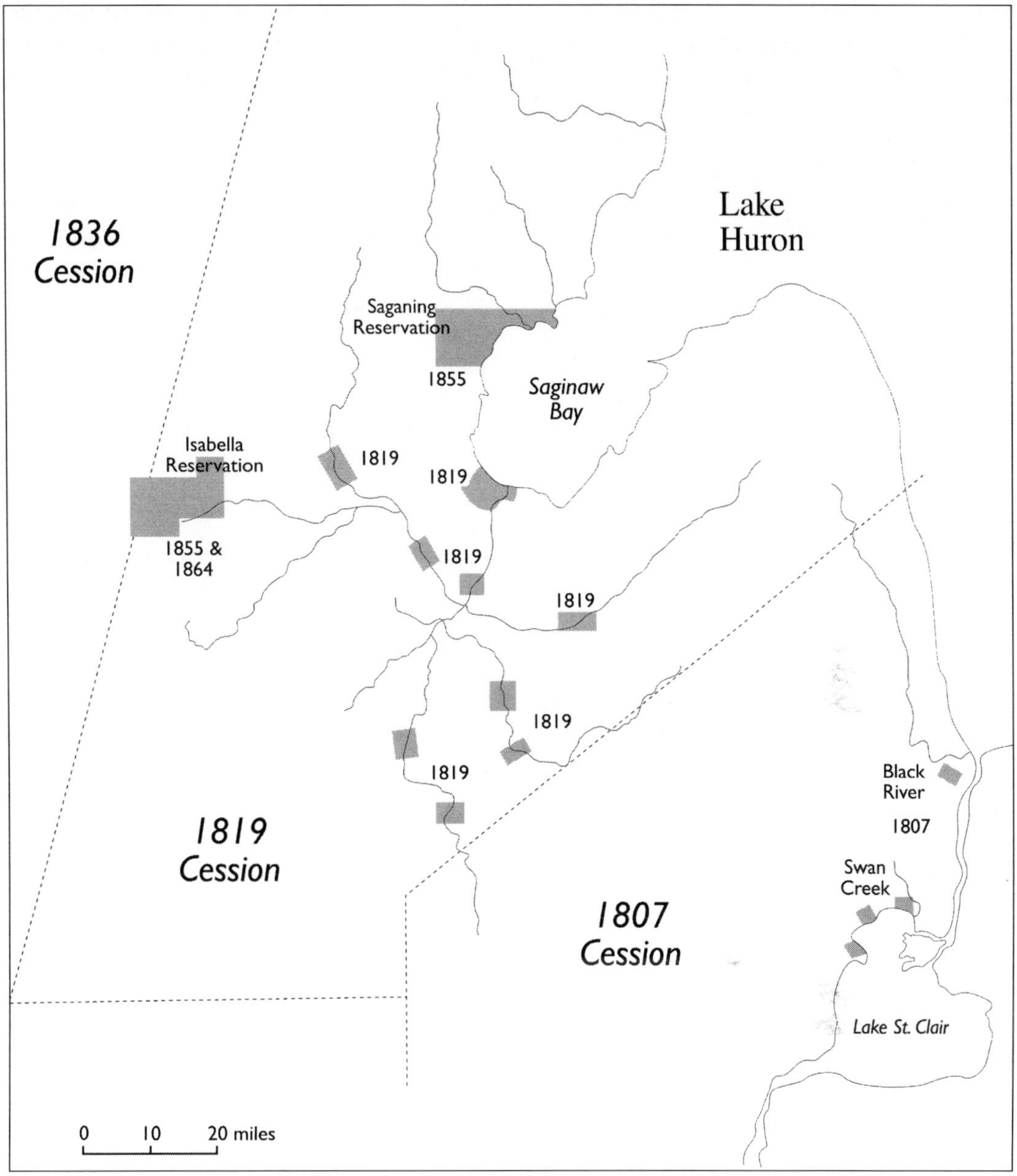

Map 24. Approximate locations of land cessions and reservations under treaties of 1807 and 1819

serves, since on January 23, 1838, the Saginaw chiefs negotiated a new agreement that set the minimum price at five dollars per acre.[8] Once the land reserves of the 1807 cession were ceded, the Black River and Swan Creek bands moved west into the Saginaw Basin, where they gradually intermingled with the Saginaw Chippewa. After the cession of the 1819 reserves by the Saginaw Chippewa, the United States began to deal with the Black River, Swan Creek, and Saginaw Chippewa bands as a single political entity, although each band maintained its separate identity.

Although an Indian scouting party was sent west to locate lands in Kansas, the Black River, Swan Creek, and Saginaw Chippewa would not accept removal. They continued to reside on their reserves and throughout the ceded territory. However, the government proceeded to survey and sell their reserves, leaving these Chippewa exposed to expropriation of their improvements and theft of timber resources.[9]

In 1842 an Indian census showed 1,023 Saginaw Chippewa organized into nine bands.[10] The Black River and Swan Creek bands perhaps numbered five hundred or so more. They continued to receive annuities and services from the government and to be attended by Methodist missionaries. With the exception of about fifty to sixty Black River and Swan Creek Chippewa who actually removed west, the Saginaw Indian people strongly resisted removal. At the same time, it was becoming apparent to the government that removal was an impractical and expensive exercise.

By the mid-1840s, the Chippewa of southeastern Michigan were in a difficult position. Without a land base, they were subject to greater abuses by whites, and they could not be protected by the government. Since they were not citizens of the United States, they were neither subject to its laws nor protected by them. Without sure title to land, the Indians had little inducement to acquire agricultural skills or to make the improvements that were so urgently suggested by their agents and missionaries. They were, in fact, displaced persons and refugees in their own land.

By 1850 Michigan Indian affairs were a disaster. The government's efforts to remove the Indian people by squeezing them off the land failed. The poverty, conflict, and discontent that the failure created became an embarrassment to the government, a moral outrage to the missionaries, and a tragedy for the Indian people. Clearly some means had to be found to settle Michigan's Indians within the state and to make better progress at preparing them for life within, rather than outside of, American society.

This situation prevailed not only in the case of the Black River, Swan Creek, and Saginaw Chippewa but also, in large measure, in the case of the Ottawa and Chippewa communities of western and northern Michigan. Although the latter groups retained reserves made in the Treaty of 1836, the reservations would expire in 1842 by the five-year residence limitation added to the treaty by the U.S. Senate. After that, the Ottawa and northern Chippewa, like the Black River, Swan Creek, and Saginaw Chippewa, were in limbo. Since none had chosen to remove and since land tenure in Michigan was insecure (to say the least), almost every Indian community began to appeal to the government for a new treaty. Their main objective was to secure permanent land within the state.[11] The government responded to the Ottawa-Chippewa by periodically renewing tenure to their reserves, which was a very unsatisfactory solution and certainly a temporary measure. The Saginaw Chippewa, who had no reserves, did not have even temporary reprieve.

The desperate plight of the Michigan Ottawa and Chippewa, as well as the Black River, Swan Creek, and Saginaw Chippewa, ultimately led to the treaties made on July 31 and August 2, 1855. These treaties attempted to resolve the Michigan Indian problem by concentrating Indians on reservations located within their tribal estate. It was hoped that these new reservations would provide stability, protection, and a means to civilize these tribal people. The 1855 and 1864 treaties must be understood against the backdrop of both local historical conditions and contemporary U.S. Indian policy. Accordingly, before discussing the specific provisions of these two treaties, it is necessary to review such conditions and policies.

American Settlement in Michigan, 1815–50

Lands acquired from the Black River and Swan Creek Chippewa in 1807 were not surveyed until after the War of 1812. By 1825 most of the southern third of lower Michigan was surveyed, and by 1840 the survey extended to most of the Lower Peninsula.[12] By the Land Act of 1820, Congress set land prices at $1.25 per acre and permitted minimum purchases of eighty acres from the public domain. Michigan land offices opened in Detroit (1818), Monroe (1825), White Pigeon (1831), and both Ionia and Flint (1836). At these land offices, lands could be "entered" for cash or bank drafts, and after the sale was registered with the General Land Office in Washington, a "patent," as original deeds were called, was issued.

Non-Indian settlement in Michigan generally proceeded from east to west and south to north. In 1820 there were 8,765 non-Indians in the territory, which was surely a drastic undercount. By 1830 the number had grown to 31,640. During the next four years, the non-Indian population of the Michigan Territory nearly tripled, to 87,278 people. Of these, 85,856 lived in the southern part of the Lower Peninsula. By 1837, the year of statehood, there were 174,543 people in Michigan, and by 1840 the federal census listed a population of 212,267 people.[13] The huge influx of population in the 1830s was mostly settler farmers from the eastern states who moved into the southern tier of lower Michigan counties.[14]

Federal land sales in Michigan reached an early peak in 1825 in the Detroit area and declined somewhat until 1830, when there was a significant increase in demand for land.[15] This land boom was the result of easy credit and speculation in land, leading to pressure to open the new land acquired by the Treaty of Washington in 1836 and the cessions of Saginaw Chippewa reserves in 1836 and 1837. Shortly after, immigrant settlers began moving into the Saginaw Basin and the Grand River valley in great numbers, and Indian people found themselves suddenly overwhelmed by the newcomers.

The Panic of 1837 and the failure of the U.S. Bank killed the Michigan land boom. By 1839 land sales and the price of land fell dramatically. Congress responded in 1841 by passing the Distribution and Preemption Act, which made permanent a land sale scheme first passed in 1830 called the Graduation Act. Under provision of the Graduation Act, the price of public land dropped with the length of time it remained unsold, falling until the cost per acre reached twenty-five cents. When the Saginaw Chippewa ceded their reserves in 1836 and 1837, the land boom was at its height, and on this basis, the government made very optimistic predictions on how much they would make from the sale.[16] Of course, the government could not foresee the crash in land sales or the fact that settlers would eventually be able to purchase the ceded lands at much reduced costs under the Graduation Act.

Since central Michigan was part of the winter hunting territory of the Saginaw Chippewa, they knew something of the country in and around Isabella County where their reservation was to be established in 1855.[17] The Saginaw Chippewa bands normally conducted their winter hunts in the upper reaches of the rivers that drained the Saginaw Basin (see map 25). The Salt, Chippewa, and Pine rivers, tributaries of the Tittabawassee, drain modern Gratiot, Isabella, and Clair counties, and all were prime Chippewa hunting grounds. In the typical subsistence cycle, the Saginaw Chippewa occupied the lower part of the Saginaw Valley in the summer, congregating in large villages. Following the harvest of crops in the fall, the villages broke up as families left for their winter hunting territories upstream. After spending the winter dispersed, they would gradually reassemble at their villages in the spring. This pattern continued after the Treaty of 1819, which explicitly protected the Saginaw Chippewa's access to vital game, fish, and gathered foods.

Like the rest of interior Michigan, Isabella County was not known to whites at the mid-nineteenth century. Even though surveys had been run, contemporary maps show a rather poor notion of river drainages, distances, and proportions. It was for precisely this reason that the land was selected for an Indian reservation. In fact, white settlement commenced in this area at almost exactly the same time as the land was withdrawn from the market for Indian purposes. It is possible that some settlement might have taken place as early as 1851, when immigrant farmers cut a crude road along the Pine River from Midland County to the east, but the first real settlement took place in November 1854. During that month, a road was completed to the southeast corner of the county, from Gratiot County to the south. Late in 1854 seven pioneer families entered Coe Township of Isabella County and began to clear farms. The nearest settlements where supplies or mail could be obtained were forty-five miles distant.[18]

Isabella County had been named at the time Michigan entered the Union on January 26, 1837, but it was not formally organized until 1859. Coe Township was organized in 1855 and originally comprised townships 13 and 14 north of range 3 west. The remaining parts of the county comprised the townships of Chippewa and Isabella. Chippewa Township was to the north of Coe, in the north half of township 14 north of range 3 west, and Isabella Township consisted of the remaining parts of the county.[19] See map 26. The federal census of 1850 does not show any population in Isabella County, but by 1860 the census

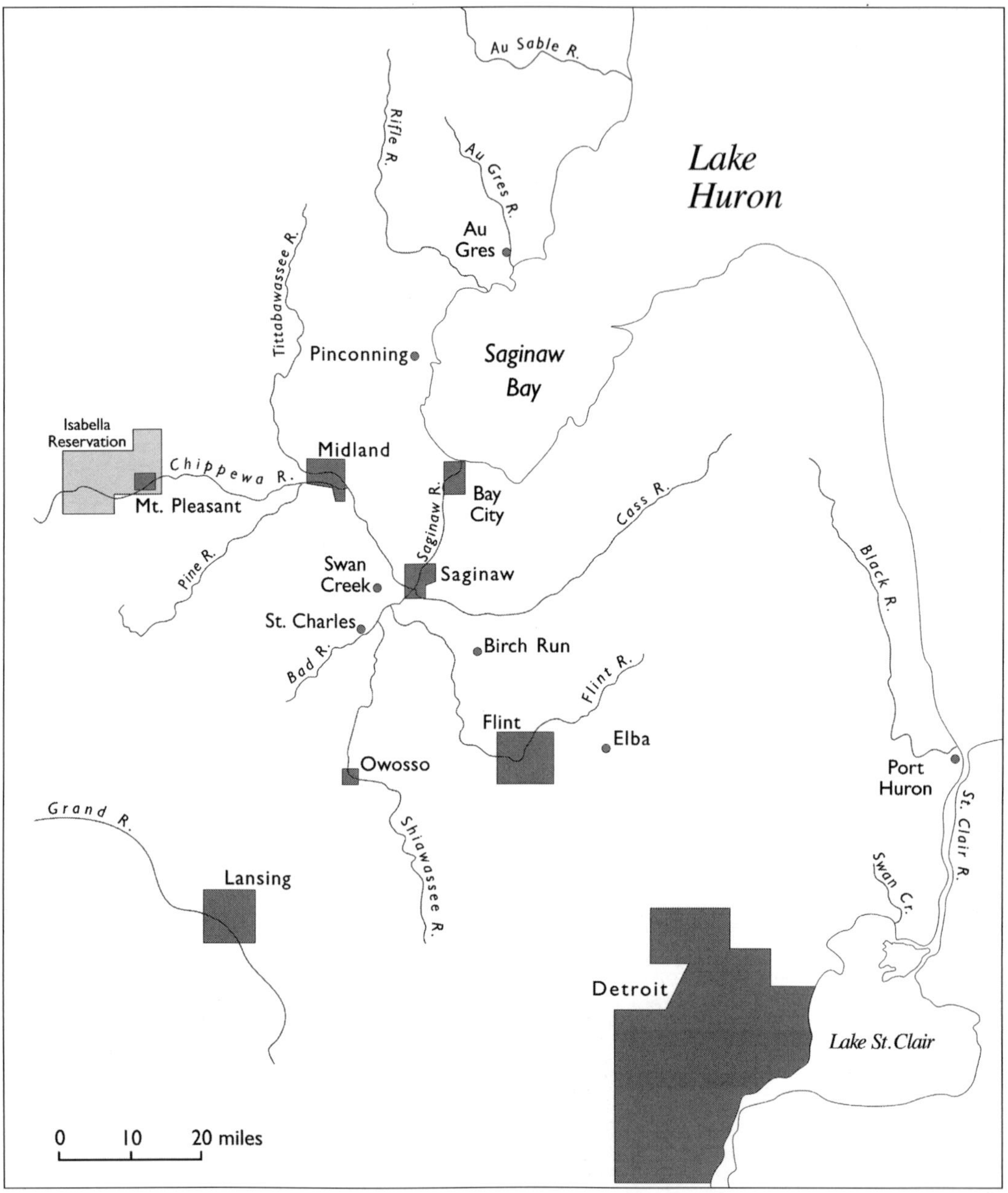

Map 25. Territory of the Saginaw, Black River, and Swan Creek Chippewa

lists 577 whites and 856 Indians residing there.[20]

After establishment of the Indian agency and gristmill in 1857, known locally as "Indian Mills," a small town grew up nearby, called Isabella City. This settlement was gradually abandoned in favor of Mt. Pleasant, which was platted a mile up the Chippewa River in 1863. By the early 1870s, Mt. Pleasant was an active civic and commercial center.[21] See map 27.

In the mid-nineteenth century, Isabella County land was subject to a great deal of land speculation. Prior to the presidential executive order of May 14, 1855, that withdrew the entire county for Indian purposes, timber and land speculators purchased some sizable tracts under the Graduation Act at fifty cents per acre. In addition to these cash entries, land was acquired by using "military warrants." The latter were trans-

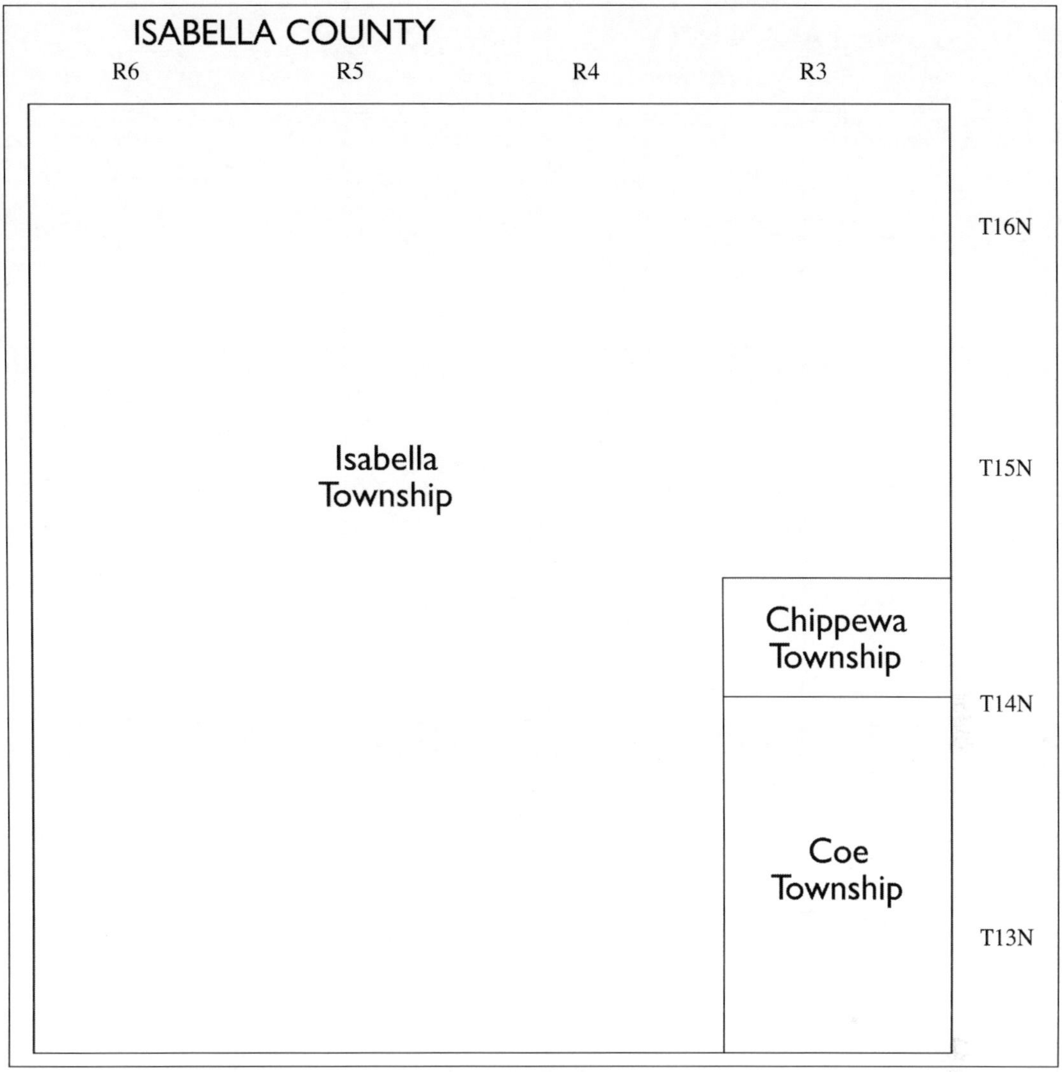

Map 26. Original charter townships of Isabella County

ferable vouchers for specific quantities of public land that were used to partially compensate for military service during the early years of the Republic. Speculators often purchased large numbers of warrants at discount from veterans and used them together to acquire blocks of land.

The Saginaw Valley produced a spectacular lumber boom during the 1850s and 1860s. White pine, which flourished on the sandy soils of the region, was highly prized for building material. Not only was it easy to cut, but it could be floated with little difficulty down the braid of streams that flowed through the valley. From the downstream mills, lumber could be transported down the Great Lakes to eastern markets. In 1854 there were already twenty-nine sawmills, with a combined capacity of one hundred million board feet per year, operating on the Cass, Shiawassee, and Tittabawassee rivers. By 1860 the number had increased to seventy-two mills, and the valley saw a wholesale immigration of lumbermen from the east. The demand for pine timber soared.[22]

Despite land and timber speculation, Isabella County remained an Indian hunting ground in 1855. Other than the feeble beginning of less than a dozen small farms started in the winter of 1854–55, Isabella County was devoid of evidence of settlement. Those scattered farmsteads and the rude cabins of white settlers were concen-

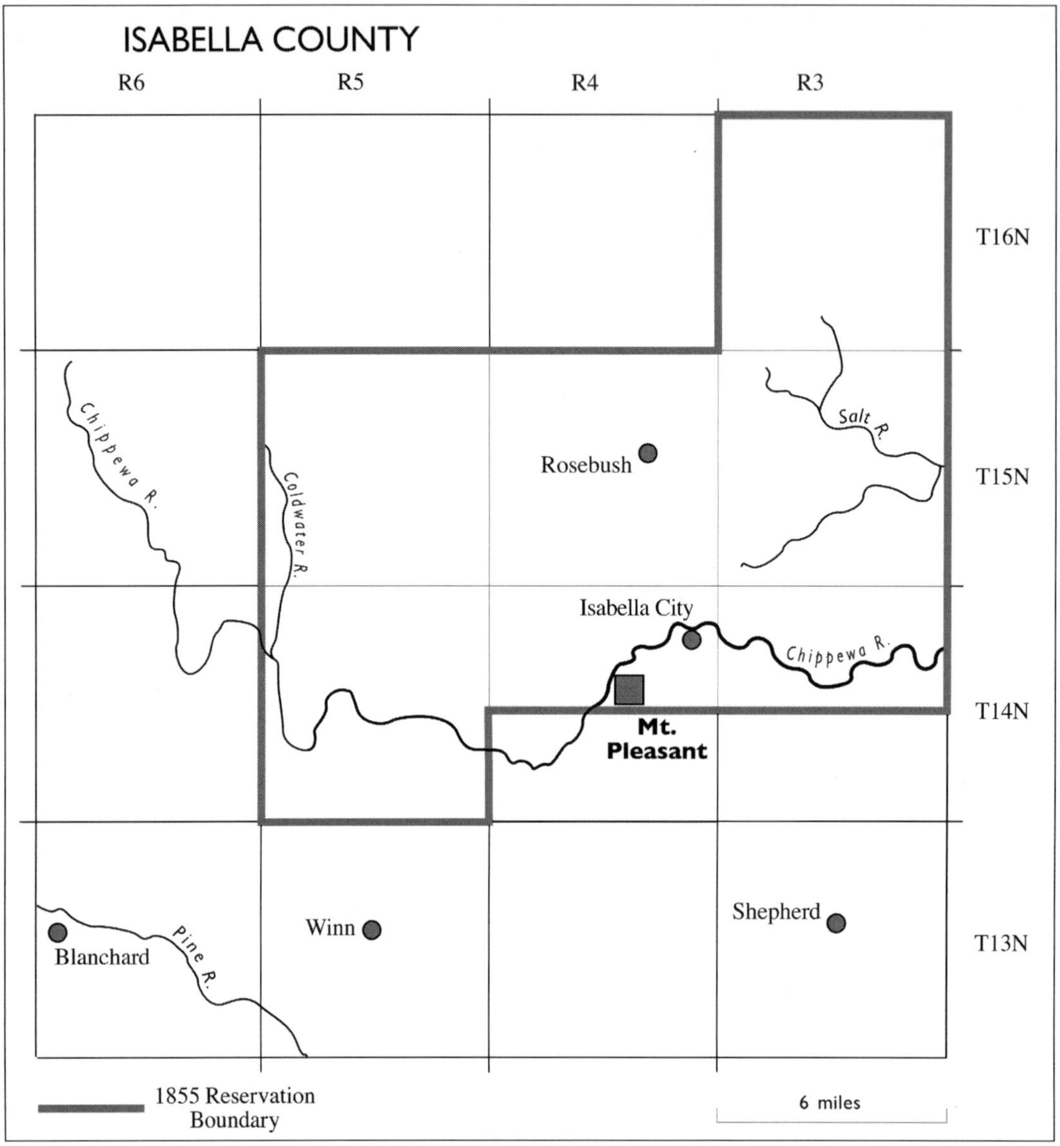

Map 27. Major rivers and towns of Isabella County

trated in the extreme southeastern part of the county. This was the situation when, on May 14, 1855, President Franklin Pierce ordered the withdrawal of all the "vacant land in Isabella County for Indian purposes."[23] There was every reason to believe that the county was virtually all "vacant" land.

The desperate plight of the Michigan Chippewa and Ottawa and the Saginaw Chippewa ultimately led to the treaties made on July 31 and August 2, 1855. Both treaties were negotiated at Detroit by the commissioner of Indian affairs, George Manypenny, and Michigan Indian agent Henry Gilbert, as treaty commissioners for the United States.[24] Both treaties attempted to resolve Michigan Indian problems by concentrating Indians on a few large reservations.[25] As early as 1854, Henry Gilbert wrote to Commissioner Manypenny that the Saginaw Chippewa should be supplied with a suitable tract of land "as far removed from white settlement as possible" and that "no white person should be permitted to locate or live among them except as teachers, traders or mechanics."[26] In the case of the Saginaw Chippewa, now having incorporated the Black River and Swan Creek bands, their reservation was to be six contiguous townships in Isabella County.[27]

Thus, the reservation system of the 1850s attempted to accommodate Indian desires to remain on their traditional lands, promote federal assimilation objectives, and also protect Indian interests. When George Manypenny succeeded Luke Lea as commissioner in 1853, he moved rapidly to negotiate a large number of treaties that put a reservation system in place as a means of promoting civilization efforts (see chapter 2). One of the primary factors that led Manypenny and his fellow reformers to implement the reservation system was that the Trade and Intercourse Act of 1834 had proved to be inadequate to protect the person and property of the Indians.[28] By concentrating Indians on reservations, the Indians could be protected for the period during which they were expected to master the arts and skills of civilization. Manypenny believed that this process could proceed quite rapidly.

In his November 1855 report as commissioner, Manypenny specifically commented on the reservations made in the Michigan treaties of the previous summer: "By them the Indians are to have assigned permanent homes to be hereafter confirmed to them, in small tracts, in severalty. Such guards and restrictions are thrown around their lands and limited annuities as cannot fail, if faithfully regarded and respected to place them in comfortable and independent circumstances."[29] Likewise, in support of his reservation policy, Manypenny said that all non-Indians who settled on ceded lands should be made to understand "that the tribes are to be protected and remain undisturbed within the limits of their reservations, and this policy will be inflexibly adhered to by the government."[30] This position was also held by Manypenny's successors J. W. Denver and Charles Mix. Commissioner Denver went so far as to insist that "no white person should be permitted to obtain any kind of possession or foothold within the limits of reservations, nor even to enter them, except in the employ or by permission of the government, and none should be employed except such as would be actually necessary for the instruction of Indians."[31]

An important part of this policy was the allotment process. Except in rare cases, the reservations were to be held not by the tribe in common but by individual tribal members. Individual landownership, it was believed, would teach Indians the value of toil and pride in individual achievement. To protect the interests of Indian allottees in their land and to prevent their land from falling into the hands of whites as a result of fraud, the Manypenny treaties usually contained a mechanism to prevent alienation of allotments. A favorite of these involved designating Indians as either "competent" or "not so competent." Indians judged to be in the latter category were not able to speak or read English or otherwise protect their own interests. Likewise, by the time of the 1855 treaties at Detroit, Michigan Indians were well aware of their vulnerability if they did not have "strong" title to the land, that is, a patent or deed.[32] In the course of Manypenny's administration, several different allotment schemes evolved, all of which, by Manypenny's own admission, ultimately failed. In 1885 he lamented the loss of Indian land produced by his own allotment treaties: "Had I known then, as I now know, what would result from these treaties, I would be compelled to admit that I had committed a high crime."[33]

It was with these understandings of Indians and the objectives of U.S. Indian policy that George Manypenny and his Michigan agent Henry Gilbert approached the difficult problems facing Michigan Indians in 1855. It would be their task to rectify the problems created when prior administrations, anxious to acquire agricultural land, timber, and mineral resources, wrote "optional" removal treaties that left Indians without legal claim to land. Indians subject to these treaties simply continued to pursue their traditional subsistence rounds throughout the Great Lakes country.

The Treaty of August 2, 1855

In 1855 George Manypenny broke with his usual precedent of negotiating treaties in Washington to come to Detroit to negotiate with the Michigan Indians. Preliminary arrangements centered mainly on the negotiations to be held with the Ottawa and Chippewa Indians whose ancestors had signed the Treaty of Washington in 1836. Correspondence and newspaper accounts indicate that the main purpose of business was to change the terms of former treaties in order to create reservations that would permit Indians to remain in Michigan and to accomplish the assimilation objectives Manypenny saw as important to the future welfare of Indian people.[34] Unlike the Ottawa and Chippewa of western Michigan, some of whom were already living on temporary reserves made under the Treaty of 1836, the Saginaw Chippewa were landless, in the legal sense. As a result, the Saginaw Chippewa's problem was more acute, since a new reservation had to first be created.

The treaty commissioners wished to conduct the Michigan treaty business as cheaply as possible. Since the government provided room and board for delegations of chiefs, cheap also meant quick. It was for this reason that the Michigan treaty conference was held in Detroit during late July, the hottest time of the year.[35] This latter, mean-spirited strategy had its desired effect. After a week of Detroit heat and humidity, the Sault Ste. Marie chief Waubojeeg complained about the weather and voiced his desire to return to the north.[36]

Between Wednesday, July 25, and Thursday, August 2, 1855, Manypenny and Gilbert actually negotiated three treaties. From July 25 until July 31, discussion was with the Ottawa and Chippewa of western and northern Michigan. According to newspaper reports, business with these groups was concluded on the morning of August 1. In the afternoon and for part of the next day, negotiations were held with the Swan Creek, Black River, and Saginaw Chippewa bands, which resulted in the Treaty of August 2.[37] The *Detroit Daily Free Press* of August 2 reported that "a new council was commenced with the Chippewas of Saginaw separately. They have heretofore been treated with separately [from] the other bands and will be still."[38] Later that same day, Gilbert and Manypenny obtained a cession of fishing rights at the rapids of Sault Ste. Marie from the Chippewa band in that area.

It is clear that the Ottawa-Chippewa Treaty of July 31 was the main order of business at Detroit. In fact, as late as mid-July, Agent Gilbert and Saginaw Chippewa missionaries George Smith and J. Durbin, general secretary of the Methodist missions in Michigan, pled with Manypenny to deal with the Saginaw Chippewa. Gilbert warned that their matters were very unsatisfactory and unsettled and that the Saginaw Chippewa needed land to settle on more than any other Michigan Indians.[39] Perhaps Commissioner Manypenny mistakenly thought that the Saginaw people were already included as part of the Michigan Chippewa and Ottawa. Whatever the case, arrangements for the Saginaw Chippewa Treaty of August 2 were not made until mid-July and seemed almost an afterthought on the part of Manypenny.

This conclusion is also supported by the language of the August 2 treaty, which is very much a typical Manypenny treaty. In language, form, and content, it is similar to many other treaties negotiated during Manypenny's tenure as commissioner of Indian affairs between 1853 and 1857. There is no evidence that much time was devoted to learning about the special problems of the Saginaw people or that much negotiation took place. No minutes of the treaty discussions have yet been found. From the arrangements detailed in the treaty, it is clear that the special interests of the Methodist Church were discussed.

The Treaty of August 2, 1855, was, in fact, designed to merge the desire of the Chippewa for a permanent Michigan homeland with Manypenny's objective of allotting land in severalty. Prior to this treaty, the Saginaw Chippewa occupied their traditional territory but had no secure land title except in rare instances by private purchase. A short preamble to the treaty makes reference to the fact that the treaty was necessary because of the Indians' "existing condition" and their acknowledged "legal and equitable" claims against the United States. The "existing condition" refers to the fact that the Indians were without secure land tenure and scattered. The "legal and equitable claims" of the Indians derived from the promises made during the negotiations of the Treaty of January 14, 1837, that former reserves were to be sold and the proceeds paid to the Indians. Because land values dropped dramatically following the 1837 treaty, these lands, in large part, remained unsold or, if sold, were undervalued. Article 3 of the Treaty of August 2, 1855, specifically releases the United States from liability for these claims.

The first order of business for Manypenny was to create a permanent Michigan homeland for the Saginaw people. In anticipation of this objective, the president had withdrawn the whole of Isabella County from sale to the public on May 14, 1855.[40] It was thought that at least six townships would be needed for Indian purposes. At the time of the withdrawal, it was not known which Indians might be settled in Isabella County or how many; this was one of the reasons that the specific location of the Isabella Reservation remained vague at the time the treaty was signed.

The U.S. General Land Office was, however, anxious that the withdrawal of land not be prolonged, since they knew that demand for mid-Michigan land was rapidly expanding as roads and railroads began reaching the region. Land in Isabella County was also very cheap, thanks to provisions of the new Graduation Act of August 1854. Under the terms of this revised act, some land in Isabella County that had been on the market since 1833 could be acquired for only twenty-five cents per acre. The rest of the county had been on the market since 1840 and was therefore available for seventy-five cents per acre. Further, much of the county contained very valuable stands of pine timber, making the price even more attractive to speculators and timber interests.

By the early 1850s, much of the traditional lands of the Saginaw, Black River, and Swan Creek Chippewa had been purchased by white settlers. The Indian agent, the Methodist missionaries, and the Indians themselves were in a panic. They all rightly feared that there would soon be no suitable public land available to provide permanent homes for the Indians in Michigan.[41] Consultation between the General Land Office and the Office of Indian Affairs determined that the best chance of acquiring vacant public land was in the heavily forested region in the center of the Lower Peninsula. Isabella County was chosen because, while it had potential for agriculture, it was also just beyond the fringe of white settlement.[42]

Land office records showed that relatively little of this wilderness land had been sold, and at the time of the 1855 treaty, Isabella County had as few as a half-dozen settlers. These settlers were located along Isabella County's eastern border and in the extreme southeastern corner.[43] Although some of the land in the county went on the market in 1833 and the remainder in 1840, the commissioner of the General Land Office reported to the commissioner of Indian affairs in December 1854 that only two-ninths of the entire county had been "disposed of."[44] Some land in Isabella County had been purchased by immigrant farmers as cash entries, and some timberlands had been selected by speculators. Given the urgent need to make land available as part of the anticipated treaty negotiations with the Michigan Indians, the secretary of the interior, Robert McClelland, wrote to President Franklin Pierce on April 12, 1855, suggesting that the entire Isabella County be withdrawn from sale for the benefit of the Michigan Indians.[45]

Article 1 of the August 2 treaty withdrew from sale, for the benefit of the Black River, Swan Creek, and Saginaw Chippewa, townships 17 and 18 north of ranges 3, 4, and 5 east, located at Saginaw Bay, and "all the unsold public lands" in six adjoining townships in Isabella County. The townships at Isabella were supposed to be selected by the Indians within three months. Questions have been raised in modern times about the meaning of the phrase *unsold land*. Here we must bear in mind the desires and responsibilities of the treaty commissioners. Foremost on their own agenda, as well as the Indians', was the provision for a homeland where the scattered Saginaw bands could be consolidated and protected from whites. It was also true that the treaty commissioners had to protect the landownership interests of non-Indians. The problem facing the commissioners was to find a sufficient tract of contiguous land that had not yet been sold. By 1855 Isabella County had been surveyed and on the market for some years. Government officials were aware of the fact that some land in Isabella County had already been sold and was in private hands. Although Manypenny and Gilbert knew that some parcels in Isabella County would not be available for Indian allotments, they deliberately chose this unsettled territory to reduce the chance of such conflicts. The executive order of May 14, 1855, was intended to halt all further sales.

This was not a unique problem but one handled in the same fashion in other places. An excellent illustration is found in the treaty with the Lake Superior Chippewa written at La Pointe in 1854. Here Manypenny and Gilbert created six reservations, five of which were made on unsurveyed lands, while one, that at L'Anse, was made where land survey permitted its description in terms of range and township. Since prior sale was possible in the case of this reservation alone, it was the only one of the six where the withdrawal of land for Indian purposes included the words "unsold land."

The use of the phrase *unsold land* had nothing to do with whether or not a reservation was intended to be created. The term did not exclude land from the reservation but merely recognized that certain land would not be available for allotment, thus protecting any ownership rights of those who might otherwise be unjustly displaced. Thus, in the minds of the chiefs and government officials, the phrase *unsold land* reduced neither the quantity of land reserved nor the integrity of the reservation but only the dispersal of allotted land.[46]

Allotment was but one of a long series of objectives that Manypenny and Gilbert wanted to accomplish. Manypenny believed strongly that for the allotment process to work, Indians had to be protected. Clearly it was the desire of both the United States and the Indians for the Saginaw Chippewas to be collected together and protected while they were learning the arts of civilization and the value of private property. The reservation, with its protective exterior boundaries, was integral to that goal. In the specific case of the Isabella Reservation, Secretary McClelland wrote to President Pierce on April 12, 1855, explaining the necessity of withdrawing land for the reservation in anticipation of the treaty. It was necessary, he said, to furnish these Indians "with land . . . to the greatest possible extent separated from evil example or annoyance of unprincipled whites, who might be disposed to settle in their vicinity or within their midst."[47]

In his book *Our Indian Wards,* published in 1880, Manypenny wrote, "When the tribe is permanently located on the reservation, and the integrity of the same is placed beyond question, and when those disposed to intrude upon the possessions of the red man understand, that if done, it is at their peril, and that certain and swift punishment will follow, the work of the agent may be successfully prosecuted."[48] The importance of protecting the Indian community and land base is also noted in the journal of the Treaty of July 31, 1855. On July 26, just a week before the August 2 treaty was concluded, Henry Gilbert explained to the Ottawa and Chippewa,

> The first thing I want you to determine is the location of these lands. The Government doesn't expect that all the Indians in Michigan will locate in one place and is willing to set aside tracts sufficient for small settlements in different places, but it will not permit you as individuals to locate promiscuously here and there a tract as your personal wishes may direct. It desires and will insist on your collecting into communities. It desires that these communities shall be as large as possible, because it will be cheaper in support of school, township and county organizations. Now I wish you to give me a description of the locations you wish to settle upon.[49]

In September 1855, following the signing of the treaty, the Commissioner of the General Land Office wrote that he doubted if six wholly unoccupied townships existed in Isabella County, and he suggested that the reservation idea be done away with. He believed things would go much easier if the agent took each Indian to the land office and had him or her register an appropriate selection.[50] The Office of Indian Affairs rejected this advice. The office was concerned with efficiency in the delivery of services to Indians and with the establishment of a bounded reservation so that the Indians and resources could be protected. In fact, in the following decades, the federal government often did intervene to protect the Isabella Reservation.[51]

Clearly the reservation was conceived by the government in terms of well-defined, contiguous townships, not just a quantity of land. Although the specific townships that make up the Isabella Reservation were designated in June 1856, it was not until April 1859 that Charles Mix, commissioner of Indian affairs, officially notified the commissioner of the General Land Office that the remaining parts of Isabella County could be restored to the public domain.[52] In doing so, Mix reminded the commissioner that the 1855 treaty provided for six townships of land; if there were preemption claims—that is, lands not available for Indian allotment within the selected townships—the government should retain a sufficient quantity of the *contiguous* lands to make up such deficiency" (emphasis added).[53] A further indication of the intention of the Indians and the government to create a permanent, defined reservation in 1855 is the fact that both commonly used the term *reservation* to refer to the six townships in question. Repeated use of the term *reservation* in contemporary communication from the general public, missionaries, the Indians, and government officials, both in Michigan and Washington, illustrates the common belief that the Saginaw Chippewa holdings in Isabella County were a "reservation" in the usual sense of the word.[54]

In 1860 the secretary of the interior, Jacob Thompson, described the types of treaties made between the United States and various Indian tribes during the previous decade.[55] He distinguished between treaties that created allotments within bounded reservations and those that created allotments scattered among white settlers. At Isabella there was a presumption that all land within the reservation boundary, except land that had been sold at the time of the executive order, might ultimately be needed for Indian purposes. It is worth noting here that at the time the decision was made in December 1854 to request withdrawal of the six townships in Isabella County for Indian purposes, no decision had been made about which Indians or how many Indians might be assigned to the reservation.[56] While it is true in the case of the Isabella Reservation that subsequent transfer of title from Indians to non-Indians as well as preexisting privately owned land within the reservation boundaries at the time of the treaty did create a checkerboard of Indian and non-Indian ownership, this was not the intent of the government in 1855. The clear intent was to create allotments within a bounded reservation separate from non-Indians to the greatest extent possible under existing conditions. The Treaty of August 2, 1855, did not provide for or even contemplate the sale of land within the reservation to non-Indians.

Article 6 of the Treaty of August 2 purports to dissolve the tribal organization of the Black River, Swan Creek, and Saginaw Chippewa, except as may be necessary to carry out the provisions of the treaty. This provision is a shortened version of Article 5 of the Treaty of July 31, 1855, with the Ottawa and Chippewa, which went on to explain that it was aimed at eliminating "general conventions" of the tribe. Clearly the government wished to avoid the costly and time-consuming necessity of calling together all of the political representatives of the Ottawa and Chippewa to transact business that only affected those "immediately interested."[57] In fact, this article was explained to the Ottawa and Chippewa by Manypenny in the treaty negotiations at Detroit. In answer to Chief Waubojeeg's complaint that the Ottawa and Chippewa interests were different and that the Chippewa wished to be separated from the Ottawa, Manypenny replied, "The very case you suggest is met in the treaty [in Article 5]—you are separated as you desire. This treaty [of July 31, 1855] you and the Ottawa must sign together because the old treaty of 36 [the 1836 Treaty of Washington] was made in that way, but here we have followed your suggestion and provided that money shall be paid to different bands and that no general council shall be called."[58]

Manypenny's statement, made eight days prior to the signing of the August 2 treaty, clearly indicates that the United States did not intend to dissolve the Saginaw, Black River, and Swan Creek body politic but intended only to economize the efficiency with which the Indians would deal with the United States in the future. Ironically, the government was suggesting a return to band-level politics that the Indians had, in fact, always maintained, despite the fiction of the larger political groupings created by the United States for its own purposes. Further support for the proposition that the political existence of the Indians continued after 1855 and that the government continued to recognize the tribal organization is found in the Treaty of October 18, 1864, with the Chippewa of Saginaw, Swan Creek, and Black River, discussed later in this chapter.

The Intertreaty Period, 1855–64

Within a matter of months after the Treaty of August 2, 1855, was negotiated, the problems of putting Manypenny's idealism into actual practice became apparent. In fact, the decade following the treaty was filled with frustration for government officials and Indians alike.

The Treaty of 1855 provides that the specific townships of Isabella County that would make up the reserve were to be selected by the Indians within three months. In February 1856 Agent Henry Gilbert wrote to Manypenny and suggested that township 15 north of ranges 3, 4, 5, and 6 west and township 14 north of ranges 3 and 4 west be designated as the reserve (see map 28).[59] In early April, the commissioner of the General Land Office, Thomas Hendricks, wrote to Manypenny informing him that some land within the suggested townships had been claimed by David Ward on military bounties. Although these claims had been canceled, they were about to be reinstated.[60] Manypenny objected strongly, and the argument went to the secretary of the interior for resolution.[61] Incredibly, the secretary ruled that the presidential order of May 14, 1855, that withdrew the whole of Isabella County from public sale was not effective until it was received at the land office in Ionia Michigan on May 23, 1855.[62] Since the Ward claim was made after May 14 but before May 23, his claim was reinstated.

Not only would non-Indian landownership within the reservation boundaries interfere with the government's policy of civilizing the Saginaw Chippewa, but such ownership would also reduce the quantity of land available for allotment to the Indians. Consequently, Agent Gilbert made another selection; by adjusting the reservation lines, he was able to avoid most of the Ward lands. Township 16 north of range 3 west was substituted for township 15 north of range 6 west, and township 14 north of range 5 west was added to replace the southern half of township 14 north of ranges 3 and 4 west. Thus the Isabella Reservation took its modern form, with the intention of excluding non-Indian ownership from within the boundary. See map 28.[63]

Late in the summer of 1856, the Methodist missionary William Brockway brought one hundred Indians to Isabella County for the purpose of making allotment selections as well as to select a mill site.[64] Allotment selections were submitted by Gilbert to Manypenny on April 4, 1857.[65] Apparently the first Indian residents of the reservation appeared that summer, because by November 1856, the new Indian agent A. W. Fitch reported that the Isabella Indians were starving.[66]

In April 1859 the commissioner of Indian affairs, Charles Mix, officially notified the commissioner of the General Land Office of the six townships selected under the provision of the first clause of the first article of the Treaty of 1855. These were the same lands recommended earlier by Agent Gilbert. Mix also requested release of the remaining land in Isabella County that had been withdrawn from public sale by the presidential order of May 14, 1855, and he suggested to Commissioner Hendricks that if any preemption claims had been admitted upon the selected townships, "it will be necessary to retain a sufficient quantity of the contiguous lands to make up such deficiency."[67] Since the General Land Office was aware that the Saginaw Chippewa were advancing a claim for lands within the six townships that had been sold and that were not available for allotment under the treaty, the General Land Office decided not to reopen county lands to public sale. The government calculated the amount of land to be 35,695.06 acres.[68]

Five years after the 1855 treaty, the land allotment process was hopelessly snarled. Because of conflicting claims and selections, mistakes in recording, and other errors, land selections had been made and canceled. No certificates of selection—let alone patents—had been issued to the Indians. In fact, no certificates were issued until 1864, nine years after the treaty.

Both the Indians and the government officials were becoming extremely frustrated. Non-Indian speculators were beginning to infringe on the lands and resources guaranteed by the treaty. Timber thefts and swindles on reservation land were a growing problem. When these problems were reported by Agent Fitch in November 1860, the commissioner of Indian affairs directed him to vigorously investigate the thefts.[69] Agent Fitch did indeed conclude that the Saginaw Chippewa were being collectively and individually exploited by certain timber interests.[70] There were other problems as well. The Chippewa also came to realize that the actual amount of land available for allotment within the six townships was reduced by swampland and school section claims made by the state of Michigan and a railroad claim made by the Grand Haven and Pere Marquette railroads.[71]

While the Indian agents and the commission-

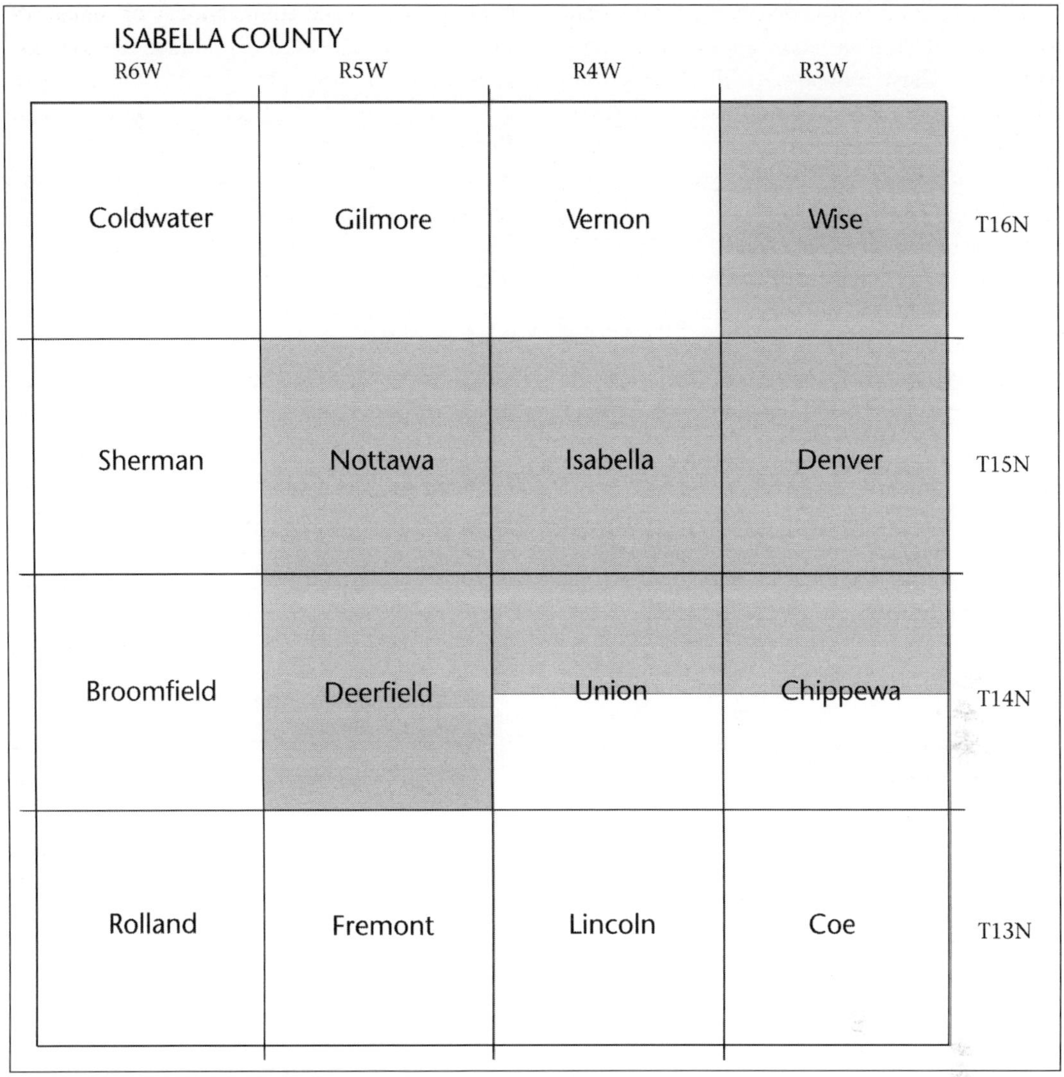

Map 28. Modern townships of Isabella County and Isabella Indian reservation

ers of Indian affairs did try to represent the best interests of the Saginaw Chippewa, they were up against an extremely powerful business lobby that was supported by Michigan's political delegation. The Indians became dissatisfied and distrustful of the government and its agents. The Saginaw chiefs called for a new treaty to straighten out land issues.[72] Given pending land claims, the dispersal of the Chippewa on two reservations and elsewhere, and the fact that Isabella County continued to be withdrawn from the market, the Indian Office supported the chiefs' request.[73]

The Treaty of 1864

In 1864 the Black River, Swan Creek, and Saginaw Chippewa numbered 1,581 people. These were divided among fourteen autonomous bands centered at the Isabella Reservation, at the Saginaw Bay Reservation, and in scattered groups that continued to reside along the Saginaw River and its tributaries. There were three bands of almost 400 people at Saginaw Bay and approximately seven bands of somewhat over 1,000 people at Isabella. The remaining four bands were scattered through the ceded territory. Of these, at least one band of 150 people was identified with the Black River Chippewa.[74] Perhaps the result of factionalism due to Christian conversions and acculturation, there were, in fact, more bands in 1864 than there had been in 1855.

The Saginaw chiefs wanted to accomplish two main objectives by a new treaty: to provide that future land allotments would be available to their children as they came of age and to privately purchase land within the six townships, a right guaranteed by the 1855 treaty but never permitted by the government. The Saginaw chiefs hoped to exercise this right collectively with money due the tribe as the final payments under the 1855 treaty. Considering the previous decade's record of white encroachment, the chiefs expressed their apprehension: "If the land is brought into market and white men come and settle among us, we fear it will disturb us very much and break up our settlement."[75] In other words, the Saginaw chiefs wished to secure a stable land base free from the interference of whites. To a large extent, this was also the intent of the government in agreeing to treat with the Saginaw Chippewa in 1864. The United States hoped to concentrate the Chippewa bands on one reservation and to reaffirm the reservation's integrity by making sure that land was available for selection until the six townships were all taken up by Indian allotments.[76]

The Treaty of October 18, 1864, was therefore supplementary to the Treaty of August 2, 1855.[77] The first article of the 1864 treaty called for the release of the reservation on Saginaw Bay created under the 1855 treaty. The Indians also relinquished their rights to "locate lands in lieu of lands sold or disposed of by the United States upon their reservation at Isabella and also the right to purchase unselected lands in said reservation as provided for in the first article of said treaty [the Treaty of August 2, 1855]."

In exchange for the relinquishment of six townships of land on Saginaw Bay and the Indians' right to select 35,695 acres of land outside the reservation at Isabella, the United States agreed to expend twenty thousand dollars in support of a manual labor school to be built by the Methodist Episcopal Church. The Saginaw Chippewa of the reservation at Isabella County agreed to absorb their kin from Saginaw Bay as well as several bands of Grand River Ottawa, Chippewa, and Potawatomi and gave up a quarter section of land to the Methodist Church. The last two payments under the 1855 treaty were to be set aside as an agricultural fund. This money could not be used for land purchases as the chiefs had hoped, because the government believed it would be unfair to make them purchase their own lands.[78] This magnanimous gesture later worked havoc on the Saginaw Chippewa land base.

Political concerns also motivated the government's negotiation of the 1864 treaty. As an active Republican politician, Agent DeWitt Leach was keenly aware that support for the administration of President Lincoln and Governor Austin Blair was eroding. In Michigan the governor's margin of victory fell from twenty thousand votes in 1858 to only six thousand in 1862. Two of the six Michigan congressmen elected that year were Democrats.[79] Local elections in many districts promised to be tight in the 1864 election year. In early October, a little over two weeks before the 1864 treaty was concluded and well before the November elections, Agent Leach wrote to William Dole, commissioner of Indian affairs, "We hope to make the proposed changes in the treaty of some political use to us. Our Indians are voters and their votes may be of great importance to us in the approaching election. They [the Saginaw Chippewa] reside in the closest congressional district in the State and hence, anything fair and honorable that we can do to put them in good humor and to favorably dispose them towards the Government we wish to do."[80]

The Post-treaty Era

1864–71: Land and Timber Frauds at Isabella

Theoretically, the Treaty of 1864 was intended to solve the pressing problems of the Saginaw Chippewa. In reality, the 1864 treaty marked the advent of a period of extraordinary abuse of their rights by American citizens and a betrayal of the trust responsibility of the United States. No sooner was the treaty negotiated than avaricious whites swooped in to exploit the Chippewa's newly reaffirmed land and resources. The result was that the original intent and purposes of Manypenny and others in creating a reservation for the Indians in mid-Michigan and allotting them land under the 1855 and 1864 treaties were subverted and destroyed. Timber and land frauds perpetrated against the Indians—in some instances, with the knowledge and assistance of local Indian agents—soon resulted in large quantities of land within the reservation passing to non-Indian ownership contrary to the purposes of the treaties. The defenseless Indians had little hope of changing or affecting these events.

Perhaps the disruption of the Civil War was to blame for the lack of government vigilance in the first part of the 1860s. Almost certainly the fact that the Indian Office was small and remote contributed to the problem. After all, one agent in Detroit had responsibility for thousands of Indians scattered widely across Michigan's huge and largely roadless wilderness. On top of these factors, Agent Richard Smith, who served from April 1865 to April 1869, and Agent William Brockway, who was appointed in April 1869 and served to June 1869, were both utter incompetents. In a surprisingly candid appraisal of his predecessor's performance, Agent Major James Long said that rather than ascertaining the government's position and trying to honestly explain it to his charges, Smith preferred to make endless promises to the Indians and then pray that the promises would be fulfilled.[81]

Shortly after the Treaty of 1864 was negotiated, the government learned of a massive land swindle on the Isabella Reservation.[82] By taking advantage of the second provision of the first article of the Treaty of August 2, 1855, which permitted Indians to purchase reservation land in fee simple, Ezra Rust hired two mixed-blood Indians to purchase fifteen thousand acres in his behalf. The purchasers, Charles Rodd and Andrew Campeau, assigned the land by quitclaim deeds to Rust. This land, which became known as the Rust Purchase, contained valuable stands of pine timber. The Rust Purchase was vigorously denounced by the local press, missionaries, agents, and the Saginaw chiefs. Despite the fact that it would be almost two years before the 1864 treaty worked its way to proclamation, the secretary of the interior, John Usher, quickly directed the commissioner of the General Land Office to cancel the sale of Isabella Reservation land to non-Indians.[83] However, Rust was politically powerful enough to enlist congressional support to uphold his purchase, and in 1869 Congress passed a bill providing him patents.[84]

In the meantime, a general assault was mounted by the local population and their congressional representatives on the Isabella Reservation and other Michigan reservations. The Isabella County fathers wrote that the reservation was an utter wilderness in the midst of civilization and that they believed it unfair and detrimental to progress that Indians could hold office and vote but did not contribute taxes.[85] In fact, the Michigan auditor general ruled that Indian lands held by certificate were liable to state and local taxes.[86] The commissioner of Indian affairs in the Grant administration, Eli Parker, vigorously disabused the state auditor general of this position by pointing out that while Indians held certificates, land selections were held by the United States in trust for the individual Indians.[87] Congressmen and citizens alike called for an end to the reservation system. They wanted patents granted to each Indian, and they wanted unallotted reservation land sold on the public market.[88]

The cause of most of the dissatisfaction of both Indians and their white neighbors, albeit for vastly different reasons, was that the federal government continued to promise the eminent delivery of patents while, in truth, the land selection and registration process was hopelessly snarled. Apparently no plat books, lists of qualified allottees, or allotment selections were kept in the agency office.[89] Each new agent had to start from scratch, but when he did so, he found that the government and state records contained conflicting entries made by previous agents. Commissioner Parker determined to straighten out this mess, a task that he assigned to new agent James Long.[90] Long, who was appointed in June 1869, was organized, competent, and at least initially respected by both the Indian and non-Indian communities.

While working to straighten out the land problems, Long reopened the question of the legality of the Rust Purchase. He was joined in this task by the Saginaw Chippewa missionary George Bradley.[91] By late 1869 Rust was preparing to strip the pine from his land within the reservation, when an insidious new twist developed. Two Saginaw timber speculators, Timothy Jerome and George Williams, drew up a contract in which they offered to sue Rust to invalidate his deeds in exchange for a ten years' option to buy pine from each allotment at a very low price. By offering ten-dollar signing bonuses, Jerome and Williams induced as many as five hundred Indian allottees to sign such contracts. Through inside information, Jerome and Williams also knew that the U.S. attorney in Detroit had been authorized to bring a suit against Rust so they would not be obliged to use their own funds to initiate the agreed-on suit.[92] Since Agent Long had not permitted Indians to register allotments on the Rust claim because of potential conflict and because it contained the best timberland, Jerome and Williams hired the trusted missionary Rev. George Bradley to induce Indians to make selections on the Rust Purchase. Bradley was able to do this because he was also temporarily in the employ of Agent Long as a land selector and registrar. Long only belatedly learned of the government's suit against Rust and of his betrayal by Bradley.[93] While the U.S. attorney was proceeding against Rust, Jerome and Williams continued to encumber timber on Indian allotments. When the U.S. District Court for the Eastern District of Michigan ruled in favor of the United States in October 1870, Rust's claim was eliminated, and Jerome and Williams controlled the majority of timber resources on the Isabella Reservation.[94]

When Agent Long resigned in early 1871, the government announced the reappointment of former agent Rev. Richard Smith. The Saginaw chiefs were aghast at the prospect. In a petition to the commissioner of Indian affairs, they complained that they had still not received a single patent, fifteen years after the Treaty of 1855. Rather than have Smith as their agent, they would rather have no agent at all and simply end their formal relationship with the United States. The Saginaw chiefs suggested the appointment of James Long as a temporary special agent to finish up the allotment process.[95] Long liked this idea and asked several influential politicians to lobby for his appointment. In anticipation of his appointment, he left office with all the Indian land records.[96] Instead of Long, however, the hapless Richard Smith became agent in April 1871. Smith drowned in a storm on Saginaw Bay that summer, taking the agency records with him.[97]

As it turned out, the victory for the Saginaw Chippewa and the United States in the Rust case was also a victory for the land and timber speculators.[98] With the Rust pineland now open for Indian selection and with a court ruling that gave Indian allottees the right to sell timber from their allotments, the stage was set for wholesale fraud.[99] Three Saginaw brothers, Peter, E. C., and Alexander Andre, in league with "Chief" Paymawsaw and Mt. Pleasant real estate men I. E. Arnold and I. A. Francher, began to "help" Indians select and register allotments with the government. Their real interest, of course, was in acquiring rights to valuable pine timber. Essentially the Indian process of land allotment was privatized. The results were predictable.

In the fall of 1871, the U.S. attorney in Detroit wrote to the secretary of the interior, warning that land and timber fraud was out of control on the Isabella Reservation.[100] The Saginaw chiefs also sent up a distress signal.[101] Even a group of competing Saginaw lumbermen petitioned the president to do something about the Isabella timber cartel.[102] John Knox, who had been sent as a special agent to give out the first set of land patents in October 1871, was asked to investigate. Finally the secretary of interior asked the U.S. attorney to bring an end to trespass by unauthorized individuals on the Isabella Reservation, the theft of timber, and property fraud.[103]

The history of the Isabella Reservation in the period following the Treaty of 1864 shows a repetition of patterns established after the 1855 treaty. No sooner was the 1864 treaty proclaimed than its intent was subverted. The benevolence of treaty commissioners Alvord and Leach and the desires of the Saginaw chiefs were indeed swept aside by powerful real estate, railroad, and timber interests. Had the 1864 treaty been permitted to function as it was designed, the Saginaw, Black River, and Swan Creek Chippewa and their descendants would have taken allotments on the Isabella Reservation until all the available land within the boundaries of the six townships was held by Indians. After some years, they could have become educated, economically self-sufficient, Christian farmers. The fact that this promise was not fulfilled was not due to any lapse on the part of the Saginaw Chippewa. They tried their best to meet their obligations under the treaties. That they again lost hope for the bright future held out by the U.S. government in the Treaty of 1864 is a story of conspiracy, greed, and betrayal.

1871–1900: Land Fraud and Timber Trespass

During the decade after the Civil War, there was much discussion both within and outside the federal government concerning the proper way of managing Indian affairs. The old philosophy, a product of the colonial era, was that tribes were sovereign entities within the boundaries of the United States and conducted their relationship with the United States as political equals by virtue of their sovereign status and treaty agreements. Under this philosophy, the management of Indian affairs was almost entirely in the hands of the War Department, within the executive branch of government. Given the Indian wars that swept the western plains beginning in the 1860s, given charges of widespread corruption in the Indian Department during the Grant administration, and for a variety of other reasons, Congress began to take a more active role in managing Indian relations by the end of the 1860s.[104] To gain more control and to limit the Senate's authority over Indian affairs under the treaty ratification clause of the Constitution, the House of Representatives added a rider to the Indian appropriation bill in 1871 that outlawed further treaty making by the executive branch.[105] Consequently there was a major shift in philosophy about the relationship between the Indians and the United States. From the government's perspective, Indians were transformed from independent sovereigns to dependent wards of the federal government. Indians were citizens neither of a state nor of the United States; they were protected by no laws other than those passed by Congress. Where possible, Indians did continue to evoke existing treaties, which, of course, remained in effect.

In many ways, it was difficult for Indians to comprehend this shift in philosophy because, in large part, they saw politics in terms of personal relationships. The treaty relationship was a solemn agreement between themselves and the president of the United States, who was their protector as a father is to his children. Under the new arrangement, this relationship became very remote as layers of bureaucracy evolved to manage the Office of Indian Affairs within the Department of Interior. The chiefs seemed to lose contact and thereby influence with the Great Father, while the local agents became tremendously powerful in the affairs of the Indians. Matters could hardly get worse for the Chippewa of Saginaw, Black River, and Swan Creek who were involved in the tremendous confusion of their allotment process, the appointment of the inept agent Richard Smith and his subsequent drowning with the loss of agency records, and the lack of any meaningful protection against widespread fraud.[106] But the situation did get worse, much worse.

In November 1871 Rev. George Betts was appointed as Indian agent for the Mackinac Agency, an office that he held until February 1876. Betts represented what was perhaps the single contingency that treaty commissioners George Manypenny, Henry Gilbert, and their successors, H. J. Alvord and DeWitt Leach, did not consider when they designed the allotment system, with its safeguards against alienation. In placing their trust in the agent to protect the interest of Indian people, the treaty commissioners did not consider that the agent himself might be corrupt. George Betts was indeed corrupt.

The full extent of Betts's involvement in the conspiracy of real estate and lumber interests to steal Indian land on the Isabella Reservation was not appreciated for several years. During the spring and summer of 1875, the Saginaw chiefs began a campaign to have Betts and his interpreter John Collins removed from office.[107] In the midst of furious claims and counterclaims that followed the chiefs' accusations, the secretary of the interior directed the commissioner of Indian affairs to dispatch special agent Edward Kemble to investigate the chiefs' charges.[108] By February Kemble had confirmed the chiefs' claims, including the fact that Betts tried to manipulate the tribe by appointing his own "Council of Chiefs."[109] On the basis of the Kemble report, Betts was removed from office for fraud and, in December 1879, was charged with corruption.[110]

Before detailing Betts's involvement in land fraud, it is necessary to understand the enormous profits that were involved in the theft of land and timber from the Isabella Reservation. The government, with the recommendation of the agent, was issuing patents to Indians for either forty-acre individual allotments or eighty-acre parcels to heads of families. For the most part, these allottees could not read, write, or speak English. They probably had no idea how big an acre of land was, and they certainly had but the scantiest idea of the working of the real estate or lumber markets. Almost all were desperately poor and often starving.[111]

By conservative estimate, pinelands like those on the Isabella Reservation could produce fifty thousand board feet of lumber per acre. At the going rate for stumpage in the early 1870s of $1.50 per thousand board feet, the pine lumber on each acre was worth about three thousand dollars.[112] Typically, deeds for a forty-acre Indian allotment could be obtained for a ten-dollar down payment and a fifteen-dollar promissory note. Thus, for as little as ten dollars, "investors" acquired the right to cut timber worth three thousand dollars, and for fifteen dollars more, they acquired the land, which was itself worth, at a minimum, twice the twenty-five-dollar price of purchase. The potential profit to be made in defrauding Indians was so great that it became a feeding frenzy of "land sharks."[113]

According to detailed reports issued on four separate occasions between 1878 and 1886 by Edward Kemble, E. J. Brooks, and J. D. C. Atkins, who were all assigned as special agents to investigate land and timber fraud at the Isabella Reservation, George Betts conspired with a number of individuals to defraud his Indian charges.[114] On taking office, Betts quickly drew up a list of 686 selections, which he forwarded with recommendations for patents. Under the terms of the Treaty of 1864, he was to judge the "competence" of each individual Indian allottee, that is, their ability to defend their land title. Literacy in the English language was considered paramount in this regard. Betts recommended that only fifteen of the patents be restricted by the designation "not so competent." As a result, 671 of the first round of patents issued in August 1871 had no restrictions guarding against alienation of the land. Between 1872 and 1874, 101 of these patents were canceled as improper.[115] Since many of the canceled patents had already been sold to non-Indians, there was tremendous confusion over title.

Late in 1875, Betts recommended patents for 251 more selections, of which he judged two as "not so competent." In compiling the list of selections, Betts required Indians to register selections with Mt. Pleasant real estate agents J. E. Arnold and Alexander Andre. In fact, these men selected the specific parcels for each Indian. Since Arnold's and Andre's object was to acquire rights to pine timber, they selected sandy pinelands that were relatively unsuited for agriculture. Special agent E. J. Brooks later confirmed that 212 of the 251 patents issued as a result of Bett's 1875 list ended up in the hands of Andre, Arnold, or other non-Indians.[116] After making the selection, these men offered ten dollars in cash and a fifteen-dollar promissory note for each patent. Although Betts claimed he had carefully checked the list to make sure each Indian was in fact eligible to receive a patent, Brooks found that only 32 of 251 Indians were actually eligible.[117] Representative W. D. Foster wrote to the commissioner of Indian affairs in 1872 complaining that while Agent Betts reported the total population of the Saginaw, Black River, and Swan Creek Chippewa at 1,464 souls, he had authorized over 1,900 eighty-acre selections for "heads of families." Foster asked that the government spend the time and money to head off the plundering of the Isabella Reservation.[118]

In the end, Brooks reported that 1,711 selections, amounting to seventy-five thousand acres, were made and patented to Indians during the Betts era. Of these, at least 250 selections were actually purchased for H. W. Sage by I. E. Arnold. Likewise, Jerome and Williams held 322 deeds for timber and had recorded 855 deeds for thirty thousand acres of land first patented to Indians. James Leyton of Mt. Pleasant held one hundred selections obtained by having Indians sign a "receipt" that was in fact a warranty deed to their land. Brooks also observed that the Isabella Indians had no protection against such speculators. Those who spoke English did so brokenly and had no business capacity. Brooks reported that he interviewed at least one hundred Indians who were listed as "competent" and that not one was able to transact business.[119]

Over one hundred years after the fact, it is difficult to describe the extent and effect of the actions of Betts, Andre, Arnold, and their accomplices in defrauding the Saginaw Chippewa people. Not only did they rob defenseless people of their land and resources, but they also cheated them of a fair chance to emerge as equal competitors with their non-Indian neighbors. This inability to compete led directly to the poverty, sickness, and discrimination suffered by successive generations of Saginaw Chippewa. Perhaps agent Rev. George Lee expressed the outrage of many decent non-Indians when, in his 1878 annual report to the commissioner of Indian affairs, he remarked that those responsible for the frauds perpetuated against the Saginaw Chippewa at Isabella should be consigned to the penitentiary "without benefit of pardon or clergy."[120]

For all its errors, the government must be credited with moving properly and decisively when the Betts frauds were discovered. Betts was discharged and replaced by George Lee, a good, honest, competent man who took office in May 1876. Lee acted quickly to try to bring timber trespass under control. As a first step, he asked that all future allotments be restricted by the designation "not so competent."[121] Timber theft was also prosecuted, an action that was periodically recommended by the Saginaw chiefs.[122]

When Lee became acquainted with the Isabella Reservation, he found that the schools were dysfunctional. Land fraud had gone so far that the Indian schools had been acquired by non-Indians as part of the land deals.[123] The same was true even of the Indian cemetery, which Agent Lee was finally able to repurchase with a special government appropriation.[124]

More patents were issued by Lee, but despite his persistence, he was only able to slow land and timber fraud. In 1867 Lee also did an assessment of the Saginaw, Black River, and Swan Creek Chippewa settlements, which gives a different impression than might be gained from official correspondence of the previous decade indicating that nearly all of the Chippewa were settled on the Isabella Reservation. Lee estimated that only about half of the total population of about two thousand people lived at Isabella; the rest lived in widely scattered communities throughout the Saginaw Valley. Lee pointed out that many bands pooled their money to buy lands that they shared in common. These holdings ranged from a few acres to as much as five hundred acres. The Saginaw, Black River, and Swan Creek people were organized into fourteen bands under the leadership of traditional chiefs and headmen. Settlements were found at Sagining on Saginaw Bay and near the modern towns of Pinconning, Birch Run, St. Charles, and Saginaw. Small communities were also located on the Au Sable River, on Swan Creek in Saginaw County, and at Elba in Lapeer County. Lee noted that in addition to farming, the Indians depended heavily on hunting, trapping, fishing, and collecting food products, particularly berries and maple sugar, which had both subsistence and commercial value.[125] See map 25.

Agent Lee retired from office in 1882 and was replaced by Edward Allen, who seemed to have involved himself very strictly with the problems and mechanics of land allotment. In December 1885 another highly competent agent, Mark Stevens, took charge of the Michigan Agency. Among his accomplishments was the vigorous pursuit of timber trespassers. By the 1880s such theft had become so common on Indian reservations that the government had even devised an official form to report these activities.[126] Much of the new activity in this regard was related to hardwood cropping, now economically feasible as a result of the construction of the railroads. After investigations by special agents J. D. C. Atkin and, later, F. W. Worden, Agent Stevens and the U.S. attorney for the Eastern District of Michigan brought a large number of suits against timber thieves on the Isabella Reservation.[127] In 1888 they obtained convictions in several cases.[128]

Stevens faced two additional assaults on the land of the Isabella Reservation and the rights guaranteed to the Saginaw Chippewa in the Treaties of 1855 and 1864. The first challenge was the result of the long-standing problem with the levy of tax on Indian land by local units of government and the subsequent sale of such land for back taxes. Since the first Isabella lands were patented in 1871, this practice had resulted in nearly yearly tax sales.[129] Apparently tax sales in 1887 included both lands patented under "not so competent" patents and lands that had yet to be allotted. The tax sales by Isabella County were based on an opinion of the Michigan auditor general issued in December 1873. This opinion, which Agent Stevens described as "extreme," took the position that the interest of the United States in Isabella land was divested when the Treaty of 1864 became operative, because the treaty granted the land to the Indians for their "use, *ownership* and occupancy" (emphasis added).[130]

With a tax sale for 560 acres pending in 1887, Stevens went to Lansing to meet the state attorney general, who, while confirming the opinion of the former auditor general, did make some concessions. He agreed with Stevens that unselected land, which Stevens contended was held "in common," should not be subject to tax sale. He also agreed that the date of the patent, not the date of approved selection lists, ought to be crucial in determining questions of title.[131] Likewise, he admitted that treaties, unlike acts of congress, did not simply make grants of land but should be construed more broadly.

In this latter point, Stevens and the attorney general were no doubt contemplating the impact of the General Allotment Act, which had just been passed by Congress on February 8 of 1887. Among many other provisions, this act made allottees under the act subject to the laws of states and citizens of the United States.[132] In making the argument that the Isabella Indians should be subject to state tax, the attorney general pointed out that they were voters. While acknowledging that this was true, Stevens pointed out that the Indians voted under state, not federal, law and that they also maintained tribal relations. Most important, Stevens argued that by taxing and foreclosing on "not so competent" land for taxes, the state was, in fact, nullifying a treaty agreement between the Saginaw, Black River, and Swan Creek Chippewa that sought to protect their land from alienation and their security in permanent homes.[133] Despite Stevens's objections, the tax sales of "not so competent" allotments proceeded.

Another challenge to Isabella Reservation lands occurred in September 1888, when Stevens found that the Grayling land office was permitting non-Indians to make homestead entries on three thousand acres of "vacant" reservation land.[134] Stevens vigorously protested to the commissioner of Indian affairs and reported that the Indians were "very much excited."[135] Fortunately, the commissioner of the General Land Office, who recognized that reservation lands at Isabella County were not subject to entry by non-Indian homesteaders, ordered the practice to be discontinued.[136]

Late in December 1888, Stevens attempted to deal with the Saginaw Chippewa's request to allot land. A major point of contention with the Indians was that much land was lost to them because of canceled patents. Since the court in a timber trespass case ruled that the secretary of the interior had the power to cancel selections but not patents, the Saginaw Chippewa claimed they should be given fourteen hundred more acres of land, an amount equal to that lost through the return of canceled patents to non-Indians. Stevens pointed out that even this amount of new land, plus the 3,520 acres of land that remained unallotted, would not be enough to provide forty acres for the approximately eleven hundred Indians still eligible for allotments. Apparently the government also suggested that new land allotments should be made under the General Allotment Act. The Indians objected very strongly to this idea and insisted that Isabella lands be allotted under the Treaties of 1855 and 1864.[137] Among the provisions of the General Allotment Act that probably bothered the Saginaw Chippewa were a twenty-five-year trust status for allotments, a provision for the sale of surplus reservation lands, and a citizenship provision that seemed to make unallotted Indians subject to state law without the benefit of protection afforded to U.S. citizens.

Cast Adrift, 1880–1900

During the last two decades of the nineteenth century, a shift in government Indian policy assumed a level of acculturation and sophistication among Indians that did not square with reality.[138] One result was to withdraw local agents in favor of a more central administration of Indian affairs and regional boarding schools. Consequently, in 1889 the Mackinac Agency was closed.[139] In his annual report for 1886, Agent Stevens indicated clearly that the Saginaw, Black River, and Swan Creek Chippewa were far from ready for this new hands-off policy. He told the commissioner of Indian affairs that of the 98,760 acres of allottable land of the reservation provided in 1855, only 6,640 acres remained in Indian hands in the form of restricted patents. Stevens called this a "gross and wanton outrage." He went on to remark that as many as two thousand Indians may have once occupied the Isabella Reservation, but because of "the frauds, the intimidations, and the threats that have been brought to bear upon them by the whites in the vicinity, they have been compelled for their own safety and welfare to seek other places of abode." In 1886 only 540 Indians remained on the reservation.[140]

Some of the business between the Saginaw, Black River, and Swan Creek Chippewa and the federal government during the last decade of the nineteenth century and the first two decades of the twentieth century were conducted through the superintendent of the Bureau of Indian Affairs boarding school that operated at Mt. Pleasant between 1893 and 1933.[141] The scant record of correspondence for this time clearly indicates that Saginaw chiefs and individual Indian people addressed their problems directly to the commissioner of Indian affairs, the secretary of the interior, the U.S. attorney general, and the president, as well as senators and congressmen. Questions pertaining to allotment, title, and taxes, as well as hunting and fishing rights, were frequently raised.

Some modifications of the old system of tribal governance during the last decade of the nineteenth century related to a feeling on the part of the younger Indians that the system of traditional government through band chiefs was not democratic. As a result, the Saginaw, Black River, and Swan Creek people began to legitimize their chiefs by "electing" them to office. In August 1893, for example, they sent the government notice of the election of Elijah Pilcher, Andrew Jackson, and Jacob Machaba as chiefs and asked for a certification of their credentials.[142] These and other chiefs, such as Akin Bell and Joseph Bradley, continued to try to represent their people.

A new political institution, called "business committees," arose on Indian reservations in this period. These committees were developed with the encouragement of the government. Although in part competitive with the traditional political system, the business committees frequently included chiefs and represented the general interest of the bands.[143] Thus the traditional political system changed enough to accommodate new interest but continued to deal with the same problems. This was the case at the Isabella Reservation, where the Saginaw Chippewa formed a tribal business committee that began to represent the broad interests of the tribe and its members.

The federal government continued its formal relationship with the Saginaw Chippewa into the twentieth century, although the advice, services, and protection offered were greatly diminished. For example, the government continued to represent the Saginaw Chippewa in court, particularly related to land problems and timber trespass.[144] Small amounts of land also continued to be allotted on an annual basis well into the twentieth century. The Saginaw, Black River, and Swan Creek Chippewa continued to press their collective rights under the 1819, 1855, and 1864 treaties, including hunting and fishing rights and land claims.[145]

The long record of the Saginaw, Black River, and Swan Creek Chippewa to acquire and maintain a permanent home within their traditional territory was and remains the central theme in their history. Through all of the anguish, poverty, sickness, fraud, and discrimination that they have suffered, the Saginaw, Black River, and Swan Creek Chippewa have struggled to maintain their land, to protect their political and cultural integrity, and to exercise their rights over the lands, which they retained by solemn agreement with the government of the United States.

CHAPTER 21

Allotment and Land Loss on the Keweenaw Bay Reservation

How the Ojibwe Understood the 1854 Treaty

Fifty-one chiefs and headmen signed the 1854 La Pointe Treaty for the Ojibwe of Lake Superior and the Mississippi. Among these were seven chiefs representing the L'Anse and Lac Vieux Desert bands: David King, John Southwind, Peter Marksman, Nawtawmegezhick, Awseneece, Maydwayawshi, and Poshquaygin. Given the fact that the Treaty of 1854 was negotiated between people who did not speak each other's language and who were thus required to use interpreters, and given that their cultures were foreign to each other and that the traditions and practices of each side sometimes held little logic for the other, it could be expected that the treaty was not always understood in the same way by the Ojibwe as it was by its American negotiators. It could be concluded, however, on the basis of petitions and other correspondence that the Ojibwe had written on their behalf by missionaries and other literate supporters, that the Ojibwe had a good understanding of the major guarantees contained in the treaty. These documents also indicate that the Ojibwe had only a vague idea of the details and practicalities of how the treaty might be given effect. In fairness, it could also be said that the same was true of Commissioner George Manypenny and Agent Henry Gilbert, who left many of the details of the treaty to future administrative decisions. Unlike these men, however, the Ojibwe chiefs had a limited understanding of the concepts that were behind some of the treaty's provisions.

The Ojibwe did not fully appreciate such basic Western concepts as private property ownership, or the exclusive control of property by an individual. Since they conceptualized land not as an inanimate thing but, rather, as a living, organic being who they personified as Grandmother Earth, it was difficult for the Ojibwe to understand how a piece of land could be owned, let alone exclusively controlled by an individual. Even today, though modern traditional Ojibwe understand the concept of private property, they find the idea to be antithetical to their traditional belief that Grandmother Earth provides for all humans and that her resources should be used respectfully. Beyond the basic concept of private property lay a set of even more complex Western ideas, such as the subdivision of the land; allotment; individual, rather than group, initiative; and all of the administrative details embodied in deeds, registration, sale, and inheritance of land. The Ojibwe signatories had little, if any, familiarity with these ideas. Many of these same legal aspects of land and its transactions were also obscure to the average American citizen in the nineteenth century, as they are to those in modern times.

What might the Lake Superior Ojibwe of the treaty times have understood about the concepts and details of the treaty? First, a few of the Lake Superior Ojibwe may have had some comprehension of American principles of land tenure. It is known that two among the approximately five hundred Ojibwe associated with the bands that lived at or frequented Keweenaw Bay were educated and competent in the English language. These were John Street, the son-in-law of Chief David King, and Rev. Peter Marksman, an interpreter and speaker for the Methodist band. The Ojibwe also had access to several English-speaking traders who could write English and likely had some fluency in Ojibwe. Peter Crebassa, Peter Barbeau, John Holliday, and perhaps some of the other métis could be included in this category. These people were related by blood or marriage to the Ojibwe, but it should be remembered that most métis were illiterate, and those who were not probably spoke French and Ojibwe rather than English and Ojibwe. Father Baraga was an Ojibwe linguist and was certainly fluent in the language, as were most of the Catholic priests who succeeded him at the Catholic mission. In addition to the Ojibwe preachers, various Protestant missionaries and the government employees at L'Anse probably also had working familiarity with the Ojibwe language. Furthermore, the interpreters employed as translators during the treaty negotiation all seemed to be competent. Nonetheless, there is good evidence that the details of the 1854 treaty, based as they were on Western concepts, were lost on the vast majority of the L'Anse Ojibwe.

German travelogue writer Johann Kohl attended the 1855 treaty payment and later recounted Manypenny's less-than-satisfactory cultural interaction with the Ojibwe chiefs. Apparently at one of their first meetings, the Ojibwe, as the occasion demanded, were dressed in their finest regalia and face paint, which Manypenny regarded as barbaric. When he was asked to smoke a peace pipe, Manypenny not only refused to smoke but left the meeting abruptly. The chiefs were stunned and offended by this rude behavior, since smoking of the peace pipe was a necessary prelude to an important meeting. For the Ojibwe, smoking evoked a blessing, since the smoke was believed to carry their prayers for success to the Great Spirit. One of the chiefs said, "My friends: Our Father from Washington has refused to smoke the pipe of peace with us. He has rejected and despised it. My Friends! It is of no consequence to us! Let him go his road and we will go ours!"[1] On the next day, Manypenny told the chief, "See! I wish you to become like the white men, and quite give up your old pagan and bloody ceremonies. I will refuse every pipe of peace you offer me in connexion with such ceremonies, and have always done so among the other tribes of your red brethren. I wish to civilise you, and give you a lesson and an example."[2] He then invited them to smoke and to talk about cultivation of their land, the affairs of their villages, and the improvement of their households.[3] This incident alone says a great deal about the clash of cultures that characterized the nineteenth-century Lake Superior frontier.

By Articles 2, 3, and 11 of the treaty as it was explained to them by Henry Gilbert at the treaty negotiation, the Lake Superior Ojibwe believed that they had obtained their reservation lands permanently and that these homelands would be secured for them so that no whites, except for those authorized by the government or mixed bloods, could live within the reservation boundaries. They understood that their reservation would never be taken from them and that they would not be forced to leave it.[4] Their tenure on the reservation did not depend on the technical aspects of legal title to land. As Gilbert reported to Manypenny after the treaty,

> We found that the points most strenuously insisted upon by them were first the privilege of remaining in the country where they reside and next the appropriation of land for their future homes. Without yielding these points, it was idle for us to talk about a treaty. We therefore agreed to the selection of lands for them in the territory heretofore ceded.
>
> The tract for the Ance and Vieux Desert bands is at the head of Ke,wa,we,naw [*sic*] Bay in Michigan and is at present occupied by them. I estimate the quantity at about 60,000 acres.[5]

By the terms of Article 3, the United States promised to have the reservation lands surveyed and, over the course of time, to assign each head of family or single person over twenty-one years of age an eighty-acre allotment. Eventually, Indian allotments would take up all of the land within the exterior boundaries of the reservation, so that tribal members would own all of the land set apart. This is, in fact, exactly what transpired and exactly how the Indians understood the treaty. In September 1858 L'Anse chiefs David King and Awseneece, as well as Peter Marksman, all signers of the 1854 treaty, wrote to their agent Andrew Fitch explaining how they understood this aspect of the treaty: "When we made the Treaty with the agents of the Government at La Pointe in 1854, it was fully and distinctly explained to us, that the Reservations, as stated in the Treaty, was to be ours forever we were individually as stated to have our 80 acres in it, and the balance was to be ours in common."[6] This position was supported by Agent Leach in 1863 in a letter to the commissioner of Indian affairs, William Dole:

> These Indians contend that all their young men, as they come of age, are thus entitled to select land for themselves until the whole reservation is occupied.

> I have myself carefully examined the Treaty, and have no doubt the Indian construction of it is correct. Articles 2d and 3d seem to be very clear and explicit, that the *whole* reservation was to be "set apart" *for their "use"* and that "from time to time" in the discretion of the President, portions of it were to be surveyed and "assigned to each head of a family or single person over twenty-one years of age." This "*from time to time*" must refer, it seems to me, to the periods at which young people may become entitled to land.
>
> Richard M. Smith who acted as Secretary at the time of the Treaty was made, and signed the instrument in that capacity, and Rev. H. Wheeler, Missionary, who was present and signed as a witness, distinctly recollect that the Indians were told that the *whole* reservation was theirs.[7]

It should be noted here that this allotment process resulted in an entirely different kind of reservation than the one that would have resulted from the process found in the Otto-Missouri Treaty, which Manypenny sent to Gilbert as an example of an allotment process. In that case, the Otto and Missouri were to all receive an immediate allotment of their choosing, then the leftover or unallotted portion of the reservation would be sold for the benefit of the tribe. As a result, the Indian allotments would be scattered among the fee holdings of non-Indian purchasers. In other words, a reservation with a well-defined exterior boundary owned by Indians would not be created. Instead, there would be a concentration of Indian landholdings scattered among their non-Indian neighbors.

In 1864, ten years after the treaty, a group of Ojibwe leaders, frustrated by the fact that the United States had not fulfilled all of its treaty obligations, prepared a petition that set forth their understanding of their treaties. Included in this group was Chief Nawgawnegawbo, who had signed the 1854 treaty. Since their treaty history was oral rather than written, it contained not only their recollection of the formal written provisions of the treaties but also things that had been promised to them verbally by the U.S. treaty negotiators. As Agent Henry Gilbert put it, "The memory of an Indian is very tenacious. He treasures up everything that is said by a Government officer and regards his statements and verbal assurances as equally binding upon the Government as the formal stipulations of a treaty."[8] Meeting at Bad River, the Ojibwe leaders told their understanding of their various treaties to George Warren, who rendered it into phonemic Ojibwe, which was translated by Joseph Gurnoe, the agency interpreter at Bayfield, Wisconsin.[9] The resulting bilingual petition has this to say regarding the 1854 treaty:

> Then again came word of our Great Father calling his children together through Gilbert asking us for the North Shore Country. Your Great Father promises to give you Ninety Thousand Dollars to be disposed of as you may see fit, and you may distribute them same among your young men, Provided you consent to comply with his wishes, and sell him the North Shore Country. *You shall reserve the land you are inhabiting, there you shall live as long as there is one Indian left. Then you will never be removed from your reservation, nor never be ordered to leave it.* For the sake of your Graves [not being willing to abandon the burial places of their ancestors] you was [*sic*] not willing to remove when your Great Father ordered you through Watrous, which was for all the Indians. Your Mixed Bloods are expelled from your Villages, and Reservations. You will give them Six Thousand Dollars in Coin. He [a mixed blood] will then have Eighty Acres of land outside of your Reservations. Your Great Father also gives you School Teachers, the same who will teach your Children to read. You will give or mark out your School Teachers fence which he will cultivate as a Garden to live on. You shall do the same with your Black Smith who will furnish you with iron. This is what Gilbert told us.[10] (emphasis added)

This statement focuses on the content of the treaty that was immediately important to the Ojibwe. Explicitly it stated that the treaty ceded their remaining land, for which they would receive annuity benefits; that they would receive reservation lands; that these lands would be in their traditional territories and be permanent homes; and that they would not have to share the reservation lands with non-Indians.

Some reasonable inferences can also be made from what the chiefs did not say about the treaty. For example, there is no indication that the chiefs understood that the status of the reservation somehow turned on technicalities of title to the land within the boundaries, nor does it indicate that allotment in severalty was something they valued or even understood to be an important part of the treaty. To the extent that they did understand allotment, they would likely have understood it as a means to acquire security on the reservation. Certainly, they did not understand the idea of taxation as a condition of holding their permanent reservation. If Gilbert had told the Ojibwe in 1854 that they had to pay money each year to hold their land, the Ojibwe, who had very limited access to hard currency, would have most certainly objected. In fact, they would not have even signed the treaty. Gilbert made this point with Commissioner Manypenny when he reported on the draft treaty: "We found that the points most strenuously insisted upon by them were first *the privilege of remaining* in the country where they reside and next the appropriation of land for their future homes. Without yielding these points, it was idle for us to talk about a treaty. We therefore agreed to the selection of lands for them in the territory heretofore ceded."[11]

By and large, the 1854 treaty was a good agreement from the perspective of both the government and the Ojibwe. For its part, the United States acquired badly wanted mineral deposits and managed to settle the difficult dispute that had arisen between the Lake Superior and Mississippi Ojibwe. Also, by clarifying the status and territorial claims of various bands, the course of future relations with the Ojibwe was vastly improved. Last, but not least, the reservation and allotment provisions, along with the support offered for education and agriculture, advanced the new policies of the Indian Office and Congress. The Ojibwe, for their part, got the permanent homes and security they so fervently desired, by acquiring the reservation lands. Annuity payments would help them support themselves, and the trader debt provision would relieve the enormous pressure brought on them by the traders. Likewise, they were able to provide land and other benefits for the mixed bloods, who, after all, were also their sons and daughters, wives, and grandchildren.

The Broken Covenant

The major purpose of the 1854 treaty as far as the Ojibwe were concerned was to provide them with the security of permanent homes for all time by creation of the reservation lands described in Article 2. The chiefs who negotiated for the various bands at La Pointe understood that these reservation lands would include all of the land within the described boundaries and would remain so forever. Yet, by the early decades of the twentieth century, most of the children and grandchildren of these chiefs found their reservation lands largely gone, their families landless, destitute, and with few prospects for a prosperous future in American society. To a great extent, this situation was due to the fact that the United States did not fulfill all of its commitments under the 1854 treaty. Most important, it did not protect the reservation land base, thus undermining the economic, social, and political viability of the community.

There were three main avenues of involuntary alienation of the land withdrawn from sale by President Pierce in order to create the L'Anse and Lac Vieux Desert Indian Reservation in 1855. These include patenting of 2,720 acres of reservation land to the Sault Ste. Marie Canal Company; the improper restoration to market and sale of 18,427 acres of reservation land in 1871; and the improper taxation of Indian fee lands by the state of Michigan, resulting in the loss of at least fifteen hundred acres of reservation land due to its sale for unpaid taxes.

Loss of Canal Lands

At the midpoint of the nineteenth century, the great impediment to the American development of the Lake Superior country was a twenty-one-foot falls on the St. Marys River at Sault Ste. Marie that blocked effective navigation into and out of Lake Superior.[12] A canal connecting Lake Superior with the other Great Lakes was deemed to be in the national interest, and Congress passed a bill that would provide 750,000 acres of federal land in Michigan that the state could use to finance a canal around the St. Marys falls. The canal company immediately sent out teams of "land lookers" to identify the 750,000 acres that it hoped to acquire and ultimately to sell in order to reimburse construction costs. Of the 750,000 acres available to the canal company, 253,000 acres were ultimately selected in the Upper Peninsula, while the rest was selected south of the Straits of Mackinac. The Upper Peninsula land was mostly chosen to speculate on copper and iron deposits as well as timberland. Predicting that the land at the head of Keweenaw Bay would one day become an important port city, the company also selected land in a semicircle around the village of Baraga on the west side of the bay (see map 19 in chapter 14).[13]

The secretary of the interior, former Michigan governor Robert McClelland, approved the selected lands in 1855, and they were then transferred from the federal government to Michigan to await completion of the canal. The state finally accepted the completed canal on May 21, 1855, and it patented the selected canal lands to the canal company a few days later.[14] Among the lands selected by the canal company were 2,720 acres of land located within the boundaries of the L'Anse and Lac Vieux Desert Indian Reservation, which had previously been set apart when the 1854 treaty was signed on September 30, 1854. Even though the land had already been withdrawn for Indian purposes, it was deeded to the canal company in the spring of 1855 and was never to become available for Indian purposes.

Loss of Huron Bay Lands

When mineral deposits were discovered on a portion of the reservation lying west of Huron Bay in township 51 north of range 31 west, an interested citizen called the government's attention to the description of the L'Anse and Lac Vieux Desert land reserve found in the treaty. Specifically in Article 2, the reservation is described by township and range, with the proviso that in the case of township 51 north of range 31 west, it would include all the land of that township "lying west of Huron Bay."[15] The government was also reminded that President Pierce had, however, withdrawn the whole of township 51 north of range 31 west.[16] As a result, the government was asked to restore the reservation land east of Huron Bay to the market, since it was argued that this land was improperly withdrawn. The government, initially convinced of this argument, did restore this land to market, and it was quickly purchased by mineral speculators.[17]

Subsequently, an investigation by the U.S. House Committee on Indian Affairs and by Agent Betts concluded that at the time of the 1854 treaty, the L'Anse chiefs had, in fact, understood that the land west of Huron Bay was to be part of the reservation. It was the proviso in the treaty that was in error. At the time of the treaty in 1854, Peter Marksman drew a map of the proposed reservation, which was agreed to during the treaty negotiations. Early the next year, this very map, which showed the land lying west of Huron Bay to be part of the reservation, was included as part of President Pierce's order to withdraw the reservation land for Indian use. In fact, in 1855 Marksman said that he had noticed the error in the printed treaty and brought it to the attention of Agent Gilbert, who, in turn, promised to have it corrected.

With this new information, Congress decided that 18,427 acres of reservation land had been improperly restored to market, and it appropriated twenty thousand dollars in compensation. This money was placed in a trust fund to benefit the tribe.[18] In concluding its investigation of the Huron Bay affair, the House Committee on Indian Affairs concluded that "these two bands of Indians [the L'Anse and Lac Vieux Desert bands] have been unjustly dealt by and wronged, by an appropriation of valuable lands intended and supposed to have been secured to them by the terms of a formal treaty; and that they are clearly entitled to the indemnity they seek."[19]

Loss of Lands by Taxation

It should be recalled here that the 1854 treaty does not include any provision that reservation land would be subject to taxation. This is proper since the enabling legislation for the treaty expressly prohibits "taxation and execution." It should also be remembered that the written record of the negotiation of the treaty by Henry Gilbert, the treaty commissioner, and others does not mention that Gilbert ever explained taxation to the Indians or informed them that they would be required to pay taxes on reservation land. In the few instances where Indians have left records of their understanding of the treaty, they do not indicate in any way that they expected to pay taxes on reservation land. Indeed, however, all the parties indicate that security in holding reservation lands as a permanent home was the central goal of both the Indians and the United States in concluding the 1854 treaty. Article 11 of the treaty, included at the behest of the chiefs, states that "the Indians shall not be required to remove from the homes hereby set apart for them."[20] Nevertheless, the state imposed taxes on an increasing amount of reservation land as time went on.

Allotments

The Treaty of La Pointe was ratified on January 10, 1855, and proclaimed on January 29, 1855. On March 7, President Franklin Pierce issued an executive order withdrawing the townships of land mentioned in Article 2 of the treaty to "be reserved from sale or entry for any purpose not consistent with the stipulations of the 1st Clause and the 2nd Article [which describes the reservation for the L'Anse and Lac Vieux Desert bands] of the treaty with the Chippewa Indians ratified on the 10th day of January 1855."[21] On March 30, 1855, the commissioner of the General Land Office, John Wilson, notified the register and receiver of the Government Land Office in Sault Ste. Marie that township 51 north of ranges 31, 32, and 33 west and the western and eastern halves of township 50 north of range 32 west were "withheld from sale or deed for any purposes whatever, until further orders."[22]

In his annual report of 1855, Agent Gilbert wrote,

> No time should be lost. The Lake Indians [Lake Superior Ojibwe] are exceedingly anxious to select their homes, and very many will occupy them without delay. All the necessary details for carrying out this provision of the treaty [the allotment provision of the 1854 treaty] should be attended to. The form of a certificate should be determined upon, and every Indian who selects land should receive his evidence of title. They attach great importance to this, and I hope before visiting them again, that such measures will be taken as will enable me to close up this branch of the treaty with all who are ready to avail themselves of its benefits.[23]

Henry Gilbert reported to Manypenny on April 10, 1855, that since the L'Anse Reservation was already divided and subdivided, no further action was required except to see that the land was withdrawn and that allotments were made as described in the treaty. Gilbert also noted that the L'Anse community now included the Lac Vieux Desert bands.

Despite Agent Gilbert's enthusiastic pronouncement about how highly the Indians valued the prospect of owning land allotments, there appears to have been no pressure from the L'Anse chiefs for the allotment of their reservation during the years following the 1854 treaty.[24] None of their many petitions to Washington or their complaints to their agents ever mentions the failure of the government to attend to the assignment of eighty acres of land to each household head. Indeed, it would have been surprising if they had done so, since as far as the Ojibwe were concerned, the reservation was secure, and their traditions did not conceptualize land in terms of individual ownership. In fact, in the regulations for making allotments at L'Anse that were received from Washington, the agents were instructed to explain to the Indians that they were not to trespass on each other's land.[25] Presumably, this is because it was known that the idea of exclusive private use was foreign to Indian tradition and that, if not altered, Indian behavior would continue to orient to the common use of reservation land. The unallotted lands on the reservation were, in fact, open for common use.

The first real move to allot the L'Anse Reservation seems to have originated with Agent George Betts. In early 1874 Betts wrote to the commissioner of Indian affairs, Edward Smith, asking for permission to make allotments for the L'Anse, Lac Vieux Desert, and Ontonagon bands under the authority granted the president by the 1854 treaty. He reported that these Indians had already made eighty-acre land selections on an "informal basis."[26] Commissioner Smith forwarded to Betts a letter of instruction issued by the secretary of the interior describing the process by which allotments would be made on the L'Anse Reservation.[27] Permission was forthcoming, and Betts reported in December on some of the details of organizing allotment selections as well as the meeting he held with the L'Anse Ojibwe to explain the allotment process to them.

> From Marquette I proceeded to L'Anse and called a general council of the Chiefs and members of the bands referred to, and through special interpreter Kahgudaahqua read your letter of instructions and explained the treaty and the nature of the business so that they fully understood the matter, spread before them the official plats of the Reservation, and proceeded to make the allotments according to their expressed wishes, after they in each case proved their identity and age, according to the terms of the treaty and your letter of instructions herein referred to.[28]

Presumably, Betts had arranged for each eligible individual to locate a selection on a map. The description of the selections were then sent to the General Land Office to be checked for possible conflicts and to assure that the information necessary to issue a patent was supplied. Once the selection was approved by the Department of the Interior, a patent was issued, and the nearest government land office was notified to record the allotment. This process created at least four record sets: a federal tract book kept by the General Land Office, a federal tract book kept by the nearest federal land office, a local tract book kept by the state auditor general, and a tract book kept by the local Indian agency. In some cases, these various land records conflicted.

Agent Betts reported that he had found 319 L'Anse Indians qualified for allotments. Since he had been directed to "classify the Indians" as he deeded the property, so that their "material interest" could be protected, Betts examined the competency of each potential allottee to safeguard their interest in the land.[29]

> In regard to this matter, I beg to state that after carefully considering this part of my duty in light of my experience and observation with other tribes, under my care, to whom patents in fee simple had been given for their lands, and after a full discussion of the subject with the chiefs and Indians in council assembled, we came to the conclusion that except in a very few cases it would be the wisest and most desirable course to recommend the Department to place such restrictions on the power of alienation, in their patents for the lands allotted to them as would effectively prevent their disposing of them without the recommendation of the Indian Agent, Commissioner of Indian Affairs, and consent in writing or by a change of the character of the patent, by the Secretary of the Interior for the time being, when such a privilege might be desirable.
>
> I would therefore suggest that the following or some equivalent clause be inserted in the patents, viz
>
> The said (here the name of the person) is expressly prohibited from assigning, selling, transferring or attempting to convey the land herein described or any interest therein, to any person whomsoever, without the written consent of the Secretary of the Interior, for the time being, after the recommendation of the Commissioner of Indian Affairs, for the time being, under penalty of entire forfeiture thereof. The number of patents containing such a clause, in my present report to be three hundred and seven.
>
> The number of persons to whom I would recommend that patents in fee simple be issued is but twelve.[30]

Thus, Agent Betts decided that only 12 of the 319 allottees, or 3.6 percent, would be issued fee patents without restrictions against alienation.[31]

It is important to note that Betts does not say that he explained to the Indians that their unrestricted allotments were made with the condition that this land would be subject to taxation or that reservation land could be seized and sold if taxes were not paid. By issuing deeds without restrictions, the government clearly anticipated that land allotments so deeded could be sold. It is a fair assumption that the government at the time of the 1854 treaty assumed that land sales would be made between Indians, since it was probably supposed that non-Indians would not want to buy land in the midst of an Indian community. In 1857 the commissioner of Indian affairs, James Denver, speaking of allotments and how they should be restricted, said, "The title should remain in the tribe, with the power reserved to the government, when any of them become sufficiently intelligent, sober and industrious, to grant them patents for the lands so assigned to them, but leaseable or alienable only to members of the tribe, until they become so far advanced as to be fitted for enjoyment of all the rights and privileges of citizens of the United States."[32] It was also anticipated that the land within the exterior boundaries of the reservation created by the 1854 treaty would be fully allotted and would remain in Indian hands as their permanent homeland. This is how the treaty was explained to the Lake Superior Ojibwe, and this was how they understood their future. It was also the way the Department of the Interior believed the treaty would actually work.

In June 1875, twenty-one years after the negotiation of the 1854 treaty, the first 313 patents were issued to the L'Anse, Lac Vieux Desert and Ontonagon bands at L'Anse.[33] Beginning in 1858 and continuing for the next twenty-five years, the L'Anse Ojibwe sent at least one and sometimes several petitions to Washington each year complaining about their circumstances. The majority of these petitions asked that a delegation of chiefs be permitted to visit Washington to discuss their problems directly with the president or the commissioner of Indian affairs.[34] A variety of problems were cited as subjects for discussion, and most were related to issues that were supposedly solved by the 1854 treaty. Among the major complaints of the L'Anse chiefs were that whites and mixed bloods were encroaching on their reservation and that reservation land was not being protected.[35]

The Taxation of Reservation Land

There are several reasons why taxes, which were not intended to be part of post-treaty life on the L'Anse Reservation, were levied and became an important factor in the alienation of reservation land. In fact, involuntary land loss was particularly difficult for the Ojibwe community because the land most vulnerable to tax liens was the land where the majority of the Indian population actually lived, that is, fee land adjacent to the missionary and agency establishments. Most of this land was ultimately lost to the community through its sale to recover unpaid taxes.

While allotments were not taxed during the early years of the reservation, fee lands were. Most of the fee land on which Indians lived, which constituted perhaps 70 percent of the fee land within the reservation (see table 2 in chapter 14), was purchased as a hedge against removal. In a sense, this was land that was privately allotted by missionaries and government agents. As far as the Indians probably knew, except in size, these plots were not different in any way from the eighty-acre allotments made under the treaty. As far as the Indians, the agent, and missionaries who made these fee allotments were concerned, their purpose was exactly the same as the treaty allotments, that is, to provide stability and security to the L'Anse Ojibwe community. The reason that most of this fee land continued to be held by the Ojibwe during the early reservation years was because taxes on their holdings were paid by non-Indians. This fact did not affect their understanding of the 1854 treaty or their expectations of the United States in protecting their interests in the reservation.

Much of the land loss was due to a lack of vigilance on the part of the United States, which permitted the encroachment of private interests and also allowed the state of Michigan to become involved in the affairs of the Indian community. What partly permitted these encroachments was the mistaken theory that the reservation only consisted of federal trust land—in other words, land not yet allotted or land held by Indians under restricted patents. As federal officials saw it, these were the only lands for which the federal government had trust responsibilities, so they thereby constituted the reservation. Thus, rather than the L'Anse Reservation consisting of a tribal reservation with a well-defined exterior boundary as it was intended by the negotiators of the 1854 treaty, the reservation gradually became in practice a checkerboard of individual Indian landholdings. The Indian people of the L'Anse Reservation never accepted this definition and always believed that the exterior boundary as described by the townships and ranges set out in Article 2 of the 1854 treaty constituted the reservation. In 1989 the tribe's position was affirmed by the U.S. District Court for the Western District of Michigan.[36]

The taxation of land within the exterior boundaries of the L'Anse Reservation after the allotment of land in severalty was the result of a gradual transformation. Immediately after allotments were made and for some decades thereafter, allotments of either restricted or unrestricted nature were not taxed. Gradually, during the last decades of the nineteenth century, the state and federal governments began to believe that unrestricted fee lands within the reservation were subject to tax. This was likely because non-Indian fee holders, especially lumber interests, now held considerable amounts of reservation land.

After the first allotments were made in 1875, the allotment of reservation land proceeded slowly at L'Anse, with small numbers of patents being issued from time to time. By 1909, however, all the land available for allotment had been assigned.[37] With less than a dozen exceptions, these were restricted deeds, meaning that the patent to the allotment contained the following language: "That said allottee and his heirs, shall not sell, lease, or in any manner alienate said tract, without the consent of the President of the United States."[38] During the late nineteenth century, land within the boundary of the L'Anse Reservation thus consisted of several classes: federal land waiting to be allotted to individuals, allotted land, lands designated as state swamplands or school sections under federal legislation, state-held delinquent tax lands, and various categories of land held privately by fee patent (see map 29). Among the latter, there was also land that had been improperly transferred to the St. Marys Canal Shipping Company after the date of the treaty. Reservation land was, thus, held either through a patent in fee simple, which was freely negotiable, by patent with a clause restricting alienation, by the federal government in trust for the tribe, or by the state of Michigan.

From the earliest surviving tax rolls, which date to the year 1858, onward, private land or land held by fee patent on the reservation was taxed by the state of Michigan through the two townships and the county where the reservation was located.[39] There were no apparent exceptions. Indians, non-Indians, and corporate entities alike that held land in fee, including missionaries and government agents, were all taxed. The rule of taxing authorities was a simple one: if the land could be sold it was taxable. Land assigned to Indian allottees under restricted patents and unallotted land was not taxed, and neither was land held by the legal heirs or assigns of allottees. Indian allotments held in unrestricted status were taxed only if alienated by the original allottee. Further, there is no evidence that the eleven parcels of land patented in fee in 1875 to competent Indians were ever taxed during the two years they remained in Indian ownership.[40] Most of these allotments were purchased by the Silver River Company (a mining company) in 1877 and first appeared on the 1878 tax rolls under that name.[41]

Although the foregoing was the general policy from 1858 onward, things did not work so simply in practice. During the allotment era (1875–1909), land records were sometimes conflicting and always confusing. Local offices of Indian agencies did not have complete or accurate land records. After the 1890s and during the next three decades, local tax officials seem to have had little idea about who owned what land on the reservation or the status of these lands under federal law.[42]

The status of private fee land held by Indians or by non-Indians for Indian benefit was problematic in the sense that such land was, in effect, the functional equivalent of allotment. In fact, most of this land was informally allotted in small parcels or lots by the Catholic and Methodist missionaries and by Agent Fitch. The deeds for some of this class of private property clearly reflected the fact that this land was meant to be held in collective ownership. The United States even issued a rare joint patent to Chiefs Poshquaygin and Adam Nungo.[43] Reverend Baraga deeded all the Catholic land, less fourteen acres surrounding the church, to "Edward Assinines and his band." The deed named all forty-seven members of that band and gave them each an interest.[44]

Much of the Methodist land was subdivided by Agent Fitch as informal allotments with patents in fee. For example, the Rathbun lands were eventually deeded to Agent Fitch by Benjamin Rathbun's widow and daughter in September 1859.[45] Fitch then hired a surveyor to subdi-

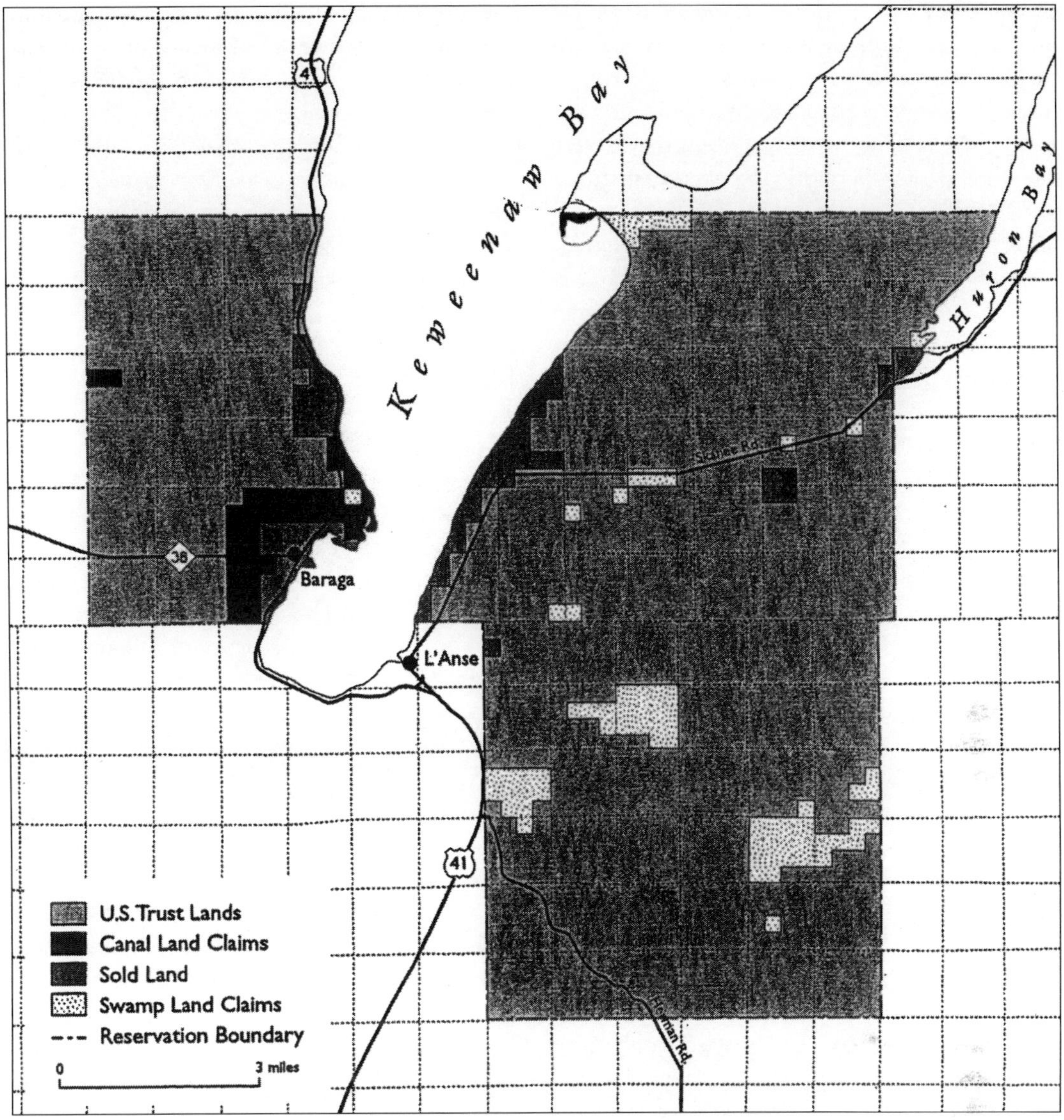

Map 29. Categories of land on the Keweenaw Bay Indian reservation, 1854

vide and plot this land into five- and ten-acre plots. Some of the Methodist Indians who received deeds to these plots were Nelson Valentine, James Holliday, Nawwandagoquay, Benjamin George, and William Bass.[46] Fitch continued to oversee the Rathbun property long after he retired from the Indian service and moved to southern Michigan. All of these private lands were taxed from 1858 onward, but not always consistently. For example, from 1877 to at least 1879, some of the land owned by Edward Assinines and his band was not taxed because the land value was classed as "poor,"[47] yet the same land owned by this band was taxed again in 1888 and 1897.[48]

A question that might be asked is, if Indians in the early days were not literate and not conversant with taxation and its procedures, how did taxes get paid on their properties? We will never be able to completely answer this question, because the early tax rolls seldom indicate who actually paid the taxes. It is likely that at least during the 1860s (if not before) and through the 1880s, taxes on Indian fee land and on the fee land held for Indian benefit were paid by non-Indians who understood both the concepts of land taxation and the consequence for not paying taxes that had been assessed. Indian "landowners" or "freeholders" such as Poshquaygin, Adam Nungo, David King, and Edward Assinines could not read tax notices, had very limited and only periodic access to cash funds (treaty annuity payments provided each Indian $2.25 per year), and would have been unfamiliar with the procedures for paying taxes.[49] Certainly, one could speculate that these men and their descendants must have gradually come to understand the concept of land taxation as time passed, but it is unlikely they had the means to pay taxes even if they understood the concept.

While this process was taking place, the Ojibwe of the L'Anse community had many sympathetic allies who were literate and did understand taxation. These included Father Baraga, Peter Barbeau, Peter Crebessa, Rev. William Brockway, Abel Hall, and Andrew Fitch, among others. Some, like Barbeau, Brockway, and Fitch eventually moved away from the reservation, so they did not actually live in the Keweenaw Bay area, but nonetheless they continued to work on the Indians' behalf in land and tax matters. From 1858 until the beginning of the twentieth century, there is documentary evidence that at least William Owen, E. A. Critchfield, and Abel Hall actually paid taxes on land owned or occupied by Indians.[50] In the case of the lands owned by Chief Poshquaygin and Adam Nungo, taxes seem to have been paid, at least sometimes, by the lawyer John Hulbert.[51] Still, there is no known case where Indians can be shown to have actually paid their own property taxes until the last decades of the nineteenth century.[52] In 1882, for instance, it was Abel Hall who actually paid delinquent taxes to redeem property owned by David King and also by Peter Marksman, yet these properties continued to be in the ownership of these individuals thereafter.[53] As such actions clearly demonstrated, Abel Hall might be described as the unofficial caretaker of the Methodist Indian land until the early twentieth century.

The major problem with the taxation of fee land within the external boundaries of the L'Anse Reservation, which was owned by or for the benefit of Indians, was that it could potentially defeat the entire purpose of the 1854 treaty and violate the Indians' understanding of what they had secured under it. The main goal of the treaty as far as the Ojibwe were concerned was to establish a secure and permanent homeland for their people. Allotment in severalty was a device designed to promote that goal. The authority of the state of Michigan to execute tax liens and to sell reservation land for unpaid taxes, if permitted to operate, had the effect of involuntarily alienating Indian land within the reservation.

The Involuntary Loss of Reservation Land through Tax Sales

One example of how land slipped from Indian ownership as a result of taxation can be drawn from the land around the Methodist mission. In 1853, prior to the 1854 treaty, Rev. Robert Dubois, a Methodist missionary, bought 71.6 acres of land for the residence of Indian parishioners. Much of this land was occupied by the followers of Chief Poshquaygin and headman Adam Nungo. In 1859 Reverend Dubois deeded this land to Indian agent Andrew Fitch. In early 1857 Fitch was engaged in securing and consolidating the "Methodist" lands by acquiring both the Dubois and the Rathbun parcels.[54] In 1859 Agent Fitch deeded the title to the Dubois land over to Chief Poshquaygin. Tax rolls show that the chief owned the 71.6 acres through the 1860s and 1870s. Taxes were paid during this time, but it is not known who paid them. In 1893 twenty acres of this property were lost to delinquent taxes, and by 1900 the entire parcel, except for eleven acres, was in non-Indian ownership, probably as a result of sale for delinquent taxes.[55] This eleven-acre parcel was then held by John and Mary Asher, who were members of the Indian community and who paid taxes on their land until the 1930s. In the fall of 1939, the auditor general erroneously bid off the Ashers' land for taxes due between 1925 and 1935.[56] A follow-up check of the tax rolls showed, however, that the Ashers had, in fact, paid their taxes during the years in question, and the auditor general consequently ordered the Michigan Department of Conservation to deed the parcel back to them.[57] Undoubtedly shaken by this incident, the Ashers promptly thereafter deeded their property to the United States to hold in trust for the Keweenaw Bay Indian Community.[58]

Another large parcel of the Methodist mission's land was purchased in March 1854 by Abel Hall, who was brought to L'Anse by the Methodist mission to teach the Indians to farm. This land was in part occupied by Indians of the mission and remained in Hall's name until his death in 1894. The property was inherited by Hall's son and daughter, who did not pay taxes on the property in 1895. Taxes were sporadically paid, but the property was sold for delinquent taxes in 1910. It was purchased by a non-Indian.

The history of the lands patented to Reverend Baraga is equally informative about the way taxation operated to involuntarily alienate Indian land during the nineteenth and early twentieth centuries on the L'Anse Reservation. Beginning in 1849 and continuing until 1852, Reverend Baraga, who was independently wealthy, began to purchase large parcels of land for the benefit of his Indian congregation. In all, he purchased seven parcels, which together constituted nearly five hundred acres of land, all within township 51 north of range 33 west, land that was later selected as part of the L'Anse Reservation. Reverend Baraga was by far the largest owner of "sold land" on the reservation, as he had patents on nearly a square mile of property.

In 1863, however, Baraga deeded all but fourteen acres of his property to Edward Assinines and named members of his band. The fourteen acres he retained were the portion of the property that surrounded the Catholic church and cemetery. Taxes were paid on the Assinines property throughout the nineteenth century, presumably by the church or by Father Baraga. In 1883, when a railroad purchased a right-of-way through both the Assinines and church property, the railroad insisted on deeds from both the band and the church for the Assinines property.[59] This seems to be the result of the fact that by paying taxes on the Assinines property for forty years, the church had acquired an equitable, if not a legal, claim to the land required by the railroad, even though it was deeded to Assinines and his band. The large property holdings deeded to the Assinines band by Baraga remained intact until the early 1900s.

Sometime between 1897 and 1902, part of the land owned by the band became exempt as church property, even though it remained deeded to Assinines. The remaining land was taxed in 1903, but the taxes were then not paid for the first time since they were patented to Baraga and deeded to the Assinines band. In 1908, 1909, and 1910, delinquent tax sales were held, and the Assinines band's land was bought by the Catholic Church. State land tax deeds from the auditor general were issued at that time to Bishop Frederick Eis of the diocese of Marquette.[60] The tax rolls, however, continued to show the lands owned by Assinines for the next twenty years. It may be inferred that in the period 1903–10, the church simply stopped paying taxes on the Assinines properties and then purchased them on tax liens. By 1945 the tax rolls showed the owner of some of this property to be the St. Joseph Orphanage.[61] In 1949 the church sold 173 acres of the Assinines land, and no corresponding deeds from the Assinines band were made. Indians continued to live on the lands, now exempt from taxes as orphanage property, and even issued deeds to each other for small plots of land. Thereafter, all land deeded to Indians either by the church or from other Indians reverted to being taxed. It can thus be seen that the landownership, land use, and tax issues related to the Baraga-Assinines land have been entangled throughout their history. It is clear that a considerable portion of these lands were alienated from Indian ownership by the Catholic Church after the church acquired title through tax deeds.

Two additional cases of the loss of Indian-owned fee land in the L'Anse Reservation illustrate the predicaments of other members of the community when faced with the improper assessment of property tax. These examples are the cases of Henry Barbano and Sam Spruce, both enrolled members of the Keweenaw Bay Indian Community. In the early 1930s, Henry Barbano purchased a 2.25-acre parcel that had earlier been part of the allotment of Jane Holliday but was then owned by Charles Hebard and Sons, a lumber company heavily invested on the L'Anse Reservation.[62] In 1933 and probably in other years, the taxes on the Barbano parcel were unpaid, and in 1938 the land was sold to the state of Michigan to recover delinquent taxes.[63] Sam Spruce was an allottee who held an eighty-acre parcel under a restricted deed.[64] In 1924 Spruce was issued a certificate of competency by the federal government. It is not known if Mr. Spruce solicited the certificate or if it was issued without his consent. At any rate, taxes were assessed on the Spruce property as a result of the certificate, and taxes were not paid during the 1930s.[65] In 1938 the allotment property was acquired by the state of Michigan for delinquent taxes.[66] The state held the property for several years and sold it to a non-Indian.

As to the question of taxation, the documentary record of the 1854 treaty shows only a single instance in which this topic was even mentioned. This is in the enabling legislation for the 1854 treaty, in which Congress specifically says that Indians receiving reservations and allotments under the treaty would not be subject to tax or execution on their land or other property. Beyond this, Commissioner Manypenny did not bring up the matter with treaty commissioners Gilbert and Herriman, nor did the commissioners raise it with Manypenny. There is no record that anyone attempted to explain taxation to the Indians assembled at La Pointe or that they thought they were going to have to pay money each year to keep their permanent homes. Given their anxiety concerning removal at the time of the treaty, had they understood that it was an intention of the United States that they pay property taxes, they would most certainly have raised strong objections and would probably not have agreed to the treaty. In the case of the Keweenaw Bay Indian Community, the treaties of 1842 and 1854 are the basis of the tribe's unique legal status. These treaties and particularly the 1854 treaty, which provided the Keweenaw Bay Indian Community with a permanent and secure tribal reservation, did not give authority for the state of Michigan to levy property taxes on members of the tribe holding land in the reservation. That the state did so was contrary to the expressed wishes of Congress and to the object of the 1854 treaty. Ultimately, the state's actions have caused and continue to result in improper taxation and the alienation of land from a federal Indian reservation.

Allotment and Timber Sales

After the 313 allotments made by Agent Betts in 1875, a few more deeds were issued in 1878, but none were seen again until 1895, when seventy-one more allotments were forthcoming.[67] This was true despite the fact that more land was available for allotment and that many young people who had come of age since the first allotments were eager to receive them. The annual report for the Mackinac Agency in 1886 states that the L'Anse and Lac Vieux Desert bands were granted a reservation "containing 58,249 acres. Since the treaty was made, 2,720 acres of the same have been used for canal purposes and sold, leaving 55,529 acres to be allotted. Thirty thousand four hundred and eighty-nine acres of the same have been patented to Indians, leaving at this time 25,040 acres subject to allotment."[68] In 1901 the state of Michigan claimed and sold 3,200 acres of reservation land under the federal Swampland Act of 1850, and the state eventually claimed another 120 acres designated as school sections.[69] This left 21,720 acres to be allotted, and presumably this was done, since it was reported by 1909 that no allottable land remained on the reservation.[70]

The reality was that at least as early as 1877, allotted Indians were anxious to sell their allotments for the value of the resources on them or, failing that, the land itself.[71] Of all the hundreds of allotments made at L'Anse, only eleven of these were ever awarded in fee. In each of those cases, the agent had judged the allottee to be capable of safeguarding his own interest. All of the rest was held by restricted patents, which required the permission of the president before either the land or timber could be sold.[72]

In 1878 special agent E. J. Brooks was sent to L'Anse to investigate reports of timber thefts from reservation land. Brooks reported not only that lumbermen were stealing timber but that Agent Betts was complicit in the thefts.[73] Agent George Lee, who succeeded Betts, also reported that a large amount of timber was being cut from unallotted portions of the reserve.[74] A few years later, in 1880, Agent Mark Stevens prosecuted several timber thieves who cut from vacant reservation land. He also noted that some timber was cut by Indians and then sold to lumbermen.[75]

During the 1880s and 1890s, the government tried to restrain logging activities on both allotted and unallotted reservation land throughout the United States, because standing lumber was regarded as trust property that was controlled by the United States as trustee for the Indian tribe.[76] Congress did not even permit the sale of dead and down timber by allottees until 1889, and the tribes themselves were not permitted to cut timber until 1910 and then only with congressional approval.[77] Indians on the L'Anse Reservation were, in fact, very anxious to sell the timber from their allotments and/or, if need be, the allotments themselves.[78] There were several good reasons why this was so:

1. The northern Ojibwe who lived on Lake Superior were, by cultural tradition and personal experience, fishermen and hunters. They did not aspire to be farmers, and the soil and climate of the area are not conducive to agricultural production.
2. The process of making allotments was complex and painfully slow. The Indians at L'Anse did not receive their first patents until 1875, twenty-one or more years after the treaty.
3. The Indian people at L'Anse did not actually live on their allotments once they were made, since they were scattered and covered with heavy timber. Instead, they lived in small lakeshore settlements located on land patented in fee, where they had access to government and mission facilities and to the water for fishing.
4. The value of allotments, once made, was almost entirely in the timber that grew on them rather than in the land itself.

Given these factors, government agents in Michigan began to find means to help Indians earn money by disposing of the allotments that they knew were worthless to the Indians as farmsteads, especially when covered by heavy stands of timber. Unfortunately, in the process, the reservations were vastly diminished in landholdings. The result of these factors was that by the early 1890s, most of the 55,529 acres of allottable land on the Keweenaw Bay Reservation had been assigned to individual Indians. By the third decade of the twentieth century, only a few thousand acres remained in Indian hands. The federal government and its officials no doubt believed at the time that they were serving both the Indian trustees and American industry.

Since the vast majority of patents issued at L'Anse were restricted, permission of the president of the United States was required to dispose of the land or timber. On November 24, 1877, the Department of the Interior issued rules and regulations to be observed in the execution of conveyances for the L'Anse, Lac Vieux Desert, and Ontonagon bands.[79] According to these regulations, deeds or conveyances had to be witnessed by the agent and supported by a certification of two chiefs as to the true identity of the Indian sellers.[80] The agent was required to explain the terms of the sale to the allottee and to obtain a certification that the purchase price had either been paid or was on deposit with a bank. Finally, it was necessary to furnish a surveyed plat to the Indian Office. Since it was obvious that these technical details could not be left to either nonliterate Indian allottees or agents for lumber companies, the responsibility fell to the government Indian agents.[81] The agents found ways to streamline the process of selling allotments or timber, which in the end defeated the reservation system.

The initial step was to compile the necessary paperwork so that deeds, either for land or standing timber sales, could be executed.[82] Usually, agents of lumber companies first offered allottees a price for their property. This offer was often unfairly low, so the government began directing the superintendent of logging to make an independent appraisal of the allotment and its timber.[83] The Indian agent then acquired the necessary paperwork and forwarded groups of requests to the Department of the Interior for further inspection. Purchase offers were occasionally rejected by the department and returned for various corrections or additional information.[84] In the end, however, nearly all, if not all, of the restricted patents were eventually approved for sale and returned with the president's signature affixed. Once approved, the lands were listed in groups and advertised for sale.[85] Bids would be received, and the land would be sold.

After the lumbering era, most of the land that remained in Indian hands was comprised of allotments where only timber deeds had been executed. Even if approved for sale, this land, with low agricultural potential, was difficult to sell once it was cleared, because the market was glutted by literally millions of acres of cutover land that was for sale in northern Michigan at the time.[86] This was land that lumber companies purchased, cut, and did not pay taxes on. It was then reclaimed by the state on tax liens and could be purchased at a very cheap price.

Why were timber companies so anxious to acquire the timber on Indian allotments, and why did they push so hard to acquire them despite the considerable government "red tape"? First, during the last decades of the nineteenth century, America's population and the population of the Upper Peninsula were growing rapidly, and thus so was the market for lumber. Second, timber on the L'Anse Reservation was, relative to other land in the areas of the Upper Peninsula, protected from the initial surge of lumbering. Thus, the reservation timber represented some of the last virgin stands in the entire region. Finally, the lumbering of allotments was very profitable.

For example, in 1902 the main lumber being marketed was hemlock, a species that abounded on the reservation.[87] At that time, many eighty-acre allotments contained an average of 240,000 board feet. Stumpage fees for hemlock averaged about $1.25 per thousand board feet.[88] This means that the hemlock timber on an average allotment could be purchased for $300, or about $3.75 per acre. Hemlock lumber sold for about $5.50 per thousand board feet, so that the average allotment would produce hemlock lumber worth $1,320.[89] Incidentally, hemlock bark was used in tanning, and this product added to the profits. Given stumpage costs alone, $1,020 could be made by purchasing hemlock stumpage from a single allotment. The standard practice of the day was to let land with no further merchantable timber revert to the state for unpaid taxes. In short, a lumberman investing $300 might expect to double his investment.

The Demise and Rebirth of the Reservation, 1900–1936

At the turn of the twentieth century, the L'Anse Indian community was in desperate condition. About eight hundred Indians lived at the head of Keweenaw Bay, most clustered at either the Methodist mission near the town of L'Anse or the Catholic mission near Baraga. As in earlier times, these people lived on fee land along the lakeshore but within the boundary of the reservation. As timber was stripped from the area, there were fewer jobs in the lumber industry, and consequently the Indian people began sinking deeper and deeper into poverty.

Day schools near the reservation, as well as distant boarding schools, were making progress in teaching young people to read, write, and do arithmetic. But these also strongly discouraged the use of the Ojibwe language as well as traditional cultural practices. By the early decades of the twentieth century, the younger generation grew impatient with the leadership of traditional chiefs and decided to elect a council of representatives to govern the tribe.[90]

During the period from about 1890 to 1903, there was very little federal government presence on northern Michigan reservations. In 1903 and 1904, the entire business of the reservation fell to two different medical doctors hired by the government to treat sick Indians. One doctor, Romulus Buckland, became the special disbursement officer for the reservation in 1904 and served until 1918. Dr. Buckland seems to have at least tried to honestly protect the interest of his charges during the period of his service. Nonetheless, Indian land was being raided without mercy by local lumber companies.

The reservation's land base was thus vastly reduced and had been all but stripped of its timber. Although the cash reserves of the agency were increased by lumber sales, individual Indians were locked in a cycle of hopeless poverty. With the failure of the United States as an effective trustee for Indian lands and resources, the state of Michigan began to exert more and more control as it involved itself in law enforcement, social services, and taxation issues on the reservation. The distressing conditions on American Indian reservations in the United States began to penetrate the public consciousness in the 1920s, and eventually Congress resolved to repudiate the disastrous allotment policy.

During the 1920s, when the rest of the country was enjoying a period of prosperity, American Indians were suffering in poverty. Their reservations and natural resources were vastly reduced by land loss under the provisions of the General Allotment Act and occasionally by corruption or indifference of public officials. Poor to nonexistent opportunities for employment led to deplorable conditions of public health and housing. Incidence of disease and starvation was appalling, and the poorly educated Indian population was caught in a hopeless cycle of poverty and despair.

Fortunately, citizens of good conscience began to organize to expose these conditions on American Indian reservations and to bring this information to the American public and to Congress. Helen Hunt Jackson's popular expose *A Century of Dishonor,* published in 1881, helped energize reform.

Citizenship and Taxation

The question of the status of Indians on federal reservations had long been complex and troubling. This was the case because while Indians were encouraged by the federal government to exercise the responsibilities of citizenship, such as voting, serving in the military, and even holding elected office, they were not afforded many of the benefits of citizenship, that is, the protection of law, security of their property, or representation in Congress. Until 1924, when Congress made Native Americans citizens of the United States, the only path to becoming a U.S. citizen was to receive an allotment under provisions of the General Allotment Act. The L'Anse Ojibwe were recognized as citizens of Michigan, but allotment under the Treaty of 1854 did not confer U.S. citizenship.

Agent Mark Stevens pointed out the unequal access Michigan Indians had to the local judicial system in regard to protecting their property.

> I desire to urge upon the Department that no more patents in fee-simple be issued to the Indians in Michigan. In case frauds and trespasses in reference to lands and timber have been perpetrated upon lands where patents have been issued in fee-simple, redress can be had for the Indians only in the State courts, which substantially means no redress at all, for the reason that the Indian has not the money nor the ability to conduct a suit. It would be an unequal contest, although doubtless there are many cases where evidence could be found sufficient to reinvest the Indian with the lands if his case could be properly presented in the State courts; but cases where trespasses have been committed upon lands and timber that were granted by restricted patents, and upon vacant lands not yet patented, are matters that should be and can only be adjusted in the United States courts.[91]

In the same report, Stevens noted the recent ruling of the U.S. District Court for the Western District of Michigan that since Michigan's Indians were entitled to hold land in severalty and were citizens in all other respects, they were subject to the same laws as whites. This being the case, the court reasoned, the law banning the sale of whiskey to Indians (a federal law) did not apply to Michigan Indians.[92] Agent Stevens strongly disagreed with this position, believing that citizenship did not remove congressional jurisdiction, since the United States claimed trusteeship for its dependent Indian wards. His position was supported by the U.S. Supreme Court in 1892 in *U.S. v. Holliday,* when the court ruled that no state could withdraw the right of the federal government to protect Indians from intoxicating beverages as long as a trust status exists, even if the Indians are voters.[93]

The line between federal and state jurisdiction was further blurred in 1886, when cases arose on the L'Anse Reservation in which allottees holding restricted patents died and left minor children as orphans. In such cases, the local probate court, as guardian of the interest of the children, ordered that allotments be sold in support of the children. The argument was made that the permission of the president was not required to sell the property because, by law, life leases could not be perpetuated and that the interest of minor heirs came within the jurisdiction of state courts. Thus, it was decided by the probate court that, through its own authority, it could alienate land set apart by Congress as an Indian reservation.[94]

One of the other land problems that arose in the late nineteenth and early twentieth centuries dealt with inheritance. As the original allottees passed away, their children and spouses inherited the land. In many cases, the large numbers of heirs gave each such a small interest in the whole that it was difficult to dispose of allotments even if permission could be obtained to sell them. In cases where the heirs were spouses or only a few children, Indians sometimes claimed that restrictions remained on the title, while the government argued that the land would be inherited in fee and thus eligible for sale as well as taxation.[95]

Three years later, in 1892, the Michigan Supreme Court issued a ruling in the case of Sarah Williams, a Saginaw Chippewa woman who sued to prevent the state of Michigan from taxing her restricted allotment on the Isabella Reservation. The court ruled that the state did not have the power to tax land over which the United States acted as a trustee for a dependent Indian.[96] As part of its opinion, the court pointed out that the enabling legislation for Michigan statehood, as in the case of all other states, prohibits the taxation of federal lands within the boundaries of the state.

Despite its setback in the Sarah Williams case, the state and its various taxing authorities continued to seek information regarding the status of various Indian properties on the L'Anse Reservation in order to determine if they believed they were subject to property tax.[97] Given this situation, Indian allottees became increasingly reluctant to have their property restrictions removed. This could be done by asking the government to issue a certificate of competency as well as a fee patent.[98] In 1911 several L'Anse Indians hired an attorney to represent them because their reservation land had been listed for taxes.[99] The exact circumstances of these listings are not known, nor is the ultimate outcome of the incident.

It was also assumed that when Indians purchased land in fee, the land would be subject to taxation, but this was not always the case, as E. B. Merritt, assistant commissioner of Indian affairs, pointed out to the auditor general of Michigan. Merritt cited the cases of Mary Stoddard, Maggie Duschaine, and Mary Sturgeon of L'Anse, who were all given restricted allotments pursuant to the 1854 treaty. The Duschaine and Sturgeon allotments and timber from the Stoddard allotment were all sold with the permission of the president. Money received was then used to purchase town lots or other land within the reservation for each woman. The land so acquired was conveyed subject to the same restrictions as the deeds to the original allotments.[100] The importance of this communication, as far as the federal government was concerned, is that competency or lack thereof was a characteristic of the individual. A person could not be made competent by acquiring land in fee. One of the restricted allotments that was put on the tax rolls in about 1913 was held by Jerry Spruce. This allotment was listed for tax sale in 1918 for unpaid taxes during the years 1913–15.[101] Again, the specific fate of this piece of land is not known.

Federal policy seemed to be inconsistent. It is worth noting again that the influence of the General Allotment Act was being felt, even though it did not apply to treaty-based allotments. In 1922 the chief clerk of the Indian Office, C. F. Hauke, wrote to the Mackinac Agency—which was under the care of Edward Clements, who was otherwise in charge of the Indian school at Mackinac—to articulate the government's policy on taxation.

> An Indian allotment held under a restricted fee patent is not taxable until after the record in the county in which the land is situated, of a certificate of competency which provides that the same shall not become effective until thirty days after the date of such record. If the land is held under a trust patent and a patent in fee is applied for and received, or if issued after the end of the trust period without application therefore, the land is taxable, even though not recorded in the county. If a patent in fee is issued during the trust period without the Indian's consent and he refuses to accept the same, or accept under ___ his land is not taxable.[102]

As if the preceding was not confusing enough, Hauke replied to an inquiry by H. C. Perrault, a member of the L'Anse Indian community, with the following further explanation: "You are advised that where land is taxable when an assessment is made, the amount remains a lien on the land until paid, even though the same may be sold to an Indian, paid for with trust funds, and conveyed with restrictions against alienation; but the government holds that assessments cannot be legally made after it is conveyed to the Indian."[103] Mr. Hauke goes on to explain that the federal courts had ruled that "such lands are taxable unless the deed shows affirmatively that such land was purchased as a home for the grantee."[104]

The Keweenaw Bay Community, 1912–22

In 1912 and 1913, Dr. Romulus Buckland, who had been the agency physical and special disbursement officer at L'Anse for eight years and knew the L'Anse Ojibwe well, characterized the community in his annual reports. According to a census prepared in 1910, Buckland reported 1,097 Indians enrolled under the L'Anse Agency; this figure included L'Anse, Lac Vieux Desert, and Ontonagon bands. Of this number, seven to eight hundred Indians actually resided at L'Anse. Of the original 55,529-acre reservation, there were now 14,000 acres remaining at L'Anse and Ontonagon combined. Only 140 acres of land on the reservation were under cultivation. Buckland noted that up until the last decade, only six or seven Indians actually lived on allotments set apart by the 1854 treaty. Most allotments had been sold for between fifty and one hundred dollars for each eighty-acre parcel.[105] These lands had little, if any, economic worth and, if taxed, would produce very little income for the schools.

Buckland went on to report in the next year that the Indians were all regarded as citizens and were allowed to vote (presumably in state and local elections). He also asserted that local non-Indians held no prejudicial feelings over the fact that Indian landholdings (allotments) were exempt from taxation.[106] He then observed that he did not think "Indians holding allotments on this reservation should have to pay taxes on their lands until such a time as the lands are improved and yield some income to the allottees."[107]

As far as Dr. Buckland was concerned, the Indians had all the rights of citizenship and depended on the protection of the federal government only insofar as their lands and timber were concerned. While he believed there were some Indians who should receive patents in fee, the majority, he reported, was incompetent, and it was essential that restrictions should be maintained on their allotments. Finally, Dr. Buckland mentioned that there was a state law prohibiting the sale of liquor to Indians but that the law was not rigidly enforced.[108]

Another extended report was prepared in 1922 by Inspector Herbert C. Creel.[109] Mr. Creel reported that 1,172 Indians were enrolled at the L'Anse Agency, with six to eight hundred actually living around Keweenaw Bay. There were still 13,547 acres of land held by Indians under restricted patents. According to Creel, only twenty-three patents in fee had ever been issued for the L'Anse Reservation, and ten of these were issued for government-owned land located off the reservation at a time when no allottable land was available within the boundaries. He also reported that most of the Indians holding restricted patents refused to accept fee patents in order to avoid taxation. Creel went on to add that if patents in fee were issued to these Indians, it would "tend to disrupt various timber sales."[110] Sale of land was slow because cutover timberland had little value. Only two sales of reservation land were reported for 1922 for which allottees received eighteen dollars per acre. About 3,200 acres of "swampland" were patented to the state of Michigan as late as 1901. However, Creel tells us that this "swampland" included some of the best and most valuable timberland on the reservation.[111] He believed that it was improperly deeded to the state because the reservation had already been set aside for the Indians.

Inspector Creel cited reliable reports that some Indians had moonshine stills on the reservation and that there was "quite a lot of drinking in this jurisdiction." These Indians, he said, greatly preferred moonshine because they could not afford to buy lemon extract and other proprietary medicines with high alcohol content sold in grocery and drug stores.[112]

Other Federal Interests

While agents at L'Anse often claimed that land and timber were the only remaining interests of the federal government and while these issues undoubtedly were of primary concern, there were, in fact, other matters that either were or should have been federal concerns. These were the use and sale of intoxicating beverages on the reservation, which were in violation of Article II of the 1842 treaty as well as state and federal prohibition laws. Likewise, Indians of the L'Anse Reservation believed they had the right, under the same article, to hunt, fish, and gather over the territory ceded by the 1842 treaty.[113]

The annual reports of the commissioner of Indian affairs for 1886 and 1892 both pointed out the damaging aspect of alcohol consumption on Michigan Indians, and this was a long-standing problem.[114] By 1915 bootleg liquor consumption was a serious problem at L'Anse, and one tribal member sued in court to establish his right to maintain a saloon.[115] It was not until the prohibition era that any real attempt was made to solve the alcohol problem at L'Anse. Unfortunately, such efforts were not effective, but they do indicate that federal officials at least recognized some lingering obligation to protect the interests of Indian wards.

The real impetus to deal with the alcohol problem came from a petition signed by David Bedell and twenty-three other L'Anse Indians asking for Indian police to be appointed in order to suppress the liquor trade.[116] This petition made its way to the federal prohibition office for the state of Michigan and also to the Office of Indian Affairs.[117] The Office of Indian Affairs responded to the L'Anse agent that the government could not afford Indian policemen; that the federal commissioner of prohibition had notified the federal director of prohibition in Michigan about the problem at L'Anse; and that he, in turn, notified special agent Edward Clements of the Mackinac Agency. Clements complained that the state of Michigan had provided little cooperation in the L'Anse area but that such cooperation was essential to catching and prosecuting moonshiners. Clements specifically dismissed David Bedell's suggestion that Indian police be appointed to address the problem, on the grounds that "the majority of our Indians [at L'Anse] were living on taxable land and the activities of tribal policemen would be limited to reservation or restricted property which would be of little assistance not to speak of the many complications that might arise."[118] In other words, the federal government believed that the L'Anse Reservation consisted of only the land held under restricted patents; obviously the Indians saw things differently.

Another area in which there was conflict over federal responsibility dealt with the continued existence of hunting and fishing rights under the 1842 treaty. The L'Anse Indians believed they had secured these rights and that it was the federal government's responsibility to protect them. Agent Buckland agreed with this position.[119] Federal officials in Washington, however, took exactly the same position they took over the prohibition issue, namely, that the only remaining federal responsibility at L'Anse was to protect land held under restricted patents. In other words, this small checkerboard of remaining allotments was all that remained of the reservation. A logical outcome of this position was that all land outside of the exterior boundaries (the ceded land) and all land held in fee within the boundaries were under the jurisdiction of the state. It was then concluded that the only Indians who could hunt under the treaty were "noncitizen Indians" who held restricted allotments and that the only place they could hunt was on such allotments. As a result, Indians were advised to obey state hunting and fishing laws.[120]

As a result of the government's policies, any Indian who had not been allotted land, any Indian who was certified as competent, or any Indian who owned fee land was disenfranchised as a Native American, as he or she held no further rights as a member of the L'Anse Lake Superior Ojibwe. In 1930 tribal member James Chosa questioned his status in a letter to the agent at Lac du Flambeau, Wisconsin, who handled the business of the L'Anse Indians at that date.[121] In reply, P. S. Everest informed him as follows:

> The census roll of the L'Anse and Lac Vieux Desert bands of Chippewa Indians formerly the jurisdiction of the now-abandoned Baraga field agency bears the name James Chosa. However, the name of James J. Chosa (provided these two names pertain to one and the same person) was removed from any further government supervision by the granting of a certificate of competency to the allottee on February 5, 1923. By reason of the granting of such certificate, James J. Chosa was removed from his status as a government ward to that of a non-ward. Such, non-ward Indians—four-fifths of the L'Anse-Baraga tribe within such classification status—have no further claim upon the Government.[122]

Mr. Chosa replied,

> I take it that the certificate of competency which was granted to me at that time does not in any way remove or interfere with my rights as a blood member of the L'Anse and Lac Vieux Desert band of Chippewa Indians or in any way effect my tribal rights as such it does not occur to me that our legal rights can be taken away just because he has become by education a little intelligent.[123]

The Indian New Deal

In 1924 the Institute for Governmental Research published the report "The Problems of Indian Administration" by Lewis Meriam, which publicized the social and economic plight of Indian communities across the country. Importantly, the Meriam report also made recommendations for sweeping changes in Indian policy. These suggestions became virtual guidelines for Congress and the executive branch until well after World War II.[124]

The most important effect of the Meriam report was, however, the Indian Reorganization Act (IRA), which was passed by Congress in 1934.[125] The IRA had two cornerstones. The first was to stop the allotment and further loss of Indian land. Indeed, the act contained a large appropriation to begin repurchasing reservation land in order to help tribes build a viable land base. Second, the IRA provided a structure so that the tribes could formalize their governmental structures. This was done by providing the opportunity to enact a constitution and bylaws that would be federally acknowledged and, thus, to constitute semisovereign governments within their various states. It was hoped that these new tribes would eventually be able to generate economic security for their members. Much of the reorganization under the IRA was supervised by John Collier, a social reformer who was the commissioner of Indian affairs from 1933 to 1945 under the Franklin Roosevelt administration.[126] Central to Collier's policy was his goal to "relieve the Indian of the unrealistic and fatal allotment system," which he claimed had "destroyed the economic integrity of the Indian estate and deprived the Indian of normal economic and human activity."[127]

At L'Anse, the people of the L'Anse, Lac Vieux Desert, and Ontonagon bands voted to reorganize under the IRA and, in December 1936, formed the Keweenaw Bay Indian Community, which was acknowledged by the federal government. The advisory committee at L'Anse described the situation on the eve of the tribe's rebirth.

At the eve of federal recognition there were about 350 Indian families living in the L'Anse-Baraga area, most of which were landless. It was no wonder that the newly acknowledged tribe was anxious to take advantage of the provision of the IRA that permitted the government to purchase land for the tribe. There was no shortage of cutover land within the boundaries of the reservation that, once acquired, could be assigned as subsistence homesteads to landless tribal members.

At the time of reorganization, the little Indian land that remained included a very small parcel of land held in trust by the United States; a few of the original allotments, by now each owned by hundreds of heirs; and some surviving parcels of Indian-owned fee land associated with the Catholic and Methodist missions. The vast majority of the reservation was owned by lumber companies, non-Indian private owners, or the state of Michigan, which had acquired title through delinquent tax liens.

During the nineteenth century, most of the land loss on the reservation was due to the Indians themselves selling allotments to lumber interests. In some cases, only the timber was sold, but allottees were led to believe they had sold the land. In these dealings, the allottees needed the permission of the United States and the cooperation of their agents to make these sales.

During the early decades of the twentieth century, local taxing authorities became more efficient in taxing private Indian landholders, who, incidentally, were mostly illiterate in English and therefore not competent to protect their property. The Catholic mission property deeded by Father Baraga to thirty-seven of his parishioners in 1863 serves as an example of the checkered history of such private Indian landholding. Apparently the taxes on these parcels were paid by the church in the early years, but in the first decade of the nineteenth century, they were seized by the state for delinquent taxes. The church redeemed these properties in about 1910 by paying the delinquent taxes, and taxes were not charged from 1916 to 1936 under the mistaken belief that these were church lands.[128] After reorganization, the United States assumed trust responsibility for these lands.

On the Methodist side of the bay, Abel Hall most likely paid the taxes on the lands that he deeded to various Indians during the nineteenth century. Taxes were apparently not paid on these lands in the 1930s, since a field agent for the Minneapolis area office of the Bureau of Indian Affairs reported in 1938 that seven of these properties had appeared on a list of parcels that were about to be sold for back taxes.[129] Since the federal government hoped to acquire the Methodist lands as part of the reorganization effort, the Michigan auditor general was asked to withhold these lands from tax sale, but the state refused to do so, thereby forcing the United States to bid for the land on the open market.[130]

The United States did, however, succeed in purchasing or otherwise acquiring land for the Keweenaw Bay Indian Community in the years before and after World War II. Today, the modern reservation consists of fifteen thousand acres, including both fee and trust land.[131]

The New Reservation

The fact that the United States reversed the loss of land occasioned by the allotment policy and began the process of creating an economically viable and politically autonomous Indian community did not lessen the tension between the tribe and state authorities. In the areas of law enforcement, taxation, treaty rights, and social services, confusion continued to exist over the relative responsibility of the state to its Indian citizens as opposed to the duty of the federal government in its responsibility over Indians as members of Native American tribes. During the sixty-five years since passage of the IRA, the process of sorting out state, federal, and tribal relationships has been ongoing and, although constantly improving, remains troublesome in some regards.

In 1939 the superintendent of the Great Lakes Indian Agency wrote to the Michigan attorney general, Thomas Read, hoping to initiate discussion of four issues that he saw as problematic in Michigan's Indian affairs. These included the limits of federal and state law enforcement jurisdiction on reservations, legislation to fully extend citizenship to Indian citizens, laws to validate traditional customs in marriage and divorce under state law, and the attitude of the state concerning the possible repeal of a federal law banning sale of intoxicating liquors to Indians.[132] This letter elicited a terse reply from Read, who maintained that there were no problems with Indians in Michigan and no legal difficulties with Indian citizens in the state, since Indians were treated exactly like all other citizens. Mr. Read took note of the fact that Michigan law already made it an offense to incite Indians to violate a treaty and that there was another law that exempted noncitizen Indians from taxation of their personal property.[133]

Unfortunately, the refusal of the state to recognize that its Indian citizens were not just like every other citizen continued to generate problems until the present time. The critical distinction is, of course, that Indians often have rights as members of tribes that non-Indian citizens do not. Among these rights are those that flow from the treaty guarantees that exist between the United States and respective tribes. In the case of the Keweenaw Bay Indian Community, the treaties of 1842 and 1854 are the basis of the tribe's unique legal status. These treaties—particularly the 1854 treaty, which provided the Keweenaw Bay Indian Community with a permanent and secure tribal reservation—did not provide authority for the state of Michigan to levy property taxes on members of the tribe. That the state did so was contrary to the expressed wishes of Congress and to the object of the 1854 treaty. Ultimately, the state's actions have caused and continue to result in the alienation of land from a federal Indian reservation.

CHAPTER 22

Keweenaw Bay Indian Community v. Naftaly, 6th Cir. 2006, Case No. 452 F.3d 514, 527

Skip Durocher
Dorsey and Whitney LLP, Minneapolis, MN

> [I]n order to accomplish the object of the 1854 Treaty, the preservation of a permanent home for the Chippewa Indians, [the Keweenaw Bay Indian Community] and its members must be relieved of every species of involuntary removal, including a levy and sale for taxes.
> —Hon. Eric L. Clay, *Keweenaw Bay Indian Community v. Naftaly*

On November 27, 2006, the U.S. Supreme Court denied the Michigan State Tax Commission's petition for a writ of certiorari to review the Sixth Circuit's resounding affirmation that the state of Michigan cannot collect property taxes from the Keweenaw Bay Indian Community (hereinafter "the Community") or its members on lands held in fee simple within the Community's reservation boundaries.[1] The decision was the final word in a property tax dispute spanning more than twenty-five years, ten judicial decisions, and four different courts.

The History of the Keweenaw Bay Indian Community and Its Treaties

The Keweenaw Bay Indian Community is a federally recognized Indian tribal government organized and operating under a constitution and bylaws approved by the secretary of the interior on December 17, 1936, pursuant to the Indian Reorganization Act of 1934.[2] The Community is the successor-in-interest of the L'Anse and Ontonagon bands of Chippewa Indians, signatories to the treaties made with the Chippewa at La Pointe on October 4, 1842 (7 Stat. 591), and September 30, 1854 (10 Stat. 1109). The 1854 treaty is at the heart of the Community's property tax litigation, but to fully understand the Community's position with respect to the tax dispute, we must start with an examination of the 1842 treaty.

The 1842 Treaty and Its Aftermath

Pursuant to the 1842 treaty, the Chippewa of Lake Superior and the Mississippi ceded the western half of Michigan's Upper Peninsula as well as portions of northern Wisconsin to the United States.[3] Most of the Chippewa continued to live and reside within the ceded area, however, and Article II of the 1842 treaty guaranteed them the right to hunt within the ceded area, with the usual privileges of occupancy unless and until required to remove by the president. Article II also assured the Community and its members of the continued protection of the federal Indian trade and intercourse laws within the ceded area.

Though the threat of removal appeared remote in 1842, the United States had surveyed and begun to sell land in the Keweenaw Bay area by the late 1840s, causing fear among the Chippewa Indians that they would be forced to remove from their residences and villages within the ceded area.[4] The Chippewa leaders sent numerous petitions and letters to the president and Indian agents, asking for the creation of permanent reservations. At the same time, to further protect against removal, religious leaders of the Chippewa, such as Father Frederick Baraga, purchased land in the Keweenaw Bay area for the Indians, as did some of the Indians themselves.[5] The local Indian agent, remarking that removal was "the great terror of [the Indians'] lives," maintained, "I hazard nothing in saying they will sooner submit to extermination than comply with it."[6]

The 1854 Treaty

As a result of the petitions and letters from the Chippewa Indians, the United States agreed to negotiate a treaty with them in 1854. The Indians strongly desired permanent homes in their present locations, and the 1854 treaty satisfied this desire of the Chippewa by creating permanent homes for them on reservations on lands that included their actual dwelling places.[7] For the L'Anse and Lac Vieux Desert bands, the United States "agree[d] to set apart and withhold from sale" the lands that became known as the L'Anse Indian Reservation.[8] The reservation consists of approximately 59,840 acres located on both sides of the Keweenaw Bay of Lake Superior in present-day Baraga County in Michigan's Upper Peninsula.

The 1854 treaty contained two additional provisions of central importance to the preservation of the Community's reservation and to its future property tax litigation. Article 11 provides:

> All annuity payments to the Chippewas of Lake Superior, shall hereafter be made at L'Anse, La Pointe, Grand Portage, and on the St. Louis River; *and the Indians shall not be required to remove from the homes hereby set apart for them.* And such of them that reside in the territory hereby ceded, shall have the right to hunt and fish therein, until otherwise ordered by the President.[9]

The other important provision is Article 3, which provides, in pertinent part:

> [T]he President may, from time to time, at his discretion, cause the whole [reservation] to be surveyed, and may assign to each head of a family or single person over twenty-one years of age, eighty acres of land for his or their separate use; and he may, at his discretion, as fast as the occupants become capable of transacting their own affairs, issue patents therefore to such occupants, with such restrictions of the power of alienation as he may see fit to impose. And he may also, at his discretion, make rules and regulations, respecting the disposition of the lands in case of the death of the head of a family, or single person occupying the same, or in case of its abandonment by them.[10]

The 1854 treaty was ratified on January 10, 1855. After ratification, the president of the United States from time to time assigned parcels of the reservation land to individual Chippewa Indians, pursuant to Article 3 of the 1854 treaty. The president did not make the assignments pursuant to the General Allotment Act of 1887 (24 Stat. 388), the Nelson Act of 1889 (25 Stat. 642), the Burke Act of 1906 (34 Stat. 182), or any other act of Congress.

In 1889, the assistant attorney general of the United States held that the General Allotment Act does not modify, repeal, or supersede Article 3 of the 1854 treaty and that the General Allotment Act makes "no express reference whatever to the treaty of 1854, and no repeal or change in terms of any of its provisions."[11] In accordance with Article 3 of the 1854 treaty, the president made the assignments in the form of patents with restrictions on alienation or, occasionally, patents in fee simple.

The Keweenaw Bay Indian Community's Property Tax Litigation History

The Community has a lengthy history of enforcing its sovereignty through litigation of its property tax disputes with state and local authorities seeking to impose property taxes on land held in fee simple by the Community or its members within its reservation boundaries (the Community's "reservation fee lands"). This history serves as the backdrop to the litigation leading to the Community's victories in the Western District of Michigan and the Sixth Circuit.

Between 1978 and 1982, the Community was engaged in property tax litigation before the Michigan Tax Tribunal. In *Baraga County Equalization Department v. Darcy,*[12] the Michigan Tax Tribunal held that lands owned by individual members of the Community within the Community's reservation created pursuant to the 1854 treaty were subject to taxation if they had been sold prior to ratification of the 1854 treaty in 1855. The decision was based in part on the language of the 1854 treaty, which reserved for the L'Anse and Lac Vieux Desert bands "all the unsold lands" in the townships at issue. It was conceded by the Michigan attorney general, as amicus, and held by the tribunal that those properties that were not sold prior to the ratification of the treaty were free from *ad valorem* taxation even though the parcels were owned in fee simple.

In 1991, in *Keweenaw Bay Indian Community v. Michigan,*[13] the federal district court in the Western District of Michigan held that the boundaries of the reservation follow the exterior lines of the townships and fractional townships described in the 1854 treaty. The court rejected the checkerboard principle upheld in *Darcy* and held that all lands within these exterior boundaries, including plots sold before ratification of the 1854 treaty in 1855, were part of the reservation and constituted Indian country. Later that year, in an unpublished decision in the Community's boundary litigation,[14] the same federal district court rejected the Community's motion to hold the state in contempt for failing to prevent Baraga Township and Baraga County from continuing to tax forty-two parcels within the reservation boundaries that had been sold prior to ratification of the treaty. The court held that the state was not liable for the actions of the local officials, that the taxation issue was outside the scope of the court's boundary decision, and that federal review of the township's actions through contempt proceedings was inappropriate.

In March 1994, after years of disputes and shifting positions by local and state officials regarding the enforcement of the Michigan General Property Tax Act[15] within the Community's reservation, the Community, L'Anse and Baraga townships, and Baraga County stipulated to the entry of a consent judgment by the Michigan Tax Tribunal, under which the parties acknowledged the lack of jurisdiction to enforce the act against the reservation fee lands. Under that consent judgment, the Community also agreed to make payments for governmental services in lieu of taxes in an amount equal to 100 percent of the taxes and any fees or charges that otherwise would be due for such properties. The parties agreed that the Community could make the payments in lieu of taxes out of the 2 percent fund from a 1993 consent judgment on gaming.[16]

From 1994 to early 2003, all of the parties to the 1994 consent judgment abided by and enjoyed the benefits of their agreement. For its part, the Community made regular and reliable payments in lieu of taxes for the reservation fee lands for all tax years from 1992 forward, equal to 100 percent of the taxes that otherwise would have been due. In return, the local governments received consistent payments and enjoyed a strong government-to-government relationship with the Community.

Despite this mutually beneficial relationship between the Community and the local government entities, the Michigan Tax Commission challenged the 1994 consent judgment in 1999 and ordered the local assessors and equalization directors to place the reservation fee lands back on the tax rolls. This order was based on the commission's perception that the U.S. Supreme Court's decision in *Cass County v. Leech Lake Band of Chippewa Indians*[17] allowed state taxation of the reservation fee lands. The two townships and the county, along with two Community members, sought a writ of mandamus in the circuit court of Baraga County to prevent the Michigan Tax Commission from interfering with the consent judgment.[18] The circuit court issued the writ of mandamus, and the Michigan Court of Appeals upheld the issuance, but the Michigan Supreme Court reversed the mandamus order on the basis that the Michigan Tax Commission was not a party to and thus was not bound by the consent judgment.[19] When the Michigan Tax Commission ordered the local tax assessor to place the reservation fee lands back on the tax rolls in early 2003 and mail out assessment notices, the Community filed suit in federal court in the Western District of Michigan to protect its rights under the 1854 treaty.

The Community's Theory of the Case

The Community filed suit against the chairman, the members, and the executive secretary of the Michigan State Tax Commission; L'Anse and Baraga townships; and the assessor for L'Anse and Baraga townships. The suit challenged the enforcement of the Michigan General Property Tax Act against the reservation fee lands. Approximately 17,810 acres of the Community's reservation at the time of the filing were owned by or for the benefit of the Community and its members.[20] The reservation fee lands included 2,947 acres of land owned in fee simple by the Community and approximately 688 acres of land owned in fee simple by the Community members.

The Community's theory of the case relied primarily on the language of Article 11 of the 1854 treaty, which provided that "the Indians shall not be required to remove from the homes hereby set apart for them." The Community argued that the 1854 treaty precludes enforcement of the Michigan General Property Tax Act against reservation fee lands by its plain language, by its necessary implications, and by its complete agreement with the objectives and intentions of the Indian signatories to establish permanent reservations. The Community argued that the 1854 treaty precluded the enforcement of the act, the tax sale provisions of which could cause the Community or its members to be required to remove from the homes set apart for them for failure to pay property taxes, in direct violation of the 1854 treaty.

The Community further argued that the *Cass County* principle that land rendered alienable by Congress is subject to taxation would be extended far beyond its intended scope if applied to the 1854 treaty, jettisoning 175 years of federal principles of Indian treaty construction. The Community also argued that even if the *Cass County* principle were applied to the 1854 treaty, removal of alienation restrictions from reservation land would not render such land taxable, because, as provided for by *Cass County* itself, Article 11 constitutes a "clear manifestation of a contrary intent" by the signatories to the treaty. The Community further argued that Congress neither abrogated nor modified the Article 11 guarantee against involuntary removal from or taxation of Indian-owned lands within the reservation.[21]

Pursuant to a separate count of its complaint based on federal common law, rather than the terms of the 1854 treaty, the Community argued that the state defendants could not tax reservation fee lands absent an unmistakably clear authorization by Congress, either by explicit language or by making such lands alienable, and that the defendants had failed to identify a single statute that satisfied the established federal common-law test. The Community emphasized that the allotments were made by the president pursuant to the 1854 treaty and not pursuant to any act of Congress.

The Defendants' Theory of the Case

The defendants' theory of the case relied heavily on the Supreme Court's holding in *Cass County v. Leech Lake Band of Chippewa Indians* that "when Congress makes reservation lands freely alienable, it is unmistakably clear that Congress intends that land to be taxable by state and local governments, unless a contrary intent is clearly manifested."[22] The defendants argued that the Supreme Court made free alienability of land the controlling principle in deciding whether reservation fee land is subject to state *ad valorem* taxes.[23] The defendants argued that the land was rendered freely alienable by federal approval of allotment and the removal of restrictions. The defendants relied on Article 3 of the 1854 treaty, which authorized allotments subject to restrictions on alienation until the allottees were deemed competent by the president. By 1912, almost all available land on the L'Anse Reservation had been allotted and assigned, to be held in fee simple by the allottees, their heirs, other members of the Community, the Community itself, or nonmembers of the Community.[24] The defendants argued that the 1854 treaty was itself "the equivalent of an act of Congress and authorized the President to allot land on the L'Anse Reservation and to remove restrictions on alienation on that land."[25] The defendants conflated Senate ratification of the 1854 treaty with congressional action rendering the reservation fee land alienable and thus taxable under *Cass County,* and they further argued that ratification of the 1854 treaty was an act of Congress because it had the effect of making the self-executing parts of the treaty the law of the land.

The defendants also argued that Congress passed several statutes that allowed the secretary of the interior to make land freely alienable within the L'Anse Reservation. Relying on *Cass County* and *County of Yakima v. Confederated Tribes and Bands of the Yakima Indian Nation,*[26] the defendants emphasized that the form of congressional authorization for removing restrictions on alienation did not control those Supreme Court cases and should not determine the outcome for the Community's reservation fee lands. According to the defendant, the only question to be answered in order to determine whether the reservation fee lands were taxable was whether Congress had authorized the president or someone else to allot the lands on the reservation. The defendants stressed the importance of the General Allotment Act[27] and cited congressional actions in 1910 and 1913 relating to the testamentary disposition of lands allotted under the 1854 treaty.[28] According to the defendants, these acts granted to the secretary of the interior the "final and conclusive right" to determine legal heirs and their competence and to issue patents to those heirs in fee simple.[29] Furthermore, in 1922, Congress passed a provision allowing the secretary of the interior to exercise the power of the president to authorize the alienation of land allotted under treaties.[30] The defendants argued that the 1922 act applied to the 1854 treaty and constituted an act of Congress authorizing alienation and thus taxation of the reservation fee lands.

The Western District of Michigan and Sixth Circuit Decisions

On May 27, 2005, the U.S. District Court for the Western District of Michigan held, in a summary judgment decision by then district court judge David McKeague,[31] that Michigan property taxes could not be imposed on fee land owned by the Community or its members within the reservation. The court decided the case on both grounds presented to it: (1) that the 1854 treaty establishing the reservation, which provided that the Indians "shall never be required to remove from" the reservation, precluded state property taxation; and, alternatively, (2) that taxation is precluded as a matter of federal common law because Congress has never authorized the taxation of the land as required by federal precedents.[32] In reaching its decision, the court emphasized, "It defies logic to believe that the Indians would have signed a treaty ceding over seven million acres to the United States, knowing that they could lose the land they kept as a reservation the following year, due to non-payment of taxes."[33]

On appeal from the district court's grant of summary judgment in favor of the Community, the U.S. Court of Appeals for the Sixth Circuit, in a majority opinion by Judge Eric Clay,[34] held that the district court did not err in granting summary judgment to the Community and enjoining enforcement of the Michigan General Property Tax Act against the Community's reservation fee lands.[35] In reaching this conclusion, the Sixth Circuit reviewed the history of the treaties and the litigation regarding property taxes. The Sixth Circuit focused on Article 11 of the 1854 treaty and its language that "the Indians shall not be required to remove from the homes hereby set apart for them."[36] Though the Sixth Circuit found this language ambiguous, the Court emphasized that it must interpret the language as the Indians themselves would have understood the treaty language, in accordance with established Supreme Court precedent.

> In our view, the language of Article 11 of the 1854 Treaty is ambiguous. It is unclear whether the provision precluded all forms of involuntary alienation, including the sale of lands in satisfaction of tax liabilities, or only the general removal of the Chippewa Indians from the reservation area. As made amply clear by Supreme Court precedent, this Court must read this ambiguity in favor of Plaintiff and its members, and against the backdrop of the Indian sovereignty doctrine and the notion that American Indian tribes enjoy quasi-sovereignty. This backdrop reinforces Plaintiff's interpretation that the treaty disallowed involuntary state tax sales, and thus state taxation, of real property held by Plaintiff or its members.[37]

The Sixth Circuit emphasized that the purpose of the treaty was to secure a permanent home for the Chippewa Indians. The Sixth Circuit confirmed the finding of the Community's expert, Dr. Charles E. Cleland, that the Chippewa Indians did not have reason to know at the time of signing the 1854 treaty that they would be required to pay property taxes on allotted lands and face the prospect of losing those lands if they did not pay the taxes.[38] Stating that the district court was required, as a matter of law, to interpret ambiguity in the 1854 treaty in favor of the Community, the Sixth Circuit held that "in order to accomplish the object of the 1854 treaty, the preservation of a permanent home for the Chippewa Indians, Plaintiff and its members must be relieved of every species of involuntary removal, including a levy and sale for taxes."[39] The Sixth Circuit upheld the district court's grant of summary judgment in favor of the Community on the basis of the 1854 treaty.

The Sixth Circuit also affirmed the district court on the basis of the federal common law.

Relying on and quoting *McClanahan v. State Tax Commission of Arizona*,[40] the Sixth Circuit held that tribal property on an Indian reservation is not subject to state taxation "except by virtue of *express authority* conferred upon the State by an *act of Congress*."[41] Emphasizing that the Indian sovereignty doctrine is the backdrop against which statutory interpretation regarding alienation of tribal land must be analyzed, the Sixth Circuit found that no act of Congress cited by the defendants manifested the "unmistakably clear" intent required by the Supreme Court in *County of Yakima v. Confederated Tribes and Bands of Yakima Indian Nation*.[42]

In reaching its decision, the Sixth Circuit rejected the defendants' argument that ratification of the 1854 treaty constituted an act of Congress rendering the Community's reservation fee lands alienable, noting that although treaties have the force of law, that "does not mean a treaty is in fact an act of Congress representing that body's will."[43] The Sixth Circuit disposed of the state defendants' other statutory arguments, emphasizing that all of the Community's land was allotted pursuant to the 1854 treaty and was not allotted pursuant to the General Allotment Act. It also emphasized that because the Community's lands were all allotted by 1912, the 1922 act allowing the alienation of treaty allotments could not have authorized allotment or alienation of those same lands.[44]

The defendants filed a timely petition with the U.S. Supreme Court seeking certiorari. The Supreme Court declined to review the decision on November 27, 2006, giving final resolution to the Community's long history of property tax litigation.

The Case's Contribution to Indian Law

From the perspective of the Keweenaw Bay Indian Community, the need for this property tax litigation in the first place was the unfortunate result of the state of Michigan's interference in a mutually beneficial government-to-government relationship between the Community and the local governments. This disruptive action did not escape the notice of the Sixth Circuit. During oral argument, one of the court's final questions was what happened to the payments in lieu of taxes that the Community agreed to pay pursuant to the consent judgment. In my capacity as counsel for the Community, I responded that the Community had consistently remitted those payments every year to the local governments. Judge Martha Craig Daughtrey then lamented that "no good deed goes unpunished."[45]

The consequence of being forced into litigation to defend its treaty and sovereignty rights ultimately yielded a favorable outcome for the Keweenaw Bay Indian Community and its members. As a result of the court's decision in the property tax litigation, neither the Community nor its members will be faced with losing their property for failure to pay property taxes. The litigation also affirmed central principles of Indian treaty interpretation, including the interpretation of treaty language according to Indian understanding, an important reassurance in an era of Supreme Court jurisprudence that might otherwise conflict with this long-standing federal doctrine of Indian law, which has evolved to protect tribes' treaty and sovereignty rights.

PART 4

Conclusions

CHAPTER 23

The Benefits of Reestablished Treaties

The affirmation of treaty rights, which have long lain dormant, has produced many and diverse benefits to the contemporary tribes, which are successors in interest to the nineteenth-century treaties. These benefits, which are economic, political, social, and religious, contribute importantly to the welfare of both the Indian people as individuals and the tribes to which they belong. Beyond these benefits, the reinstitution of treaty guarantees has also profited the non-Indian segment of our population in a number of regards. This chapter will discuss the ramifications of successful treaty litigation.

An Economic Boost

The settlement agreement between the Ottawa and Chippewa tribes of Michigan and the state of Michigan that followed the affirmation of the fishing rights under the Treaty of 1836 gave tribal fishermen exclusive access to the commercial fishery of most of the waters ceded by the treaty. The latter includes the northern portions of Lakes Michigan and Huron and the eastern part of Lake Superior south of the international boundary with Canada. These waters produce much of the Great Lakes region's whitefish and lake trout that enter the U.S. market for fresh fish.

Although treaty catch figures are difficult to obtain, it can be said that while the total number of tribal fishermen is relatively small, many of these fishermen have very large investments in equipment. In aggregate, they also catch some millions of pounds of fish per annum. Perhaps 85 percent of the catch is whitefish, with the remaining portion made up of lake trout, lake herring, salmon, walleye, and rainbow and brown trout. The quota for each species is set by joint agreement between tribal and state authorities in fishery management. Although the wholesale prices the fishermen receive is far less than the retail value, the tribal fishery is thought to be worth some millions of dollars per year.

Many Indian tribes maintain programs for hatchery stocking in addition to those of the states of Michigan, Minnesota, and Wisconsin and the U.S. Fish and Wildlife Service. Tribal hatcheries stock fish that are eventually available to non-Indian sportfishermen as well as for commercial production in the Great Lakes waters. It is also a great benefit to the public to have fresh fish available in stores and restaurants as a result of the strenuous and dangerous labors of Indian fishermen.

The Indian right to hunt, fish, and gather on land ceded in the treaties of 1836, 1837, 1842, and 1854 includes the lands that now make up northern Wisconsin and eastern Minnesota as well as the northwestern Lower Peninsula and Upper Peninsula of Michigan. Here are found other valuable resources for the many tribes that are party to these agreements. In Wisconsin and Minnesota, wild rice is produced by Indian harvesters for subsistence as well as a commercial crop. Wild rice is, of course, a very valuable commercial commodity. To some degree, the off-reservation wild rice crop is shared by non-Indian gatherers licensed by their states and Indian harvesters licensed by their tribes. Several tribes, most notably the Bad River and Mole Lake tribes in Wisconsin and the Mille Lacs tribe in Minnesota, have large productive rice stands on their reservations. Tribal regulation of rice harvest both on and off the reservation is controlled by "rice chiefs," traditional specialists that determine optimum harvest seasons for each rice lake as well as the harvest methods that are enforced to assure reseeding of the rice beds. These traditional methods of conservation, combined with rice research and replanting programs undertaken by the treaty tribes, assure an abundant rice crop in most years. Within the state of Wisconsin alone, about one hundred tribal members are licensed per year to harvest wild rice from the ceded territory (the northern one-third of the state). On average, these gatherers harvest 9.4 tons of green or freshly harvested rice. Most of this rice is thought to be for home consumption.[1]

Gathering rights under treaties all across the northern Great Lakes region produce other commercial products; for example, cedar boughs and ground pine are used in the manufacture of Christmas wreaths. Another important market for natural resources is the value-added handicraft industry, which produces such items as baskets made from birch bark and split ash, quill boxes, and other art products important to the northern tourist economy. These items are made from birch bark, sweetgrass, cedar roots, basswood fiber, porcupine quills, deer hide, antler, and many other natural products. Such materials are gathered under permits issued by the tribes and, when the gathering takes place on national forestlands, by the U.S. Forest Service. It is believed that the total value of Indian handicraft products is substantial and that the retail sale of handicraft items is an important source of income to the Indian artisans who produce them. As in the case of the sale of fresh and smoked fish and finished rice, most of the sales of Indian art and handicrafts find their way to the non-Indian market. In this way, the reaffirmation of their treaty rights is a benefit to the general public, as well as an economic asset to native people.

Tribal Sovereignty

During the 1970s, when news that the first Indian treaty cases had been filed with the federal courts appeared in the public press, many non-Indians had trouble taking the news stories seriously. Most people were, in fact, surprised to learn that Indian tribes still existed, let alone that they had any special rights under ancient treaties. At that time, few members of the public could even name one of the Indian tribes of their state, and almost all scoffed at the idea that tribal members had "rights" that superseded their own. As these treaty cases made their way through the courts during the last decades of the twentieth century, the public began to take notice of Indian affairs, Indian history, and the role of tribes in modern political life.

When it became apparent that the tribes were winning the majority of treaty cases, the first reaction of the public was divided. Generally, many people living in the southern portion of the Great Lakes states, the urbanized portions, tended to regard Indian victories as long-delayed justice for past wrongs committed by their own pioneer ancestors. Conversely, many people living in the northern more rural areas, where hunting and fishing are both a part of everyday life and important to the tourist economy, viewed the same decisions as a deep injustice, an assault committed by a small and undeserving Indian minority. In northern Michigan and especially in northern Wisconsin, these attitudes resulted in much civil unrest against Indian individuals, including even schoolchildren, which was ultimately addressed by the U.S. Civil Rights Commission. In Wisconsin, riots, assaults, and vandalism required the intervention of the Wisconsin National Guard.

Fortunately, the intervening years have brought calm and grudging acceptance of the court-mandated right of the tribes to exercise their hunting, fishing, and gathering rights under the treaties. Dire predictions about the pillage of natural resources and the ruination of the northern tourist economy at the hands of Indians have proved to be false.[2] Today, even the most vociferous opponents of treaty rights have difficulty pointing to any negative impacts of treaty harvest.

Accepting that Indian tribes are autonomous political institutions has led both citizens and officials of the various Great Lakes states to the realization that tribal governments can best be thought of as equal partners in preserving and pursuing common goals. This newfound attitude has worked well in matters of resource conservation as well as in other realms of civil affairs. In this sense, learning about the Indian tribes and the Indian people within the Great Lakes states has fostered a good working relationship that is ultimately a benefit to the non-Indian public.

As political institutions, the tribes also benefited enormously from the new relationship with the states and local governments that followed the establishment of treaty rights in the courts. While it is true that the advent of casino gaming during the last few decades has brought greater affluence to the tribes and commensurate expansion of their social and political infrastructure, they have also gained much political stature. This is a result not, as often thought, of their philanthropic giving at the local level but of their enhanced sovereign political status. Though long-denied in practice, their sovereignty was affirmed and, in fact, reestablished by the courts in order to improve the administration of newly reacquired treaty rights by the tribes.

As one example, the need to reassure the public and the courts that the tribes were capable of engaging in wildlife conservation led to the promulgation of tribal conservation codes, the appointment of tribal conservation officers, and the employment of tribal biologists to develop an enforcement and research infrastructure. This included a viable tribal court system and conservation committees to set tribal resource policy. That these new tribal institutions and their personnel have performed superbly is well recognized today by the Great Lakes states and federal government and, indeed, by the joint U.S.-Canadian International Fishery Commission. These tribal institutions provide a welcome addition to the intergovernmental effort to protect and preserve the U.S.-Canadian natural heritage, which is yet another benefit of treaty rights litigation.

Not only has treaty rights litigation enhanced the political standing of existing tribes, but the prospect of participating in the long-deferred treaty rights has itself stimulated the formation of tribal governments in some cases. One example is the Grand Traverse Band of Ottawa and Chippewa Indians located on Grand Traverse Bay in the northwest portion of the southern peninsula of Michigan. This Indian community actually sought federal recognition by the federal government so that it could join in an ongoing lawsuit to establish fishing rights under the Treaty of 1836. Since the ancestral chiefs of the Grand Traverse Band had signed that treaty and since the band's fishermen were badly in need of the protection of their rights to fish, the community sought and received federal recognition.

It is apparent that the tribes that have been successful in pursuing the recognition of treaty rights all across northern Michigan, Wisconsin, and Minnesota are stronger internally and enjoy greater status externally because they are equal partners with state and local governments in many realms of civil affairs. It should also be mentioned that the tribes that are parties to hunting, fishing, and gathering rights have formed two well-regarded organizations devoted to promoting wildlife conservation in the Great Lakes region. These are the Great Lakes Indian Fish and Wildlife Commission located in Odanah, Wisconsin, and the Chippewa-Ottawa Resource Authority in Sault Ste. Marie, Michigan. These organizations provide participating tribal governments with biological and policy expertise, as well as research on the status of many fish, wildlife, and plant species. Both organizations were, in part, created with funds derived from treaties settlements, and both are full working partners with state and international agencies of land and resource management.

An International Perspective

A largely unexplored benefit of the study of Indian treaties and their litigation is the potential to provide new ideas toward resolving the many contemporary conflicts between native people within the confines of nation-states in other parts of the world. In these instances, indigenous people are fighting the same battles to preserve their land and cultures as were waged on the American frontier during the nineteenth century. Examples include the well-publicized conflicts in the Amazon basin between native forest tribes and corporate interests involved in clearing land for agriculture and grazing. In South Asia and Southeast Asia, indigenous swidden agriculturalists struggle to maintain traditional lands in the face of state-sponsored policies that make the same land available for large-scale, commercial monoculture. In these same areas, lumbering of tropical forests and mineral extraction are displacing hunters, gatherers, and swidden agriculturalists. Likewise, tribes in sub-Saharan Africa face similar threats due to mining, lumbering, policies of land distribution, and the development of ecological tourism, as well as other causes. It would, of course, be disingenuous, given the record of the historic abuse of native people in the United States, to carry the criticism of nations of the third world too far, and this seems especially true given the unresolved plight of native Hawaiians.[3]

In the majority of contemporary cases, indigenous cultural minorities are without any rights or, at least, rights that can be fairly litigated by their country's courts. I am not suggesting that the treaty system developed in the former British colonies be exported. It is conceivable, however, that some of the attendant components that have evolved out of treaty making in the twentieth century might be helpful in other contexts where indigenous minorities face problems in nation-states in the twenty-first century. Some of these components might include the following:

1. A system for the formal acknowledgment of indigenous groups and subgroups by the national government
2. Federal mechanisms to provide and legitimize limited political rights and governmental functions for native groups
3. A system of federal laws to protect the integrity of indigenous cultural groups and the rights of native people
4. Contractual mechanisms to define homelands, preserve cultural integrity, and fund institutional stability of acknowledged cultural groups
5. Judicial standards for the interpretation of the special legal relationship between the national and indigenous governments

Whatever mechanisms may be drawn from the Great Lakes examples, it seems safe to conclude that the combination of successful litigation of treaty rights and the system of legal and political safeguards in place in the United States and Canada have at least stabilized land loss and ended forced acculturation. In this sense, the study of treaty history may be instructive for the native people in other parts of the world who are struggling with many of the same problems once faced by Native Americans.

The Ties That Bind

At one time or another, as treaties were being litigated with the Great Lakes states, it occurred to state authorities that they might defeat treaty claims by offering huge money inducements to the tribes to drop the lawsuits. During the early 1980s, the Michigan Department of Natural Resources often asked why an Indian commercial fishery producing ten million dollars per year had to be traded for a tourist-based sportfishing economy worth perhaps ten times that amount. Leaving aside the fact that commercial and sports fisheries were not and are not now mutually exclusive, Indian people were both shocked and outraged with money offers to forgo their treaty rights. The vast majority of Indian people regarded a buyout as a sellout of their ancestors who agreed to the treaties to benefit future generations. Accepting the many millions of proffered dollars would constitute not only a repudiation of their birthright but also a refutation of their heritage as Indian people. As an Indian fisherman once told me, "I fish because I am an Indian, and I am an Indian because I fish."

In earlier chapters of this book, it was noted that the general public tends to relegate Indians to the historic past and thereby to consign them and their historic relationship to pioneer Euro-Americans to the misty events of yesteryear, where they can remain obscure. Indian people, in contrast, tend to construct their historic acculturation around the misdeeds of American pioneers and the suffering of the Indian generations that followed. The chiefs who signed treaties and struggled against the abuses of colonization are Indian heroes. In this sense of history, the treaties embody a series of difficult trade-offs: land for hunting rights, reservations for protection of a few critical resources, allotments of land to avoid removal, and so forth. These tough decisions by the leaders of old were made, despite their cultural costs, in hope of protecting and enhancing the chances of survival for future generations. To Indian people, the denial of treaties, which represent a material vestige of the struggle of hero ancestors, is a denial of their own ethnic and cultural link to the past and therefore their special place in the modern world. To native people, to uphold the treaty tradition is to enhance those same values.

Many native people also feel themselves to be tied to native species in a way that is biologically inclusive; that is, they believe that their bodies have been adapted over thousands of years to the consumption of the native fish, animals, and plants that, like themselves, are indigenous to the Great Lakes ecosystem. Although this idea may lack scientific support, there is much anecdotal evidence that a diet consisting of venison, fish, wild rice, nuts, berries, and other wild foods makes Indian people feel better and more able to resist both physical and mental disease. There is certainly no doubt that native people do better on a diet of natural foods than on one high in refined sugar and fatty processed foods. It scarcely needs mentioning that many of the problems Indian people have with the metabolism of alcohol seem to be related to the lack of evolutionary experience with the brewing and fermenting of alcoholic beverages. The high rate of alcoholism, obesity, and diabetes among Indian populations seems to, at the very least, indicate that low-fat and low-sugar diets derived from wild species would be a superior diet for Indian people. A treaty right that provides these foods and promotes their incorporation into native diet thus strengthens not only their bodies but also their spirits.

From Grandmother Earth

Occasionally the complaint is voiced that Indians no longer need hunting and fishing rights because casino operations provide plenty of money for them to buy food in stores like everybody else. This is true enough, but the ability to harvest natural resources is not solely an economic issue. In fact, in the contemporary life of native people, the use of natural foods is an important religious consideration.

In the traditional conception of the natural world, which has long been the underpinnings of the education of Indian young people, the place of human beings within nature is very distinct from that taught to the children of the dominant Judeo-Christian tradition.[4] In the spiritual world of Great Lakes natives, the distinction between animal and plant species and human beings is, in many ways, ambiguous. Both are regarded as "persons," of the human and nonhuman varieties. Plants, animals, and even inorganic objects are thought to have the same qualities of spirit or souls as human persons. Moreover, the unique characteristics and capabilities of each species, including humans, are the result of historic events that transpired during creation times. In fact, traditional Indian people believe that their own family origins ultimately derived from animal progenitors, hence their membership in totemic clans.

Such a belief ties human and nonhuman persons in the tight embrace of Grandmother Earth, on whose welfare and survival they depend. Injury to Grandmother Earth, because of overharvests, waste, pollution, and other effects of human action, causes harm to the organic whole, which must be repaired. Human persons, those who have the power of conscious actions as well as willful omissions, thereby also have the power to cause offense to Grandmother Earth, when the balance and symmetry in the cycle of life are upset. But as willful creatures, humans also possess the power to cure and restore harmony. This they accomplish through organizing rites of renewal, which include, in part, purification, prayers, gifting, fasting, and feasting. Acknowledgment of the cycle of human life and its natural rhythms—in birth, naming ceremonies, weddings, ghost suppers, purification rituals, funerals, and other religious celebrations—calls for the consumption of the natural food that is believed to restore the balance of Grandmother Earth. In the very eating of such foods, the proper relationship between nonhuman and human persons is achieved.

Here is a simple but profound truth: a balanced relationship with the other species of the earth is necessary for the perpetuation of the natural world and therefore for the survival of all species, including our own. In this philosophy, we see how the access to natural foods that is provided for native people through treaty-based harvesting rights forms a vital link in their belief system. It would also seem apparent that encouraging such a religious philosophy of conservation and sustainability has great benefit for everyone on the planet.

Parting Words

As should be apparent from the preceding chapters, the history that played out between the native people of the upper Great Lakes region and its Euro-American colonizers has been marred by intense conflict and cultural turmoil. In comparison to many other regions of North America, however, the upper Great Lakes region's history has not witnessed the worst examples of all-out warfare, the forced removal of Indian people, or their complete social and political assimilation into the dominant society. Indeed, in this region, native peoples have been able to maintain a small but significant population, a sovereign political presence, and viable cultural institutions.

These not inconsequential blessings are, at least in part, due to the treaty-making process, as well as the wisdom and tenacity of the chiefs who negotiated the treaties and the willingness of modern Indian people and their leadership to fight for their reinstatement in modern times. Considering the power differential between the American state and Indian tribes at the time of the treaties, the results to date are, perhaps, as good as might be hoped for. Of course, many of the gains and stopgaps that Indian parties instituted in the original process of treaty negotiations were subsequently subverted by political intrigue, lack of performance, or simply attrition over time. Certainly the cultural conflicts that occasioned the treaties to begin with did not abate but simply took on new and more insidious forms, hence the poverty and hopelessness of Indian populations during most of the twentieth century. In this perspective, the reinstitution of at least some of the treaty-based benefits by the legal actions of our courts brings also the sense that the labor and sacrifice of previous generations of Indian people can be brought forward to benefit present and future generations. This is, of course, exactly what the chiefs of old hoped to accomplish.

Ultimately, justice under treaty law, such as it is possible to achieve at this late date, seems, in final analysis, to depend not so much on the governments of the tribes, the states, or even the United States but on the will of the public. After all, the prosperity of native peoples ultimately depends on the acceptance by our society of cultural diversity in public affairs, the ability to recontextualize our history with Indians so as to avoid both vilification and romanticism, and, finally, our willingness to protect the natural environment.

A good example of why the protection of the natural world is interlinked with the successful reinstitution of treaty-reserved rights is a right to fish in the Great Lakes. This right, guaranteed by treaty and, therefore, by the full force of federal law, is worthless if there are no fish left to catch. Surely, it would have been inconceivable for the treaty framers, both Indian and non-Indian, to envision our inland seas devoid of fish, yet ecological degradation in modern times creates just such a possibility. In an innovative paper, Singel and Fletcher address this very issue.[5] Treaties, they suggest, are important tools to rally support to fight the introduction of invasive species, the loss of native species, habitat destruction or degradation, water withdraws, and pollution in the upper Great Lakes. Singel and Fletcher reason that treaty rights trump state and private property rights without a takings concern. In addition, they suggest that treaty law that recognizes tribal property interest on public (and sometimes private) land and water and that is enforceable through tribal-federal agreement should be part of a strategy to save the Great Lakes.[6]

In fact, the same argument, though never formally filed as part of a lawsuit, was used to help defeat the Crandon Mine proposal in northern Wisconsin during the first decade of this century. This project involved the opening of a huge copper sulfide mine located near the Forest County Potawatomi Reservation, a short distance upstream from the Mole Lake Ojibwe Reservation's wild rice beds and at the headwaters of the Wolf River, which flows through the Menominee Reservation. During the time that these tribes fought powerful international mining corporations on environmental issues, the underlying premise was that the impacts of the mine would severely limit the ability of the tribes to harvest and consume wild foods. In this way, environmental impact would be extremely detrimental to the core beliefs and identity of these Indian people. Before this proposition could be tested in court, the tribes ended the matter by purchasing the mine site.

Given the close ties between native people and the natural world, cultural and biological welfare are, of necessity, closely intertwined. For this reason, native communities are not only to be trusted in matters of conservation but should be the bellwether in efforts to maintain a healthy natural environment.[7] Protecting the harvest rights of Indians under treaties is a benefit to everyone.

Aside from direct and indirect benefits to Indian people, treaty litigation has also witnessed the edification of ethnohistory as a means of understanding the past, particularly in the context where the courts have, for the sake of fairness, mandated that treaties must be understood as they were by their Indian negotiators. Orthodox historical analysis has fallen short in the attempts to achieve this goal. Indian understanding in the contextural sense demanded by legal precedent is not immediately visible from written records that were not produced by Indians or from the invariably erroneous firsthand accounts left by those who had little knowledge or appreciation of the cultures of the people they described. Indeed, the outcome of these cases shows that the documentary record must be read through the prism of ethnography and comparative ethnology.

Likewise, the litigation described herein has initiated some notable legal innovations. For example, through the combined cases of *United States v. Michigan, Lac Courte Oreilles Band v. Wisconsin,* and *Mille Lacs Band of Chippewa Indians et al. v. State of Minnesota et al.,* the courts have provided practical means for both treaty and nontreaty harvesters to share the same natural resources by means that do not damage wildlife populations or provoke conflict. While incorporating different means to accommodate treaty-based harvest rights, the courts have solved some difficult problems, such as how to interface treaty rights with private property rights and how to regulate and enforce two different but interrelated strategies of wildlife management. In *Keweenaw Bay Indian Community v. Michigan,* the court defined the KBIC reservation as it was described in the 1854 treaty, that is, composed of all the land within its boundaries whether or not it was owned by tribal members. This precedent is now being used in several ongoing legal actions over the boundaries of other reservations. Following the KBIC boundary case, *Keweenaw Bay Indian Community v. Naftaly* successfully challenged the well-established legal precedent that Indian-owned land that was alienable was also taxable, that is, that if an owner could sell his or her land without restriction, it could be taxed by the state. The decision in *Naftaly* challenged this proposition on the grounds that land within treaty-created reservations was being alienated from Indian control by tax sale. This decision will likely have broader application.

Overall, the litigation of treaty rights has brought about a resurgence of interest in Indian affairs, as well as an improved relationship between native and nonnative segments of the region's population. Successful litigation of treaties in our courts has recharged the sovereignty of tribes as political institutions and thereby helped to make them more internally effective governments and more influential in civil affairs in general. The ability of Indian people to participate in treaty harvests on their own terms and to control their own reservations has given native people a renewed sense of well-being and has strengthened their identity. Finally, the confirmation of treaty rights by our courts has given all of our citizens a reason to address the unpleasant details of the history of the United States in respect to Indian affairs.

Notes

CHAPTER 1

1. I later published this work in 1982 in the journal *American Antiquity.* "The Origin and Development of the Inland Shore Fishery and Its Importance in Prehistory of the Upper Great Lakes Region," *American Antiquity* 47, no. 4 (1982): 761–84.

2. Helen H. Tanner,"History v. the Law: Processing Indians in the American Legal System," *Law Review,* University of Detroit Mercy, 67, no. 3 (1999): 693–708.

3. Sherry B Ortner, "Theory in Anthropology since the Sixties," in *Culture/Power/History,* ed. N. B. Dirks, G. Eley, and S. B. Ortner (Princeton, N.J.: Princeton University Press, 1994), 402–3; Emicko Ohnuki-Tierney, *Culture through Time* (Stanford: Stanford University Press, 1990).

4. F. Broudel, *On History* (Chicago: University of Chicago Press, 1980); Maurice Bloch, "The Long Term and the Short Term: The Economics and Political Significance of the Morality of Kinship," in *The Character of Kinship,* ed. Jack Goody (Cambridge: Cambridge University Press, 1974); Emmanuel Le Roy Ladurie, *Times of Feast, Times of Famine: A History of Climate since the Year 1000* (New York: Doubleday, 1971).

5. The Annual Reports of the Commissioner of Indian Affairs are replete with references touting civilized behavior by Indian agents. They are cited throughout this volume as ARCOIA. Reprints of originals from U.S. Government Printing Office (New York: AMS Press).

6. R. G. Thwaites, ed., "A Wisconsin Fur-Trader's Journal, 1803–04, by Michael Curot," in *Wisconsin Historical Collections* (Madison: Wisconsin Historical Society, 1911), 20:396–472.

7. Thomas McKenney, *Sketches of a Tour of the Lakes,* facsimile ed. (Minneapolis: Ross and Haines, 1959), 469–76.

8. Lewis Cass, "Removal of the Indians," *North American Review* 30 (1830): 72.

CHAPTER 2

1. Lewis Cass, "Removal of the Indians," *North American Review* 30 (1830): 83.

2. Ibid., 80.

3. Ibid., 80.

4. *Johnson v. McIntosh,* 21 U.S. 543 (1823); D. H. Getches, C. F. Wilkinson, and R. A. Williams, *Federal Indian Law* (St. Paul: West Publishing, 1998), 41–72.

5. Appropriation for Indian Department, March 3, 1871, 16 Stat. 566.

6. ARCOIA, November 26, 1862.

7. Indian Removal Act, May 28, 1830, 4 Stat. 411–12.

8. Ronald N. Satz, *American Indian Policy in the Jacksonian Era* (Lincoln: University of Nebraska Press, 1975).

9. Robert M. Kvasnicka and Herman J. Viola, *The Commissioners of Indian Affairs, 1824–1977* (Lincoln: University of Nebraska Press, 1979), 57–67.

10. Francis P. Prucha, *The Great Father: The United States Government and the American Indians* (Lincoln: University of Nebraska Press, 1984), 325–27.

11. ARCOIA 1857, Senate of the United States, 35th Cong., 1st sess., Exec. Doc., Report of the Secretary of the Interior, 293; ARCOIA 1856, U.S. House of Representatives, 34th Cong., 3rd sess., 1856–57, Exec. Doc., Report of the Secretary of the Interior, 575.

12. An act making appropriation for the current and contingent expense of the Indian Department, March 3, 1871, 16 Stat. 566.

13. General Allotment Act, February 8, 1891, 26 Stat. 494–96.

14. Christine Bolt, *American Indian Policy and American Reform* (London: Unwin Hyman, 1987), 59–60.

15. Indian Reorganization Act, June 18, 1934, 48 Stat. 984–88.

16. ARCOIA1934.

17. Constitution of the United States, art. 2, sec. 2.

CHAPTER 3

1. Helen H. Tanner, *Atlas of Great Lakes Indian History* (Norman: University of Oklahoma Press, 1987), map 22, 123.

2. Ibid.; Charles E. Cleland, *Rites of Conquest: The History and Culture of Michigan's Native Americans* (Ann Arbor: University of Michigan Press, 1992), map 4.

3. Lewis Henry Morgan, *League of the Ho-de-no-saw-nee or Iroquois* (Rochester: Sage and Brothers, 1851).

4. Marshall Sahlins, *Stone Age Economics* (Hawthorn, N.Y.: Aldine deGruyter, 1972), 30–32.

5. Charles E. Cleland, "From Ethnohistory to Archaeology: Ottawa and Ojibwa Band Territories of the Northern Great Lakes," in *Text Aided Archaeology,* ed. Barbara Little (Boca Raton: CRC Press, 1992), 97–102.

6. Marshall Sahlins, *Tribesmen* (Englewood Cliffs, N.J.: Prentice-Hall, 1968), 82–83.

7. Alanson Skinner, "The Mascoutens or Prairie Potawatomi: Part I, Social Life and Ceremonies," *Bulletin of the Public Museum of the City of Milwaukee* 6 (1924): 17–20.

8. R. David Edmunds, *The Potawatomis—Keepers of the Fire* (Norman: University of Oklahoma Press, 1978), 116–36.

9. The history of the fur trade and the participation of Indians within it are well told in a number of excellent histories. The chronology used here is drawn from the following sources:

Harold A. Innis, *The Fur Trade in Canada* (Toronto: University of Toronto Press, 1956); Arthur J. Ray, *Indians in the Fur Trade: Their Role as Hunters, Trappers, and Middlemen in the Lands Southwest of Hudson Bay, 1660–1870* (Toronto: University of Toronto Press, 1974); Bruce G. Trigger, *Natives and Newcomers* (Montreal: McGill Queens University Press, 1985); Richard White, *The Middle Ground—Indians, Empires, and Republics in the Great Lakes Region, 1650–1815* (Cambridge: Cambridge University Press, 1991); Eric Wolf, *Europe and the People without History* (Berkeley: University of California Press, 1982).

10. Colin G. Galloway, *Crown and Cabinet: British-Indian Relations, 1783–1815* (Norman: University of Oklahoma Press, 1987).

11. Charles E. Cleland, *Rites of Conquest: The History and Culture of Michigan's Native Americans* (Ann Arbor: University of Michigan Press, 1992).

12. Loring B. Priest, *Uncle Sam's Stepchildren: The Reformation of United States Indian Policy, 1865–1887* (New Brunswick: Rutgers University Press, 1942).

13. Frederick E. Hoxie, *A Final Promise: The Campaign to Assimilate the Indians, 1880–1920* (Cambridge: Cambridge University Press, 1989).

14. Christine Bolt, *American Indian Policy and American Reform* (London: Unwin Hyman, 1987), 103–45; Donald L. Fixico, *Termination and Relocation: Federal Indian Policy, 1945–1960* (Albuquerque: University of New Mexico Press, 1986); Francis P. Prucha, *The Great Father: The United States Government and the American Indians* (Lincoln: University of Nebraska Press, 1984), 948–68.

15. Marshall Sahlins, *Tribesmen* (Englewood Cliffs, N.J.: Prentice-Hall, 1968), 14–20.

16. Ibid.

17. William W. Warren, *History of the Ojibway People* (St. Paul: Minnesota Historical Society Press, 1984), 188.

18. Ibid., 165.

19. Emma H. Blair, *The Indian Tribes of the Region of the Great Lakes* (Lincoln: University of Nebraska Press, 1996), pt. 1, 145.

20. Ibid., 145.

21. Wilbur R. Jacobs, *Diplomacy and Indian Gifts* (Stanford: Stanford University Press, 1950), 17.

22. William W. Warren, *History of the Ojibway People* (St. Paul: Minnesota Historical Society Press, 1984), 197–98.

23. Ibid., 197–98.

24. Emma H. Blair, *The Indian Tribes of the Region of the Great Lakes* (Lincoln: University of Nebraska Press, 1996), pt. 2, 21; Vernon Kinetz, *Indians of the Western Great Lakes* (Ann Arbor: University of Michigan Press, 1965), 250.

25. Emma H. Blair, *The Indian Tribes of the Region of the Great Lakes* (Lincoln: University of Nebraska Press, 1996), pt. 1, 91, 182–83, 361.

CHAPTER 4

1. Richard White, *The Middle Ground: Indians, Empires, and Republics in the Great Lakes Region, 1650–1815* (Cambridge: Cambridge University Press, 1991).

2. Treaty of Saginaw, September 29, 1819, 7 Stat. 203; Charles P. Avery, "The Treaty of Saginaw of 1819," in *Indian and Pioneer Directory and Business Advertizer for 1866–68* (Saginaw: Thomas and A. E. Galatin, 1866).

3. Treaty of Fond du Lac, August 26, 1826, 7 Stat. 290.

4. Thomas L. McKenney, *Sketches of a Tour to the Lakes*, facsimile ed. (Minneapolis: Ross and Haines, 1959), 475–76.

5. James McClurken, "We Wish to Be Civilized: Ottawa-American Political Contest on the Michigan Frontier" (PhD diss., Michigan State University, 1988).

6. Mary Black-Rodgers, "Varieties of 'Starving': Semantics and Survival in the Subarctic Fur Trade, 1750–1850," *Ethnohistory* 33, no. 4 (1986): 353–83.

7. Ibid.

8. Ibid.

9. Ibid.

10. Treaty of Washington, March 28, 1836, 7 Stat. 491.

11. NAM M234 R. 422:146–47, January 27, 1836, Noahquageshik et al. to A. Jackson.

12. NAM T494 R. 3:548–68, July 20, 1837, Proceedings of the Council held by Gov. Henry Dodge with the Chiefs and Principal Men of the Chippewa Nation of Indians near Fort Snelling at the Confluence of the St. Peter and Mississippi Rivers, manuscript copy, 21; Treaty of St. Peters, July 29, 1837, 7 Stat 536.

13. Alfred Brunson, *A Western Pioneer, or Incidents of Life and Times of Rev. Alfred Brunson* (Cincinnati: Hitchcock and Walden, 1879), 83.

14. John D. Nichols, *"Statement Made by the Indians": A Bilingual Petition of the Chippewas of Lake Superior, 1864* (London: Centre for Research and Teaching of Canadian Native Languages, University of Western Ontario, 1988).

15. Ibid., 15.

16. Ibid., 17.

17. Johann Kohl, *Kitchi-Gami: Life among the Lake Superior Ojibway* (St. Paul: Minnesota Historical Society Press, 1985), 25; Richard Morse, "The Chippewas of Lake Superior," in *Wisconsin Historical Collections* (Madison: Wisconsin Historical Society, 1857), 3:344.

18. NAM M234 R. 404–90, December 10, 1853, H. Gilbert to G. Manypenny.

19. NAM M234 R. 162:60–70, February 25, 1875, Council with a Delegation of Mille Lacs Chippewa, Office of Indian Affairs, Washington, D.C.

20. Haldimand Papers, Michigan Pioneer and Historical Collections 10:537, November 5, 1781, A. DePeyster to Gen. F. Haldimand.

21. Arthur T. Adams, ed., *The Explorations of Pierre Esprit Radisson* (Minneapolis: Ross and Haines, 1961), 128–29.

22. Treaty of Washington, March 28, 1836, 7 Stat. 491.

23. Treaty of LaPointe, October 4, 1842, 7 Stat. 591.

24. ABCFM Ms. BA10.A512b, May 3, 1843, D. Greene to L. H. Wheeler.

25. Ibid., 1.

26. Ibid., 1–2.

27. Ibid., 2.

28. Ibid., 15.

29. NAM T494 R. 5:321, Documents Relating to the Negotiation of the Treaty of February 22, 1855.

30. Herman J. Viola, *Diplomats in Buckskin: A History of Indian Delegations in Washington City* (Washington, D.C.: Smithsonian Institution Press, 1981).

CHAPTER 5

1. *Worcester v. Georgia*, 31 U.S. (6 pet.) 515 (1832).

2. *Cherokee Nation v. Georgia*, 30 U.S. (5 pet.) 1 (1831).

3. Felix S. Cohen, *Felix S. Cohen's Handbook of Federal Indian Law* (Charlottesville, VA: Michie Bobbs-Merrill, 1982), 207.

4. *Cherokee Nation v. Georgia*, 30 U.S. (5 pet.) 1 (1831).

5. Felix S. Cohen, *Felix S. Cohen's Handbook of Federal Indian Law* (Charlottesville, VA: Michie Bobbs-Merrill, 1982), 207.

6. *Worcester v. Georgia*, 31 U.S. (6 pet.) 515 (1832).

7. Ibid.

8. Felix S. Cohen, *Felix S. Cohen's Handbook of Federal Indian Law* (Charlottesville, VA: Michie Bobbs-Merrill, 1982), 208.

9. Ibid., 468; *Ward v. Race Horse*, 163 U.S. 504 (1896); *Menominee Nation v. United States*, 391 U.S. 404 (1968).

10. *Menominee Nation v. United States*, 391 U.S. 404 (1968).

11. Felix S. Cohen, *Felix S. Cohen's Handbook of Federal Indian Law* (Charlottesville, VA: Michie Bobbs-Merrill, 1982), 223.

12. Ibid., 444.

13. David Getches, C. Wilkinson, and R. Williams, *Cases and Material on Federal Indian Law*, 4th ed., American Case Book (St. Paul: West Group, 1998), 137–38.

14. *United States v. Winans*, 198 U.S. 371 (1905).

15. *Whitefoot v. United States*, 293 F.2d 648, 659 (CT. Cl. 1961); *United States v. Washington*, 520 F.21d 676 (9th Cir. 1975).

16. Felix S. Cohen, *Felix S. Cohen's Handbook of Federal Indian Law* (Charlottesville, VA: Michie Bobbs-Merrill, 1982), 451–52.

17. *Jones v. Meehan*, 175 U.S. 1 (1899). See also *Choctaw Nation v. United States*, 318 U.S. 423 (1943); *Alaska Pacific Fisheries Co. v. United States*, 248 U.S. 78 (1918).

18. *Worcester v. Georgia*, 31 U.S. (6 pet.) 515 (1832).

19. *Winters v. United States*, 207 U.S. 564 (1908).

20. *McClanahan v. Arizona Tax Commission*, 441 U.S. 164 (1973).

21. *Alaska Pacific Fisheries Co. v. United States*, 248 U.S. 78 (1918); *Choctaw Nation v. Oklahoma*, 397 U.S. 620 (1970); *Worcester v. Georgia*, U.S. (6 pet.) 515 (1832).

22. *United States v. Winans*, 198 U.S. 371 (1905).

23. *Choctaw Nation v. United States*, 318 U.S. 423 (1943).

24. *Choctaw Nation v. Oklahoma*, 397 U.S. 620 (1970).

25. Ibid.

26. *Jones v. Meehan*, 175 U.S. 1 (1899).

PART 2

1. *People v. Chosa*, 252 Mich. 154, 162, 233, N.W. 205, 207 (1930).

2. *People v. LaBlanc*, 248 N.W. 2d at 214, n 17 (1976).

3. Treaty of St. Peters, 1837, 7 Stat. 536.

4. *Lac Courte Oreilles Band v. Voigt*, 700 F.2d 341 (7th Cir.), *cert. denied;* 464 U.S. 805 (1983).

5. Ibid.

6. Larry Nesper, *The Walleye War: The Struggle for Ojibwe Spearfishing and Treaty Rights* (Lincoln: University of Nebraska Press, 2002).

7. 10 Stat. 1165.

8. *Minnesota v. Mille Lacs Band*, 526 U.S. 172 (1999).

CHAPTER 6

1. Wiley Sword, *President Washington's Indian War: The Struggle for the Old Northwest, 1790–1795* (Norman: University of Oklahoma Press, 1985).

2. Treaty of Greenville, August 3, 1795, 7 Stat 49.

3. Ibid., art. V

4. Ibid., art. V.

5. Ibid., art. VI.

6. Report of the Committee on Indian Affairs, October 15, 1783, *Journals of the Continental Congress* 25:681–83, 693; Indian Trade and Intercourse Act of 1790, 1 Stat. 137–38; Indian Trade and Intercourse Act of June 30, 1834, 4 Stat.729–35; Ordinance for the Regulation of Indian Affairs, August 7, 1786, *Journals of the Continental Congress* 31:490–93; Indian Trade and Intercourse Act of March 30, 1802, 2 Stat. 39–46.

7. Treaty of Greenville, August 3, 1795, 7 Stat 49, art. VII.

8. Ibid.

9. NAM M1 R. 69:72, October 15, 1834, H. Schoolcraft to S. T. Mason.

10. Treaty with the Ottawa, etc., 1807, 7 Stat. 105; Treaty with the Chippewa, etc., 1808, 7 Stat. 112; Treaty with the Ottawa, etc., 1816, 7 Stat. 146; Treaty with the Wyandot, etc., 1817, 7 Stat. 160.

11. Treaty with the Wyandot, etc., 1815, 7 Stat. 131.

12. Treaty with the Chippewa, 1819, 7 Stat. 203; Treaty with the Ottawa, etc., 1821, 7 Stat. 218; Treaty with the Ottawa, etc., 1807, 7 Stat. 105; Treaty with the Wyandot, etc., 1817, 7 Stat. 160.

13. Treaty with the Chippewa, 1819, 7 Stat. 203; Treaty with the Ottawa, etc., 1821, 7 Stat. 218.

14. Treaty with the Chippewa, 1820, 7 Stat. 206.

15. Treaty with the Chippewa, 1820, 7 Stat. 206, art. 3.

16. Sketch of the Claims to Land on the River St. Marys at Pouwayteeg, July 6, 1823, National Archives of the United States, Cartographic Collection Record Group 77, drawer 137, sheet 10.

17. Charles Cleland, "Cass, Sassaba and Ozhawguscodaywaquay: History, Ethnohistory, and Historical Reality," in *Entering the Nineties: The North American Experience,* ed. Thomas Schirer (Sault Ste Marie: Lake Superior State University Press, 1991).

18. Mentor Williams, ed., *Narrative Journals of Travels through the Northwest Regions of the United States Extending from Detroit through the Great Chain of American Lakes to the Source of the Mississippi River in the Year 1820,* by Henry R. Schoolcraft (East Lansing: Michigan State College Press, 1953), 83.

19. Treaty with the Ottawa and Chippewa, 1820, 7 Stat. 207.

20. Territorial Papers, 11:36–37, June 17, 1820, L. Cass to J. Calhoun.

21. Treaty of Greenville, August 3, 1795, 7 Stat. 49, art. VI.

22. NAM M1 R. 12:565–67, August 7, 1824, G. Boyd to L. Cass.

23. HRSP LCM Papers R. 47:30591, May 27, 1833, to September 30, 1837, Private Journal of Indian Affairs.

24. NAM M1 R. 69:78, October 25, 1834, H. Schoolcraft to E. Herring.

25. NAM M1 R. 27:232–35, September 22, 1830, H. R. Schoolcraft to L. Cass.

26. Treaty of Greenville, August 3, 1795, 7 Stat. 49.

27. NAM M1 R. 71:52, June 13, 1833, Biddle and Drew to H. Schoolcraft.

28. NAM M1 R. 71:59–60, June 20, 1833, G. Johnston to H. Schoolcraft.

29. NAM M1 R. 69:67, September 30, 1834, Notice from H. R. Schoolcraft.

30. NAM M1 R. 69:72, October 15, 1834, H. Schoolcraft to S. T. Mason.

31. Lee R. Dice, *The Biotic Provinces of North America* (Ann Arbor: University of Michigan Press, 1943).

32. J. E. Potzger, "Phytosociology of the Primeval Forest in Central Northern Wisconsin and Upper Michigan and a Brief Post-Glacial History of the Lake Forest Formation." *Ecological Monographs* 16 (1946): 211–50.

33. Charles E. Cleland, "The Prehistoric Animal Ecology and Ethnozoology of the Upper Great Lakes Region" (Anthropological Paper 29, Museum of Anthropology, University of Michigan, Ann Arbor, 1966), fig. 1.

34. Richard Yarnell, "Aboriginal Relationships between Culture and Plant Life in the Great Lakes Region" (Anthropological Paper 23, Museum of Anthropology, University of Michigan, Ann Arbor, 1964), map 4.

35. Nancy N. Cleland, "Natural Vegetation c. 1600," in *Atlas of Great Lakes Indian History,* ed. H. H. Tanner (Norman: University of Oklahoma Press, 1987), map 3, 13–17.

36. V. O. Veatch, "Presettlement Forests in Michigan" (East Lansing: Department of Resource Development, Michigan State University, 1959).

37. Clever Bald, "Some Myths about Michigan," *Michigan History* 28, no. 4 (1944): 600.

38. Ibid., 601.

39. Ibid., 601.

40. Ibid., 601.

41. Dallas L. Jones, "The Survey and Sale of Public Land in Michigan 1815–1862" (master's thesis, Cornell University, 1952), 67–68.

42. Richard Morris, ed., *Encyclopedia of American History* (New York: Harper & Brothers, 1953), 178.

43. Philip Mason, *Schoolcraft's Expedition to Lake Itasca* (East Lansing: Michigan State University Press, 1958), xxiv.

44. Richard G. Bremer, *Indian Agent and Wilderness Scholar: The Life of Henry Rowe Schoolcraft* (Mt. Pleasant: Clarke Historical Library, Central Michigan University, 1987), 180, 187.

45. Rhonda Gilman, "The Last Days of the Upper Mississippian Fur Trade," *Minnesota History* 42, no. 4 (1970): 129.

46. NAM M1 R. 41:51–73, n.d. 1836, K. Pritchette to S. Mason.

47. NAM M1 R. 35:511, November 21, 1833, H. Schoolcraft to G. Porter; HRSP LCM Papers R. 47:30591, February 5, 1834, Private Journal of Indian Affairs; NAM M234 R. 421:722–25, December 5, 1835, A. Hamlin to L. Cass.

48. NAM M234 R. 421:768–73, November 18, 1835, F. Rese to J. Norwell.

49. NAM M1 R. 72:217, August 29, 1835, E. Herring to H. Schoolcraft.

50. HRSP LCM Papers R. 6:2077, March 12, 1834, R. Stuart to H. Schoolcraft.

51. BBC MF 66-2, A-421 LSA XIV/VI, 35:1–4, June 26, 1834, F. Baraga to Leopoldine Foundation.

52. Richard G. Bremer, *Indian Agent and Wilderness Scholar: The Life of Henry Rowe Schoolcraft* (Mt. Pleasant: Clarke Historical Library, Central Michigan University, 1987), 192.

53. Ibid., 173.

54. HRSP-LCM Papers R. 47:30591, February 5, 1834, Private Journal of Indian Affairs.

55. NAM M1 R. 69:140, November 3, 1835, H. Schoolcraft to E. Herring.

56. NAM M1 R. 36:218, September 7, 1835, H. Schoolcraft to S. Mason.

57. NAM M234 R. 421:768–73, November 18, 1835, F. Rese to J. Norwell.

58. NAM M1 R. 69:72, October 15, 1834, H. Schoolcraft to S. T. Mason, Enclosure—August 18, 1834, Petition to President Jackson by Ottawa and Chippewa Chiefs.

59. NAM M1 R. 68, July 6, 1834, F. Audrain to H. Schoolcraft.

60. NAM M1 R. 69:51, August 18, 1834, H. Schoolcraft to S. T. Mason; NAM M1 R. 69:72, October 15, 1834, H. Schoolcraft to S. T. Mason, Enclosure—August 18, 1834, Petition to President Jackson by Ottawa

and Chippewa Chiefs; NAM M1 R. 69:72, October 15, 1834, H. Schoolcraft to S. T. Mason, Enclosure—August 18, 1834, Speech by Pabanmitabi of L'Arbre Croche.

61. NAM M1 R. 69:72, October 15, 1834, H. Schoolcraft to S. T. Mason, Enclosure—August 18, 1834, Speech by Pabanmitabi of L'Arbre Croche.

62. Ibid.

63. NAM M1 R. 67:121, September 23, 1835, H. Schoolcraft to Major Cobbs.

64. NAM M1 R. 69:143, November 7, 1835, H. Schoolcraft to Major Cobbs.

65. NAM M1 R. 72:217, August 29, 1935, E. Herring to H. Schoolcraft.

66. NAM M1 R. 36:218, September 7, 1835, H. Schoolcraft to S. Mason.

67. NAM M1 R. 69:140, November 3, 1835, H. Schoolcraft to E. Herring.

68. NAM M1 R. 72:323–24, November 17, 1835, W. Johnston to H. Schoolcraft.

69. Richard G. Bremer, *Indian Agent and Wilderness Scholar: The Life of Henry Rowe Schoolcraft* (Mount Pleasant: Clarke Historical Library, Central Michigan University, 1987), 159.

70. NAM M234 R. 421:722–25, December 5, 1835, A. Hamlin to L. Cass.

71. HRSP LCM Papers R. 7:2298, December 29, 1835, H. Schoolcraft to J. Schoolcraft.

72. NAM M234 R. 422:146–47, January 27, 1836, Noahquageshik et al. to A. Jackson; NAM M1 R. 69:140, November 3, 1835, H. Schoolcraft to E. Herring.

73. NAM M1 R. 72:348, December 28, 1835, H. Schoolcraft to J. Clitz.

74. HRSP LCM Papers R. 25:13853, February 16, 1836, W. Johnston to H. R. Schoolcraft.

75. HRSP LCM Papers R. 24:13635–636, December 29, 1835, Petition of Northern Chiefs, J. Clitz to H. Schoolcraft.

76. HRSP LCM Papers, R. 25:13930:5–18, March 1836, Journal of Ottawa and Chippewa Treaty of Washington, 1836, 12.

77. Ibid.

78. LLL, vol. 27:466–67, December 25, 1835, L. Lyon to R. Robinson; and December 26, 1835, L. Lyon to J. Drew.

79. NAM M1 R. 72:388, January 25, 1836, C. Trowbridge to H. Schoolcraft.

80. HRSP LCM Papers R. 7:2298, December 29, 1835, H. Schoolcraft to J. Schoolcraft.

81. There is some controversy about the relationship between Waishkey and Waubojeeg, but they were either brothers or father and son.

82. Henry Schoolcraft, *Information Respecting the History, Condition, and Prospects of Indian Tribes in the United States* (Philadelphia: Lippincott, Grambo, 1851), 532–33; HRSP LCM Papers R. 24:13879, March 9, 1836, J. Schoolcraft to H. Schoolcraft.

83. HRSP LCM Papers R. 25:13853–55, February 16, 1836, W. Johnston to H. Schoolcraft.

84. Ibid.

85. AMFCP-CMU Micro Mss. R. 23:49, February 23, 1836, W. Brewster to R. Crooks.

86. AMFCP-CMU Micro Mss. F-49, R. 23:1350, March 5, 1836, M. Holliday to R. Crooks; AMFCP-CMU Micro Mss. F-49, R. 23:1866, March 11, 1836, M. Holliday to R. Crooks; AMFCP-CMU Micro Mss. F-49, R. 23:1398, March 22, 1836, M. Holliday to R. Crooks.

87. *United States v. Michigan*, M-26-73CA, Exhibit 233A, March 17, 1836, M. Holliday to R. Crooks.

88. NAM M1 R. 72:462, March 14, 1836, L. Cass to H. Schoolcraft.

89. HRSP LCM Papers R. 25:13930:5–18, March 1836, Journal of the Ottawa and Chippewa Treaty of Washington, 1836, transcript copy, 4.

90. Ibid., 8.

91. Ibid.

92. AMFCP-CMU Micro Mss. F-49 R. 23:1398, March 22, 1836, M. Holliday to R. Crooks.

93. AMFCP-CMU Micro Mss. F-49 R. 23:1411, March 22, 1836, R. Robinson to R. Crooks.

94. Commission Finding on the Chippewa Indians of the Indian Claims Commission, *Finding of Fact Red Lake Band Including Bay Mills Indian Community and the Ottawa and Chippewa of Michigan v. United States*, Findings of the Indian Claims Commission (New York: Garland, 1974), 199.

95. Treaty with the Ottawa, etc., 1836, 7 Stat. 491.

96. ARCOIA 1837.

97. Richard G. Bremer, *Indian Agent and Wilderness Scholar: The Life of Henry Rowe Schoolcraft* (Mount Pleasant: Clarke Historical Library, Central Michigan University, 1987), 173.

98. Ibid., 219–29.

99. Ibid.

100. Ibid., 389.

101. NAM T494 R. 3:362–64, March 30, 1836, H. Schoolcraft to L. Cass; NAM M21 R. 18, April 1, 1836, L. Cass to President of the United States.

102. *United States v. Michigan*, MI-26-73CA, Exhibit 234A, March 28, 1836, H. Schoolcraft to J. Schoolcraft.

103. Henry Schoolcraft, *Personal Memoirs of a Residence of Thirty Years with the Indian Tribes of the American Frontier* (Philadelphia: Lippincott, Grambo, 1851), 534.

104. Ibid.

105. NAM M1 R. 72:478, May 20, 1836, Resolution of the Senate of the United States.

106. Ibid.

107. HRSP LCM Papers R. 26:14317–19, June 27, 1836, R. Robinson to H. Schoolcraft.

108. NAM M21 R. 19:111–13, July 1, 1836, L. Cass to H. White.

109. NAM M668 R. 8:89–117, Treaty with the Ottawa and Chippewa at Washington, March 28, 1836; and supplemental articles, March 31, 1836.

110. HRSP LCM Papers R. 26:14439, July 18, 1836, H. Schoolcraft to L. Cass.

111. The *Random House College Dictionary* (1984 edition) defines the word *indefinite* as "(1) not definite; without fixed limit (2) not clearly defined or determined."

112. HRSP LCM Papers 1851:180–94, November 13, 1836, Petition of Chiefs to President Andrew Jackson.

113. LLC-WLCL, Box February–August 1837, February 13, 1837, S. Smith to L. Lyons.

114. NAM M234 R. 402:356–60, June 8, 1837, J. McDonell and J. Clark to C. Harris.

115. NAM M1 R. 42:177, February 20, 1837, D. A. Lyman, A. D. Rathbone, and A. H. Finney to H. Schoolcraft.

116. NAM M1 R. 37:171, February 27, 1837, H. Schoolcraft to D. A. Lyman, A. D. Rathbone, and A. H. Finney.

117. Dallas L. Jones, "The Survey and Sale of Public Land in Michigan 1815–1862" (master's thesis, Cornell University, 1952), 116.

118. NAM M1 R37:134, January 13, 1837, H. Schoolcraft to C. A. Harris.

119. NAM M1 R. 42:93, January 27, 1837, C. Harris to H. Schoolcraft.

120. NAM M1 R. 37:168, February 27, 1837, H. Schoolcraft to C. Harris.

121. NAM M21:204, March 23, 1837, C. Harris to J. Poinsett.

122. NAM M234 R. 36:12, April 20, 1837, B. F. Butler to J. Poinsett.

123. Lewis Cass, "Removal of Indians," *North American Review* 30 (1830): 83.

124. Opinion of the U.S. Attorney General No. 3, 126, June 21, 1836.

125. Treaty with the Ottawa, etc., 1836, 7 Stat. 491.

126. HRSP LCM Papers R .26:14439, July 18, 1836, H. Schoolcraft to L. Cass.

127. Lewis Cass, "Removal of Indians," *North American Review* 30 (1830): 83.

128. Ibid., 80.

129. Ibid.

130. Ibid., 83.

131. Treaty of Greenville, 1795, 7 Stat. 49.

132. Treaty with the Ottawa, etc., 1807, 7 Stat. 105.

133. Treaty with the Wyandot, etc., 1817, 7 Stat. 160.

134. Treaty with the Chippewa, 1819, 7 Stat. 203.

135. Treaty with the Ottawa, etc., 1821, 7 Stat. 218.

136. Treaty with the Wyandot, etc., 1817, 7 Stat. 160; Treaty with the Chippewa, 1819, 7 Stat. 203; Treaty with the Ottawa, etc., 1821, 7 Stat. 218.

137. NAM M1 R. 72:348, December 28, 1835, H. Schoolcraft to Capt. J. Clitz.

138. HRSP LCM Papers R. 24:13635–36, December 29, 1835, Petition of Northern Chiefs, J. Clitz to H. Schoolcraft.

139. NAM M1 R.37:168, February 27, 1837, H. Schoolcraft to C. A. Harris.

140. NAM M234 R. 245:518–21, October 2, 1842, P. Dougherty to R. Stuart.

141. HRSP LCM Papers 1851:180–94, November 13, 1836, Petition of Chiefs to President Andrew Jackson.

142. HRSP LCM Papers R. 26:14439, July 18, 1836, H. Schoolcraft to L. Cass; NAM M1 R37:171, February 27, 1837, H. Schoolcraft to D. A. Lyman, A. D. Rathbone, and A. H. Finney.

143. NAM M234 R. 422:632–34, February 27, 1837, H. Schoolcraft to C. Harris.

144. Ibid.

145. NAM M1 R. 37:171, February 27, 1837, H. Schoolcraft to D. A. Lyman, A. D. Rathbone, and A. H. Finney.

146. Henry Schoolcraft, *Personal Memoirs of a Residence of Thirty Years with the Indian Tribes of the American Frontier* (Philadelphia: Lippincott, Grambo, 1851), 534.

147. HRSP LCM Papers R. 26:14439, July 18, 1836, H. Schoolcraft to L. Cass.

148. ARCOIA 1839, 477.

149. ARCOIA 1837, 532.

150. NAM M1 R. 72:323–24, November 17, 1835, W. Johnston to H. Schoolcraft.

151. Marshall Sahlins, *Tribesmen* (Englewood Cliffs, N.J.: Prentice-Hall, 1968), 76.

152. NAM M234 R422:632–34, February 27, 1837, H. Schoolcraft to C. Harris.

153. Henry Schoolcraft, *Personal Memoirs of a Residence of Thirty Years with the Indian Tribes of the American Frontier* (Philadelphia: Lippincott, Grambo, 1851), 534.

154. HRSP LCM Papers R. 25:13930:5–18, March 1836, Journal of Ottawa and Chippewa Treaty of Washington 1836, transcript copy, 7.

155. ARCOIA 1838.

156. Richard G. Bremer, *Indian Agent and Wilderness Scholar: The Life of Henry Rowe Schoolcraft* (Mt. Pleasant: Clarke Historical Library, Central Michigan University, 1987), 195–203, 262–69.

157. ARCOIA 1837, 1839, 1840, 1841, 1842, 1845, 1847, and 1849.

158. ARCOIA 1838.

159. ARCOIA 1839.

160. HRSP LCM Papers R. 30:16149–50, March 1, 1838, H. Schoolcraft to C. Harris.

161. NAM M1 R. 37:491, May 22, 1838, H. Schoolcraft to J. Schoolcraft.

162. *United States v. Michigan,* M-26-73CA, Exhibit 92-A, June 5, 1838, J. Ord to H. Schoolcraft; NAM M234 R. 415:611–14, June 9, 1838, J. Schoolcraft to C. Harris.

163. NAM M234 R. 415:624–26, June 26, 1838, J. Schoolcraft to C. Harris.

164. NAM M1 R. 37:515, June 23, 1838, H. Schoolcraft to I. McCoy.

165. Ibid.

166. NAM M1 R. 37:515, June 23, 1838, H. Schoolcraft to I. McCoy.

167. Indian Removal Act, May 28, 1830, 4 Stat. 411–12.

168. NAM M234 R. 415:636–43, August 29, 1838, J. Schoolcraft to C. Harris.

169. NAM M1 R. 45:47, July 27, 1838, I. McCoy to H. Schoolcraft.

170. NAM M234 R. 402:889, September 29, 1838, H. Schoolcraft to C. Harris.

171. ARCOIA 1840, 340; NAM M234 R. 424:165–70, July 15, 1840, H. Schoolcraft to H. Crawford.

172. Treaty with the Ottawa, etc., 1836, 7 Stat. 941.

173. NAM M21 R. 22:52, July 1, 1837, C. Harris to H. Schoolcraft; NAM M1 R. 37:265, July 25, 1837, H. Schoolcraft to J. Mullett.

174. NAM M1 R. 37:265, July 25, 1837, H. Schoolcraft to J. Mullett.

175. NAM M1 R. 50:495, April 1, 1841, E. Hains to J. Witcomb.

176. NAM M234 R. 424:50–53, May 23, 1840,

Apakosigan et al. to President; PHSC, Box 7, 3:46, September 14, 1840, P. Dougherty to D. Wells.

177. NAM M234 R. 427:570–71, August 10, 1840, J. Whitcomb to H. Crawford; HRSP LCM Papers R. 28:1602–22, January 8, 1838, Contract of J. Brink and H. Schoolcraft.

178. NAM M21 R. 29:359, November 4, 1840, H. Crawford to H. Schoolcraft; NAM M1 R. 49:415, November 4, 1840, H. Crawford to H. Schoolcraft.

179. NAM M1 R49:415, November 4, 1840, H. Crawford to H. Schoolcraft.

180. ARCOIA 1839, 477.

181. Ibid.

182. Treaty with the Chippewa, 1842, 7 Stat. 591.

183. NAM M1 R. 46:383, May 22, 1839, J. Schoolcraft to H. Schoolcraft.

184. James M. McClurken, "We Wish to Be Civilized: Ottawa-American Political Contest on the Michigan Frontier" (PhD diss., Michigan State University, 1988).

185. NAM M234 R. 424:50–53, May 23, 1840, Apakosigan et al. to President.

186. Ibid.

187. James M. McClurken, "We Wish to Be Civilized: Ottawa-American Political Contest on the Michigan Frontier" (PhD diss., Michigan State University, 1988).

188. Richard G. Bremer, *Indian Agent and Wilderness Scholar: The Life of Henry Rowe Schoolcraft* (Mt. Pleasant: Clarke Historical Library, Central Michigan University, 1987), 205–7.

189. NAM M234 R. 598:16, June 4, 1851, P. Dougherty to W. Lowrie.

190. NAM M234 R. 403:603–4, July 15, 1851, W. Richmond to L. Lea; GNS-LCM R. 1, August 11, 1851; NAM M21 R. 44:425, June 4, 1851, L. Lea to E. Murray.

191. NAM M21 R. 44:425, June 4, 1851, L. Lea to E. Murray.

192. NAM M234 R. 598:51–54, July 31, 1851, Kanapima to Chiefs.

193. NAM M234 R. 598:41, September 2, 1851, E. Murray to L. Lea.

194. ARCOIA 1853.

195. Ibid.; NAM M234 R. 404:646–49, May 22, 1855, H. Gilbert to G. Manypenny.

196. NAM M234 R. 598:16, June 4, 1851, P. Dougherty to W. Lowrie.

197. *United States v. Michigan*, MI-26-73CA, Plaintiff Exhibit Pl. 19, July 25, 1855, Proceeding of a Council with the Chippeways and Ottawas of Michigan Held at the City of Detroit by the Hon. George W. Manypeny [*sic*] and Henry C. Gilbert, Commissioners of the United States, 10–14, 57.

198. *United States v. Michigan*, MI-26-73CA, Plaintiff Exhibit Pl. 19, July 25, 1855, Proceeding of a Council with the Chippeways and Ottawas of Michigan Held at the City of Detroit by the Hon. George W. Manypeny [*sic*] and Henry C. Gilbert, Commissioners of the United States, 26.

199. NAM M234 R. 403:701–3, April 7, 1852, Resolution of the Senate of the United States.

200. Treaty with the Ottawa and Chippewa, July 31, 1855, 11 Stat. 621; Treaty with the Chippewa of Saginaw, August 2, 1855, 11 Stat. 633.

201. NAM M234 R. 404:840–41, April 26, 1855, Sec. McClelland to G. Manypenny; NAM M234 R. 404:842–43, May 21, 1855, Sen. McClelland to G. Manypenny.

202. NAM M234 R. 404:368–80, March 6, 1854, H. Gilbert to G. Manypenny; NAM M234 R. 404:844–51, May 21, 1855, G. Manypenny to Sec. McClelland.

203. ARCOIA 1855.

204. Francis P. Prucha, *The Great Father: The United States Government and the American Indians* (Lincoln: University of Nebraska Press, 1984); ARCOIA 1856, U.S. House of Representatives, 34th Cong., 3rd sess., Exec. Doc., 574–75.

205. Robert M. Kvasnicka and Herman J. Viola, eds., *The Commissioners of Indian Affairs, 1824–1977* (Lincoln: University of Nebraska Press, 1979), 57–67.

206. Treaty with the Ottawa and Chippewa, July 31, 1855, 11 Stat. 621; Treaty with the Chippewa of Sault Ste. Marie, August 2, 1855, 11 Stat. 631; Treaty with the Chippewa of Saginaw, etc., August 2, 1855, 11 Stat. 633.

207. ARCOIA 1855, 1.

208. Ibid., 19.

209. ARCOIA 1857, 293.

210. *United States v. Michigan*, MI-26-73CA, Plaintiff Exhibit Pl. 19, July 25, 1855, Proceeding of a Council with the Chippeways and Ottawas of Michigan held at the City of Detroit by the Hon. George W. Manypeny [*sic*] and Henry C. Gilbert, Commissioners of the United States.

211. NAM M234 R. 404:368–80, March 6, 1854, H. Gilbert to G. Manypenny.

212. NAM M234 R. 404:625–27, April 12, 1855, H. Gilbert to G. Manypenny.

213. Charles Kappler, ed., *Indian Affairs: Laws and Treaties* (Washington, D.C.: U.S. Government Printing Office, 1904), 2:846.

214. LRMS 131, April 25, 1855, G. Manypenny to R. McClelland.

215. NAM M234 R. 404:840–41, April 26, 1855, Sec. McClelland to G. Manypenny; NAM M234 R. 404:842–43, May 21, 1855, Sec. McClelland to G. Manypenny; NAM M234 R. 404:844–51, May 21, 1855, G. Manypenny to Sec. McClelland.

216. NAM M234 R. 404:844–51, May 21, 1855, G. Manypenny to Sec. McClelland.

217. NAM M21 R. 51:485–86, June 6, 1855, G. Manypenny to H. Gilbert; NAM M234 R. 404:705–7, June 9, 1855, H. Gilbert to G. Manypenny; NAM M234 R. 404:708–10, June 13, 1855, H. Gilbert to G. Manypenny; NAM M234 R. 404:711–12, June 19, 1855, H. Gilbert to G. Manypenny.

218. Treaty with the Ottawa and Chippewa, July 31, 1855, 11 Stat. 621.

219. *United States v. Michigan*, MI-26-73CA, Plaintiff Exhibit Pl.19, July 25, 1855, Proceeding of a Council with the Chippeways and Ottawas of Michigan held at the City of Detroit by the Hon. George W. Manypeny [*sic*] and Henry C. Gilbert, Commissioners of the United States.

220. *Detroit Daily Free Press*, July 26, 1855.

221. *Detroit Daily Free Press*, July 29, 1855.

222. *United States v. Michigan*, MI-26-73CA, Plaintiff Exhibit Pl. 19, July 25, 1855, Proceeding of a

Council with the Chippeways and Ottawas of Michigan Held at the City of Detroit by the Hon. George W. Manypeny [*sic*] and Henry C. Gilbert, Commissioners of the United States, 27.

223. Ibid., 5.

224. Ibid., 6.

225. For example: Treaty with the Oto and Missouri, 1854, 10 Stat. 1038; Treaty with Omaha, 1854, 10 Stat. 1043; Treaty with the Chippewa of Saginaw, etc., August 2, 1855, 11 Stat. 633; Treaty with the Creeks, etc., 1856, 11 Stat. 699.

226. *United States v. Michigan*, MI-26-73CA, Plaintiff Exhibit Pl. 19, July 25, 1855, Proceeding of a Council with the Chippeways and Ottawas of Michigan held at the City of Detroit by the Hon. George W. Manypeny [*sic*] and Henry C. Gilbert, Commissioners of the United States, 5.

227. NAM M234 R. 404:368–80, March 6, 1854, H. Gilbert to G. Manypenny.

228. *United States v. Michigan*, MI-26-73CA, Plaintiff Exhibit Pl. 19, July 25, 1855, Proceeding of a Council with the Chippeways and Ottawas of Michigan Held at the City of Detroit by the Hon. George W. Manypeny [*sic*] and Henry C. Gilbert, Commissioners of the United States, 5.

229. Treaty with the Chippewa, 1854, 10 Stat. 1109.

230. Treaty with the Chippewa of Sault Ste. Marie, August 2, 1855, 11 Stat. 631.

231. *United States v. Michigan*, MI-26-73CA, Plaintiff Exhibit Pl. 19, July 25, 1855, Proceeding of a Council with the Chippeways and Ottawas of Michigan Held at the City of Detroit by the Hon. George W. Manypeny [*sic*] and Henry C. Gilbert, Commissioners of the United States, 26–27.

232. Ibid., 65.

233. Ibid.

234. Treaty with the Ottawa and Chippewa, July 31, 1855, 11 Stat. 621.

235. *United States v. Michigan*, MI-26-73CA, Plaintiff Exhibit Pl. 19A, August 7, 1855, G. Manypenny and H. Gilbert to C. Mix.

236. NAM M21 R. 52, August 23, 1855, C. Mix to H. Gilbert; NAM M234 R. 404:953–55, October 12, 1855, W. Richmond to G. Manypenny.

237. NAM M234 R. 404:950–52, September 3, 1855, W. Richmond to G. Manypenny.

238. H-211, January 2, 1856, G. Manypenny to R. McClelland; H-211, January 3, 1856, R. McClelland to the President.

239. NAM M234 R. 405:60–63, February 18, 1856, H. Gilbert to Unidentified.

CHAPTER 7

1. *People v. LeBlanc*, 399 Mich. 31, 248 N.W.2d 199 (1976).

2. *Jones v. Meehan*, 175 U.S. 1 (1899); *United States v. Shoshone Tribe*, 304 U.S. 111 (1938); *Starr v. Long Jim*, 227 U.S. 613 (1913); *Choctaw Nation of Indians v. United States*, 318 U.S. 423 (1943); *McClanahan v. Arizona Tax Com'n*, 411 U.S. 164 (1973); *Carpenter v. Shaw*, 280 U.S. 363 (1930); and *Winters v. United States*, 207 U.S. 564 (1908).

3. See Indian Removal Act, May 28, 1830, 4 Stat. 411.

4. *United States v. Michigan*, 471 F. Supp. 192 (W.D. Mich. 1979), *aff'd*, 653 F.2d 277 (6th Cir.), *cert. denied*, 102 S.Ct. 971 (1981).

5. *United States v. Washington*, 384 F. Supp. 312 (1974), *aff'd*, 520 F.2d 676 (9th Cir. 1975), *cert. denied*, 423 U.S. 1086 (1976).

6. Treaty of Medicine Creek, 10 Stat. 1132. During 1854 and 1855, Governor Isaac Stevens of the Washington territory negotiated several treaties with the Indians residing in the Puget Sound area, all of which contained this same language. *See Washington v. Washington State Commercial Passenger Fishing Vessel Ass'n*, 443 U.S. 658 (1979).

CHAPTER 8

1. *United States v. Michigan*, 471 F. Supp. 192, 203 (W.D. Mich. 1979), *aff'd in part and remanded*, 653 F.2d 277 (6th Cir. 1981), *cert. denied*, 454 U.S. 1124 (1981).

2. *United States v. Michigan*, 471 F. Supp. at 278.

3. *United States v. Michigan*, 471 F. Supp. at 279.

4. *United States v. Michigan*, 653 F.2d at 278.

5. See, e.g., *United States v. Michigan*, 12 Indian L. Rptr. 3079 (W.D. Mich. 1985).

CHAPTER 9

A more extended version of this chapter was published in *Fish in the Lakes, Wild Rice, and Game in Abundance: Testimony in Behalf of Mille Lacs Ojibwe Hunting and Fishing Rights*, comp. James M. McClurken (East Lansing: Michigan State University Press, 2000).

1. William W. Warren, *History of the Ojibwa People* (St. Paul: Minnesota Historical Society Press, 1984).

2. Harold Hickerson, *The Chippewa and Their Neighbors* (Prospect Heights, Ill: Waveland Press, 1970), 77.

3. Helen H. Tanner, *Atlas of Great Lakes Indian History* (Norman: University of Oklahoma Press, 1987), map 13.

4. Harold Hickerson, *The Chippewa and Their Neighbors* (Prospect Heights, Ill.: Waveland Press, 1970).

5. Ibid., 70.

6. MCT, Docket 18C, 18S, 18T, Letter Received, Michigan Superintendency, April 16, 1825, J. Barbour to L. Cass.

7. MCT, Docket 18C, 18S, 18T, June 30–August 22, 1825, Journal of Proceedings, Treaty of Prairie du Chien.

8. Treaty of Prairie du Chien, 1825, 7 Stat. 272.

9. NAM M234 R. 757:64–66, July 30, 1830, L. Taliaferro to J. Eaton.

10. MN 008089, Defendant Exhibit, *Mille Lacs v. Minnesota*, February 20, 1837, Z. Taylor to R. Jones.

11. NAM T494 R. 1, Treaty 139, June 30–August 22, 1825, Journal of the Proceedings of the Treaty of Prairie du Chien, 9.

12. Treaty of Prairie du Chien, 1825, 7 Stat. 272.

13. NAM M21 R .3:95–96, May 24, 1826, J. Barbour to L. Cass and T. McKenney.

14. Thomas L. McKenney, *Sketches of a Tour of the Lakes*, facsimile ed. (Minneapolis: Ross and Haines, 1959).

15. NAM T494 R. 1:835–54, August 2, 1826, Journal of the Commissioners.

16. NAM T494 R. 1:835–54, August 2, 1826, Journal of the Commissioners.

17. Charles E. Cleland, "Economic and Adaptive Change among the Lake Superior Chippewa of the Nineteenth Century," in *Approaches to Cultural Contact: Ethnohistorical and Archaeological Perspectives on Change*, ed. J. Rodger and S. Wilson (New York: Plenum Press, 1993).

18. Treaty of Fond du Lac, August 26, 1826, 7 Stat. 290.

19. NAM M234 R. 757:64–66, July 30, 1830, L. Taliaferro to J. Eaton.

20. MCT, Docket 18C, November 11, 1835, J. Bean to W. Clark; MCT, Docket 18C, September 2, 1835, L. Taliaferro to W. Clark.

21. Taliaferro Papers R. 3:369, 6, May 22, 1832; MCT, Docket 18C, Exhibit 41, March 4, 1834, H. Schoolcraft to L. Warren.

22. MCT, Docket 18C, Exhibit 41, March 4, 1834, H. Schoolcraft to L. Warren; 4 Stat.729–35, Trade and Intercourse Act of 1834.

23. MCT, Docket 18C, Exhibit 56, September 30, 1834, H. Schoolcraft—circular.

24. NAM M21 R. 18:76–77, March 7, 1836, L. Cass to M. Van Buren; NAM M21 R. 21:200, May 13, 1837, C. Harris to H. Dodge and W. R. Smith.

25. NAM T494 R. 3, March 25, 1837, J. Poinsett to H. Dodge.

26. NAM M21 R. 21:200, May 13, 1837, C. Harris to H. Dodge and W. R. Smith.

27. NAM M21 R. 22:364–65, October 2, 1837, C. A. Harris to H. R. Schoolcraft.

28. Indian Removal Act, May 28, 1830, 4 Stat. 411–12.

29. MN 006415 M951 R. 4:109, Defendant Exhibit, *Mille Lacs v. Minnesota,* July 26, 1842, J. Doty to H. Crawford; NAM T494 R. 3:548–68, July 20, 1837, Proceedings of the Council Held by Gov. Henry Dodge with the Chiefs and Principal Men of the Chippewa Nation of Indians near Ft. Snelling at the Confluence of the St. Peters and Mississippi Rivers, manuscript copy, 25–26.

30. NAM T494 R. 3:540–45, August 7, 1837, H. Dodge to C. Harris.

31. NAM M21 R. 18:76–77, March 7, 1836, L. Cass to M. Van Buren.

32. MN 007529 M951 R. 4:067, Defendant Exhibit, *Mille Lacs v. Minnesota,* October 18, 1839, H. Dodge to H. Crawford.

33. NAM T494 R. 3:548–68, July 20, 1837, Proceedings of the Council Held by Gov. Henry Dodge with the Chiefs and Principal Men of the Chippewa Nation of the Indians near Ft. Snelling at the Confluence of the St. Peter and Mississippi Rivers, manuscript copy, 5.

34. Ibid., 13.

35. Ibid., 2, 18.

36. Treaty of Fond du Lac, August 26, 1826, 7 Stat. 290.

37. NAM T494 R. 3:548–68, July 20, 1837, Proceedings of the Council Held by Gov. Henry Dodge with the Chiefs and Principal Men of the Chippewa Nation of the Indians near Ft. Snelling at the Confluence of the St. Peter and Mississippi Rivers, manuscript copy, 31.

38. ABCFM Ms. BA10.A512b, MHS MSS 141, No. 192, October 4, 1837, F. Ayer to D. Green; NAM M234 R. 387:100–105, September 30, 1837, F. Ayer to M. Van Buren, Speeches of Nodin et al.

39. NAM T494 R. 3:548–68, July 20, 1837, Proceedings of the Council Held by Gov. Henry Dodge with the Chiefs and Principal Men of the Chippewa Nation of the Indians near Ft. Snelling at the Confluence of the St. Peter and Mississippi Rivers, manuscript copy, 29.

40. Ibid., 21.

41. Ibid., 25–26.

42. Ibid., 29.

43. Ibid., 27.

44. 7 Stat 536, Treaty of St. Peters.

45. Marshall Sahlins, *Tribesmen* (Englewood Cliffs, N.J.: Prentice-Hall, 1968).

46. ABCFM Ms. BA10.A512b, August 17, 1837, W. Boutwell to D. Greene.

47. NAM T494 R. 3: 548–68, July 20, 1837, Proceedings of the Council Held by Gov. Henry Dodge with the Chiefs and Principal Men of the Chippewa Nation of the Indians near Ft. Snelling at the Confluence of the St. Peter and Mississippi Rivers, manuscript copy, 23.

48. NAM T494 R. 3:548–68, July 20, 1837, Proceedings of the Council Held by Gov. Henry Dodge with the Chiefs and Principal Men of the Chippewa Nation of the Indians near Ft. Snelling at the Confluence of the St. Peter and Mississippi Rivers, manuscript copy, 24.

49. Ibid., 19.

50. Ibid., 7.

51. Ibid., 20–21.

52. Ibid., 21.

53. NAM M234 R. 948:251, May 18, 1838, H. Dodge to C. Harris.

54. NAM M234 R. 948:226, July 6, 1838, H. Dodge to C. Harris.

55. NAM M234 R. 948, October 1, 1838, H. Dodge to C. Harris.

56. NAM M234 R. 948, February 13, 1839, D. Bushnell to H. Dodge.

57. ARCOIA, December 1, 1837, C. Harris to J. Poinsett; MN 007620, February 15, 1838, Hole in the Day to Major Pympton; ABCFM Ms. BA10.A512b, October 8, 1838, F. Ayer to D. Greene; ARCOIA 1838.

58. ABCFM Ms. BA10.A512b, MHS MSS Nos. 74, 75, and 76, May 1833, S. Hall to W. T. Boutwell.

59. ABCFM Ms. BA10.A512b, MHS MSS 141, No. 194, October 8, 1838, F. Ayer to D. Green.

60. MN 007497, July 25, 1839, T. H. Crawford to L. Lyons.

61. MN 007529, M951 R. 4:067, October 18, 1839, H. Dodge to T. H. Crawford.

62. MCT, Docket 18C, Plantiff Exhibit 72, July 27, 1842, R. Stuart to J. C. Spenser.

63. NAM M1 R. 53, August 1, 1842, H. Crawford to R. Stuart.

64. Ibid.

65. ABCFM Ms. BA10.A512b, May 3, 1843, L. H. Wheeler to D. Greene, Journal of the 1842 Treaty Negotiated at La Pointe.

66. NAM M234 R. 389:61–67, September 29, 1842, Speech at La Pointe by Robert Stuart, Enclosed with NAM M234 R. 389, March 29, 1844.

67. ABCFM Ms. BA10.A512b, May 3, 1843, L. H. Wheeler to D. Greene, Journal of the 1842 Treaty Negotiated at La Pointe.

68. NAM M234 R. 389:61–67, September 29, 1842, Speech at La Pointe by Robert Stuart, Enclosed with NAM M234 R. 389, March 29, 1844; ABCFM Ms. BA10.A512b, May 3, 1843, L. H. Wheeler to D. Greene, Journal of the 1842 Treaty Negotiated at La Pointe.

69. ARCOIA, November 16, 1842; NAM M234 R. 425:146–54, October 28, 1842, R. Stuart to H. Crawford.

70. NAM M234 R. 389:61–67, September 29, 1842, Speech at La Pointe by Robert Stuart, Enclosed with NAM M234 R. 389, March 29, 1844.

71. Ibid.

72. Treaty of La Pointe, 7 Stat. 591.

73. ABCFM Ms. BA10.A512b, May 3, 1843, L. H. Wheeler to D. Greene, Journal of the 1842 Treaty Negotiated at La Pointe; MCT, Docket 18C, Exhibit 72, July 27, 1842, Robert Stuart to J. Spencer.

74. ABCFM Ms. BA10.A512b, May 3, 1843, L. H. Wheeler to D. Green, Journal of the 1842 Treaty Negotiated at La Pointe.

75. Treaty of La Pointe, 7 Stat. 591.

76. NAM M1 R. 53, August 1, 1842, H. Crawford to R. Stuart.

77. ABCFM Ms. BA10.A512b, May 3, 1843, L. Wheeler to D. Greene, Journal of 1842 Treaty.

78. NAM M234 R. 388:390–407, January 8, 1843, A. Brunson to H. Doty, Enclosure by Marten.

79. ABCFM Ms. BA10.A512b, December 8, 1842, R. Stuart to D. Greene; Senate Document 403 (29-1) 477, June 24, 1846, Message from the President of the United States—Letter by R. Stuart.

80. *Lac Courte Oreilles Band v. Wisconsin*, Exhibit 1, November 6, 1851, Chief Buffalo et al to L. Lea.

81. NAM M234 R. 390 M784, March 26, 1850, J. Livermore to A. Ramsey.

82. Hon. James Doyle, Opinion and Order, *United States v. Bouchard*, 464 F. Supp. 1316 (1978) at 1327.

83. MN 06427, Defendant Exhibit, *Mille Lacs v. Minnesota*, June 30, 1850, A Chippewa Address by Chief Hole in the Day; MN 003366, January 21, 1851, S. Treat to L. Lea; NAM M234 R. 767:131–41, January 28, 1851, W. Warren to A. Ramsey (enclosure); ABCFM Ms. BA10.A512b, Box 5, August 27, 1851, S. Hall to S. Treat.

84. MN 007661, March 18, 1852, J. Watrous to A. Ramsey; MN 0068-0074, Defendant Exhibit, *Mille Lacs v. Minnesota*, May 10, 1850, J. Livermore to Braun.

85. NAM M234 R. 404:183–90, December 10, 1853, H. Gilbert to G. Manypenny.

86. John D. Nichols, "*Statement Made by the Indians*": *A Bilingual Petition of the Chippewas of Lake Superior, 1864* (London: Centre for Research and Teaching of Canadian Native Languages, University of Western Ontario, 1988).

87. NAM M234 R. 394:485–88, September 12, 1869, Speech by Blackbird in Council at Bad River.

88. ABCFM Ms. BA10.A512b, MSS 141, No. 223, 12, May 3, 1843, L. H. Wheeler to D. Greene, Journal of the 1842 Treaty Negotiated at La Pointe.

89. ABCFM Ms. BA10.A512b, October 8, 1838, F. Ayer to D. Greene.

90. Treaty of La Pointe, 1842, 7 Stat. 591, art. 3.

91. Senate Document 403 (29-1) 477, June 24, 1846, Message from the President of the United States—Letter by R. Stuart.

92. NAM M234 R. 949, November 28, 1846, H. Dodge to J. Hays; NAM M234 R. 949, November 30, 1846, H. Dodge to J. Hays; NAM M234 R. 949, March 26, 1847, H. Dodge to W. Medill.

93. NAM M234 R. 46, June 4, 1847, W. Medill to I. Verplank and C. Mix.

94. Ibid.

95. Ibid.

96. Ibid.

97. Ibid.

98. Ibid.

99. Ibid.

100. Ibid.

101. Treaty of Fond du Lac, August 2, 1847, 9 Stat. 904; Treaty of Leech Lake, August 21, 1847, 9 Stat. 908.

102. NAM M236 R. 46, August 2, 1847, I. Verplank to W. Medill.

103. NAM M234 R. 389, August 21, 1847, Nagonabe et al. to President; NAM M234 R. 389, September 3, 1847, Nodin et al. to President; NAM M234 R. 390, November 14, 1848, Nagonabe to J. Livermore; NAM M234 R. 390:79–80, September 13, 1848, J. Livermore to W. Medill.

104. ABCFM Ms. BA10.A512b, Box 5, October 9, 1848, S. Hall to S. Treat.

105. NAM M234 R.390, February 5, 1849, Chippewa to President; NAM M234 R. 390, n.d. 1849, Chiefs to President.

106. NAM M234 R. 390, December 5, 1848, J. Livermore to T. Ewing; NAM M234 R. 390, n.d. 1849, Chiefs to President; NAM M234 R. 390, December 5, 1848, J. Livermore to T. Ewing.

107. ABCFM Ms. BA10.A512b, Box 5, February 10, 1849, S. Hall to S. Treat.

108. NAM M234 R. 390, November 20, 1848, Shingoop et al. to J. Hays.

109. *Congressional Globe* 30 (December 14, 1854): 53–54.

110. Rhonda Gilman, "The Last Days of the Upper Mississippi Fur Trade," *Minnesota History* 42, no. 4 (Winter 1970): 125.

111. Ibid.

112. Ibid., 129.

113. Ibid., 133.

114. Ibid., 134.

115. Ibid., 135.

116. AR M203 R. 4, December 1, 1849, H. Rice to A. Ramsey; AR M203 R. 4, March 14, 1850, H. Rice to A. Ramsey.

117. Robert Trennert, "Orlando Brown 1849–

1850," in *The Commissioners of Indian Affairs, 1824–1977*, ed. Robert M. Kvasnicka and Herman J. Viola (Lincoln: University of Nebraska Press, 1979), 41–46.

118. AR M203 R. 4, December 1, 1849, H. Rice to A. Ramsey.

119. NAM M842 R. 1:10–12, June 27, 1849, W. Medill to A. Ramsey.

120. AR M204 R. 2:10, September 4, 1849, Message of the Governor.

121. NAM M234 R. 428:124–28, November 7, 1849, Joint Resolution of the Minnesota Territorial Assembly.

122. Ibid.

123. NAM M234 R. 43:23, February 6, 1850, O. Brown to A. Ramsey.

124. NAM M234 R. 390, November 14, 1848, Nagonabe to J. Livermore.

125. "Indians to Be Removed from Lake Superior," *Lake Superior Journal*, May 22, 1850.

126. MCT DEF, Exhibit 60, July 30, 1850, J. R. Giddings to President; NAM M234 R. 6, June 3, 1851, L. Lea to Acting Secretary of Interior; NAM M234 R. 168, December 26, 1851, A. Ramsey to L. Lea; MCT, Plaintiff Exhibit 400, May 24, 1850, C. Mendenhall to Z. Taylor.

127. ARCOIA 1847, J. Hays to H. Dodge, September 15, 1847.

128. NAM M234 R. 390, March 26, 1850, J. Livermore to A. Ramsey.

129. *Lac Courte Oreilles Band v. Voigt*, Exhibit 1, November 6, 1851, Chief Buffalo et al. to L. Lea.

130. Ibid.; NAM M234 R. 767:61–72, January 6, 1851, C. Mendenhall to L. Lea; NAM M234 R. 388:390–407, January 6, 1843, A. Brunson to J. Doty, Enclosure by Wabijeshi (Martin).

131. *Lac Courte Oreilles Band v. Voigt*, Exhibit 1, November 6, 1851, Chief Buffalo et al. to L. Lea.

132. NAM M234 R.390, March 26, 1850, O. Brown to A. Ramsey; NAM M21 R. 2:1171, July 2, 1850, A. Ramsey to J. Watrous; ABCFM Ms. BA10.A512b, Box 5, December 30, 1850, S. Hall to S. Treat.

133. James A. Clifton, "Wisconsin Death March: Explaining the Extremes in Old NorthWest Indian Removal," *Transactions of the Wisconsin Academy of Science, Arts, and Letters* 75 (1987): 1–39.

134. MN 003394, Defendant Exhibit, *Mille Lacs v. Minnesota*, August 29, 1851, T. Abraham to L. Lea; NAM M21 R. 45, August 25, 1851, L. Lea to J. Watrous.

135. Francis P. Prucha, *The Great Father: The United States Government and the American Indians*, abridged ed. (Lincoln: University of Nebraska Press, 1986), 112–15.

136. Harold Hickerson, *Chippewa Indians III: Ethnohistory of Chippewa of Lake Superior* (New York: Garland Publishing, 1974), 243.

137. AR M203 R. 4, December 1, 1849, H. Rice to A. Ramsey.

138. NAM M234 R. 150:222, February 16, 1855, W. Gorman to G. Manypenny.

139. MN 008243, Defendant Exhibit, *Mille Lacs v. Minnesota*, June 4, 1855, W. Gorman to Little Hill.

140. James M. McClurken, "The 1837 Treaty of St. Peters Preserving the Rights of the Mille Lacs Ojibwa to Hunt, Fish, and Gather: The Effects of Treaties and Agreements since 1855," in *Fish in the Lakes, Wild Rice, and Game in Abundance: Testimony in Behalf of Mille Lacs Ojibwe Hunting and Fishing Rights*, comp. James M. McClurken (East Lansing: Michigan State University Press, 2000); Bruce White, "Stereotypes of Minnesota's Native People," *Minnesota History* (Fall 1992): 99–110; Frances Densmore, "Narrative of Nodiens," in *Chippewa Customs* (Minneapolis: Ross and Haines, 1970), 119–23.

CHAPTER 10

1. 7 Stat. 536.

2. 7 Stat. 591.

3. Treaty of September 30, 1854, 10 Stat. 1109.

4. *United States v. Ben Ruby*, Case No. 72-C-366.

5. *United States v. Bouchard*, 464 F. Supp. 1316 (W.D. Wis. 1978).

6. Ibid.

7. *United States v. Bouchard*, supra, at 1322.

8. *State of Wisconsin v. Baker*, 524 F. Supp. 726 (W.D. Wis. 1981).

9. Ibid.

10. *Lac Courte Oreilles Band v. Voigt*, 700 F.2d 341 (7th Cir. 1983). This is *Lac Courte Oreilles I*.

11. *Menominee Tribe v. U.S.*, 391 U.S. 404 (1968); *Mattz v. Arnett*, 412 U.S. 481 (1973).

12. *Lac Courte Oreilles Band v. Wisconsin*, 760 F.2d 177 (7th Cir. 1985). This is *Lac Courte Oreilles II*.

13. *Lac Courte Oreilles Band v. Wisconsin*, 653 F. Supp. 1420 (W.D. Wis. 1987). This is *Lac Courte Oreilles III*.

14. *Lac Courte Oreilles Band v. Wisconsin*, 116 F.R.D. 608 (W.D. Wis. 1987) Muskies, Inc. denied intervention.

15. *Washington v. Washington State Commercial Passenger Fishing Vessel Ass'n*, 443 U.S. 658, 682 (1979).

16. *Lac Courte Oreilles Band v. Wisconsin*, 668 F. Supp. 1233 (W.D. Wis. 1987). This is *Lac Courte Oreilles IV*.

17. *Lac Courte Oreilles Band v. Wisconsin*, 686 F. Supp. 226 (W.D. Wis. 1988). This is *Lac Courte Oreilles V*.

18. *Lac Courte Oreilles Band v. Wisconsin*, 707 F. Supp. 1034 (W.D. Wis. 1989). This is *Lac Courte Oreilles VI*.

19. *Lac Courte Oreilles Band v. Wisconsin*, 740 F. Supp. 1400 (W.D. Wis. 1990). This is *Lac Courte Oreilles VII*.

20. *Lac Courte Oreilles Band v. Wisconsin*, 758 F. Supp. 1262 (W.D. Wis. 1990). This is *Lac Courte Oreilles IX*.

21. *Lac Courte Oreilles Band v. Wisconsin*, 749 F. Supp. 913 (W.D. Wis. 1990). This is *Lac Courte Oreilles VIII*.

22. *Blatchford v. Native Village of Noatak*, 501 U.S. 775 (1991).

23. *Lac Courte Oreilles Band v. Wisconsin*, 775 F. Supp. 321 (W.D. Wis. 1991). This is *Lac Courte Oreilles X*.

CHAPTER 11

1. 7 Stat. 536.
2. 7 Stat. 591.
3. 700 F.2d 341 (7th Cir.), *cert denied,* 464 U.S. 805 (1983).
4. 471 F. Supp. 192 (W.D. Mich. 1979), *aff'd,* 653 F.2d 277 (6th Cir.), *cert. denied,* 454 U.S. 1124 (1981).
5. *People v. LeBlanc,* 399 Mich. 31, 248 N.W.2d 199 (1976); *State v. Gurnoe,* 53 Wis. 2d 390, 192 N.W.2d 892 (1972).
6. *United States v. Bouchard,* 464 F. Supp. 1316 (W.D. Wis. 1978).
7. 10 Stat. 1109.
8. 10 Stat. 1165.
9. *Mille Lacs Band v. Minnesota,* 853 F. Supp. 1118 (D. Minn. 1993).
10. *Mille Lacs Band v. Minnesota,* 861 F. Supp. 784 (D. Minn. 1994).
11. 11 Stat. 285.
12. *Mille Lacs Band v. Minnesota,* 952 F. Supp. 1382 (D. Minn. 1997).
13. *Mille Lacs Band v. Minnesota,* 124 F.3d 904 (8th Cir. 1997).
14. *Minnesota v. Mille Lacs Band,* 526 U.S. 172 (1999).

CHAPTER 12

1. Walter J. Hoffman, *The Menominee Indians,* Fourteenth Annual Report of the Bureau of American Ethnology, Smithsonian Institution (Washington, D.C.: U.S. Government Printing Office, 1896), 40; Leonard Bloomfield, *Menomini Texts,* Publication of the American Ethnological Society, vol. 12 (New York: G. E. Stechert, 1928), 71–73.
2. Walter J. Hoffman, *The Menominee Indians,* Fourteenth Annual Report of the Bureau of American Ethnology, Smithsonian Institution (Washington, D.C.: U.S. Government Printing Office, 1896), 41.
3. Ibid.
4. I. Goddard, "Central Algonquian Languages," in *Handbook of North American Indians,* ed. B. Trigger, vol. 15, *Northeast* (Washington, D.C.: Smithsonian Institution, 1978), 584.
5. Carol I. Mason, *Introduction to Wisconsin Indians* (Salem, Wis.: Sheffield Publishing, 1988), 66–69; R. G. Thwaites, ed., *The Jesuit Relations and Allied Documents,* vol. 18, *Hurons and Quebec: 1640* (New York: Pageant, 1959), 231.
6. Charles E. Cleland, *Rites of Conquest: The History and Culture of Michigan's Native Americans* (Ann Arbor: University of Michigan Press, 1992); Carol I. Mason, *Introduction to Wisconsin Indians* (Salem, Wis.: Sheffield Publishing, 1988), 69–73; Ronald Mason, "Rock Island, Historical Indian Archaeology in the Northern Lake Michigan Basin," *Midcontinental Journal of Archaeology,* Special Paper 6 (Kent, Ohio: Kent State University Press, 1986).
7. Felix Keesing, *The Menomini Indians of Wisconsin* (Madison: University of Wisconsin Press, 1987), 58–62.
8. Ibid.
9. P. Ourada, *The Menominee Indians* (Norman: University of Oklahoma Press, 1979), 17–19.
10. Ibid., 29–39.
11. Ibid., 40.
12. Ibid., 36.
13. Jeanne Kay, "Wisconsin Indian Hunting Patterns, 1634–1836," *Annals of the Association of American Geographers* 69, no. 3 (1979): 402–18.
14. D. Beck, "The Importance of Sturgeon in Menominee History as Viewed through Documentary Sources," manuscript on file with the Treaty Protection Office of the Menominee Tribe of Wisconsin, Keshena (n.d.).
15. Jeanne Kay, "Wisconsin Indian Hunting Patterns, 1634–1836," *Annals of the Association of American Geographers* 69, no. 3 (1979): 414–16.
16. Jeanne Kay, "The Fur Trade and Native American Population Growth," *Ethnohistory* 31, no. 4 (1984): 281.
17. Jeanne Kay, "Wisconsin Indian Hunting Patterns, 1634–1836," *Annals of the Association of American Geographers* 69, no. 3 (1979): 402–18.
18. Felix Keesing, *The Menominee Indians of Wisconsin* (Madison: University of Wisconsin Press, 1987), 39–40.
19. Walter J. Hoffman, *The Menominee Indians,* Fourteenth Annual Report of the Bureau of American Ethnology, Smithsonian Institution (Washington, D.C.: U.S. Government Printing Office, 1896), 44–60.
20. Ibid.
21. NAM M668 R. 41:312–17, March 30, 1817, Treaty with the Menominee at St. Louis.
22. *Journals of the Continental Congress* 32:340–41.
23. Treaty of Prairie du Chien, 1825, 7 Stat. 272.
24. Ibid.
25. Treaty of Fond du Lac, August 26, 1826, 7 Stat. 290.
26. Treaty of Butte des Morts, 1827, 7 Stat. 303.
27. Jedidiah Morse, *Report to the Secretary of War on Indian Affairs* (New Haven: S. Converse, 1822).
28. Ibid., table 1, 362.
29. Ibid., 15, 49.
30. Ibid., 47.
31. Ibid., 47–48.
32. Ibid., 52.
33. Ibid., 51–52.
34. NAM M234 R. 315:3–7, September 1, 1824, H. Brevoort to T. McKenney.
35. Ibid.
36. A. Grignon, "Seventy-two Years' Recollections in Wisconsin," in *Wisconsin Historical Collections* (Madison: Wisconsin Historical Society, 1857), 3:226–30.
37. Ibid.; Walter J. Hoffman, *The Menominee Indians,* Fourteenth Annual Report of the Bureau of American Ethnology, Smithsonian Institution (Washington, D.C.: U.S. Government Printing Office, 1896), 44–60.
38. J. Peterson, "Prelude to Red River: A Social Portrait of the Great Lakes Metis," *Ethnohistory* 25, no. 1 (1978): 41–69.
39. Jedidiah Morse, *Report to the Secretary of War*

on Indian Affairs (New Haven: S. Converse, 1822), 56, app.

40. A. Grignon, "Seventy-two Years' Recollections in Wisconsin," in *Wisconsin Historical Collections* (Madison: Wisconsin Historical Society, 1857), 3:226–30.

41. Ibid.

42. Ibid.

43. Jedidiah Morse, *Report to the Secretary of War on Indian Affairs* (New Haven: S. Converse, 1822), 50, app.

44. Ebenezer Childs, "Recollections of Wisconsin since 1820," in *Wisconsin Historical Collections* (Madison: Wisconsin Historical Society, 1859), 4:61–62.

45. Alice Smith, *The History of Wisconsin* (Madison: State Historical Society of Wisconsin, 1973), 1:163.

46. Jedidiah Morse, *Report to the Secretary of War on Indian Affairs* (New Haven: S. Converse, 1822), 46.

47. A. G. Ellis, "Advent of the New York Indians into Wisconsin," in *Wisconsin Historical Collections* (Madison: Wisconsin Historical Society, 1856), 2:415.

48. Jedidiah Morse, *Report to the Secretary of War on Indian Affairs* (New Haven: S. Converse, 1822), 26.

49. Ibid., 55, app.

50. Ibid., 15.

51. GWL-CHS, Box 6, Folder 2, Mss. 2359, partial document.

52. NAM T494 R. 2, August 6, 1827, Journal of the Treaty of Butte des Morts, 19.

53. A. G. Ellis, "Advent of the New York Indians into Wisconsin," in *Wisconsin Historical Collections* (Madison: Wisconsin Historical Society, 1856), 2:428.

54. Ibid., 429–30.

55. NAM T494 R. 2, August 4, 1831, S. Stambaugh to Secretary of War, 12.

56. 2 Stat.139–46.

57. NAM T494 R. 2, August 4, 1831, S. Stambaugh to Secretary of War, 17.

58. Treaty of Fond du Lac, August 26, 1826, 7 Stat. 290.

59. Treaty of Butte des Morts, 1827, 7 Stat. 303.

60. Ibid.

61. NAM T494 R. 2, August 6, 1827, Journal of the Treaty of Butte des Morts, 19.

62. Ibid., 19.

63. Treaty of Butte des Morts, 1827, 7 Stat. 303.

64. A. G. Ellis, "Advent of the New York Indians into Wisconsin," in *Wisconsin Historical Collections* (Madison: Wisconsin Historical Society, 1856), 2:431–32.

65. Treaty of Butte des Morts, 1827, 7 Stat. 303.

66. NAM M234 R. 315:207–17, June 9, 1830, J. Eaton to E. Root, J. McCall, etc.

67. NAM M21 R. 1:377, February 25, 1825, T. McKenney to T. Dean; NAM M21 R. 1:393, March 8, 1825, T. McKenney to H. Brevoot.

68. NAM T494 R. 2, August 6, 1827, Journal of the Treaty of Butte des Morts, 4.

69. Ibid., 5–6.

70. NAM M21 R. 4:253, January 15, 1828, T. McKenney to T. Ogden.

71. NAM M21 R. 6:209, December 28, 1829, T. McKenney to T. Ogden.

72. NAM M21 R. 6:254, February 6, 1830, T. McKenney to J. Eaton.

73. NAM M21 R. 6:424, May 18, 1830, T. McKenney to J. Eaton.

74. NAM M21 R. 6:463–67, June 9, 1830, J. Eaton to E. Root, J. McCall, and J. Mason, 2–4.

75. A. G. Ellis, "Advent of the New York Indians into Wisconsin," in *Wisconsin Historical Collections* (Madison: Wisconsin Historical Society, 1856), 2:432.

76. NAM M234 R. 315:147–48, 188–89, October 30, 1830, W. Hunt to J. Eaton.

77. NAM M234 R. 315:289–300, September 5, 1830, S. Stambaugh's account of his talk with the Menominee.

78. Ibid.

79. Ibid.

80. Ibid.

81. Ibid.

82. A. G. Ellis, "Advent of the New York Indians into Wisconsin," in *Wisconsin Historical Collections* (Madison: Wisconsin Historical Society, 1856), 2:433.

83. Treaty with the Menominee, 1831, 7 Stat. 342.

84. Ibid.

85. A. G. Ellis, "Advent of the New York Indians into Wisconsin," in *Wisconsin Historical Collections* (Madison: Wisconsin Historical Society, 1856), 2:434.

86. NAM T494 R. 2, August 4, 1831, S. Stambaugh to Secretary of War, 44.

87. Ibid., 32 and app. B, 6–7.

88. Treaty with the Menominee, 1831, 7 Stat. 342.

89. Ibid.

90. Treaty with the Menominee, 1831, 7 Stat. 342. See also NAM T494 R. 2, September 11, 1832, Treaty Journal, 10; NAM M234 R. 315:526–40, August 16, 1831, S. Stambaugh to Secretary of War, 7.

91. Treaty with the Menominee, 1831, 7 Stat. 342.

92. Ibid.

93. Ibid.

94. NAM M234 R. 320:972–73, October 1, 1850, General Land Office to R.W. Thompson.

95. NAM T494 R. 2, July 18, 1831, S. Stambaugh to Secretary of War, 10.

96. S. Stambaugh, "Report on the Quality and Condition of Wisconsin Territory, 1831," in *Wisconsin Historical Collections* (Madison: Wisconsin Historical Society, 1900), 15:433. See also NAM M234 R. 315:566–608, November 8, 1831, S. Stambaugh to Secretary of War.

97. S. Stambaugh, "Report on the Quality and Condition of Wisconsin Territory, 1831," in *Wisconsin Historical Collections* (Madison: Wisconsin Historical Society, 1900), 15:432.

98. Ibid., 434.

99. NAM T494 R. 2, September 11, 1832, Treaty Journal, 11.

100. Ibid., 13–14.

101. Ibid., 26.

102. Ibid., 17–18.

103. Ibid., 25.

104. Treaty with the Menominee, 1831, 7 Stat. 342.

105. Ibid.

106. Treaty of La Pointe, 1842, 7 Stat. 591; Treaty of Greenville, August 3, 1795, 7 Stat. 49.

107. Treaty with the Menominee, 1831, 7 Stat. 342.

108. Ibid.

109. A. G. Ellis, "Advent of the New York Indians into Wisconsin," in *Wisconsin Historical Collections* (Madison: Wisconsin Historical Society, 1856), 2:437.

110. Treaty with the Menominee, 1831, 7 Stat. 346.

111. Treaty with the Menominee, February 17, 1831, 7 Stat. 346.

112. A. G. Ellis, "Advent of the New York Indians into Wisconsin," in *Wisconsin Historical Collections* (Madison: Wisconsin Historical Society, 1856), 2:439–40.

113. NAM T494 R. 2, September 11, 1832, Treaty Journal.

114. NAM T494 R. 2:65–66, January 24, 1833, G. Porter to L. Cass, 2.

115. Ibid.

116. Ibid.

117. NAM T494 R. 2, July 18, 1831, S. Stambaugh to Secretary of War, 11.

118. Ibid., 16.

119. Editor, "The Territorial Census for 1836," in *Wisconsin Historical Collections* (Madison: Wisconsin Historical Society, 1895), 13:249; Editor, "Population of Brown County June 1830," in *Wisconsin Historical Collections* (Madison: Wisconsin Historical Society, 1895), 13:469–70.

120. Henry S. Baird, "Recollections of the Early History of Northern Wisconsin," in *Wisconsin Historical Collections* (Madison: Wisconsin Historical Society, 1859), 4:99.

121. Ebenezer Childs, "Recollections of Wisconsin since 1820," in *Wisconsin Historical Collections* (Madison: Wisconsin Historical Society, 1859), 4:161–62.

122. Henry S. Baird, "Recollections of the Early History of Northern Wisconsin," in *Wisconsin Historical Collections* (Madison: Wisconsin Historical Society, 1859), 4:165.

123. Walter Kuehnle, "Appraisal of Royce Area 242 in the States of Wisconsin and Minnesota," Docket 18C before the Indian Claims Commission for the Department of Justice (1966), 149.

124. Ibid., 156.

125. Ibid., 166.

126. Juliette M. Kinzie, *Wau Bun, the "Early Day" in the North-West* (Chicago: Lakeside Press, 1932), 50–62.

127. Walter Kuehnle, "Appraisal of Royce Area 242 in the States of Wisconsin and Minnesota," Docket 18C before the Indian Claims Commission for the Department of Justice (1966), 161; Ebenezer Childs, "Recollections of Wisconsin since 1820," in *Wisconsin Historical Collections* (Madison: Wisconsin Historical Society, 1859), 4:187.

128. Rubin G. Thwaites, "The Fur Trade in Wisconsin. Agreement of A. Grignon et al. and R. Crooks. August 24, 1821," in *Wisconsin Historical Collections* (Madison: Wisconsin Historical Society, 1911), 20:206–10.

129. John Haeger, "Western Town Growth: A Study of the Development of Towns on the Western Shore of Lake Michigan, 1815–1845" (PhD diss., Loyola University, Chicago, 1969), 89.

130. Ibid.

131. Walter Kuehnle, "Appraisal of Royce Area 242 in the States of Wisconsin and Minnesota," Docket 18C before the Indian Claims Commission for the Department of Justice (1966), 183.

132. Ebenezer Childs, "Recollections of Wisconsin since 1820," in *Wisconsin Historical Collections* (Madison: Wisconsin Historical Society, 1859), 4:186.

133. John Haeger, "Western Town Growth: A Study of the Development of Towns on the Western Shore of Lake Michigan, 1815–1845" (PhD diss., Loyola University, Chicago, 1969), 237.

134. NAM M234 R. 315:608–10, March 2, 1831, J. Street to J. Eaton.

135. Treaty with the Menominee, 1831, 7 Stat. 342.

136. NAM M234 R. 315:354–56, April 8, 1831, W. Clark to J. Eaton.

137. NAM M234 R. 315:611–22, August 1, 1831, J. Street to Secretary of War.

138. NAM M234 R. 315:357–58, August 26, 1831, W. Clark to Secretary of War.

139. Charles Whittlesey, "Recollections of a Tour through Wisconsin in 1832," in *Wisconsin Historical Collections* (Madison: Wisconsin Historical Society, 1855), 1:71.

140. GWL-CHS, Box 1, Folder 6, July 23, 1832, G. Boyd to S. Stambaugh et al.; GWL-CHS, Box 1, Folder 6, September 1, 1832, G. Boyd to S. Stambaugh; Ebenezer Childs, "Recollections of Wisconsin since 1820," in *Wisconsin Historical Collections* (Madison: Wisconsin Historical Society, 1859), 4:185–86.

141. George Boyd, "Papers of Indian Agent Boyd 1832. Aug. 13, 1832. G. Boyd to G. Porter," in *Wisconsin Historical Collections* (Madison: Wisconsin Historical Society, 1892), 12:287.

142. GWL–CHS, Box 1, Folder 6, September 1, 1832, G. Boyd to S. Stambaugh.

143. NAM M234 R. 316:62–64, September 25, 1834, G. Boyd to E. Herring; Henry S. Baird, "Recollections of the Early History of Northern Wisconsin," in *Wisconsin Historical Collections* (Madison: Wisconsin Historical Society, 1859), 4:213.

144. Felix Keesing, *The Menomini Indians of Wisconsin* (Madison: University of Wisconsin Press, 1987), 137.

145. P. K. Ourada, *The Menominee Indians: A History* (Norman: University of Oklahoma Press, 1979), 95.

146. Walter J. Hoffman, *The Menominee Indians*, Fourteenth Annual Report of the American Bureau of Ethnology, Smithsonian Institution (Washington, D.C.: U.S. Government Printing Office, 1896), pt. 1, 11–328; P. K. Ourada, *The Menominee Indians* (Norman: University of Oklahoma Press, 1979), 94.

147. NAM M234 R. 2, July 18, 1831, Journal of a Council by Col. Stambaugh, 10.

148. John Humins, "George Boyd: Indian Agent of the Upper Great Lakes, 1819–1842" (PhD diss., Michigan State University, East Lansing, 1975), 110.

149. NAM M21 R. 14:281, December 17, 1834, L. Cass to R. Cadel; NAM M21 R. 10:251–54, April 16, 1833, E. Herring to G. Porter.

150. John Humins, "George Boyd: Indian Agent of the Upper Great Lakes, 1819–1842" (PhD diss., Michigan State University, East Lansing, 1975), 164.

151. Ibid., 116.

152. Ibid., 173.

153. NAM M21 R. 14:17–21, October 8, 1834, E. Herring to G. Boyd.

154. NAM M234 R. 316:177–81, December 5, 1834, G. Boyd to G. Brooke.

155. NAM M21 R. 14:282–85, December 18, 1834, E. Herring to G. Boyd; NAM M21 R. 17:145, September 29, 1835, E. Herring to G. Boyd.

156. John Humins, "George Boyd: Indian Agent of the Upper Great Lakes, 1819–1842" (PhD diss., Michigan State University, East Lansing, 1975), 178–79.

157. NAM M234 R. 320:30–34, June 2, 1848, A. Ellis to H. Dodge, Petition of Menominee Chiefs.

158. John Humins, "George Boyd: Indian Agent of the Upper Great Lakes, 1819–1842" (PhD diss., Michigan State University, East Lansing, 1975), 176–77.

159. George Boyd, "Papers of Indian Agent Boyd 1832. Aug. 13, 1832. G. Boyd to G. Porter," in *Wisconsin Historical Collections* (Madison: Wisconsin Historical Society, 1892), 12:295.

160. H. H. Tanner, *Atlas of Great Lakes Indian History* (Norman: University of Oklahoma Press, 1987), 143 and map 27.

161. NAM M21 R. 20:339, December 27, 1836, C. Harris to Secretary of War.

162. 4 Stat. 411, sec. 4-7.

163. Ronald N. Satz, "Carey Harris (1831–1836)," in *The Commissioners of Indian Affairs, 1824–1977*, ed. Robert M. Kvasnicka and Herman J. Viola (Lincoln: University of Nebraska Press, 1979), 17–22.

164. ARCOIA 1837, 575.

165. NAM M21 R. 17:116, September 22, 1835, E. Herring to G. Boyd.

166. NAM M21 R. 17:274, November 16, 1835, E. Herring to G. M. Brooke.

167. NAM M21 R. 18:143, March 7, 1836, L. Cass to M. Van Buren.

168. L. P. Kellogg, "The Menominee Treaty at the Cedars, 1836," *Transactions of the Wisconsin Academy of Science, Arts, and Letters* 26 (1931): 131.

169. NAM M668 R. 8:211–34, August 29, 1836, A Journal of the Proceedings of a Treaty Held by Gov. H. Dodge and the Menominee Nation at Cedar Point, August 29, 1836, 2.

170. Ibid.

171. Ibid., 3.

172. Treaty with the Menominee, 1831, 7 Stat. 342.

173. NAM M668 R. 8:211–34, August 29, 1836, A Journal of the Proceedings of a Treaty Held by Gov. H. Dodge and the Menominee Nation at Cedar Point, August 29, 1836, 4.

174. Ibid.

175. Ibid., 4–5.

176. Ibid., 20.

177. Ibid., 14, 18, 21.

178. Ibid., 16.

179. Treaty with the Menominee, 1836, 7 Stat. 506.

180. NAM M21 R. 20:339, December 27, 1836, C. Harris to Secretary of War.

181. Ibid.

182. Editor, "The Territorial Census for 1836," in *Wisconsin Historical Collections* (Madison: Wisconsin Historical Society, 1895), 13:247; R. C. Ostergren, "Geographic Perspective and the History of Settlement in the Upper Midwest," *Upper Midwest History* 1 (1981): 27–39.

183. NAM M21 R. 20:339, December 27, 1836, C. Harris to Secretary of War.

184. NAM M234 R. 320:27–29, June 3, 1848, A. Ellis to H. Dodge.

185. NAM M234 R. 320:88–90, September 6, 1848, Unidentified to A. Ellis.

186. Treaty with the Menominee, 1836, 7 Stat. 506, art. 3; NAM M668 R. 8:211–34, August 29, 1836, A Journal of the Proceedings of a Treaty Held by Gov. Dodge and the Menominee Indians at Cedar Point, August 29, 1836, 15.

187. J. Humins, "George Boyd: Indian Agent of the Upper Great Lakes, 1819–1842" (PhD diss., Michigan State University, East Lansing, 1975), 225–26.

188. Ibid., 214–16; NAM M234 R. 317:237–38, February 28, 1838, Petition of Menominee Chiefs; NAM M234 R. 318:240–65, October 31, 1840, M. Martin to M. Van Buren.

189. GWL-CHS, Box 2, Folder 3, September 3, 1839, H. Dodge to G. Boyd; NAM M234 R. 317:516–26, October 31, 1839, M. Martin to J. Poinsett.

190. NAM M21 R. 21:234–35, March 31, 1837, C. Harris to H. Dodge; J. Humins, "George Boyd: Indian Agent of the Upper Great Lakes, 1819–1842" (PhD diss., Michigan State University. East Lansing, 1975), 242.

191. NAM M234 R. 318:240–65, October 31, 1840, M. Martin to M. Van Buren; J. Humins, "George Boyd: Indian Agent of the Upper Great Lakes, 1819–1842" (PhD diss., Michigan State University. East Lansing, 1975), 252.

192. NAM M234 R. 318:542, September 30, 1841, Statement of Green Bay Agent G. Boyd.

193. ARCOIA 1843, 433–34.

194. ARCOIA 1845, 494; J. Humins, "George Boyd: Indian Agent of the Upper Great Lakes, 1819–1842" (PhD diss., Michigan State University, East Lansing, 1975), 216–18.

195. ARCOIA 1843, 434.

196. ARCOIA 1843, 435.

197. Increase A. Lapham, "A Winter's Journey from Milwaukee to Green Bay, 1843," *Wisconsin Magazine of History* 9 (1925–26): 93.

198. ARCOIA 1846, 256.

199. NAM M234 R. 319:640–45, April 15, 1846, A. Ellis to J. Doty.

200. NAM M234 R. 318:902, January 19, 1843, G. Lawe to J. Doty.

201. ARCOIA 1846, 256.

202. Charles E. Cleland, "The Inland Shore Fishery of the Northern Great Lakes: Its Development and Importance in Prehistory," *American Antiquity* 47, no. 4 (1982):761–84; GWL-CHS, Box 1, Folder 7, March 7, 1835, R. Crooks to J. Lawe.

203. Jeanne Kay, "Wisconsin Indian Hunting Patterns, 1834–1836," *Annals of the Association of American Geographers* 69, no. 3 (1979): 402–18.

204. ARCOIA 1846, 256.

205. ARCOIA 1847, 830–31.

206. ARCOIA 1846, 256.

207. NAM M234 R. 318:472–82, July 26, 1841, H.

Dodge to H. Crawford; NAM M234 R. 320:154–56, February 23, 1842, A. Ellis to H. Dodge; NAM M234 R. 320:157–59, March 30, 1848, W. Medill to H. Dodge.

208. GWL-CHS, Box 2, Folder 6, October 30, 1842, Oshkosh to G. Lawe.

209. ARCOIA 1843, 432; GWL-CHS, Box 3, Folder 3, October 17, 1843, G. Lawe to J. Doty.

210. NAM M21 R. 32:89, April 7, 1842, H. Crawford to J. Doty; NAM M234 R. 319:168–70, February 16, 1844, J. Doty to H. Crawford.

211. NAM M234 R. 319:688–89, August 10, 1846, W. Lynde to A. Ellis.

212. NAM M21 R. 15:184–86, March 20, 1835, E. Herring to G. Boyd.

213. NAM M234 R. 316:193–95, December 24, 1834, G. Boyd to E. Herring; NAM M21 R. 15:184–86, March 20, 1835, E. Herring to G. Boyd; NAM M234 R. 318:18–19, July 27, 1837, Affidavits of Menominee Indians; NAM M21 R. 25:154, August 30, 1838, C. Harris to B. Boyd.

214. ARCOIA 1845, 491.

215. Ibid., 494.

216. Robert Trennert, "William Medill (1845–49)," in *The Commissioners of Indian Affairs, 1824–1977*, ed. Robert M. Kvasnicka and Herman J. Viola (Lincoln: University of Nebraska Press, 1979), 29–39.

217. Alice Smith, *The History of Wisconsin* (Madison: State Historical Society of Wisconsin, 1973), 1:260.

218. Ibid.

219. ARCOIA 1846, 251.

220. ARCOIA 1847, 822.

221. Treaty with the Chippewa of the Mississippi and Lake Superior, 1847, 9 Stat. 904.

222. NAM M234 R. 319:695–96, September 10, 1846, A. Ellis to H. Dodge; ARCOIA 1846, 251; NAM M234 R. 319:692–94, September 26, 1846, H. Dodge to W. Medill.

223. GWL-CHS, Box 4, Folder 4, January 28, 1847, R. Crooks to J. Mead; ARCOIA 1846, 251.

224. NAM M234 R. 319:692–94, September 26, 1846, H. Dodge to W. Medill; NAM M21 R. 40, October 21, 1847, W. Medill to H. Dodge.

225. NAM M21 R. 39:90, December 31, 1846, W. Medill to H. Dodge and J. Cottrell.

226. Jeanne Kay, "Wisconsin Indian Hunting Patterns, 1634–1836," *Annals of the Association of American Geographers* 69, no. 3 (1979): 402–18.

227. NAM M234 R. 319:744–46, n.d. 1847, Unidentified to H. Dodge (incomplete letter); NAM M234 R. 949, n.d. 1847, Memoranda; NAM M234 R. 319:740–41, October 4, 1847, L. Verplank to W. Medill.

228. H. Hickerson, *The Chippewa and Their Neighbors* (Prospect Heights, Ill.: Waveland Press, 1970).

229. Jeanne Kay, "Wisconsin Indian Hunting Patterns, 1634–1836," *Annals of the Association of American Geographers* 69, no. 3 (1979): 402–18.

230. NAM M234 R. 319:370–74, July 7, 1845, H. Dodge to H. Crawford; NAM M234 R. 319:345–48, September 24, 1845, A. Ellis to H. Dodge.

231. NAM M234 R. 949, November 23, 1846, H. Dodge to W. Medill.

232. Report of Senator Walker to the United States Senate, Rep. Com. No. 410, 32nd Cong., 2nd sess. (1853).

233. GWL-CHS, Box 4, Folder 4, January 28, 1847, R. Crooks to J. Meade.

234. NAM M234 R. 320:35–37, July 20, 1848, H. Dodge et al. to House of Representatives.

235. Ibid.

236. NAM M21 R. 39:90, December 31, 1846, W. Medill to H. Dodge.

237. Ibid.

238. NAM M234 R. 319:695–96, September 10, 1846, A. Ellis to H. Dodge.

239. Treaty with the Chippewa of the Mississippi and Lake Superior, 1847, 9 Stat. 904; Treaty with the Pillager Chippewa, 1847, 9 Stat. 908.

240. NAM M234 R. 319:740–41, October 4, 1847, L. Verplank to W. Medill.

241. NAM M21 R. 40, October 18, 1847, W. Medill to L. Verplank.

242. NAM M21 R. 41, September 9, 1848, W. Medill to A. Ellis.

243. NAM M234 R. 320:82–84, November 11, 1848, A. Ellis to W. Medill; NAM M234 R. 320:967–71, December 12, 1848, W. Medill to W. Marcy.

244. NAM M234 R. 320:936–66, October 11, 1850, R. Thompson to Secretary of Interior A. Stuart.

245. NAM M234 R. 320:990, October 9, 1849, Affidavit of A. Dodge.

246. ARCOIA 1851, 36.

247. NAM M234 R. 320:1001–3, May 29, 1849, Affidavit of E. Saywer.

248. Ibid.

249. Ibid.

250. Ibid.

251. Ibid.

252. NAM M234 R. 320:995–96, October 10, 1849, Affidavit of G. Wright.

253. Ibid.

254. NAM M234 R. 320:295–304, July 25, 1849, Proceedings of a Council at Powawhaykonnay.

255. Treaty of Lake Powawhaykonnay of 1848, 9 Stat. 952.

256. Ibid.

257. Ibid.

258. Ibid.

259. Ibid.

260. Ibid.

261. Ibid.

262. Ibid.

263. NAM M234 R. 319:345–48, September 24, 1845, A. Ellis to H. Dodge; NAM M234 R. 319:695–96, September 10, 1846, A. Ellis to H. Dodge.

264. Treaty of Fort Armstrong, 1832, 7 Stat. 370; Treaty with Winnebago, 1837, 7 Stat. 544; Treaty of St. Peters, 1837, 7 Stat. 536.

265. NAM M234 R. 320:967–71, December 12, 1848, W. Medill to W. Marcy.

266. Ibid.

267. Report of Senator Walker to the United States Senate, Rep. Com. No. 410, 32nd Cong., 2nd sess. (1853).

268. NAM M234 R. 320:967–71, December 12, 1848, W. Medill to W. Marcy.

269. Report of Senator Walker to the United States Senate, Rep. Com. No. 410, 32nd Cong., 2nd sess. (1853).

270. Ibid.

271. Ibid.

272. Treaty of Lake Powawhaykonnay of 1848, 9 Stat. 952.

273. Report of Senator Walker to the United States Senate, Rep. Com. No. 410, 32nd Cong., 2nd sess. (1853).

274. NAM M234 R. 320:936–66, October 11, 1850, R. Thompson to A. Stuart.

275. Treaty of Lake Powawhaykonnay of 1848. 9 Stat. 952.

276. Treaty with the Winnebago, 1846, 9 Stat. 878.

277. Ibid.

278. NAM M234 R. 320:295–304, July 25, 1849, Proceedings of a Council at Powawhaykonnay.

279. Ibid.

280. Ibid.

281. Ibid.

282. NAM M234 R. 321:76–80, n.d. 1851, Petition of J. Doty to President from the Christian Menominees.

283. NAM M234 R. 320:997–98, October 15, 1849, Notarized Statement of Charles Geisey.

In this unusual and aptly chosen idiomatic expression, Oshkosh refers to the habit of the crawfish, which can move forward only with great caution but can retreat backward with a great burst of speed using its powerful tail. Medill presumably understood Oshkosh's meaning.

284. Ibid.

285. Ibid.

286. NAM M234 R. 321:184–87, August 27, 1849, O. Brown to W. Bruce; GWL-CHS, Box 4, Folder 6, May 27, 1850, G. Lawe to O. Brown; GWL-CHS, Box 4, Folder 6, June 10, 1850, O. Brown to G. Lawe.

287. NAM M234 R. 321:123–25, March 22, 1850, J. Ewing to O. Brown; NAM M234 R. 321:96–99, March 30, 1850, W. Rathburn to W. Bruce; HSB-WHS Wis Mss V, Box 2, August 28, 1849, O. Brown to G. Crawford.

288. HSB-WHS Wis Mss V, Box 2, August 1, 1850, W. Powell to W. Bruce; NAM M234 R. 320:773–77, August 5, 1850, E. Childs to W. Bruce; NAM M234 R. 320:784–99, August 5, 1850, C. Tallair to Oshkosh.

289. NAM M234 R. 320:770–72, August 1, 1850, W. Powell to W. Bruce.

290. ARCOIA 1851; NAM M234 R. 321:76–80, n.d. 1851, J. Doty to President for Christian Menominee.

291. C. Cleland, *Rites of Conquest: The History and Culture of Michigan's Native Americans* (Ann Arbor: University of Michigan Press, 1992).

292. Francis P. Prucha, *The Great Father: The United States Government and the American Indians*, abridged ed. (Lincoln: University of Nebraska Press, 1986), 106.

293. ARCOIA 1855, 17–19; ARCOIA 1856, 571–72.

294. GWL-CHS, Box 4, Folder 8, September 29, 1851, G. Lawe to Sir (Unidentified).

295. NAM M234 R. 321:189–91, March 22, 1851, W. Bruce to L. Lea.

296. ARCOIA 1849.

297. ARCOIA 1849.

298. Treaty of Lake Powawhaykonnay of 1848, 9 Stat. 952.

299. ARCOIA 1851, 5.

300. GWL-CHS, Box 3, Folder 3, December 14, 1843, G. Lawe to J. Doty.

301. NAM M234 R. 321:628–30, April 1, 1852, R. Thompson to L. Lea.

302. NAM M234 R. 321:272–74, May 10, 1851, Wisconsin Citizens to President Fillmore; NAM M234 R. 321:340–46, March 1, 1851, Petition to President Fillmore; NAM M234 R. 321:628–30, April 1, 1852, R. Thompson to L. Lea.

303. ARCOIA 1851.

304. Ibid., 38.

305. Ibid.

306. NAM M234 R. 321:277–79, January 8, 1851, J. Doty to L. Lea.

307. ARCOIA 1851, 38.

308. Report of Senator Walker to the United States Senate, Rep. Com. No. 410, 32nd Cong., 2nd sess. (1853).

309. NAM M234 R. 321:277–79, January 8, 1851, J. Doty to L. Lea.

310. NAM M234 R. 321:189–91, March 22, 1851, W. Bruce to L. Lea.

311. GWL-CHS, Box 4, Folder 8, July 8, 1851, W. Powell to E. Murray and G. Lawe.

312. NAM M234 R. 321:404–6, October 2, 1851, W. Powell to E. Murray.

313. GWL-CHS, Box 5, Folder 3, October 3, 1852, E. Murray to Menominee Chiefs.

314. NAM M234 R. 321:594–96, December 3, 1852, Menominee Chiefs to President.

315. NAM M234 R. 322:286–87, February 1, 1853, Resolution of Wisconsin Senate and Assembly.

316. NAM M234 R. 322:177–79, July 14, 1853, J. Wilson to G. Manypenny.

317. Treaty of the Wolf River, 1854, 10 Stat. 1064.

318. Ibid.

319. Ibid.

320. NAM M234 R. 322:409–11, May 30, 1854, F. Huebschmann to G. Manypenny.

321. Treaty of the Wolf River, 1854, 10 Stat. 1064.

322. Treaty of La Pointe, 1854.

CHAPTER 13

1. 10 Stat. 1064.

2. 7 Stat. 342, *supplemented*, February 17, 1831; 7 Stat. 346, *amended*, October 27, 1832; 7 Stat. 405.

3. 7 Stat. 509.

4. 9 Stat. 952.

5. "[T]he United States, as the party with presumptively superior negotiating skills and superior knowledge of the language in which the treaty is recorded, has a responsibility to avoid taking advantage of the other side." *Washington v. Washington Passenger Fishing Vesel Ass'n*, 444 U.S. 658, 675–76 (1979). "But the document [the treaty] is not to be read as an ordinary contract agreed upon by the parties dealing at arm's length with equal bargaining positions." *McClanahan v. Arizona State Tax Comm'n*, 411 U.S. 164, 174 (1973).

6. "The Indian nations did not seek out the United States and agree upon an exchange of lands in an

arms-length transaction. Rather, treaties were imposed upon them and they had no choice but to consent." *Choctaw Nation v. Oklahoma,* 397 U.S. 620, 630–31 (1970).

7. Treaties "are not to be interpreted narrowly, as sometimes may be writings expressed in words of art employed by conveyancers, but are to be construed in the sense in which naturally the Indians would understand them." *United States v. Shoshone Tribe of Indians,* 304 U.S. 111, 116 (1938).

8. Because of the differing backgrounds and experiences of the tribal leaders and the U.S. treaty commissioners, treaties "must therefore be construed, not according to the technical meaning of its words by learned lawyers, but in the sense in which they would be naturally understood by the Indians." *Jones v. Meehan,* 175 U.S. 1, 11 (1899).

9. "It is our responsibility to see that the terms of the treaty are carried out, so far as possible, in accordance with the meaning they were understood to have by the tribal representatives at council and in a spirit which generously recognizes the full obligation of this nation to protect the interests of a dependent people." *Tulee v. Washington,* 315 U.S. 681, 684–85 (1942).

10. "Doubtful expressions [in treaties] are to be resolved in favor of the weak and defenseless people who are the wards of the nation, dependent upon its protection and good faith." *Carpenter v. Shaw,* 280 U.S. 363, 367 (1930).

11. *Menominee Indian Tribe of Wisconsin v. Thompson,* 161 F.3d 449 (7th Cir. 1998).

12. *Menominee Indian Tribe of Wisconsin v. Thompson,* 161 F.3d at 460.

13. 700 F.2d 341 (7th Cir. 1983).

14. Ibid., at 345.

15. *Jones v. Meehan,* 175 U.S. 11.

16. *Menominee Indian Tribe of Wisconsin v. Thompson,* 943 F. Supp. at 1015–16.

17. 526 U.S. 172 (1999).

18. 7 Stat. 536.

19. 10 Stat. 1165.

PART 3

1. Felix Cohen, *Felix S. Cohen's Handbook of Federal Indian Law* (Charlottesville, Va.: Michie Bobbs-Merrill, 1982), 282.

2. 18 U.S.C. 1151–65.

3. *Santa Clara Pueblo v. Martinez,* 436 U.S. 49 (1978); *Byron v. Itaska County,* 426 U.S. 373 (1976).

4. PL 280, August 15, 1953, 67 Stat. 588–90.

5. 18 U.S.C. 1152; 18 U.S.C. 1153, 3242.

6. *U.S. v. John,* 437 U.S. 634 (1978).

7. *Montana v. Blackfeet Tribe of Indians,* 471 U.S. 759 (1985).

8. *Keweenaw Bay Indian Community v. Naftaly,* 370 F. Supp. 2d 620 (W.D. Mich. 2005).

CHAPTER 14

1. William W. Warren, *The History of the Ojibwe People* (St. Paul: Minnesota Historical Society Press, 1984), 327–67; Harold Hickerson, *The Chippewa and Their Neighbors* (Prospect Heights, Ill.: Waveland Press, 1970).

2. Frederick Baraga, *Chippewa Indians as Recorded in 1847* (New York: Studies Slovenica, League of Slovenian Americans, 1976); Charles E. Cleland, "The Inland Shore Fishery of the Northern Great Lakes: Its Development and Importance in Prehistory," *American Antiquity* 47, no. 4 (1982).

3. Johann Kohl, *Kitchi-Game: Life among the Lake Superior Chippewa* (St. Paul: Minnesota Historical Society Press, 1985); Mentor Williams, ed., *Narrative Journals of Travels through the Northwest Regions of the United States Extending from Detroit through the Great Chain of American Lakes to the Source of the Mississippi River in the Year 1820,* by Henry R. Schoolcraft (East Lansing: Michigan State University Press, 1953).

4. Charles E. Cleland, "Economic and Adaptive Change among the Lake Superior Chippewa of the Nineteenth Century," in *Approaches to Cultural Contact: Ethnohistorical and Archaeological Perspectives on Change,* ed. J. D. Rodgers and S. M. Wilson (New York: Plenum Press, 1993), 111–12.

5. Edward E. Hill, *The Office of Indian Affairs, 1824–1880: Historical Sketches* (New York: Clearwater Publishing, 1967).

6. Edmund J. Danziger, *The Chippewas of Lake Superior* (Norman: University of Oklahoma Press, 1979), 78.

7. Edward E. Hill, *The Office of Indian Affairs, 1824–1880: Historical Sketches* (New York: Clearwater Publishing, 1967).

8. Virgil L. Vogel, *Indian Names in Michigan* (Ann Arbor: University of Michigan Press, 1986), 134–36.

9. Philip P. Mason, ed., *Schoolcraft's Expedition to Lake Itasca* (East Lansing: Michigan State University Press, 1958), 172–73.

10. ARCOIA, September 20, 1852.

11. NAM M234 R. 390, January 30, 1849, Keasheaush et al. to President.

12. Philip P. Mason, ed., *Schoolcraft's Expedition to Lake Itasca* (East Lansing: Michigan State University Press, 1958), 170–75; NAM M234 R. 77, September 24, 1824, Trading Licenses Granted by H. R. Schoolcraft; NAM M1 R. 54:52–53, February 15, 1843, G. Brown to R. Stuart.

13. Philip P. Mason, ed., *Schoolcraft's Expedition to Lake Itasca* (East Lansing: Michigan State University Press, 1958), table V, 158.

14. Dorothy Reuter, *Methodist Indian Ministries in Michigan, 1830–1990* (Michigan Area United Methodist Historical Society, 1993).

15. Antoine I. Rezek, *History of the Diocese of Sault Ste. Marie and Marquette* (Houghton, Mich., 1907), chap. 19.

16. Dorothy Reuter, *Methodist Indian Ministries in Michigan, 1830–1990* (Michigan Area United Methodist Historical Society, 1993), 45; NAM M1 R. 56:299–300, December 29, 1843, G. Brown to R. Stuart; NAM M1 R. 39:161, April 20, 1844, R. Stuart to J. Ord.

17. Dorothy Reuter, *Methodist Indian Ministries in Michigan, 1830–1990* (Michigan Area United Methodist Historical Society, 1993), 16–48.

18. NAM M234 R. 388, July 12, 1843, J. Doty to A. Brunson.

19. NAM M234 R. 388, September 30, 1843, Annual report of A. Brunson to J. Doty.

20. "Annuity Payment at La Pointe," *New York Herald Tribune*, August 27, 1847.

21. Dorothy Reuter, *Methodist Indian Ministries in Michigan, 1830–1990* (Michigan Area United Methodist Historical Society, 1993), 353.

22. NAM M574 R. 16, September 3, 1855, Claim No. 66—Marksman.

23. ARCOIA 1853, Report of James Shaw, 282.

24. 31st Annual Report of Methodist Missionary Society of the Methodist Episcopal Church, 1850, 69.

25. MHS, Manuscript relating to Northwest Missions, January–February 1849, 2–3.

26. 31st Annual Report of Methodist Missionary Society of the Methodist Episcopal Church, 1850, 69.

27. ARCOIA, September 20, 1851, J. Watrous to A. Ramsey.

28. MHS, Manuscript Relating to Northwest Missions, January–February 1849, 2.

29. NAM M234 R. 771, March 31, 1849, W. Pratt to W. Richmond.

30. NA RG 279, Indian Claims Commission, Docket 18-S, Defendant Exhibit CR-2-24, n.d. 1836, Annuity roll for 1863.

31. NAM M574 R. 22:278, September 10, 1855, Claim No. 64.

32. Treaty with the Sioux, etc., August 19, 1825, 7 Stat. 272; Treaty with the Chippewa, August 5, 1826, 7 Stat. 290; Treaty with the Chippewa, etc., August 11, 1827, 7 Stat. 303.

33. Thomas McKenney, *Sketches of a Tour of the Lakes*, facsimile ed. (Minneapolis: Ross and Haines, 1959).

34. Treaty with the Chippewa, August 5, 1826, 7 Stat. 290.

35. Ibid.

36. Francis P. Prucha, *The Great Father: The United States Government and the American Indians* (Lincoln: University of Nebraska Press, 1984), 183–208.

37. Indian Removal Act, May 28, 1830, 4 Stat. 411–12.

38. Treaty with the Chippewa, July 29, 1837, 7 Stat. 536.

39. Ibid.

40. Charles E. Cleland, "Preliminary Report for the Ethnohistorical Basis of Hunting, Fishing, and Gathering Rights of the Mille Lacs Ojibwe," in *Fish in the Lakes, Wild Rice, and Game in Abundance: Testimony in Behalf of Mille Lacs Ojibwe Hunting and Fishing Rights*, comp. James M. McClurken (East Lansing: Michigan State University Press, 2000).

41. MN 007529 M951 R4:067, October 18, 1839, H. Dodge to T. H. Crawford.

42. NAM M21 R. 359–63, August 1, 1842, H. Crawford to R. Stuart; NAM M234 R. 389, September 29, 1842, Speech of R. Stuart to Indians.

43. Treaty with the Chippewa, October 4, 1842, 7 Stat. 571.

44. Ibid., art. III.

45. Charles E. Cleland, "Preliminary Report for the Ethnohistorical Basis of Hunting, Fishing, and Gathering Rights of the Mille Lacs Ojibwe," in *Fish in the Lakes, Wild Rice, and Game in Abundance: Testimony in Behalf of Mille Lacs Ojibwe Hunting and Fishing Rights*, comp. James M. McClurken (East Lansing: Michigan State University Press, 2000), 36–41.

46. Ibid.

47. NAM M234 R. 388, March 9, 1843, A. Brunson to J. Doty.

48. NAM M234 R. 388, July 12, 1843, J. Doty to A. Brunson.

49. NAM M234 R. 388, September 30, 1843, Annual report of A. Brunson to J. Doty.

50. John D. Nichols, *Statement Made by the Indians: A Bilingual Petition of the Chippewas of Lake Superior, 1864* (London: Centre for Research and Teaching of Canadian Native Languages, University of Western Ontario, 1988).

51. NAM T494 R. 3:548–68, July 20, 1837, Proceedings of the Council held by Gov. Henry Dodge with the Chiefs and Principal Men of the Chippewa Nation of Indians near Fort Snelling at the Confluence of the St. Peter and Mississippi Rivers, 2, 18, 27; ABCFM Ms. BA10.A512b, May 3, 1843, L. H. Wheeler to D. Green, Journal of the 1842 Treaty Negotiated at La Pointe.

52. Lewis Cass, "Conditions of the Present State of the Indians, and Their Removal" (1830; repr., New York: Arno Press, 1975), 80.

53. Treaty with the Chippewa of the Mississippi and Lake Superior, August 2, 1847, 9 Stat. 904.

54. Charles E. Cleland, "Preliminary Report for the Ethnohistorical Basis of Hunting, Fishing, and Gathering Rights of the Mille Lacs Ojibwe," in *Fish in the Lakes, Wild Rice, and Game in Abundance: Testimony in Behalf of Mille Lacs Ojibwe Hunting and Fishing Rights*, comp. James M. McClurken (East Lansing: Michigan State University Press, 2000), 51–53.

55. NAM M236 R. 46, June 5, 1847, W. Medill to I. Verplank and C. Mix.

56. NAM M234 R. 389, September 3, 1847, Nodin et al. to President; NAM M234 R. 390, November 14, 1848, Nagonabe to J. Livermore.

57. Charles E. Cleland, "Preliminary Report for the Ethnohistorical Basis of Hunting, Fishing, and Gathering Rights of the Mille Lacs Ojibwe," in *Fish in the Lakes, Wild Rice, and Game in Abundance: Testimony in Behalf of Mille Lacs Ojibwe Hunting and Fishing Rights*, comp. James M. McClurken (East Lansing: Michigan State University Press, 2000), 54–72.

58. U.S. House of Representatives, 30th Cong., 3rd sess., February 7, 1849, Misc. Doc. 36, Petition of Lake Superior Chiefs.

59. NAM M1 R. 62:58, May 11, 1848, C. Bineshi and E. Assinins to W. Richmond.

60. NAM M234 R. 390, October 8, 1848, Chippewa Chiefs to President.

61. N.d. 1849, Three deed records U.S. to Nicholas Menclear to Baraga and two deeded U.S. to Baraga.

62. NAM M1 R. 40:66, July 4, 1848, W. A. Richmond to P. B. Barbeau.

63. Ibid.

64. BBC-NA-OIA-M, July 22, 1858, Lac Vieux Desert Indians to A. Fitch.

65. Ibid.

66. Bruce White, "The Regional Context of the

Removal Order of 1850," in *Fish in the Lakes, Wild Rice, and Game in Abundance: Testimony in Behalf of Mille Lacs Ojibwe Hunting and Fishing Rights,* comp. James M. McClurken (East Lansing: Michigan State University Press, 2000), 141–328.

67. NAM M21 R. 43:25, February 6, 1850, O. Brown to A. Ramsey.

68. ABCFM Ms. M55245 No. 87, February 25, 1850, S. Hall to S. B. Trent; MCT Plaintiff Exhibit 400, May 24, 1850, C. Mendenhall to Z. Taylor; "Indians to Be Removed from Lake Superior," *Lake Superior Journal,* May 22, 1850.

69. James A. Clifton, "Wisconsin Death March: Explaining the Extremes in Old Northwest Indian Removal," *Transactions of the Wisconsin Academy of Science, Arts, and Letters* 75 (1987): 1–39.

70. NAM M234 R. 771, May 31, 1850, D. Aitken to C. Babcock; NAM M234 R. 390, July 30, 1850, J. Beedon et al. to President; ARCOIA, September 20, 1851, J. Watrous to A. Ramsey.

71. NAM M234 R. 777, June 28, 1850, D. Aitken to O. Brown; NAM M234 R. 771, July 15, 1850, D. King to D. Aitken.

72. MN 003394, August 25, 1851, T. Abraham (Graham) to L. Lea.

73. NAM M842 R. 8, August 10, 1852, A. Ramsey to Buffalo and Oshaga.

74. Charles E. Cleland, *Rites of Conquest: The History and Culture of Michigan's Native Americans* (Ann Arbor: University of Michigan Press, 1992), 198–203.

75. Francis P. Prucha, *The Great Father: The United States Government and the American Indians* (Lincoln: University of Nebraska Press, 1984), 325–27; Robert M. Kvasnicka and Herman J. Viola, eds., *The Commissioners of Indian Affairs, 1824–1977* (Lincoln: University of Nebraska Press, 1979).

76. ARCOIA 1856, U.S. House of Representatives, 34th Cong., 3rd sess., 1856–57, Exec. Doc., Report of the Secretary of the Interior, 575.

77. ARCOIA 1857, Exec. Doc. of the Senate of the United States, 35th Cong., 1st sess., 1857–58, Exec. Doc., Report of the Secretary of the Interior, 293.

78. Ibid., 290–93.

79. Treaty with the Chippewa, 1819, 7 Stat. 203; Treaty with the Chickasaw, 1834, 7 Stat. 450.

80. Treaty with the Oto and Missouri, March 15, 1854, 10 Stat. 1038; NAM M21 R. 49:454–57, August 11, 1854, G. Manypenny to H. Gilbert.

81. Treaty with the Oto and Missouri, March 15, 1854, 10 Stat. 1038.

82. Treaty with the Omaha, March 16, 1854, 10 Stat. 1043; Treaty with the Miami, June 5, 1854, 10 Stat. 1093.

83. Treaty with the Iowa, May 17, 1854, 10 Stat. 1069; Treaty with the Sauk and Foxes of Missouri, May 18, 1854, 10 Stat. 1074; Treaty with the Kickapoo, May 18, 1854, 10 Stat. 1078.

84. Treaty with the Kaskaska and Peoria, etc., May 30, 1854, 10 Stat. 1082.

85. ARCOIA 1854.

86. Charles E. Cleland, "Preliminary Report for the Ethnohistorical Basis of Hunting, Fishing, and Gathering Rights of the Mille Lacs Ojibwe," in *Fish in the Lakes, Wild Rice, and Game in Abundance: Testimony in Behalf of Mille Lacs Ojibwe Hunting and Fishing Rights,* comp. James M. McClurken (East Lansing: Michigan State University Press, 2000), 82–86.

87. ARCOIA 1851.

88. NAM M234 R. 404:184–90, December 10, 1853, H. Gilbert to G. Manypenny.

89. *Journal of the House of Representatives,* March 7, 1854.

90. *Congressional Globe,* May 1, 1854, 1032–37.

91. *Journal of the House of Representatives,* December 19, 1854.

92. Ibid.

93. ARCOIA 1854.

94. NAM M21 R. 49:454–57, August 11, 1854, G. Manypenny to H. Gilbert.

95. Ibid.

96. NAM M21 R. 49, August 10, 1854, G. Manypenny to D. Herriman.

97. NAM M21 R. 49:454–57, August 11, 1854, G. Manypenny to H. Gilbert.

98. Ibid.

99. NAM M21 R. 49:475–76, August 14, 1854, G. Manypenny to H. Gilbert.

100. Treaty with the Chippewa, September 30, 1854, 10 Stat. 1109.

101. NAM T494 R. 5, October 17, 1854, H. Gilbert to G. Manypenny.

102. Ibid.

103. Treaty with the Chippewa, September 30, 1854, 10 Stat. 1109.

104. Treaty of La Pointe, September 30, 1854, 10 Stat. 1109; NA RG 75, Executive Orders Relating to Indian Reservations, March 7, 1855.

105. John D. Nichols, "*Statement Made by the Indians*": *A Bilingual Petition of the Chippewas of Lake Superior, 1864* (London: Ontario Center for Research and Teaching of Canadian Native Languages, 1988).

106. NAM M574 R. 21, September 3, 1855, Claim No. 11—Baraga; NAM M574 R. 21:1169–71, December 20, 1855, Gilbert Affidavit.

107. NAM M574 R. 16, September 5, 1855, Claim No. 32—Rathburn.

108. NAM M234 R. 405:101–2, May 21, 1856, H. Gilbert to G. Manypenny.

109. BCC-RD, Deeds, L3:95–97, Warranty Deed, July 2, 1863, F. Baraga to "Edward Assinnes Chief of the Catholic Band of Indians and the following indivuals of the band . . ."

110. BBC-NA-OIA M95-3, January 31, 1857, S. Caley to A. Fitch.

111. BBC-NA-OIA-M, July 22, 1858, Lac Vieux Desert Indians to A. Fitch.

112. Ibid.

113. Treaty of La Pointe, 1854.

114. BBC-NA-OIA-M, July 22, 1858, Lac Vieux Desert Indians to A. Fitch.

115. Treaty with the Chippewa, September 30, 1854, 10 Stat. 1109.

116. Ibid.

117. NAM T494 R. 5, October 17, 1854, H. Gilbert to G. Manypenny.

118. Treaty with the Chippewa, September 30, 1854, 11 Stat. 1109.

119. Report of the Secretary of the Interior, 1860.

CHAPTER 15

1. 10 Stat. 1109.
2. 7 Stat. 591.
3. 10 Stat. 1109.
4. 18 U.S.C. 1153.
5. 18 U.S.C. 1151.
6. *Keweenaw Bay Indian Community v. Michigan*, 784 F. Supp. 418, 427 (W.D. Mich. 1991).
7. "Swamplands, canal lands, and school lands" refers to lands the title to which had passed to the state prior to the 1854 treaty by operation of federal grants made under various acts of Congress. See, e.g., Canal Lands Act, chap. 92, August 26, 1852, 10 Stat. 35; Swamp Lands Act of 1850, chap. 84, sec. 2, 9 Stat. 519 (codified at 43 U.S.C. 983); and *Minnesota v. Hitchcock*, 185 U.S. 373 (1902).
8. *Keweenaw Bay Indian Community v. Michigan*, 784 F. Supp. at 427.
9. *Jones v. Meehan*, 175 U.S. 1 (1899); *United States v. Shoshone Tribe*, 304 U.S. 111 (1938); *Starr v. Long Jim*, 227 U.S. 613 (1913); *Choctaw Nation of Indians v. United States*, 318 U.S. 423 (1943); *McClanahan v. Arizona Tax Com'n*, 411 U.S. 164 (1973); *Carpenter v. Shaw*, 280 U.S. 363 (1930); and *Winters v. United States*, 207 U.S. 564 (1908).
10. *Keweenaw Bay Indian Community v. Michigan*, 784 F. Supp. at 421.
11. Ibid., 424.
12. Ibid., 425.

CHAPTER 16

1. Indian Removal Act, May 28, 1830, 4 Stat. 411–12.
2. Ronald N. Satz, *American Indian Policy in the Jacksonian Era* (Lincoln: University of Nebraska Press, 1975).
3. Charles E. Cleland, *Rites of Conquest: The History and Culture of Michigan's Native Americans* (Ann Arbor: University of Michigan Press, 1992), 202–50.
4. Treaty with the Seneca, etc., July 20, 1831, 7 Stat. 351.
5. Treaty with the Shawnee, August 8, 1831, 7 Stat. 355.
6. Treaty with the Chippewa, etc., September 26, 1833, 7 Stat. 431.
7. Treaty with the Winnebago, September 15, 1832, 7 Stat. 370.
8. Treaty with the Ottawa and Chippewa, March 28, 1836, 7 Stat. 491.
9. Treaty with the Chippewa, October 4, 1842, 7 Stat. 591.
10. Treaty with the Stockbridge Tribe, November 24, 1848, 9 Stat. 955.
11. Treaty with the Chippewa, July 29, 1837, 7 Stat. 536.
12. Treaty with the Menominee, October 18, 1848, 9 Stat. 952.
13. *Journals of the Continental Congress* 32:340–41.
14. ARCOIA 1838, 497.
15. J. M. McClurken, "We Wish to Be Civilized: Ottawa-American Political Contest on the Michigan Frontier" (PhD diss., Michigan State University, East Lansing, 1988); James A. Clifton, *The Prairie People* (Lawrence: Regents Press of Kansas, 1977), 252–54.
16. James W. Oberly, *A Nation of Statesmen: The Political Culture of the Stockbridge-Munsee Mohicans, 1815–1972* (Norman: University of Oklahoma Press, 2005).
17. Treaty with the Stockbridge and Munsee, September 3, 1839, 7 Stat. 580.
18. ARCOIA 1840.
19. ARCOIA 1844.
20. James W. Oberly, *A Nation of Statesmen: The Political Culture of the Stockbridge-Munsee Mohicians, 1815–1972* (Norman: University of Oklahoma Press, 2005), provides a full narrative history of the Stockbridge-Munsee tribe in Wisconsin. Also included are the full texts of many of the documents mentioned in this more abbreviated account.
21. Act of 1843, 5 Stat. 645.
22. MMLM NA RG 75 SC 42-S611, January 3, 1872, Memorial to the U.S. Senate and House of Representatives.
23. NA RG 46 B56, F 2-3, April 18, 1855, J. Wilson to R. McClelland.
24. ARCOIA 1847.
25. Preamble to Treaty of 1848, 9 Stat. 955.
26. ARCOIA 1847.
27. Treaty with the Stockbridge Tribe, November 24, 1848, 9 Stat. 955.
28. ARCOIA 1854.
29. ARCOIA 1854.
30. NA RG 46 B56 F2-3, January 7, 1856, G. Manypenny to F. Huebschmann.
31. Ibid.
32. Ibid.
33. Treaty with the Stockbridge and Munsee, February 5, 1856, 11 Stat. 663.
34. Treaty with the Stockbridge and Munsee, February 5, 1856, 11 Stat. 663.
35. ARCOIA 1853.
36. NAM M1166 R. 1:358–59, April 28, 1854, G. Manypenny to J. Quinney and Z. Peter.
37. NAM M1166 R. 1:282–83, December 29, 1853, F. Huebschmann to G. Manypenny; NAM M1166 R. 1:309–10, January 14, 1854, F. Huebschmann to G. Manypenny; NAM M1166 R. 1:337–38, March 20, 1854, F. Huebschmann to G. Manypenny.
38. Treaty with the Ottawa and Chippewa, July 31, 1855, 11 Stat. 621.
39. Treaty with the Chippewa, September 30, 1854, 10 Stat. 1109.
40. Treaty with the Stockbridge and Munsee, February 5, 1856, 11 Stat. 663.
41. NAM M234 R. 327:825–84, May 18, 1870, Bourn to Parker, Trial transcript of *U.S. v. Wybro*, 54.
42. NAM M234 R. 325:132, August 21, 1865, Petition to M. M. Davis.
43. Treaty with the Stockbridge and Munsee, February 5, 1856, 11 Stat. 663; February 23, 1856, Letter appended to treaty, F. Huebschmann to G. Manypenny.
44. Treaty with the Menominee, May 12, 1854, 10 Stat. 1064.

45. NAM M234 R. 325:212–18, June 5, 1865, J. Edmunds to J. Harlan.

46. NAM M234 R. 325:210–11, June 26, 1865, J. Harlan to COIA.

47. Francis P. Prucha, *The Great Father: The United States Government and the American Indians* (Lincoln: University of Nebraska Press, 1984), 482.

48. Ibid.

49. Ibid., 525.

50. Francis P. Prucha, *Documents of the United States Indian Policy* (Lincoln: University of Nebraska Press, 1975), 136.

51. Treaty with the Menominee, February 11, 1856, 11 Stat. 679.

52. ARCOIA 1859, 1860, and 1865; Richard Yarnell, "Aboriginal Relationships between Culture and Plant Life," Anthropological Paper 23, Museum of Anthropology, University of Michigan (Ann Arbor, 1964), 127–37.

53. ARCOIA 1859 and 1862.

54. ARCOIA 1863 and 1870.

55. ARCOIA 1866, 287.

56. ARCOIA 1859; MMLM NA RG 75 SC 42 P762 R. 1, March 9, 1858, Z. Peters and J. Hendricks to C. Mix; MMLM NA RG 75 SC 42 B55 R. 1, September 10, 1859, A. D. Bonsteel to A. B. Greenwood.

57. ARCOIA 1862.

58. ARCOIA 1863.

59. NAM M234 R. 325:132, August 21, 1865, Petition to M. M. Davis; NAM M234 R. 325:944–52, June 28, 1867, Oneida chiefs to President; NAM M234 R. 327:360–61, August 3, 1870, D. Charles to COIA.

60. NAM M234 R. 325:346, March 5, 1866, M. Davis to COIA Cooley; NAM M234 R. 327:507–9, January 7, 1870, J. Manley to COIA Parker.

61. Francis P. Prucha, *The Great Father: The United States Government and the American Indians* (Lincoln: University of Nebraska Press, 1984), 889.

62. NAM M234 R. 325:710–11, November 27, 1866, L. Bogy to M. Martin.

63. NAM M234 R. 327:564–65, February 7, 1870, J. Manley to E. Parker.

64. NAM M234 R. 327:825–84, May 18, 1870, W. R. Bourn to E. Parker, Trial transcript of *U.S. v. Wybro*, 52–53.

65. Treaty with the Stockbridge and Munsee, February 5, 1856, 11 Stat. 663; NAM M234 R. 327:564–65, February 7, 1870, J. Manley to E. Parker.

66. NAM M234 R. 325:132, August 21, 1865, Petition to M. M. Davis.

67. Ibid.

68. NAM M234 R. 325:988–89, October 21, 1867, J. Hendricks to COIA; NAM M234 R. 325:642–47, July 20, 1866, M. Martin to D. Cooley.

69. NAM M234 R. 325:521–22, November 19, 1866, D. Charles to COIA.

70. NAM M234 R. 327:540–44, February 3, 1870, J. Manley to E. Parker.

71. NAM M234 R. 325:1029–30, January 5, 1867, M. Martin to L. Bogy; NAM M234 R. 327:530–33, February 1, 1870, J. Manley to E. Parker.

72. NAM M234 R. 227:549–53, February 7, 1870, J. Manley to E. Parker.

73. NAM M234 R. 327:567–69, February 9, 1870, J. Manley to COIA Parker.

74. George Gary, "Hon. Philetus Sawyer," *Magazine of Western History Illustrated* 10, no. 1 (1889): 469.

75. Richard N. Current, *Pine Logs and Politics A Life of Philetus Sawyer 1816–1900* (Madison: State Historical Society of Wisconsin, 1950), 71–74.

76. George Gary, "Hon. Philetus Sawyer," *Magazine of Western History Illustrated* 10, no. 1 (1889): 465.

77. Ibid., 465.

78. Ibid.

79. NAM M234 R. 325:350–51, March 12, 1866, E. S. Hammond to J. R. Doolittle.

80. Ibid.

81. NAM M234 R. 327:564–65, February 7, 1870, J. Manley to E. Parker.

82. NAM M234 R. 327:540–44, February 3, 1870, J. Manley to E. Parker.

83. NAM M234 R. 327:760, December 20, 1869, D. Charles to P. Sawyer, Enclosed with January 15, 1870, P. Sawyer to COIA Parker; NAM M234 R. 327:427, January 18, 1870, D. Charles to P. Sawyer.

84. NAM M234 R. 327:651–54, March 7, 1870, J. Manley to COIA Parker.

85. NAM M234 R. 327:549–53, February 7, 1870, J. Manley to E. Parker.

86. NAM M234 R. 327:395–97, March 27, 1870, S. Gillett to COIA Parker.

87. NAM M234 R. 327:549–53, February 7, 1870, J. Manley to E. Parker.

88. NAM M234 R. 327:536–38, February 1, 1870, Certification of petition of November 29, 1869, by J. Manley; NAM M234 R. 327:530–33, February 1, 1870, J. Manley to E. Parker.

89. NAM M234 R. 327:382–83, February 5, 1870, S. Davids et al. to COIA Parker.

90. NAM M234 R. 327:770–71, February 9, 1870, S. Gardner to P. Sawyer.

91. Ibid.

92. NAM M234 R. 327:762–67, February 12, 1870, P. Sawyer to COIA Parker containing Petition to Congress, February 1, 1870, from S. Davids et al. and Petition to U.S. Senate and U.S. Congress assembled, February 1, 1870, S. Davids et al.

93. NAM M234 R. 327:931–32, February 17, 1870, P. Sawyer to S. Gardner enclosed with March 6, 1871, S. Gardner to Secretary of Interior.

94. Francis P. Prucha, *The Great Father: The United States Government and the American Indians* (Lincoln: University of Nebraska Press, 1984), 550–51.

95. NAM M234 R. 327:507–9, January 7, 1870, J. Manley to COIA Parker.

96. NAM M234 R. 327:757–60, January 15, 1870, P. Sawyer to E. Parker.

97. NAM M234 R. 327:520–23, January 22, 1870, J. Manley to E. Parker.

98. NAM M234 R. 327:781–86, February 19, 1870, P. Sawyer to J. Cox.

99. NA RG 46, B99, 41st Congress, SB 610, March 2, 1870.

100. MMLM NA RG 75 SC 42 R. 1, December 15, 1873, W. Richardson to E. Smith.

101. MMLM NA RG 75 SC 42.I811 R. 1, August 2, 1875, E. Pierpoint to C. Delano (incomplete), "The Stockbridge Difficulty" (Newspaper clipping enclosed); MMLM NA RG 75 SC 42 B666 R. 1, May 4, 1875, Petition of Citizens.

102. MMLM NA RG 75 SC 42-S114, January 24, 1871, D. Charles et al. to COIA; NAM M234 R. 327:923–26, February 1, 1871, S. Gardner to Secretary of Interior.

103. MMLM NA RG 75 SC 42 R. 40, February 14, 1871, W. Richardson to E. Parker.

104. MMLM NA RG 75 SC 42-P189, March 25, 1871, J. Hendricks et al. to President Grant; NAM M234 R. 327:927–32, March 6, 1871, S. Gardner to C. Delano.

105. MMLM NA RG 75 SC 42-P189, March 25, 1871, Hendricks et al. to President Grant.

106. LOC Presidential Papers, Microfilm, U.S. Grant Papers Series 2:R.3, Letterbook vol. 1, 272, January 25, 1871, O. Babcock to Secretary of Interior.

107. RBH, Grant Papers LS.OFH, January 30, 1871, C. Delano to U. S. Grant.

108. NAM M234 R. 327:923–26, February 1, 1871, S. Gardner to Secretary of Interior.

109. LOC Presidential Papers, Microfilm, U.S. Grant Papers Series 2:R.3, Letterbook vol. 1, 280, February 6, 1871, H. Porter to H. Fish.

110. NA RG 46 B56 F14 S712:F4, February 16, 1871, P. Sawyer to J. Slingerland.

111. MMLM NA RG 75 SC 42.K316 R. 1, November 12, 1877, E. Kemble to E. Hayt; NA RG 46 B56 F14 5712:F.4, August 26, 1887, Affidavit of Orlin Andrews; NA RG 46 B56 F14 5712, April 27, 1888, J. D. C. Atkins to Secretary of Interior.

112. MMLM NA RG 75 SC 42-216 R. 2, December 29, 1885, G. Bennett to Secretary of Interior; MMLM NA RG 75 SC 42.2967 R. 2, January 16, 1888, W. Parsons to J. D. C. Atkins.

113. MMLM NA RG 75 SC 42.K316 R. 1, November 12, 1877, E. Kemble to E. Hayt; NA RG 46 B56 F14 S912:F4, July 8, 1878, W. Leeds to Secretary of Interior.

114. Treaty with the Menominee, February 11, 1856, 11 Stat. 679.

115. MMLM NA RG SC 42-W1003 R. 1, May 29, 1873, E. Smith to C. Delano.

116. MMLM NA RG 75 SC 42 P235 R. 1, July 12, 1873, S. Gardner et al. to Great Father.

117. MMLM RG 75 SC 42 R. 1, December 15, 1873, W. Richardson to E. Smith.

118. Ibid.

119. MMLM NA RG 75 SC 42 B1230 R. 1, August 2, 1875, J. Bridgman to J. Smith; MMLM NA RG 75 SC 42 B1348 R. 1, November 18, 1876, J. Bridgman to J. Smith.

120. MMLM NA RG 75 SC 42 B1404 R. 1, December 14, 1876, J. Bridgeman to J. Smith.

121. MMLM NA RG 75 SC 42 [30] R. 1, June 18, 1875, T. Chase to J. Smith.

122. MMLM NA RG 75 SC 42.K316 R. 1, November 12, 1877, E. Kemble to E. Hayt.

123. Ibid.

124. Ibid.

125. Ibid.

126. MMLM NA RG 75 SC 42 R. 1, April 13, 1877, S. Gardner to C. Shurz; MMLM NA RG 75 SC 42 R. 1, July 19, 1879, J. Adams to C. Shurz; MMLM NA RG 75 SC 42 B799 R. 1, July 25, 1879, G. Bennett to R. Breck; MMLM NA RG 75 SC 42.21962 R. 1, September 9, 1885, S. Gardner to F. Miller; MMLM NA RG 75 SC 42.12388 R. 2, April 30, 1886, J. Chicks et al. to COIA; MMLM NA RG 75 SC 42.40083, October 21, 1895, J. P. Hendricks et al. to Great Father.

127. MMLM NA RG 75 SC 42.4020 R. 2, February 4, 1886, T. Jennings to COIA, Enclosed clipping from *Appleton Crescent* and *Oshkosh Times.*

128. Ibid.

129. "Stockbridge Indians," *Chicago Tribune,* June 29, 1882.

130. Ibid.

131. Laws of Wisconsin 1883:327–328; MMLM NA RG 75 SC 42.31620 R. 2, n.d. 1886, Memorial of State of Wisconsin.

132. MMLM NA RG 75 SC 42.3868 R. 2, n.d. 1892, Petition of the Stockbridge and Munsee tribe.

133. ARCOIA, August 17, 1903.

134. Ibid.

135. MMLM NA RG 75 SC 42.31620 R. 2, November 16, 1886, S. Gardner to Secretary of Interior.

136. U.S. House of Representatives Hearings on Senate Bill 335, February 29, 1904, Hearings before Committee on Indian Affairs.

137. MMLM NA RG 75 SC 42 S321 R. 1, February 10, 1879, Davids et al. to COIA; MMLM NA RG 75 SC 42 R. 1, January 20, 1880, HR 3678.

138. NA RG 46 B56, SD V2 N76, 51st Congress Committee Papers, Sensia-F14 S712:F4, April 1, 1884, U.S. House of Representatives, Report 1054; NA RG 46 B56 F2-3, September 20, 1888, Report of the Senate Committee on Indian Affairs.

139. U.S. House of Representatives, Committee on Indian Affairs, 51st Cong., 1st sess., May 2, 1890, Report 1856.

140. MMLM NA RG 75 SC 42 R. 2, November 23, 1887, Petition of A. Miller and 22 others.

141. Files of U.S. Atty. of Wisconsin, Correspondence on Indian matters, n.d. 1906–8, W. Wheeler to S. Young, *State v. Gardner and Read.*

142. NA RG 75, Letters Received 45815, June 1, 1910, Tousey to COIA.

143. Ibid., Tousey to COIA.

144. NA RG 21, U.S. Dept. of Interior, U.S. Atty. for Western Dist. of Wisconsin, Case Files 1900–1902, July 23, 1901, OIA Circular L.

145. CCF 2709-1911, 170 Keshena Agency, January 24, 1911, F. Abbott to E. Henning.

146. General Allotment Act of February 8, 1887, 24 Stat. 388–91.

147. An Act for Relief of the Stockbridge and Munsee Tribe of Indians in the State of Wisconsin, March 3, 1893, 27 Stat. 744.

148. Ibid.

149. MMLM NA RG 75 SC 42.39915 R. 2, September 29, 1893, Petition by Hendricks, Gardner and 64 others, Enclosed in Lynch to COIA, October 26, 1893.

150. CCF 95218-1916, 170 Keshena Agency, August 30, 1916, E. B. Merritt to Secretary of Interior.

151. NA RG 75 Letters sent—land LB663, P.49, V.332, March 21, 1904, COIA to H. K. Butterfield.

152. U.S. House of Representatives, Committee on Indian Affairs, 58th Cong., 2nd sess., January 7, 1904, Report 173.

153. Allotment of the Stockbridge and Munsee Tribe of Wisconsin, June 21, 1906, 27 Stat. 745, vol. 1, 500.

154. Ibid.

155. Ibid.

156. CCF 78952-1909, 313 Keshena Agency, October 1, 1909, COIA to Secretary of Interior.

157. CCF 8436-1908, 313 Keshena Agency, February 8, 1908, Acting COIA to E. A. Morse.

158. CCF 49832-1910, 313 Keshena Agency, 1907–39, June 8, 1910, Petition of Stockbridge to President (partial copy).

CHAPTER 17

1. We will refer to the tribe by its modern name, as stated in its current constitution. The treaty was entered into with the "Stockbridge and Munsee tribes."

2. 25 U.S.C. 461 et seq.

3. *State v. Davids*, 94 Wis. 2d1, 386 (1995).

4. 25 U.S.C. 2701 *et seq.*

5. 25 U.S.C. 2719(b)(1)(A).

6. *Solem v. Bartlett*, 465 U.S. 463, 470, 104 S. Ct. 1161, 79 L. Ed. 2d 443 (1984465 U.S. at 470).

7. 465 U.S. at 470.

8. 465 U.S. at 471.

9. Ibid.

10. Ibid.

11. 465 U.S. at 472.

12. *Hagen v. Utah*, 510 U.S. 399 (1994).

13. *South Dakota v. Yankton Sioux Tribe*, 522 U.S. 329, 357 (1998).

14. E.D. Wis. 1999.

15. *State v. Stockbridge-Munsee Community and Chicks*, 366 F. Supp. 2d 698 (E.D.Wis. 2004).

CHAPTER 18

1. Charles E. Cleland, "Preliminary Report on the Ethnohistorical Basis of the Hunting, Fishing, and Gathering Rights of the Mille Lacs Chippewa," in *Fish in the Lakes, Wild Rice, and Game in Abundance: Testimony in Behalf of the Mille Lacs Ojibwe Hunting and Fishing Rights*, comp. James M. McClurken (East Lansing: Michigan State University Press, 2000), 89.

2. NAM T494 R. 5:307, February 12, 1855, Documents Relating to the Negotiation of the Treaty of February 22, 1855, 335.

3. Ibid., 336.

4. Treaty with the Chippewa, February 22, 1855, 10 Stat. 1165.

5. HW-MNHS, Box 3, February 28, 1863, Emnegahbowh (J. Johnston) to H. Whipple; HW-MNHS, Box 3, February 16, 1863, J. Johnston to H. Whipple.

6. HW-MNHS, Box 3, March 31, 1862, C. Blood to H. Whipple; HW-MNHS, Box 3, May 8, 1862, M. Wilkinson to H. Whipple; HW-MNHS, Box 3, September 1862, H. W. Whipple to President.

7. Robert Utley, "Indian-United States Military Situation 1848–1891," in *Handbook of North American Indians*, vol. 4, *History of Indian-White Relations*, ed. W. E. Washburn (Washington, D.C.: Smithsonian Institution, 1988).

8. Mark Diedrick, *The Chief Hole-n-the-Day of the Mississippi Chippewa* (St. Louis Park, Minn.: Coyote Books, 1986), 34–36.

9. HW-MNHS, Box 3, September 6, 1862, Rev. Peake to H. Whipple; HW-MNHS, Box 3, September 10, 1862, Rev. Peake to H. Whipple; HW-MNHS, Box 3, September 10, 1862, Rev. Peake to H. Whipple.

10. HW-MNHS, Box 3, September 6, 1862, Rev. Peake to H. Whipple; HW-MNHS, Box 3, September 10, 1862, Rev. Peake to H. Whipple; HW-MNHS, Box 3, September 10, 1862, Rev. Peake to H. Whipple.

11. Congress did not permit the sale of even dead and down timber on Indian reservations until 1889, and it was not until 1910 that tribes were able to cut timber with congressional approval. Francis P. Prucha, *The Great Father: The United States Government and the American Indians* (Lincoln: University of Nebraska Press, 1984), 889.

12. NAM T494 R. 5:307, February 12, 1855, Documents Relating to the Negotiation of the Treaty of February 22, 1855.

13. NAM M234 R. 153:220, Shobaushkum et al. Affidavit, March 17, 1863.

14. NAM T494 R. 6:541–653, Documents Relating to the Negotiation of the Treaty of March 11, 1863, with the Mississippi, Pillager, and Lake Winnibigoshish Bands of Chippewa Indians, 50–51; HW-MNHS, Box 3, February 16, 1863, J. Johnson to H. Whipple; HW-MNHS, Box 3, February 28, 1863, Emmegahbowh (J. Johnson) to H. Whipple.

15. HW-MNHS, Box 3, March 18, 1863, H. Rice to H. Whipple.

16. NAM T494 R. 6:541–653, Documents Relating to the Negotiation of the Treaty of March 11, 1863, with the Mississippi, Pillager, and Lake Winnibigoshish Bands of Chippewa Indians, 44.

17. LROIA 20033-1890, February 5, 1890, "Poor Show-Bosh-King. Bishop Whipple Pays a Gentle Tribute to the Memory of a Famous Indian," newspaper article.

18. NAM M234 R. 162:60–70, February 25, 1875, Council with a Delegation of Mille Lacs Chippewa, Office of Indian Affairs, Washington, D.C.

19. Treaty with the Chippewa of the Mississippi and the Pillager and Lake Winnibigoshish Bands, 12 Stat. 1249, March 11, 1863.

20. NAM M234 R. 155:658, December 2, 1867, Me no me ne kary et al. to Secretary of Indian Department.

21. Special Case 109, May 12, 1870, J. Roberts to G. Atcheson.

22. Special Case 109, March 22, 1880, Chiefs to President R. B. Hayes.

23. "The Mille Lacs Reservation," *Minneapolis Tribune*, July 18, 1883.

24. NAM T494 R. 6:541–653, Documents Relating to the Negotiation of the Treaty of March 11, 1863, with the Mississippi, Pillager, and Lake Winnibigoshish Bands of Chippewa Indians, 44.

25. NAM M234 R. 153:408, March 14, 1864, Shobaushkum et al. to H. Whipple.

26. NAM T494 R. 5:321, Documents Relating to the Negotiation of the Treaty of February 22, 1855.

27. NAM M234 R. 162:60–70, February 25, 1875, Council with a Delegation of Mille Lacs Chippewa, Office of Indian Affairs, Washington, D.C., February 1875.

28. Ibid.

29. U.S. House of Representatives 247 (54-1) 2747, March 6, 1890, 163 Chippewa Indians of Minnesota, Message from the President of the United States Transmitting a Communication from the Secretary of the Interior Relative to the Chippewa Indians in the State of Minnesota.

30. Treaty with the Chippewa of the Mississippi, March 19, 1867, 16 Stat. 719.

31. NAM M234 R. 155:687, July 25, 1867, Kawnodowinwinzo et al. to COIA.

32. Ibid.

33. HW-MNHS, Box 5, n.d. 1868, Report of H. Whipple.

34. MN 002213, October 29, 1867, Bassette to Taylor; LROIA 4778-1886, February 9, 1886, J. Roberts to Hon. W. Holman.

35. Special Case 109, May 12, 1870, J. Roberts to G. Atcheson; HW-MNHS, Box 5, September 23, 1867, Enmegahbowh to H. Whipple; NAM M234 R. 155:658, December 2, 1867, Menomenekary et al. to Secretary of Interior.

36. NAM M234 R. 166:343–44, March 19, 1878, C. Ruffee to E. Hoyt; Special Case 109, March 31, 1871, E. P. Smith to E. Parker.

37. Special Case 109, August 25, 1882, Inspection Report on Mille Lacs Reservation—George M. Chapman.

38. Ibid.

39. LROIA 11832, April 26, 1883, Special Case 109, H. Price to Secretary of Interior.

40. Ibid.

41. Special Case File 109, November 10, 1882, Petition from Mille Lacs Chiefs to OIA.

42. MNHS-FE96, C6R6, Joseph Roberts Papers 1826–1886, List of Chippewa Indians at Mille Lacs circa 1880.

43. Special Case 109, August 25, 1882, Inspection Report on Mille Lacs Reservation, August 25, 1882, George M. Chapman; Special Case 109, June 27, 1883, Report of Special Agent John Wright.

44. Special Case 109, March 31, 1871, E. P. Smith to E. Parker.

45. LROIA 2564, February 2, 1884, L. Hubbard to H. Price; Special Case 109, March 31, 1871, E. Smith to E. Parker.

46. Special Case 109, March 31, 1871, E. Smith to E. Parker.

47. Ibid.

48. NAM M234 R. 164:494–97, April 1877, Petition of Citizens of Morrison County, Minnesota.

49. NAM M234 R. 164:494–97, April 14, 1877, Petition of Mille Lacs Chiefs.

50. LROIA 2733-1888, January 30, 1888, E. Rice to J. Atkins.

51. LROIA 2587-1884, January 21, 1884, Affidavit of O. Sylvester, J. Stillwell, and R. Worthington.

52. LROIA 2354-1883, December 22, 1883, L. Hubbard to C. P. Luce; LROIA 2587-1884, January 23, 1884, Affidavit of J. Robert; LROIA 2587-1884, January 21, 1884, Affidavit of O. Sylvester, J. Stillwell, and R. Worthington.

53. LROIA 2564-1884, February 2, 1884, L. Hubbard to H. Price.

54. LROIA 2564-1884, February 2, 1884, L. Hubbard to H. Price; LROIA 2587-1884, January 23, 1884, Affidavit of Joseph Roberts.

55. LROIA 961-1884, January 11, 1884, C. Luce to H. Price.

56. LROIA 7217-1890, March 5, 1890, B. Shuler to COIA; LROIA-16695-1889, June 22, 1889, R. Gardner to J. Oberly; LROIA 9861-1890, March 24, 1890, D. Robbins to J. Noble.

57. House Documents 110 (50-1) 2558, January 20, 1888.

58. LROIA 2733-1888, January 30, 1888, Chiefs to Great Father.

59. An Act for the Relief and Civilization of the Chippewa Indians in the State of Minnesota, January 14, 1889, 25 Stat. 642.

60. ARCOIA 1890, XLII.

61. An Act for the Relief and Civilization of the Chippewa Indians in the State of Minnesota, January 14, 1889, 25 Stat. 642.

62. U.S. House of Representatives 247 (54-1) 2747, March 6, 1890, 163 Chippewa Indians of Minnesota, Message from the President of the United States Transmitting a Communication from the Secretary of the Interior Relative to the Chippewa Indians in the State of Minnesota, 5.

63. Ibid.

64. Ibid., 163.

65. Ibid., 164.

66. Ibid., 165.

67. Ibid., 169.

68. Ibid.

69. Ibid., 175.

70. ARCOIA 1990, XLIII.

71. U.S. House of Representatives 247 (54-1) 2747, March 6, 1890, 163 Chippewa Indians of Minnesota, Message from the President of the United States Transmitting a Communication from the Secretary of the Interior Relative to the Chippewa Indians in the State of Minnesota, 173.

72. Ibid., 168.

73. LROIA 29144-1889, October 12, 1889, H. Rice to COIA.

74. U.S. House of Representatives 247 (54-1) 2747, March 6, 1890, 163 Chippewa Indians of Minnesota, Message from the President of the United States Transmitting a Communication from the Secretary of the Interior Relative to the Chippewa Indians in the State of Minnesota, 45.

75. Ibid., 71.

76. Ibid., 169.

77. Ibid., 168.

78. Ibid., 165.

79. Ibid.

80. 26 Stat. 290.

CHAPTER 19

1. 10 Stat. 1165, February 22, 1855.
2. 12 Stat. 1249, March 11, 1863.
3. 13 Stat. 693, May 7, 1964.

4. 23 Stat. 76, 89, July 4, 1884.

5. Felix S. Cohen, *Felix S. Cohen's Handbook of Federal Indian Law,* 2005 ed. (Newark, N.J. LexisNexis, 2005), 77–78.

6. 25 Stat. 642, January 14, 1889.

7. U.S. House of Representatives, 50th Cong., 1st sess., March 1, 1888, Report 789.

8. Ibid.

9. *Congressional Record* 19 (October 3, 1888): S 9129—32.

10. *Congressional Record* 19 (October 3, 1888): S 9130.

11. U.S. House of Representatives, 51st Cong., 1st Sess., March 6, 1890, Exec. Doc. 247 at 163–64.

12. Ibid., 165.

13. Ibid., 168.

14. Ibid., 169.

15. Ibid.

16. Ibid., 166–67, 169–70.

17. Ibid., 171–75.

18. Ibid., 45–46.

19. Ibid.

20. Ibid., 22.

21. Ibid., 22–23.

22. Ibid., 24–25.

23. S. M. Brosius, *The Urgent Case of the Mille Lacs Indians* (Indian Rights Ass'n, 1901), 3.

24. 28 Stat. 576, December 19, 1893.

25. 30 Stat. 745, May 27, 1898.

26. 35 Stat. 619, February 15, 1909.

27. *Mille Lac Band of Chippewa Indians v. United States,* 47 Ct. Cl. 415, 457 (Ct. Cl. 1912).

28. *United States v. Mille Lac Band of Chippewa Indians,* 229 U.S. 498, 503, 506–07, 509–10 (1913).

29. 38 Stat. 582, August 1, 1914.

30. The county attorney's memorandum is filed in the court record in *County of Mille Lacs v. Melanie Benjamin,* No. 02-CV-407 (D. Minn.).

31. *Minnesota v. Mille Lacs Band,* 526 U.S. 172, 196 (1999).

32. Ibid.

33. Ibid., 200.

34. *South Dakota v. Yankton Sioux Tribe,* 522 U.S. 329, 343 (1998).

35. *Solem v. Bartlett,* 465 U.S. 463, 470 (1984).

36. *Yankton Sioux,* 522 U.S. 345, *citing Mattz v. Arnett,* 412 U.S. 481, 497 (1973), and *Seymour v. Superintendent,* 368 U.S. 351, 355–56 (1962).

37. *Yankton Sioux,* 522 U.S. at 345, *citing Solem v. Bartlett.*

38. *Yankton Sioux,* 522 U.S. at 345.

39. *Solem v. Bartlett,* 465 U.S. at 469.

40. Ibid., 471.

41. Ibid.

42. Ibid., 471–72.

43. *Yankton Sioux,* 522 U.S. at 356.

44. *Solem v. Bartlett,* 465 U.S. at 472.

CHAPTER 20

1. NAM M21 R. 18:179–80, March 14, 1836, L. Cass to H. Schoolcraft; NAM M21 R. 18:431, May 17, 1836, L. Cass to H. Schoolcraft; NAM M21 R. 19:492, September 30, 1836, C. A. Harris to H. Schoolcraft.

2. 7 Stat. 491.

3. NAM M21 R. 18:179–80, March 14, 1836, L. Cass to H. Schoolcraft.

4. Charles Kappler, ed., *Indian Affairs: Laws and Treaties* (Washington, D.C.: U.S. Government Printing Office, 1904), 2:461–62 (7 Stat. 503).

5. 7 Stat. 528.

6. Charles Kappler, ed., *Indian Affairs: Laws and Treaties* (Washington, D.C.: U.S. Government Printing Office, 1904), 2:482–85 (7 Stat. 503).

7. NAM M21 R. 22:364–65, October 2, 1837, C. A. Harris to H. Schoolcraft.

8. Charles Kappler, ed., *Indian Affairs: Laws and Treaties* (Washington, D.C.: U.S. Government Printing Office, 1904), 2:516–17 (7 Stat. 565).

9. NAM M21 R. 22:510–11, November 7, 1839, C. A. Harris to H. Schoolcraft.

10. NA RG 75 BIA Civilization Division. Census of Indians within the Superintendency of Michigan in 1842.

11. James M. McClurken, "We Wish to Be Civilized: Ottawa-American Political Contest on the Michigan Frontier" (PhD diss., Michigan State University, East Lansing, 1988).

12. Willis Dunbar, *Michigan: A History of the Wolverine State* (Grand Rapids: W. B. Eerdmans Publishing, 1970).

13. Ibid., 249–50.

14. Kenneth E. Lewis, *West to Far Michigan* (East Lansing: Michigan State University Press, 2002).

15. Ibid., 246; NAM M234 R. 404:497–98, April 12, 1854, J. Wilson to G. Manypenny.

16. NAM M21 R. 52, July 12, 1855, C. Mix to H. Schoolcraft; H-211, August 7, 1855, G. Manypenny and H. Gilbert to C. Mix.

17. Charles Cleland, "From Ethnohistory to Archaeology: Ottawa and Ojibwa Band Territories of the Northern Great Lakes," in *Text Aided Archaeology,* ed. Barbara Little (Caldwell N.J.: Telford Press, 1991).

18. Anonymous, *Portraits and Biographical Album of Isabella County, Michigan* (Chicago, 1884), 536.

19. Ibid., 537.

20. Ibid., 540; J. D. B. DeBox, *Statistical View of the United States* (Washington, D.C.: A. O. P. Nicholson Publishing, 1854), 256.

21. Anonymous, *Portraits and Biographical Album of Isabella County, Michigan* (Chicago, 1884), 566.

22. Willis Dunbar, *Michigan: A History of the Wolverine State* (Grand Rapids: W. B. Eerdmans Publishing, 1970).

23. Charles Kappler, ed., *Indian Affairs: Laws and Treaties* (Washington, D.C.: U.S. Government Printing Office, 1904), 2:847 (Executive Order, President Franklin Pierce, May 14, 1855).

24. NAM M234 R. 404:840–41, April 26, 1855, Secretary McClelland to G. Manypenny; NAM M234 R. 404:842–43, May 21, 1855, Secretary McCleland to G. Manypenny.

25. NAM M234 R. 404:368–80, March 6, 1854, H. Gilbert to G. Manypenny; NAM M234 R. 404:844–51, May 21, 1855, G. Manypenny to Secretary McClelland; NAM M 234 R. 404:713–14, July 3, 1855, H. Gilbert to G. Manypenny.

26. NAM M234 R. 404:368–80, March 6, 1854, H. Gilbert to G. Manypenny.

27. Charles Kappler, ed., *Indian Affairs: Laws and Treaties* (Washington, D.C.: U.S. Government Printing Office, 1904), 2:847 (Executive Order, President Franklin Pierce, May 14, 1855).

28. Francis P. Prucha, *The Great Father: The United States Government and the American Indians* (Lincoln: University of Nebraska Press, 1984); U.S. House of Representatives, 34th Cong., 3rd sess., 1856, Exec. Doc., 1856 Report of the Commissioner of Indian Affairs, G. Manypenny, 574.

29. ARCOIA 1855, 1.

30. ARCOIA 1857, 19.

31. Ibid., 1857, 293.

32. *United States v. Michigan,* MI-26-73CA, Plaintiff Exhibit Pl. 19, July 25, 1855, Proceeding of a Council with the Chippeways and Ottawas of Michigan Held at the City of Detroit by the Hon. George W. Manypeny [*sic*] and Henry C. Gilbert, Commissioners of the United States.

33. Loring B. Priest, *Uncle Sam's Stepchildren: The Reformation of United States' Indian Policy, 1865–1887* (New Brunswick: Rutgers University Press, 1942), 178.

34. NAM M234 R. 404:844–51, May 21, 1855, G. Manypenny to R. McClelland; H-211, June 6, 1855, G. Manypenny to H. Gilbert; *Detroit Daily Free Press,* July 26, 1855.

35. NAM M234 R. 404:708–10, June 13, 1855, H. Gilbert to G. Manypenny.

36. *Detroit Daily Free Press,* July 29, 1855.

37. 11 Stat. 633.

38. *Detroit Daily Free Press,* August 2, 1855.

39. NAM M234 R. 404:705–7, June 9, 1855, H. Gilbert to G. Manypenny; NAM M234 R. 404:713–14, July 3, 1855, H. Gilbert to G. Manypenny; NAM M234 R. 404:978–79, July 7, 1855, G. Smith to G. Manypenny; NAM M234 R. 404:574–76, July 14, 1855, J. Durbin to G. Manypenny.

40. Charles Kappler, ed., *Indian Affairs: Laws and Treaties* (Washington, D.C.: U.S. Government Printing Office, 1904), 847 (Executive Order, President Franklin Pierce, May 14, 1855).

41. NAM M234 R. 404:368–80, March 6, 1854, H. Gilbert to G. Manypenny; NAM M234 R. 404:516–19, March 14, 1854, G. Smith to G. Manypenny.

42. NAM M234 R. 404:625–27, April 12, 1855, H. Gilbert to G. Manypenny; NAM M234 R. 404:915–17, September 8, 1855, T. Hendricks to C. Mix.

43. Anonymous, *Portrait and Biographical Album of Isabella County, Michigan* (Chicago, 1884), 536.

44. Charles Kappler, ed., *Indian Affairs: Laws and Treaties* (Washington, D.C.: U.S. Government Printing Office, 1904), 2:846 (J. Wilson to R. McClelland, December 20, 1854).

45. Charles Kappler, ed., *Indian Affairs: Laws and Treaties* (Washington, D.C.: U.S. Government Printing Office, 1904), 2:846 (R. McClelland to President, April 12, 1855).

46. H-211, C. Mix to I. Hendricks, April 14, 1859.

47. Charles Kappler, ed., *Indian Affairs: Laws and Treaties* (Washington, D.C.: U.S. Government Printing Office, 1904), 2:846 (R. McClelland to President, April 12, 1855).

48. G. W. Manypenny, *Our Indian Wards* (New York: DaCapo Press, 1972).

49. *United States v. Michigan,* MI-26-73CA, Plaintiff Exhibit Pl. 19, July 25, 1855, Proceeding of a Council with the Chippeways and Ottawas of Michigan Held at the City of Detroit by the Hon. George W. Manypeny [*sic*] and Henry C. Gilbert, Commissioners of the United States.

50. NAM M234 R. 404: 915–17, September 8, 1855, T. Hendricks to C. Mix.

51. *East Saginaw Courier,* July 12 1860; NAM M234 R. 406:994–95, July 10, 1861, D. C. Leach to W. P. Dole.

52. NAM M234 R. 405:119–20, June 19, 1856, H. Gilbert to G. Manypenny.

53. H-211, April 14, 1859. C. Mix to I. Hendricks.

54. NAM M234 R. 405:633–34, April 4, 1857, H. Gilbert to G. Manypenny; NAM M234 R. 406:463–66, June 21, 1859, A. Fitch to A. B. Greenwood; NAM M234 R. 406:569–73, June 21, 1859, Saginaw Chiefs to President J. Buchanan; NAM M234 R. 406:706–7, June 8, 1860, A. Fitch to A. B. Greenwood; NAM M234 R. 406:906–7, September 10, 1860, A. Fitch to W. P. Dole; NAM M234 R. 406:1019–23, April 3, 1861, C. Smith to Commissioner of General Land Office; NAM M234 R. 407:134–36, November 28, 1862, J. M. Edmunds to W. P. Dole; NAM M234 R. 407:197–99, May 27, 1863, G. Bradley to J. M. Edmunds; NAM M234 R. 407:470–71, February 15, 1864, Saginaw Chiefs to President A. Lincoln; NAM M234 R. 407:467–69, April 9, 1864, D. C. Leach to W. P. Dole.

55. Exec. Doc., 36th Cong., 2nd sess., Report of the Secretary of the Interior, 1860 (Washington, D.C.: G. W. Bowman Printer, 1861), 34–35.

56. Charles Kappler, ed., *Indian Affairs: Laws and Treaties* (Washington, D.C.: U.S. Government Printing Office, 1904), 2:846 (J. Wilson to R. McClelland, December 20, 1854); NAM M234 R. 404:516–19, May 14, 1854, G. Smith to G. Manypenny.

57. Charles Kappler, ed., *Indian Affairs: Laws and Treaties* (Washington, D.C.: U.S. Government Printing Office, 1904), 2: 729 (Treaty, July 31, 1855).

58. *United States v. Michigan,* MI-26-73CA, Plaintiff Exhibit Pl. 19, July 25, 1855, Proceeding of a Council with the Chippeways and Ottawas of Michigan Held at the City of Detroit by the Hon. George W. Manypeny [*sic*] and Henry C. Gilbert, Commissioners of the United States.

59. NAM M234 R. 405:244–51, February 25, 1856, H. Gilbert to G. Manypenny.

60. NAM M234 R. 405:295–97, April 2, 1856, T. Hendricks to G. Manypenny.

61. NAM M234 R. 405:307–8, April 9, 1856, T. Hendricks to G. Manypenny.

62. NAM M234 R. 405:237–38, April 14, 1856, Sec. of Interior to G. Manypenny.

63. NAM M234 R. 405:119–20, June 19, 1856, H. Gilbert to G. Manypenny.

64. NAM M234 R. 405:154–55, August 14, 1856, W. Brockway to H. Gilbert.

65. NAM M234 R. 405:633–34, April 4, 1857, H. Gilbert to G. Manypenny.

66. NAM M234 R. 405:559–60, November 2, 1857, A.W. Fitch to J. Denver.

67. H-211, April 14, 1859, C. Mix to I. Hendricks.

68. NAM M234 R. 406:547–49, August 30, 1859, Commissioner of General Land Office to A. Greenwood.

69. NAM M234 R. 406:755–57, November 19, 1860, A. Fitch to A. Greenwood.

70. NAM M234 R. 406:994–95, July 10, 1861, D. Leach to Dole.

71. NAM M234 R. 404:833, December 6, 1855, H. Gilbert to Anonymous; NAM M234 R. 406:1018, October 31, 1861, J. M. Edmunds to COIA; NAM M234 R. 407:134–36, November 28, 1862, J. M. Edmunds to W. P. Dole.

72. NAM M234 R. 407:470–71, February 15, 1864, Nottawa et al. to President Lincoln; NAM M234 R. 407:467–69, April 9, 1864, D. Leach to W. Dole.

73. NAM M234 R. 407:467–69, April 9, 1864, D. Leach to W. Dole; NAM M21 R. 75:181–82, September 3, 1864, W. Dole to H. J. Alvord.

74. NAM M234 R. 407:677–707, n.d. 1864, Pay List for 1855 Treaty Payment.

75. NAM M234 R. 407:470–71, February 15, 1864, Nottawa et al. to President A. Lincoln.

76. NAM M21 R. 75:181–82, September 3, 1864, W. Dole to H. J. Alvord.

77. 14 Stat. 657.

78. NAM M21 R. 75:181–82, September 3, 1864, W. Dole to H. J. Alvord.

79. Willis Dunbar, *Michigan: A History of the Wolverine State* (Grand Rapids: W. B. Eerdmans Publishing, 1970), 460–61.

80. NAM M234 R. 407:538–40, October 4, 1864, D. Leach to W. P. Dole.

81. NAM M234 R. 408:877–93, November 13, 1869, J. Long to E. Parker.

82. NAM M234 R. 407:371–74, December 1, 1864, W. Nelson to H. J. Alvord; NAM M234 R. 407:368–70, December 6, 1864, G. Bradley to H. J. Alvord.

83. NAM M234 R. 407:1006–8, December 2, 1864, J. Usher to J. Edmunds.

84. NAM M234 R. 408:894–97, November 4, 1869, G. Bradley to E. Parker.

85. NAM M234 R. 408:667–74, n.d. 1869, N. Mosher et al., Petition of Citizens of Isabella County.

86. NAM M234 R. 408:858–62, September 29, 1869, H. R. Patt(?) to J. Long.

87. NAM M21 R. 92:350–53, October 21, 1869, E. Parker to J. Long.

88. NAM M234 R. 408:424–29, June 5, 1868, T. Ferry to O. Browning.

89. NAM M234 R. 408:877–93, November 13, 1869, J. Long to E. Parker.

90. NAM M21 R. 91, July 30, 1869, E. Parker to J. Long.

91. NAM M234 R. 408:877–93, November 13, 1869, J. Long to E. Parker; NAM M234 R. 408:894–97, November 4, 1869, G. Bradley to E. Parker.

92. NAM M234 R. 409:148–53, n.d. 1870, Contract of Jerome and Williams; NAM M234 R. 409:121–33, February 4, 1870, J. Long to E. Parker.

93. NAM M234 R. 409:121–33, February 4, 1870, J. Long to E. Parker.

94. NAM M234 R. 409:421–24, October 31, 1870, G. Bradley to President U. S. Grant.

95. NAM M234 R. 409:462–64, n.d. 1871, A. Osawwapon et al. to E. Parker; NAM M234 R. 409:903–9, December 19, 1870, Ahkojin et al. to Secretary of Interior.

96. NAM M234 R. 409:968–69, June 15, 1871, R. Smith to E. Parker.

97. H-211, October 19, 1871, J. Long to H. Clum.

98. *Saginaw Weekly Enterprise*, November 3, 1870; NAM M234 R. 409:421–24, October 31, 1870, G. Bradley to U. S. Grant.

99. NAM M234 R. 409:303–9, November 8, 1870, J. Long to E. Parker.

100. NAM M234 R. 409:634–36, September 14, 1871, A. Maynard to C. Delano.

101. NAM M234 R. 409:896–98, September 16, 1871, A. Osawwabon et al. to Secretary of Interior.

102. H-211, 5434, May 27, 1872, Charles Eddy et al. to President.

103. NAM M234 R. 409:639–41, September 18, 1871, C. Delano to A. Akerman.

104. Loring B. Priest, *Uncle Sam's Stepchildren: The Reformation of United States Indian Policy, 1865–1887* (New Brunswick: Rutgers University Press, 1942), 95–105; Francis P. Prucha, *The Great Father: The United States Government and the American Indians* (Lincoln: University of Nebraska Press, 1984).

105. 16 Stat. 566.

106. H-211, 5435, n.d. 1872, P. Pahahmoshshe et al. to Hon. F. Walker.

107. NAM M234 R. 411:546–51, May 28, 1875, Mishahquaknahuw et al. to Great Father in Washington; NAM M234 R. 411:552–59, August 2, 1875, Lyman Bennett et al. to Our Great Father in Washington.

108. NAM M234 R. 411:760–62, January 25, 1876, J. Q. Smith to E. Kemble.

109. H-211, 2496, February 22, 1876, E. Kemble to COIA.

110. H-211, 4875, February 26, 1876, J. Smith to G. Betts; NAM M234 R. 414:124–25, November 6, 1879, W. W. Upton to COIA.

111. NAM M234 R. 411:9–47, January 18, 1878, E. J. Brooks to E. A. Hayt; NAM M234 R. 411:876–80, June 30, 1876, G. Lee to J. Smith; NAM M234 R. 412:152–54, January 22, 1877, G. Lee to J. Smith

112. LROIA 22911-1885, September 26, 1885, Mrs. G. Owen to President.

113. NAM M234 R. 413:304–9, January 15, 1878, G. Lee to COIA.

114. H-211, 2496, February 22, 1876, E. Kemble to COIA; NAM M234 R. 411:9–47, January 18, 1878, E. J. Brooks to E. A. Hayt; NAM M234 R. 414:34–44, October 25, 1879, E. J. Brooks to COIA; LROIA 10005-1891, May 15, 1886, J. D. C. Atkins to Secretary of Interior.

115. NAM M234 R. 414:34–44, October 25, 1879, E. J. Brooks to COIA.

116. Ibid.

117. Ibid.

118. NAM M234 R. 410:479–81, July 6, 1872, W. D. Foster to F. Walker.

119. NAM M234 R. 411:9–47, January 18, 1878, E. J. Brooks to E. A. Hayt.

120. ARCOIA 1878.

121. NAM M24 R. 412:280–86, March 28, 1877, G. Lee to J. Q. Smith.

122. H-211, 5421, n.d. 1878, Sawwabon et al. to Secretary of Interior; NAM M234 R. 411:939–41, October 30, 1876, G. Lee to J. Q. Smith; H-211, 5420, February 18, 1878, G. Lee to COIA; NAM M234 R. 413:730–32, June 22, 1878, Sawwabon et al. to Secretary of Interior; NAM M234 R. 415:175–79, March 18, 1880, G. Lee to R. E. Trowbridge; NAM M234 R. 414:639–40, June 19, 1880, Attorney General to C. Shurz; LR Mackinac Agency (1870–1877), April 21, 1881, J. Welsh to G. Lee; H-211, May 7, 1881, J. Welsh to J. A. Williamson.

123. NAM M234 R. 411:876–80, June 30, 1876, G. Lee to J. Q. Smith.

124. NAM M234 R. 414:172–73, April 1, 1878, G. Lee to COIA; NAM M234 R. 414:170–71, January 18, 1879, C. Shurz to COIA.

125. ARCOIA 1867.

126. LROIA 132120-1886, May 15, 1886, Acting Commissioner of the General Land Office to J. D. C. Atkin.

127. LROIA 10005-1891, May 15, 1886, J. D. C. Atkins to Secretary of Interior; LROIA 15646-1886, June 11, 1886, M. Stevens to J. D. C. Atkins; H-211, June 30, 1886, Report, U.S. Dist. Attorney, Eastern District of Michigan, to Commissioner of General Land Office; LROIA 17295-1886, July 2, 1886, Commissioner of General Land Office to J. D. C. Atkins; LROIA 18819-1886, July 14, 1886, M. Stevens to J. D. C. Atkins.

128. LROIA 17497-1888, July 5, 1888, M. Stevens to J. D. C. Atkins.

129. LROIA 26252-1887, October 3, 1887, M. Stevens to J. D. C. Atkins; LROIA 22911-1885, September 26, 1885, G. Owen to President.

130. LROIA 26252-1887, December 4, 1873, Report of the Auditor General of Michigan 1874.

131. LROIA 26252-1887, October 3, 1887, M. Stevens to J. D. C. Atkins.

132. 24 Stat. 288–91.

133. LROIA 26252-1887, October 3, 1887, M. Stevens to J. D. C. Atkins.

134. LROIA 23713-1888, September 20, 1888, M. Stevens to J. D. C. Atkins.

135. LROIA 23932-1888, September 22, 1888, M. Stevens to COIA.

136. LROIA 24195-1888, September 22, 1888, Commissioner of General Land Office to J. D. C. Atkins.

137. LROIA 30040-1888, December 1, 1888, M. Stevens to J. H. Oberly.

138. Frederick E. Hoxie, *A Final Promise: The Campaign to Assimilate the Indians, 1880–1920* (Cambridge: Cambridge University Press, 1989).

139. LROIA 13600-1889, May 20, 1889, M. Stevens to J. H. Oberly.

140. ARCOIA 1886, 166–67.

141. Alice Littlefield, "The BIA Boarding School: Theories of Resistance and Social Reproduction," *Humanities and Society* 13, no. 4 (1989): 428–41.

142. LROIA 32393-1893, August 23, 1893, J. Williams to COIA.

143. LROIA 229905-1895, July 16, 1895, P. Gruett to Department of Interior; LROIA 1479-1896, January 9, 1896, Fancher and Sangster to COIA; LROIA 50639-1900, October 9, 1900, Superintendent of the Indian School in Mt. Pleasant to COIA.

144. LROIA 45149-1894, November 16, 1894, Attorney General to Secretary of Interior; LROIA 48026-1894, December 6, 1894, Attorney General to Secretary of Interior; LROIA 45020-1899, September 20, 1899, T. Ryan to COIA; LROIA 36407-1906, April 21, 1906, Attorney General to Secretary of Interior.

145. An Act for the Relief of the Saginaw, Swan Creek and Black River Band of Chippewa Indians in the State of Michigan, June 25, 1910, in *Senate Document 53*, Serial Set 8849, ed. Charles Kappler (Washington, D.C.: Senate Committee on Printing, 1929), Vol. 4:415; CCF Mackinac 90122-1920, 115, November 4, 1920, L. Walker Demsey to Cato Sells.

CHAPTER 21

1. Johann Kohl, *Kitchi-Gami: Life among the Lake Superior Ojibway* (St. Paul: Minnesota Historical Society Press, 1985), 25.

2. Ibid., 25–26.

3. Ibid., 26.

4. John D. Nichols, *"Statement Made by the Indians": A Bilingual Petition of the Chippewas of Lake Superior, 1864* (London: Centre for Research and Teaching of Canadian Native Languages, University of Western Ontario, 1988).

5. NAM T494 R. 5, October 17, 1854, H. Gilbert to G. Manypenny.

6. NA RG 75, Mackinac LR, BBC, M95-4, September 1858. Chiefs to A. Fitch.

7. NAM M234 R. 407:238–39, February 25, 1863, D. Leach to W. Dole.

8. NAM M234 R. 404:184–90, December 10, 1853, H. Gilbert to G. Manypenny.

9. John D. Nichols, *"Statement Made by the Indians": A Bilingual Petition of the Chippewas of Lake Superior, 1864* (London: Centre for Research and Teaching of Canadian Native Languages, University of Western Ontario, 1988).

10. Ibid., 23–24.

11. NAM T494 R. 5, October 17, 1854, H. Gilbert to G. Manypenny.

12. Irene Neu, "The Building of the Sault Canal: 1852–1855," *Mississippi Valley Historical Review* 20 (1954): 25–46.

13. Ibid.

14. Ibid., 44.

15. Treaty with the Chippewa, September 30, 1854, 10 Stat. 1109.

16. NAM M234 R. 394, August 12, 1870, A. Whittlesey to E. Parker.

17. U.S. House of Representatives, 43rd Cong., 1st sess., April 11, 1874, Report 396.

18. NAM M234 R. 411, October 6, 1874, S. S. Binath to E. Smith; NAM M234 R. 411:138–43, November 3, 1874, G. Betts to COIA.

19. U.S. House of Representatives, 43rd Cong., 1st sess., April 11, 1874, Report 396.

20. Treaty with the Chippewa, September 30, 1854, 10 Stat. 1109.

21. NA RG 75, Executive Order relating to Indian Reservations, March 7, 1855.

22. NAM M234 R. 391, March 30, 1855, J. Wilson to Register and Receiver.

23. ARCOIA 1855.

24. ARCOIA 1855.

25. NA RG 75 E91, LR-1881-1907, November 24, 1877, Printed Rules and Regulations for Land Conveyances at L'Anse.

26. NAM M234 R. 411, February 11, 1874, G. Betts to COIA (Enclosed with Cowen to COIA, February 16, 1874).

27. NAM M21 R. 116, March 21, 1874, E. Smith to G. Betts.

28. NAM M234 R. 411:159–66, December 11, 1874, G. Betts to COIA Smith.

29. Ibid.

30. Ibid.

31. Of this number only 11 were approved in Washington.

32. ARCOIA 1857, Senate of the United States, 35th Cong., 1st sess., 1857–58, Exec. Doc., Report of the Secretary of the Interior, 292.

33. NAM M234 R. 411:513–14, July 21, 1875, S. Burdett to E. Smith.

34. NAM M234 R. 407:401–2, September 8, 1864, D. King et al. to COIA.

35. NAM M234 R. 404:670–71, January 7, 1865, D. King et al. to W. Dole; NAM M234 R. 407:729, February 23, 1865, D. Leach to W. Dole; NAM M234 R. 409:914–15, March 21, 1871, D. King et al. to President.

36. *Keweenaw Bay Indian Community v. Michigan,* 784 F. Supp. 418 (W.D. Mich 1991).

37. CCF 49380-09 Mackinac 313, July 8, 1909, J. Dortch to J. LaBrecque; CCF 56562-09 Mackinac 313, July 14, 1909, J. LaBrecque to Secretary of Interior.

38. BCC-RD, Deeds, L25:178, July 19, 1875, U.S. to Catherine Asher.

39. In 1854 the reservation was part of L'Anse Township of Houghton County, but in 1870 Baraga Township was formed so that the reservation now lies within both L'Anse and Baraga Townships of Houghton County. Baraga County was formed from part of Houghton County in 1875, and the townships remained the same.

40. The tax assessment rolls for 1875, 1876, and 1877 show these lands were not taxed, even though patents in fee were issued for all of these on July 19, 1875. See BCC-TO-TAR, Baraga County, 1875, 1876, and 1877. SAM RG 65-5-A, Box 2, F1, n.d. to 1924, Abstracts of "lands set apart for the L'Anse and Vieux de Sert bands of Chippewa Indians of Lake Superior Michigan under treaty of September 30, 1854."

41. BCC-TO-TAR, Baraga County, 1878. The Silver River Company was later renamed the Silver River State and Mining Company.

42. NA RG 75 E91, LR-1892-12408, March 31, 1892, Supervisor of L'Anse Township to COIA; CCF 9048-11 Chippewa Lake 300, October 19, 1911, H. Smith to COIA; CCF 55182-13 Mackinac, May 10, 1913, C. Hauke to Buckland.

43. BCC-RD, Deeds, L7:318, August 18, 1853, Patent, United States to Pushquagin and Adam Nungo.

44. BCC-RD, Deeds, L3:95–7, Warranty Deed, July 2, 1863, F. Baraga to "Edward Assinnes Chief of the Catholic Band of Indians, and the following individuals of the band . . ."

45. BCC-RD, Deeds, L3:33–34, September 21, 1854, Caroline Rathbun to A. M. Fitch.

46. BCC-RD, Deeds, L3:46, September 6, 1860, Deed, A. M. Fitch to N. Valentine; BCC-RD, Deeds, L3:130–31, March 17, 1865, Warranty Deed, A. & S. Fitch to J. Holliday; BCC-RD, Deeds, L3:129–30, May 9, 1865, Warranty Deed, A. & S. Fitch to Nawwandagoquay; BCC-RD, Deeds, L3:187–88, July 21, 1866, Deed, A. & S. Fitch to W. Bass; BCC-RD, Deeds, L3:365–67, March 28, 1866, Deed, A. & S. Fitch to B. George.

47. BCC-TO-TAR, Baraga County, 1877, 1878, and 1879.

48. BCC-TO-TAR, Baraga County, 1888 and 1897.

49. NAM M234 R. 394, December 10, 1867, L. Webb to N. Taylor.

50. For example, William Owen is shown paying taxes on land owned by James Holliday. BCC-TO-TAR, Baraga County, 1875. E. A. Critchfield was a non-Indian businessman who lived in Baraga and is shown on tax assessment rolls as acting as "agent for Peter Marksman" and paying taxes for Marksman from 1866 to 1868. SAM (MTU) RG77-105, Box 67, File 4, Houghton County Tax Assessment Rolls, L'Anse Twp., Taxes Paid and Unpaid, 1866, 1867, 1868, and 1869.

51. BCC-TO-TAR, Baraga County, 1879.

52. BCC-TO-TAR, L'Anse Township, 1884 and 1895.

53. BCC-RD, Deeds, L5:464, December 17, 1881, Auditor General to Abel Hall, State Land Tax Deed; BCC-RD, Deeds, L8:199–200, February 11, 1892, Abel Hall to Auditor General, Release of Tax Title. Marksman held title to the north seven acres of Lot 2 until after 1897, while the David King estate retained ownership of Lot 2 until well into the twentieth century. SAM (MTU) RG77-105, Vols. 101 and 102, Houghton County Assessment Rolls, Baraga Twp., 1873–74; and BCC-TO-TAR for years 1875–79, 1888, 1897, and 1910.

54. BCC NA-OIA M95-3, January 31, 1857, S. Caley to A. Fitch.

55. BCC-RD, Deeds, L5:143, May 1, 1893, Deed, Auditor General to W. J. Law.

56. BCC-RD, Deeds, L.53:97, November 29, 1939, Deed, Auditor General to State of Michigan.

57. BCC-RD, Deeds, L.52:484, April 21, 1941, Deed, Dept. of Conservation, State of Michigan, to J. W. Asher.

58. BCC-RD, Deeds, L.52:485, April 29, 1941, Warranty Deed, J. & M. Asher to U.S. in Trust for KBIC.

59. BCC-RD, Deeds, L.4:431–32, June 1, 1883, Quit Claim Deed, Rev. J. Yerten to M. H. Borr Co.; BCC-RD, Deeds, L8:409–10, May 29, 1883, Quit Claim Deed, E. Assinins, E. Kebeossaday et al. to M. H. Borr Co.

60. BCC-RD, Deeds, L.24:179–236, October 28, 1908, and September 16, 1909, Auditor General to Rev. F. Eis.

61. BCC-TO-TAR, Baraga County, 1945 and 1956.

62. BCC-TO-TAR, L'Anse Township, 1933.

63. BCC RD, Deeds, L.53:96, Deed, Auditor General to State of Michigan, November 29, 1939.

64. SAM RG 65-5-A, Box 2, File 1, n.d. to 1924, "Abstract of lands set apart for L'Anse & Lac Vieux De Sert Bands of Chippewa Indians . . . under Treaty of September 30, 1854."

65. BCC-TO-TAR, Baraga Twp., 1924 and 1935.

66. BCC-RD, Deed, L53:106, November 29, 1939; BCC-TO-TAR, Baraga Twp., 1942.

67. NA RG 75 LR-BIA, January 17, 1884, J. B. Crebassa to E. Breitung; NA RG 75 LR-BIA, May 4, 1885, L. Harrison to COIA.

68. ARCOIA 1886.

69. CCF 1922-101393-300 Mackinac, December 22, 1922, Report of Inspector H. Creel.

70. CCF 49380-09 Mackinac 313, June 21, 1909, L. LaBrecque to COIA.

71. The Silver River Company, aka Silver River Mining Company, bought nine of the eleven allotments that were awarded in fee. See BCC-TO-TAR, Baraga County, 1878; and SAM RG 65-5-A, Box 2, File 4, n.d. to 1924, "Abstract of lands . . . set apart under Treaty 1854."

72. CCF1922-101393-300 Mackinac, December 22, 1922, Report of Inspector H. Creel.

73. NAM M234 R. 415:18–20, January 27, 1880, P. Crebassa to COIA C. Shurs.

74. NAM M234 R. 415:138, February 12, 1880, G. Lee to COIA.

75. NA RG 75 LR-BIA Mackinac Agency No. 17201, June 29, 1886, M. Stevens to COIA J. D. C. Atkins.

76. NA RG 75 Mackinac LR, B14, F., June 5, 1903, Acting COIA to D. McIntyre.

77. Francis P. Prucha, *The Great Father: The United States Government and the American Indians* (Lincoln: University of Nebraska Press, 1984), 889.

78. NA RG 75 E91, LR-1903-60309 Authority 78611, October 6, 1902, F. Conser to COIA.

79. NA RG 75 E91, LR-1881-1907, November 24, 1877, Rules and Regulations for the Approval of Deeds and Conveyances.

80. NA RG 75 E91, LR-1899-43046, January 7, 1899, Affidavit of Chiefs; BCC-RD, Deeds, L39:506–7, John and Charlotte Tawyosh to John Campbell, August 11, 1891.

81. NA RG 75 E91, LR-1905-90606, November 6, 1905, Secretary of the Interior to the President.

82. NA RG 75 E91, LR-1903-36777, June 24, 1903, Secretary of the Interior to COIA.

83. NA RG 75 E91, LR-1905-90606, November 6, 1905, Secretary of the Interior to the President.

84. NA RG 75 E91, LR-1905-94643, November 25, 1905, Secretary of the Interior to COIA; NA RG 75 E91, LR-1906-10556, February 1, 1906, Secretary of the Interior to COIA; NA RG 75, MA-PCLS, SDA, B1, January 13, 1906, R. Buckland to COIA.

85. NA (GLR) RG 75, MA-PCLS, SDA, B1:1904–6, July 31, 1906, R. Buckland to COIA.

86. CCF 1922-101393-300 Mackinac, December 22, 1922, Report of Inspector H. Creel.

87. NA RG 75 E91, LR-1903-60309, October 6, 1902, F. Conser to COIA.

88. Ibid.

89. Ibid.

90. CCF 87670-1915 Mackinac Agency, July 27, 1915, D. Bedell to COIA C. Sells.

91. ARCOIA 1886, 167–68.

92. Ibid., 165; An Act to Regulate Trade, March 31, 1947, 9 Stat. 203–4.

93. ARCOIA 1892.

94. NA RG 75 LR-BIA, December 23, 1886, M. Stevens to J. D. Atkin.

95. NA (GLR) RG 75, MA-GCS, "R" Misc. 1922–1927, September 8, 1926, V. Raiche to E. Clements; NA (GLR) RG 75, MA-GCS, "R" Misc. 1922–1927, September 10, 1926, E. Clements to V. Raiche.

96. *Auditor General v. Sarah Williams*, 53 NW 1097 (Mich. 1892).

97. NA RG 75 E91, LR-1982-12408, March 31, 1892, Supervisor to COIA; NA (GLR) RG 75, MA-GLS, M Misc. 1911–1917, Auditor General Bradley to T. Nester.

98. LROIA 172, November 22, 1907, R. Buckland to COIA.

99. LROIA 37812, April 26, 1911, C. R. Brown to Dept. of the Interior.

100. State of Michigan Tract Book, June 27, 1922, E. B. Merritt to Auditor General.

101. CCF 26510-1918 Mackinac Agency 302, March 25, 1918, R. Buckland to COIA.

102. CCF 36837-1922 Mackinac Agency 302, May 13, 1922, C. F. Hauke to E. Clements.

103. CCF 22120-23 Mackinac Agency 302, March 29, 1923, C. F. Hauke to H. C. Perrault.

104. Ibid.

105. CCF 109358-1913 Mackinac Agency, November 8, 1913, R. Buckland to COIA.

106. NA (GLR) RG 75, MA-PCLS, SDA, B2:1911–13, R. Buckland to COIA.

107. Ibid.

108. Ibid.

109. CCF 101388-1922 Mackinac Agency 170, December 22, 1922, Report of H. M. Creel.

110. Ibid.

111. Ibid.

112. Ibid.

113. Treaty of La Pointe, October 4, 1842, 7 Stat. 571.

114. ARCOIA 1886 and 1892.

115. CCF 47985-1915 Mackinac Agency 300, April 25, 1915, L. Michael to COIA.

116. CCF 78979 Mackinac Agency 126, November 5, 1924, Special Agent to Mr. Haynes.

117. CCF 789-1924 Mackinac Agency 126, November 5, 1924, Asst. COIA to D. Bedell; CCF 78979-1924 Mackinac Agency 126, November 28, 1924, E. B. Merritt to E. Clements; CCF 78979-1924 Mackinac Agency 126, November 5, 1924, Petition of D. Bedell et al.

118. CCF 78979-1924 Mackinac Agency 126, December 2, 1924, E. Clements to COIA.

119. CCF 18724-10 Mackinac Agency 175, March 24, 1910, R. Buckland to COIA; CCF 115932-15 Mackinac Agency 115, March 27, 1916, R. Buckland to COIA.

120. CCF 32301-1926 Mackinac Agency 115, June 28, 1926, E. Clements to COIA; CCF 115932-1915

Mackinac Agency 115, February 1, 1917, Warner to Secretary of Interior.

121. NA (GLR) RG 75, BDC, Row 361:057, June 2, 1930, J. Chosa to Indian Department.

122. NA (GLR) RG 75, BDC, Row 361:057, June 3, 1930, P. Everest to J. Chosa.

123. NA (GLR) RG 75, BDC, Row 361:057, October 27, 1934, J. Chosa to U.S. Indian Agent.

124. Francis P. Prucha, *The Great Father: The United States Government and the American Indians* (Lincoln: University of Nebraska Press, 1984), 941–68.

125. The Indian Reorganization Act of June 18, 1934, 48 Stat. 984–988.

126. Robert M. Kvasnicka and Herman J. Viola, eds., *The Commissioners of Indian Affairs, 1824–1977* (Lincoln: University of Nebraska Press, 1979), 273–82.

127. ARCOIA 1933. Quoted in Francis P. Prucha, *Documents of the United States Indian Policy* (Lincoln: University of Nebraska Press, 1975), 225.

128. KBIC-ROA, Box 2, File "Mission Lands," September 11, 1940, J. C. Caville to F. H. Daiker; KBIC-ROA, Box 1, File "Church Lands," August 10, 1973, G. W. Hood to Rev. R. Jenks.

129. KBIC-ROA, Box 2, File "Land Purchase Project," April 22, 1938, E. J. Warren to A. L. Hook; KBIC-ROA, Box 2, File "Land Purchase Project," n.d. circa 1938, E. J. Warren to A.C. Hook.

130. KBIC-ROA, Box 2, File "Land Acquisition," May 14, 1938, J. C. Cavill to A. L. Hood.

131. Charles E. Cleland, *Rites of Conquest: The History and Culture of Michigan's Native Americans* (Ann Arbor: University of Michigan Press, 1992), 290.

132. KBIC-ROA, Box 2, File "Law and Order," November 17, 1939, J. C. Cavill to Attorney General.

133. KBIC-ROA, Box 2, File "Law and Order," November 21, 1939, T. Read to J. C. Cavill.

CHAPTER 22

The quotation at the beginning of the chapter is from *Keweenaw Bay Indian Community v. Naftaly* 452 F.3d 514, 527 (6th Cir. 2006).

This chapter was prepared with the assistance of Christopher Duggan and Mary Streitz.

1. *Naftaly v. Keweenaw Bay Indian Community*, 127 S.Ct. 680 (Mem.) (2006).

2. 25 U.S.C. 476.

3. *Keweenaw Bay Indian Community v. Michigan*, 784 F. Supp. 418, 421 (W.D. Mich. 1991).

4. Ibid.

5. Ibid., 421–22.

6. Ibid., 421.

7. Ibid., 426; see also *United States v. Thomas*, 151 U.S. 577, 582 (1894) (1854 Treaty created "permanent reservations" for the Chippewa); *Wisconsin v. Hitchcock*, 201 U.S. 202, 213 (1906) (same).

8. 1854 Treaty, art. 2.

9. Ibid., art. 11.

10. Ibid., art. 3.

11. 9 Land Dec. 392, 396–97 (September 23, 1889).

12. Mich. Tax Tribunal Docket 29713 (February 23, 1982).

13. 784 F. Supp. 418 (W.D. Mich. 1991).

14. *Keweenaw Bay Indian Community v. State of Michigan*, No. 2:87-CV-00278-RHB (W.D. Mich. 1991).

15. Mich. Comp. Laws 211.1 *et seq.*

16. In 1993, the federal district court entered a gaming consent judgment between the governor of Michigan and various Michigan tribes, including the Keweenaw Bay Indian Community, under which the tribes agreed to pay 8 percent of the net win at each casino from all class III electronic games of chance to the state. The gaming consent judgment also provided that the tribes would pay 2 percent of such net win to "any local units of state government in the immediate vicinity of each tribal casino."

17. 524 U.S. 103 (1998).

18. *Baraga County v. State Tax Commission*, File 99-4607-AW (Baraga Cty. Cir. Ct., June 8, 1999).

19. Ibid.; *Baraga County v. State Tax Commission*, 622 N.W.2d 109 (Mich. Ct. App. 2000); *Baraga County v. State Tax Commission*, 645 N.W.2d 13 (Mich. 2002).

20. The remaining 42,030 acres of the reservation are owned by nonmembers of the Community.

21. The community's 1854 treaty arguments constituted count II of the community's federal complaint. The community prevailed on its motion for summary judgment on the basis of these arguments in the Western District of Michigan.

22. 524 U.S. 103, 113 (1998) (internal quotations and citations omitted).

23. Brief of Defendant—Appellant, *Keweenaw Bay Indian Community v. Naftaly* at 14–19, No. 05-1952 (6th Cir., September 13, 2005).

24. Ibid., 10.

25. Ibid., 19.

26. 502 U.S. 251 (1992).

27. 24 Stat. 388 (1887).

28. Brief of Defendant—Appellant, at 29–31.

29. Ibid., 30–31 nn.76–78 and accompanying text.

30. Ibid., 31, 31 n.79.

31. After his decision in this case, Judge McKeague was elevated to the U.S. Court of Appeals for the Sixth Circuit. Judge McKeague did not sit on the Sixth Circuit panel that reviewed his district court decision in this case.

32. *Keweenaw Bay Indian Community v. Naftaly*, 370 F. Supp.2d 620 (W.D. Mich. 2005).

33. Ibid., 628.

34. Honorable Eric L. Clay, United States Judge for the U.S. Court of Appeals for the Sixth Circuit.

35. *Keweenaw Bay Indian Cmty v. Naftaly*, 452 F.3d 514, 524 (6th Cir. 2006).

36. Ibid.

37. Ibid., 525.

38. Ibid., 525–26.

39. Ibid., 527.

40. 411 U.S. 164, 170–171 (1973).

41. *Keweenaw Bay Indian Cmty v. Naftaly*, 452 F.3d at 528.

42. Ibid., 530–32 (citing *County of Yakima v. Confederated Tribes and Bands of Yakima Indian Nation*, 502 U.S. 251, 258 (1992).

43. Ibid., 531.

44. Ibid., 532–33. The Sixth Circuit went on to agree with the district court that the 1922 act "appears to be more of an 'administrative housekeeping measure' than an act that was intended to abrogate or change the rights under the 1854 Treaty or address the alienability of such land."

45. Oral argument in *Keweenaw Bay Indian Community v. Naftaly,* 05-1952 (6th Cir., April 26, 2006), at 29:55–30:30.

CHAPTER 23

1. Estimate supplied by the Great Lakes Indian Fish and Wildlife Commission, Odanah, Wisconsin.

2. Anonymous, "Fact Sheet on Economic and Tourism Growth in the 1837 and 1842 ceded Territories of Wisconsin," Great Lakes Indian Fish and Wildlife Commission, Odanah, Wisconsin, April 1, 1997.

3. Jon Van Dyke, *Who Owns the Crown Lands of Hawaii?* (Honolulu: University of Honolulu Press, 2008).

4. Charles R. Menzies, ed., *Traditional Ecological Knowledge and Natural Resource Management* (Lincoln: University of Nebraska Press, 2006).

5. Wanona Singel and Matthew L. M. Fletcher, "Indian Treaties and the Survival of the Great Lakes" (Research Paper 04-14, Legal Studies Research Paper Series, Michigan State University College of Law, East Lansing, 2006).

6. Ibid., 4, 12, 15.

7. L. Nesper and James H. Schlender, "The Politics of Cultural Revitalization and Intertribal Resource Management: The Great Lakes Indian Fish and Wildlife Commission and the States of Wisconsin, Michigan, and Minnesota," in *Native Americans and the Environment: Perspectives on the Ecological Indian,* ed. Michael Harkin and David Lewis (Lincoln: University of Nebraska Press, 2007).

Acronyms and Bibliography

Compiled by Nancy N. Cleland

ABCFM. American Board of Commission of Foreign Missions.

Adams, Arthur T., ed. 1961. *The Exploration of Pierre Esprit Radisson.* Minneapolis: Ross and Haines.

AMFCP-CMU. Records of the American Fur Company on Mackinac Island, 1810–48. Microfilm. Mt. Pleasant: Clarke Historical Library, Central Michigan University.

Anonymous. 1884. *Portraits and Biographical Album of Isabella County, Michigan.* Chicago.

Anonymous. 1997. "Fact Sheet on Economic and Tourism Growth in the 1837 and 1842 ceded Territories of Wisconsin." Great Lakes Indian Fish and Wildlife Commission, Odanah, Wisconsin, April 1.

AR. Alexander Ramsey Papers. Microfilm. St. Paul: Minnesota Historical Society.

ARCOIA. Annual Reports of the Commissioner of Indian Affairs. Washington, D.C.: U.S. Government Printing Office.

Avery, Charles P. 1866. "The Treaty of Saginaw of 1819." In *Indian and Pioneer Directory and Business Advertizer for 1866–68.* Saginaw: Thomas and A. E. Galatin.

Baird, Henry S. 1859. "Recollections of the Early History of Northern Wisconsin." In *Wisconsin Historical Collections,* 4:197–221. Madison: Wisconsin Historical Society.

Bald, Clever. 1944. "Some Myths about Michigan" *Michigan History* 28, no. 4: 595–609.

Baraga, Frederick. 1976. *Chippewa Indians as Recorded in 1847.* New York: Studies Slovenica, League of Slovenian Americans.

BBC. Bishop Baraga Collection. Typescript of originals in Almanac Manuscripts. Marquette: Bishop Baraga Collections.

BBC-NA-OIA-M. Baraga County Courthouse, National Archives, Office of Indian Affairs.

BCC-RD. Baraga County Courthouse, Register of Deeds.

BCC-TO. Baraga County Courthouse, Treasurer's Office.

BCC-TO-TAR. Baraga County Courthouse, Treasurer's Office, Tax Assessment Records.

Beck, D. n.d. "The Importance of Sturgeon in Menominee History as Viewed through Documentary Sources." Manuscript on file with the Treaty Protection Office of the Menominee Tribe of Wisconsin, Keshena.

Black-Rodgers, Mary. 1986. "Varieties of 'Starving': Semantics and Survival in the Subarctic Fur Trade, 1750–1850." *Ethnohistory* 33, no. 4: 353–83.

Blair, Emma H. 1996. *The Indian Tribes of the Region of the Great Lakes.* Lincoln: University of Nebraska Press.

Bloch, Maurice. 1974. "The Long Term and the Short Term: The Economics and Significance of the Morality of Kinship." In *The Character of Kinship,* ed. Jack Goody. Cambridge: Cambridge University Press.

Bloomfield, Leonard. 1928. *Menomini Texts.* Publication of the American Ethnological Society, vol. 12. New York: G. E. Stechert.

Bolt, Christine. 1987. *American Indian Policy and American Reform.* London: Unwin Hyman.

Boyd, George. 1892. "Papers of Indian Agent Boyd 1832." In *Wisconsin Historical Collections,* 12:266–98. Madison: Wisconsin Historical Society.

Bremer, Richard G. 1987. *Indian Agent and Wilderness Scholar: The Life of Henry Rowe Schoolcraft.* Mt. Pleasant: Clarke Historical Library, Central Michigan University.

Broudel, F. 1980. *On History.* Chicago: University of Chicago Press.

Brunson, Alfred. 1879. *A Western Pioneer, or Incidents of Life and Times of Rev. Alfred Brunson.* Cincinnati: Hitchcock and Walden.

Cass, Lewis. 1830. "Conditions of the Present State of the Indians, and Their Removal." Reprint, New York: Arno Press, 1975.

Cass, Lewis. 1830. "Removal of the Indians." *North American Review* 30.

CCF. Central Classified Files. Correspondence received, Office of Indian Affairs, 1904–38. Record Group 75. Washington, D.C.: National Archives of the United States.

Chicago Tribune.

Childs, Ebenezer. 1859. "Recollections of Wisconsin since 1820." In *Wisconsin Historical Collections,* 4:153–95. Madison: Wisconsin Historical Society.

Cleland, Charles E. 1966. "The Prehistoric Animal Ecology and Ethnozoology of the Upper Great Lakes Region." Anthropological Paper 29, Museum of Anthropology, University of Michigan, Ann Arbor.

Cleland, Charles E. 1982. "The Inland Shore Fishery of the Northern Great Lakes: Its Development and Importance in Prehistory." *American Antiquity* 47, no. 4: 761–84.

Cleland, Charles E. 1991. "Cass, Sassaba, and Ozhawguscodaywaquay: History, Ethnohistory, and Historical Reality." In *Entering the Nineties: The North American Experience,* ed. Thomas Schirer. Sault Ste. Marie: Lake Superior State University Press.

Cleland, Charles E. 1992. "From Ethnohistory to Archaeology: Ottawa and Ojibwa Band Territories of the Northern Great Lakes." In *Text Aided Archaeology,* ed. Barbara Little. Boca Raton: CRC Press.

Cleland, Charles E. 1992. *Rites of Conquest: The History and Culture of Michigan's Native Americans.* Ann Arbor: University of Michigan Press.

Cleland, Charles E. 1993. "Economic and Adaptive Change among the Lake Superior Chippewa of the Nineteenth Century." In *Approaches to Cultural Contact: Ethnohistorical and Archaeological Per-*

spectives on Change, ed. J. Rodgers and S. Wilson. New York: Plenum Press.

Cleland, Charles E. 2000. "Preliminary Report for the Ethnohistorical Basis of Hunting, Fishing, and Gathering Rights of the Mille Lacs Ojibwe." In *Fish in the Lakes, Wild Rice, and Game in Abundance: Testimony in Behalf of Mille Lacs Ojibwe Hunting and Fishing Rights*, comp. James M. McClurken. East Lansing: Michigan State University Press.

Cleland, Nancy Nowak. 1987. "Natural Vegetation c. 1600." In *Atlas of Great Lakes Indian History*, ed. H. H. Tanner. Norman: University of Oklahoma Press.

Clifton, James A. 1977. *The Prairie People*. Lawrence: Regents Press of Kansas.

Clifton, James A. 1987. "Wisconsin Death March: Explaining the Extremes in Old NorthWest Indian Removal." *Transactions of the Wisconsin Academy of Science, Arts, and Letters* 75:1–39.

Cohen, Felix S. 1982. *Felix S. Cohen's Handbook of Federal Indian Law*. Charlottesville, Va.: Michie Bobbs-Merrill.

Cohen, Felix S. 2005 *Felix S. Cohen's Handbook of Federal Indian Law*, 2005 ed. Newark, N.J.: Lexis-Nexis.

Commission Finding on the Chippewa Indians of the Indian Claims Commission. *Finding of Fact Red Lake Band Including Bay Mills Indian Community and the Ottawa and Chippewa of Michigan v. United States*. Findings of the Indian Claims Commission 7. New York: Garland Publishing.

Composite Map of the United States Land Surveyors' Original Plates and Field Notes. 1966. Minnesota: J. W. Trygg.

Congressional Globe.

Current, Richard N. 1950. *Pine Logs and Politics: A Life of Philetus Sawyer, 1816–1900*. Madison: State Historical Society of Wisconsin.

Danziger, Edmund J. 1979. *The Chippewas of Lake Superior*. Norman: University of Oklahoma Press.

DeBox, J. D. B. 1854. *Statistical View of the United States*. Washington, D.C.: A. O. P. Nicholson Publishing.

Densmore, Frances. 1970. "Narrative of Nodiens." In *Chippewa Customs*. Minneapolis: Ross and Haines.

Detroit Daily Free Press.

Dice, Lee R. 1943. *The Biotic Provinces of North America*. Ann Arbor: University of Michigan Press.

Diedrick, Mark. 1986. *The Chief Hole-in-the-Day of the Mississippi Chippewa*. St. Louis Park, Minn.: Coyote Books.

Dunbar, Willis. 1970. *Michigan: A History of the Wolverine State*. Grand Rapids: W. B. Eerdmans Publishing.

East Saginaw Courier.

Editor. 1895. "Population of Brown County June 1830." In *Wisconsin Historical Collections*, 13:468–72. Madison: Wisconsin Historical Society.

Editor. 1895. "The Territorial Census for 1836." In *Wisconsin Historical Collections*, 13:247–70. Madison: Wisconsin Historical Society.

Edmunds, R. David. 1978. *The Potawatomi—Keepers of the Fire*. Norman: University of Oklahoma Press.

Ellis, A. G. 1856. "Advent of the New York Indians into Wisconsin." In *Wisconsin Historical Collections*, 2:415–49. Madison: Wisconsin Historical Society.

Fixico, Donald L. 1986. *Termination and Relocation: Federal Indian Policy, 1945–1960*. Albuquerque: University of New Mexico Press.

Galloway, Colin G. 1987. *Crown and Cabinet: British-Indian Relations, 1783–1815*. Norman: University of Oklahoma Press.

Gary, George. 1889. "Hon. Philetus Sawyer." *Magazine of Western History Illustrated* 10, no. 1: 469.

Getches, D. H., C. F. Wilkinson, and R. A. Williams. 1998. *Cases and Material on Federal Indian Law*. St. Paul: West Publishing.

Gilman, Rhonda. 1974. "The Last Days of the Upper Mississippian Fur Trade." *Minnesota History* 42, no. 4: 122–40.

GNS MIHC. George N. Smith Papers. Diaries 1842–45, 1849, and 1857. Ms. AA, Aa 1608, 4507, 4572. Ann Arbor: Bentley Library, University of Michigan.

Goddard, I. 1978. "Central Algonquian Languages." In *Handbook of North American Indians*, ed. B. Trigger, vol. 15, *Northeast*. Washington, D.C.: Smithsonian Institution.

Grignon, A. 1857. "Seventy-two Years' Recollections in Wisconsin." In *Wisconsin Historical Collections*, 3:195–295. Madison: Wisconsin Historical Society.

GWL-CHS. George W. Lawe Papers, Chicago Historical Society.

GNS-LCM. George N. Smith Papers. Microfilm. Library of Congress.

HBS-WHS. Henry S. Baird Papers, Chicago Historical Society.

Haeger, John. 1969. "Western Town Growth: A Study of the Development of Towns on the Western Shore of Lake Michigan, 1815–1845." PhD diss., Loyola University, Chicago.

Haldimand Papers. Michigan Pioneer and Historical Collections.

Hickerson, Harold. 1970. *The Chippewa and Their Neighbors*. Prospect Heights, Ill.: Waveland Press.

Hickerson, Harold. 1974. *Chippewa Indians III: Ethnohistory of Chippewa of Lake Superior*. New York: Garland Publishing.

Hill, Edward, E. 1967. *The Office of Indian Affairs, 1824–1880: Historical Sketches*. New York: Clearwater Publishing.

Hoffman, Walter J. 1896. *The Menominee Indians*. Fourteenth Annual Report of the Bureau of American Ethnology, Smithsonian Institution. Washington, D.C.: U.S. Government Printing Office.

Hoxie, Frederick E. 1989. *A Final Promise: The Campaign to Assimilate the Indians, 1880–1920*. Cambridge: Cambridge University Press.

HRSP LCM Papers. Henry Rowe Schoolcraft Papers. R. 47:30591. May 27, 1833, to September 30, 1837. Private Journal of Indian Affairs.

H-211. U.S. Court of Claims Case H-211, *Saginaw, Swan Creek, and Black River Chippewas vs. the*

United States of America, Docket 3444. Suitland, Md.: Federal Records Center.

Humins, John. 1975. "George Boyd: Indian Agent of the Upper Great Lakes, 1819–1842." Ph.D. diss., Michigan State University, East Lansing.

HW-MNHS. Henry Whipple Papers, 1833–1934. St. Paul: Minnesota Historical Society.

Innis, Harold A. 1956. *The Fur Trade in Canada*. Toronto: University of Toronto Press.

Jacobs, Wilbur R. 1950. *Diplomacy and Indian Gifts*. Stanford: Stanford University Press.

Jones, Dallas L. 1952. "Survey and Sale of Public Land in Michigan 1815–1862." Master's thesis, Cornell University.

Journals of the Continental Congress.

Journal of the House of Representatives.

Kappler, Charles, ed. 1904. *Indian Affairs: Laws and Treaties*. 2 vols. Washington, D.C.: U.S. Government Printing Office.

Kappler, Charles, ed. 1929. *Senate Document 53*. Serial set 8849. Vols. 3–5. Washington, D.C.: Senate Committee on Printing.

Kappler, Charles, ed. 1972. *Indian Treaties, 1778–1883*. Mattituck, N.Y.: Amereon House.

Kay, Jeanne. 1979. "Wisconsin Indian Hunting Patterns, 1634–1836." *Annals of the Association of American Geographers* 69, no. 3: 402–18.

Kay, Jeanne. 1984. "The Fur Trade and Native American Population Growth." *Ethnohistory* 31, no. 4: 265–87.

KBIC-ROA. Keweenaw Bay Indian Community, Real Estate Office Archives.

Keesing, Felix. 1987. *The Menomini Indians of Wisconsin*. Madison: University of Wisconsin Press.

Kellogg, L. P. 1931. "The Menominee Treaty at the Cedars, 1836." *Transactions of the Wisconsin Academy of Science, Arts, and Letters* 26:127–35.

Kinetz, Vernon. 1965. *Indians of the Western Great Lakes*. Ann Arbor: University of Michigan Press.

Kinzie, Juliette M. 1932. *Wau Bun, the "Early Day" in the North-West*. Chicago: Lakeside Press.

Kohl, Johann. 1985. *Kitchi-Gami: Life among the Lake Superior Ojibway*. St. Paul: Minnesota Historical Society Press.

Kuehnle, Walter. 1966. "Appraisal of Royce Area 242 in the States of Wisconsin and Minnesota." Docket 18C before the Indian Claims Commission for the Department of Justice.

Kvasnicka, Robert M., and Herman J. Viola, eds. 1979. *The Commissioners of Indian Affairs, 1824–1977*. Lincoln: University of Nebraska Press.

Ladurie, Emmanuel Le Roy. 1971. *Times of Feast, Times of Famine: A History of Climate since the Year 1000*. New York: Doubleday.

Lake Superior Mining Journal.

Lapham, Increase A. 1925. "A Winter's Journey from Milwaukee to Green Bay, 1843." *Wisconsin Magazine of History* 9:90–97.

Lawrence Taliaferro Papers, 1813–1818. Microfilm. St. Paul: Minnesota Historical Society.

Lewis, Kenneth E. 2002. *West to Far Michigan*. East Lansing: Michigan State University Press.

Littlefield, Alice. 1989. "The BIA Boarding School: Theories of Resistance and Social Reproduction." *Humanities and Society* 13, no. 4: 428–41.

LLC-WLCL. Lucius Lyon Collection, W. L. Clements Library.

LLL. Letters of Lucius Lyon, Michigan Pioneer and Historical Society, *Michigan Historical Collections*.

LOC. Library of Congress, Presidential Papers.

LRMS 131. United States, Bureau of Indian Affairs. RG 75. Letters Received by the Michigan Superintendency and Mackinac Agency, 1849–69. Entry 1131. National Archives, Washington, D.C.

LROIA. Letters Received, Office of Indian Affairs.

Manypenny, George. 1972. *Our Indian Wards*. New York: DaCapo Press.

Mason, Carol I. 1988. *Introduction to Wisconsin Indians*. Salem, Wis.: Sheffield Publishing.

Mason, Philip. 1958. *Schoolcraft's Expedition to Lake Itasca*. East Lansing: Michigan State University Press.

Mason, Ronald. 1986. "Rock Island, Historical Indian Archaeology in the Northern Lake Michigan Basin." *Midcontinental Journal of Archaeology*, Special Paper 6. Kent, Ohio: Kent State University Press.

McClurken, James M. 1988. "We Wish to Be Civilized: Ottawa-American Political Contest on the Michigan Frontier." PhD diss., Michigan State University.

McClurken, James M., comp. 2000. *Fish in the Lakes, Wild Rice, and Game in Abundance: Testimony in Behalf of Mille Lacs Ojibwe Hunting and Fishing Rights*. East Lansing: Michigan State University Press.

McClurken, James M. 2000. "The 1837 Treaty of St. Peters Preserving the Rights of the Mille Lacs Ojibwa to Hunt, Fish. and Gather: The Effects of Treaties and Agreements since 1855." In *Fish in the Lakes, Wild Rice, and Game in Abundance: Testimony in Behalf of Mille Lacs Ojibwe Hunting and Fishing Rights*, comp. James M. McClurken. East Lansing: Michigan State University Press.

McKenney, Thomas. 1959. *Sketches of a Tour of the Lakes*. Facsimile ed. Minneapolis: Ross and Haines.

MCT, DEF. *Minnesota Chippewa Tribe, et al. v. United States*. Dockets 18C, 18S, 18T. Defendant Exhibits, In Support of Defendant's Motion for Summary Judgment. National Archives Records Service, Suitland, Maryland.

MCT. *Minnesota Chippewa Tribe, et al. v. United States*. Dockets 18C, 18S, 18T. Plaintiff Exhibits, In Support of Plaintiffs' Motion for Summary Judgment. National Archives Records Service, Suitland, Maryland.

Menzies, Charles R., ed. 2006. *Traditional Ecological Knowledge and Natural Resource Management*. Lincoln: University of Nebraska Press.

MHS. Minnesota Historical Society.

Minneapolis Tribune.

MMLM NA RG 75 SC 42. Records of the Bureau of Indian Affairs. Miller Memorial Library Microfilm Special Case 42.

MN. This indicates that the document was obtained from the state of Minnesota's (defendant) exhibits. It may have come from many sources.

MNHS. Minnesota Historical Society.

MNSA. Minnesota State Archives, Governors' Archives. Microfilm. St. Paul: Minnesota Historical Society.

Morgan, Lewis Henry. 1851. *League of the Ho-de-no-saw-nee or Iroquois*. Rochester: Sage and Brothers.

Morris, Richard, ed. 1951. *Encyclopedia of American History.* New York: Harper & Brothers Publishing.

Morse, Jedidiah. 1822. *Report to the Secretary of War on Indian Affairs*. New Haven: S. Converse.

Morse, Richard. 1857. "The Chippewas of Lake Superior." In *Wisconsin Historical Collections,* 3:338–69. Madison: Wisconsin Historical Society.

NA RG 21. Record Group 21, Department of the Interior, National Archives.

NA (GLR) RG 75, BDC. Birth and Death Census Rolls, Tribal Relations.

NA (GLR) RG 75, MA-GCS. National Archives, (Great Lakes Region) (Chicago) Record Group 75, Mackinac Agency—General Correspondence Superintendency.

NA (GLR) RG 75, MA-PCLS. National Archives, (Great Lakes Region) (Chicago) Record Group 75, Mackinac Agency—Press Correspondence Superintendency.

NA RG 46. National Archives and Records Service, Records of the United States Senate Manuscript Copies, Committee on Indian Affairs. Washington, D.C.: National Archives Microfilm.

NA RG 75 E91, LR-1881-1907. National Archives Record Group 75, Letters Received, Bureau of Indian Affairs, 1881–1907.

NA RG 75, BIA Civilization Division. Census of Indians within the Superintendency at Michigan in 1842.

NA RG 279. National Archives and Records Service, Indian Claims Commission. Washington, D.C.: National Archives Microfilm.

NA RG 75 LR-BIA. Letters Received, BIA.

NA RG 75 Mackinac LR. Letters Received, Mackinac Agency.

NAM. National Archives Microfilm.

NAM M1. National Archives and Record Service. Letters Received and Sent by Superintendent of Michigan Superintendency, 1814–51. Record Group 75. Washington, D.C.: National Archives Microfilms.

NAM M21. National Archives and Records Service, Correspondence of the Office of Indian Affairs (Central Office) and Related Records, Letters Sent 1824–81. Record Group 75. Washington, D.C.: National Archives Microfilms.

NAM M234. National Archives and Records Service, Correspondence of the Office of Indian Affairs (Central Office) and Related Records, Letters Received, 1824–81. Record Group 75. Washington, D.C.: National Archives Microfilms.

NAM M236. National Archives and Records Service, Records Relating to Territories, Territorial Papers of the United States, Wisconsin, 1836–48. Record Group 75. Washington, D.C.: National Archives Microfilms.

NAM M574. National Archives and Records Service, Special Files, 1807–1904. Records Related to Claims and Investigations. Record Group 75. Washington, D.C.: National Archives Microfilms.

NAM M668. National Archives and Record Service, Records Relating to Indian Treaties, Ratified Indian Treaties, 1722–1869. Record Group 75. Washington, D.C.: National Archives Microfilms.

NAM M842. National Archives and Records Service, Records of the Superintendencies and Agencies of the Office of Indian Affairs, Records of the Minnesota Superintendency, 1849–56. Record Group 75. Washington, D.C.: National Archives Microfilms.

NAM M1166. National Archives and Records Service, Records of the Northern Superintendency, 1851–76, Bureau of Indian Affairs. Washington. D.C.: National Archives Microfilms.

NAM T494. National Archives and Records Service, Documents Relating to the Negotiation of Ratified and Unratified Treaties with Various Indian Tribes, 1801–69. Record Group No. 75. Washington, D.C.: National Archives Microfilms.

Nesper, Larry. 2002. *The Walleye War: The Struggle for Ojibwe Spearfishing and Treaty Rights*. Lincoln: University of Nebraska Press.

Nesper, Larry, and James H. Schlender. 2007. "The Politics of Cultural Revitalization and Intertribal Resource Management: The Great Lakes Indian Fish and Wildlife Commission and the States of Wisconsin, Michigan, and Minnesota." In *Native Americans and the Environment: Perspectives on the Ecological Indian,* ed. Michael Harkin and David Lewis. Lincoln: University of Nebraska Press.

Neu, Irene. 1954. "The Building of the Sault Canal: 1852–1855." *Mississippi Valley Historical Review* 20: 25–46.

New York Herald Tribune.

Nichols, John D. 1988. *"Statement Made by the Indians": A Bilingual Petition of the Chippewas of Lake Superior, 1864*. London: Centre for Research and Teaching of Canadian Native Languages, University of Western Ontario.

Oberly, James W. 2005. *A Nation of Statesmen: The Political Culture of the Stockbridge-Munsee Mohicans, 1815–1972*. Norman: University of Oklahoma Press.

Ohnuki-Tierney, Emicko. 1990. *Culture through Time*. Stanford: Stanford University Press.

Ortner, Sherry B. 1994. "Theory in Anthropology since the Sixties." Reprinted in *Culture/Power/History,* ed. N. B. Dirks, G. Eley, and S. B. Ortner. Princeton, N.J.: Princeton University Press.

Ostergren, R. C. 1981. "Geographic Perspective and the History of Settlement in the Upper Midwest." *Upper Midwest History* 1:27–39.

Ourada, P. 1979. *The Menominee Indians*. Norman: University of Oklahoma Press.

Peterson, J. 1978. "Prelude to Red River: A Social Portrait of the Great Lakes Metis." *Ethnohistory* 25, no. 1: 41–69.

PHSC. *American Indian Correspondence: The Presbyterian Historical Society Collection of Missionaries' Letters, 1833–93*. Microfilm. Westport, Conn.: Greenwood Press.

Potzger, J. E. 1946. "Phytosociology of the Primeval Forest in Central Northern Wisconsin and Upper

Michigan and a Brief Post-Glacial History of the Lake Forest Formation." *Ecological Monographs* 16:211–50.

Priest, Loring B. 1942. *Uncle Sam's Stepchildren: The Reformation of United States Indian Policy, 1865–1887.* New Brunswick: Rutgers University Press.

Prucha, Francis P. 1984. *The Great Father: The United States Government and the American Indians.* Lincoln: University of Nebraska Press.

Prucha, Francis P. 1986. *The Great Father: The United States Government and the American Indians.* Abridged edition. Lincoln: University of Nebraska Press.

Prucha, Francis P. 1990. *Documents of United States Indian Policy.* Lincoln: University of Nebraska Press.

Ray, Arthur J. 1974. *Indians in the Fur Trade: Their Role as Hunters, Trappers, and Middlemen in the Lands Southwest of Hudson Bay, 1660–1870.* Toronto: University of Toronto Press.

RBH. Rutherford B. Hayes Library.

Reuter, Dorothy. 1993. *Methodist Indian Ministries in Michigan, 1830–1990.* Michigan Area United Methodist Historical Society.

Rezek, Antoine I. 1907. *History of the Diocese of Sault Ste. Marie and Marquette.* Houghton, Mich.

Saginaw Weekly Enterprise.

Sahlins, Marshall. 1968. *Tribesmen.* Englewood Cliffs, N.J.: Prentice-Hall.

Sahlins, Marshall. 1972. *Stone Age Economics.* Hawthorn, N.Y.: Aldine deGruyter.

SAM (MTU) RG 77–105. State Archives of Michigan, Michigan Technological University, Record Group 77.

SAM RG 65-5-A, Box 2, F1. State Archives of Michigan, Record Group 65, Auditor General Department, Register of Court Cases Related to Sale of Land Subject to Delinquent Taxes.

Satz, Ronald N. 1975. *American Indian Policy in the Jacksonian Era.* Lincoln: University of Nebraska Press.

Satz, Ronald N. 1979. "Carey Harris (1831–1836)." In *Commissioners of Indian Affairs, 1824–1977,* ed. Robert M. Kvasnicka and Herman J. Viola. Lincoln: University of Nebraska Press.

Schoolcraft, Henry. 1851. *Information Respecting the History, Condition, and Prospects of Indian Tribes in the United States.* Philadelphia: Lippincott, Grambo.

Schoolcraft, Henry. 1851. *Personal Memoirs of a Residence of Thirty Years with the Indian Tribes on the American Frontier.* Philadelphia: Lippincott, Grambo.

Singel, Wanona, and Matthew L. M. Fletcher. 2006. "Indian Treaties and the Survival of the Great Lakes." Research Paper 04-14, Legal Studies Research Paper Series, Michigan State University College of Law, East Lansing.

Sketch of the Claims to Land on the River St. Marys at Pouwayteeg. July 6, 1823. National Archives of the United States. Cartographic Collection Record Group 77. Drawer 137, Sheet 10.

Skinner, Alanson. 1924. "The Mascoutens or Prairie Potawatomi: Part I, Social Life and Ceremonies." *Bulletin of the Public Museum of the City of Milwaukee* 6, no. 1: 17–20.

Smith, Alice. 1973. *The History of Wisconsin.* Vol. 1. Madison: State Historical Society of Wisconsin.

Special Case 109 [Minnesota Chippewa?]. Record Group 75. Washington, D.C.: National Archives.

Stambaugh, S. 1910. "Report on the Quality and Condition of Wisconsin Territory, 1831." In *Wisconsin Historical Collections,* 15:399–438. Madison: Wisconsin Historical Society.

Sword, Wiley. 1985. *President Washington's Indian War: The Struggle for the Old Northwest, 1790–1795.* Norman: University of Oklahoma Press.

Tanner, Helen H. 1987. *Atlas of Great Lakes Indian History.* Norman: University of Oklahoma Press.

Tanner, Helen H. 1999. "History v. the Law: Processing Indians in the American Legal System." *Law Review,* University of Detroit Mercy, 67, no. 3: 693–708.

Thwaites, R. G., ed. 1911. "A Wisconsin Fur-Trader's Journal, 1803–04, by Michael Curot." In *Wisconsin Historical Collections,* 20:396–472. Madison: Wisconsin Historical Society.

Thwaites, R. G. 1911. "The Fur Trade in Wisconsin. Agreement of A. Grignon et al. and R. Crooks." August 24, 1821. In *Wisconsin Historical Collections,* 20:206–10. Madison: Wisconsin Historical Society.

Thwaites, R. G., ed. 1959. *The Jesuit Relations and Allied Documents.* Vol. 18, *Hurons and Quebec: 1640,* New York: Pageant.

Trennert, Robert. 1979. "Orlando Brown 1849–1850." In *The Commissioners of Indian Affairs, 1824–1977,* ed. Robert M. Kvasnicka and Herman J. Viola. Lincoln: University of Nebraska Press.

Trennert, Robert. 1979. "William Medill (1845–49)." In *The Commissioners of Indian Affairs, 1824–1977,* ed. Robert M. Kvasnicka and Herman J. Viola. Lincoln: University of Nebraska Press.

Trigger, Bruce G. 1985. *Natives and Newcomers.* Montreal: McGill Queens University Press.

Utley, Robert. 1988. "Indian-United States Military Situation 1848–1891." In *Handbook of North American Indians,* vol. 4, *History of Indian-White Relations,* ed. W. E. Washburn. Washington, D.C.: Smithsonian Institution.

Van Dyke, Jon. 2008. *Who Owns the Crown Lands of Hawaii?* Honolulu: University of Hawaii Press.

Veatch, V. O. 1959. *Presettlement Forests in Michigan.* East Lansing: Department of Resource Development, Michigan State University.

Viola, Herman J. 1981. *Diplomats in Buckskin: A History of Indian Delegations in Washington City.* Washington, D.C.: Smithsonian Institution Press.

Vogel, Virgil L. 1986. *Indian Names in Michigan.* Ann Arbor: University of Michigan Press.

Warren, William W. 1984. *History of the Ojibway People.* St. Paul: Minnesota Historical Society Press.

White, Bruce. 1992. "Stereotypes of Minnesota's Native People" *Minnesota History,* Fall.

White, Bruce. 2000. "The Regional Context of the Removal Order of 1850." In *Fish in the Lakes, Wild Rice, and Game in Abundance: Testimony in Behalf of the Mille Lacs Ojibwe Hunting and Fishing Rights*, comp. James M. McClurken. East Lansing: Michigan State University Press.

White, Richard. 1991. *The Middle Ground: Indians, Empires, and Republics in the Great Lakes Region, 1650–1815*. Cambridge: Cambridge University Press.

Whittlesey, Charles. 1855. "Recollections of a Tour through Wisconsin in 1832." In *Wisconsin Historical Collections*, 1:64–85. Madison: Wisconsin Historical Society.

Williams, Mentor, ed. 1953. *Narrative Journals of Travels through the Northwest Regions of the United States Extending from Detroit through the Great Chain of American Lakes to the Source of the Mississippi River in the Year 1820*, by Henry R. Schoolcraft. East Lansing: Michigan State College Press.

Wolf, Eric. 1982. *Europe and the People without History*. Berkeley: University of California Press.

Yarnell, Richard. 1964. "Aboriginal Relationships between Culture and Plant Life in the Great Lakes Region." Anthropological Paper 23, Museum of Anthropology, University of Michigan, Ann Arbor.

Index

Aagwonay, 275
Abbott, F. H., 255, 261
aboriginal title, 13
abrogation of treaties, 41
acculturation, 232
Act of 1843, 234
Act of 1846, 234
Act of 1871, 246, 247, 249, 252, 253
Act of July 4, 1884, 280
Act of March 3, 1893, 256
Act of June 21, 1906, 257
Adams, J. C., 252
Adams, John Quincy, 151
Aishkebogekoshe (Flat Mouth), 107, 109, 110
Aitken, William, 119, 205
alewife, 90
Allen, Edward, 305
allotment of land, 15, 16, 26, 84, 86, 199, 216–17, 234, 236, 238, 247, 276–77, 280–82, 293, 296, 304, 309, 314–16, 321
American Fur Company, 63–64, 118–19, 165, 181, 205
Anderson, Marge, 139
Andre brothers, 302, 304
Anishnabe (Anishnabeg), 19, 20
Apokisigan (Smoking Mixture), 54, 65
Arnold, I. E., 302
Arnold, J. E., 304
Assagon (Little Ant), 84–85
Assiginac (Blackbird), 59
Assinines, Edward, 212, 213, 317, 318, 319
Atkins, J. D. C., 304
Awseneece (Small Stones), 206, 308
Ayamataw (Fish Spawn), 155, 169, 171

Bad River band, 111, 127, 310
Baird, Henry, 170
bands, 23
Baraga, Frederick, 205, 213, 223, 308, 316, 318, 319, 327
Baraga Township, MI, 331
Barbano, Henry, 319
Barbeau, Peter, 205, 213, 308, 318
Bartelme Township, WI, 258
Bass, William, 317
Bay de Noc, 140
Bay Mills Indian Community, 89, 94
Bedell, David, 326
Bell, Akin, 307
Benjamin, Melanie, 284
Betts, George, 303, 304, 312, 313–14, 320
Biddle, Edward, 54, 66
Binnayshi, Charles, 206, 209
Black Hawk War, 167, 177
Black River, 145, 180, 181
Black River band, 286, 293
Blair, Austin, 300
Blatchford, Henry, 12
Bois Blanc Island, 54
Bois Forte band, 217
Bonduel, F. J., 177, 186
Borup, Charles, 119, 121
Boutwell, William, 109
Boyd, Brenda, 135
Boyd, George, 149, 167, 168–69, 174–76, 232
Bradley, George, 301
Bradley, Joseph, 307
Bresbois, Bernard, 119
Brevoort, H. B., 146, 151
Brewster, William, 64
British period, 25
Brockway, William, 205, 223, 298, 318
Brooks, E. J., 304, 320
Brothertowns (Munsee), 149, 150, 161
Brown, Orlando, 186
Brunetti, Dominick, 147
Brunson, Alfred, 113
Buchanan, James, 267
Buckland, Romulus, 324–25
Buffalo (Kechewaishke or Peshekee), 113, 121
Burket, George, 205
Bushnell, David, 108, 110, 204
Butler, B. F., 70

Cadotte, Louis, 84
Cadotte, Michael, 205
Calhoun, John, 146
Campeau, Andrew, 301
canal lands, 311–12, 316
canons of treaty construction, 42, 228
Carron, Glode (Konot), 141, 145, 169
Carron, Josette, 148, 151, 153, 167, 168, 186
Cass, Lewis, 13, 30, 51, 59, 61, 70–72, 85, 101, 103, 145, 151, 153, 209, 212, 286
Cass Lake, 101
Catlin, George, 167–68
Central Algonquian, 140
Chakauchokama (Old King), 141, 145, 148
Chandler, Zachariah, 279
Chapman, George, 272–73
Chappues, Stanislaus, 147
Charles, Darius, 242, 245, 247
Chase, Thomas, 251
checkerboarded reservations, 199, 226–27, 234, 297
Chemebowme, 176
Chequanmegon Bay, 204
Chipman, I. L., 84
Chippewa, 19, 20
Chippewa-Dakota warfare, 100, 103
Chippewa Nation, 107, 115, 117, 210
Chippewa of Lake Superior, 107, 112, 117, 122, 219
Chippewa of the Mississippi, 105, 107, 111, 112, 117, 265, 271
Chippewa-Ottawa Resource Authority (CORA), 339
Chippewa River, 180, 181

cholera, 167, 187
Chosa, James, 326
Citizens Party, 233, 234, 235, 237, 238, 242, 245, 258, 260
Civil War, 177
clans, 13, 23, 27, 140, 144, 204, 341
Clark, John, 69
Clark, William, 101, 145
Clay, Eric, 333
Cleland, Charles, 135, 192, 262, 333
Cleveland, Grover, 274
Clifton, James, 214, 262
Clitz, John, 62
Clothier, Charles, 205
Cohen, Felix, 200
Collier, John, 327
commercial Indian fishing, 337
commercial rice harvest, 337–38
"competent" Indians, 293, 304
congressional intent, 259, 260–61, 284–85
Conner, Henry, 154
Copeway, George, 205
Cox, Jacob, 240, 246
Crabb, Barbara, 129, 196
Crawford, T. Hartley, 77, 79, 111, 113, 187
Crebassa, Peter, 205, 213, 308, 318
Creel, Herbert, 325
Crooks, Ramsey, 63, 64, 119, 165, 191
Crow Wing, MN, 100, 116, 219, 266
Curot, Michael, 9

Dakota (Sioux), 20, 100–101
Dakota uprising of 1862, 267, 268
Daughtrey, Martha Craig, 334
Davids, Bert, 258
Davis, Michael, 137
Dawes, Henry, 280
Dawes Act, 17
de Langlade, Charles, 141, 148
Delano, Columbus, 240, 248
Denver, J. W., 83, 293, 315
Dodge, Henry, 105, 107, 108–11, 170, 172, 179, 188, 210
Dole, William, 267, 300, 309
domestic rice harvest, 338
Doty, James, 151, 169, 189
Dougherty, Peter, 73
Dousman, Hercules, 118
Doyle, James, 125–29
Drew, John, 60, 62, 64, 65, 66
Drummond Island, 59, 61
Dubay, Jean, 205
Dubois, Robert, 214, 223, 318
Duck Creek, 151
Dunkley, Joseph, 135
Durbin, J., 294
Duschaine, Maggie, 324

Eaton, John, 153, 155
Edmonds, John, 66
egalitarianism, 23
Eighth Circuit Court of Appeals, 285
Ellis, Albert, 177, 178, 179, 184, 234
equal footing doctrine, 126, 137–38, 139
ethnohistory, 5, 8–9, 101, 342
Ewing, Thomas, 119
Executive Order 7868, 258

faith in paper, 37, 269
Feley, Laurent, 146
Fillmore, Millard, 122
Fitch, A. W., 298, 309, 316
five-year reservations, 79–80
Follies Avoines, 140
Fond du Lac, 100, 103, 104, 105, 108, 111, 112
Fond du Lac band, 107, 111, 117, 118, 122, 217
forts
  Brady, 61, 63
  Crawford, 167
  Drummond, 209
  Howard, 148, 164, 167
  La Baye, 141
  Mackinac, 52, 60, 62, 141, 209
  Michilimackinac, 28, 30, 74
  Snelling, 107, 110, 123, 132, 204
Fox, Noel P., 91–92
Fox River, 141, 143, 157, 159, 161
"fradulent treaty," 192
Francher, I. A., 302
fur trade, 15, 22, 24–25, 31, 33, 58, 63, 64, 73, 95, 118, 119, 141, 148, 203, 213

Gahbow, Art, 134–35
Gallup, Albert, 233
Gardner, Stephen, 245, 248
General Allotment Act (1887), 17, 199, 254, 256, 280, 306, 322, 323, 332
gens de lac, 203
gens de terre, 203
George, Benjamin, 317
gift exchange, 28, 36
Gilbert, Henry, 82, 85, 88, 89, 90, 122, 216, 228, 292, 293, 298, 308, 309, 310, 313
gill nets, 88, 89, 90
Gilman, Rhonda, 119
Godfroy, John, 94
Gorence, Patricia, 262
Gorman, Willis, 123
Graduation Act (1830), 289
Graduation Act (1854), 295
Grand Kaulaulin, 146
Grandmother Earth, 308, 341
Grand Portage band, 117, 208, 217, 220, 275
Grand River Ottawa, 58, 59, 65, 70, 84, 85, 300
Grand Traverse band, 59, 90, 93, 339
Grant, U. S., 240, 245, 248, 249, 253, 303
Great Father, 35, 63, 64, 65, 83, 103, 104, 269, 303
Great Lakes Indian Fish and Wildlife Commission (GLIFWC), 339
Greeley, Horace, 56
Green, Dan, 3
Green Bay, 141, 143, 157, 159, 161
Green Bay Company, 165
Greene, Bruce, 3, 4, 6
Greene, David, 109
Grignon, Augustin, 148, 161, 165
Grignon, Charles, 154, 171
Grignon, Louis, 165

Grignon, Pierre, 165
Gull Lake band, 117, 268
Gurnoe, Joseph, 310

HR 293, 218
Hall, Abel, 223, 318, 319, 327
Hall, Sherman, 111, 118
Hamlin, Augustin (Kanapima), 61, 64, 65, 81, 84
handicraft industry, 338
Harris, Carey, 69, 70, 73, 74, 76, 79, 106, 110, 169, 170, 286
Harrison, William H., 282
Hauke, C. F., 324
Hayes, James, 118
Hayes, Rutherford B., 269
Hayt, E. H., 251
Herriman, David, 218
Herring, Elbert, 59, 61
Hickerson, Harold, 100
Ho Chunk (Winnebago), 20, 102, 103, 116, 119, 120, 209, 230, 231
Hole in the Day (elder), 37, 107, 112
Hole in the Day (younger), 37, 117, 265, 267, 269
Holliday, James, 317
Holliday, John, 62, 64, 65, 205, 308
Holliday, Mary, 64, 65
Holliday, William, 205
Howe, Timothy O., 246, 247
Hubbard, L. R., 274
Huebschmann, Francis, 189, 235, 236, 237, 238
Hulbert, John, 64, 66
Hull, William, 72

Indian country, 227, 263, 266
Indian Gaming Regulatory Act, 259
Indian Party, 233, 234, 235, 238, 241, 242, 245, 251, 258, 260
Indian Peace Commission, 240
Indian Removal Act, 15, 65, 78, 95, 106, 169, 174, 210, 215, 230
Indian Reorganization Act, 17, 26, 258, 327, 329
Indian sovereignty, 200
Indian title, 13
indigenous treaties, 27
inland consent decree, 98
interpreters, 9, 33, 34, 37, 38, 76, 84, 112, 171, 174, 308
Iroquois, 20
Irwin, Samuel, 147
Isabella County, 291, 295, 298
Isabella Reservation, 296, 297, 301, 302, 305
Iskkininew, 169
Iwyematan (Iometah), 147, 148

Jackson, Andrew, 64, 68, 73, 77, 92, 153, 154, 155, 230, 307
Jackson, Helen Hunt, 323
James, Bill, 3
Jannetta, Jim, 3, 193
Jawbawadic (Waishkey) (Young Caribou Buck), 63
Jerome, Timothy, 301, 302, 304
Johnston, George, 54, 58, 66, 84, 204
Johnston, John, 61, 65, 84
Johnston, Susan (Ozhawguscodaywaquay), 63, 66
Johnston, William, 58, 61, 62, 63, 66, 75
judicial power, 284

Kachakawasheka (Notch Maker), 141
Kafura, Fred, 262
Kauskkaunonaive (Grizzly Bear), 141, 153, 155, 159, 160, 164, 168
Kawgayosh (Gull), 63
Kaygwaydash (The Attempter), 265, 271
Keeshketawwug (Cut Ear), 206, 209
Kegg, Herman, 135
Kelly, Lawrence, 262
Kemble, Edward, 250, 251, 303
Kesewaaush (Little Eagle), 206
Kewayqwaskum, 78
Keweenaw Bay band, 127
Keweenaw Bay Indian Community, 200, 324–25
Keweenaw Bay Reservation, 201, 203, 205, 207, 209, 225
King, David, 205, 212, 308, 318
Kirkwood, Samuel, 272
Kitchimeheegun (Big Wolf), 118
Kohl, Johann, 309
Komanikin (Big Wave), 151, 155, 169, 171
Komanikeenoshah (Little Wave), 155, 169, 171

Lac Courte Oreilles band, 46, 105, 107, 113, 114, 124, 125, 126, 127, 131
Lac du Flambeau band, 46, 106, 107, 127, 203, 209, 228, 326
La Chat, 141
Lac Vieux Desert band, 206, 213, 226, 308, 312
Lake Poygon, 177
Lake Winnebago, 140, 159, 230
Lake Winnebago Reservation, 236, 237, 241, 243, 250, 258
La Motte, 141, 189
L'Anse, 204, 205, 206, 207–8, 214, 321
L'Anse band, 114, 205, 211, 226, 308, 312
L'Anse Catholic mission, 205
L'Anse Methodist mission, 205
L'Anse Reservation, 206, 221–23, 313, 321, 322
Lapham, Increase, 176
La Pointe subagency, 204
L'Arbre Croche band, 59
Lasley, William, 64, 65
LaVake, Henry, 64, 65
Lawe, George, 176, 178, 188
Lawe, John, 146, 148, 165
Lay, Donald, 138
Lea, Luke, 81, 82, 122, 188, 189, 293
Leach, DeWitt, 300
LeBlanc, Abe, 88, 91
Lee, George, 305, 320
Leech Lake, 100, 107, 109, 111, 268, 271
Leech Lake band, 102, 107, 111, 275
Leeds, William, 250
legal cases
Alaska Pacific Fishery Co. v. United States, 43
Baraga County Equalization Department v. Darcy, 330
Cass County v. Leech Lake Band of Chippewa Indians, 331
Cherokee Nation v. Georgia, 41

legal cases (*continued*)
Choctaw Nation v. Oklahoma, 43
County of Mille Lacs v. Melanie Benjamin et al., 279–85
County of Yakima v. Confederated Tribes and Bands of Yakima Indian Nation, 332–34
Fond du Lac Band v. Carlson, 138
Hagen v. Utah, 260
Johnson v. MacIntosh, 13
Jones v. Meehan, 42
Keweenaw Bay Indian Community v. Michigan, 203, 226–29, 330–31, 343
Keweenaw Bay Indian Community v. Naftaly, 203, 329–34, 343
Lac Courte Oreilles v. Wisconsin (Voigt), 46, 124–31, 132, 196, 203, 343
McClanahan v. Arizona State Tax Commission, 43, 334
Menominee Indian Tribe of Wisconsin v. Thompson, 192–97
Michigan v. LeBlanc, 91, 126
Mille Lacs Band of Chippewa Indians v. State of Minnesota et al., 132–39, 196, 203, 343
Solem v. Bartlett, 260
South Dakota v. Yankton Sioux Tribe, 260
United States v. Ben Ruby, 125
United States v. Bouchard, 125
United States v. Celestine, 255
United States v. Kiya, 255
United States v. Michigan, 45, 46, 88–92, 93–99, 126, 132, 343
United States v. Sutton, 255
United States v. Washington, 42, 92
United States v. Winans, 41, 43
United States v. Wybro, 238, 242
Whitefoot v. United States, 42
Williams v. Michigan, 324
Wisconsin v. Baker, 126
Wisconsin v. Davids, 258–59
Wisconsin v. Doxtuter, 255
Wisconsin v. Gardner, 254, 256
Wisconsin v. Stockbridge-Munsee Community and Robert Chicks, 258–64
Worchester v. Georgia, 40, 41, 42, 43
legislative resolution of 1851, 80–81
Lincoln, Abraham, 267, 269, 270, 300
Little River band, 93
Little Traverse Bay band, 59, 93
Livermore, James, 118
Livermore, John, 113, 114, 121
Long, James, 301, 302
Lund, Tom, 135
Lyon, Lucius, 56, 62, 69

Machaba, Jacob, 307
Mackinac Indian Agency, 58, 77, 204, 286, 306, 320
Mackinac Island, 49, 54, 65, 68, 168, 204, 286
Madeline Island, 204
Maghegabo (La Trappe), 108, 109, 110
Mahconseweamence, 54
Mahgekewis, 275
Mahungance, 275, 276, 277
Major Crimes Act, 200
Manitoulin Island, 80
Manypenny, George, 15, 16, 38, 82–87, 114, 122, 187, 199, 235, 237, 238, 292, 293, 308
Marksman, Peter (Gahgodahahquah), 205, 206, 212, 213, 223, 308, 309, 312, 318
Marshall, John, 13, 40, 41, 43
Martin, Morgan, 181, 234, 241, 242, 245, 248
Marty, Martin, 275
Mason, John, 153
Mason, Stevens T., 56, 58
Matakosega, 212
Maucautaubee, 147, 148
Mawbawzo, 176
Maydwayawshi, 206, 308
McCall, James, 153
McClelland, Robert, 84, 235, 295, 296, 312
McClurken, James, 135
McDonell, John, 69
McKeague, David, 333
McKenney, Thomas, 31, 104, 151, 153, 209
meaning of "settlement," 76, 96
Medill, William, 116–17, 179, 181–83, 184
Megisinini (Power Shell Man), 64, 65, 78
Mendenhall, Cyrus, 114
Menogeshick (Fine Day), 271
Menomenkeshin (Rice Maker), 265, 267, 271
Menominee, 19, 20, 102, 103, 116–17, 140–45
Menominee bands, 142, 143, 144, 155, 167, 177, 187
Menominee removal, 178, 185, 186
Menominee Reservation, 190, 191, 196, 200, 236, 239, 244, 247, 342
Menominee River, 20, 140, 146, 147, 159, 165, 169, 176, 188
Meriam, Lewis, 327
Merritt, E. B., 324
métis, 25, 33, 36, 148, 150, 152, 166, 204–5, 206, 207, 212, 222, 308
Miami, 230
Michigan Department of Natural Resources, 88–90
Michigan Indian Superintendency, 204
Michigan Supreme Court, 91
Michigan Tax Tribunal, 330
Mihehwehna (Minevavana), 28
Milanowski, John P., 88, 91
military warrants, 290
Mille Lacs band, 107, 123, 127, 265, 268, 281
Mills Lacs County Board of Commissioners, 282
Mille Lacs Lake, 101, 133, 134, 136, 265, 267, 268, 279
Mille Lacs Reservation, 20, 136, 140, 146, 147, 159, 204–5, 206, 207, 212, 222, 228, 282, 285, 308
Miller, Glen, 192
Mississauga Ojibwe, 21, 51
Mississippi River, 15, 20, 56, 65, 100, 105, 106, 111, 115, 116, 155, 174, 205, 210, 214, 217
Mix, Charles, 82, 83, 87, 116, 187, 199, 293, 296, 298
mixed bloods, 58
Mohican, 230
Mole Lake band, 127
Mongozid (Loon's Foot), 103, 105, 118
Monroe, James, 150
Morgan, Lewis H., 21
Morse, Jedidiah, 52, 146, 147, 148
Morse, Samuel, 56
Moseomannay, 267, 269, 275
Mt. Pleasant, MI, 290

Mt. Pleasant Indian School, 307
Mukudaybenasi (Blackbird), 64
Munsee, 21, 149, 150, 154, 161, 164, 200, 230, 232–33, 243, 245, 249, 256, 258
Murphy, Diana E., 135–37
Murray, Elias, 81
muskellunge, 129

nadoways, 149
Nagonabe (Feather's End), 102, 118, 121
Nawgawnegawbo (Stands First), 310
Nawtawmegezhick (First Sky), 206, 308
Nawwandagoquay, 317
Nebawnaygezhick (Night Sky), 87, 105
Nelson, Knute, 280
Nelson Act (1889), 271, 274, 275–77, 280, 283, 284
Newell, Alan, 262
New York Indians, 150, 155, 159
Nezeegum, 275
Nichols, John, 135
Nicolet, Jean, 140
Noahquageshik, 33
Nolin, Louis, 205
Northwest Ordinance (1787), 145, 232
"not so competent" Indians, 293, 304
Nungo, Adam, 213, 316, 318

Oberly, James, 233, 262
Oberly, John, 281
O'Connor, Sandra Day, 138
Odawa, 19, 20, 22, 23, 24, 28, 33, 34, 46, 199
off reservation rights, 126, 127, 194, 197, 250, 274, 277
ogamagigido (speaker), 84, 205
ogamaw (chief), 23
Ogden, David, 149
Ogden Land Company, 150, 151, 155
Ohopashah (Little Whoop), 155
Ojibwe, 4, 5, 7, 8, 9, 19, 20, 21, 23, 24, 31, 34, 46, 102, 104, 199, 201, 203–10, 220, 225, 308
Ojibwe removal, 207, 214–15
Ojininin, Curtis, 213
Okimase (Young Chief), 205
Okundekun (Buoy), 206, 211
Okwemaw, 144
Old Carron, Thomas, 141, 145
"Old Citizens," 239, 243, 251
Oneida, 20, 21, 149, 150, 151, 154, 171, 230, 242, 254
Ontonagon band, 206, 321
oral history, 7, 34, 35, 40
oratory, 28
Osawwishkeno (Yellow Bird), 141
Oshawano (Shawono) (South), 61, 63
Oshkishhenayniew, 189
Oshkosh (Bear Claw), 141, 146, 148, 151, 153, 164, 169, 171, 172, 183, 186, 188, 196

Pabamatabi, 55, 60
Pagoonakeezhig (Hole in the Day), 107
Panic of 1837, 77, 289
Parker, Eli, 240, 301
patrilineal kinship, 9, 23, 35, 37, 144, 204
Paybahmesay (Walks Around), 84
Paymawsaw, 302
Pedudence (Muskrat's Liver), 265, 271
Perrault, H. C., 324
Peter, Ziba, 237
Pierce, Franklin, 292, 295, 312
Pierre Chouteau Company, 119
Pilcher, Elijah, 307
Pillager Chippewa, 100, 101, 107, 112, 117
Pitezel, John, 204, 205
plenary power, 38
Pokegoma Lake band, 111, 268
Polk, James, 179, 183
Porter, George, 59, 161
Portier, Jacques, 146, 165
Poshquaygin (Leather), 206, 213, 223, 308, 316, 318
post-treaty era, 26
Potawatomi, 5, 15, 19, 20, 22, 23, 24, 28, 33, 49, 51, 103, 140, 141, 143, 145, 155, 159, 166, 176, 209, 231, 300
Powell, William, 187
power of sale, 62–63, 73, 96
Powless, Sheila, 262
Preemption Act (1841), 289
preemption claims, 69
Price, Hiram, 272
Pritchette, Kintzing, 58
"privilege of occupancy," 71, 72
property taxes, 201, 243, 318, 320, 328, 329, 330, 332, 333, 334
Prucha, Francis, 240
public law, 200, 280
Puggwonaygeshik, 275
Puthuff, Willliam, 149

Quinney, Austin, 238
Quinney, John, 237

Rabbit Lake band, 268
Rainy Lake band, 105
Rainy River, 100
Ralette, Joseph, 118
Ramsey, Alexander, 113, 119, 122, 214, 267
Rathburn, Benjamin, 223, 316
Ratstetter, Bill, 3
reciprocal sharing, 22
Red Cliff band, 127
Red Lake, 100
Red Lake Reservation, 199
Red Springs Township, 258
Removal Act (1830), 106, 169–70, 174, 230
Removal Order (1850), 79, 121–22, 126, 133, 136
removal policy, 195, 230
Renaitenow (The Rain), 159
required for settlement, 65, 66, 68, 70, 71, 73, 74, 76, 89, 93, 94, 97
reservation policy, 215–17
reservation types, 225
reserved rights doctrine, 41
res judicata, 197, 259
ribbon farms, 164
Rice, Henry, 117, 118, 119, 186, 267, 268, 271, 275, 276, 281
rice chiefs, 337
Richardson, William, 246, 248–49, 251
"right of hunting," 46, 61, 65, 68, 70, 71, 89, 93, 102, 113, 124, 211

Roberts, Joseph, 269
Robinson, Rix, 63, 64, 65, 66, 68
Rodd, Charles, 301
Root, Erastus, 153
Rum River, 101, 105, 123, 265
Rust, Ezra, 301

Sabin, Dwight, 279
Saginaw band, 286, 293, 295
Saginaw Bay Reservation, 299
Saginaw Valley, 291
St. Croix band, 105, 107, 127
St. Croix River, 101, 105
St. Regis Mohawk, 150
salmon, 90
Sandy Lake affair, 214, 225
Sandy Lake band, 106, 107, 111, 268
Sandy Lake payment, 122
Santee Dakota, 267
Sauk Rapids, 120
Sault Ste. Marie, MI, 51, 56, 60–64, 75, 76, 78, 88, 148, 204, 209, 223, 294, 311, 313, 339
Sault Ste. Marie band, 19, 63, 84, 85, 86, 87
Sawyer, Philetus, 243, 245, 246, 247
Schoolcraft, Henry, 56, 59, 62, 63, 70, 71, 72, 75, 77, 78, 79, 87, 105, 204, 286
Schoolcraft, James, 63, 66, 78
Schoolcraft, Jane (Johnston), 62
Schurz, Carl, 279
sea lamprey, 90
seasonal round, 22, 203, 289
Senate amendments—1836 treaty, 97
Seventh Circuit Court of Appeals, 127, 132, 263
Sferrazza, Peter, 124
Shagobi (Little Six), 108, 267
Shauwanopenessee (South Bird), 176
Shawanodin (John Southwind), 205, 221, 308
Shawwannoh (The South), 171
Shingoop (Balsam), 105, 118
Shobaushkum (He That Passes under Everything), 35, 265, 267, 268, 270, 271, 272, 273, 275, 276
Shonene, 183, 186
Sibley, Henry, 118, 119, 121
Six Nations, 150
Sixth Circuit Court of Appeals, 93, 329, 333
Skakautcheokemaw, 147, 148
Slater, Leonard, 64, 65, 69
Slingerland, Jeremiah, 242, 245, 247, 249
smallpox, 111, 167, 168, 169, 266, 308
Smith, E. P., 35, 251, 268, 270
Smith, George, 294
Smith, Richard, 84, 301, 302, 303, 310
Smith, W. R., 105, 107
Snake River, 105, 111
Snake River band, 105, 108, 111
Southwind, John, 205, 221, 308
sovereignty, 26, 40, 41, 44, 102, 107, 200, 330, 333, 334
Spencer, John, 111
Spruce, Sam, 319–20
Stambaugh, Samuel C., 153, 154, 155, 157, 161, 164, 168, 172
state jurisdiction, 200, 201, 257, 280, 323
Stevens, Mark, 305, 306–7, 320, 323
Stockbridge (Mohekunnucks), 149, 161
Stockbridge-Munsee, 21, 201, 258
Stockbridge-Munsee Reservation, 192, 200, 239, 250
Stockbridge-Munsee rolls, 247
Street, John, 308
Stuart, Robert, 64, 66, 73, 79, 80, 111–15, 204, 210–11
Sturgeon, Mary, 324
Sunday, John, 205
supremacy clause, 41
surplus land, 199, 217, 225, 238, 247, 254, 256, 259, 260, 280, 284, 285
Swan Creek band, 286, 293
Swan Lake band, 107
Sylvester, William, 54

Taft, William H., 257
Tanner, H. S., 56
Tanner, Helen H., 4, 100, 135
Tanner, Howard A., 90
Taunchey, John, 205
taxation on reservations, 311, 312, 315, 316
Taylor, Zachary, 103, 120, 122, 125, 132, 196
Tedawkaymosay (The Pacer), 271
Teller, Henry, 280
territorial claims, 20, 22, 102, 103, 145, 151, 201, 209, 311
Thompson, Jacob, 225, 266, 297
Thompson, R. W., 182, 184, 188
Tierney, Kathryn, 3, 91
Tody, Wayne, 90
Tomah, 141, 144, 145, 148, 149, 153
touching the pen, 37–38
Trade and Intercourse Act (1802), 150
Trade and Intercourse Act (1834), 293
trade and intercourse acts, 55, 73, 105
trader-debt system, 32
treaties (in chronological order)
  Treaty of Greenville (1795), 14, 49–52, 54, 55, 56, 72, 76, 85, 160
  Treaty of Detroit (1807), 51, 286
  Treaty of Springwells (1815), 51
  Treaty of St. Louis (1817), 146
  Treaty of Miami Rapids (1817), 51, 72
  Treaty of Saginaw (1819), 30, 51, 72, 286
  Treaty of Sault Ste. Marie (1820), 51, 52, 58, 85–86
  Treaty of Chicago (1821), 51, 72
  Treaty of Prairie du Chien (1825), 101, 102, 103, 105, 110, 145, 209
  Treaty of Fond du Lac (1826), 31, 103–5, 209
  Treaty of Butte des Morts (1827), 145, 146, 151, 209
  Treaty of Washington (1831), 155, 160, 161, 166, 192, 233
  Treaty of Chicago (1833), 166
  Treaty of the Cedars (1836), 169–74, 192
  Treaty with Ottawa and Chippewa (1836), 49, 62–69, 72–78, 86, 88, 93, 286
  Treaty with the Saginaw Chippewa (1836), 286
  Treaty with the Chippewa (1837), 294
  Treaty of Flint (1837), 294
  Treaty of St. Peters (1837), 34, 46, 105–11, 125, 132, 196, 210, 273, 274, 279
  Treaty of La Pointe (1842), 34, 36, 46, 111–16, 125, 132, 210–11, 226, 320, 329

Treaty of Washington (1846), 184
Treaty of Fond du Lac (1847), 116, 212
Treaty of Leech Lake (1847), 117
Treaty with the Stockbridge (1848), 235
Treaty of Lake Poygan (1848), 179–86, 192
Treaty of Wolf River (1854), 186–87, 192
Otto-Missouri Treaty of 1854, 216
Treaty of La Pointe (1854), 86, 117, 125, 133, 200, 203, 216, 220, 224–25, 226, 308, 309–11, 320, 329–30
Treaty of Washington (1855), 133–34, 265, 268, 276, 278, 279
Treaty of Detroit (July 31, 1855), 84–87, 98, 238
Treaty of Detroit with the Saginaw Chippewa (August 2, 1855), 82, 97, 293–97
Treaty of Detroit with Sault Ste. Marie Chippewa (August 2, 1855), 294
Treaty with the Stockbridge and Munsee (1856), 235, 236–37
Treaty of Keshena (1856), 241
Treaty of Stockbridge (1856), 239, 240, 259, 260
Treaty of Washington (1863), 268, 269, 272, 279
Treaty of Saginaw (1864), 286, 297, 299–300
Treaty with the Chippewa of the Mississippi (1864), 270, 272, 284
Treaty with the Chippewa of the Mississippi (1867), 268, 271
treaty ceremony, 38
treaty era, 25
tribal conservation codes, 339
tribal factionalism, 25, 232, 233, 234, 236, 300
tribal harvest regulation, 126, 137
tribal rights, 42
tribal sovereignty, 338
Tribble, Fred, 124
Tribble, Mike, 124
tribes, 3, 5, 6, 7, 8, 9, 13, 14, 15, 16, 17, 23, 24, 26, 27, 28, 40, 41, 45, 46
Tuscarora, 150

United States Civil Rights Commission, 338
United States Court of Claims, 282, 283
United States Fish and Wildlife Service, 337
United States Forest Service, 338
United States Supreme Court, 138, 282, 285, 329, 334
Usher, John, 301
usufructuary activity, 45, 46, 50, 51, 55, 59, 62, 69, 70, 73, 75, 77, 95, 124, 125, 126, 128, 130, 132, 133, 135, 137, 138, 139, 160, 178, 192, 194, 195

Valentine, Nelson, 317
Van Antwerp, Ver Planck, 105, 107, 110
Van Tassell, William, 207
Vermilion Lake band, 105
Verplank, Isaac, 116, 117, 181
Voigt, Lester, 124
Voigt task force, 127

Wabijeshi (Marten), 113
Wahpeton Dakota, 100
Wahweyaycum, 275
Wainesaut, 169
Waishkey (First Born), 61, 63
walleye, 129
Warren, Lyman, 119
Warren, William, 27
Washaskkokone (Muskrat's Liver), 107
Wasson, 84
Watrous, John, 114, 122
Waubojeeg (White Fisher), 63, 85, 294, 297
Waukechon, 189
Waupesepin, 145
Wawnawco, 176
Wells, H. R., 250
Wheeler-Howard Act, 17
Whipple, Henry, 267, 268, 269
White, Bruce, 135
White Crow, 113, 114
White Earth Reservation, 134, 271, 274, 277, 280
Whiting, Henry, 66
Whiting, Joseph, 275, 276
Whittlesey, Charles, 167
Wilder, Amherst, 279
Wiley, John, 124
Williams, Eleazer, 149, 150, 151, 154, 160
Williams, George, 301, 302, 304
Winnebago, 20, 102, 103, 116, 119, 120, 140, 141, 143, 146, 151, 168, 177, 180, 181, 184, 212, 231
Winnibigoshish Lake, 100, 116, 268
Wisconsin Department of Natural Resources, 124, 127
Wolf River, 140, 157, 159, 165, 176, 186, 189, 191, 192, 243, 342

Yellow Lake band, 111